Social Change and the City in Japan

# SOCIAL CHANGE and the CITY in JAPAN

*From earliest times through the Industrial Revolution*

*By* Takeo Yazaki
*Professor of Sociology, Keio University*

JAPAN PUBLICATIONS, INC.

Translated by David L. Swain

Published by Japan Publications, Inc.
Distributed by Japan Publications Trading Company
1255 Howard Street, San Francisco, Calif., 94103
175 Fifth Avenue, New York, N.Y. 10010
Central P.O. Box 722, Tokyo

Library of Congress Catalog Card No. 67–28969
First Printing, December 1968

MADE AND PRINTED IN JAPAN BY DAI NIPPON PRINTING CO., LTD.

# Foreword

When I first went to the University of Chicago in 1949 many of those scholars who have since become famous in the history of sociology were still arrayed there as a most impressive constellation—E. W. Burgess, Louis Wirth, William Ogburn, P. M. Hauser, Everett C. Hughes, Robert Redfield, Lloyd Warner, Herbert Blumer, Donald C. Bogue, Otis Duncan, Albert Reiss, Jr., and Thomas Shibutani. It was my privilege to study sociology, and especially urban sociology and human ecology, under their genial and exacting leadership for three years. Nineteen years have passed since those days so memorable for me.

Upon returning to Japan I felt it was my first obligation to introduce the training which I had received in advanced urban sociology to the Japanese academic world. I strained every energy in this effort, while using this knowledge to carry out my own studies of urban Japan, particularly in performing an analysis of the Japanese city with the methods of human ecology which was at that time the most underdeveloped phase of basic research in Japanese urban sociology.

Urban research consists not only of human ecology, however, but of analysis of social structures as well. The structure of Japanese society being considerably different from that of America, use of the analytical tools of American urban sociology can elucidate certain aspects of the Japanese city but leaves the total perspective lacking in a number of crucial points. Without denying the definite superiority of American urban sociology, I felt painfully the need for urban sociology in Japan to have the same close connection with the realities of social development as that enjoyed by urban studies in America. Delving deeply into the exploratory urban research made by various Japanese scholars in different fields and taking note of certain inadequacies in the body of existing research, I was able somehow in the next ten years to work out my own analytical methods and conceptual framework for the study of the Japanese city.

As a working and living member of Japanese society, I came to realize that inquiry into the interrelations of cities themselves and of cities to the remote villages of Japan should focus first on the preurban conditions of primitive society. The communities of the earliest times were structurally related to the Japanese city's development, in both the establishment of the feudal cities and their structures and in the emergence of the modern city accomplished through the industrial revolution. In 1962

I published a volume describing that historical process, titled *Nihon Toshi no Hatten Katei* (The Process of Development of the Japanese City. Tokyo: Kōbundō, 1962). To my delight this book was highly evaluated as a major contribution to systematic knowledge of the contemporary Japanese city from a broad theoretical perspective by both scholars and journalists in Japan and abroad in many fields, such as sociology, history, geography, demography, economics, public administration and cultural anthropology. From time to time limited portions of this work were translated into English and introduced abroad when I received invitations to speak at universities and conferences overseas.

A research project of such broad scope as this necessarily must make the fullest possible use of the accumulated research of others, and this I had tried to achieve. Yet, from the standpoint of theory it did not embody a fully satisfactory range of data or research references. Taking into consideration the criticisms that appeared after the original volume was published, I began making revisions, adding new data, and incorporating new research results. I particularly felt a need to enlarge the descriptive materials on the modern city. At this point Dr. R. J. Smith, Chairman of Anthropology Department of Cornell University, took a keen interest in my work and arranged for financial assistance for the translation from the Wenner Gren Foundation for Anthropological Research. With this stimulus I was able to complete revision of large portions of the book and prepare it for publication in English under the present title. It seemed to me that there was great value in making available in English a systematic analysis of Japanese society, for specialists in urban studies, of course, but also for non-Japanese scholars. This seemed especially true as a comprehensive survey such as this was previously unavailable even in the Japanese language.

Publication of a book in English on the history of urban development without precedent in the history of Japan has been an extremely difficult task for all involved, and I am deeply indebted to Messrs. Kinjiro Ōtsuka and David L. Swain, without whose devoted and energetic labors it would surely have been impossible. Particularly for the taxing work of rendering into English a vast range of previously untranslated terms dealing with Japanese politics, economics, society and culture and for the accurate articulation of their meaning so that these terms and meanings can be properly understood by English speaking people—not only a most difficult but an exceedingly important work—I am especially grateful to Mr. Swain for his persistent efforts. Also I have only the highest regard and appreciation for Mr. Iwao Yoshizaki, chief editor of Japan Publications, Inc., for undertaking the exacting task of seeing this publication to its completion with genuine professional competence and commitment. Indeed, it has taken three years of unrelenting cooperation on the part of all of us to reach this final goal.

At this point the general reader may wish to move directly to the first chapter; but I would like to offer a few comments for those interested in the methodology and structure of the book. To carry out sociological analysis of the Japanese city and present the range of systematic knowledge attempted in this book, it was obviously necessary to have an appropriate methodology. It is quite impossible to spell it out in detail here in the limited space of a few pages. Those interested in the theoretical aspects of that methodology can refer to the translation of an earlier work of mine, *The Japanese City: A Sociological Analysis* (Tokyo: Japan Publications Trading Co., Ltd., 1963); though the general reader will very likely grasp the basic outlines of the methodology for himself as he works through the book chapter by chapter. A few remarks recorded here may, however, make it much easier to grasp it comprehensively.

For a long time students of culture have touched on aspects of the city from the various viewpoints of history, philosophy and general cultural analysis. In the beginnings of sociology as a science such classical sociologists as Karl Marx, Max Weber, Werner Sombart, Ferdinard Tönnies, and Georg Simmel in Germany and Emile Durkheim in France dealt with features of the city as part of their structural analysis of civilization. It was in the twentieth century that sociology was established as an empirical science, particularly from the 1920's, through the work of scholars centered in the University of Chicago and Columbia University. Urban studies were no longer based upon philosophical speculation, but were now founded upon exact analysis rooted in empirical observation. The city became a laboratory for the empirical analysis of human behavior.

Once this stage was reached, countless empirical observations were performed, the data was organized conceptually, and both empirical investigation and theoretical formulation were greatly enhanced. Attempts were made at formulating the theoretical structure of the city as a whole and the urban sociological theory developed in America began to exert a profound influence throughout the world.

The first sociological research performed on the Japanese city was that of Okui Fukutaro, who published his *Gendai Daitoshi Ron* (Theory of the Modern Metropolis. Tokyo: Yūhikaku, 1941) and introduced the empirical methods of urban research of R. E. Park, E. W. Burgess and R. D. McKenzie. His pioneering efforts are widely recognized in the field of sociology. Japanese sociology remained in an undeveloped state during and immediately after World War II, when the chief concern of Japanese sociologists was with the introduction and assimilation of the more philosophically oriented social theories of the West. Moreover, total mobilization for war left little margin of time or energy for empirical investigations and, hence, no urban studies of an empirical or systematic nature were carried out for a decade or more. Following the war the more strictly scientific sociology of America was introduced, attracting widespread attention. It became generally acknowledged that sociological research of the city must have its foundation in observable, verifiable factual data. Empirical investigation of the Japanese city was activated through the labors of such men as Suzuki Eitaro who followed the theories of Galpin and Sanderson, Isomura Eiichi working with the ideas of Wirth and Gist, and Ariga Kizaemon and Nakano Tadashi who applied their earlier studies of the extended family system to analysis of the city. Kitagawa Ryūkichi and Shimazaki Minoru applied the criteria of Marxist analysis to urban problems, and Tachi Minoru carried out extensive population studies. Others active in this period of the revival of sociological research were Hayase Toshio, Daidō Yasujiro, Kurasawa Susumu, Ōmi Tetsuo, Ōhashi Kaoru, and Suzuki Hiroshi. Through the combined efforts of these scholars, empirical observation of urban data and organization of the data into theoretical systems experienced rapid progress.

Sociological research on the Japanese city has not been comprehensive, however, and while there are excellent studies on particular dimensions of the city, adequate theories dealing with the totality of the city have yet to be formulated. Urban research in America is more voluminous and has a much longer history; in theory and observational techniques it is unquestionably superior. Hence, while any inquiry into the Japanese city must rely heavily on the work of Japanese researchers in sociology, economics, politics, history, geography, technology, population and culture, it must at the same time draw on the observational methods and systematic theories of American scholarship.

Theory and techniques are developed in relation to the object of investigation and it is quite natural that the methods and concepts of American sociology cannot always be readily applied to the realities of the Japanese city which is rooted in a different socio-cultural system. When notable differences appear, some reformulation of theories is inescapable. So long as empirical studies of the processes of change in socio-cultural structures of the various regions of the world were not sufficiently advanced, the notion was widespread that the Western pattern of civilized society was that which other societies would follow. Until the end of World War II, there was a tendency in urban sociology to measure all societies with other cultural backgrounds by the same yardstick, revealing a kind of intellectual ethnocentrism which regarded theories gained from the results of observation of American cities as universally applicable. In the postwar years America's world position changed considerably and her contacts with different cultures were greatly extended. As research progressed, exchange was heightened between the comparative cultural studies of sociology and anthropology and the historical investigations of the processes of social development. Geography advanced from descriptive studies of community patterns to a more functional approach. To deal with the diverse structures and the problems of growth and decline in cities of different cultural spheres, there arose a demand for theories that held good in the face of cultural relativity, beginning with R. H. Lee, G. Sjoberg and others.

In Japan as well postwar interest has shifted from social theory to social science and there is an awareness of the need for more than simply the direct importation of American theories. While the theories, concepts and observational techniques of American sociology can still be usefully appropriated, our basic task is that of reorganizing these theories, concepts and techniques on the basis of factual data derived from investigations of the Japanese city, and of attempting the conceptual reformulations necessary for acquiring a theoretical grasp of the Japanese city through empirical analysis.

At the same time, it should be remembered that scientific research has among its purposes the need to make classifications and comparisons that permit the formation of general theory. Hence, one must be careful not to abstract only the unique aspects of the Japanese city, but seek to understand it cross-culturally in terms applicable to all sociology and strive to make possible meaningful comparisons of the Japanese city with cities of other regions and times. Acknowledgement of the importance of comparison and generalization need not, however, lead to the exclusion of the fact that Japanese culture and social structure are, after all, different from those of the West. In tracing the lines of emergence, development and decline in the history of the Japanese city we shall try to mark clearly the reasons for distinct patterns of structural change. It will be evident, for example, that throughout the succeeding generations there is a considerable degree of cultural continuity; that is, many cultural traits have been preserved for a long time through successive stages of development. While some of these traits fell by the wayside in times of transition, others were incorporated into the new cultural complexes resulting from major structural changes. Thus, to understand the reasons for the emergence of the modern Japanese city and for the changes that have led to its present social structure, a socio-cultural approach to the processes of historical change was mandatory.

For this purpose we have used not a narrow sociological approach to the city but a broad approach to the structural relations of rural and urban sectors and of these to the national structure. We have tried to view the social, political, legal, economic, geographical, demographic and cultural dimensions of the city from a comprehensive angle of vision. This kind of research is exceedingly complex. Historically the feudal character of Japanese society has been very strong, but from the primitive and ancient societies that preceded feudalism to the modern age that followed it there runs a comparatively continuous cultural stream within the discrete history of this island nation. Through the aggregate aid of the many disciplines of the social sciences it is not impossible, if one has an appropriate conceptual framework, to comprehend the structural processes of change and development of the city in its interrelations with the rural sector and with the overall national structure.

For so comprehensive a task I have been forced, far beyond my own personal studies, to reliance on the scholarly results of many others. For the methods of analysis and systematization it has been necessary to construct a theoretical framework by drawing on the work of many, especially European and American sociologists, and by adopting their concepts as closely as possible to the realities of Japan. The scholars whose works have been most helpful to me in one way or other form a long list; but I would like to mention, in addition to those named in the opening paragraphs of this foreword, those to whom I feel a special indebtedness: Robert E. Park, Robert D. McKenzie, Sol Tax, Amos Hawley, August B. Hollingshead, Gideon Sjoberg, Julian Stewart, Rose Hum Lee, K. Ishiwaran, Irne Taeuber, Nels Anderson, Kingsley Davis, James Quinn, Talcott Parsons, Solomon Levy, Noel P. Gist, Stuart A. Queen, David B. Carpenter, Floyd Hunter, Reinhard Bendix, C. Wright Mills, Calvin Schmidt, Paul K. Hatt, Walter Firey, William S. Whyte, Robert J. Smith, Robert E. Dickinson, Maurice R. Davie, Ronald Freedman, Oscar Luis, Morris Janowitz, Seymour M. Lipset, Peter Blow, Joseph A. Schumpeter, William A. Kohnhouser, Thorstein Veblen, Henri Pirrene, Lewis Mumford, Donald L. Foley, Marvin B. Sussman, Scott Greer, Lloyd Rodwin, John Dyckman, Martin Meyerson, Irwin T. Sanders, Svend Reimer, R. Centers, E. Gordon Erickson, Norton Ginsberg, David Kornhouser, Ernest Manheim, Peter H. Rossie, Raymond Vernon, Charles P. Loomis, Pitirim Sorokin, Robert M. MacIver, Charles H. Page, Marion J. Levy, Jack P. Gibbs, Werner J. Cohnman, Alvin Boscoff, Robert A. Nibset, Alex Inkeles, Sigmund Diamond, Harlan W. Gilmore, Joseph Maier, Tamme Wittermans, Bryce Ryan, Robin M. Williams, William A. Robson, C. K. Yang, Ronald P. Dore, James Abeglen, Robert N. Bellah, Habert Passin, William Lebra, Douglas Yamamura, Shunzo Sakamaki, C.K. Cheng, George Yamamoto, Robert Sakai, Richard K. Bearsley, John W. Hall, Robert Faris, Frank Miyamoto, Chester Hunt and Edwin O. Reischauer.

The works of these scholars have been invaluable in comprehending the general structure of the city in terms of metropolitan, satellite, and surrounding rural communities, as well as in treating both the rural and urban sectors within the total national structure in each historical period, and in dealing with the problems of class and power structures throughout the processes of social change relative to the city in Japan.

Tokyo, September 1968 — TAKEO YAZAKI

# Translator's Preface

For a long and difficult translation a translator needs, I believe, far more motivation than idle curiosity or a mere sense of obligation. Mine has derived from a firm conviction that (1) the major external, i.e., objective factor of Japanese culture in the present and coming age is massive urbanization, (2) the major internal factor of Japanese culture in the days ahead is the pervasive influence of scientific knowledge and inquiry, and (3) the implications of these two find a happy coincidence in the life work of Professor Yazaki. Ever since my translation of his shorter theoretical work, *The Japanese City: A Sociological Analysis*, was published in 1963, it has been my personal and keen desire that his longer and more detailed study of the historical process of development of the Japanese city, *Nihon Toshi no Hatten Katei*, would be made available in English translation—hopefully by someone more qualified than myself.

Only after the initial spadework of putting the many difficult terms for persons, places, institutions and historical happenings into workable English was performed by Mr. Kinjiro Ōtsuka could I be persuaded to venture the full translation of this material, which forms the foundation of all of Professor Yazaki's subsequent and prolific labors. I can hardly express adequately my appreciation to Mr. Ōtsuka for his help in getting this project started. Responsibility for the English text, imperfect as it surely is, is mine; though the content, happily, is entirely Professor Yazaki's province.

Most of the historical terms employed in the original Japanese text are learned by every Japanese schoolboy and girl long before reaching the university level; they rarely appear in most Japanese-English dictionaries. The routine terminology of sociology and other social sciences are picked up in introductory courses in these disciplines early in a university career; hence, they are generally excluded from academic dictionaries, which concentrate on the specialized terminology relevant to graduate and professional requirements. Not a few of the more difficult Chinese characters used to express technical concepts and remote historical data simply are not found in most Chinese character dictionaries. Far from pleading innocence, I can only hope that the final English text adequately and accurately reflects the meaning of the original Japanese material. If it also conveys the sense of historical significance of the original, it bespeaks the helpfulness of Mr. Ōtsuka's initial work and the sustained cooperation of Professor Yazaki and of Mr. Iwao Yoshizaki, chief editor of Japan Publications, Inc. The entire project has been a most rewarding learning experience for me, and they have been my valued tutors.

A meticulous and direct translation (were it possible) would have greatly exceeded, if not doubled, the 464 pages of the Japanese text. In the interests of economy and, more important, readability, it was agreed by both author and publisher that certain liberties were to be taken in condensing portions of the original material where possible and feasible. This was necessitated partly by the need to accommodate additions of new data by the author and partly by the need to provide some supplementary explanations of historical and cultural items not generally familiar or comprehensible to the non-Japanese reader.

In general I have tried to follow established conventions for rendering Japanese into English; though, as anyone who has set his hand to the task knows, there is no single universally accepted set of such conventions. I have found the Style Sheet for Publications of the East Asian Research Center of Harvard University a very helpful guide in many instances, and a doctoral graduate of that same university, Dr. J. David Reid, a close personal friend, saved me from numerous violations of the delicacies of both the Japanese and English languages by going over the working draft of the translation with an impassionate scrutiny. Neither the Center nor Dr. Reid should be held accountable, however, for any deviations from their standards. My appreciation for both, nonetheless, remains.

It may be of some value to record some of the working principles which I have tried to follow consistently. An effort has been made to adhere to preferred spellings of *Webster's New Collegiate Dictionary* (1949) in English and to Kenkyūsha's *New Japanese-English Dictionary* (1954) in the romanization of Japanese terms. As a general rule, Japanese words are italicized. Exceptions include well-known terms such as samurai, shogun and daimyō, which are found in most English dictionaries; and proper names are not italicized, whether persons, places, or organizations.

A word on the use of macrons over long vowels may be in order. They are used, of course, in both common terms, as in *kenkyū*, and in proper names, as in *Jōmon*. Departure from usual practice will be noticed in two cases: (1) inasmuch as this book is a specialized and authoritative study of the Japanese city, macrons have been retained in the names of all cities, even the more familiar ones like Tōkyō, Ōsaka and Kyōto, to assure an accurate reading of all city names; (2) the macron has been kept in the word daimyō, though it is not italicized, as it appears in many combinations, such as *kunimochi-daimyō*, *shiromochi-daimyō*, *fudai-daimyō* and *tozama-daimyō*, which require italics.

Regarding Japanese terms, an attempt has been made to give a clear translation or conceptual equivalent in all cases of initial occurrence, and in occasional recurrences far removed from the first appearance. Terms appearing in italics are incorporated, with page references, in the Index for convenient reference. In cases of initial occurrence of proper names, full names have been entered in the text. All Japanese names appear in the normal Japanese order, i.e., family name first.

The practice usually followed with proper names of castles, temples, rivers, and the like, has been to retain the suffix—such as *-jō* for castle, *-ji* for temple, and *-kawa* (or *-gawa*) for river—and the English word following is in lower case letters; e.g., Hachigatajō castle, Zenkōji temple, and Arakawa or Sumidagawa rivers. In rare cases where the Japanese suffix element is not retained, the English part of the proper name has a capital letter, as in the River Saho. This practice should prove helpful to those who would follow up their reading with visits or conversations with a Japanese person, who would certainly recognize "Hōryūji temple" but might balk at "the Temple Hōryū."

Parentheses in the text include translations or other explanatory materials; brackets mark the author's or translator's addition to a quotation. Brief tables have been used to avoid long and difficult passages, especially those involving substantial statistical data. Japanese terms for weights and measures have been consistently italicized, and where possible approximate equivalents have been provided. The reader should be warned, however, that weights and measures varied with historical periods in many instances, and the equivalents given are not necessarily precise. Monetary values constitute a major problem in Japanese historical research and, rather than be too misleading, few equivalent values have been ventured.

As a rule, all dates appear according to the Western calendar, except when the name of an era is important for clarity or style. The dates of a given era are provided in parentheses on initial occurrence, or again when the era name appears after a long absence.

Finally, it would definitely be amiss to conclude without mentioning my deep indebtedness to Professor Masayoshi Sugimoto of Kanagawa University whose collaboration with me in the study of Japanese intellectual history over the past decade has, more than anything else, prepared me for whatever ability I have had in comprehending the sweep of Japanese history which Professor Yazaki elucidates so well from his own vantage point. My wife Betty's deep commitment to making a fuller understanding of Japanese culture a richer and more common experience for others has been a constant and sustaining source of energy and insight.

Tokyo, July 1968 DAVID L. SWAIN

# Contents

# List of Illustrations

# Chapter I

# Transformation of Primitive Life and the Rise of the City as a Political Center

# 1. Pre-urban Society

The development of the city as a social process and phenomenon can be seen from several perspectives. The historian treats the stages of development from ancient to modern societies with greater emphasis on process, referring to the status of the city at each stage. The social anthropologist centers more on the structural analysis of urban phenomena, with the city at the core of civilized society. The sociologist shares the concern for process and phenomenon, but seeks in his own ways to draw out the identifying characteristics of the urban in contrast to rural ways of life. The sociologist also pays close attention to the process of expansion of the city within the context of structural relationships of rural and urban society; and he tries to see both rural and urban sectors as part of a larger social system.

As part of the process in which the city gradually emerges from pre-urban communities into the cities of ancient, feudal, and modern times, a considerable degree of cultural continuity is operative throughout the generations. That is, the modern city can be understood fully only by referring back into earlier stages, such as medieval and ancient. Hence, even when the emphasis is primarily on the description of the urban characteristics of human society, it is important not to overlook the historical roots of the process in pre-urban conditions.

To grasp properly, then, the process of development of the city in a particular society, it seems most appropriate to begin with an investigation of the emergence of pre-urban society and then trace the developmental process through each succeeding historical stage. We shall look not only into the contrast between urban and rural ways of life at each stage, but shall seek also to observe the overall functional relationships obtaining among urban and rural communities. Finally, we shall endeavor to see how urban-rural interrelationships constitute integral parts of the larger social system.

Our study begins with a description of that complex of elements which constituted pre-urban society in the initial phases of Japan's cultural history. These phases were the Jōmon (*circa* 5000–150 B.C.), the Yayoi (150 B.C.–A.D. 250), and the Kofun (A.D. 250–552) periods. Close attention will be given to those elements that changed the earlier forms of society into societies with living centers that can justifiably be called cities. A comparison of these social and historical elements and their processes of change will, we believe, help enrich our understanding of what is meant in sociological studies by "city" and "urban."

*Jōmon period.*——It is not entirely clear just when or how the Japanese people originated, or from what racial sources. We have only certain remains of the Jōmon culture which is assumed to have continued for some five or six thousand years until the 2nd century B.C. at least. The name "Jōmon" derives from archaeological discoveries of earthenware exhibiting surface patterns made by impressing straw rope upon these clay utensils. As there are no indications of the use of megaliths or domesticated farm animals, the evidence so far indicates but an incomplete pattern of neolithic culture. Remains of Jōmon-style pottery have been found all over Japan, including Hokkaidō and Okinawa, though they are especially dense in the eastern half of Japan, that is, the Kantō (eastern plain) and Tōhoku (northeastern) districts.

Jōmon culture appears to have shifted originally from the western part of Japan to the east and to have disappeared in the west when succeeded by the Yayoi culture around the 2nd century B.C. Yayoi culture arose, it seems, in the northern part of Kyūshū island and spread from there onto the main island, though Jōmon culture continued to survive in the eastern part of the main island of Honshū long after Yayoi culture became dominant elsewhere.[1]

Lacking techniques for controlling nature, the people of the Jōmon period inhabited areas with easy access to water and other natural resources necessary to their livelihood, such as wooded tablelands in the hills convenient for defense and effective lookout, or beaches fronting on ocean shallows where fish and edible shells could be had with relative ease. That their economic livelihood depended upon hunting and fishing is concluded from such remains as arrowheads, fishhooks, harpoons and nets, as well as such evidences of their diet as shells, fishbones, and the bones of animals and birds.

In the early part of the Jōmon period simple dwellings were fashioned from bamboo and vines as found in their natural environment. Later caves were dug and secured with cut saplings and bamboo poles.

In their food-gathering economy the natural materials available in a given area could be easily depleted, especially if there was any population increase; hence, limited numbers of people lived in small, scattered settlements and moved about frequently, as can be discerned from the paucity of settlement traces found in any given location.[2]

As deer, wild boar and badger were among the game sought, cooperative effort was required to some extent. On the whole, though, it is thought that each man hunted independently, his catch being dedicated to the tribal deity after which, in accordance with custom, it was shared and consumed by all in the settlement.[3]

Some increase in population and, accordingly, in manpower resources may be inferred from improvements in the techniques of procuring food and materials, from some division of labor, and from the breeding of dogs for use in hunting. At any rate, these developments are indicated by the increase in quantity of bone remains and the discovery of large whale bones in historic sites.

Technical improvements, materials procurement, and relative systematization of cooperative endeavor naturally led to the trend, about the middle of the Jōmon era, to remain longer in a fixed location and for the size of the unit group to expand. Living sites shifted to the seashore or to river banks where men could fish with greater ease, indicating greater dependence upon fishing than upon hunting.[4]

The size of the unit group in the Jōmon period has not yet been fully clarified, but it was definitely limited by the rudimentary techniques of hunting and fishing and by natural conditions of weather, topography, and available flora and fauna. Located on hills, near the seashore, or near rivers and springs, early Jōmon dwellings were shallow pits of square shape covered by a roof supported by wooden poles, large enough to accommodate five or six persons. Changed to circular shaped structures about the middle of the Jōmon period, these pit-dwellings were arranged in a horseshoe arc of twenty to thirty pits, with the open space in the center for meetings and ceremonial performances. From such an arrangement is inferred a level of community development involving the unifying function of a primitive religious cult.

In the latter days of the Jōmon period the horseshoe-shaped groups of dwellings disappeared as there occurred a substantial increase in both the size of the settlements and their number. Originally based on genuine kinship relations, the village groups increasingly regarded the land they occupied as the bond of their union.[5] This resulted not only from population expansion but also from the acquisition of elementary techniques of land cultivation. The existence of a hearth in each dwelling suggests that they lived in individual family groups, although the kinds of beasts and deep-sea fish remains found in their sites indicates that hunting and fishing were increasingly cooperative ventures. In the very late Jōmon period communal systems of cooperative work requiring division of labor by sex and age appeared, and lands were jointly owned.

In the division of labor women were responsible for child-rearing, the gathering of fruits and vegetables, and the making of woven goods and earthenware; men were responsible for hunting, fishing, and defense of the village territory. Despite this elementary division of labor, no distinctions based on wealth occurred as there were as yet no methods of storing surplus goods. Tools were made by hand, but no persons specializing in handicrafts appeared in this stage.

In this pre-literate society past experience served as the basis of coping with the rigors of nature. Past experience being accessible only through memory, men of ripe years and rich experience naturally assumed positions of leadership in the group as chiefs. From the late Jōmon custom of pulling certain teeth,[6] it is supposed that some form of age group distinctions existed, denoting differences in social rank, rights and duties.

Controls over individual behavior were necessary to the life of the group. Such power was symbolized by the group's deity, the *kami*, and punishment for anti-social behavior was meted out in the name of the deity. The chief was a priest-ruler, serving at once as the representative of the deity's will and, because of the belief that they were all of one blood, as the parent-ruler of the group.

The same stone slabs and tombs accommodated all members of the group for burials, and no significant differences have been found in the kinds of goods buried with the dead, all being everyday objects. Moreover, pit-dwelling remains fail to establish the existence of any special class of people, leading to the conclusion that the economy of the Jōmon period was a communal economy with no rigid status system or any independent position for the individual families.

If inventions, discoveries, and cultural influx are taken as causes of social change, then the changeless and stable persistence of Jōmon culture over several thousands of years was doubtless closely connected with its insularity, self-sufficiency and near absence of cultural transmission from the outside. Insularity and self-sufficiency are relative matters, however, and the remains of earthenware and shell bracelets show a basic correspondence in design and decoration in widely dispersed geographical areas, and similar patterns of change are evident in widely separated places. Though not completely self-sufficient, these communities were able to meet their needs as regards food, clothing, and other staples, without depending upon outside sources for services or supplies, and they were free from extraneous controls.

In summary, the Jōmon culture embraced but a small population, living within the limits of a largely self-sufficient collective economy by means of the simplest tools and techniques. The level of socio-economic differentiation remained low in a society that was classless except for sex and age groupings. Kinship relations lay at the heart of the simple social order. Individual behavior coincided with conventionalized sacred norms, engendered by a strong sense of group solidarity. Unpossessed of a written language, communication with outside communities was limited to face-to-face contacts. The possibilities of receiving outside influence being thus severely limited, society in the Jōmon period remained virtually autonomous in its mode of life, and changes that occurred did so at an exceedingly slow pace.

*Yayoi period.*——In the second and third centuries B.C., while Jōmon culture still prevailed in the Japanese islands, the Han dynasty came to power on the continent and extended its influence into most of the surrounding countries. During the second and first centuries B.C., metal-working techniques were transmitted to Japan along with rudimentary methods of farming, spinning and domestic crafts. Coming initially to northern Kyūshū, these techniques then spread into southern Kyūshū and later onto the main island of Honshū, precipitating remarkable changes in the configuration of the culture. Thus began the Yayoi cultural period, characterized by newer and simpler designs on pottery, and named after a site in Tōkyō where remains of such pottery were first recorded archaeologically.

The effect of this cultural influx was both sudden and revolutionary, being developed not from within Jōmon culture but derived from the expanding culture of the continent. While crude farming was not altogether lacking in late Jōmon culture, the emergence of Yayoi culture brought the technique of wet-field rice cultivation and made possible the reclamation of dry lands through irrigation. This meant an enormous decrease in the extent to which nature determined the conditions of economic life and the very location of community sites, now that men possessed new means of controlling and utilizing nature.

Owing to technical improvements in cultivation, rice came eventually to constitute the most important food product in the Yayoi period, though hunting and fishing tool discoveries at shell mound sites reveal the continued importance of these pursuits. Metal instruments were uncommon in the early days of the Yayoi period and, in addition to stone implements, hoes and plows made of wood have been found at Karako in Nara Prefecture[7] and at Toro in Shizuoka Prefecture,[8] together with wooden mortars and handmills for threshing. In the latter part of the Yayoi period iron sickles, hoes and plows were introduced. In time wet-land rice cultivation was diffused, and the villagers moved from the hillsides to leveler plains.

These agricultural developments, permitting prolonged residence and larger population concentrations, precipitated an expansion in the size of villages to some 500–600 houses, as found in the sites at Karako and at Kugahara in present-day Tōkyō.[9] Hillside residents retained the pit-dwellings, but in the plains there appeared houses constructed at ground-level, with the bare ground as floors, the precursors of farm houses of later eras. Some houses with elevated floors also appeared, forerunners of more aristocratic architecture as reflected in engravings on old *dōtaku* (copper bells). Here, again, one finds evidence of progress in domestic techniques.

Cooperative work patterns came more naturally with prolonged residence at fixed places, as did differentiation of social functions and the resultant stratification according to authority. An extraordinarily large pit, which seems to have been a meeting place, was found at the Karako site of early Yayoi days, and in the Toro site of later Yayoi times the paddy fields are in units of 400–600 *tsubo* (1 *tsubo*=36 sq.ft.) in a chessboard pattern. Irrigation ditches framed with wooden planks and piles (*azekuro*) requiring sizable and plenteous supplies of Japanese cedar (cryptomeria) also indicate more advanced levels of technique and more extensive cooperation in work patterns. These data lead to the conclusion that remarkable progress in work organization was made by the people of the Yayoi period, in contrast to the level of cooperative labors of the Jōmon period.

Lands reclaimed for cultivation in the Yayoi period were jointly owned by the villagers, no individual or family being allowed to own land privately. Each family engaged in farming was no longer simply a unit of consumption based on consanguinity, as in the Jōmon period, but became a unit of production and consumption. The local connection of unions of families in the villages and the coordination of their activities became inevitable in the allocation of lands, irrigation projects, and the manufacture of farm tools.

In the Toro site there are remains of warehouses constructed with elevated floors for storing harvested rice and twelve homesites of the ground-level type. A typical group was comprised of four or five houses, with a comparatively large one at the center. This appears to have been a hierarchically structured cluster of kinship dwellings, with the main family occupying the center place. The pattern is that of the clan society that emerged in the late Yayoi period as powerful families took advantage of improved methods of farming to accumulate private wealth. Groups of families included some not in kinship relations with the head family, though the latter governed land and labor by exercising its rule over the entire extended kinship group (*dōzoku*) as the core structure of the clan society.

Rice crops were influenced, of course, by natural phenomena such as seasons and climate. The people felt grateful when blessed by nature, and they were likewise awed by its dreadful power, believing piously in deities who controlled crops and land. There were believers, for instance, in Amaterasu-Ōmikami, a sun deity, and in Susano-no-mikoto who symbolized the blessings and awesomeness of nature. Another deity, Ubusunagami, who protected the community, became identified with ancestor worship. The head of the village, as priest, conveyed the will of a particular deity to the villagers and their wishes to the deity, thus bolstering the village head's authority over the people.

Villages were gradually differentiated in function as the cooperative system expanded and the social structure became more complicated. Groups of craftsmen were, in time, formed into local communities for the production of earthenware, stone implements, and metal utensils. In northern Kyūshū[10] and the Kinki[11] districts workshop sites have been found that exhibit remains of polished stone axes and knives clearly differing from the more homely artifacts of the Jōmon period. In a site at Sugu in Fukuoka Prefecture casting furnaces for bronzeware[12] have been found that contain wide halberds of copper. From the location of these sites of different types of production we can assume that there was a degree of interdependence among villages extending over a fairly wide area, with some important transportation point in a central location.

The introduction of agrarian culture from the continent, then, precipitated changes not only in the methods of procuring materials necessary to daily living and in the location and shape of villages, but also in the social organization of Japan itself. The accumulation of wealth that began in the Yayoi period gave impetus to the establishment of social classes and stratification according to status, a radical departure from the classless society of the previous Jōmon period.

Such changes are explicitly indicated in the changing patterns of graveyards. While it is not known what kind of cemetery was common in the central part of the main island (Kinai), the eastern region of Japan had communal graveyards. This seems to have been the common style of cemetery all over Japan, and in it there appeared no special graves for individuals or families. From the middle of the Yayoi period, however, the number of earthen burial urns in northern Kyūshū increased, and one copper sword was found in one out of ten such urns in the Sugu site in Kyūshū.[13] At a site in the city of Iizuka a group of urns was unearthed in the highest place of a community cemetery, set apart from other graves by large stones. This shows something of the differences between Jōmon and Yayoi organization, though the material underlying this inference is limited to the northern part of Kyūshū where the large influence of continental culture is first discerned. Hence, such social distinctions cannot be said to have been common to all areas throughout the Yayoi period.

Preparatory to contrasting the organizational differences between socio-economic life throughout the Jōmon and Yayoi periods and the urban life that developed in the succeeding Kofun era, we may summarize the socio-economic characteristics of the culture that began in the Jōmon period and extended into the Yayoi period in the following paragraphs.

In conjunction with progress made in the acquisition of staple materials there occurred changes in the methods of utilizing nature. The materials-gathering economy of Jōmon culture gave way to the agrarian economy of Yayoi villages. As the migratory life of the Jōmon period shifted to the more sedentary ways of the Yayoi period, village construction was promoted and the complexities of an expanded system of cooperative labor emerged. With the assimilation of continental modes of rice cultivation, the family function became clearly defined as a unit for production, in addition to its original consumptive function of the Jōmon era. The cooperation necessary to the farm life of the Yayoi settlements of families led to the constitution of a unified and extended kinship system further regulated by religious sanctions. This society was based upon a consistent value system articulating the sacred association among the families.

Advancing notably beyond Jōmon culture in technology and socio-economic differentiation, Yayoi culture remained basically self-sufficient and insular, as the village itself constituted a total society with almost all its needs being met within the territory controlled by the village.

With increasing social complexity, social stratification tended to become fixed, although it was limited to the appearance of men of authority within the cooperative system of the village structure. Persons possessed of culture or status differing in kind from the ordinary villagers had not yet appeared. It was a society of low productive skills and a low level of differentiation of socio-economic functions; it was a cooperative union characterized by relative self-sufficiency on a small scale wherein the positions of authority had not been solidified.

It was hardly possible in such a society for a city to evolve that would consist of a large population enjoying a variety of social roles and styles of living. Such an evolution depended upon an adequate farm surplus permitting an advanced differentiation of socio-economic functions, with a nucleus of integrative organs for controlling political, economic, military, and cultural activity over a vast region on the basis of solidified relations of superordination and subordination.

## 2. The Rise of the City as a Political Capital

Complex family structures had already appeared in the Yayoi period in answer to production demands, binding together those of blood relations, collateral relations, and even those not in blood relations, under a single head of an extended family. The contrast between small and large dwellings at the Yayoi period site of Toro and the status distinctions presumably connected with that contrast in dwelling sizes have already been mentioned. In the succeeding period, archaeologically designated as the Kofun period because of large sepulchral mounds built during the period, there was a noticeable and rapid increase in these distinctions.

Dwelling sites of the Kofun period are rarely discovered due to the increase in wood construction dwellings of the ground-level type during this period, as indicated, for instance, by *haniwaya* or clay images of houses dating from this period. A clay model found in Gunma Prefecture, indicates a main house of 3 *ken* by 2 *ken* ($6 \times 4$ yds.), flanked on both sides by annexes of like measurements covered with *ajiro* (wickerwork of split bamboo or wood), together with four warehouses and a shed. This reflects, it is thought, an extended family organization with the master's house in the center.[14] According to Wajima Seiichi's research into the Shimura site in Tōkyō, differences in the dwelling sizes there suggest the existence of a large household consisting of several pit-dwellings.[15]

Although individuals and families engaged in farming worked separate fields, the cooperation so necessary to a mode of life centered in agriculture meant that there was also, over the households, a cooperative organization for controlling the cooperative labors, namely, the village. The village, called *uji*, was a hierarchically structured union of extended kinship families, living on and working the same land area, sharing the same name and customs, worshipping the same deity, and often including those not in direct blood relations with them.[16] As this *uji*, the village, was not simply a cooperative organization for production but was united by religion as well, the status of the head of the village was further secured by his equally important role as priestly mediator, *uji-no-kami*, between the deity and the people, and to him was awarded the authority to collect all farm surplus. Under the supervision of the *uji-no-kami* lived and worked the many *ujibito*, or villagers.[17]

As a village became established, the notion of property ownership emerged with the clarification of the boundaries of its farmland, in the sense that the lands were regarded as belonging to the *uji-no-kami*, the priest-ruler of the village. In time his political and military power grew as more primitive ritualistic controls diminished, and differences in the relative power among villages appeared.[18] The ruler's secular powers were reinforced by the production of arms, such as swords, helmets, and shields; his authority was promoted by technical advances in farming. There gradually emerged a pattern of weaker villages held in subordination by the more powerful ones.

In such a pattern the more powerful rulers formed, through their control over lesser rulers, a union of villages known as *ōuji* (i. e., greater *uji*), while the subordinate villages were known as *be*.[19] Existing in half-slave conditions, the *be* villagers were engaged in farming, handicrafts, and other labors for the sake of the superordinate rulers and their people. Displaying exceptional skills in crafts production, the *be* villagers took on specialized functions in the differentiation of work that developed later.

As population increases in the villages strained their low productive capacities, political controls were weakened and some split off from their original village groups, moving elsewhere. In some cases such as the Soga, Kose, and Katsuragi houses descended from the extended family of Takenouchi-no-Sukune, each unit that split and moved became independent. The majority of cases were like the sub-groups of the Inbe clan, made up of the descendants of Futodama-no-mikoto. This clan became the ancestral house, while in Kii (Wakayama Prefecture), Izumo (Shimane Prefecture), Awa (Tokushima Prefecture), Awa (Chiba Prefecture), Sanuki (Kagawa Prefecture) and elsewhere, subsidiary or branch families subordinate to the ancestral houses were formed.[20]

One by one the villages were combined into associations of villages through the efforts of the more powerful rulers, whose patron deities were made to comprehend the local deities of subordinate villages, producing a kind of primitive village state. Extending over admittedly small areas, there were many such village states.

A significant distinction between the distribution of swords and halberds in northern Kyūshū as over against bells found in the Kinki district indicates that these primitive states did not constitute a single, uniform cultural region. At any rate, with the advent of the Iron Age rapid cultural progress was made in the Kinki district, where a powerful state centering in the Yamato court emerged, unifying the village unions all over Japan politically, militarily, and economically. People belonging to the various villages became also, though indirectly, constituents of the state, working partly to fulfill its functions, inasmuch as the governance of a local ruler over his own people obligated him to pay tribute and to offer men for *corvée* labor and military service to the state.

By reflecting upon the extensive labor and material resources required for the construction of gigantic burial mounds such as the Takatsuka mound—which had not existed prior to the emergence of this state—we can see how powerful were the rulers of the unified state under the Yamato court. The extent of the political power of those buried in the great tombs can be judged from the location of the imposing structures, overlooking the residential areas of great masses of people, while their important religious roles in the state can be inferred from the items buried with them, such as mirrors, stone wheels, bracelets of jasper and spiral shells, and mattock-shaped stones. These were items, not of normal daily use, but those treasured for their magical significance.[21]

By the latter half of the 3rd century A.D., the unification achieved in the era of the Emperor Sujin, called the "Emperor who opened and ruled the country," extended from Kyūshū in the west through Shikoku island and across the Kantō plain of Honshū island northward, including almost all of present-day Japan, except Hokkaidō.

The expanding power and prosperity of the Yamato court from the latter half of the 4th century A.D. through the 5th century are indicated in the gigantic burial mounds of the Emperors Ōjin and Nintoku. According to Saitō Tadashi, there were, counting only the large ones, 1,087 mounds of the *zenpo-koen* (square in front, round in back) type constructed by powerful nobility in imitation of the emperors. The wide distribution of these sepulchral mounds witnesses to the penetration of Yamato power throughout the whole of Japan.

At his capital in the Yamato region the Emperor Ōjin constructed a palace surrounded by moats and ponds that involved considerable civil engineering skill, and the remains uncovered there remind us that here the oldest city in our country was built. Under the reigns of Emperors Ōjin and Nintoku the Japanese sphere of influence was extended to the southern tip of the Korean peninsula, for which the port of Naniwa (in present-day Ōsaka) was developed to control traffic on both land and sea. These emperors erected forts there, along with road and moat systems. But imperial headquarters were returned to the Yamato region in the Nara basin under the next emperor as the center of high culture had remained there in its original stronghold.

Official contacts with the mainland of China were fostered during this era. Through these channels came men schooled in the culture of the continent, many of them becoming "naturalized citizens" (*kikajin*) of Japan. Technically skilled men among these immigrants were employed by the Yamato court in projects of sericulture, spinning, architecture, and pottery, as well as land reclamation and riparian works. Scholars trained in Chinese thought and literature were used in matters relating to foreign affairs and the compilation of court records. The elements of the more advanced continental civilization as introduced by the naturalized citizens were assimilated to some extent, the literary skills by members of the ruling class, and the technical skills by members of the lower classes, introducing new complexities into the socio-cultural configuration of the native culture.

As the Yamato court strengthened its political hold over the many *uji* villages, the central administration expanded in scale, necessitating some differentiation of political, military, and religious functions. Accordingly, central and provincial offices were apportioned out to the *uji-no-kami*, the heads of the village states. Key posts in the central administration went to those with surnames of Omi and Muraji, such as Ōtomo-no-muraji, Mononobe-no-muraji, Heguri-no-omi, Kose-no-omi, and Soga-no-omi, the Omi group being descendants of the aforementioned house of Takenouchi-no-sukune.

Provincial positions went to those with surnames of Kuni-no-miyatsuko, Agatanushi, and Inagi; their primary responsibilities were providing *corvée* labor and tribute for the imperial court. The common people were not direct subjects of the state, but were bound to it through their leaders, the *uji-no-kami*. The kinship concept deriving from the relation of the *uji-no-kami* to his people, the *ujibito*, was extended to the relation of the imperial family and the local clans, binding them together in the idea that the state consisted of one large, unified family.

Cultural development did not advance concomitantly with the progress of political unification. Some areas remained at the level of Jōmon culture, although most of the provinces enjoyed the more advanced agricultural economy of Yayoi culture. In consequence of the employment of iron implements, however, the method of cutting rice near the roots developed, oxen and horses were utilized, and productivity steadily climbed. Agriculture was dominated by the more powerful rulers, who distributed farm tools to weaker clans, requiring commensurate services of them. The Yamato authority promoted irrigation projects and, in turn, imperial needs were met on an apportionment basis. Some division of labor was achieved, and a fairly high level of proficiency in special crafts was attained. Nonetheless, the villages remained largely self-sufficient, possessing neither the population nor the productive surplus to permit the setting apart of specialists solely for crafts production.

Both farm production gains due to technological progress and an expanding range of village contacts enhanced by unification served to stimulate bartering, and market places appeared at convenient locations. "Cities are made by merchants," the saying goes; and, needless to say, the market played its part in the development of the Japanese city.

Certain scholars have advanced theories regarding the origin of the market in Japan, notably Yokoi Tokifuyu, Nishimura Shinji, Honjo Eijiro, and Kuromasa Iwao. Here it is sufficient to note that limited bartering occurred on the occasion of religious festivals for the tutelary deities of various localities, or at other times of gathering at the political centers. In any case, the essential condition for a market was a suitable location at a traffic junction relatively near to the places of production and consumption.

In time a number of fixed market places developed. According to the *Nihon Shoki* (the oldest extant record of Japan), market places were set up at the following places during the reigns indicated:

| *Market name* | *Location* | *Imperial reign* | *Dates* |
|---|---|---|---|
| Karu-ichi | Kawachi | Ōjin | d. A.D. 310 |
| Ega-ichi | Kawachi | Yūryaku | 456–479 |
| Tsubaki-ichi | Yamato | Buretsu | 498–506 |
| Atokuwa-ichi | 〃 | Bitatsu | 572–585 |
| Asuka-ichi | 〃 | 〃 | 〃 |
| Iwayo-ichi | 〃 | 〃 | 〃 |
| Miwa-ichi | 〃 | 〃 | 〃 |
| Tatsuta-ichi | 〃 | 〃 | 〃 |

Given the basic orientation to self-sufficiency in agriculture, however, no surplus in staples was available for exchange. Barter centered in luxuries, such as sweet rice wine and bear hides collected by the clan heads as tribute from provincial subordinates and then put up by the same clan heads for exchange at outdoor markets. There was insufficient basis, either in the volume of exchange or in population concentration, to support professional merchants or for the market to function as a primary factor in the formation of cities.[22]

In the early stage of unification Japan possessed no city with a large population or complex organization. The imperial residence was called *miya*, meaning the center of political integration of the state or province; and the term *miyadokoro*, signifying the residential site of the ruler, was later converted into *miyako*, meaning capital city.

Politically the state of Yamato was a union of lesser village states. The imperial seat had no complex organization or bureaucracy requiring a heavy concentration of people in its immediate vicinity. The chief retainers to the court resided in their own villages to govern their people as the *uji-no-kami*, visiting the court only to administer affairs of state. Residences of these leading families were as follows:[23]

| *Family* | *Location* |
|---|---|
| Ōtomo | Tsukisaka, Yamato |
| Mononobe | Shibukawa, Hatsuse, Ishigami |
| Inbe | Inbe |
| Soga | Katsuragi, Soga, Ishikawa, Amasu, Shima |
| Nakaomi | Fujiwara |

In this basically agricultural society there were no essential differences between the styles of life in the political centers and in the farm villages. The residence of the Emperor Yūryaku, the *Asakura-no-miya* at Hatsuse (in Nara), constructed with the aid of the naturalized citizens from the continent was, it is true, a lofty structure in its day. Nevertheless, traditional features remained intact, such as the *katsuogi* (decorative rods on the ridge pole of the roof), pillars sunk directly into the earth, warehouses for food and weapons, a gatehouse, thatched-roof of miscanthus, and a surrounding hedge.[24] In short, while there were differences in degree, there were none in kind between the imperial residence and those of the provincial nobility.

Being relatively isolated from the Asian mainland and, by this historical stage, racially homogeneous, invasion dangers were rare and, hence, defense needs low, for which natural materials sufficed during the earlier half of the Kofun period. Later on, internal contentions prompted the construction of earthen barriers, stone walls, and moats.[25]

Economic needs of the people for clothes, household utensils and furniture were met by themselves. All surplus was absorbed by the nobility, who themselves performed the bartering functions, for which luxury items were in highest demand. Thus, a merchant class failed to emerge and no concentration of population occurred by reason of market developments.

The imperial seat, *miyako*, was merely the center of the association of clans and was often transferred for various reasons. It was not yet the site for concentrating large-scale integrating organs to supervise the overall political, military, economic, and religious life of the entire country. Therefore, it required no great concentration of population.

With reference to capital transfers, it may be instructive to introduce some of the explanations suggested by Kida Teikichi. In accordance with the then common practice either of matrilocal residence or of separately maintained residences for husband and wife, the emperor did not always share the same residence with the empress. Children of the empress became members of the maternal house, and it was customary for a prince to accede to the throne at the palace of the empress, though some actually lived at the emperor's palace. From this conflux of customs may have arisen reasons for transfer of the capital, in that residence prior to accession to the throne need not have remained the same after accession. Another possible reason may have derived from the notion that associated death with contamination, hence requiring a fresh palace for a new emperor; this would have resulted, however, more often in reconstruction of the palace itself than in transfer of the capital.

Greater significance attaches, rather, to other details noted by Kida. In the first place, the foundation pillars were sunk directly into raw earth, and the wood framing was bound by straw ropes, requiring replacement about every twenty years. At those times, then, the palace, *miya*, was transferred if not the capital city, *miyako*.

In the second place, there were political factors, such as campaigns against "outsiders" from Kumaso in Kyūshū and the Ezo power in northern Honshū (migrated later to Hokkaidō), to say nothing of defense measures against a feared invasion from the Three Kingdoms of Korea: Silla, Paekche, and Koguryō. A location close to defense efforts and covenient to internal communication routes was necessary, and the capital was moved often, sometimes as much as two or three times in the same generation.[26]

Though referred to as "moving the capital," the fact is that no great distances were involved but, rather, short-distance shifts within the central Yamato region at the easternmost end of the Inland Sea (Seto-nai-kai), which was the focal center for all political and cultural activity among the top stratum of the ruling class. Inasmuch as the whole populace did not move each time a transfer was made, what is traditionally termed "moving the capital" is better understood as "relocating the imperial residence."

In the era of the Empress Suiko, when Shōtoku Taishi was Prince Regent, both domestic and foreign affairs received a great stimulus from opening up direct diplomatic channels with the continent and the increase in the number of immigrants bringing its culture, on the one hand, and from the intensification of cultural and political activity in the capital and in provincial centers, on the other hand, in accordance with the enforced unification of all Japan. Moreover, the fixation of the imperial palace site in the Asuka district (southern part of Nara basin) served as a further impetus to cultural development.

Immigrants from the continent settled in the Asuka district, making it the central locus for the introduction of Chinese-style culture. By the thirty-second year of the Empress Suiko's reign, the number of Buddhist temples had reached forty-six, with 1,385 monks and nuns. Near the Toyoura palace in Oharita were constructed the five major Asuka temples—Arahaka, Kawara, Toyoura, Sakata, and Omiya—in addition to others. The ruling elite in the area became the key figures in the attempt to incorporate into the pattern of their daily lives the political and economic systems, the thought and religion, the fine arts and crafts, and the architectural styles and skills of continental culture. They were the *avant garde* of their time and Yamato district was the new frontier of cultural progress.

One example of architectural achievement was the Itabuta palace of the Emperor Kōgyoku (642–645), said to have been erected on a construction schedule of only four months, and the first structure in Japan to have a roof of wood shingles. Built by laborers assembled from provinces as far east as Totomi (present Aichi Pref.) and Aki in the west (present Hiroshima Pref.), it boasted twelve gates, each guarded by a contingent of soldiers—a large-scale project quite impressive in its day.[27]

At the center of the political, military, and religious unification achieved throughout the country at this stage, then, stood a capital region of increased magnitude. While the continued self-sufficiency of the villages rendered this stage of national integration incomplete, the villages had the shell of their insularity broken as they became parts of an increasingly integrated whole. In comparison with earlier periods of primitive society, the total society assumed greater complexity in the Kofun period and began to be structured on a larger scale.

The process of unification inevitably demanded that agencies, differentiated by functions, be established and administered from the capital. The noble families taking up leadership roles in these integrative activities, and those dependent upon and subordinate to them—people of differing status and customs—gradually concentrated in the capital district.

Thus, the capital was transformed. Though still shaped by the clan system, life in the capital no longer had its former flavor of an agricultural society with its small-scale system of intimate face-to-face relationships. These features gave way to larger structures of formalized bureaucratic relationships. While the ordinary people's lives advanced little beyond the primitive conditions of earlier days of the pit-dwellings, the nobility now occupied new continental style homes with elevated floors, dressed stylishly in the new continental modes, and surrounded themselves with the splendid products of the fine arts and crafts of Chinese origin. The distinction between rural and urban ways of life was greatly intensified.

# Chapter II | THE CITY IN ANTIQUITY (A.D. 645–1180)

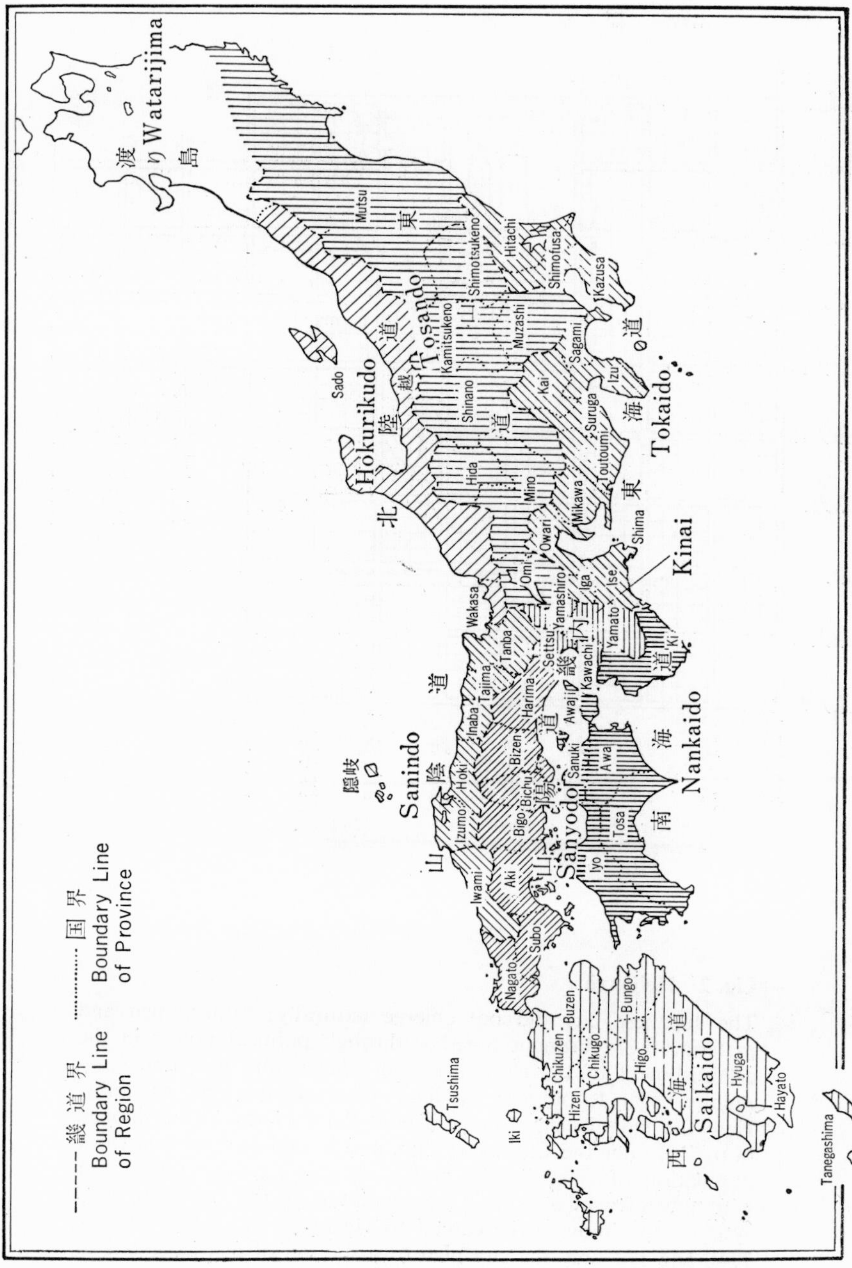


**Fig. 1 Map of Japan during the Ritsuryō Period**
(adapted from *Nihon Rekishi Chizu*)

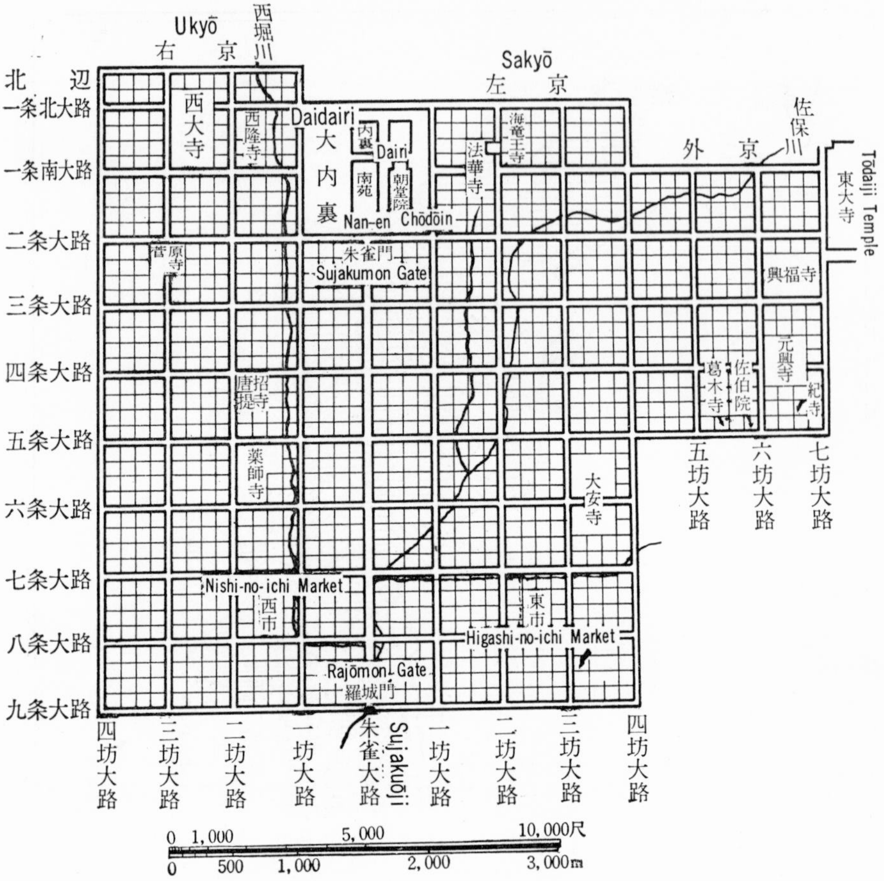


**Fig. 2 Heijōkyō**

The Japanese city did not emerge naturally; rather, men and materials were brought together through political power in the establishment of the *ritsuryō* system long before the rural community began to outgrow the limits of a self-sustaining economy. Here the magnificent *ritsuryō* capital (later Nara) was fashioned (A.D. 710) after the Chinese system, and is said to have boasted a population of 200,000. The pattern of this city was taken over with only a few alterations in the attempt to reconstruct the *ritsuryō* system when moving the capital to Heiankyō (later Kyōto) (A.D. 794), and not only the city plan (distribution of districts), but in many instances the same names were used.

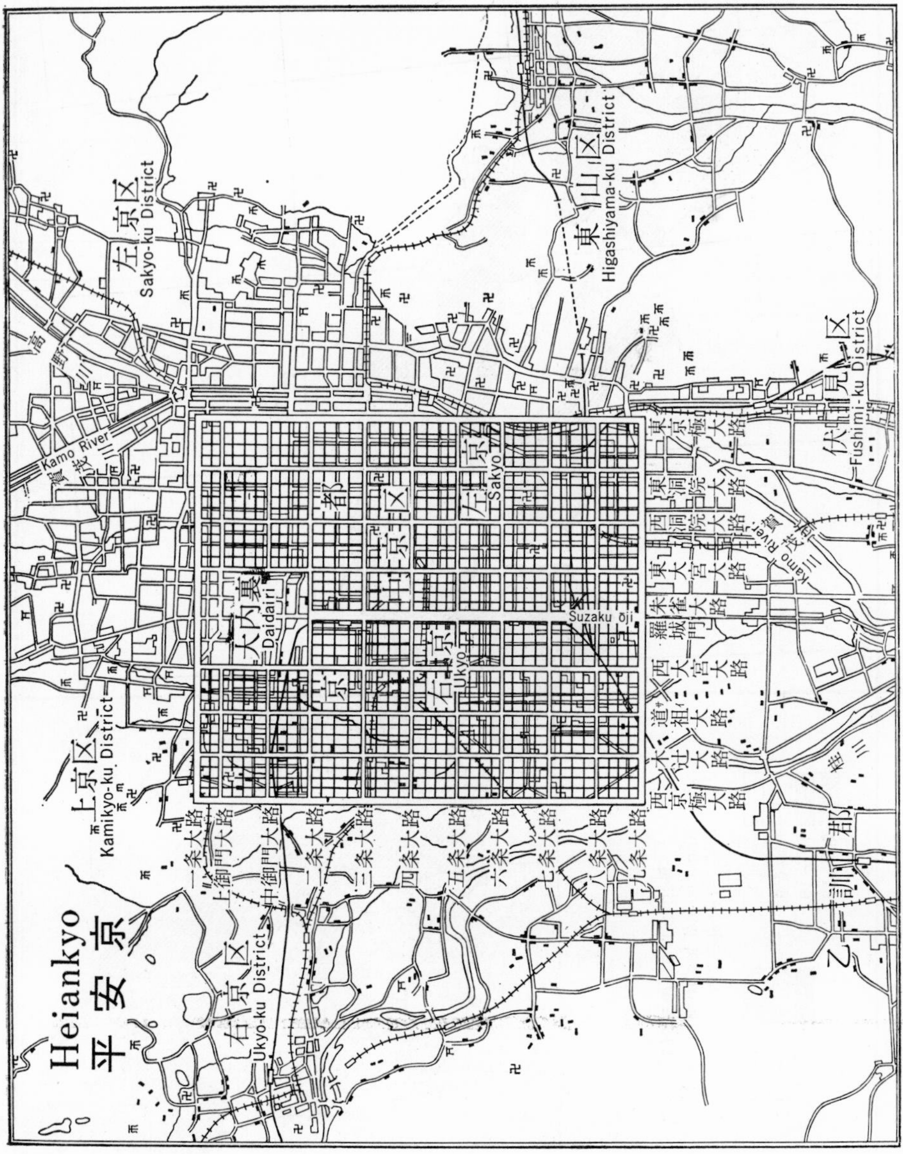


**Fig. 3 Plan of Heiankyō Superimposed on Map of Present-day Kyōto**
(drawn by Toshio Fukuyama)

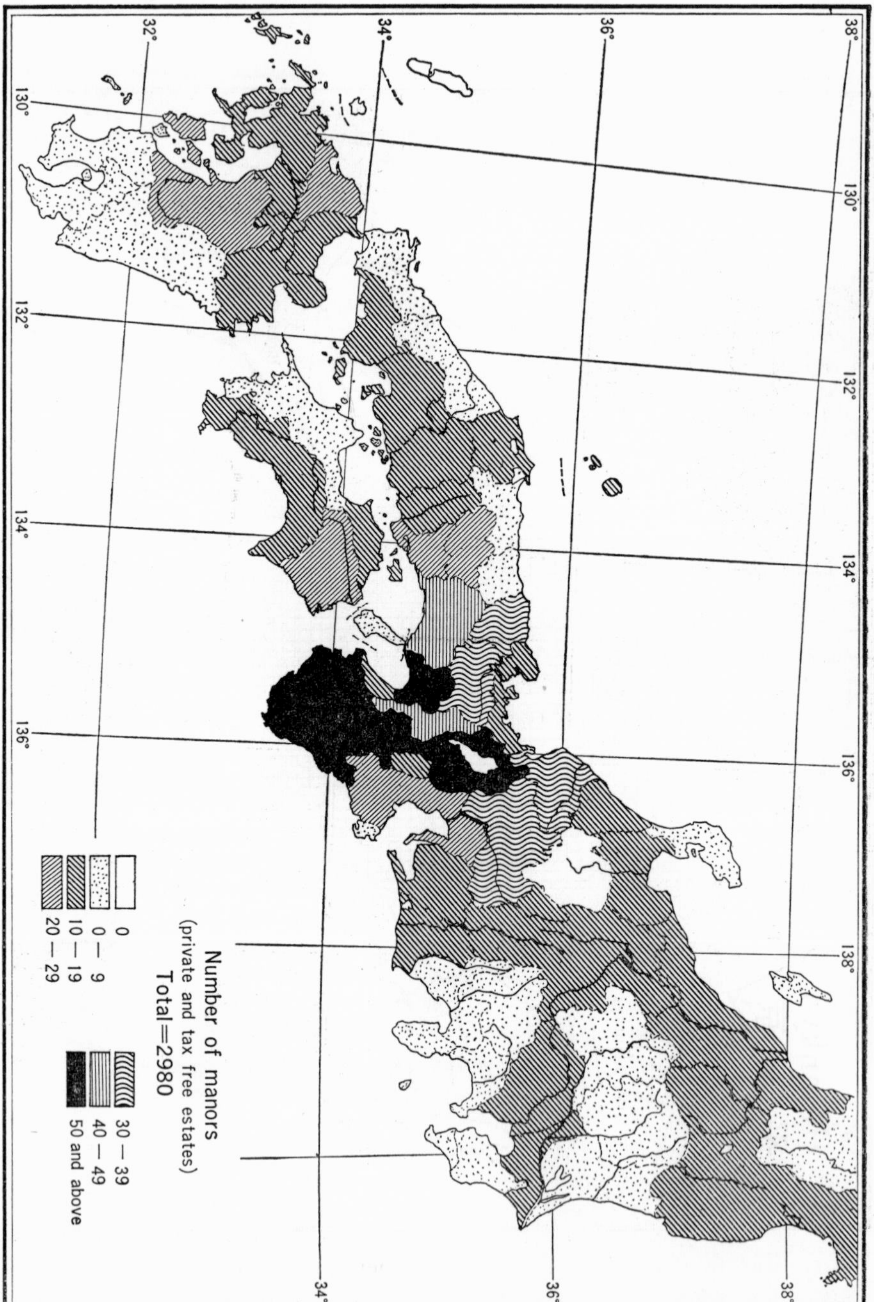


**Fig. 4 Distribution of Manors in Antiquity** (drawn by Masao Shimizu)

# 1. The Total Social System of the Nation as the Foundation of the Ancient City

Primitive society in Japan had more or less the character of a folk society as defined by Robert Redfield. Such a society is small, isolated, nonliterate, and homogeneous, with a strong sense of group solidarity. The ways of living are conventionalized into that coherent system which we call culture. Behavior is traditional, spontaneous, uncritical and personal; there is no legislation or habit of experiment and reflection for intellectual ends. Kinship, its relationships and institutions, are the type categories of experience and the familial group is the unit of action. The sacred prevails over the secular; the economy is one of status rather than market. These and related characterizations may be restated in terms of "folk mentality." Redfield's typology is superior as a general concept of folk society for research into the process of change in the structures of civilization and community. However, inasmuch as a low level of differentiation of socio-economic functions is basically important and closely related to the above-mentioned characteristics, this factor should be included in his typology.

Various societies at a certain level of development, while preserving environmental and cultural traits, undergo ecological adaptation to the regional environment. As technological advances resulting from diffusion and invention yield surplus produce, the population increases and differentiations of simple, insular socio-economic functions occur in the self-supporting system. A process emerges in which an advanced hierarchical power system is organized over a wide regional area, generally involving competition and conflict. In this process, the city is born as the locus of the concentration of organs which perform the functions of the total integrative system in the geographical and cultural center of the region. To the extent that an integrating system organized on the basis of power concentrated through the process outlined above is enlarged in scale, the hierarchical order is intensified.

The initial processes of differentiation, while seen to some extent in the Jōmon and Yayoi periods, were accelerated in the Kofun period by extensive utilization of the technological innovations of metal-working and rice cultivation imported from mainland China. Increased surpluses were used by the village rulers to strengthen and firmly fix their superordinate status relations with respect to the villagers. In similar fashion, larger villages brought smaller ones into subordination, consolidating them into small village states. These village states were unified into a single state by the Yamato court, which introduced from contemporary China an extensive, complicated social system for integration and control of the whole country. This total social system is known as *ritsuryō-seido*, which refers literally to the administrative and penal code that undergirded the entire system.

In this process of change in social organization there developed certain larger integrative organs in the geographical center of the total unified integrated area, marking the first stage in the emergence of the capital city as a political center. There did not appear at this stage, however, a really big city with a large population concentration and large-scale integrative organs. The level of socio-economic differentiation was insufficient and agricultural surplus inadequate to support an urban mode of life for a large non-agricultural population. Urban development at this stage coincided more singularly with the role of the city as the national integrating center and the population expanded only to the level required by the political, military, and religious organs of the new administrative system, though these were of heretofore unprecedented size. The overall development was an expression of the expansion of Yamato power throughout the entire land, and was accelerated by the necessities of controlling foreign affairs and of doing away with private ownership of lands and peoples by the village state heads, bringing them under the strict controls of the central government It was centralization of political power that constituted the foundation of the new state and likewise freed the people from the insularity of controls by unions of the *uji* clans.

The *ritsuryō* administrative system brought large amounts of taxes and *corvée* labor from the farming villages into the city to meet the demands of the ruling class and the integrative organs. On the basis of this concentration of goods and labor for the purposes of the ever-enlarging organs of state, the capital cities, national and provincial, grew in scale and magnificence along lines imitative of continental patterns in ecological structure, modes of living, and administrative system. It was a revolutionary change from small, self-sufficient and insular patterns of life of the primitive villages. The new modes were visible also in the provincial capitals, *kokufu*, established throughout the country to strengthen the controlling power of the central government, and connected with the central area by newly-developed communications routes.

After original unification was achieved, the Yamato state continued to expand its power over other clan groupings, extending its influence even to the southern tip of the Korean peninsula. The *uji*-oriented village states, for their part, also grew in strength, struggled with each other, and sometimes even opposed the central Yamato power. The Yamato position was based on a balance of power among the provincial states. By the turn of the 7th century the loss of its foothold in Korea seriously weakened the Yamato state's position at home, necessitating stronger steps both to preserve unification and to retain its own centrality. These pressures led to the epoch-making plans for reforming internal organization and regulating foreign affairs, namely, the overall adoption of the administrative system of centralized bureaucratic controls of the T'ang dynasty (A.D. 618–907), with which the Yamato state had been in frequent contact since the loss of its Korean territory. This plan was initiated with the announcement by imperial edict in 646 of the Taika Reforms.

The basic thrust of the reform edict was to deny independence to the old clan states, bringing all lands and peoples under the central authority. Thenceforth, all lands were to be distributed according to T'ang inspired principles of equity, for which commensurate taxes and labor services would be due the central government.

The highest organ of the central government, under the emperor, was a Grand Council of State (*Dajōkan*), which included a Grand Minister of State (*Dajō Daijin*), Ministers of the Left (*Sadaijin*) and Right (*Udaijin*), and other high officials. *Dajōkan* officials supervised eight ministries, *sho*, responsible for ceremonials, civic affairs, public works, defense, justice, and finance, as in the T'ang model, as well as a central bureaucratic agency and a special ministry of the Imperial Household. In addition to the Imperial Household agency, an Office of (Shinto) Deities (*Jingikan*) was instituted on the level of the Grand Council of State, retaining the traditional politico-religious duality rooted in *uji* society.

There were eight administrative divisions, namely, the central capital region called Kinai (later Kinki), and seven regions described by the routes (*dō*) constructed to reach them from the capital. These seven regions, or circuits, were called:

Tōkaidō, or "East Sea Route" along the Pacific coast from the capital district of Kinai to, and including most of, the Kantō plain;

Tōsandō, or "East Mountain Route" including provinces in the mountain area between the Pacific Ocean and the Japan Sea east of the Kinai district;

Hokurikudō, or "Northland Route" including provinces on the Japan Sea coast northeast of Kinai;

Sanyōdō, or "Sunny Slopes Route" including provinces along the Pacific coast west of Kinai;

Sanindō, or "Shady Slopes Route" including provinces on the Japan Sea side of the western end of the main island, opposite the Sanyōdō region;

Nankaidō, or "Southern Sea Route" of provinces circled by the route along the Kii peninsula due south of Kinai and including also four provinces on Shikoku ("four states") island; and finally,

Saikaidō, or "West Sea Route" including provinces on present-day Kyūshū ("nine states") island.

Kinai district itself embraced the Yamato, Yamashiro, Settsu, Kawachi, and Izumi provinces, and had the largest population concentration of the time for economic and political support of the Yamato authority. These administrative regions were divided into more than sixty provincial states, *kuni*, which were further divided into districts and townships called *gun* and *ri* respectively. Each administrative unit had its designated head, *kokushi* over the *kuni*, and *gunshi* and *richō* over the *gun* and *ri* respectively. In the document *Engishiki* (compiled in 927), which describes conditions up to the beginning of the Heian era, the many states are grouped together under four area names: Kinai, Kingoku, Chūgoku, and Engoku (for central, neighboring, intermediate, and distant states). Kingoku extended from Tōtomi to Harima; Chūgoku from Izu, Shinano, and Etchū in the east to Izumo, Bitchū, Sanuki, and Awa in the west; all other provinces belonged to the Engoku group. This classification indicates the extent of the controlling power exercised by the Yamato central government.

In Saikaidō the special regional capital of Dazaifu (see p.41) was established over all the provinces in that region, and it served as an advance base for political, military, and cultural contacts with the continent. Central government controls reached as far as Hyuga (present-day Miyazaki) on this island, though Ōsumi and Kagoshima on the southern end of the island remained outside its administrative range until the second year of the Taihō era (702). Iwaki and Iwase in the northeast sector of the main island were the eastern boundaries of the Yamato state; the Japan Sea coastline, of course, was the western frontier, where fences were built to prevent illegal entry into the country. Official guards were appointed and stationed in the Settsu province, gateway to the capital district, and at Sakyō and Ukyō inside the capital city to secure the city's position within the overall system of controls.

The transformation of the state through the Taika Reforms brought changes in ideas as well as in social organization. Administratively, religion and politics were separated, although the emperor was empowered to supervise both realms. The emperor was regarded as the high priest of the *ujigami* of the Yamato clan, and this deity came to be venerated as the progenitor of the many *ujigami* of local clans all over Japan, an arrangement affording a nation-binding religious sanction that enabled people in the various localities to retain their own traditional *ujigami* unaltered.

Buddhism was introduced from the continent as the medium for spiritual promotion of the new order in society, and its universal qualities provided the state with a new context of integration free of traditional localism. Finally, Confucian morality—emphasizng filial piety, respect for elders, male superiority with reference to women in general and wives in particular—was also appropriated as a means of entrenching further the traditional family system as the foundation of the social order.

The most important innovations of the Taika Reforms, with respect to strengthening the emperor's hold on the concentration of power, were the systems of land distribution and social status (the laws of *kōchi-kōmin* and *handen-shūju* respectively) which undergirded the nation's finances and bureaucracy. The T'ang-developed formula of land reform stipulated that "equal fields" (*kōchi-kōmin*) were to be distributed on a basis of 2 *tan* (1 *tan*=0.245 acre) per man, 1.33 *tan* per women, and 0.67 *tan* per slave, after reaching age six. For these grants in land, designated taxes in agricultural and textile produce (*so*, *yō*, and *chō*) and *corvée* services were to be paid to the government. *So* taxes were levied on government-distributed lands, claiming about 3% of the crops; *yō* taxes were levied by the head on adults, and were collected in local products such as silk and cotton threads and fabrics, dyestuffs, and oil, etc.; *chō* taxes were also levied by the head on adults, payable in linens. While these measures were taken to release people and lands from local *uji* ownership and while individuals were counted as discrete units for tax calculation purposes, the extended family group (*ko*) was expected to engage in farming as a collective unit. The familial units were responsible for the actual cultivation of lands allocated on an individual-unit basis.

In principle the *ritsuryō* system rejected the old *uji* clan system, and formal provision was made for the appointment of any qualified person to bureaucratic posts regardless of family standing. In actual practice, though, the traditionally ascribed family status patterns proved more powerful than reform policies, as it was the established noble families that had put the emperor on the throne and who actually ruled over lands and peoples. The imperial family and those with court rankings of third class or above were granted estates (*shokuhō*), and fifth-rank families and above received lands and stipends. Nomination to official posts gave these families further aristocratic privileges of additional lands, stipends, and services.

The *gunshi*, heads of provincial subdivisions, were selected from among the former *uji-no-kami*, so that these clan heads continued to consititute the ruling class and occupied the important posts in central and provincial administration, even after losing their former independence. Under this ruling stratum there were two main status groups, the ordinary peasants (*ryōmin*, or "good people") and servants and slaves (*senmin*, or "lowborn"). The *ryōmin* class comprised the majority of former members of *uji* and *be* villages, who now worked the government-distributed lands and paid the *so*, *yō* and *chō* taxes. Legally they were eligible for bureaucratic appointment, but the burden of heavy taxes left them little or no surplus wealth or energies, and they remained fixed in their traditional status. The lowest sub-group in the *ryōmin* class, the *zōshiki*, were not freed by the Taika Reforms; they continued in their role of producing goods required by the imperial court.

The *senmin* consisted of five classes, *ryōko*, *kanko*, *yahahito*, *kunuhi*, and *shinuhi*. The upper three groups were permitted families, though the lower two were slaves and were regarded as the private property of temples and high-ranking families. They were used in cultivation of their owners' lands and the manufacture of high-quality handicrafts demanded by their masters.

Thus, the Taika Reforms resulted in a drastic reorganization of the political order designed to strengthen centralized control over the state, by means of a legally-structured bureaucratic system manifesting, at all levels, the singular and supreme authority of the emperor. Compromise with the old heads of powerful clans, however, was inevitable in appointments to high office and administration was heavily influenced by traditional ideas and customs. The common people, far from experiencing improvement in their livelihood, found that the heavy tax burdens left them more miserable than before.

The Reforms did precipitate the emergence of a much larger capital, a greatly expanded city as the location of large-scale integrating organs for political, military, and religious functions. It was, hence, the locus of a large concentration of members of an expanded ruling class and their subordinates. The influx of continental culture effected great changes not only in administrative patterns, but in stimulating the growth of urban community structures and modes of living. Nevertheless, the majority of the populace remained, as always, peasants engaged in farming under traditional socio-economic conditions and cultural patterns. This very traditionalism in their lives, and especially in the way they were controlled, proved crucial to the formation of the city, as they constituted the broad base of financial and human resources of the state, enabling the ruling group to develop and sustain urban ways of living while operating the integrative organs in the city.

The Taika plan for partitioning land, *jōrisei*, allocated fields to commoners (*ryōmin*) according to standard units laid off in checkerboard fashion. Known as *kubunden*, these allotted fields carried also the tax obligations mentioned earlier. Evidence of these land divisions observable even today indicate that this system was applied all over Japan in the implementation of the Taika Reforms, excluding mountainous regions. It also suggests the degree of power available then for enforcing such a system on a nationwide basis.

The operational unit in farming after the Taika Reforms was not the village but *gōko*, a union of families including their dependents and slaves, in which the numbers of persons varied from as few as a dozen to more than a hundred. Although living quarters, daily necessities such as food and clothing, and marital arrangements varied for separate families (*bōko*) within the union, the head of the *gōko* controlled all lands belonging to the larger unit. He was also responsible for paying the *so*, *yō*, and *chō* taxes levied against all the lands of those families unified in the extended family group. The Taika reformers were able to disregard the power of the village as a unit in land distribution due to the fact that the custom of communal ownership of land by the village had already weakened, as separate and specific ownership by families had gradually become accepted practice. A strong sense of community remained, however, nurtured by such customs as cooperative planting of rice and joint management of communal grass crops and irrigation facilities.

As agriculture constituted the sole financial basis of the *ritsuryō* government, the latter utilized its own labor and financial resources in sponsoring irrigation and land reclamation projects to acquire new arable lands needed to overcome shortages due to an ever-increasing population. Increased productivity on available lands was achieved, moreover, through the importation of advanced agricultural techniques from the continent, such as the introduction of products other than rice, distribution of more efficient iron tools, new methods of rice planting and harvesting, and the diffusion of sericulture, animal husbandry (cattle) and methods of processing marine products.

All surplus from the new productivity, though, was absorbed by taxes due the central government and the common people were left poor as ever, trapped within the limits of the older self-sustaining economy. For themselves they managed to weave cloth from jute and other fibers, and subsisted on natural rice and miscellaneous grains, supplemented by wild vegetables, game and fish. Houses of about 10 *tsubo* (39.5 sq. yds.) with wooden floors and grass roofs replaced the former pit-dwellings, though the latter still sufficed in remote areas. Silk for clothing, thick grass mats for flooring, and paper for sliding doors and windows (so common to later periods and so typically "Japanese") were limited as yet to the homes of the nobility, commoners possessing at best thin straw pads for use on wooden-plank floors.

With no surplus available, a free exchange of goods naturally failed to develop. In hard times even the precious iron tools might be surrendered in lieu of tax payments, though returned in part by the government. In such times, members of the family unions shared with those who could not provide for themselves. The union of families was the unit of a kind of self-sustaining economy. Though the market, *ichi*, existed from ancient times as a place for bartering where goods offered as taxes were exchanged (the medium being rice and cloth), this was controlled by government officials in both the central district and the provinces, and commoners could hardly afford to buy anything for themselves.

## 2. Description of the Capital City of Heijōkyō (later Nara), the Regional Capital of Dazaifu, and Provincial Capitals, *Kokufu*

Most of the populace in Japan were engaged in supplying their own needs in food, clothing, housing and utensils through their own labor, and society remained largely undifferentiated in economic and social functions. Given this localized structure of relative self-sufficiency and insularity, it is hardly to be expected that the city should develop as a center of commerce and industry, although there was some exchange of goods such as cooking pots and pans, farm tools and other ironware among local provinces where natural resources differed.

Following establishment of the *ritsuryō* system for achieving political unification along Chinese lines, the central administrative organs inevitably increased in size and complexity. The orientation of the former heads of powerful clans shifted to operation of the central organs of state, for which they were directly responsible to the emperor. They found it necessary to have stable and permanent headquarters in the capital city, as effective administration involved an hitherto unprecedented volume of contacts to be made both abroad and with the local provinces. Responding to these urgent demands, the city as political center of the state swelled to gigantic proportions, supported, of course, by the heavy taxes levied on the peasant population.

Prior to this evolution of a major city, the imperial residence had long been in the Asuka district, drawing nobility, officials, temples and shrines into its environs and forming a kind of city. After imperial controls were extended over western Japan, including Kyūshū, however, a new and larger capital was envisaged that would be both suitable for administration through a larger organizational framework and free from the age-old controls of the former provincial clans in the narrow confines of the Asuka district. In 645 the Emperor Kōtoku constructed the Nagara-no-toyosaki-no-miya Palace at Naniwa, an important control point for land and sea traffic situated along the Yamatogawa and Yodogawa rivers and at the junction of main roads connecting the Yamato and Yamashiro basins. Naniwa also served as the main port for dispatching the important diplomatic and trade missions to the T'ang court on the continent.

The ancient city of Naniwa was laid out according to the *jōbō*, i.e., checkerboard design, of the Chinese capital of Chang'an under the supervision of a man named Aratai-no-Hirabu. In addition to the buildings for the top administrative organ, the *Dajōkan*, there were also constructed offices for the eight major ministries, *shō*, and hundreds of subsidiary offices. Residential lots were allocated according to the stratification of nobility and commoners, with accompanying differences in sizes and shapes of houses. Reform measures included an imperial edict appointing a responsible head for each city block, *bō*, and supervisors, *rei*, for every four *bō*, who were responsible for peace and order throughout the city.[1] Unable to attract sufficient numbers of leaders of the temples and shrines, and of the scholars and technicians attached to the powerful clans who remained in Asuka, the capital was forced to give up its new base in Naniwa after only seven years and return to the Asuka district.

The Emperor Tenchi in 667 attempted once more to transfer the capital, this time to Ōtsu in the Ōmi district (Shiga Pref.), so as to control communications leading to the northern regions under his control, Tōhoku, Hokuriku, and Oshima of Hokkaidō. Locating his residence far from the coast at the foot of Mt. Ōsaka, with water routes open across nearby Lake Biwa, he sought security from possible dangers in his campaign against the T'ang and Silla powers on behalf of Paekche, as well as freedom from traditionalistic pressures of the Asuka clans. He too failed to withstand their opposition and after five years was forced to return to Asuka, specifically by the Jinshin rebellion.[2]

Efforts to overcome clan influences and centralize power in the imperial throne were fruitless, in view of the fact that imperial authority had been established initially through support of the clans. Their Asuka stronghold was the richest area in Japan, further strengthened by being the center of advanced cultural forms imported from China. Unable to abandon Asuka, the imperial family finally built the Fujiwara capital city in the southeastern corner of the Yamato plain, surrounded by the three mountains of Unebi, Miminashi, and Kagu, in 694 under the Empress Jitō.

The Fujiwara capital city, like the earlier Naniwa, was patterned after the socio-ecological structure of the T'ang capital of Chang'an. Encompassed about by twelve gates, the new imperial site boasted palace buildings on a scale equalling the later Heijōkyō (Nara) and Heiankyō (Kyōtō) structures, plus other official buildings. Temples were transferred to this city and its population is said to have reached 1,505 households.[3]

The imperial palace was situated centrally in the north end of the city. From its main entrance (at the south end of the imperial compound) ran the main street of Sujaku to the south end of the city, dividing the whole into two equal halves, Sakyō (left) and Ukyō (right). Each half was subdivided into twelve parts from north to south called *jō*, each being cross-divided into four more *jō*, yielding a total of 96 subdivisions called *bō* in the entire city. Powerful clans living throughout the Kinai district were granted lots commensurate with their rank and family size. Markets were placed in Sakyō and Ukyō in imitation of T'ang institutions, though not based on demands of an exchange economy. They were supervised by officially appointed market masters, and supply was controlled by the demands of noblemen and bureaucrats. The same market system occurred later in the cities of Heijōkyō.

In time the Fujiwara capital site, hemmed in by mountains in the more remote southern end of the narrow Yamato plain, became wholly inadequate as a location for the concentration of the expanded integrative organs necessary to effective administration. Life had become considerably more complex as power sufficient to control all Japan was attained and the appointment of *kokushi* for governing local provinces necessitated greater convenience in communications internally, as did the increased frequency of contacts with the continent. Thus, in the era of the Emperor Genmei in 710 the capital was transferred to the famous Nara site, ending a period of 120 years of imperial residence in the Asuka district since the time of Empress Suiko. The Heijōkyō capital in Nara flourished as a big city for some 70 years spanning the reigns of seven emperors.

Imperial attempts to relocate the capital away from the Asuka district had failed not only because of opposition by powerful clans entrenched there, but also because of resistance on the part of the influential temples equally entrenched there. The Nara site was a suitable compromise choice, being situated in the same Yamato plain yet affording greater travel conveniences. The Tōsan and Hokuriku regions could be reached via the Yamashiro plain just beyond the hills of the Yamato plain; the Yamatogawa river afforded easy access to Naniwa, and a road was constructed along this access route later to connect with the east-west highway, the Tōkaidō.

The concilatory approach of the Heijōkyō transfer resulted in many Asuka temples being moved to the new city. These included *ujidera* (family-sponsored temples) of powerful clans such as Kōfukuji belonging to the Fujiwara house, Katsuragiji of Katsuragi clan connection, Kidera co-sponsored by Ki and Soga groups, in addition to other big temples like Daianji, Genkōji, Hōkōji, Yakushiji and so on. In re-establishing these temples in Heijōkyō steps were taken to leave the main temples in Asuka standing to pacify the feelings of the people in the old city who were dissatisfied with the transfer of the capital to Nara.[4]

Into the new city of Heijōkyō moved many bureaucrats, priests, and their subordinates from the Asuka district, plus not a few ordinary families moving under government orders. After establishment the new capital's population swelled further with the arrival of rootless people seeking employment, such as merchants to work in the markets of Sakyō and Ukyō, technicians employed in the construction of Buddhist temples and statues, laborers for palace and temple projects, peasants used in transporting goods received as taxes, and other landless peoples in search of new jobs. Most of them came from the nearby Kinai region, though some, with and without families, came from the Kantō and Shikoku regions.[5] Heijōkyō thus emerged as the first truly large-scale city in Japan, complete with the highest civilization available in its time and an estimated population of 200,000.[6]

Life in Heijōkyō was overwhelmingly dominated by the aristocratic bureaucracy fostered by the *ritsuryō* social order. Noblemen holding the fifth rank or above numbered over 130 and the total number of officials is said to have reached 10,000 or one out of twenty of the total estimated population. Almost all non-official people, though, had some connection with the government or the temples. There developed in Heijōkyō a mode of urban life that served to regulate the behavior of this highly concentrated population of diverse socio-economic positions and customs.

The self-sufficiency and lack of goods exchange systems in the rural areas in this historical stage prevented cities from evolving naturally or spontaneously. The conditions enabling the construction by the Japanese nobility of this cultured model of the Chinese city, even though the productivity level was inferior to that of China, were complex yet interconnected. They included the extensive controls exercised over rural labor and productivity by the integrative organs of the *ritsuryō* system, the strength and wealth accruing to the nobility though grants in land (*shokuhō*) and official stipends (*iroku*), plus the resources of funds and labor supplied by priests of large temples with great wealth and labor reserves, including slaves. Every corner of Japan was drawn upon in the mobilization of these resources poured into the construction of the new capital city of Heijōkyō.

The city plan was almost identical to that of the Fujiwara capital, yet larger in scale as demanded by the expanded administrative system.

The checkerboard-type layout measured about 32 by 36 *chō* east to west and north to south (approx. 2.5×3.1 mi.). The main street, Sujakuōji, ran from Sujakumon (gate) in the north to Rajōmon (gate) in the south, dividing the capital area as before into equal halves. Its width was 150 *shaku* (50 yds.). Perpendicular to the main street ran nine major city streets, and parallel to it eight other streets, forming city blocks that were 4 *chō* square (approx. 476 sq. yds.). The city blocks, called *bō*, were subdivided into 16 equal square sections termed *tsubo*.[7] While copied after the Chinese capital city, there were no ramparts surrounding the entire city as in China; only the structure of the Rajōmon gate and the adjacent barriers reflected the style of the heavy walls found at Chang'an.

The emperor's palace, Daidairi, focal point of the capital, was situated at Sujakumon in the north end of the city. Markets were operated in the east and west sections; temples transferred from the Asuka district graced the city here and there. The great Buddha image of Hōryūji temple, the Daibutsuden, was one of the most prominent structures in the city. Housing lots for nobles, officials, and ordinary citizens were dispersed throughout the capital.

The emperor's palace grounds measured 8 *chō* (approx. 0.5 sq. mi.) and its boundaries were marked by mud walls topped by a miniature roof. Each of the four walls around the palace had three gates, twelve in all, protected by a special palace guard. Inside were the court hall, Chōdōin, and twelve other buildings divided among the main offices of government on one side, and on the other side the imperial residential buildings, or Dairi. The main office of the court hall was named Daigokuden, of which some six feet of stage in an oblong area of 15 *jō* 6 *shaku* (52 yds.) by 8 *jō* 5 *shaku* (28 yds.) can still be seen. It is thought to have been constructed in the *shichū-zukuri* style with vermilion-lacquered pillars, white plaster walls, and roofing tiles, producing a magnificent appearance. The absence of roofing tile remains at the Dairi site indicates, however, that the residential buildings of the palace were fashioned after the traditional Japanese style using round pillars set in holes, uncolored, and a roof thatched with bark from the Japanese cypress. From evidence in the layout of the later capital of Heiankyō (Kyōto) it is further surmised that Chinese-style construction was indeed limited to the court hall, Chōdōin, and other government buildings; but even the imperial residential structures, by virtue of their size, added to the overall imposing aura of authority of the central government, as compared to the humbler dwellings of the citizenry.

Residential land grants for noblemen and officials were made for life, though areas available were only half the size of former Fujiwara capital lots, and the increased density of Heijōkyō led to more urbanized patterns of life.[8] Nobles holding the third rank or above were allocated 1 *chō* (2.45 acres), fourth and fifth rank holders 1/2 *chō*, and lower ranks only 1/4 *chō*. Nobles of the first group were allowed frontage on the main street of the city, and their gates and homes reflected their wealth and positions. In the eleventh month of the first year of the Jinki era (724) an order was issued for all houses in Heijōkyō to be plastered white, and to have vermilion columns and tiled roofs, although traditional architectural standards as manifested in the Ise Shrine called for polished natural-wood timbers and cypress-shingled roofs. The main house of a residence had living and sleeping rooms, with the nearby buildings for storing grain and other purposes having grass-thatched roofs. Gardens with ponds, including small islands, grass and trees, all surrounded by fences or hedges, completed the lot's development. These structures were prototypes of the *shinden-zukuri* style of the later Heian era, though buildings were not yet joined by corridors.

Lots granted officials varied in size according to rank. With population increases and the intensification of urban ways, lot sizes were decreased by eliminating the warehouses and workrooms more appropriate to rural modes of living. Commoners' lots of only 1/16, or sometimes only 1/32 *chō*, allowed only about 1 *tsubo* (3.95 sq. yds.) per head; hence, their humble dwellings, with a common oven for several families, differed little from former rural conditions. Protected by grass-thatched roofs, their occupants sat on grass pads strewn on wooden floors or, in poorer homes, on straw or bamboo spread directly on the ground.[9]

Buddhism consitituted a fundamental principle in politics and social work, exercising political power directly, and the imperial government provided large appropriations in the state budget for construction of official temples. Tōdaiji became the center of state Buddhism, being known as *Sōkokubunji* (Great State Temple), and its massive Daibutsuden was constructed on a scale considered superior to all wooden structures in the history of the world, consuming for that time a stupendous outlay of funds. It is said that in the year Yōrō 4 (720) there were 48 temples in Heijōkyō, and the priests moved in the upper circles of society.

A typical temple might include: a tiered tower (pagoda) with sacred bones of the Buddha or some saint, or some other relic as an object of worship inside; the main hall, *kondō*, where statues were erected; a lecture hall, *kōdō*, for training novitiates; residential and dining halls, *sōbō* and *jikidō* respectively, plus warehouses for use of the priests; headquarters for social work, *keidenin;* and clinics for adults, *seyakuin*, and children, *hidenin*. Many priests and worshippers were involved in the overall program of a temple unit.

As with residences, the evolving urbanity showed clearly in clothing styles, which were also utilized to express formally the stratification of social classes. Official wear for bureaucrats adopted the three sartorial classes of T'ang practice, *reifuku*, *chōfuku*, and *seifuku* appropriate to ceremonies, court attendance and official business respectively. All officials wore headgear, *kanmuri*, and jewelled ornaments, women wearing hair ornaments. Common people continued wearing the common old-style clothes, or even primitive styles of southern origin.

Thus, not only in the material culture of the day such as architecture, civil engineering, and apparel, but also in the non-material culture of politics, art, religion, education, and literature, the upper classes were greatly influenced by the influx of continental culture. For the most part the common people lived in quite another world from those who governed them, rooted unchanged in the traditional, indigenous ideas, customs, and styles existing in the islands long before this revolutionary epoch.

While the lives of those in the various status strata in heavily populated areas became increasingly urbanized, it cannot be said that even nobles and officials were completely so. Officials were each given a fifteen-day leave in the fifth and eighth months for tending their farm lands, at which time it was quite common for them to return to their rural residences. The women often remained in the rural homesteads. These customs tended to preserve the power and structure of the clans, and the officials' positions within them.[10] All those living in the city were allocated lands on the outskirts of the city, or even in the city itself. Those governed remained clearly under the direct governance of specific members of the ruling class. The basis of urban life in this period lay clearly in its connection with the land, its control and use, distinguishing the socio-economic structure of the ancient city markedly from that of the modern city.

The state structured around a status system defined in the *ritsuryō* laws, as well as the refinement and brilliance it achieved culturally, were made possible by concentrating in the capital city the labor and products drawn from the farming areas. The economic flow was strictly one-way, city prosperity being premissed upon the impoverishment of the rural districts. Goods meant for city consumption, such as rice and other foodstuffs, woven and finished cloth goods, ironware, utensils and raw materials, left the farmers' hands as taxes, though it was the latters' burden to provide transport to the insatiable urban coffers. In certain fields necessary to high-level aristocratic life in the city, technicians of proven abilities in continental crafts were able to receive good wages of some 10 *mon* to 60 *mon* per day, as such skilled craftsmen were scarce. Working under orders from government officials, these artisans employed their own assistants to help meet the heavy demands of the nobility.[11] Given the self-supporting economy of this period, these technicians were engaged originally as peasants in the cultivation of government-allotted lands. Those demonstrating exceptional skills enjoying strong demands were released wholly or partially from the *chō*, *yō*, and *zatsuyō* (miscellaneous) taxes to give definite terms of service in the workshops of their respective crafts. Imported from the continent and patronized in the capital region, these high-level techniques were not diffused further across the country. The technicians, then, resided in the city area to supply this specialized market.

Non-skilled workers used in the construction projects included ordinary laborers, *ninpu,* and those forcefully assembled from the Kinai district and vicinity, known as *kofu*. Forced employment, known as *koeki,* was common in the first half of the Nara period, though in the latter half of this era, these laborers came voluntarily to earn money to pay their taxes, and were called *wako*. Another type of compulsory employment, *jicho*, demanded one man per every fifty households in a village. *Wako* and *jicho* laborers received 10 *mon* per day, or enough to buy between 2 and 3.6 *go* (0.76 US pts.–1.36 US pts.) of unhulled rice.[12]

Artisans and their apprentices, as well as skilled slaves, under government officials or temples or shrines, were required by government order to process materials collected as *chō* and *yō* taxes to meet the demands of the ruling class. Officials, priests, and nobles released any excess products thus attained in the Sakyō and Ukyō markets, thereby securing items short in their own stocks. Such exchange enabled them to enjoy a sustained high level of living. Increased demands spurred remarkable advances in techniques such as metal-processing, architecture, dyeing, and weaving, which in turn stimulated the demand for exchanged goods.

Though incomplete, the urbanized environment resulting from the emergence of a large city in turn produced new modes of behavior. This process had been accelerated by a complex of many social forces; namely, the expansion of the political mechanism, wealth accumulation, quantitative increase and proliferation of demands, technical progress, increased differentiation of socio-economic functions, and larger population concentrations. Access to the expanded exchange markets freed the imperial court and government agencies from dependency upon their own artisans, who consequently were freed from conditions of slave-like employment. Construction projects requiring large numbers of skilled workers to be retained in continuous employment, as in the case of large shrine and temple buildings, prompted the erection of special workshops that permitted technical specialists to work more independently. With the advances in occupational differentiation and the increased number of independent technicians, the framework of the self-supporting economy was undermined.[13] In time contractual arrangements for employment of the independent technicians appeared, whereby they received wages only when employed to meet specific demands, and patterns of temporary employment of laborers increased, as a result of the population concentration in the city.

Kishiro Shūichi points out that a considerable number of copiers of Buddhist scriptures are mentioned in records preserved in the Shōsōin (national museum in Nara) who had no guarantee for their positions but were paid according to the number of copies delivered. He regards this as one element in the emerging urbanization of human behavior in this period. The highest official rank held by these scribes was *sho-rokui*, ordinary sixth grade, though most of them were lower ranked officials. Their work in copying the Buddhist sutras was done independently to supplement their low incomes as minor officials. Their status was but a little above the common people, and copying was actually their primary source of income. The supply of sutras was inadequate to provide good incomes for all seeking supplemental income, and it is reported that the scribes once petitioned their superiors for the following:

1. That employment of new copyists be suspended until such time as the sutra supply increased to accommodate them:

2. That leave on the fifth day of each month be granted; and,
3. That food and clothing allowances be improved in both quality and quantity.

The same documents record also an instance of a copyist's fellow scribes petitioning their superior to lighten the punishment meted to him because of errors in his work.[14]

Once a city matures and varieties of behavior peculiar to an urban environment appear, activities become relatively free from the restrictions imposed by the fixed status and organization of the village. Among the more liberalized and individualized actions in the total range of human behavior, there emerge, though not on a general scale by any means, modes of conduct of an increasingly disintegrative impact with respect to the social order of the city. The most serious problem that arose in the capital city of the *ritsuryō* system was the large influx of vagabonds from the rural areas, where heavy taxes and the dreadful menace of frequent famines due to primitive agricultural techniques made life unbearable for many peasants. The flow of such peasants from the villages into the city was greatly accelerated by the provisions of the land distribution system that allowed wealthy aristocrats and powerful temples to extend their estates over wider ranges of arable land.

In the year Hōki 4 (773) the number of poor citizens given alms in the capital city is said to have reached 9,703 in the east sector, Sakyō, and 9,042 in the west sector, Ukyō. This figure includes both those improvident citizens resident in the city and those migrating in. A ratio of nearly 20,000 poor with respect to an estimated total population of 200,000 in the capital represents a sizable proportion and a serious social problem.[15]

Under such circumstances there inevitably occurred a rise in immoral conduct and crime. Some exhausted their assets in gambling (*sugoroku*, a kind of backgammon), others robbed for money in the streets, and some even burned houses in the city. Finally, in the Enryaku era (782–806) an order was issued that all gamblers and vagrants were to be arrested or expelled from the city.[16]

The birth of an age that included (1) a new social class embracing workers with some intellectual background, technicians, and wage laborers, all independently employed, (2) the initiation of cooperative action by employees for improving their working conditions, and (3) the evolution of a large population of poor people, appeared as part of the urbanizing process that resulted from bringing together so many varieties of people with differing ways of life, so recently released from the powerful social controls of the previous age. It is not surprising that what resulted from this drastic change was quite different from the traditional social relations that existed in the stable rural scene of an immediate yesterday.

The economic foundation of the *ritsuryō* city lay in the taxes gleaned from the common citizenry, and not in the marketplace. Bartering itself, though, was promoted by the tax collection system as products made on the farms were used to pay taxes, or exchanged in the city for other goods with which to make tax payments. Moreover, nobles and priests released their excess products into the city's markets. Copying the system of the T'ang dynasty, government-controlled markets were set up in Heijōkyō. Various goods were exchanged in the east and west markets, such as cloth, linen, rice, paper, iron and porcelain ware, fruits and vegetables. Sources for these goods were government releases, excess of items collected from estates of aristocrats, and products offered for exchange by farmers living near the city. The greater portion, though, came through the channels of the government, nobility, and the larger temples.

Laws governing social status and financial positions of the people imposed restrictions upon those permitted to engage in this commerce. Such privileges extended to those of the fifth rank and above, who dispatched their attendants or slaves to carry on their business. The temples had their own servants, *kōekishi*, to manage their commercial ventures. Only those lower than the fifth rank were allowed to open shops personally in the markets.

Rural folk were too absorbed in farming to have time to develop marketing practices professionally, and the east and west markets of the capital city were opened for only half of each month. Consequently, there failed to emerge at this historical stage a professional class given solely to marketing.[17]

Cloth and rice were the major items in the government's financial system, and it was the economic stage of commodity circulation of rice, cloth, silk and cotton, and farm tools, that succeeded the original stage of exchanging miscellaneous goods. The T'ang system of coinage was introduced eventually and *wadōkaihō* coins were minted in Japan in the year Wadō 2 (709). In both markets of Heijōkyō thereafter all commodities were pricemarked, official commodity prices being firmly fixed by the market master. Court and government employees, such as *kofu* and *jicho*, were also paid in coins. Coin circulation was stimulated by the local tax payment system which permitted tax remittance by coins only in Heijōkyō or the surrounding Kinai district. Coins included *dōsen* (copper coins) and *yōsen* (coins acceptable in lieu of labor obligations); those desiring coins applied for government employment as *wako* (volunteers).

Even after coins came into circulation the economy remained essentially a self-supporting one, barter channels being used only for goods scarce within one's own productive range. Individual activity was most meager, and the market was dominated by copper and tax products required by government programs. On the whole commodity circulation sufficed and coin circulation was limited to the Yamato, Yamashiro, Ōmi, and Settsu areas around the capital. Marketing in more remote areas was not yet advanced sufficiently to need or accommodate coin circulation.

Markets had been established, of course, in various places throughout the country prior to, or during the *ritsuryō* period. They were under the supervision of local governors and were dominated by goods of the local governments. Rural people lived in self-sufficiency, exchanging only such goods as were not needed. The markets opened either from time to time irregularly, or at definite times but for limited periods only.

Cities could hardly develop under such adverse rural conditions as the absence of a large population, self-sufficient modes of living, no separation of commerce and industry, not to mention restrictions on movements of people and goods imposed by poor transportation facilities, and failure of an exchange economy to develop. Only limited urbanization occurred at such places as the Kyūshū regional capital of Dazaifu, the northern defense center called Chinjufu, or the various provincial *kokufu*, which were developed by the central authorities for political or defensive purposes.

The term *kokufu* refers to the provincial capitals established in each of the provinces (*kuni*) provided for in the Taihō Reform laws and patterned after T'ang models. Classified into three grades, large, medium, and small (*jō*, *chū*, and *ge*), each *kokufu* was allotted officials in numbers and ranks commensurate with its grade, for the political administration of the province. *Kokufu* sites were selected according to farm productivity of the area, defense advantages, centrality, and convenient access to the national capital. Facilities included an administrative office for control of the farmers, *kokuchō*, the provincial temple, *kokubunji*, and shrine, *sōja*, a militia, *gundan*, and finally, the provincial school, *kokugaku*. These organs drew together a consuming population of officials, priests, and their servants. Markets to serve their needs were founded under the supervision of the *kokuchō*. Though far smaller in scale, the *kokufu* were planned cities like the capital; for example, the *kokufu* of Suho, Echizen, and Ise had areas ranging from 4 *chō* to 8 *chō* (1 *chō*=2.45 acres). Surrounded by moats and embankments, the checkerboard patterns of the *kokufu* cities contained considerable lands under cultivation within their bounds.[18]

Due to the great importance of overseas contacts with the T'ang court during the *ritsuryō* period, north Kyūshū became a district of significance in political, cultural, and military affairs second only to the capital region, and the provincial capital of Dazaifu located there was the most important city in the nation next to the central capital. Its plan was similar to the *kokufu*, though it was much larger. Its defense was well provided for, with a castle on a mountain fastness and another on the seashore to defend the bay entrance. In addition to foreign affairs, it functioned as the administrative center for all Kyūshū, containing a religious center, Kannonji, a regional college, Gakugyōin, and other necessary facilities.[19]

In order to complete its defense lines to the north on the main island, the central government in the year 724 erected the castle fortress of Tagajō (near present-day Sendai in Miyagi Pref.) on a hill in Mutsu (most of present-day Miyagi, Iwate, and Aomori Prefectures) for keeping the Ezo tribes of northern Japan under safe control. Later in the Heian era a defense port farther north was constructed at Tanzawa, though it had no political function such as did Dazaifu in Kyūshū. The Tanzawa castle grounds encompassed 8 *chō* (19.60 acres) protected by moats and embankments, and a garrison for *tondenhei*, soldiers who farmed when not fighting. Placements within inner precincts were patterned after the main administrative structures of Fujiwarakyō and Heijōkyō, though smaller, with the office of the governor, *seiden*, set apart by its own fence and gateway.[20]

From the above descriptions it should be clear that the provincial cities did not emerge as spontaneous aggregates of people assembled for purposes of their own. Rather, they were cities planned and constructed by the central government for local administration of the *ritsuryō* political system, linked to and centering in the top integrative organs in the national capital. They were "bureaucratic cities."

As for the communication routes so necessary to the implementation of the centralization policies, there were main highways connecting the central Kinai district with the seven regions of Tōkai, Tōsan, Hokuriku, San-in, San-yo, Nankai, and Saikai. The *Engishiki* records classify the western route through the San-yo region connecting the capital with the next most important city, Dazaifu, as the "main road," or *tairo*. The two eastern routes by the sea or over the mountains, the Tōkaidō and Tōsandō respectively, were regarded as "secondary roads," or *chūro*. All others were grouped together as "lesser roads," or *shōro*. Along these routes were founded rest stations at points about 5 *ri* apart (approx. 12 mi.; laws called for one at least every 30 *ri*), where replacements of manservants and horses, food and lodging could be had. Distances between stations varied with the lay of the land, flat or steep, the availability of grass and water. A station master, *ekichō*, supervised each station, and he was responsible to the provincial governor of his area, who had appointed him. The *ekichō* was generally a man of wealth and talent who, as *ekichō*, was granted *ekifu* and *ekiden*, lands and paddy fields, to acquire funds to operate the station, and all this was tax-exempt. Under the station master were certain employees, *ekiko*, who were also exempted from compulsory labor services, *yōeki*. (The *eki* in *yōeki* refers to public duty, and is different from the *eki* in *ekichō*, *ekifu*, *ekiden*, and *ekiko*, all of which refer to the station.)[21]

Twenty horses were allotted each station along the primary Sanyōdō route to Dazaifu, ten to stations on the secondary Tōkaidō and Tōsandō routes, and only five to stations along lesser roads. The horses, of course, were not available to the common people but only to bearers of court ranks of the fifth grade and above, or to messengers bearing urgent or other official letters and their attendants.

Where these official roads crossed large rivers, ferry services were provided. The roads also had barriers at select points to serve as checking stations against undesirable movements of people and goods; for instance, barriers were set up at Kikuta of Shirakawa and at Nenjugaseki to halt invasions of the Ezo southward. Defense ports were also established at Nuttari and Iwabunesaku. To guard the access roads to the capital city, checking stations were set up at Suzuka of Ise, Fuha of Mino, and Arachi of Echizen (later removed to Ōsaka of Ōmi) where militia served on a rotation basis.

Despite the obligations of ordinary households to deliver goods to government agencies in payment of *chō* and *yō* taxes, station facilities along the highways were reserved strictly for officials and high ranking nobility. Travel presented great difficulties as local residents were most reluctant to open their homes to strangers. If food supplies carried on a journey ran out, it was equally difficult to replenish one's rations. Highway robbers compounded the misery, and to pass the checking stations common travelers had first to apply for permission and then submit to inspection of their persons and all goods.

In short, social controls added to natural difficulties and dangers made travel extremely troublesome for commoners. In the year Wado 5 (712), though, there was issued a law that allowed rice provisions to be supplied such travelers, and the priest Gyōki founded simple inns, *fuseya*, in Yamashiro, Kawachi, Settsu, and Izumi for the comforts of commoners when journeying.[22]

Rugged terrain as well as political necessities had made travel by sea most important to the Japanese at an early stage in their history, in fact, more important than overland traffic. If land routes were closed, then the *kokufu* could be reached by sea. If the *kokufu* were landlocked, nearby ports served them. A large port was even developed at Ōtsu to service transportation across Lake Biwa. Both Ōtsu and Naniwa served at one time as capital cities, and at the same time were good ports. Traffic was prosperous on the Inland Sea of Seto as many provinces in the Nankai and San-yō districts forwarded their *chō* and *yō* taxes by sea to the capital. The port cities attracted considerable populations, the most densely populated port being Naniwa (present-day Ōsaka).

Trade relations with the T'ang regime in China accounted for a portion of sea traffic in this period. Goods from the mainland were first received by the central authorities, and then released through local government offices for sale. Art objects comprised a great portion of the imported goods destined for sale to noblemen, this trade having little to do with the common classes. Hakata in north Kyūshū was the main service port for the influential regional capital of Dazaifu, and here facilities for entertaining foreign envoys were constructed. The Kyūshū ports of Hirato, Tsushima, Kanzaki, and Karatsu also prospered. Later, the Hokuriku port of Tsuruga also came into some prominence in trade relations that developed with the Sung dynasty (960–1279) that succeeded the T'ang court.[23]

# 3. Changes in the *Ritsuryō* System and Transfer of the Capital to Heiankyō (later Kyōto) in 794

The development of the city in Japan, and the forms that development took, were decided fundamentally by the following processes; (1) expansion of the centralizing functions following upon national unification and the concentration of the integrative organs in a central place; (2) appropriation of the large-scale city plan as developed in continental culture; and (3) the dependence of a cultured urban minority upon the productivity of a rural majority, an economic structure sustained by the strict stratification of status in an aristocratic society.

In the early days of the Nara era, the guidelines of the *ritsuryō* system were followed rather faithfully. Land was under state ownership, tax burdens were fairly evenly distributed, and the agriculturally based way of living seemed even more promising as continental contacts afforded impressive improvements in cultivating methods and farm equipment, as well as the diffusion of sericulture, and new ore mines were opened. Farmers released from the suppressive clan systems of old now took more initiative as their livelihood improved and their numbers increased. Compared to the luxurious lives of the aristocrats, priests, and bureaucrats in the city, though, the farmers' lot was yet miserable, heavily burdened by taxes, and not far above a subsistence level.

Though fairly distributed originally, the paddy fields granted men for the duration of their lives, the *kubunden*, were often assumed as private properties by their heirs, after the original owners died. The unit of *kubunden* allocation was the individual person, though this yielded several allotments to a single household. In time there emerged owners of vast land areas whose estates contained many families and slaves. Wealth differences among individual families widened greatly. The old and powerful clans that filled the official positions of government were in particularly advantageous positions for acquiring vast landholdings. Likewise, the temples acquired great estates. Lands available for distribution to the common people—in an estimated population of 6–7 millions toward the end of the Nara era—became increasingly scarce.[24]

Land scarcity rendered implementation of the equal-land plan virtually impossible. On top of this, food shortages suffered by the peasants caused some of them to give up farming, thereby diminishing to that extent the tax resources of the nation. The state, however, required greater resources than ever for constructing the imperial capital and for providing itself with the political, military, and other facilities necessary to realization of its goals of unification and emulation of the advanced culture of the continent. The new and expensive modes of living acquired by the nobility and officials further intensified the tax burdens on the peasants, which included compulsory labor in the capital city, or fighting the Ezo on the northern frontier. In a word, the farmers fell into a worse plight than ever.

To alleviate these circumstances, the central government initiated projects to reclaim waste lands in the year Yōrō 6 (722); but these projects realized only meager results. Consequently, the government extended the privileges of land reclamation to private citizens and agencies. Such projects involved large-scale irrigation facilities and, thus, it was the landed nobility and temples who could and did direct large numbers of their workers and funds into extensive reclamation works. Their estates became greatly extended through these measures, as well as through the willingness of poor farmers to sell their lands when they could no longer bear the tax burdens, including debts incurred in borrowing rice plants on a crop percentage basis. The displaced peasants became roving vagabonds, or tenant farmers on the aristocrat's reclaimed lands, or else migrated into the cities. The "equal land" system introduced by the Taika Reforms began to crumble. When it was formally and judicially recognized that land could be owned personally and when that ownership was further extended, the system was virtually doomed.

As men of power expanded their estates through reclamation all over the country, the lesser landowners became threatened with complete absorption. Some avoided this deprivation by taking the initiative in donating their lands to noblemen or to the temples. Productive capacities of the larger estates were certainly increased, but the land system fell into serious confusion. The concentration of lands in the hands of a limited number of powerful landowners, moreover, seriously impaired the authority of the central government. Wealthy noblemen, powerful clans, and temples in many districts, including the central region, consolidated their localized powers into vast manors, *shōen*. These manors were more or less free of central controls, and were protected by locally organized groups of feudalistically loyal soldiers. There gradually emerged thereafter a new feudal order of privately owned estates, protected by a new system of privately maintained and commanded troops, that rendered the *ritsuryō* program of equally distributed though centrally controlled lands ineffective. Furthermore, the financial basis of the central government was gravely jeopardized as the overall volume of taxable lands was greatly diminished.

Deprived of funds, the power of the integrative political organs necessary to centralized administration could not be effectively maintained. As the *ritsuryō* ideals collapsed, the strengthened powers of clan and nobility moved in to exploit the vacuum. Powerful families like the Fujiwara overpowered older ones such as the Ōtomo family and others, while appealing to its own history of distinguished service to the imperial family since the time of Fujiwara Kamatari, progenitor of the Fujiwara household and chief instigator, with Prince (later Emperor) Tenchi, of the Taika Reforms in 645. The temples and shrines were also able to take advantage of special state privileges, and of newly acquired land wealth, to enhance their positions in political affairs. Rivalry among these powers precipitated a very unstable situation in the political arena.

The imperial throne was balanced precariously on the fluctuating support of three groups: the imperial family itself; the nobility; and the priests;—the emperor being regarded as spiritual head of the national family, even when it was busy quarreling. His residence, central symbol of national unity, was often subject to relocation as the balance of power shifted.

The Fujiwara family had maintained a strong position at court since the time when Fujiwara Kamatari controlled the court council. Once, when smallpox inflicted the Fujiwara household, a rival named Tachibana-no-moroe was appointed to the post of chief councillor. In reaction to this move, Fujiwara Hirotsugu provoked a rebellion against him in Dazaifu. Tachibana-no-moroe responded by advising the emperor to move the imperial palace in 741 to a new location called Kuni (different ideograph from the word for "state"). Though approved and done, the new location could not be maintained and the palace was removed to Naniwa in 744 on the advice of the Fujiwara family. In the following year it was moved again to Shigaraki, southeast of Kyōto in the Ōmi district, on the recommendation of the priest Gyōki, as this district was a center of Buddist development. This mountainside location proved too remote from the center of political controls, however, and the imperial residence was returned once again to Heijōkyō in 746.

Three years after restoration of the palace to Heijōkyō, Fujiwara Tanetsugu announced that the palace was to be transferred to Nagaoka just southwest of present-day Kyōto, a move designed to get rid of the influences of the rival powers of the Ōtomo, Saeki, and other families. The Nagaoka site offered greater command of waterways, being situated on the Yodogawa river. Construction of the Nagaoka *miyako* continued for some ten years, supported by generous donations from the Hata family which had maternal relations with the Fujiwara household. Naturalized families from the continent also lent support to this effort, until the assassination of Fujiwara Tanetsugu brought an end to the endeavor.[25]

These transfers of the imperial residence occurred frequently in the prevailing unstable political situation. The Fujiwara leaders sought to overcome their weakness in political struggles by propagating the idea that they were in blood relation with the imperial family and thus directly linked to the central figure in the Japanese theocracy.[26]

The Fujiwara maneuvers were opposed by Wake-no-kiyomaro, who submitted a plan to the emperor for moving the palace and capital to a new site where no contending power had any claim and the emperor's position would be neutral with respect to all rival families. This plan, adopted in 749, was motivated by a desire to correct the defects that had vitiated the Taika Reforms; and, as a visual demonstration of the determination to fulfill the ideal of a fully integrated nation, the proposal envisaged a more magnificent capital city than ever before.

In its straitened economic circumstances the central government could hardly afford anything more ambitious than the Nagaoka plan, which had failed. Even greater funds and a larger land area were required if the plan was to be successful. Help came from wealthy immigrant families from China whose skill in weaving had made great fortunes for them. Some fourteen out of twenty-five such related families living in the Yamashiro district gave lands as well as funds for construction of the new capital. In addition, political support came from Fujiwara Kokuromaro, who had married a daughter of one of these naturalized families.[27] In 794, then, the emperor decided to transfer the *miyako* from Heijōkyō to Uda, in Kuzuno district of the Yamase region, where the capital city of Heiankyō was developed. His edict stated that "The rivers and mountains of the imperial site in Kuzuno are beautiful to behold; may our subjects from all over the country come to see them." It was indeed a beautiful site for the capital, and better situated than Heijōkyō for political strategem and transportation conveniences.

Following the transfer to Heiankyō a campaign was carried out to cleanse the government operations of accumulated, deeply-rooted evils that blocked the way to development of a social order true to the *ritsuryō* ideals. Pressures were brought to bear on landowners who had absorbed too much land, maladministration of provincial governors was checked, official promotions went more often to men of talent, land controls and distribution were more strictly handled, and defenses against the Ezo threat in the north were strengthened. The imperial capital was restored to its position as the nucleus of the centralized integrative system, ruled over by the emperor, as originally projected in the *ritsuryō* laws. The centrality of the imperial capital was thus maintained for another century.

Traffic routes to the new capital were convenient and it became an economically advanced area. Many families were drawn there from the Nara basin, as the imperial family, aristocrats, and bureaucrats moved in with their subordinates, followed by technicians and merchants who supplied their needs. Peasants working off labor obligations and refugees from tax-burdened farms—taxes in the capital were lighter than in the rural areas—added to the overall population increase.[28]

The population of Heiankyō is not clearly established. The capital measured 1,580 *jō* (2.9 mi.) from east to west and 1,753 *jō* (3.5 mi.) from north to south. Some 1,215 towns were incorporated in the municipal system, although full construction of all houses in all towns was never accomplished. The total area of 580 *chō* (1,421 acres) could have accommodated a very sizable populace. When a large fire broke out in the year Jishō 1 (1177) several tens of thousands of dwellings were ravished over an area of 180 *chō* (451 acres). In the year Meiō 9 (1500) some 15,000 homes were destroyed by fire, and this followed the devastations of the Ōnin War that ended in 1477. On the basis of these considerations, Harada

Tomohiko estimates a minimum population of 100,000, as against a maximum capacity of 200,000 judging from the size of the city.[29]

In Heijōkyō Buddhism had been made the official basis of politics, thought, and religion. Heijōkyō was, as it were, a Buddhist city, and its temples acquired extensive landholdings and exercised great influence over politics and economic life. In the transfer of the capital an attempt was made to eliminate this influence from the political sphere, and construction of temples was limited to as few as possible at first. Very few temples were permitted to move to Heiankyō, so as to strengthen the direct control of the emperor himself in government affairs.

Heiankyō was planned after continental patterns the same as Heijōkyō had been. A large agency, named *zōeishi*, with 150 staff officers in its various sections, was formed for construction of the city. Government officials of the fifth rank and over were ordered to supply laborers for construction work. Gates for the palace were to be built by local provinces. As many as 24,000 laborers are said to have been provided by the Tōtomi, Suruga, Shinano, and Izumo provinces in the year Enryaku 16 (797). Land and building distribution were determined by the *zōeishi*.[30]

The projected scale of Heiankyō was much larger than that of Heijōkyō, but the subdivision into towns and even the names given them were, except for a few alterations, quite the same. The main street was the same, Sujakuōji, and it split the city into two equal parts, these being subdivided again by 9 *jō* and 8 *bō*, as in Heijōkyō. The city was surrounded by earthen walls 6 *shaku* (approx. 6 ft.) thick and by a belt of land 7 *shaku* wide, encompassed by a moat 1 *jō* (3.3 yds.) wide. A city castle, *rajō*, was built in imitation of T'ang structures, *rakakujō*, for defending outskirts of towns in China, though actually the fence and moat of Heiankyō's *rajō* was of little value defensively, being merely a mud wall marking the boundary line of the city castle.

The main street of Sujakuōji was 28 *jō* (92 yds., 2 ft.) wide, and ran north and south, with the typical left and right halves, Sakyō and Ukyō, on either side. Other streets, *ōji*, ran parallel and perpendicular to the main street, from 8 *jō* to 12 *jō* wide, intersected by smaller roads, *kōji*, of 4 *jo* width. Nine east-west subdivisions called *jō* were further divided into four *bō*. One *bō* consisted of 16 *chō*, four of these forming one *hō*. Housing lots were granted for life to nobles, officials, and even common citizens. A lot for a family of common status was 1/32 of a *chō*, and was called *henushi*.[31]

The imposing government building, Daidairi, at the north end of the main thoroughfare measured 394 *jō* (1,306.5 yds.) by 460 *jō* (1,525.3 yds.). It was surrounded by roofed mud walls with 14 gates, including the main entrance, Ōtemon. Before it stood the Chōdōin, a complex of structures for official state ceremonies. Included were the Daigokuden, the main palace, and Hōrakuin, the largest hall for state celebrations, well-appointed offices of state administration, and five-tiered pagodas on the east and west sides commanding magnificent views. These structures all had elevated floors, white plaster walls, pillars in Chinese vermilion, and roofs of greenish-glazed tiles. It was a splendid reproduction of T'ang-styled architecture.

The imperial residence, Dairi, was located northeast of Chōdōin, surrounded by a wall. Its compound included the official palace, Shishinden, the residential palace, Seiryoden, and residences for the court nobility as well as for imperial consorts. The Dairi buildings were built according to age-old Japanese architectural styles, with exposed natural lumber and thatched roofs of cypress bark. The unadorned simplicity of these structures stood in stark contrast to the ornate splendor of the T'ang-styled government buildings. In Sakyō was located the government institute for training bureaucrats, Daigakuryō, and in Ukyō the national granary, Kokusōin. To the east of Daigakuryō was Shinsenen, where the emperor held garden parties. Both Sakyō and Ukyō contained special facilities for entertaining official guests from foreign countries, Kōrokan. Beyond the Kōrokan were the markets of east and west, opened alternately a half a month each, where cloth and finished goods, foodstuffs, utensils, and furniture were bought and sold. At the far end of the main street opposite the palace stood the castle-like city gate, an impressive sentinel on guard at the end of highways leading in from Nara and Saikoku.

Thus, the city of Heiankyō was clearly oriented around the main thoroughfare, Sujakuōji, as its axis. The political sector occupied the important north end, the cultural and economic sectors shared the middle area. The east and west parts of the city gave it a simple symmetry, and the subdivisions an appearance of good order. Noblemen's residences were equally distributed east and west, averaging 1 *chō* (2.45 acres) per lot. Mansions of the upper class nobility were located near the Daidairi, and constructed in a distinctive style known as *shinden-zukuri*. Sizes varied, of course, with ranks, only state councillors and nobility of the third rank or above being permitted entrances facing the main street.

The *shinden-zukuri* style consisted of simple round pillars and a hipped roof with gables, or *irimoya* style, of Japanese cypress bark. The center structure, *shinden*, was for the master of the house, and was flanked on both sides by *tainoya*, residences for the other members of the family. The area in front was given to a sandstrewn garden, a pond spotted with small islands, and a small mound beyond. The flanking *tainoya* were connected to the *shinden* and to smaller garden pavilions on the opposite sides by covered corridors. Midway in one of the corridors was an inner gate, *chūmon*, used by the steward and other attendants to the family. The rooms of the master's house, *shinden*, were not divided by panels, but remained open for meetings. Latticed doors encompassed the rooms, inside of which hung huge screens of bamboo strips. The floors were made of wooden planks. The master's private quarters were curtained off, supplied with straw floor mats, and round straw cushions for sitting.

In the early days of the Heian era commoners were not permitted to operate shops in their homes; their houses were solely for living. As land was limited, a commoner's lot facing a side street occupied an area of only 3 *ken* (6 yds.) in width by 4 *ken* (8 yds.) depth. Resembling rural homes of ancient times, the roofs were saddleback shaped, and thatched with wooden strips. Of the 3 *ken* width, 1 *ken* was left bare ground, permitting passage to the rear of the lot; the remaining 2 *ken* were covered with wooden planks. Windows were placed high in the walls, covered by movable shutters.[32]

In such a city as Heiankyō, the movements of a populace with such varying backgrounds and modes of life necessarily had to be put under a system of controls. Such a system was required also to effect a transition from rural to urban patterns of living. The system established for the sake of Heiankyō was in addition to the social order set up on a national scale. The Sakyō and Ukyō sectors of the city were assigned officials equivalent to provincial governors in the administrative hierarchy. Under them were ward managers, *bōchō* and *tone*, who controlled the *bō* and *hō* subdivisions respectively. Tax levies and militia recruitment were administered according to census registrations. Civil order was maintained at the local level through a system of organizing every five neighboring households into a group, *goko* (different from *gōko*) and the groups were responsible to a ward leader, *hochō*. This system enforced joint responsibilities for registering, policing, tax-collecting, and agricultural work. It also provided for checks on illegal movements of the citizens themselves or vagrants, and for the prevention of crimes and the apprehension of criminals.

It was difficult to expedite such a system in a society based on status stratification, where people of different status mixed in the same geographical area. Accordingly, the civil order system was carried out only among commoners and low grade officials in the early phase of this era. Nobility of court ranks of the fifth grade and over were exempted, particularly as they belonged to the ruling class, and not the ruled. From the year Jōgan 4 (862) on, the system applied to upper nobility as well, although they did not participate personally in its operations. Their attendants were given these jobs, to be performed on behalf of their masters.[33]

The development of Heiankyō stimulated movement in and out of the city, necessitating controls over mobility. The *Engishiki* records mention some of the restrictions. Nobles of the third court rank and above alone were privileged to have their residential entrances facing the main street. The sections of the city nearest the palace and the main thoroughfare were cleaned by laborers who were inspected by officials twice annually. People whose homes faced on the city streets were instructed to tidy up the streets daily and to see that trees were planted along them. Transients succumbing to illness unexpectedly were sent to the government operated clinics. Thus the developing urban order sought to maintain public neatness and hygiene as part of the increasingly complex patterns of life.[34]

The process of accelerated urbanization, centered in the governing agencies of the nobility and the bureaucrats, was founded upon, and made possible by, a state system of finance soundly supported by the *ritsuryō* framework of authority. According to Abe Takeshi's studies in the economic structure of Heiankyō, state finances depended upon the *so*, *chō*, and *yō* taxes, various labor services, interest on rice seed loans, and rents from public paddy fields. *Chō* and *yō* taxes were collected by provincial governors and district chiefs and sent to the capital. These covered the expenses of operating the integrative machinery across the nation. A part of the *so* tax receipts and the land rents also went into the capital city budget. Certain court officials living in Heiankyō received monthly payments, mainly in rice. Others of different ranks procured their incomes from paddy fields granted them. Officials of yet other ranks, living in the Kinai district, received stipends upon submission of applications to the Ministry of Finance. All holding official ranks had a certain number of tax payees, *fugo*, under their control, and the officials could keep half of the *so* taxes and the full amount of the *chō* and *yō* taxes collected. From this it is clear that the incomes of persons holding various court ranks formed the basis of the economic activity of Heiankyō, and constituted its primary purchasing power.[35]

The capital city, even from the time of its location in Heijōkyō, was not merely a center of administration and consumption. Under governmental auspices, as well as by demands of the nobility and temples, various goods were produced there. We have already noted the constricted conditions of the work shops in Heijōkyō. In Heiankyō as well, the technicians employed in government workshops preserved the high quality of their manufacturing techniques, although production itself was retarded. While they supplied items not only to their masters but to common people as well, the raw materials for their products were furnished by those placing orders, and the technicians were paid in commodities, such as silk and other cloths, thread and rice. Toward the end of the Heian era, though, some of the technicians attained independence from subordinate relations, and were able to procure necessary raw materials for their products, which they then sold in the markets themselves.[36]

The economic foundation for urban life was laid, therefore, in the production and consumption processes indicated. Moreover, this foundation was buttressed by the regional structures and social control patterns inherent in the socio-cultural framework of the *ritsuryō* status system. But the social order as planned and institutionalized failed to comply with changing realities in the daily lives of the people.

Physically, Heiankyō was planned as a balanced, symmetrical city, but the plan was too expansive ever to be completed. Indeed, five or six years after the transfer was made from Heijōkyō to Heiankyō, the palace was still unfinished. Subduing the Ezo tribes in northern Honshū was a constant drain on human and financial reserves. The people's strength was exhausted in efforts to pay the taxes and provide the labor services required. In return, the ruling class were unable to overcome the serious instability of the political arena. Restricted by the circumstances, the government suspended its plans for completion of the *miyako*, in the year Enryaku 24 (805).[37]

As the manors grew in strength, the powerful clans pilfered the goods paid as taxes by the common people, then transported the pilfered goods to the capital as their own private property. Land purchases in the capital city were monopolized by the influential temples, who retained much of the properties under temple ownership. At the foot of a hill called Higashiyama these wealthy elite erected many villas, and small and private clan temples, as well as some gigantic temples. Yet all such structures were formally prohibited by official regulations drawn up to govern relocation of the capital in Heiankyō. Such, however, was the extent of their power and the luxury of their lives.

Nobility who were denied good government posts due to the monopolization of political power by the Fujiwara family went instead into local government positions. After their terms of service expired some declined to return to the capital, working instead to build up the power of local clans. Some refused to go to provincial posts at all, staying in the capital to build personal fortunes dealing in farm products. Their frequent success was plainly visible in their splendid *shinden*-type houses of aristocratic class and their own well-stocked warehouses. The common people, though, often denied them the honor due true aristocrats, calling them "upstarts."[38]

Peasants that had been pauperized, through loss of their government land grants to the expanding manors, flowed into the capital seeking jobs. Their influx sharpened the contrast between wealth and poverty in the city. Often they committed arson as acts of revenge against their former, tyrannical rulers. Under such pressures the social order of the *ritsuryō* city tended to disintegrate. Magistrates (*tone*) were appointed over the *hō*, the smallest unit of social organization for maintaining order, as countermeasures, and these officers were later put under the stricter authority of officials who acted as both police and judge, the *kebiishi*. From the 10th century on, though, the powers of the *kebiishi* were seriously weakened by the political confusion that prevailed. Even an order by Fujiwara Sanesuke, issued in the year Kannin 3 (1019), that lookout stations, *dōshusha*, be constructed throughout the country to check arson activity, was not implemented. The magistrates experienced considerable difficulty in attempting to control the gambling activities of lower class employees of the wealthy households. In time the magistrates themselves could not be expected to yield full obedience to their superiors. Thus the neighborhood network for dispelling disorder and guaranteeing person and property became functionally ineffective.[39]

Changing political, economic, and social circumstances naturally precipitated deviations from the original community structure of the city as planned in the *ritsuryō* society based on class stratification and hierarchical controls. For instance, population movement was activated by an interesting set of circumstances. The right sector of the symmetrically designed city, the Ukyō, was rather swampy, damp ground, and technically too difficult to drain dry. The left sector, Sakyō, on the other hand, was higher and drier ground. Several rivers ran southward, including the connecting Kamogawa and Yodogawa rivers, lending added transportation advantages. In addition to such natural merits, the idea that "left" (*sa*) is to be preferred over "right" (*u*) was introduced from the continent.[40] For such reasons many nobles transferred their large mansions to Sakyō, as did a number of temples and shrines. Land requirements for these large structures displaced an inordinate number of common citizens from their lots to lower riverside areas and elsewhere.

In the famine year of Tengyō 5 (942) relief monies were distributed among the people according to density in a given area. It is recorded that sums distributed in Sakyō and Ukyō were 40 and 20 *kan* respectively. Remembering that most of the wealthy families not needing relief lived in Sakyō, the fact that its relief dole was double that of Ukyō indicates how dense the population concentration there had become.[41] The relative scarcity of houses in Ukyō left vacant lots unused. It was prohibited in the *Engishiki* to cultivate paddy fields in the city, so the government proposed that parsley and lotus be grown in the vacant lots by the citizens. The gap between the original plan and the actuality of the city grew larger and larger.

Imbalance in the population of the two city sectors understandably affected the markets there. According to the *Engishiki*, the markets functioned under the strict supervision of the market masters, who exercised controls over quality, prices, and measurements of the goods marketed. The east (Sakyō) market opened regularly during the first half of the month, the west (Ukyō) market during the latter half. The merchants dealt in various commodities, ranging from basic necessities such as clothes and foods, to expensive luxuries. Living in a section of the city restricted to their own kind, the merchants were all registered and controlled by government offices and were tax-exempt. In the market the shops clustered in an area of 12 *chō* (29.4 acres) at the junction of the seventh *jō* and the second *bō*, or about midway in each sector. The shops carried the names of the provinces related to their wares, and were grouped around the market master's office in the center of the area. In the east market there were 51 *ten* of shops, and 33 *ten* in the west. *Ten*, according to Abe Takeshi's research, seems to have been a unit of shops dealing in the same product.[42]

The markets flourished in the Heian era, but especially the east market. The loss of population from the west sector, Ukyō, naturally meant a loss of customers, and a concomitant gain for the east market. A market master of the west market is reported to have commented, "The people are all moving to the eastern sector, and our shops are empty. Both officials and merchants stand to lose from this."

The government attempted to direct business to the west market by giving it monopoly rights over sales of special items, such as cotton, silk, special silk fabrics, hand-woven cloth and threads in the Shōwa era (834–848), forty years after the capital was transferred to Heiankyō. Such artificial government devices failed to level the unbalanced population problem, especially as the east market master vigorously opposed the measure.[43]

The decline of the west market and prosperous business in the east market represented only a part of the changes taking place. Both markets were intended originally to handle the excess of goods collected as taxes by the government, the nobility, the shrines and temples. When the original *ritsuryō* system weakened and the manors flourished all over the country, official operations in both markets dropped off, though the overall volume of bartering did not necessarily decline. Although the *Engishiki* forbade any but officially approved transactions, the market master's authority over the market weakened, and free bartering appeared. Commodity transportation was handled by common porters, and many merchants coming into the city also purchased products on their own to take back to the city for resale, or to the provincial markets for sale. Such movement by merchants accelerated free bartering patterns. Craftsmen grouped together in certain blocks of the city where they could do piece work—besides their main jobs of servicing the nobility, the shrines and temples—and sell their products directly in the markets.

The conversion of commerce and industry from completely government-controlled orders and marketing to part-time peddling by semi-independent craftsmen was only a transitional phase toward a more settled pattern, in which goods were produced and marketed in townships organized around a specific commodity, and were freed from bartering only in the east and west markets. Along the third, fourth, and seventh *jō* there were clustered shops handling foodstuffs and clothing goods, managed by merchants (connected with the official markets), lower class officials, minor landowners (e.g., the Hata family), and even peddlers. The seventh *jō* also had shops selling craftsmen's wares. In the Horikawa riverside district there gathered merchants dealing in wood materials.[44] Nonetheless, no clear and complete separation of commerce and industry developed. It can hardly be said that there were many merchants dealing solely in the marketing of goods bought and sold with an eye singularly focused on profits. Marketing was, rather, a sideline to the yet dominant place of production.

As the center of gravity shifted gradually away from Heiankyō as the apex of the national integrative structure to the provincial manors, the control of the ruling class over the people weakened somewhat. Local markets flourished with tacit approval as long as they were situated in front of a shrine or temple gate, or in important cities such as Dazaifu in the west and Chinjufu in the north of Japan. Local markets also sprang up in the provincial capitals, *kokufu*, or in smaller administrative towns, as well as at junctions along the well-run highway system.

As the importance of local administrative divisions such as prefectures and districts dwindled due to expansion of the great manors, *shōen*, markets were opened within the manorial grounds on festival and other special days, though only irregularly. They did not, at this stage, assume any regularized sequence, such as opening on the second, twelfth, and twenty-secondth of the month, a custom known later as *hikiri-ichi*, or "market on set days."

As the barter economy developed, goods flowed in exchange between the capital city and the provinces, and between the provincial cities. From among peasants who previously engaged in part-time peddling there emerged merchants specializing solely in the marketing of goods. Their customers were mainly the aristocrats and priests in the cities, and to supply them the merchants relied necessarily on products made at the large manors. This served to bind the provinces closer to life in the cities, including the capital city.

The great bulk of merchandise was transported by waterways, enhancing the importance of the Yodogawa river in the Nara era. Along this river there sprouted numerous depots, such as Yodo, Kayo, Yamazaki, Esaki, Kanzaki, and Kanishima, which spawned many shops themselves. Beyond, along the coasts of the Inland Sea of Seto, harbor towns like Ōkawajiri and Ōwada developed warehouses, *tsuya*, where goods were handled on a consignment basis. Dazaifu, of course, enjoyed trade contacts with foreign vessels, and its markets and merchants were organized to handle this trade, until the collapse of the *ritsuryō* system and discontinuance after 894 of official contacts with the continent diminished it considerably. During the Sung period (960–1279) in China, Chinese vessels continued calling at Japanese ports, such as Imazu, Hirato, Tsushima, Kanzaki, and Karatsu in Kyūshū and even Tsuruga in the Hokuriku district. The introduction of coins of the Sung dynasty resulted from these contacts, and the circulation of Sung-made coins was destined to replace the commodity exchange medium of the barter economy eventually.

Whereas foreign trade declined after cessation of official relations with China at the end of the 9th century, intermanorial trade flourished especially in response to the demands of the priests, officials and nobility living in the capital and provincial cities. Along the roads connecting the capital and provincial cities, such as the famous Tōkaidō, or "East Coast Route," markets were set up by merchants gathering at the rest stations. These eventually were converted into permanent shops that lined the streets of the towns that later emerged.[45]

# Chapter III

# Cities and Towns in the Early Middle Ages (A.D. 1180–1273)

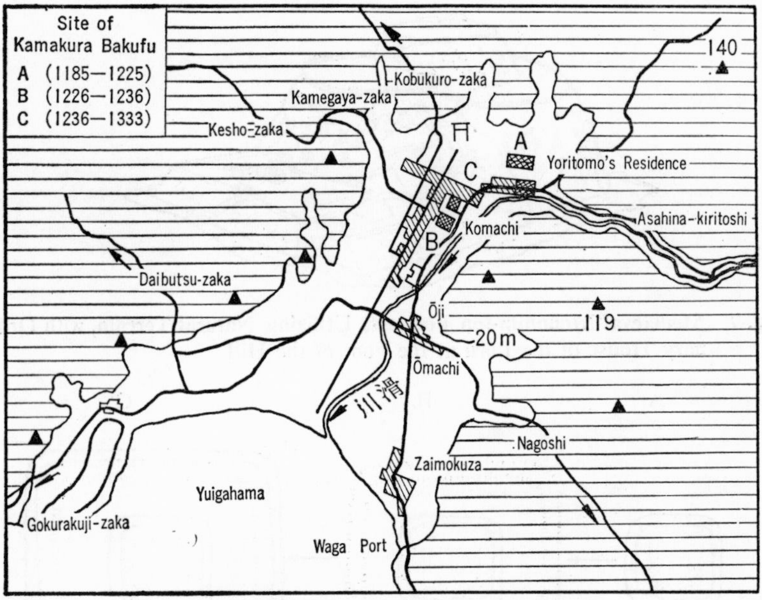


**Fig. 5 Diagram of Kamakura** (drawn by Kenjiro Fujioka)

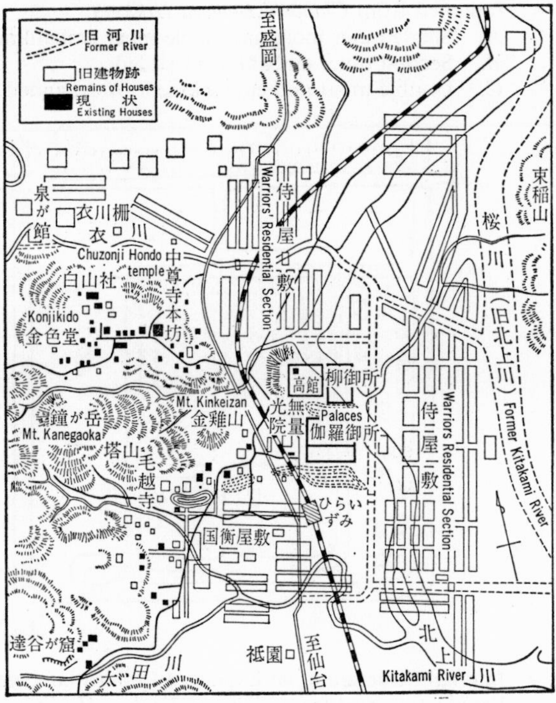


**Fig. 6 Hiraizumi** (a apted from *Meiji Izen Nihon Doboku Shi*)

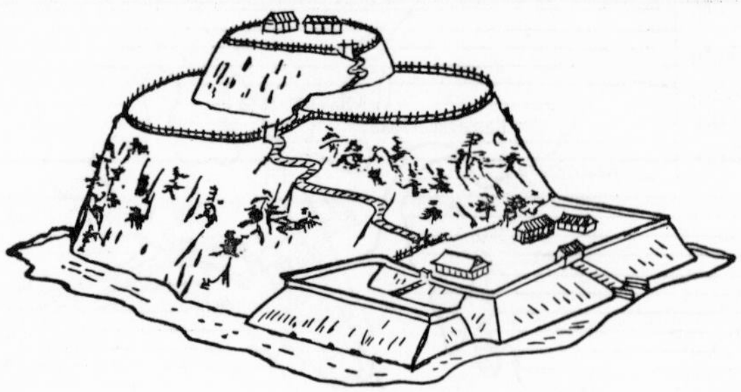

**Fig. 7 Mediaeval Mountain-top Fortress, Utilizing Natural Terrain, with Ordinary House of the Lord at the Foot of the Hill**

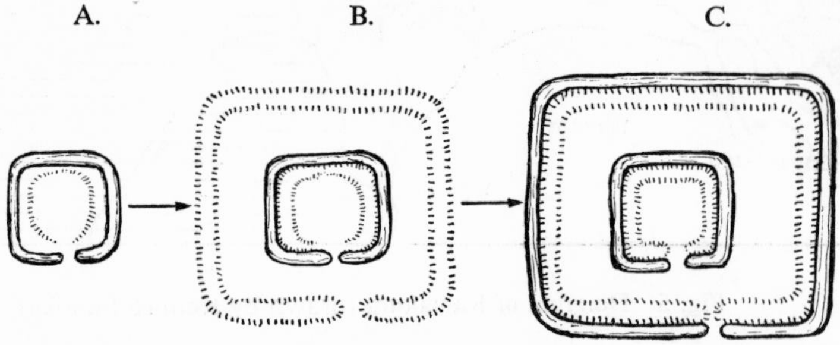


**Fig. 8 Expansion of the Residential Compounds of Powerful Provincial Families** (adapted from *Chihōshi Kenkyu Hikkei*)

A. Single outer moat and single inner embankment.
B. Second outer embankment added.
C. Double moat and embankment of expanded compound.

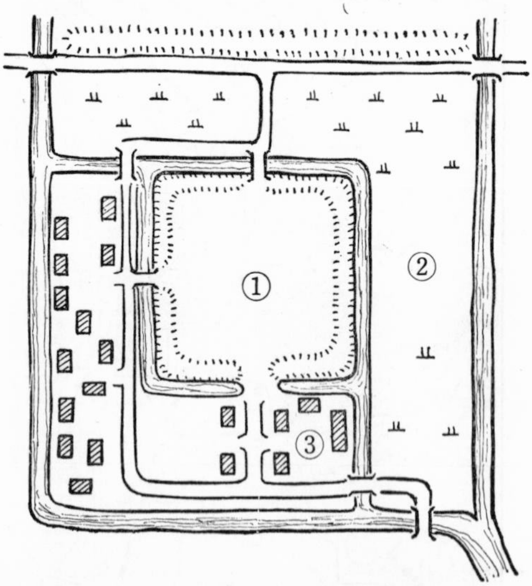


**Fig. 9 Internal Structure of an Expanded Residential Compound of a Provincial Family** (adapted from *Chihōshi Kenkyu Hikkei*)

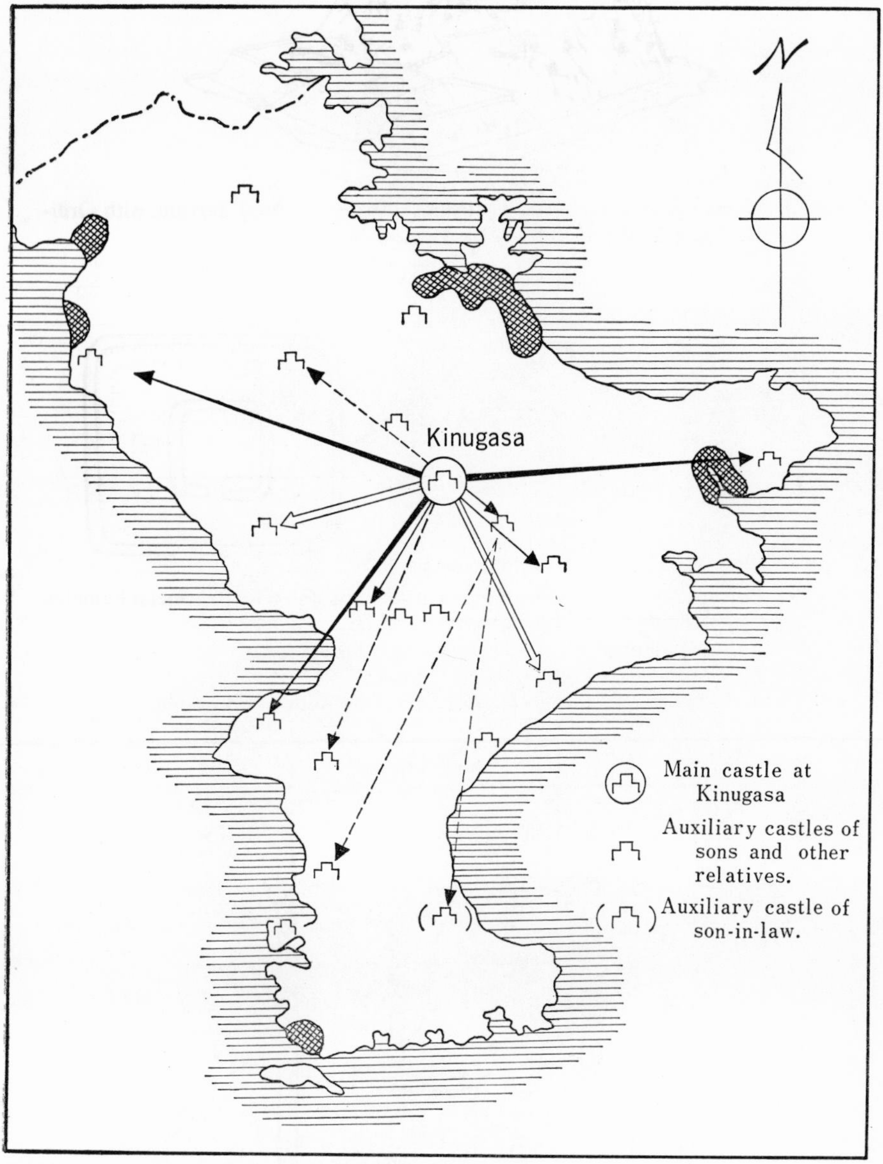


**Fig. 10 Regional Castle Network, Typical of the Kantō Plain**

## 1. Decline of the Ancient Political System (*Ritsuryō Seido*) and Emergence of the Feudal System

The *ritsuryō* system of centralized government aimed at realizing the T'ang ideals of state ownership of all lands and creation of a bureaucratic system in which men were promoted according to ability rather than family status, thereby depriving the powerful clans of political power. These established families could not be easily set aside, however, and a limited number of them actually pre-empted the socio-economic privileges of the new system. As their power solidified, their hold over the important positions of government became hereditary and they became firmly entrenched in the socio-political order.

By the middle of the 10th century the nobility, temples and shrines had acquired vast landholdings, concentrated into private, tax-free estates. The provincial governors (*kokushi*) appointed under the *ritsuryō* system,—most of them originally local clan heads—had also accumulated considerable power after settling into their posts. Some no longer even resided in their assigned provinces, delegating power instead to local deputies. Master-subordinate relations were formed between these men of power, that were regulated through fictitious systems of religious and consanguine relationships.

It was the eventual recognition of private property rights, releasing lands from government controls, that most weakened the centralized power of the state, and accelerated the emergence of provincial concentrations of power. From their bases of strength in the large estates, these powers were gradually capable of standing against the central government.

The tax measures designed to bolster up the flagging strength of the central government became unbearable burdens for the peasantry, who sought relief by subjecting themselves, and their lands, to powerful local leaders. Originally assigned for life, their lands, *kubunden*, had come to be regarded as personal property inherited by the family line. The *gōko* grouping of families as an administrative unit underwent change when the constituent families, *bōko*, assumed personal ownership of lands previously held in common by the *gōko*. As the decomposition of *gōko* took place, minor *gōko* were absorbed by larger ones.

The *gōko* master who extended his territory thusly by absorption of other lands was called *myōshu*. Lands cultivated by his own, or his subordinates' relatives were *myōden*, and the aggregate of these consanguineous units formed a village under the *myōshu*, master of the main family. Although personal ownership of property was still formally prohibited by the now weakened legal code, the *myōshu* secured their *de facto* property rights by aligning themselves with powerful estates capable of countering the central government. This they did by donating part of their landholdings to the large estates, for which the *myōshu* received, in return, the protection of the manorial power.

Government officials of noble rank brought the *myōden* lands further under the manorial system of private ownership by appointing the *myōshu* to positions on their estates, completely destroying the system of government land controls. Not only lands but the populace as well passed from national to manorial citizenship. Thus did transformations in the power structure lead to the decisive weakening of the central government and its system of controls.

Struggles for control of the new aggregates of lands and people naturally occurred and to retain power it was necessary for estate owners to assume the political authority and military strength once belonging to the court aristocracy. Armed units were formed by the *myōshu*, consisting of sons, relatives, retainers and serfs, for policing the estates and providing the joint security that replaced the weakened power of the central government for enforcing peace and order. Formation of these armed units resulted in the emergence of a rural military aristocracy, *buke*, which served the estate lords in extending their domains by exerting power over lesser lords.

Regional governors (*kokushi*) originally appointed by the central government acted on their own to build up vast estates with powerful military forces. Some of these acquired especially large concentrations of land and power comparable to those of the older aristocratic powers. Notable among these were the Genji, Heishi, and Fujiwara (Ōshu region) families.

Gradually a new mode of political integration displaced the rapidly dissolving *ritsuryō* integrative system. Nakamura Takaya, in his study of the social conditions of the medieval period, analyzes the changes in the political regions of that period, and a summary of some of his views is given below.

The Kinki district had been the political center of the nation when the imperial family, along with the Fujiwara family and other court aristocrats, retained administrative authority and control. The center of traditional culture as well, this district consumed beyond its ability to produce, being dependent upon absorption of productive surplus from both western and eastern Japan. When political power shifted into the hands of the provincially-based military cliques, the fortunes of this district gradually declined.

The region west of Kyōto is rather mountainous, without wide plains, and political life centered around the Inland Sea of Seto. The economy of this region was based not only upon farming but also upon fishing, salt production, and marine transportation. The last-mentioned, especially, had been developed since antiquity, and the arrival of vessels from

Koguryō (in Korea) and Sung (in China) brought additional wealth into this district. Seafaring capabilities added to the military prowess of leaders in this region, such as the Fujiwara fleet of pirate ships that assaulted provinces along the Inland Sea coastline, including the San-yō district and the large island of Shikoku. Daring to attack even the regional capital of Dazaifu in Kyūshū, this marine marauding was a real threat to the central government, although the houses of Ono Yoshifuru and Minamoto-no-Tsunemoto counterattacked and destroyed the Fujiwara pirate fleets.

Turning to the Kantō plain in eastern Japan, the situation was reversed. Here there were wide plains but no good ports, making sea connections with the capital region difficult. Marine traffic in this region was not developed much beyond small crafts and primitive navigational techniques, and frontal exposure to the high waves of the Pacific Ocean added to the difficulties. Steep mountain passes and wide, unruly rivers made overland communications with the capital region problematic.

Agriculture and cattle-breeding had been the economic mainstays of the Kantō region since ancient times, though vast land areas remained yet undeveloped. Powerful clans contested with each other for control over these lands, amassing huge estates and great military strength. The Heishi clan settled and commanded the area from the 9th century, though it was upset by an alliance of Taira-no-Sadamori, of the same clan, and a member of the Fujiwara line, Hidesato. In the 11th century, the Heishi regained control of the Bōso (Chiba) peninsula in the eastern coastal area, only to be overturned by troops of the Genji clan commanded by Minamoto-no-Yorinobu acting under orders of the imperial court. Genji control of the Kantō plain, added to its strength in the Kinki district, posed the most formidable power in the country at that time.

The remoteness and the mountainous terrain of the northeastern Tōhoku region afforded it a degree of independence from the central government. Gold resources and horse-breeding added to the strength of this region, though it was brought under control by the Genji clan in the 11th century and power was exercised by Fujiwara Kiyohira who had collaborated in the subduing of this region.

Meanwhile, warrior cliques consolidated in the local areas, on which the central government relied for support of its authority. Actually the central authority was not, in this stage, so weak as to permit independence for the provincial powers, and the military factions were subordinate to the imperial family and its mainstay, the Fujiwara household.

From the end of the Heian era on, the warrior groups, while acting on the one hand to support the central government, proceeded to extend their own power toward the central capital area by absorbing lesser *myōshu* and estates. Endeavoring to salvage the *ritsuryō* system, the court aristocracy vied with each other in efforts to gain the backing of the rural military factions, resulting in struggles such as the Wars of Hogen (1156) and Heiji (1159–60). This process served to make the warrior cliques indispensable to the security of the entire country. For a time the Heishi clan, based in Ise and Iga, gained ascendancy in the struggles and, when Taira-no-Kiyomori came to power in the central government, the court aristocrats were retired from administrative controls.

Kiyomori's succession to power was followed, however, by intense contests between the Heishi and Genji clans for command over the provincial warrior cliques. After Heishi power in the capital declined, they were overthrown by the Genji forces, while the Fujiwara group in Hiraizumi (in Ōshu) administered the *coup de grâce* to the Heishi forces. The Genji brought most of the warrior cliques into subjection, consolidating its power over the entire land and creating a new structure of political integration. This structure had the Genji leaders, of course, at the top, and under them the *myōshu* and *shōkan* (estate managers), who were served by their farmer-warriors. These master-subordinate relationships were articulated in terms of fictitious clan and family relationships, in which the *myōshu* and *shōkan* were "sons" of their overlords, and the peasant-warriors "sons" of the *myōshu.* Subordination had its reward in the added security of land ownership under the protection of powerful overlords. Individualism was completely submerged, of course, in such strong loyalty-protection relations.

Warrior leaders swearing allegiance to the military government, or *bakufu*, were called *gokenin*, that is, "honorable members of the household," inasmuch as the relationship was deemed an extension of the family's blood-relationship. It was not a contractual arrangement in which the subordinate agreed to be loyal if he received adequate lands; the relation demanded absolute loyalty even to death, as the first priority, and land was granted as a "reward" for fealty. The basic concept in this relationship was that of *on*, meaning "favor" or "benefit," though its significance derived not only from the fact that the absolute authority exercised by the lord on the subordinates was socially accepted. *On* was the highest moral principle both for the lord, who as benefactor was obligated to bestow benefit, and for the subordinate, whose gratitude as beneficiary was to be expressed in loyalty.

From among the *gokenin*, the military regime appointed estate supervisors, *jitō* (lit., "land head") to administer controls, collect taxes, and safeguard the estates. From among the *jitō*, and to rule over them, regional governors, *shugo* ("guardians of order") were appointed, who commanded special security troops. Throughout the country there remained, from the old *ritsuryō* system, older hierarchical relationships similar to the new military chain of command that had been cultivated in groups related to the imperial household, the nobility, and the major religious orders. These two familial structures continued to exist side by side, so that in one village the effective leader might be the military-oriented *jitō* and in a neighboring village an official related to the older system.

National integration continued to be symbolized by the emperor as the "father" of the national "clan" and the chief religious authority, although actual political and military controls were in the hands of the

Genji leaders. Imperial sovereignty was acted out in formal appointments of the top military leaders as shogun (generalissimo) and of the regional governors and estate managers to their posts, which, in effect, legitimized the military regime's exercise of authority in the emperor's name. Deprived of real power in the liquidation of the *ritsuryō* system, the emperor yet occupied the "highest" position in the land.

## 2. Description of Kamakura, Kyōto and Hiraizumi as Semi-feudal Cities

*Kamakura.*——When Minamoto-no-Yoritomo consolidated his power in Kamakura in the fourth year of Jishō (1180), marking the final dissolution of the *ritsuryō* system and the effective removal of the nation's political center away from Kyōto, Kamakura was but a small village. This move was prompted by the desire to establish a new political order away from the center of traditional patterns, and to exercise greater controls over provincial warrior groups not yet fully unified under the new military regime. Though the Genji had won ascendancy the struggle with the Heishi had not fully ended.

The Genji family history had long been connected with Kamakura. Yoritomo's father, Yoshitomo, had ruled eastern Japan (*Tōgoku*) from his base in Kamegaya in the Kamakura district, and there were many relatives and subordinates among the powerful clans near Kamakura. Its defense was enhanced by mountains surrounding all sides except the western shore, which afforded passage, through the port of Waga, to important points along the Pacific coastal regions.

In contrast to the former elaborate administrative structures of Kyōto, the Kamakura government's integrative organs were few and simple. The most important was the *Samurai-dokoro*, an office for controlling and supervising activities of the retainers, *gokenin*, to the military regime. In addition to determining duties, this bureau also meted out rewards and punishments. The administrative office was *Kumonjo*, later changed to *Man-dokoro*, which acted as the main policy-making bureau. The *Monchūjo* was the court of justice of the *bakufu*, operating on the basis of the Genji family's customs and values.

To Kamakura came the leading retainers of the regime, including the powerful regional governors, *shugo*, with their own supporting warriors. A capital guard, *Oban-yaku*, was founded in 1225, drawn from the ranks of the retainers, adding to the concentration of military personnel in Kamakura, and coming from all points east and west. Administrative personnel with ability were also needed and a number of experienced men came up from Kyōto. Through them a certain cultural continuity was retained with the older capital, strongly influencing the formation of Kamakura as a city.[1]

Construction of many temples and shrines in Kamakura naturally followed its establishment as the effective center of the nation. The Hachiman Shrine, originally located in the southern sector of the Kamakura area, built a large new structure in the northern part of the village soon after Yoritomo founded his government there. Centrally placed in the new city, public ceremonies, such as celebration of the New Year in the presence of the generalissimo (shogun), were performed in the Hachiman Shrine grounds. There was also constructed the Ebara Tenjinsha Shrine and the Zen Buddhist temple-complex known as *gozan* including Kenchōji, Enkakuji, Jufukuji, Jōchiji, and Jōmyoji, similar to the *gozan* complex on the outskirts of Kyōto. These, and many other temples and shrines, brought a sizable concentration of clerical personnel to Kamakura.

Large amounts of annual tribute poured into Kamakura from the nine provinces controlled by the military government, namely, Izu, Sagami, Kazusa, Shimo-Osa, Shinano, Échigo, Musashi, Suruga and Bungo, as well as from the estates owned by powerful warriors and landholding shrines and temples. Tribute came too from estates previously under the control of the subdued Heishi. Craftsmen and merchants were brought into Kamakura to process these goods, and to fulfill the needs of the new government in architecture, temple equipment, weapons and armor, and the necessities of daily life of the expanded population. The military government employed its own craftsmen, who were rewarded with fields to cultivate. Records show that Enkakuji temple and Hachiman Shrine also retained their own artisans, as did, presumably, other large shrines and temples.[2]

The workmen were not free laborers under contract but bonded workmen, strictly controlled by the military and religious groups in both the kinds and quantities of goods produced. Products were for fulfilling government and religious needs and not for consumption by the common people. As was the case formerly in Kyōto, the city of Kamakura prospered as the construction of both mansions for the ruling elite and temples and shrines brought into being thriving shops of merchants and craftsmen.

Although the population of Kamakura is not clearly known, according to the *Azuma-kagami* ("Mirror of the Eastland," based on official records of the Kamakura shogunate and covering the years 1180–1266) a census was worked out on the basis of the number of *sake* (rice wine) bottles consumed. The count was 37,274 when the sale of *sake* was ordered to cease temporarity in 1252. Yoshida Tōgo estimates that there were 10,000 households in Kamakura on the basis of this figure. Some 23,204 dead were reported after an earthquake damaged the city in 1293, from which we can suppose that the population in this era was between 50,000 and 60,000.[3]

The irregular terrain and vastly different social conditions governing the founding of Kamakura both worked against imitation of the checkerboard design of Kyōto, producing a different topographical layout in Kamakura. Yoritomo founded a road maintenance bureau in 1187 to repair old roads and build new ones. This office also handled necessary work on ditches, rivers, and the ocean shoreline. City planning in Kamakura was not done in advance to accommodate an estimated population, but was carried out in response to needs as they arose for an expanding populace.

The main axis of the city was a street running from the Hachiman Shrine south to the shore, lined by *Okura-yakata*, mansion of the shogun, and residences of his retainers in the northeastern sector. The *bakufu* changed locations three times, from Ōkura to Utsunomiya to Wakamiya-kōji.[4] Temples and shrines were situated on the hills in the northern sector. Along the Yuigahama shore to the south were gathered the merchants' shops. Residential areas for commoners were not clearly separated according to occupation and status, though merchants tended to congregate in the southeastern, and craftsmen in the northeastern sectors.[5]

The population of Kamakura increased in proportion to the strengthening of the military administration. The port of Waga was developed to accommodate an expanded sea traffic transporting bulky cargoes of lumber, rice, and other goods from outlying provinces. This was the sole source of lumber for the many construction jobs in Kamakura, including greatly increased demands for housing. Large warehouses were built for handling the lumber supply by the guild of lumber merchants at a place bearing the name of their guild, Zaimoku-za.

Communication routes leading to outlying districts were cut through the mountains surrounding Kamakura at seven points—Gokurakuji, Daibutsu, Keshōzaka, Kamegaya, Kobukurozaka, Asahina and Nagoshi. These routes and their locations added to the defense measures of the city.

The seriousness with which the military regime viewed the internal administration of the city is indicated in the appointment of one of the high-ranking officers of the regime, Chikugonokami Toshikane, as governor of the city. After actual power in the military government passed to a group of regents, political consultants to the shogunate, one of them occupied the governor's post. The powers of these governors extended even to high-ranking warriors and priests resident in the city, as can be seen in the restrictions placed by one of them upon extravagance in residential construction for warriors and priests, as well as upon undue currying of favors from the shogunate. Compared to the city managers under the later Tokugawa Shogunate, these governors were nearly almighty.

In the early days of the Kamakura regime the position of the city's administration was neither formalized nor specifically named, the work simply being assumed by one of the high executives of the government. In the middle of the Kamakura era municipal administration was consolidated under two official posts, that of *hokendan-bugyō*, inspector-general, and *ji-bugyō*, supervisor of roads and housing. In Kyōto the minimal unit of municipal administration had been the *hō* (groups of several families) under a leader called *tone*. Kawakami Tasuke suggests that a similar system existed in Kamakura,[6] the controlling office being *hōho-bugyō*, although Endo Motō believes this was simply a comprehensive term covering both *hokendan-bugyō* and *ji-bugyō*.[7]

Administrative controls for the city of Kamakura were exercised through the *bugyō* in the following manner:

Public safety through police security was given priority. Not only were strange travelers, unemployed men, robbers and plain rascals watched carefully, but ordinary citizens were also ordered to burn bonfires in the streets each evening, to avoid walking the streets at night, and to bring torch lights in case of reported crimes.

Once, when it was reported that a subordinate household, the Miura, had rebelled against the shogunate in 1247, the latter ordered warriors—who had rushed to Kamakura to help, but had no official status there—to return to their neighboring provinces. As in other capital cities, vagabonds were attracted to Kamakura, but the shogunate returned to the rural districts those not actually engaged in production in the city.

Buddhist temples were enlisted in the effort to maintain social order, for instance, through the enforcement of religious restrictions such as prohibitions on eating fish and game, on soliciting women, and on drinking bouts.

As housing became congested, prohibitions were issued against protruding eaves and against erecting small sheds over drainage ditches that lined the streets. Families were ordered to clean the streets in their communities, which were often congested with people and cattle. Hitching areas were designated at certain points to prevent soiling by oxen used for hauling.

Population growth in the city naturally stimulated commerce, which had got its start with the settlement of craftsmen and merchants, the development of Waga port, and coin circulation. To avoid upsetting the status structure of the city, however, the *bakufu* constantly tried to curb the growing enterprises in various ways.

For example, the number of merchants' households was limited, and transfer into the city by merchants was restricted. Rice-wine sales were suspended when poor rice crop yields reached famine levels. Commodity prices were fixed as much to suppress the merchants as to stabilize the economy or help the average citizen, and forceful merchandizing was prohibited. Dimensions of lumber sizes in heavy demand were standardized. Finally, pawnbrokers were regulated, requiring registration of the pawner's name and address to prevent pawning of stolen goods.

The process of locating shops along the streets of Kamakura had proceeded haphazardly from the beginning, resulting in confusion as the city expanded. Hence, the *bakufu* designated seven areas as market places, four of them along the street of Ōmachi-kōji, namely, Ōmachi, Komachi, Yonemachi, and Waga port. The other three lay along the travel route starting at a pass in the northeastern part of the city and ending in Yoko-ōji, namely, Kamegaya-tsuji, Okura-tsuji, and Keshōzaka-yamane. Not long afterward development of new housing areas necessitated a revision in the seven designated areas to Ōmachi, Komachi, Uomachi, Kokucho, Musashioji-shita, Sujigaebashi and Ōkura. These control measures over commercial activity stimulated the formation of cooperatives similar to the guild system in the seven areas called "Kamakura Hichiza," dealing in silk, charcoal, rice, wooden containers, medicine, salted or dried fish, and horses.

Although marketing areas were fixed in Kamakura, residential areas were not segregated according to status or occupation as in the castle towns of the later Edo era. *Bakufu* leaders, retainers, merchants, craftsmen and farmers lived in mixed communities, the various control measures being introduced only after expansion of the city itself.

The city of Kamakura emerged as the center of a new political order of feudalistically related cliques of warriors, but retained a specific character continuous with ancient cities, in that it remained dependent upon annual tribute collected mainly from the estates. The ranks of its leadership elite were composed chiefly of *kenin* who were managers, *jitō*, of the estates. Its prominent citizens were these warriors and their followers, and the religious and technical personnel who served them. There was no group of citizens whose lives were independent of the dominant military class.

*Kyōto.*——The displacement of the *ritsuryō* system by an expanded manorial system followed by the relocation of the political center of gravity in Kamakura rendered the ancient city of Kyōto far less important in the political, integrative life of the country. Imperial authority had been preserved, though, and Kyōto retained its functions as the center of traditional culture, religion and national economy, much as it had for the previous four centuries.

Here were gathered the imperial and aristocratic mansions, the stately temples and shrines. Many of the upper class nobility had erected their own temples, not for purely religious motives, but also as meeting places for pursuit of their social and cultural interests. Government-owned lands and private estates provided an abundant flow of products into Kyōto for their absentee landlords resident there. Of rather low quality, these materials were then further processed to meet the standards of their high-class consumers, thus requiring many craftsmen and merchants to handle the processing and distribution to noblemen, priests and warriors. The high-grade *Ayaori*-style silks and wide variety of refined handicrafts were but symbols of the busy economic activity.

The deviation from the original checkerboard plan has already been noted, as affluent families congregated in the more desirable Sakyō section along the Kamogawa river. It is said that the Heishi martial households that prospered in the Wars of Hogen and Heiji in the latter part of the Heian era built some 5,200 houses in the area between Kamogawa river and the hills of Higashiyama at the height of their roles as defenders of the capital. The Genji households were located in Rokujo Horikawa and Muromachi near the centers of commerce and industry in Hichijō. There were many artisans resident there who supplied the warriors' needs (i.e., in addition to craftsmen serving the nobility).

Natural disasters damaged this thriving city several times in this period. A big fire in the last year of the Angen era (1177) burned down about one-third of the city, leaving several thousands dead (and the national "University" of the *ritsuryō* period in ruins). Another big fire in 1178, a severe typhoon in 1180, a serious famine from 1181 to 1182, and a great earthquake in 1185 came in rapid succession to plague the city. Frequent skirmishes between the Genji and Heishi warriors added to the damages left by these natural calamities. Many gorgeous structures erected under imperial and aristocratic auspices were destroyed in the above disasters, including Hōseiji and Hōzenji temples and the Daigokuden palace building, none of which were reconstructed. Famine conditions sometimes led to the thoughtless selling of cultural treasures stored in temples and shrines, and many people dependent upon the aristocracy were impoverished. Some turned to robbery, and it is said that the priests of Enryakuji temple jeopardized public peace by inciting vagabonds to violence.[8] Some of the poor court nobility sought to salvage their fortunes by marrying their sons and daughters into the warrior households or into wealthy merchant families in the Kantō district.

After assuming power, Yoritomo worked to restore Kyōto, ordering repairs for the imperial palace, the Kamo Shrines, Tōji temple and other structures. His retainers were commanded to take turns at guard duty in the city. Following the Shōkyū War (1221) commissioners were appointed to the Rokuhara sector, at Nanden south of Rokuhara Mitsuji temple and at Hokuden north of it, as the representatives of the Kamakura *bakufu* in Kyōto for liaison with the imperial court. Kyōto citizens were directed to build watch-fires at night to reinforce police monitoring, as part of the shogunate's efforts to maintain order in the city.

The establishment of markets in the east and west sectors of Kyōto and the subsequent decline of the west market were mentioned in the previous chapter. The east market also suffered from the distintegration of the *ritsuryō* system. Control over materials shifted to estate owners, and craftsmen employed by the landed aristocracy and priestly class took advantage of weakened government controls to sell their own goods. In the Sanjō, Shijō and Hichijō sections were clustered shops of pawnbrokers and merchants, the latter dealing freely in foodstuffs and clothing. Commodity exchange was monopolized by merchants' guilds, whose shops eventually converged into sizable commercial areas.[9]

In effect, the aristocracy were ruined by the dislocation of political power to Kamakura. Even though temple institutions received *bakufu* protection, those built under aristocratic auspices became overrun by the warrior groups, and the aristocratic social order in Kyōto declined drastically. With the overall elevation of economic activity, the consumptive activity of the common people increased. To lend succor to the threatened fortunes of the nobility whose lives were dependent on the land, the *bakufu* sought to block the circulation of coins, but in vain, as the momentum of commercial development surpassed the force of the prohibition act.

At the same time public recognition of occupational cooperatives was given to such guilds as *kirikawa-za* (hides and leather), *wata-za* (cotton) handled by *jinin*, acolytes at the Gion Shrine, *kinu-za* (silk) and *uo-za* (fish). Wholesalers, pawnbrokers and *sake* brewers also prospered in the Sanjō and Hichijō areas. Recognition of their place in the power structure came partly in the form of taxes levied on them to bear some of the expenses of government. Funds derived from such tax measures accelerated the reformation of Kyōto as a feudal city.[10]

Eventually the protection of governmental authority served to strengthen the foundations of commerce and industry. Maintenance of public order under the military organization was conducive to economic development and, although there were no citizens' councils for community security, individual households sometimes acquired weapons for self-defense against attacks made by groups of thieves prevalent in those days.[11]

*Hiraizumi.*——Boasting the highest cultural level and the largest city structure in Japan, Kyōto was gradually transformed from an ancient aristocratic to a feudal city structure. Kamakura flourished as the integrative center of an emerging feudal order, though it manifested many characteristics of the declining ancient social order. In the provinces where administrative power of the central government was weakest there appeared feudalistically-organized regional groups. Around the residences of those local authorities, who integrated the surrounding areas, grew local cities with relatively complex structures. The most typical was Hiraizumi, situated in the Kita-kamigawa river basin halfway between present-day Sendai and Morioka, a city that thrived late in the Heian period.

In this northeastern region most of the administrative and military posts had, since the Heian era, been controlled hereditarily by the leading families of the area. To safeguard their estates the lesser families affiliated with the powerful Fujiwara family in Hiraizumi, where that clan had located its office of estate management through four successive generations, under Kiyohara, Motohira, Hidehira and Yasuhira. The integrative function of the Fujiwara family over many powerful warrior cliques in the northeastern Ōshu district led to the development of a city around its family residence in Hiraizumi. The site was blessed with convenient travel routes along the Kita-kamigawa river south to Shirakawa on the Pacific shore, and north to Sotogahama on Mutsu Bay (near present-day Aomori). The city's controlling powers extended over tens of thousands of villages throughout Ōshu.

Brilliantly described in the book *Azuma-kagami*, a picture of Hiraizumi painted by Kasai in the Kamakura era is still extant. The mansion of the lord of Hiraizumi, in the city's center, was surrounded by warriors' residences and to the west there were situated many temples on the Kinkeizan and Kanegaoka hills. Among them was Chūsonji, a fine example of late Heian architecture. In the northern sector of the city merchant dwellings were clustered at Muika-ichi, Nanoka-ichi, and Yōka-ichi (sixth, seventh and eighth-day markets). Such distribution of official structures, temples, and residences indicates that Hiraizumi functioned as the political, religious, and economic nucleus of the region. The community classification of the citizenry according to feudal status is similar to that seen in the castle towns of the daimyō in the Edo era.

Although there were many temples in Hiraizumi it was not a city established on religious foundations. The administrative organs made formal use of the Buddhist institutions, rather, to compensate for the limitations experienced in military administration after the Wars of Zenkunen (1056–62) and Gosannen (1083–87).[12]

The feudalistic character of Hiraizumi was evident also in the defense facilities of the city. Natural barriers flanked the city, hills to the west and the river on the east side, while lookouts were constructed at strategic land and river sites. Street intersections were T-shaped to confuse intruders advancing toward the Izumigajō castle in the western sector. From the viewpoints of both community layout and social structure, Hiraizumi had been converted from an ancient into a feudal city.

As mentioned earlier, this city flourished late in the Heian era as the center of integrative organs governing the extensive Ōshu region. Once destroyed by the troops of Yoritomo in 1188, as Genji power effected its unification over the entire country, it was never again rebuilt, being unable to recover any economic or cultural functions independent of the dominant political movement. Dependent upon the fortunes of the Fujiwara family for its existence, it was crushed with the latter's downfall.

After Kamakura replaced Kyōto as the political center of the country, there were two main focal points of national life, namely, Kamakura as the base of political activity, and Kyōto as the center of traditional culture. The highway and relay station system along the east coast, oriented to Kyōto alone, now had to serve the two central areas. Yoritomo of the Genji clan ordered a revision in the relay system in 1185, as well as new road construction. Travel increased considerably, for now in addition to the usual messengers there were added large movements of Genji troops.

There were three main routes connecting the two cities, the Tōkaidō, Tōsandō, and Hokurikudō. Sixty-three relay stations were built along the 120 *ri* (293 mi.) distance of the Tōkaidō, supervised by a *bakufu* office that issued licenses for authorized travelers. Local supervision was put under powerful local families, and lodging and food were supplied at the stations. Towns flourished at some of the station points, called *shukuba-machi*, such as Ōtsu, Kayatsu, Atsuta, Yabase, Akasaka, Hashimoto, Kikukawa, Maejima and Mishima. From descriptions in *Kaidōki* and *Tōkan Kikō*, it is learned that large numbers of prostitutes worked in Akasaka, Hashimoto and Mishima, indicating considerable prosperity in these towns.[13]

Yoritomo ordered Sasaki Hidetsuna, governor of Ōmi, to install a ferry system over the Inland Sea in 1187, chiefly for messengers' use. Road construction and maintenance was good, and in 1188 an express mail service was opened that covered the Tōkaidō route between Kyōto and Kamakura in seven days, and this was shortened to four days by 1239. Such speed was utilized, however, only in emergencies and the route normally required much longer. For example, Yoritomo is said to have taken sixteen days from Kyōto to Kamakura in 1190 and twelve days in 1195. Fujiwara Yoritsune spent seventeen days on the same route in 1238.[14] According to the *Kaidōki*, Mitsuyuki of the Genji household arrived in Kamakura from Kyōto after fourteen days in 1223. Commoners needed about half a month for the route, while a nun named Abutsu, authoress of *Izayoi Nikki*, needed only fourteen days even as a woman.[15]

The Kamakura military government improved the relay station system, keeping it in good repair after the death of Yoritomo in 1199. Moreover, the attempted invasions of the Mongol forces in 1274 and 1281 weakened the integrative strength of the shogunate and it is reported in the *Taiheiki*, or "Chronicle of Grand Pacification" covering the continuous wars between 1318 and 1367, that "there were many robber groups prowling about on land and sea, with no masters in the station houses and no guards in the checking stations."

Though warriors and messengers on official missions were fairly well cared for, commoners experienced many difficulties in traveling. The Tōkaidō route crossed a number of wide rivers, and the mountain passes through Hakone and Ashigara were steep and difficult to transverse. Commoners had access only to temples, shrines, and other commoners' houses for lodging, and when these were unavailable, they passed the night in the fields. They had to carry their own food, and oil paper or leather sheeting for protection against the weather. Estate managers often collected fees for passage along private roads, or across bridges or open streams. Peddlers traveled in groups of five to fifty members, bearing not only burdens of goods to exchange, but swords for defense against bandits.[16]

## 3. The Development of Castle and Commercial Centers

*Castle centers.*——We have seen how Kamakura and Kyōto developed in different ways, each with its own characteristic features yet closely connected with each other, and how the mutual relation expedited improvements in the highway system, especially the Tōkaidō linking the two cities.

Commercial activity expanded in both cities, yet the prominent citizens of each were the estate lords, their retainers, and other followers, plus the priestly class. They remained centers of consumption, dependent upon taxes and goods from the land. No independent civilian community had emerged yet, as these cities were founded upon the political and religious controls of the warriors, aristocracy, and priests. Agricultural productivity had not progressed sufficiently to permit separation of commerce and industry. Hence, there existed only two types of local communities, one the political centers, the other relatively isolated rural districts.

In these rural districts, though, there emerged castle centers which were the prototypes of the castle towns that developed later. Such castle centers were made possible by expanded production in agriculture, development in the exchange economy, structural changes in political life, and expansion of the integrated regions in the country. Development of markets near large temples and traffic junctions, land and sea, as well as increased activities of the craftsmen and merchants, all served to accelerate the emergence of new city centers.

Certain changes that occurred in the rural districts after the 10th century have already been noted, specifically the breakdown of government land controls, accumulation of vast land tracts by powerful families and temples through reclamation, and the tendency for landlords of the increased number of estates to move their residences from the central area to their estates. Weakened central controls endangered the security of the estates so that estate landlords and managers were forced to enlarge local militia to guard their lands and secure social order within them. Strengthened militia also enabled some estates to expand their holdings.

Estates belonging to powerful families living in the central area were not neatly located in one place, but were scattered here and there over the country. Each of the three large power groups, (1) the court aristocracy, (2) the major temples and shrines, and (3) the military cliques, owned an almost equal share of all the estate lands in Japan in this period. Managers were appointed to exercise actual control over the multiple land areas of each estate. Peasants on these lands were obligated to render military service as well as to pay taxes. Families living for generations on these lands were grouped together as large "families" under the martial managers (*myōshu*), to whom they "belonged" as much as the land did. The village communities which they formed together operated as self-sufficient economic units.

The nucleus of each village was its manager's residence, and the most influential leader among the managers was appointed as the head, *jitō*, and he actually governed as lord of the estate. His residence was constructed to meet the practical demands of a warrior, though some features of the aristocratic *shinden-zukuri* were added for style. In the immediate vicinity, barns and warehouses were built to store goods collected from the lands as tribute. The residence housed the master, his family, and their servants. Usually erected on a small hill near the main road of his village, commanding a good view of his territory, turrets were built around his residence compound to prevent intrusion by robber gangs and to dispel any other confusion. Further defensive measures included construction of earthen embankments about 1–2 *ken* (2–4 yds.) in height and moats of 2–8 *ken* (4–16 yds.) in width in square lines, double or single, around the residence. These facilities gave the name *horinouchi* (from the moat) or *doi* (from the embankments) to their residences. Imai Rintaro reports on examples of such places in Hatakeyama, Kawagoe, Beppu and Narita. Similar warriors' sites are also known in Musashi and other locations in the Kantō district.[17]

As a rule, the manager's residential compound included fields for dry and wet-land cultivation, tilled by his subordinates and exempted from taxes due the absentee landlord living in the capital city. In the vicinity of his residence were the village temples and shrines, as well as homes of craftsmen engaged in production of domestic products and military equipment. In payment the latter were given fields to work, *kyūden*. Common peasants living in the village area were under the direct control of the martial managers whose functions in the early middle ages were not clearly separated. Specialization of the farmer and warrior functions was to come later. Peasants were required to make tribute payments to the managers in the form of products and labor; but on fulfilling these obligations, any surplus products were at their own disposal. Cultivation rights granted for lands included also freedom to sell the lands.

Actual land area under cultivation increased by the middle of the Kamakura era as the managers (*myōshu*) extend their privately-owned lands (*myōden*) into estates, but the struggle between these powerful leaders to extend their own territories seriously diminished the stability of the social order. This was the primary provocative condition behind the construction of castles on hills near the manager's residence.

The hilltop castles took advantage of natural topography as much as possible, leveling the summits for construction and terracing the hillsides at several levels. Mountain ridges were made steeper and the courses of hillside paths altered to give the defenders more advantageous positions. In most cases, the village dwelling of the *myōshu* and the hilltop castle where he stayed during times of fighting were separately constructed. His neighbors in the village were his followers and we see no merchants' dwellings as they appeared in the later Edo era in the castle towns of that period.

Ōrui Noboru and Toba Masao characterize the castle features of this period in comparison with those of the succeeding era as follows:[18]

Limited to defensive uses, these castles were smaller than the imposing structures of the daimyō in the Edo period, being occupied only during battles. Combat was usually one to one on horseback with bows and arrows, in contrast to the massive encounters of the daimyō period. Actual fighting occurred more often in open fields than as ordered sieges of artificially-constructed fortresses or castles. Defense facilities utilized natural materials, such as moats or densely-planted, sharpened stakes.

Provincial families and *myōshu* extended their power after the decline of centralized controls and the resultant weakening of the state's armed might, especially when local disturbances upset public security. In times of confusion and danger the common people turned to the powerful *myōshu* for protection, surrendering their lands as a "donation." Status differentiations arose, distinguishing the men of power, their followers and subordinates. The latter were armed by their masters for defensive action. In time, the stronger *myōshu* commanded many others, and emerged as lords of large domains.

The constituency of the families of such *myōshu* was quite varied. Primary among the family group was the eldest son, who assumed by hereditary right the leadership of the whole family. Branch families were established separately from the main family, in which other sons and followers with records of distinguished service exercised control over various family members and lands. Within the complicated organization were some not in direct blood-relationship to the main family, yet all were tightly bound together by the values of loyalty and filial piety, *chūkō*, toward the head family.

In the early days of their rise to power in the Kamakura era, the warriors were in direct social relations to the *myōshu* residence. As land reclamation added to the territory under his control, the manager placed members of his family group, both direct and non-blood-relation members, in important locations throughout his domain. An integrative system emerged in which the sub-managers rendered taxes and services, both in military matters and land reclamation, and the head manager gave protective support in emergencies. The subordinates owed personal allegiance to the head of the "family," who extended his favors to them equally.

The Miura Peninsula, south of present-day Yokohama and southeast of Kamakura, is a case in point. A group of Heishi warriors, descendants of the Emperor Kanmu (781–806), organized initially around a single *myōshu*, later extended their territory to cover the entire peninsula. This warrior clique, composed of consanguine and non-consanguine members, had its castle center in Kinugasa, with outposts at important locations on the peninsula.[19]

Expansion by the military class in this period was limited in zonal extent, in that actual fighting did not last very long and was limited in scope. After combat the warriors returned to their own homes. That the *myōshu* castles were small in scale is noted in the studies of Asaka Yukio. For example, that of the Muraoka family, leader of the Heishi group in Sagami, measured only about five *tan* (1.2 acres), and that of Tsunemoto of the Seiwa Genji only about eight *tan* (2 acres). The Miura clique had some twenty castles, including the main one in Kinugasa, in the fifty-nine villages of the Miura district, which amounted to only one-third of the villages under Miura control. Such castle density was common in the south Kantō district.[20]

Although some of these castle centers were the predecessors of later Edo castle towns, they controlled only limited areas in this period, never occupying central positions for integrative control over an entire domain. Lacking in the organizational elements conducive to larger city development, most of them vanished in the Muromachi era in the face of larger integrative movements. Cities in this period developed, rather, in centers of economic activity and at travel junctions providing access to wider regions.

*Commercial centers.*——Land reclamation projects in the end of the Heian era stimulated a degree of progress in agriculture in local areas. The more advanced areas secured biannual crops, with improvements in fertilizers and cattle-breeding adding to elevation of overall productive capacity. After the military class acquired new strength in the Kamakura era, greater precision and diversification was introduced into cultivation methods, further promoting productivity.

Since Heian times, farm surplus had been sold in public markets, but these markets were freed from government supervision and placed under direct controls of powerful temples and local cliques for periodic opening.

Development of exchange markets did not benefit the rural peasantry, who had no freedom to bargain with the farm surpluses of their masters. Confined within the self-sufficient estates, with no local merchants catering to their needs, only occasional visits by wandering peddlers and craftsmen to the periodic markets brought any new items into their lives.

Increased production in agriculture did afford a measure of freedom, however, to the craftsmen engaged by the court aristocracy and the major temples and shrines. The landlords preferred tax and tribute payments in goods and coins rather than services. Specialization among the craftsmen was fostered by the granting of monopoly rights over their particular products by their masters. Authorization to market their own products contributed to their growing independence, although very limited capital holdings forced craftsmen to band together to prevent bankruptcy due to keen competition after gaining independence. Licenses were needed for clearance at checking stations when they sought to distribute their products to other regions, and these checking stations increased after the Heian era, and especially from the middle of the Kamakura era. Even after successfully passing the checking stations, the craftsmen were subject to natural dangers and to attacks by robbers, an added incentive to the formation of guilds, *za*, for mutual protection under the patronage of their lords.[21]

There were many famous *za* in the Kamakura era, dealing in oil, silk, salt, dyes, dried fish, iron utensils, wood and lumber, and these flourished in accordance with growth in commerce and industry. While farm surplus was not effectively utilized to improve the lot of the peasantry, it was skillfully exchanged in the markets by the estate managers for processed goods from other areas, expediting the development of the commodity market.

As commodity exchange increased in quantity and scope, the circulation of coins was stepped up. Imported originally for use in the capital region, coin circulation spread throughout the land as estate managers sought to sell their products to Kyōto-based merchants coming to the local markets. Local products to be forwarded to the capital were converted into coin currency and, by the middle of the Kamakura period, a system of money orders was established to replace transporting great quantities of the heavy coins. Craftsmen not bound to the land, and even a portion of the farmers, became active in the marketing network, primarily in collecting rural surplus and delivering it to the central areas. This network developed especially in the Kinai district where lines of exchange converged toward the highly consumptive capital populace. By the end of the Kamakura era, commodity markets were distributed all over Japan.[22]

Formerly, market locations had been limited to temple and shrine sites, towns of government offices, and travel junctions and ports. Under the manorial system, local estate markets emerged which were free from government controls, although three market days per month sufficed in these self-sufficient socio-economic units.

Toward the end of the Kamakura period, some of the *myōshu*, active since Heian times in the collection and transfer of tribute goods, began selling the products collected and sending the money to their lords. In time they accumulated great personal wealth by expanding their exchange functions, gradually becoming less dependent on their masters. Specializing in brokerage and transport activity, they emerged as independent merchants handling commodity transport and sales on consignment as their main business. Increasingly wealthy, many of the *myōshu* also opened *sake* breweries and loan firms as secondary enterprises.

Social confusion and lawlessness resulting from the breakdown of the central administrative system made land transportation more and more difficult. Estate managers turned increasingly to waterways to deliver rice and other products to the landowners, utilizing ports such as Yodo, Ōtsu, Sakamoto, Hyōgo, Onomichi, Mitajiri, Ōminato, Kohama, Tsuruga and Hakata, where goods imported from the continent were also received. Wealthy landlords often bought needed goods from the warehouses at these ports, and the facilities were improved as business thrived. The storage business, the inns built to entertain customers, and the increased personnel employed, made up the commercial centers in these ports.

It is said there were over 1,800 houses in Hakata in 1151, and 2,853 homes were destroyed by fire in Ōtsu in 1177.[23] More than 1,000 houses in Yodo are reported for the Entoku era (1489–1492), and about 1,000 houses burned in Onomichi in 1319.[24] These figures indicate not only the prosperity of port towns, but the degree of commercial activity in western Japan.

Commercial centers did develop, it is true, in districts far removed from Kamakura and Kyōto on the basis of the movement of annual tribute collected in the provinces. This development was influenced by the chronic restrictions of self-sufficiency in the manorial economy, though, and these commercial villages were quite limited in both appearance and socio-economic structure.

The self-sufficient economy continued to dominate the lives of most of the common people, whose demands were restrained. As the market opened only thrice monthly there was no opportunity to support oneself solely by profits acquired in the exchange business. Merchants operated on a part-time basis, sustaining themselves either in agricultural or handicraft work. Even the large warehouse operators were generally *myōshu* whose economic strength lay in estate management. The whole of commercial and manufacturing activity was under the control of the lords of the estates, and there were in this period no markets embracing the larger regional or social structures of the city.

# Chapter IV | Cities in the Late Middle Ages (a.d. 1274–1572)

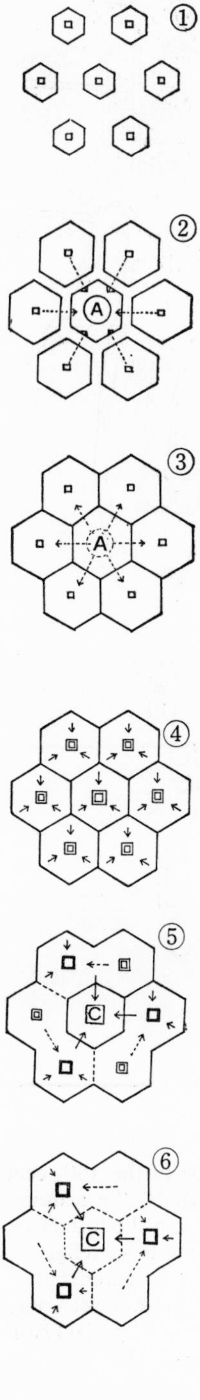

**Fig. 11 The Process of Expansion of Castle Towns in relation to Establishment of the Provinces** (drawn by Masao Toba)

① Indicates the virtual insularity of each village after the breakdown of the *ritsuryō* system.

② Signifies the strengthening of a central military town following the rise of the military class, *buke*, and hence the relativization of village independence.

③ Implies that, while the insularity of the villages broke down gradually, the towns did not grow much.

④ Shows how in the middle of the 15th century the villages became stronger as a result of the increase in agricultural productivity, and how the military left their rural estates to concentrate in the towns, exercising control over the peasants.

⑤ Indicates the process in which the stronger military groups dominated the weaker, forming fiefs extending over wide areas, the center of which was a rather large castle town.

⑥ Shows how the whole became one large fief with the main castle at the center, while smaller secondary castles were set up in strategic places for defense, with subordinates of the feudal lord in residence in the secondary castles. The single large fief was integrated completely into a self-sufficient system.

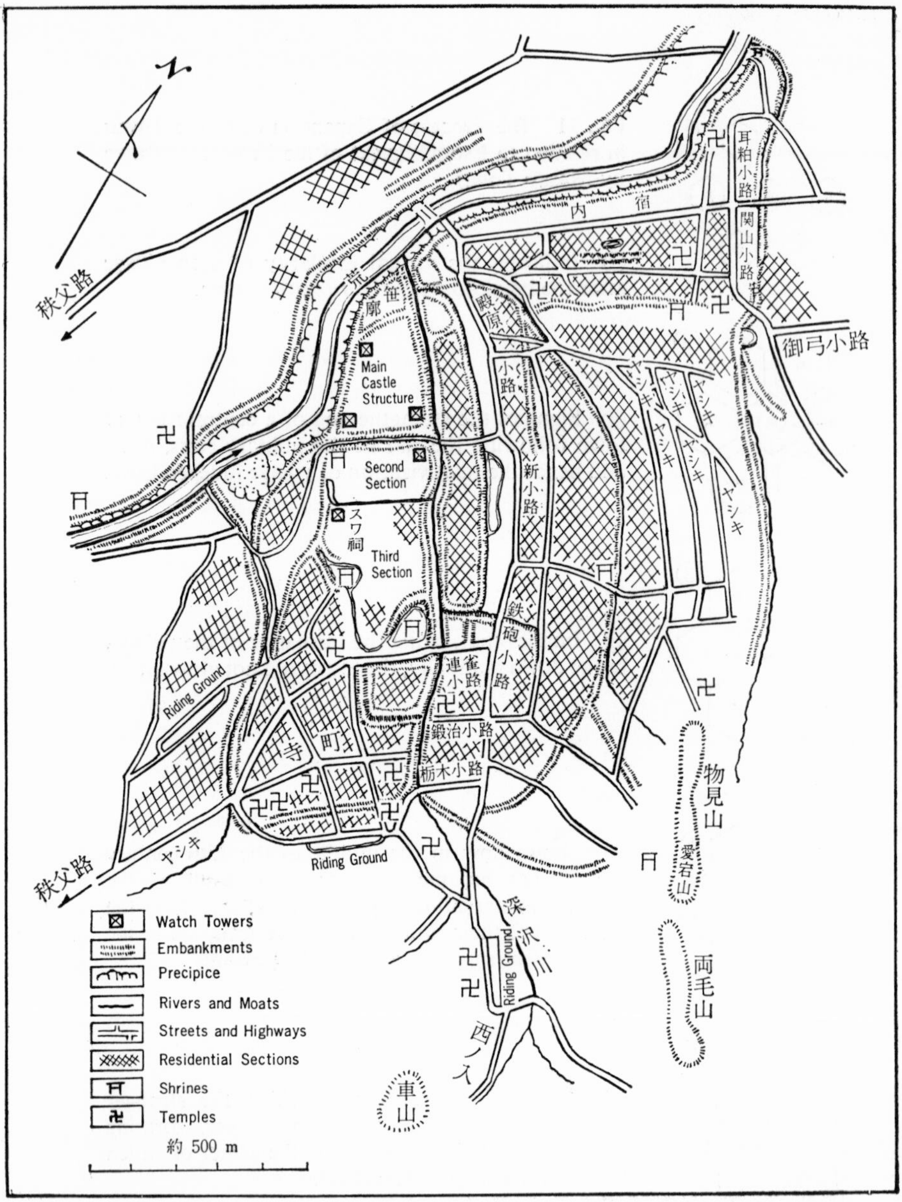


**Fig. 12 A Castle Town in the Middle Ages**

As the domains were consolidated by the daimyō in the latter part of the 16th century, the samurai concentrated in the castle towns. To meet their needs, the artisans and merchants also gathered, and temples and shrines were relocated from the former locales of the military leaders. The castle town became the political, military, religious and consuming center of a large surrounding area. The castle was at the center, but as the differentiation between farmers and the artisans and merchants was not yet complete, the residential areas were mixed. That the peasants were included in a special feature of this multiple-function mediaeval city. (adapted from *Saitama Kenshi*)

# 1. Transformation of the Feudal System

The feudal structure of the Kamakura era had its foundation in the estates controlled by the martial managers, *jitō*, who were vassals of the central military government. Changes in the socio-economic structure made it increasingly difficult to maintain the system.

One source of change was the expansion of cultivated areas through improvements in agricultural techniques, irrigation, and land reclamation. Greater quantities of fertilizer made from cut grass were required, driving the farmers into the hills and wastelands. This activity, together with the collection of animal manure, prompted expansion in the cooperative labors of the villagers. The parallel decline of manorial self-sufficiency and development of an exchange economy increased the demand for raw materials used in crafts production, further widening the scope of the exchange trade. Tenant farming practices for providing the needed raw materials was added to the system of farming under direct *jitō* controls, thus strengthening the independence of the individual family economy.

The system of controls of the absentee landlords was weakened as the local managers, *myōshu*, were gradually recognized as the actual owners of estate lands, rather than the supervisors, *jitō*, appointed by the landlords. People resident in estate lands were directly responsible to the local leaders, and the warrior cliques originally formed to protect the lands on behalf of the landlords took advantage of the socio-economic changes to strengthen their actual control over the lands. Increasingly larger factions of these warrior groups eventually exercised control over the total society.

It was just at this time of shifting fortunes of the Kamakura *bakufu* that the aggressive and rapidly expanding Mongol power in China (Yüan dynasty) made two attempts, in 1274 and 1281, to bring Japan into its vast empire. Very bad weather conditions in the invasion area of north Kyūshū (Hakata) seriously hampered the Mongols' assault forces, though the mobilized reserves of military strength of the Kamakura regime are given due credit for stiff resistance. In any event, Japan retained her independence in this critical moment.

The Kamakura regime maintained a defensive posture in western Japan for some time, fearing another attack. This placed a heavy burden on the *bakufu*, in that its warriors could not be compensated with lands won in battle, nor could the government compensate its own expenditures, as there were no spoils of war. The dissatisfaction of the vassals charged with this responsibility added to the process of weakening controls already aggravated by development of the exchange economy and structural changes in local administration.

Heightened coin circulation and sales of surplus by estate managers and, in lesser quantities, the farmers themselves, led to greater autonomy in the farming districts. Transition from self-sufficiency in the estates served to elevate the warriors' standard of living. Some of the *myōshu* accumulated great profits as middlemen in tribute collection and money-lending, and through monopolization of land transactions. In the process the less successful warriors, on fixed incomes from their lands, were pauperized and forced either to sell their lands or impose heavier taxes on resident farmers. The farmers, in turn, relinquished their lands, moved to other regions, or even rose against their masters. Sometimes they petitioned their creditors for cancellation of debts incurred. In all, relations between the leaders and the inhabitants of farm villages were increasingly marked by tension and opposition.

Amid such circumstances, it was the *shugo*, overlords of large warrior factions, who were able to lend succor to lesser warriors facing bad times and to give the protection to retainers of the *bakufu* that the *bakufu* itself could not provide. This strengthened the *shugo* positions to the extent that they could now oppose the authority of the *bakufu.*

Encouraged by the diminishing authority of the Kamakura regime and the appearance of insubordination in its ranks, the court nobility in Kyōto sought to deprive the military government of its power and restore the former *ritsuryō* system, which had been the basis of their traditional status and culture. They aligned themselves with the rebellious war lords, in the name of the emperor, whose "divine" authority transcended the *bakufu.* The Kamakura regime was defeated by these unified powers, and was replaced by a government known by the term "Kenmu Restoration." This coalition of noblemen and warriors was not, however, a restoration of *ritsuryō* institutions inasmuch as both the noble and military parties to the coalition continued to hold much land and many people under their direct control.

Although named the "Kenmu Restoration," the imperial office was by no means the central focus or power of this new government. Indeed, the primary powers, that is, the nobility and the military, contended strenuously with each other for actual power and for valid claim to imperial sanction. The court nobility and the minor cliques of warriors supporting their efforts to realize actual restoration of imperial authority are known historically as the "Southern Dynasty," or *Nanchō.* The "Northern" counterpart, or *Hokuchō*, consisted of large factions of warriors with newly-attained power, under the leadership of the Ashikaga family. Warrior cliques in the provinces were forced to choose sides between them as their wars of contention spread all over the country.

In the changing social scene, the minor warrior cliques allied with the nobility could not easily maintain control over rural bases. The contest was lost to the larger faction of warriors headed by the Ashikaga family and the "Kenmu Restoration" vanished after only three years of administration. A new military regime was formed in Kyōto, called the Muromachi *bakufu*, after the location of its headquarters.

Modeled after the Kamakura *bakufu*, the Muromachi organization even at its peak never reached the administrative or financial power of the former. Its integrative control over the whole country was inferior to that of Kamakura, as it lacked direct control over local warlords. The tightly-knit master-subordinate relations between *shugo* and *jitō* and their followers who led the local military cliques were missing in the Muromachi government's set-up. The new central authority in Muromachi represented a balance of power among a number of powerful warrior groups, mediated at the top by the Ashikaga leaders. Each major faction had its own subordinates among the minor warrior cliques, forming various provincial domains. In short, it was a more decentralized form of government.

Late in the Kamakura era the powerful provincial protectors, *shugo*, had rendered the estate supervisors, *jitō*, their subordinates, thus intensifying their powers. In the confusion of civil wars, estate owners had relinquished control of their lands to the *shugo*, who collected taxes on behalf of the owners. This extension of the territorial scope of *shugo* power led to the virtual collapse of the estate system, and to the firm fixation of expansive domains under the *shugo*.

Rural districts were released from the isolation of former days and connected anew by the expansion of economic activity. Local military power vanished as the integrative power over whole provinces was made secure. Hardly needing *bakufu* assistance, the *shugo* became self-sustained feudal lords, daimyō, under whom the former constituents of *bakufu* rule, the *jitō*, the powerful families and the warrior cliques, now rallied. Thus, the central *bakufu* was deprived of its controlling powers.

The political weakness of the Muromachi government was closely connected with the fragility of its economic foundations. Lands from which it could draw income were few and scattered, acquired mainly through confiscation of remote areas during the civil wars. Compensation was sought by levying extra taxes on lands and households, but the peasants' opposition was often severe enough to prevent enforcement of tax collections.

The Ashikaga government turned next to tax levies on prominent merchants in the capital district who dealt in *sake* and money-lending. Even travel taxes were tried. Such taxes only served to impoverish further the warriors and peasants. The Ashikaga leaders also opened formal trade relations with the Ming dynasty in China, though it was unpopular with the patriotic generals who disliked its formal character as "tribute" to the continental emperor. Ming reluctance in this trading venture imposed stringent limitations on this arrangement, and advantages accruing to the central *bakufu* were few, as the bulk of the trading was monopolized eventually by powerful lords in western Japan.

The Muromachi *bakufu* was always short of funds to bolster up its weak integrative controls, and its feudal structure gradually disintegrated.

## 2. Structural Changes in Kyōto, Kamakura and Hiraizumi

*Kyōto.*——During six decades of civil wars between the northern and southern powers (1336–92), both of which claimed to represent the imperial authority, the pattern of political integration had been considerably altered. The political organization finally established was one that functioned, though imperfectly, as an aggregate of powerful military groups under Ashikaga leadership. This integrative system had its headquarters in the Muromachi section of Kyoto.

The city of Kyōto had suffered damage several times from the internecine wars, yet had recovered its position as the integrative nucleus of the whole country. It had benefited from the growing exchange economy, which also enhanced its functions as a traditional center of religion. Under the reactivated movement of goods and people during the rule of the Ashikaga shogun, Yoshimitsu, Kyōto regained its position as the largest city in Japan.

There were seven entrances to the city, namely, Awata-guchi, Kihata-guchi, Toba-guchi, Tōji-guchi, Tanba-guchi, Yase-guchi and Kita-shirakawa-guchi. Traffic along highways leading from these entrances increased under stimulation of the new political order. Checking stations placed at each of the entry points collected duty on the flow of commodities, into and out of the city, constituting a basic source of income for the Muromachi *bakufu.*

The community structure of Kyōto in this period consisted of two political zones, the "upper" or northern sector, Kamikyō, and the "lower" or southern sector, Shimokyō. In the northern zone were located both the imperial and *bakufu* buildings, the court nobility residing near the imperial structures and the military personnel living close to their own headquarters. In the southern part were dwellings of people of the middle class or below, where the commercial area, mostly merchants' shops, was also located. There were definite differences in the ways of life of Kamikyō and Shimokyō.

The imperial palace, Tsuchimikado-dairi, at Tōdōin was modest compared to the new *bakufu* structures, its grounds measuring only four *cho*(9.8 acres), with four gates, two on the west side, one each north and east. Among the Ashikaga shoguns, Takauji built his residence in the Nijōtakakura section, and Yoshiakira transferred it first to Takakura-anenokōji, then to Sanjōmarinokōji. Yoshimitsu erected his mansion in the Imadegawa-kita section of Muromachi in 1379, a place so gorgeously planted as to be known as "the palace of flowers," *hana-no-gosho*. Succeeded early in his career by his son, Yoshimochi, Yoshimitsu retired to a mansion built in Kitayama, the famous gold-foil decorated Gold Pavilion (Kinkaku). Here he spent the rest of his days in luxury, unconcerned for the confused political situation. Adopting the ways of the decadent nobility, he even entertained the politically inactive emperor in his beautiful mountain retreat.

Kamikyō was an upper class section for the court nobility, ranking warriors, and the prominent temples. Merchants catering to upper class tastes for high-grade fabrics, artifacts, and other luxuries, were also located in Kamikyō, as were rich pawnbrokers active in the development of the money economy. Common people of the middle class and below were concentrated in Shimokyō around the Sanjō and Shijō junctions. There were many shops supplying the daily needs of commoners, and it is thought that people of the lowest social classes lived near Shijō-ōmiya, as a *hinin-buro* (beggar's public bath) was located there.[1]

Houses of merchants and craftsmen of the middle and lower classes were very small, rarely two-storied, and generally measuring no more than two *ken* square (16 sq.yds.). Roofs were of simple wooden shingles, supported by pillars stood on stones. In the six-foot wide entrance way was hung the *noren* half-curtain with the family trademark on it, and the front half of the house was furnished with shelves exhibiting commodities for sale. By the end of the Muromachi era one shop generally handled one commodity, indicating considerable progress toward occupational differentiation. These simple dwellings boasted no gardens and the backyard was shared with a dozen or more houses, in the center of which was a communal well. (This description comes from pictures on a folding screen depicting scenes in and outside Kyōto, owned by the Sanjō family.)

In addition to established shops, goods were peddled in the crowded streets. Free movement in the city streets was both caused by, and itself influenced, the changes in community and marketing patterns in this period. Even so, paddy fields were cultivated close by the city streets and even the backyard areas were often cultivated. There was little distinction between urban and rural districts.

From the standpoint of social structure, the characteristic features of the medieval city can be said to have intensified since the end of the Kamakura era. Private power increased as ancient authority declined. Rich pawnbrokers and *sake* merchants had acquired great wealth since the early Middle Ages, and controlled the city's economy. The gap between the rich and the poor broadened seriously, precipitating rebellious uprisings, *ikki*, among the latter.

The money economy had advanced after the Kamakura period, as shrewd managers of estates converted the annual taxes into currency. Gleaning personal profits from the transactions, they extended their wealth through the operation of pawnshops and breweries, gradually freeing themselves from superordinate controls. By the end of the Muromachi era as many as 400 money-lending agencies existed in Kyōto, many of them run by former estate managers from provinces near Kyōto, who had come into the city and opened pawnshops or *sake* breweries.

The court nobility and priests who had lost control of their lands depended increasingly on these money-lenders, and the official keeper of the imperial warehouses was chosen from among owners of the largest lending agencies and breweries. Quite naturally, the *bakufu* became closely associated with these *nouveaux riches*, appointing the more powerful ones as officials for collecting taxes from the rest. These enterprising merchants won from the *bakufu* a prohibition against importing *sake* brewed in the provinces, thus monopolizing that business in the capital city. In return, they became the most influential financial supporters of the *bakufu*'s municipal government, and subsidized the imperial family as well.[2] Rice and other foodstuffs as well as textiles were monopolized by several established guilds, *za*, some of which also donated funds to the imperial family. Some of the rice merchants became "millionaires."[3]

Subsequent to the acquisition of wealth and power by the merchant class, the culture of the city, formerly dominated by the court aristocracy and ranking military men, was adjusted more to the tastes of the merchants and, hence, to the interests of the citizenry. Religious institutions utilized their roles as leading cultural agents to popularize religious life, emphasizing practical values and aesthetic interests in their expanded activities among the people.

While the upper class citizens could elevate themselves culturally and economically above the stricter controls of the ruling class, the lower classes had no such possibilities, and remained culturally and economically deprived and dependent. As the divergence of economic status between rich and poor worsened, the money-lenders became indispensable to the livelihood of the poor people. In times of extreme distress the outrages of rebellion broke out, followed by pleas for cancellation of debts, *tokusei*.

Riots occurred mainly among peasants under masters in the vicinity of the city, simultaneously with the development towards greater autonomy in the remoter rural districts. After repeated rebellious uprisings, peasants, beggar priests, and vagabonds often combined forces to invade the city, killing and robbing the wealthy of their fortunes. In 1428 the pack-horse laborers in Sakamoto arose, inflicting injury upon the money-lenders, *sake* brewers, and economically active shrines by refusing to transport goods. Their petition for cancellation of debts was initially rejected by the *bakufu*, though the government later acceded to their requests. Seizing the opportunity afforded by the weakening of the Ashikaga leaders' power over the daimyō, as well as over the masses, peasants in the vicinity of Kyōto, numbering several tens of thousands, revolted in 1441, invaded the city and occupied the buildings of major temples and shrines. When the money-lenders' shops in Kamikyō were attacked by rioters in 1451, the *bakufu* ordered the daimyō to put down the riot but they refused. The owners of the pawnshops even failed to defend themselves.[4]

The growing might of citizens' movements accelerated the decline of the *bakufu*'s control over the overall network of aristocrats and warriors. A special capital guard was charged with the responsibility for maintaining public order in Kyōto, and its guardsmen were used to quell riots. The Gion Shrine employed a special security guard to patrol and secure the safety of its territory in the Sanjō and Shijō area. Gradually the idea arose among the citizens that they themselves should preserve order in the city where they lived. Thus, they expanded their activities beyond road construction and repairs to include defense of the city when riots threatened.

Self-protection by the citizens began at the local level by mobilizing neighborhood units. In town meetings, *yoriai*, problems of public safety were discussed, though implementation of specific actions was hampered by the variety of class, status and occupation differences in a given community. Unification of all citizens in one area was rather difficult, inasmuch as such a group included money-lenders and others whose opinions ran counter to those of most of the ordinary citizens.[5]

Economic growth in Kyōto enhanced the power positions of the citizenry, forcing changes in the socio-economic structure to compensate for the loss of political authority by the *bakufu*. Its organs for integration of the total society were established on fragile foundations. That is, the Ashikaga *bakufu* was originally based on a balance of power among powerful military factions, and the seeds of disintegration were inherent in the process from the start. The first break came when the *bakufu* commissioner for the Kantō region split away, throwing his area into confusion and, at the same time, stimulating the formation of other more or less independent warrior groups.

On the occasion of a succession of the shogunate the unstable situation erupted into the Civil War of Ōnin in 1467. Kyōto became the main battlefield for the two large warrior factions. The Ashikaga government, unable to deal with the situation, lost all authority. It could subdue neither the military cliques nor the peasant uprisings occurring concomitantly, and the entire city was thrown into confusion.

While the leading factions fought in the capital area, warrior cliques in local areas sought to expand their own territories, taking advantage of the disrupted political conditions. The old social order gave way to an age of powerful war lords and persistent strife. Provincial areas removed from the capital district came under the domination of former *shugo* now independently established as daimyō with their own feudal domains. Even in the central area, the nobility were replaced one by one by new leaders, called *Sengoku Daimyō*, or "Lords of the Warring States" era (1467–1568). Their counterparts in the rural regions, who also pre-empted the authority of their superiors, were the *jizamurai* (local warriors) who elevated themselves to positions of actual control.

Warriors engaged in the fighting in and around Kyōto gradually lost their motivation to continue, as there was little chance to gain new territory plus the fear of losing estates already held, and the War of Ōnin came to an indeterminate end. The contest for the central shogunate authority was transposed into a more general struggle in which each lord endeavored merely to secure or extend his own territory.

Lasting for eleven years, the War of Ōnin left Kyōto heavily damaged. Most of the houses in the more densely populated Sakyō section were burned. When the residence of Inokuma Isshikigoro at Nakamikado in Sakyō was set afire in 1467, nine conflagrations were spotted at the same time in other places. Soon the fire spread over a vast area, enveloping several hundred small townships of the city, including Nijō to the south, Mitamanotsuji to the north, Muromachi in the east and Ōtoneri in the west, spurred on by a wind from the south. Destroying over thirty thousand houses, this fiery scourge left much of Kyōto an open, scorched field.[6]

Besides this big fire, others occurred several times in Kyōto, burning down the homes of noblemen, warriors, and commoners alike, as well as temples and shrines, leaving only the imperial palace and *bakufu* office buildings. Finally, these too were partially destroyed. Merchants and craftsmen fled the city, especially after the textile industry was temporarily suspended. Kyōto's thriving prosperity was spoiled and its developed areas transformed into waste lands.

Having partially survived the ravages of war, the imperial palace became badly deteriorated late in the Sengoku era. Standing on the Sanjō bridge, lanterns in the rooms of ladies-in-waiting of the palace could be seen at night across the barren distance in between. Children played on the broken remains of the roofed mud wall surrounding the Shishinden, and peddlers sold hot tea in stalls under the bridge of Ukon. Life among the warriors and nobility was similarly humbled, and the common people fared even worse.

The Ōnin wars had left the scope of *bakufu* power severely restricted and many of the provincial domains, such as Ōmi, Mino, Owari, Tōtōmi, Mikawa, Hida, Noto, Kaga, Echizen, Yamato and Kawachi, no longer met their annual tribute obligations. Others such as Kii, Settsu, Ettchū and Izumi, were prevented from transporitng their tribute goods by continuing civil strife. Provinces remaining under *bakufu* control were Harima, Bizen, Mimasaka, Bittchū, Bingo, Ise, Iga, Awaji and Shikoku, though even these provinces did not accede easily to the demands of the shogunate. In time these once obedient areas reversed their positions, leaving the *bakufu* without any provinces forwarding tribute payments.[7]

Complicating the confusion caused by the collapse of central controls was the recurrence of many peasant revolts throughout the land. The shgounate was busy, though, with repeated relocations of its own headquarters. Despite the obvious need for restoration of the city, little expectation was placed in the old authority. A new system of power was needed and an autonomous organization of citizens appeared to fill this need.

Kyōto was the locus of the divinely-sanctioned authority of the emperor, and historically it had served as the most important nucleus of national unity through the traditional integrative organs for politics, economy, cultural movements and communications. Quite naturally the dominant provincial cliques vied with each other to displace the older authorities and assume positions of control over the whole country. It was only after one of these factions was successful that the age of turmoil called the "Warring States" era was brought to an end.

*Kamakura.*——Even at the height of its days as the site of the ruling military regime, Kamakura was not free from opposition in Kyōto. This opposition made the political situation unstable throughout the Kamakura era, and the restlessness in the nation eventually shifted the center of gravity in political life away from Kamakura.

After the integrative functions were transferred to the Muromachi *bakufu*, a commissioner (*kanrei*) for the Kantō area was assigned to Kamakura for supervision of local government affairs. Kamakura possessed no large land base in the surrounding region for its economic support, nor was it well situated for growth as a center of communications connecting other provinces. It survived only as a local center drawing upon established religious institutions for support, thoroughly deprived of national administrative functions.

The Ashikaga leaders of the Muromachi *bakufu* had appointed members of its own faction as commissioners of the Kantō district, but they were not always loyal to the central group, forcing the Muromachi *bakufu* to subdue the city of Kamakura militarily. Many of the great temples and shrines, remaining symbols of the city's former glory, were burned to the ground, and the city gradually fell into decay. Political appointments were transferred to the Uesugi family, though it dissipated its potential in intrafamilial struggles. The city completely lost its functions as a city, surviving only as a historical site. By the beginning of the Edo era, it was just one of the rural districts with a few houses here and there in the valley.[8]

*Temple towns.*——An important category in this historical period was that of towns emerging around major temples and shrines, a development with roots in ancient times. The undergirding strength of these religious institutions lay in the patronage of the aristocracy and the possession of tax-free estate lands. Many of the temples and related monasteries drew together skilled workers in handicrafts who produced goods not only for use by the temples but also for exchange. The temple towns developed, then, as residential centers of the craftsmen and merchants clustered there.

Although many of the estate lands of the temples, along with those belonging to the aristocracy, were lost to the rising daimyō in the social changes described above, the more powerful temples in the capital district managed to hold on to their lands through exercise of their traditional authority and formation of their own armed forces. The unstable political moorings of the Muromachi *bakufu* led to an ambivalent attitude toward the religious groups, at times oppressive, at other times compromising. Protective measures beneficial to the temples included an order that no *shugo* were to tamper with estates under temple ownership, although this order became void after the War of Ōnin.

Rural life in the Muromachi era was liberalized as production increased and peasants acquired relatively more freedom of movement. Development of the commodity economy in the central Kinai district promoted visits to shrines and temples, as it also activated the markets. Temples that lost their estate holdings grasped after the markets to assure their political independence and financial prosperity. Advertising their markets as "divine places" where fair transactions were guaranteed, they also managed to receive protection from the daimyō and exemption from orders for cancellation of debts due them. Market days were fixed and inns built for those patronizing them. Commercial activity became a characteristic function of the temple towns, and population increases furthered their development into cities.

When Nara was the integrative center of the *ritsuryō* system, its large size was commensurate with the multiple functions of the nobility, bureaucracy, and major shrines and temples concentrated there. After the capital was transferred to Kyōto, only the religious function remained, converting it into a temple town. Tōdaiji and Kōfukuji were central to this function and the latter, with extensive lands in the Yamato district, was able to prevent intrusions by military cliques in that district. According to Ono Akitsugu's study of "Temple Markets in Nara," the main gate of Kōfukuji marked off two distinct sectors, *jinai* and *jigai*, the inner and outer precincts of the temple. In both sectors there were many pagodas, halls and other temple structures, with some 3,000 monks in residence. The boundaries of Nara were Mt. Kasuga in the east, the Hannyazaka slope in the north, and the Saho river in the west. Most of the inhabitants within these bounds were under the Kōfukuji. In a village around the Kasuga Shrine, enshrining the local deity of Kōfukuji, there were between 7,000–8,000 people controlled by the shrine, including peasants, merchants, craftsmen, porters, prostitutes and beggars.

To supply the demands of an increased populace, a third market was added to the two older markets in northern and southern Nara. In the early Middle Ages, the markets usually opened thrice each month, but in Nara, the three markets took turns opening, one each day. As exchange volume swelled, the market shops began receiving goods continuously. The market supervisor had placed prohibitions on merchants from outside the fixed areas, but a reversal occurred in which the shops took the initiative in marketing activity and the market supervisor's office became a supplementary agency.

According to the records of the Tenmangu shrine, there were 391 lots in Kosatsuki-gō, one of the villages where it solicited funds for performances of Noh drama in the shrine festivals. One-third of the lots were occupied by merchants and craftsmen, and some fifty merchandizing and handicraft shops are listed. These figures indicate that major weight lay more with the small shops than with the official market organization itself.[9]

On temple-owned estate lands there was a variety of persons pursuing non-agricultural occupations, and goods and services collected as tribute from these persons, as well as the usual tribute from peasants were increasingly converted into money. City-based temples acquired new income from taxes levied on merchants and craftsmen operating under their auspices. The religious institutions gradually shifted from the traditional function of controlling land and agricultural production to that of controlling markets.[10]

While Nara was completely transformed from an ancient capital into a major temple town, the shrine town of Uji-yamada, east of Nara on the Ise-Shima peninsula, developed as a center for the shrines of the imperial family, the Kōtai-jingu and Toyouke-daijingu. In addition to these main shrines, there were branch shrines, called Betsugu, Sessha and Massha. Here Shinto priests and subordinate personnel lived off tribute due the deities, *shinryō*.

The head of the shrine management organization was designated by the imperial family up to the time of the Emperor Godaigo (1318–39). The appointment usually went to one of the princesses. She was assisted by Negi, Uchindo, and Monoimi, i.e., Shinto priests and assistants performing the religious rites. In the management office there were officials called *itsuki-no-miya* (master of priests in the Ise Shrine), *gūji* (priests of government-founded shrines), and other priestly officials administering shrine lands. According to the *Engishiki*, there were 1,325 farm households which delivered about 17,000 *koku* (119,340 U.S. bu.) of rice to the shrine annually. Donations of land to the shrine in 1185 increased the number of households to 2,874, constituting the largest shrine estate in Japanese history.

As local warriors acquired new powers toward the end of the Heian period, official discipline became degraded, and shrine estates suffered attacks from local military groups. In the latter half of the 13th century shrine income fell off drastically, and festivals and rites were sometimes cancelled due to lack of funds. Even the head priest of the Ise Shrine lost control of the shrine's estate after the Ōnin War, retaining only his position in the shrine proper.

By the end of the Eikyō era (1429–41) the shrine's estate had dwindled to only the Sōka-gō, Itsukinomiya-ato, and five villages east of Miyakawa. In addition to conflict between the priests and the administrative officials of the shrine, peasants on its lands refused to pay the *so*, *chō*, and *yō* taxes levied on them. Impoverishment of the Ise Shrine was furthered in that its special relation to the imperial family had included a restriction against receiving contributions from commoners, who naturally visited the shrine less during hard times. When this restriction was lifted late in the Middle Ages, visits by military leaders and commoners increased. In contrast to a reported 100,000 visitors in 934, it is said that the number reached several tens of millions in 1287. At any rate, the increase must have been enormous.[11]

Some 6,000 houses are said to have burned down in 1534, indicating a population of over 30,000 in Uji-yamada. Also, there were fifteen *za* in the Tenshō era (1573–92).[12] These figures show that Uji-yamada began as a shrine town supported originally by ancient aristocratic religious authority, though shifting its base later to commercial activity.

Another thriving temple town grew up around the Zenkōji temple in the Shinano district (present-day Nagano). It boasted many well-constructed buildings centered around the *Kondo* ("Golden Hall"), commanded a vast area, and drew many worshippers to its precincts. A fire in 1179 destroyed many of its structures, though they were rebuilt through help from neighboring estates and government holdings in the Shinano area by order of the reigning shogun, Yoritomo. After that, the temple grew by extending its own estates, as well as by increased donations. It is said that visitors to Zenkōji in 1362 were so numerous that the temple grounds resembled a crowded marketplace. Around 1400 the belief spread that this temple was the holiest place in all Japan, being the bridge connecting the "paradise in the West" and the temporal world, and a pilgrimage there assured passage over into "paradise." Merchant shops mushroomed along the gently sloping street leading down into the town from the temple's main gate. The multiplicity of trades plied in these shops is demonstrated by the wide variety of social positions represented there, for there were also many *geisha* and *shakufu* (low class prostitutes). Zenkōji was a flourishing town in those days.[13]

In the temple town of Tennōji in Settsu (now Hyōgo Pref.) it is said that there were 7,000 houses in the Bunmei era (1469–87), indicating a population of about 35,000 at that time.[14] Set between Mt. Hiei to the west and Lake Biwa to the east, the town of Sakamoto is thought to have had a populace of several thousands. There were thirty-nine money-lenders' shops there in the early days of the Muromachi period. Several thousand homes are reported to have burned in the Bunki period (1501–4), assuring a population of at least 15,000 in Sakamoto.[15] The town of Ōtsu at the southern end of Lake Biwa developed around the Enryakuji temple, and a population of some 15,000 by the end of the Heian era is estimated from a reported 2,800 houses destroyed in a fire in 1180. Population centers with over 10,000 people were also located at the temple sites of Zuisenji in Ettchū, Ishidera in Ōmi, and Honganji in Settsu. These centers included not only residential communities developed near the temples but trading and crafts' districts near markets, traffic junctions, and even ports.

There was another category of towns connected with the temples, classified as *jinai-machi* (lit., towns built within the temple compounds) by Makino Shinnosuke. Such towns were found in Yoshizaki of Echizen, Honganji of Yamashina, and Honganji of Ishiyama, all belonging to the True Pure Land Sect of Buddhism. These towns differed from other temple towns or even castle towns, in that they lay wholly within the moats or walls surrounding the temples. The walls and moats were constructed to ward off attacks by followers of other sects or by the forces of the ruler of the province in which the temple was located. These towns were directly under the religious and political control of the temple's chief abbot.

The town of Yoshizaki consisted of some 1,200 *nagaya*, multiple-unit dwellings, each one capable of accommodating many families. At each end of the main north-south street, large gates were erected. In Honganji of Yamashina an eight-*cho* area (19.6 acres) of *nagaya*, centering around the magnificent Buddhist temple, was protected by moats and embankments. The Ishiyamadera town of Ōsaka had six inner towns (Kita, Nishi, Minami, Shimizu, Shin-yashiki, and Himonoya). Similar towns were located in the following places: Tondabayashi of Kawachi, Kaizuka of Izumi, Yamada of Ōmi, Terauchi of Ōmi, Kofu of Ettchū, Inami of Ettchū, Johana of Ettchū, Kuhōji of Kawachi, Yaoterauchi of Kawachi, Tenma of Settsu, Imai of Yamato, and Himida of Ise.

People in these inner-towns lived under the strict regulations of the main temples of the sects, although they were permitted some autonomy in electing elders (*machi-doshiyori*) to represent their interests as consultants to the heads of the towns.[16]

The *jinai-machi* was the prototype of the castle towns of the feudal era. Besides combining religious and military functions under the direction of the chief abbot, the town structure had the temple at the center and the moats and embankments at the extremities. The checkerboard street plan had the added features of curved or offset streets and shuttered fences to obstruct long-range vision and rapid entry into the town.[17]

## 3. Formation of Feudal Domains and Castle Towns

Against the background of *bakufu* power giving way to rising provincial lords, and of continuing civil wars, the necessity for local integration and defense was intensified. To meet this necessity the lords of each domain founded castle towns as the centers of their integrative systems.

Depending upon the relative conditions of local estates, local warriors were either conquered and absorbed by powerful daimyō, or else took the initiative in merging under one of the more powerful lords in their regions. In the process, the local clans of rural areas were unified under a single daimyō, under whom they assumed various administrative responsibilities, bringing each region its own unification.

Initially the status of the powerful local clans remained virtually unchanged, the region being integrated merely for military and political aims. In time the newly-integrated regions progressed toward greater mutuality, not only in military and political activities, but also in economic and communications systems, thereby diminishing the independence of the subordinate vassal estates. Conversely, movement toward greater centralization of feudal domains under the daimyō was accelerated.

Throughout the Age of Civil Wars (*Sengoku*) the daimyō were kept busy with the reorganization of the administrative framework of their domains. They neither expected assistance from the central military government, nor bothered to obey its orders. The overlords' concern was primarily to strengthen their military, administrative, and juridical controls over as large a territory as possible. Their territories became essentially autonomous local states, with the castle towns serving as the capitals of each large domain, focal points of the business of reorganization of integrative structures. The integrative functions of the castle towns compensated for the decline of power in the central capital of Kyōto.

The base units of administration under the daimyō were the rural villages. Hence, the formation of castle towns depended upon changes in the rural districts, as well as upon differentiation in the modes of commerce and industry, including market developments. Changes in these areas of domestic life were required to support the formation of non-agricultural centers for the new political structures. The population of the castle towns was drawn from the warriors, merchants, and craftsmen formerly dispersed in the rural districts of its territory.

As the administrative controls of the daimyō extended over large areas containing many villages, economic activity expanded beyond the limits of the village units, wherever expansion of agricultural productivity permitted. Farming needs, such as irrigation and the use of communal grounds for growing fodder for fertilizer, could be handled within the domains on a scale exceeding local village limits, providing added agricultural yields. Upgraded productivity gave a surplus in raw materials for processing in handicrafts as tools and consumer products. This, in turn, accelerated the development of the local exchange economy beyond village boundaries.

The warrior groups under minor lords in the rural districts gathered agricultural surplus to convert into funds for military use, affording greater freedom to contend with other minor lords, thus extending their territories when victorious. Often their efforts were eclipsed, however, by the integrative thrust of major daimyō and they chose, instead, to join the larger domains and live in the greater security of the castle towns, losing their identity as minor lords.

Under the impetus of extended activities, the rural villages underwent reorganization, both in terms of enlarged operations and as integral parts of the larger domains. Village heads, *shōya* or *nanushi*, were chosen from established families with long traditions of village leadership, or from the prominent local military men. Just as the villagers were now considered citizens of the larger domains, so the village heads were now the landlords of the unit villages.

Cultivation rights were granted for land areas encompassing several villages, promoting thereby mutual responsibility among them, especially for paying taxes. This system, known as *hyakushō-uke*, was chiefly for the convenience of the feudal lords in collecting taxes. The mutual obligations of estate managers and the peasants under them brought them closer together than ever before. Their tight solidarity was further buttressed by vows before their local deities to stand or fall together.

Local autonomy was reinforced through village organizations, *sō*, under leadership of the village head. Officers of the organization administered village affairs, such as *tōban-hyakushō*, (farmer-in-charge), *nanushi-satanin* (judicial affairs), *otona* and *chōrō* (elders), and other minor leaders. These men were known as *hikan*, followers of the daimyō, and handled all negotiations with the latter on behalf of the peasants.[18] Another kind of village organization, related to local shrines and called *miyaza*, played an important role in stabilizing status stratification and exercising regulatory controls over all behavior and movement of the villagers.[19]

In times of civil wars the villages sometimes took action independently of their daimyō overlords, especially when demands upon them were unreasonable. They rose particularly to defend their immediate rights in irrigation facilities and fodder fields.[20] Autonomous and united action among villages developed notably in the economically and culturally more advanced regions of Yamashiro, Ōmi, and Nara, near the national capital. Such action also created pressures toward transformation of existing social structures, (1) by inciting armed peasant revolts against authority, such as attacks on money-lenders, and (2) by submitting requests for cancellation of debts (*tokusei*) to the provincial lords.

Local autonomy, then, tended to be strengthened by elevation of political integration to a higher, more remote level. Likewise, local economies were strengthened, and altered, through connections with a larger regional market centering in the castle towns.

In agriculture it became common to reap two crops per year, cultivating rice and barley. Crop yields increased year by year. During the Muromachi era large amounts of funds and labor were spent improving irrigation and flood control facilities, with an eye to increasing government tax receipts. Remarkable growth was achieved through introduction of methods for utilizing land space between the rows of other crops (e.g., for beans), and promotion of production of raw materials for crafts manufacture. In addition to an increase in landowners not engaged personally in cultivation, the Kinki district (without any single powerful lord) experienced an increase in contracted tenant-farming. Many of the tenants eventually became landowners.

Market developments were closely related to the *gōson* system of independent village associations. Increases in both agricultural surplus and the degree of local autonomy inevitably led to the promotion of local markets. Even in more remote areas, where local military power left the peasants less freedom, the practice of large-scale management of farm lands dwindled. The *gōson* village associations increasingly exchanged their own goods, activating the local market.

Tax payment in coins, instead of produce, became more common, adding further inducement to market development. Conversely, the farmers grew more dependent on the market as its structure and functions were strengthened. Markets opened at least three times a month and, after the middle of the 15th century, many opened on definite dates six times per month. The markets thrived as agents in the exchange of farm produce and craft products, and in tax payment transactions in coins. Rural markets were set up at average distances of 2–3 *ri* (4.9–7.3 mi.) for the peasants' convenience in making one-day trips with laden carts. Pawnshops in the markets became indispensable to poor farmers and to the operations of the *gōson* village associations.[21]

Toward the end of the Sengoku era, the daimyō authorized the establishment of new markets, with tax exemptions, for any new villages founded within their domains. Promoters of the new markets collected operating fees, *basen* or *zasen*, from merchants opening shops; and there were market bosses who exacted handling charges, *unjō*, from the merchants.[22]

In castle towns and highway rest towns, where goods were consumed though not produced, the role of the market was crucial, both to the life of these towns and to the entire domain. The market supplied not only the channel for tax collections, but served as well to make up for losses sustained by wholesalers and retailers. It was the regular, effective link between the town-based military class and the producing rural districts.

The importance of the markets was evident in the strong protection they received from the daimyō. To maintain peace and order in the markets, forceful merchandizing, quarrels and other disturbances were prohibited. Demands on debtors could not be pressed by creditors on market days. Town residents could be mobilized, if necessary, to impress upon merchants their civic responsibilities, including participation in municipal administration. Prompt payment in cash was promoted as credit systems were yet non-existent, and weights and measures were standardized. Market zones were clearly fixed so as to stimulate and control prosperity. In short, it was not a fully "free" market.[23]

The daimyō fostered a kind of free market, *raku-ichi*, by granting certain tax exemptions, for it was clearly advantageous to have as many successful merchants as possible in their domains. The foundation of the castle and highway station towns lay not only in the military and political functions, but also in healthy economic activity, which was well served by having a large consumer population.

Changes were forced upon the small-scale systems of management by village units, according to consanguine relations of ruling military cliques, by two significant factors. One of the factors was the shift from local to more broadly regional forms of political structure, and the other was a similar expansion in both the volume and the territorial scope of economic activity.

The structural changes in political power arose from (1) increased might of the daimyō supplanting the dwindling power of the central government, (2) the incompetency of local military leaders caused by inter-village cooperation, and (3) the growing autonomy of the villages, as noted earlier.

The second factor of expanded commercial activity resulted mainly from (1) increased agricultural productivity and (2) progress made in the production of finished commodities. Trends towards local autonomy and free exchange were greatly impeded by the estate-absorbing activity of the daimyō and by the persistence of estates owned by the court nobility and temples, the latter eventually evolving into feudal domains.

In the continuing contention over territories among the daimyō during the Age of Civil Wars, castles of the expanding domains grew commensurately larger. Those constructed temporarily on smaller scales for purely militaristic purposes vanished in the fluctuations of victories and defeats. It was the larger ones that survived which became the nuclei of the castle towns.

With the rise to power of the military class at the end of the Heian period, Kamakura emerged as such a provincial center of military control removed from Kyōto. Indeed, it ranked in size and power with the ancient capital. Yet, during the two hundred years' span of the Kamakura era, there did not, and could not, appear any similar population centers. Such a process had to wait upon the kinds of social changes that sufficiently reduced the integrative power of the central government, permitting the rise of provincial towns.

During the Muromachi era the *shugo* and *jitō* ascended to partial independence, and it was in the Tenmon era (1532–54) of the Age of Civil Wars that fluidity with respect to feudal domains reached its peak. That is, overall civil disorder provided the opportunities for powerful domains to enlarge their realms of control in the local areas. Locally-based warriors, until now closely tied to local programs of village protection and management, and who alternately served in the defense of boundary zones or of the main castle, were now ordered to move into the castle town in view of the prospects of extended warfare. Inter-village cooperation had already begun to relieve them of immediate duties anyway, though formally the domain embraced a collection of dispersed village units.[24]

Among the warriors appeared some who were salaried and without specific estate connections. Land-based warriors rose to arms of their own account when threatened, but the salaried mercenaries were directly responsible to the daimyō, who bore all their expenses. It was the latter who constituted the consumer population of the castle towns, adding this function to the original political and military dimensions of the castle centers.

Another factor gave impulse to expansion of the castle towns through large concentrations of warriors, namely, a shift in the basic modes of combat. Relying previously on mounted troops, the tactics of battle in the Age of Civil Wars shifted to mass confrontations on open plains, necessitating large forces of foot soldiers armed mainly with long lances. The introduction of muskets (specifically, harquebuses) in the latter half of the 16th century accentuated the role of the *ashigaru*, foot soldiers. Not only the tactical changes, but constant fear of either invasion from without or rebellion within his domain forced each daimyō to maintain well-trained and regimented standing armies within the castle town bounds. Only thus could he adequately protect his home base and also move out in defense of his domain.

Inescapable tax collecting necessities for supporting consumer battalions tied the farming districts ever more tightly to the castle centers. In the concentration of salaried troops there was an irresistible attraction to merchants and craftsmen seeking to profit from supplying their needs. Such interaction simply served to expand the castle towns even more.

Hachigata-jō castle in the north Musashi district was an example typical of those days. The main castle fronted on a river bank, the other sides being protected by moats and embankments. Around the castle were the dwellings of samurai, merchants, and craftsmen (especially those engaged in arms production), and peasants. The inner sector of the town was filled with inns, markets, and shops, while on the edges of the town were temples and shrines. Thus did such a castle town exhibit a more complicated structure embracing the multiple functions of the military, politics, market economy, travelers' facilities and religious institutions.[25]

The expansive activities of the Hōjō family in the Musashi region resulted in castle relocations several times. The Ōishi household moved castles from Ninomiya-yakata to Takatsuki-jō, Takiyama-jō, and finally to Hachiōji-jō, all in the Musashi area. Each time the number of castles decreased but the size of new castle towns was enlarged. Odawara, the castle town of the Hōjō family, continued to expand since the time of Hōjō's entering it in 1495. It grew seven or eight times the original area by the time of its peak prosperity in the Tenshō era (1573–92).[26]

After the War of Ōnin development of castle towns was more prominent in the Chūbu and Kantō districts than in the more tradition-oriented Kinki district, where the economy was still largely dependent upon estates owned by court nobility and major temples. Important castle towns developed at the following locations:

| *Town* | *Present Area* | *Lord* | *Estimated Population (date)* |
|---|---|---|---|
| Ichinoritani | Fukui | Asakura | —— |
| Odawara | Kanagawa | Hōjō | —— |
| Sunpu | Shizuoka | Imagawa | —— |
| Kiyosu, Owari | Aichi | Oda | 7,500 (1580's) |
| Funai, Bungo | N. Kyūshū | Ōtomo | 5,000 (1571) |
| Suho, Yamaguchi | Yamaguchi | Ōuchi | 10,000 (1577) |
| Kōfu | Yamanashi | Takeda | —— |
| Kagoshima | S. Kyūshū | Shimazu | —— |
| Kasugasan, Echigo | Niigata | Uesugi | 30,000 (1570's) |

From the Kamakura era on, castles tended to be situated on hilltops, with the daimyō's retainers living at the foot of the hill, giving the lower region its name of *yamashita*, or sometimes *negoya*, "cottages at the base."

Population expansion eventually forced transfer of the castles to open plains, after which they were called *hirayamajiro* or *hirajiro*. On the plains, the residence of the daimyō and his castle became unified.

In the typical castle layout in the period here under review, the main castle structure, *Honmaru*, was in the center, surrounded in concentric circles by the second and third sections, *Ninomaru* and *Sannomaru* respectively. Beyond the outer circle were attached towers known as *Nishinomaru* and *Kitanomaru* (western and northern parts respectively), while deep in the inner courts stood the keep (*Tsumemaru*), the final defense position against invading forces.

Areas encompassed by the castle structures were 2–3 *cho* (1 *cho* = approx. 120 yds.) by 5–6 *cho*, though they later became larger. The inner compound of the Odawara castle measured 15–16 *cho* east-west by 10 *cho* north-south. After the introduction of muskets (1543) and cannon (1576) castle walls were reinforced, and later castles were built with more permanent durability. Thick solid earthen battlements, mixed with even harder substances, were fitted with stone gates. Roofing tiles lent added grace to the imposing fortresses.[27]

At this stage the castles built on open plains had not yet appeared, and the hill sites were chosen for advantages in controlling both traffic and economic activity. Often there was some distance between the castle and the lower-lying town, as in the Ichinoritani-jō castle in Echizen, the Ōmikannon, Shigiyama-jō, and Sawa-jō castles in Yamato and their towns, and the Ashikaga-jō castle in Shimotsuke and its town.

To facilitate the integrative functions of the castle in controlling political, economic, and social life throughout each domain, the castles were sometimes located at already established towns such as temple towns (*monzen-machi*), highway stations (*shukuba-machi*), port (*minato-machi*) and market (*ichiba-machi*) towns. In other cases, these towns were relocated around the lord's headquarters. In still other instances, both castle and other functional communities were brought together in a wholly new location. In any case, the relation of topography to defense was of crucial importance. Whenever the economic and communication systems developed in conjunction with the political and military organs, the merchant and craft communities settled in front of the fortresses—even when the latter were situated atop hills, as in the examples of Kasugasan town in Echigo (Niigata) and Akama town in Chikuzen (N. Kyūshū).

Kasugasan expanded rapidly after the castle was constructed there, becoming one of the bigger cities in Japan at that time. Military residences occupied the area below the middle of the hill, surrounded by houses of merchants and craftsmen, the whole forming the nucleus of the town. In the commoners' residential area, wholesale houses and inns flourished, especially along the west coast highway, Hokuriku Kaidō, running through the town. A Zenkōji temple was built and attracted many worshippers. In the immediate vicinity was the port town of Naoetsu, always crowded with ships sailing to and from ports along Japan's northwestern seaboard.[28]

Castle towns in these days expanded spontaneously as their functions and organs expanded, in contrast to the planned construction of castle towns in the later Edo period. In pre-Edo times residences of warriors, peasants, merchants and craftsmen often were mixed together in the same areas. In the more stratified society of the Edo era, towns were laid out from the beginning with clear divisions of residential areas according to social status. When the warrior class swelled in the town of Kasugasan, its members simply crowded in between the castle and the town there.[29] Or, in the case of the town of Kōriyama, under the Mōri family, it was formed by drawing three markets together. Commercial houses lined the main road connecting the markets, and the residences that filled the side and back streets included warriors' houses interspersed among others.[30]

Castle and town were not fully united in the Middle Ages and, when wars broke out, the town's houses were often burned to the ground to obstruct the enemy's advance or cut off his supply routes. The sacrificed towns were rebuilt only when the integrative functions of economy and transportation were resumed. Castle towns built solely for political aims tended, if destroyed, not to be restored, having had only an unstable basis to begin with.

The social structure of the castle town was greatly influenced by the fact that, since the Muromachi era, the military and farming functions became gradually differentiated. This yielded an upper class of warriors not directly related to specific lords and a lower class of land-based militia. Other classes in castle town communities were the Shinto and Buddhist priests, merchants, craftsmen, and large numbers of peasants.

The ruling class was comprised of:

daimyō—the provincial lord, often derived from former provincial protectors, or *shugo*;

*kyūnin*—upper class warriors who possessed their own estates, vassals to the daimyō;

*gokenin* and *hikan*—middle class warriors, ranking subordinates under the *kyūnin*; and,

*ashigaru*, *komono*, and *chūgen*—lowest ranks of the military class.

Temples, shrines and their immediate communities made up as much as one-fifth to one-third of the castle towns, and the priests constituted an important segment of castle town population structure. In Odawara there were some forty-eight temples; in Yamaguchi, nineteen. The strong allegiance of the warrior groups to the religious institutions gave them a steady basis of support.

The priestly hierarchy was as follows:

*monseki*—hereditary head of a sect;

*shamu* and *shashi*—Shinto priests managing the shrines;

*gakuryo* and *shūto*—ordinary priests of middle-class standing;

*kōjin* and *dōshu*—trained priests of the lower classes.

The civilian population was composed of the following sub-groups:

—a ruling class of landlords (originally warriors, but now settled

on the land), *tonya* (wealthy wholesalers), and *dosō* (money-lenders);
—under these came the ordinary merchants, craftsmen, and farmers;
—and finally, the lowest class of citizens, including *totei* and *tedai* (apprentice merchants and clerks respectively), *kosakunin* (tenant farmers), and *kanaikenin* (servants held in near-slavery).

At the very bottom of the civilian class were entertainers, porters in transportation services, shamanistic medicine men and women, foreigners, and the rest of the lowly, poor, and outcast.[31]

Maintenance of peace and order by the daimyō in each sector of the domain was very difficult yet most important, especially to the prosperity and security of the castle towns. Strict regulations were placed on the behavior and movement of people to prevent disorder and arson by invading enemies or rebellious citizens within. Wholesalers and innkeepers in Odawara, for instance, were required to register reports on all entering or leaving their premises to the castle office.[32] In the Yamaguchi town of the Ōuchi family, such prohibitions as the following were imposed:
—against traffic in the main street at night;
—against *sumo* exhibitions in the town streets;
—against procuring women in the streets;
—against hiring fugitives from other provinces or others without suitable references as to prior status and location. In the Takeda family's town of Fuchū in Kai (Yamanashi), commoners, priests, and lower class soldiers were organized for joint patrol duty throughout the town. These are examples of ways in which local organizations and order were promoted to undergird the integrative network of the daimyō with political and economic aims held central.[33]

The concentration in the castle towns of both wealth and a large non-farming military class under the daimyō was a strong stimulus to commercial enterprises. The lord depended increasingly on the merchants to supply the large consumer class with food, clothing, and weapons. Those merchants operating on a large scale were based in Kyōto and Sakai, distributing their goods from there to the local regions. This naturally elevated the social positions of leading merchants (cf. Ito in Kiyosu of Owari, Anibe in Miyaichi of Suho, Sakata in Kōfu, Matsuki and Tomono in Sunpu, and Yanada in Wakamatsu of Aizu).

The castle town in the Age of Civil Wars served as (1) the distribution point for goods from central areas, and (2) the nucleus of local exchange economies, especially in rice consumption. Merchants were given financial aid and police protection, and merchants' ships were often exempted from various port duties, to encourage the circulation of goods from other provinces. Losses sustained from theft were often passed on to the villages where pilfering occurred.[34]

Market activity was promoted on fixed dates and at fixed places in front of the castle compounds. Shops and peddlers were frequently favored with tax exemptions (*rakuichi* or *rakuza*), as has been mentioned. Merchants were "freed" from monopolistic controls to deal directly with each other, which means, actually, that the daimyō took commerce and industry out from under special temple and shrine privileges and placed them under his own control.

From among the more powerful merchants the provincial lords appointed certain officials who were authorized to (1) collect sales taxes from peddlers, (2) oversee market festivals, (3) allocate shop sites, (4) collect operating fees from retailers occupying fixed sites, and (5) exercise policing controls over all market activity. Their authority applied not just to the castle towns, but extended over the entire domains of their lords. These merchant officials were treated virtually the same as the top military vassals of the lord who were granted estates. In times of all-out war, they joined the family and military followers in common defense of lord and domain.[35]

Commodity demands resulting from population increases precipitated rapid development of retail shops, and wholesalers became even wealthier supplying them. Some of the wholesalers came into possession of large tracts of land outside the town, further extending their control over both town and country.

Thus did the castle town come to function not only as the center of political integration, but as the nucleus of integrative commercial activity as well.

The most important of the castle town organs for comprehensive territorial integration were the systems of military and civil administration. A supporting network of auxiliary castles, *shijō* and *edashiro*, and smaller outposts, *hajiro*, were constructed to secure both internal order and defense against external attacks. These fortresses formed a defense line around the main castle, called *honjō* or *nejiro* (base castle). Along the boundary line of the domain's territory were built such aptly-named castles as "boundary eye," *sakaimeshiro*, and "watchman," *banteshiro*. Other defense structures included *tsunaginoshiro* (connected, as by tunnels) and *tsutaenoshiro* (communications), *tsumenoshiro* (reconnaisance, from battle fields), and assault positions called *mukaishiro* (attack), *tsukejiro* (lookouts), and *tainoshiro* (encounter points).[36]

These auxiliary and outlying structures were simple and temporary in the early days of this period, although they became larger in scale and more numerous during the Age of Civil Wars. In the Wakasa fortification there were ten forts of Takeda Magohachiro and forty-eight forts in the Nanbu complex. In the Hyuga province under the Itō house, lord of Obi, there were forty-eight forts around the castle. The Uesugi family had a total of 120 forts in three separate fortification sites, Kami (2), Naka (36), and Shimo (72). The Ōuchi family of Suho had four forts, the Hosokawa family of Kamogata eleven, and the Kikuchi family of Higo eighteen fortresses.[37]

Technical measures promoted by the diamyō to strengthen territorial controls included (1) progress in production, (2) standardization of weights and measures, (3) road improvements, (4) bridge construction, and (5) development of highway station facilities. Just as the scope of economic activity had expanded beyond the village unit to encompass the entire domain, so the military, administrative, and judicial controls of the daimyō gradually transcended the subdivisions of his domain. The whole territory merged into a single local state.

Because of almost total concentration of each daimyō on the needs and advantages of his own domain, the domains tended to be fairly insular. But the centers of supply for many items, especially ammunition for the new muskets and cannon, were grouped in the central traffic junctions in and around Kyōto. Merchants supplying the daimyō and his people had to go beyond their own territories to secure their merchandise. Local cooperatives, *za*, rooted in the estates soon vanished as the estates were absorbed into larger feudal domains. Merchants working under direct patronage and protection of the daimyō prospered, and their domination of the market greatly expedited development in the transportation system and, at the same time, spurred greater differentiation in specific items in local production. Under these conditions, the separate domains gradually lost their insularity.

## 4. Development of Highway and Port Towns

Within and between the relatively independent domains there existed no uniform, standard system of highway stations and relay under strict regulation such as had characterized that of the central government at its zenith in the Heian era. Travel was heavy between Kyōto and Kamakura in the days of ascendancy of the latter. With regional dispersion of political power from the Muromachi period on, the national system of transportation fell into disrepair. The provincial lords cared for needs in their own domains, neglecting the overall national system. Traffic networks were altered to serve the regional systems centered around the castle towns.

To advance the political, military and economic integration of his own territory, each daimyō endeavored to bring all traffic internal to his domain under his control. Fortifications, roads, bridges, and express messenger systems were organized to serve the central castle. Top priority went to the effective mobility of troops and supplies between the main castle and auxiliary forts, among the forts, and to and from battlefields.

Along the network of highways serving the base castle, relay stations were constructed that served more than military purposes. They were the operational bases for tax collections, and merchants and innkeepers were attracted to these station junctions. The towns that grew up at the relay points were called *machimura* style.

Local leaders, generally village heads or estate managers, usually became the agents (*toiya*) for supplying horses, porters, food, and overnight lodging. They acted as official suppliers of the lord's needs, and had authority to collect duty on movements through their stations, part of which they kept. Nor were they, in their good positions, taxed by their lords.[38]

These facilities were primarily for political and military use, although movements of merchants to and from the domain were encouraged. Peasants were bound to the land, and their movements carefully watched. Communication with neighboring friendly domains was fostered, though passage to or through unfriendly territories was not easy.

Under the disruptive civil war conditions, all but military transportation was suspended. The *bakufu* and the daimyō erected checking stations along roads and rivers to supervise the logistics of both battle and finance. It was necessary not only to provide protective cover for one's own territory, but to prevent leakages of information concerning military movements as well. Various forms of intercourse with folk of other domains, especially hostile ones, was forbidden; e.g. employment of, or marriage to outsiders, or sending and receiving letters. Permits were issued even for travel within the domains, and those passing check points paid duty.

To political obstacles were added material and social hindrances. The roads themselves were poor, and bandits rendered free movements of people and cargo most difficult. Merchants provided armed groups for their own protection, but otherwise poor travel conditions kept the domains in mutual isolation.

Land transportation was far inferior to the waterways. The relay stations, in fact, served more as markets and tax collection bases than as facilities for travelers. Poor roads, a rugged terrain, and the lack of social uniformity from domain to domain made the water routes particularly desirable for transporting heavy cargoes. By this stage movements of merchandise had taken precedence over shipments of tribute by estates to Kyōto. Port towns emerged all along the Inland Sea, in Kyūshū and Shikoku islands, and on both the Japan Sea and the Pacific shores of the main island of Honshū.

The Inland Sea was heavily infested with pirates, usually operating under the control of powerful local families. Merchant ships sailed in fleets, with guards employed to protect their cargoes on board. Kyōto and Sakai merchants often compromised with the pirates, buying "protection" at fixed rates.[39] Though large craft existed, most boats were small, and preferred the safer river trips to hazardous sea voyages. Small port towns developed along the rivers, where warehouses were built for larger stocks than the small craft could carry.

As inter-territorial commodity exchange became more widespread the importance and size of the ports increased. The ports of Hyōgo, Sakai, and

Onomichi flourished, moreover, under the Tally Trade Agreement with the Ming dynasty on the mainland. Sakai registered a population of 30,000 by 1532, and Onomichi already had 5,000 in 1320. Coastal ports with complicated community structures developed at Muro and Akamagaseki on the Inland Sea; at Tsuruga, Kohama, Mikuni, Naoetsu, and Sakata on the Japan Sea; and at Kuwana and Ōminato on the Bay of Ise. Wealthy *toinin* who operated warehouses and wholesale firms emerged in these port towns. As business expanded, they tended to specialize.

Kyōto, of course, was a forwarding point for goods produced all over the land, for here was the great consumers' haven of absentee estate owners, including the wealthy religious orders. Dealer specialization in salt, fish, and rice was notable, governing price levels throughout the entire country. Wholesalers even diversified, operating inns and warehouses. Shops handling bills of exchange emerged, the origin of this practice in Japan. Specialization also occurred among those handling commodity production and distribution. Such specialization was made possible by the growing scale of economic activity.

Within this context, *toinin* who served feudal lords in procurement and sales transactions for their lords gradually gained independence as brokers and forwarding agents. They assumed regular middlemen roles between the provinces and large city wholesalers and retailers, taking over the distribution services originally performed by markets with fixed days for opening.

Promotion of commerce thus passed into the hands of private entrepeneurs engaged in wholesale and money-lending firms, especially in Kyōto, Nara, Uji-yamada, and castle towns in the capital district, as well as in key ports. From these new positions of power, commercial interests gradually assumed control of municipal affairs formerly administered by and for primarily political interests. The cities now possessed well-ordered self-governing agencies.

There were efforts in Kyōto toward greater involvement in government by citizens even before the War of Ōnin. After that war left the city in ashes, and the *bakufu* authority was lost, citizens' autonomy was intensified. Groups of tax-paying citizens moved into the upper class section of Kamikyō, and mobile peddlers' shops cropped up here and there to serve them. The areas near the older markets in the Shimokyō section were the first to be rebuilt there. The waterfront district of Toba resumed its specialized port functions, with independent transport groups being formed.

All subdivisions of Kyōto thus developed as towns. One block surrounded by larger streets consisted of five or six *chō* (townships), and several of such *chō* units formed *oyamachi*, or larger townships. The townspeople, *machishū*, were mainly merchants and their helpers, craftsmen and some deposed nobility. Money-lenders and *sake* brewers generally held dominant positions in the management of town affairs and security, which, in any case, the townspeople managed themselves. The townships were organized into larger autonomous bodies, *machigumi*, which, again were brought into even larger unions of the Kamikyō, Nakakyō, and Shimokyō (upper, middle, and lower sections of Kyōto). Town managers for the *machigumi* were chosen for a month at a time (*tsukigyōji*), and the larger unions were under administrative councils, *sō*, constituted of ten representatives, *sōdai*.[40]

Official communications from the central government were channeled through the town managers (*tsukigyōji*) and elders (*shukurō*), as, for instance, a notice issued in the tenth year of the Tenmon era (1533–55) that taxes on land in and outside Kyōto must be paid without delay. In the twentieth year of the same era, rivalry between Kamikyō and Shimokyō residents was settled by the town elders, with reference to permission to campaign for temple-reconstruction funds.[41]

Towns developed under the auspices of temples and shrines had always been relatively free of the oppressive influences of powerful clans. Self-governing bodies arose in these towns whenever the local economy advanced sufficiently.

It is instructive to refer to the excellent study of freedom in the city of Nara made by Nagashima Fukutarō. A temple town controlled by the aristocratic estate-rich temples of Tōdaiji, Genkōji, and Kasuga-dera, it embraced a core of commercial houses at its center called *gō*. Its several sectors were combined in a complex city boasting a population of 10,000 in the Muromachi era, and 20,000 at the beginning of the Edo period.

As in other towns, set-day markets for merchants and peddlers under official supervisors were developed from the Heian era guilds, *za*, by the time of the Kamakura government. Population increases swelled the ranks of merchants and craftsmen who, in time, gained independence from temple and shrine controls. By the end of the Kamakura era, the market was actually under the direct control of self-governing councils of merchants.

Growth in consumer demands enabled peddlers to become settled retailers, merchants to become wholesalers, and wholesalers to become money-lenders and wealthy absentee landlords. Hostelries for visiting worshippers were also a lucrative business in Nara. The merchants formed the core of the commoners operative in the self-governing *gō*, and their land wealth was tax-exempt, as merchants paid only per capita taxes. Nonetheless, while the self-governing system on horizontal lines tightened, their vertical loyalties to their lords were never abolished.

In the Muromachi era, administrative units for festival observance were formed by neighborhoods, *gō*, comprising fifty households per group. These groups were under the immediate guidance of councils of elders, who governed through community meetings.

In the contest over imperial succession in the War of the Southern and Northern dynasties (1336–92), the monk soldiers of Nara wrested control from the court nobility, controlling the village *gō* much as the military class ruled provincial areas. The relation of the common people to the monk rulers did not take on the status characteristics found usually in provincial domains, and the people gained more independence for themselves whenever the monk soldiers fell into dissension among themselves. The *gō* community councils gradually became the effective governing bodies, with elected elders and responsible sub-groups. A combined council of leaders, *sōjū*, from the administratively separate southern and northern sectors of Nara was composed mainly of merchants and craftsmen.

Autonomy in Nara did not evolve further, however, as the people did not wish to relinquish their tax-exemptions as merchants in formal relations of subservience to the religious bodies, of which they were quite proud. Hence, their court superiors were not expelled, nor did they take steps toward creation of a self-governing local state.[42]

Similar movements toward autonomy emerged in the shrine town of Uji-yamada. Although a provincial governor, *shugo*, was appointed in the Heian era, he never exercised actual control over this town, this resting rather with the head priest, *kannushi*. Under him were nine administrative units (*gō*) for the Uji (6) and Yamada (3) sections. Government appointees to assist the *kannushi*, called *gunji* and *tone*, were eventually replaced by priests and their assistants, *kami-yakunin* and *jinin* respectively, who increased considerably in numbers after the Heian period.[43] Following a revolt in 1429, the *tone* administrators were replaced by a private council of *kami-yakunin* in all land control administration.

The priests and their assistants performed in their priestly roles not only for visitors to the shrine town, but maintained pastoral relations with loyal supporters all over the country. Of course, they took a leading role in the inn services for those on pilgrimages to the shrine, in marketing and money-lending, and all town administration.

Uji was administered by a council of forty-eight elders from six districts; Yamada similarly by a council of twenty-four from three districts. Uji was not so large as Yamada, actually, and pressures toward local autonomy were less there than in the latter. Yamada worked hard at securing self-rule, and an order for cancellation of debts (*tokusei*) from its local council in 1582 is known, as is the assumption of certain judicial prerogatives in the Bunmei era (1469–86).[44]

Self-government through citizens' councils was most prominent, however, in the port towns. Rich marine transporters living there did not depend on the land-economy of the domains, and could more easily stand against troublesome minor lords. Accordingly, feudal controls over large port towns tended to be weak. The freest of the port towns was the flourishing city of Sakai, for which there are two good study references, *Sakai*, by Toyota Takeshi, and the two-volume study of *The History of Sakai City*, by Miura Kaneyuki.

Early recognized as a fine fishing port, Sakai flourished as a commercial port especially after establishing trading contacts with the Yüan dynasty in the 14th century and the Ming dynasty in the 15th century. At that time it was controlled by the Ōuchi family, though it was placed under the Hosokawa family after the Ashikaga rulers took control of the *bakufu*. Later, the southern part of Sakai, Nansō, was given over to the head priest of the Shōkokuji temple. About that time the administration of the city was put in the hands of the people resident there under a system, called *jigeuke*, in which they gave fixed taxes in return to the owner. Although Sakai was later governed directly by the *bakufu*, the experience gained in the *jigeuke* arrangement was the primary factor that led to the establishment of self-government in Sakai.

Sakai was an important source of income for the Muromachi *bakufu*, and its possession was hotly contested in the War of Ōnin. After the war, Sakai became the key terminal port in the Tally Trade Agreement with the Ming Court, being equally accessible to the Kyōto and Nara districts. Merchants there were unbound by guild connections, and its craftsmen did a thriving business in textiles, lacquerware, metal casting and forging. Periodical markets, warehouses, wholesalers, money-lenders, transporters, and exchange brokers all functioned in its prosperous business, especially in the large quantities of rice, lumber, and salt unloaded there for distribution in the capital region.

A great impetus to the prosperity of Sakai was given by the Tally Trade missions to the Ming dynasty—four missions in forty years—though after cessation of this formal arrangement the China trade continued through the agency of *wako*, Japanese pirates operating in the East China Sea. Trade relations with Korea and the Ryūkyū islands were expedited. The population of Sakai reached over 20,000 at the summit of its prosperity.

Sakai's main street, Chūō-ōji, was divided into two distinct sectors, north and south. The southern sector was densely populated, with two-storied houses, while much of the northern sector was under cultivation. Merchant houses facing the street were often no more than 3–4 yards in width. The northern and southern sectors had separate town councils of thirty-six elected elders and appointed administrative officials. The local council paid for festival expenses and tended to the town's defensive needs.

In the confusion following the Ōnin War, military cliques extorted huge sums of money from the Sakai citizenry, who obliged the warriors to keep peace. But they also dug moats and erected city gates for self-defense. Leading merchants procured weapons and hired lordless warriors (*rōnin*). The merchants turned portions of their wealth to the city's defense and, when Oda Nobunaga demanded a certain military tax (*yasen*) of the Sakai merchants in 1568, the town council stood resolutely and unanimously in its decision to reject the demands.[45]

In the Hirano district adjacent to Sakai was a town, Hichichō, base of the Sueyoshi family that prospered in foreign trade. This town had some of the characteristics of a free city, a council of elders, and surrounding moats for defense. Its elders sought the help of Sakai when the latter stood against Nobunaga.[46]

Amagasaki on the Inland Sea had a self-rule system of administration even before the War of Ōnin. This town was burned to the ground by Nobunaga in 1569 for refusing to pay the *yasen* tax. Another port town, Hakata in north Kyūshū, contained many rich traders who largely eliminated feudal structures. Their wealth, as in Sakai, enabled them to ward off undue damage from the civil wars. Its citizens even rose against the provincial lord of the Ōuchi family in 1559. Likewise, the towns of Kuwana and Ōminato, connected with Ise Shrine, and the town of Atsuta Shrine, all on the Ise Bay, flourished as port towns, and have their own histories of spirited resistance against feudal lords.

The rise of these more or less free cities was rooted not only in growth in the domestic economy, but in the added accumulation of wealth through overseas trading ventures. However, these cities lacked sufficient range in their available markets, especially a truly international trade. Nor did they have adequate weapons or solidarity among the total citizenry to successfully resist and defeat the feudal powers of Japan. Certainly they were not equipped to administer the death blow to feudalism that the European merchants and craftsmen did to the feudal system there. Genuine freedom did not exist in the "free cities" of Japan; rather, it was but a degree of local autonomy shared not by wide segments of the populace, but monopolized by a limited number of wealthy merchants who dominated the local administration.

The degrees of change toward limited local autonomy, in town or country, constituted but an intermediary stage of reorganization of the overall feudal order in the period of civil disorder. A select group of wealthy merchants stood temporarily against the unsettled feudal barons struggling toward a new order. When the most powerful of the feudal warlords succeeded in giving the nation its most thoroughgoing unification in the pre-modern history of Japan, these merchants were swiftly disarmed and swept to the bottom of a rigidly-controlled social scale.

# Chapter V

# Restoration of National Unity in the Centralized Feudal System (A.D. 1572–1868)

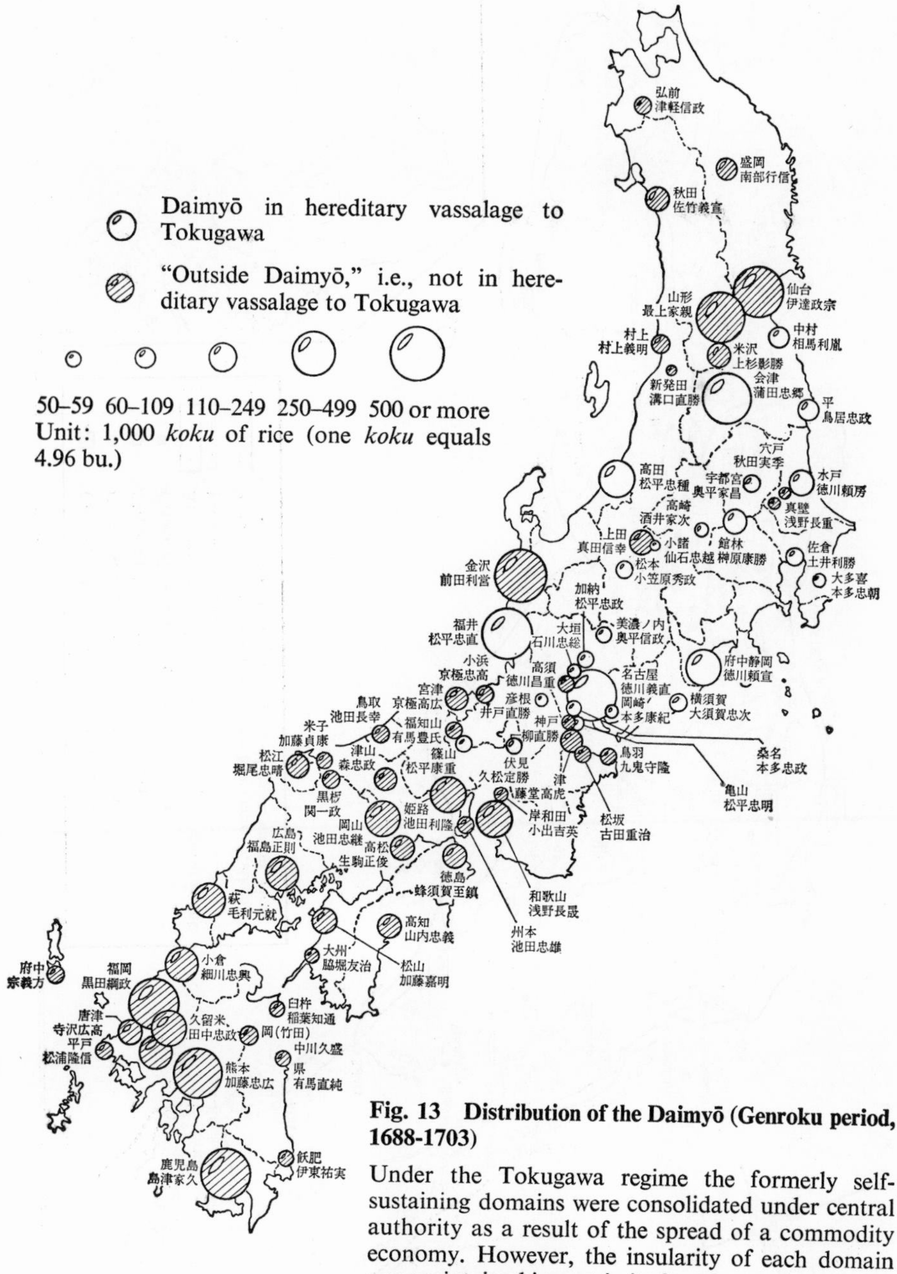


**Fig. 13 Distribution of the Daimyō (Genroku period, 1688-1703)**

Under the Tokugawa regime the formerly self-sustaining domains were consolidated under central authority as a result of the spread of a commodity economy. However, the insularity of each domain was maintained in part in its function as the political and economic administrative unit. Therefore, the castle town developed as the integrating center of each domain, and the size of the domain was largely determined by the quantity of the rice yield. (adopted from *Nihon Rekishi Chizu.*)

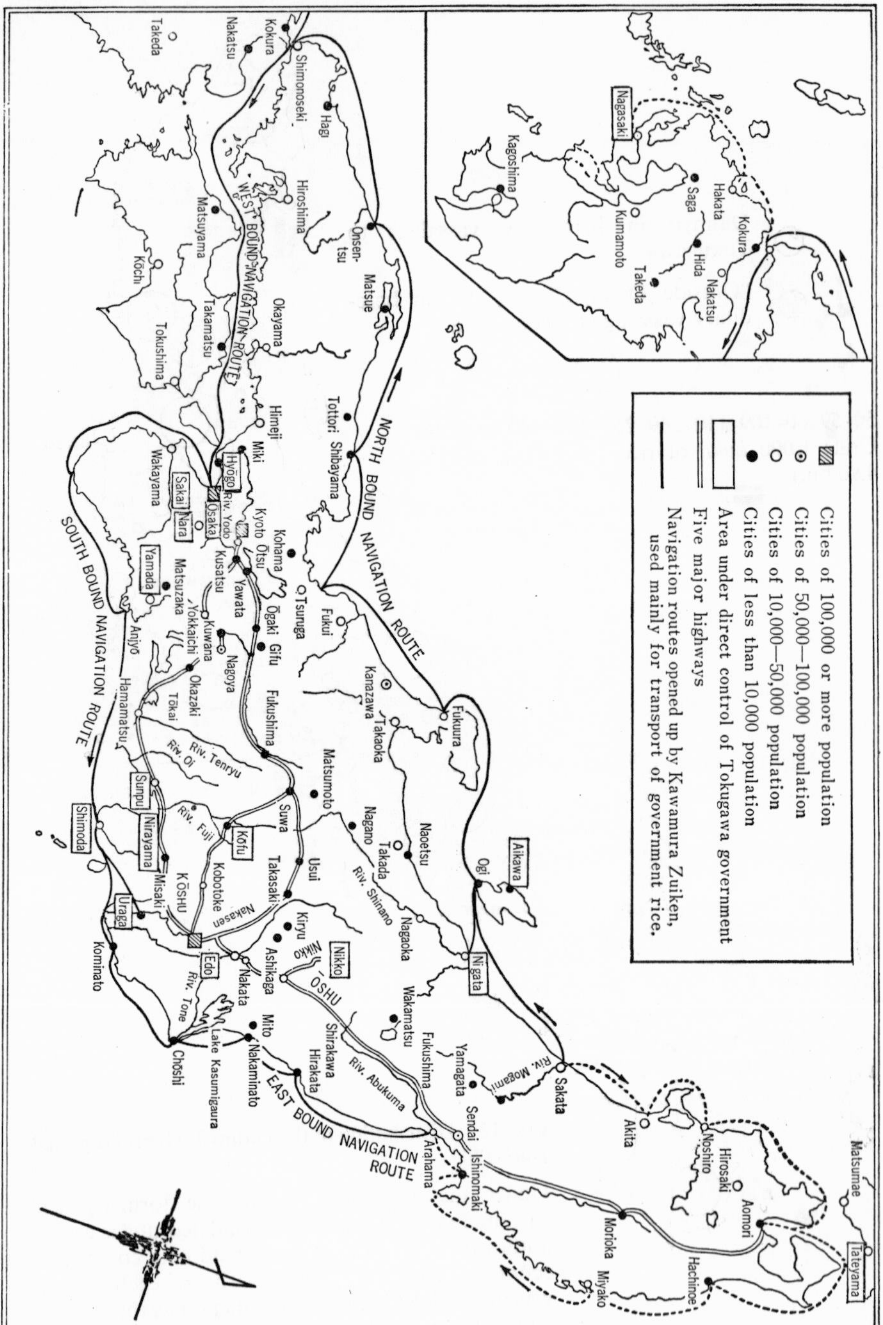


**Fig. 14 Major Cities and Travel Routes in the Edo Period**

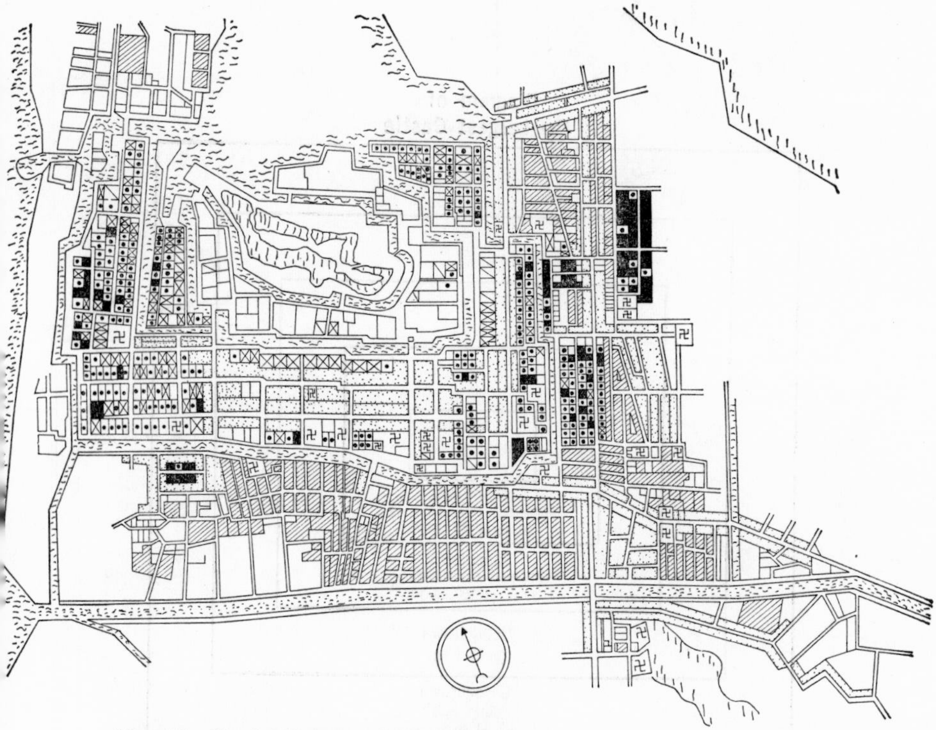

**Fig. 15 Spatial Pattern of the Castle Town**

Whenever the castle town was located the castle was central, and the structure of the town was schematically determined through the exercise of power in consideration of defense needs and status. As is clear from the illustration, the upper military class was close to the castle, while the lower military class was located on the town's periphery. The artisans and merchants were settled in definite sections. In contrast to the former (medieval) period, the town was clearly distinguished from the rural area, the peasants living on the outside. It was also different from the modern city in that it included all functions essential to its role as the integrating center of a self-sustaining domain. (drawn by Kazuhiko Yamori.)

Temples and shrines
Townsmen (artisans and merchants)
Lower class warriors
50 *koku*
100 〃
300 〃
500 〃
1,000 〃
} Warrior classes by ranks as indicated by yearly rice stipend (one *koku* equals 4.96 bu.)
Streams and moats
Hills and dirt embankments

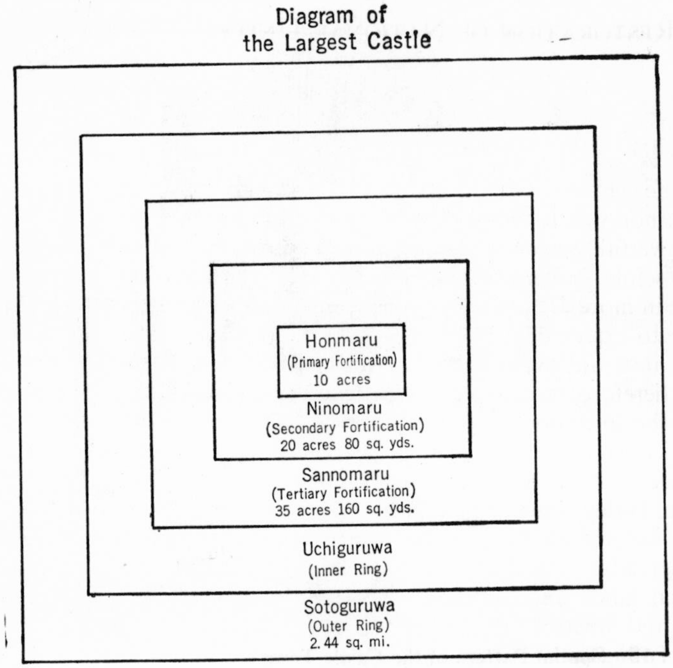


**Fig. 16 Diagram of a Large Edo Period Castle** (drawn by Masao Toba)

## 1. Restoration of National Unity

During the century of civil wars up to the second half of the 16th century (1572) minor warrior cliques were gradually absorbed by a few of the more powerful warlords, whose policy was to overpower neighboring domains while seeking to maintain friendly relations with other mighty warlords in more distant regions. No single man of great power, however, was able to extend his sphere of influence sufficiently to tie all domains together into an overarching national unity. The dominant warlords sought, therefore, to make use of the traditional authority of the emperor, wherein the lord would swear allegiance to the throne in order to gain governance of the entire country. In the process of struggle for total integrative control, Oda Nobunaga rose first to pre-eminence, followed by Toyotomi Hideyoshi and Tokugawa Ieyasu.

This was not the kind of integrative pattern found in modern states. It was a feudal system in which the leading daimyō exercised controls over local lands and peoples, while the central military government's strength and function lay in integration of the daimyō themselves.

The Tokugawa *bakufu*, which rose to unchallenged supremacy, was itself the ruling family over extensive lands, commanding about one-fourth of the total income of Japan measured in *kokudaka*, or rice crop yields. It expanded its control over eight provinces in the Kantō region, as well as over certain important big cities, port towns and mining operations, placing commissioners (*bugyō*) and deputies (*daikan*) over its holdings. The rest of the country was governed directly by the top daimyō.

The Tokugawa *bakufu* thus reorganized the once decentralized feudal order into a centralized system again. Many of the feudal domains were in direct allegiance to the Tokugawa regime and were called *hatamoto* (lit. under the flag of the *bakufu*), and retainers (*gokenin*) to the Tokugawa regime constituted its immediate source of military strength.

The total number of authorized daimyō was about 260, the large majority of whom held direct relations of hereditary vassalage to the Tokugawa family. In return for recognized control over lands and people, the daimyō owed fealty to the *bakufu*, including military duty, contributions of laborers, goods, and wealth to *bakufu* programs. To assure constancy of allegiance, the daimyō were required to spend every other year in residence in the Tokugawa capital of Edo, a requirement called *sankin-kōtai*. All of these measures were part of the absolutistic system of master-subordinate relationships promoted to prevent disintegration back into the patterns of independent land controls and indeterminate status relations which the Tokugawa powers had fought so hard to overcome. The stability of the Tokugawa political integration depended fundamentally on this system of unconditional feudal loyalty of the daimyō to the *bakufu.*

Temples and shrines also came under the overall supervision of the *bakufu.* The emperor retained his role of divinely-sanctioned authority, and the court nobility their's as his councilors. This authority was not likely to vanish as long as the status of the Tokugawa generalissimo (shogun) was based on the traditional patriarchal system and the shogun took advantage of the emperor's role as "head of the Japanese nation," though "orders" were received from the emperor only as a formal courtesy.

Three factors were of special importance in the process of accomplishing a centralized system as begun by Oda Nobunaga, furthered by Toyotomi Hideyoshi, and brought to completion by Tokugawa Ieyasu. One was stabilization of the villages in their trend toward greater agricultural productivity. Secondly, the fixation of all classes into a rigid status system was achieved. Finally, the development of towns, especially castle towns, as the nuclei of integrative organs completed the process. With the military class resident in the castle towns, regional activity among the villages was intensified. Village associations, *gōson*, unified under powerful local leaders, *nanushi*, acted cooperatively to resist both heavy tax levies by the lords and excessive interest rates imposed by the moneylenders. In time, the expanding activities of village associations came under the total governance of the daimyō.

One of the first steps taken after Oda Nobunaga and his successor, Toyotomi Hideyoshi, succeeded in unifying controls over the daimyō, was to restrict the progress made at the local level toward a free exchange economy of raw materials for crafts production, farm implements, and fertilizers. Fixing the villages in their developmental stages, this move was designed to divert the flow of farm surplus away from regional exchange and into the *bakufu* treasuries. Not only were farmers prohibited from free sale or exchange of crop yields; they were instructed as to the kinds of crops to be cultivated. Household finances were disengaged from community economies by utilization of a money system. Local rulers not only inspected lands and crops regularly, but carried out a census of each village to confirm faithful adherence to cultivation regulations. Such measures bound the farmers to their lands and assigned crops, preventing any mobility of occupation or residence. Peasants' swords were confiscated (*katanagari*) to prevent revolts, and families were organized locally into units of five (*gonin-gumi*) to enforce joint responsibility in tax payments and crime prevention. The controlling power of the feudal lords was greatly strengthened thus through official and effective stabilization of village life against socio-economic changes which might otherwise occur.

Continued growth in agricultural productivity led, just the same, to greater differentiation in manufacture and barter transactions, stimulating market activity in the castle, port, and highway station towns. As the warlords depended upon the prosperity of commodity dealers and brokers for funds necessary to military expansion, they promoted the free flow of goods in markets, farm cooperatives and ports within the context of domain controls. Their policies served to free the merchants and artisans from the relationships binding them to the medieval temples, shrines, and court aristocracy. The inconveniences of checking stations (*sekisho*) and tolls (*sekisen*) were abolished. Roads and bridges were constructed and kept in good repair, and highway distances were marked every *ri* (2.4 mi.) with *ichirizuka* (one-*ri* markers). Currency standardization facilitated commodity exchange on a nationwide basis. All of these factors enhanced integrated rule of the entire country.

The kind and extent of freedom enjoyed in commerce in this period were quite different, however, from that of modern times. Freedom was permitted only within the strict confines of the feudal system. Wealthy merchants who dared oppose the feudal leaders were often ruined. The separation of commerce from its basis in agriculture was as rigidly restrained as was the flow of foreign trade in this age of international seclusion. Commercial growth was confined to the domestic markets, and any merchant attempting to overstep these bounds was brought quickly into line. The city of Sakai was taxed heavily and its townsmen were disarmed. On the other hand, leading townsmen throughout the country were promoted to warrior status, and merchants and craftsmen were concentrated in the castle towns for more direct service to, and control by, the rulers.

By the time the integrative processes instituted by Nobunaga and Hideyoshi were formalized by Ieyasu, all freedom of movement in agricultural and commercial activities was suspended, and these activities were placed under rigid regulations. To strengthen its controls over these social functions, the *bakufu* introduced an equally rigid status system to control the people involved. Warriors, farmers, artisans, and merchants were fixed within a descending hierarchy in that order, and all social and regional mobility were firmly forbidden.

The warrior class was composed of the daimyō and their retainers, at the top of which stood the *bakufu*. They had surnames, bore swords, and were granted lands in reward for services—all distinguishing marks of the warrior class. The master-subordinate relations required of all social classes were exemplified especially in the absolute allegiance the warriors owed to the *bakufu*. The principle of total obligation, *chō-on*, held that the warriors' existence depended upon the continued favor of his lord (and the latter's successors), a notion quite different from the more immediately realized merit-award pattern of the Age of Civil Wars. The entire military class were expected to be paragons of virtue for the rest of society. Their speech, customs, houses and residential areas were different from those of other classes, and cultural refinement along with strict military discipline were required of them. They were to display pride in belonging to the warrior class, and if their honor as warriors was insulted by non-warriors, they were authorized to kill them on the spot, for which no excuse was needed—a privilege clearly stated in Article 71 of the criminal code (*Osadamegaki*), known as *kirisutegomen*.

Shinto and Buddhist priests supplemented the ruling function, mediating between the military class and the people, particularly in implanting the ideas and ethics that stabilized the feudal order. This function was shared by scholars, most of whom were members of the warrior group.

Farmers constituted the bulk of the ruled. Their cultivation rights (and obligations) were guaranteed, although proceeds were divided largely among the *bakufu* first, then the daimyō, and finally the retainers. In addition to taxes, they were subject to compulsory labor, demands that were easily extracted from a class that could not leave the land or sell it, or change professions. They barely managed to subsist within the severe restrictions placed on them. They were forbidden to eat the rice they grew, living mainly on miscellaneous cereals, and enjoyed only the humblest clothes and homes. Theatrical performances and *sumo* wrestling exhibitions were closed to them. The strict regulation of their entire existence was symbolized in an official instruction to farmers issued in the Keian era (1648–52): "You are expected to obey strictly the laws of the *bakufu*. Yield allegiance to the local governor (*jitō*) and deputies (*daikan*), and consult the village heads (*nanushi*) and his assistants (*kumigashira*), as if you were approaching your own father." The moral overtones of such relations are obvious. Again, in the preface to a manual for village administration, there appears this directive: "Every village must be organized into neighborhood units of five families (*gonin-gumi*). Should there be some who do not obey the laws and regulations, they must be reported immediately to the governmental authorities. Such cases shall be treated the same as criminal acts on the part of any members of the family units." In this system farmers were mutually responsible for their behavior under the supervision of an appointed warrior.

The merchants and artisans likewise were under military supervision, though they too received protection in return for the taxes (*myōgakin*) paid to their overseers. Nonetheless, their daily lives were strictly confined to the limits prescribed for their specific status. Commodity prices, wages, and the kinds of goods permitted to enter market sales were thoroughly regulated. These townsmen were prohibited, moreover, from constructing three-storied houses, from possessing luxury goods such as *makie* (high grade gold or silver-lacquerware), from wearing silk garments, and restrictions were placed even on certain kinds of footgear.

In the various occupational groups, guilds (*nakama*) were established. Membership in some guild was a prerequisite for doing business in Edo society. These guilds were operated, of course, on status terms like all the rest of society, and adherence to traditional methods and human relations was promoted here as elsewhere. As affluence led gradually to influence, the merchants sometimes asserted themselves against the warrior's hierarchical ethic, as is reflected in a book titled *Yugiri Awano Naruto*, "The warrior is not always noble nor the merchant humble;

one thing only is truly precious, the heart." Such an embryonic form of egalitarian values could be found among the townsmen, though it rarely was universal enough to include the "class-less" group of outcasts below all other classes, who could not even claim legitimate citizenship.

Within the rigid stratification of status, the basis of all existence became hereditary. Warriors inherited their stipends, farmers succeeded to their lands, and townsmen assumed their trades through family lineage. The obedience imposed on household members according to sex and age left little independence to individual members. As a matter of fact, the imperial household and the court nobility enjoyed relatively little influence under the same stratified system, even though they ranked as members of the ruling class and held special status with relation to the traditional system of national and local deities, *ujigami*. In actual practice they were virtually impotent.

In such a social order, individuals were deprived not only of freedom but of personality as well. The occupational groups were fixed, and within them each person's place fell to him mechanically according to his or her sex and age, predetermining not only one's relative place in society but the mode of behavior acceptable in that place.

The continuation of this social structure for generations deeply instilled in the people of all classes the ideas and feelings appropriate to master-subordinate relations, such as *onko* (master's favor), *hōkō* (sacrificing personal rights to public obedience), *giri* (personal obligations), and *chūgi* (loyalty due superiors). Changes in attitudes, customs, and standards were geared to status, as can be seen in each area of life, spoken language, dietary and sartorial habits, residential facilities, and so on. Shinto, Buddhism, and Confucianism were accommodated to the demands of the feudal system, their moral teachings giving guidance to proper attitudes and behavior in the minute details of living. In time the criteria derived from the external order penetrated deeply into the consciousness of the people, forming the central core of their sentiments.

While Buddhism had dominated the moral consciousness of the Japanese up through the medieval period, it was replaced now by Confucian precepts, promoted by the ruling class in support of the new system of stratification. Priests of the Pure Land (Jōdoshū) and Zen sects who became learned in Confucian thought served as consultants to the *bakufu*. All religious institutions were forced to cooperate with the *bakufu* through the commissioner of shrines and temples (*jisha-bugyō*). In regulations concerning temples (*jiin hatto*), relations between the head temples (*honzan*) and branch temples (*matsuji*) were stipulated. The suppression of Christianity begun under Hideyoshi late in the 16th century was carried out relentlessly under Ieyasu early in the 17th. A system requiring each citizen to register according to his religious sect, *shūshi-ninbetsu-aratamecho*, provided at once a basis of support for the religious institutions through their registrants (*danka*), and an effective means of control over the religious bodies by the *bakufu*.

## 2. The Three Largest Cities, Edo, Ōsaka, and Kyōto, and Other Cities: Population Size and Composition, Horizontal Mobility

The muscle in the centralized system that held both rural districts and social classes in fixed positions were the integrative organs developed for total national control. The nerve centers for this system were the major cities of Edo, Ōsaka, and Kyōto, and the provincial castle towns.

One of the strongest sinews in the newly-shaped national body was the formation of a national economy. The insular character of self-supporting village economies had broken down as regional economies were fostered in each domain. These, in turn, were drawn into the framework of an overall national economy.

In knitting together a nationwide economy, however, the *bakufu* took pains not to obliterate the regional units of the feudal economic order. The *bakufu* depended on the successful continuation of the domains as the functional units in its system of total integration. Accordingly, the *bakufu* sought to abolish existing barriers between the local provinces through such measures as releasing the merchants from the binding forces of local monopolies (*za*), construction and maintenance of good travel facilities, and standardization of currency, weights and measures, while preserving the integrity of each domain. On the other hand, commerce and agriculture were clearly differentiated in line with the policy of keeping status groups distinct and hierarchically ordered. This was also an age of self-imposed isolation from the world in which Tokugawa Ieyasu prohibited all Japanese from engaging in overseas travel and trade; only a limited foreign trade was permitted with the Chinese and Dutch through the port of Nagasaki. Sakai, for instance, lost its potential as a free port, being confined thoroughly within the domestic economy. Trade was "free" only in the sense that the unit domains were encouraged to prosper mutually.

The castle centers in the various domains of some 260 feudal lords were more or less evenly distributed throughout the land. Although these towns varied in size, each served as the nucleus of the integrative network in its own domain. From these castle centers, the network extended to port towns for inter-island transport, and to new markets and highway station towns developed in connection with the new system of highways.

Although castle towns appeared, as we have seen, towards the end of the medieval period, their functions were primarily military and political.

The claims of these earlier castle centers on agricultural products ran about one-half the total yield; the ratios varied from 60% for the government vs. 40% for the people (*rokkō-shimin*) to the reverse of this (or, *shikō-rokumin*). The government's share was for support of the daimyō, his vassals and troops. Merchants moved into these castle towns, though, as agents of the necessary commodity exchange, adding another function to these early castle towns. The population growth was in proportion to the ratio of crop yields.

Military purposes being primary in the medieval castle centers, unassailable topographical conditions governed the choice of sites. When the integrative functions multiplied under the centralized system of the Edo period, the castle locations were moved to more central positions in open plains or basins, facilitating integrative contacts with the whole domain. The castle's purpose shifted, that is, from mere defense of the stronghold itself to securing the entire territory against encroachment, a transition reflected in the successive terms used, from *shiro-kengo* to *tokoro-kengo* to *kuni-kengo*. These imply, first, "castle defense," then "place" and "province defense." This trend toward castle site changes received a concrete stimulus from Oda Nobunaga's directive (*ikkoku-ichijōrei*) in 1580 that there was to be but one central castle in each province. The medieval castles were disembled, especially after this edict was implemented with thoroughness under Tokugawa power in the Genna era (1615–24).

The following are some examples of key castle moves:

| *Daimyō* | *Date* | *From* | *To* | *Purpose* |
|---|---|---|---|---|
| Toyotomi Hideyoshi | 1574 | Kotani | Nagahama | To control north Ōmi by commanding Lake Biwa waterways |
| Shibata Katsuiye | 1575 | Ichinoritani | Kitanosho (Fukui) | To control Echizen |
| Oda Nobunaga | 1576 | Gifu | Azuchi | To command the strategic junction of Tōkaidō, Tōsandō, and Hokuriku highways, near Lake Biwa |
| Toyotomi Hideyoshi | 1576 | Miki | Himeji | To govern Harima by controlling seaways and ports |

| | | | | |
|---|---|---|---|---|
| Toyotomi Hideyoshi | 1583 | Himeji | Ōsaka | To command the most important site in Kinki, center of land and sea routes |
| Kobayagawa Takakage | 1587 | Dazaifu | Nashima | To govern the Chikuzen area |
| Gamō Ujisato | 1588 | Matsugashima | Matsusaka (of Ise) | ——— |
| Mōri Terumoto | 1589 | Yoshida | Hiroshima | ——— |
| Tokugawa Ieyasu | 1590 | Odawara | Edo | To control the central plain of the Kantō area[1] |

In the reference to "central locations" chosen for carrying out the expanded functions of castle towns in the Edo era, the strictly geometrical center is not intended so much as the functional center of each domain. Numerous factors combined to determine functional centrality, such as political and economic affairs, and existing and potential means of transportation and communication. Nor were completely new towns always constructed; often former port, temple, shrine, market, or highway station towns were rebuilt to accommodate the more diverse needs of a castle town. Of course, some instances involved combining two or more nearby towns of different sorts.

In his studies of feudal cities of Japan, Harada Tomohiko has drawn the following comparisons between castle towns of the medieval and Edo eras. The medieval castles were for military defense and, thus, were often poorly related to economic and traffic facilities. If the lords of these castles were defeated, or moved, the castle centers were quickly reduced to mere villages or ghost towns. Others were better situated with relation to communicative and commercial activities and, hence, survived after loss of the political and military functions as commercial towns. Examples of the latter category include: Naoetsu, Gifu, Kiyosu, Yawata, Hino, Kanbara, Hachiōji, Fukaya, Yoshida, Ōsaka, Hirano, Kanō, and Funabashi.

Drawing on Harada's findings further, we note that some of the medieval castle centers survived as castle towns in the Edo period. Their advantageous situations with respect to economic and traffic conditions kept these towns alive even when their lords' powers declined. Nagoya, for example, had a population of 55,000 in 1654, and it retained a population of 60,000–70,000 up to the end of the Edo period. Kagoshima sustained a population level of 60,000–70,000 from the end of the 16th century up to modern times. Kōfu was the most important castle center in the defense of the western part of the Kantō district, with a popualtion of about 10,000 from the second half of the 17th century. Other cities that survived conversion from medieval to Edo period castle towns included: Wakamatsu, Utsunomiya, Ashikaga, Odawara, Yūki, Kawagoe, Umayabashi, Uotsu, Fukui, Fuchū of Echizen, Ōno, Fuchū of Noto, Komatsu, Inuyama, Takatō, Takatsuki, Kameyama, Tottori, Nakamura, Ōmura, Hitoyoshi, and Obi.

Kanazawa was an example of a medieval temple town converted into a castle town. Stronghold of Kaga before conversion, this town boasted an annual income of one million *koku* of rice, and a population of 56,000 early in the 19th century. Other former temple towns made into castle towns in the Edo era were Suwa, Chōfu, Shingū, and Sakaki.

Those converted from port towns were Hakata, castle town of Fukuoka with a population of 50,000 at the turn of the 18th century, and Yodo, Kuwana, Tsu, Amagasaki, Hirado, and Shimabara. Castle towns originating from highway stations were Shirakawa, Takasaki, Annaka, Sekijuku Ueda, Toyama, Hamamatsu, Yoshida, Tawara, and Mitsugi. Some which appear to have been built originally as castle towns of this era, but were actually developed around older residential centers of the military, were Yonezawa, Okazaki, Mito, Oshi, Iwatsuki, Ōgaki, and Iida.[2]

Regardless of developmental pedigree, it was important for castle towns to have ready access to travel routes by land, river, or sea. Civil engineering projects were initiated to fulfill this basic requirement. For example, roads were sometimes re-routed to castle sites, as in the cases of Ōmi-hachiman, Hikone, Okayama, Shōnai, and Tsuruoka. Castle towns near, but without direct access to the sea, were connected by roadways with some port. Shizuoka, post-retirement residence of Ieyasu, was connected with the port of Shimizu; Tsuruoka of Shōnai in the Tōhoku district with the port of Sakata; Kanazawa with Kaneishi; Fukui with Mikuni; Kubota with Tosakie; Sendai with Shiogama; Himeji with Shikamatsu; and so on. Occasionally waterways were dug directly from the coast to the castle areas, as in Edo, Himeji, and Funai.

Initially the choice of castle sites took into consideration the natural advantages of local terrain for integrating the local domains, or the topography was altered to suit the situation. But the castle towns of the Edo era were more than local centers; they were units in a nationwide network of controls, and sites were chosen that served the total national needs of the central *bakufu*.

Among the numerous daimyō distributed throughout the land there were some who were very powerful, with annual incomes of over 200,000 *koku* of rice. Most of these were *tozama-daimyō*, or lords outside the circles of hereditary vassalage to the Tokugawa clan, except for three powerful households of Tokugawa lineage, called *gosanke*. The *tozama-daimyō* were placed outside the central Kansai and Kanto districts. The domains of Tokugawa-related lords, *shimpan*, and of those in hereditary vassalage, *fudai-daimyō*, were densely congregated along the main highways, such as the Tōkaidō, Nakasendō, and Kōshūkaidō, that led into Edo. In this way the Tokugawa *bakufu* built up a defense line of loyal lords in the central zone encompassing the castle towns of Odawara, Sunpu, Hachiōji, Umayabashi, Utsunomiya, Shirakawa, and Mito.[3]

The effective functioning of the castle towns was of crucial importance to the successful implementation of the integrative organs centered in Edo. Thus it was that the castle towns were heavily favored over rural districts, in terms of political protection, economic advantages, and all other facilities. Quite drastic measures were taken to assure the prosperity of the castle towns.

Such measures applied, for instance, to the merchants who were prohibited from setting up independent residence in the rural districts and from independent dealings in the villages. Commodity exchange was controlled through authorized wholesalers (*tonya*) and warehouses for storage of strategic goods such as rice, salt, and lumber. While merchants were exempted from land taxes, they were not included in the occasional moratoria declared on debts. In a word, they were at once protected by, and strictly tied to the castle town authorities.

Stringent controls were equally evident in the development and maintenance of all highways and ports. In these, as in the economic channels, the interests of the castle towns, numbering over 300 throughout the land, were consistently foremost.

Some contradictions existed between the effort to centralize the feudal structure and the persistent insularity of feudal domains, although this was partially overcome in the larger cities whose functions extended across the boundaries of one or more domains. Another contradiction arose from the primary dependence, on the one hand, of the *bakufu* on agricultural products for its economic stability, and its need, on the other hand, for money instead of bulk rice in supporting the warriors concentrated in the castle centers. The latter need was particularly keen in the movements of all daimyō and their retinues back and forth to Edo in alternate years under the *sankin-kōtai* regulation.

Just as local castle towns drew together merchants and craftsmen to supply the military-political elite, so the new national center of Edo, on a grander scale, drew upon the entire Kinki district (Ōsaka, and surrounding region) as its chief base of supply. Other domains were made subservient to this primary relationship of the older and newer capital regions, serving to break down the stubborn insularity of the provinces. The sheer distances involved placed a premium on currency as the medium of exchange. Local daimyō sought to achieve a favorable balance of exports from their territories over imports from others to increase their currency holdings, and this outward thrust for increased exports also worked to reduce the isolation of domains. Not only in the central capital, then, but in each locality there was an overall momentum toward a national economy.

The nation became the operational field but the domains remained the functional units of the economy. Each one established warehouses (*kura-yashiki*) in the two major consuming centers of Edo and Ōsaka to which goods were shipped for sale, and from which local daimyō could gain the needed currency. The national economy took on an elliptical shape around the two foci of Edo and Ōsaka. The latter especially developed as the major distribution point for receiving and dispatching shipments to and from the various domains. Specific shipping services to this great commercial center were developed, either with respect to particular commodities such as *sake* (*tarukaisen*) or sundries (*higaki-bune*), or in relation to specific ports, as the *Kanzaki-bune* (ships from Kanzaki) for that port town. Others ran from such ports as Ozaki, Akashi, Onomichi, Awa, Uwajima, Chikugen, Higo, and Matsumae. The wholesale houses and markets of Ōsaka became the control centers for the whole range of specific commodities all over the country.[4]

The organic relationships manifested in shipping were equally evident in the highway system that converged from all corners of the land on Edo, Ōsaka, and Kyōto. The highway station towns, like the port towns, emerged, survived and thrived in terms of their relevance to the national network centering in the three major cities.

The population of Japan in the Tenshō era (1573–92) has been estimated at 18 million by Yoshida Tōgo, this figure being based on annual rice yields of 18 million *koku.* A census taken 150 years later in the Kyōhō era (1716–36) reports a population of 26 million, indicating an actual populace over 30 million.[5] While no separate rural and urban counts were made, the status system indicates that between 80%–90% of the total were in farming families. In contrast to population increases in the towns, famines, epidemics, and human efforts to restrain increases served to diminish the rural populace, assuring a 10%–15% urban segment, composed chiefly of those in castle towns.[6]

The difficulty in arriving at accurate population figures arises mainly because the number of warriors is unknown. Townsmen tabulations were not uniform as some included, while others excluded, those under fifteen years of age. In any event, the population was always in proportion to the income of feudal lords in rice *koku* counts, the key to the extent of his power in the castle towns where political factors took precedence over economic factors. Population growth in Edo appears to have been quite rapid in its early stage, although there are no accurate records. Social problems resulting from the sudden and heavy concentration of people in Edo made it difficult even to take a census.

On the basis of official documents of Ōoka Echizen-no-kami, a town commissioner in Edo in the Kyōhō era (1716–36), Kōda Shigetomo has derived a population figure of 501,394 for Edo in 1721, excluding warriors and those related to temples and shrines, and a similar count of 472,496 for the year 1725. The actual population would have been much larger than these figures covering only those under the control of the town commissioner. For the year 1733 Kōda reports Edo's population at 536,380, this time including some 60,859 attached to temple communities.

Judging from these listings we can assume, then, a population for Edo of 500,000 to 600,000, representing the townsmen. This figure is not thought to have varied significantly up to the end of the Edo period of

Tokugawa rule.[7] To this must be added both the warriors and their families allied to the Tokugawa clan by kin or fealty relations, plus the other lords and their families living semi-permanently in Edo under the *sankin-kōtai* rule of alternate-year's residence. These warriors brought also a host of followers such as lower class troops (*ashigaru*) and household servants (*chūgen*) and other subordinates. Then, there were the unattached, lord-less warriors (*rōnin*), as well as the large numbers in shrine and temple communities, not to mention untabulated non-citizens, the outcasts. All in all, the total population of Edo must be adjusted to a figure nearer 1.4 million.

Yoshida Tōgo corroborates this total from the average annual transport of 1.4 million *koku* of rice to Edo, late in the age of the Tokugawa *bakufu*.[8] The adjusted total issues from the supposition that warriors and their retinues constituted 60% of Edo's population. Perhaps it is safer to say that there was a total population of over one million in Edo in the later part of the period that bears its name.

No population exceeding one million is reported for any European city at the beginning of the 19th century. The largest, London, is said to have had a population of 864,000 by 1801, while Paris is credited with 547,000, Vienna and Moscow 250,000 each, and 170,000 for Berlin. It seems clear, then, that Edo was the largest city in the world at that time, although it was not a modern but a feudal metropolis.

Next to Edo in population came Kanazawa, castle center of the lord Maeda, with an annual income of 1.02 million *koku*. Some 55,106 townsmen in 9,878 households are reported for the year 1664, with an increase to 56,355 in 14,907 households by the Kansei era (1789–1801). An additional population of 1,086 warrior households, plus about 1,000 senior class warrior households of direct Tokugawa lineage, raise the total population estimate of Kanazawa to 110,000–120,000.[9]

Close behind was Nagoya, whose lord claimed an annual income of 620,000 *koku*. Townsmen amounted to 54,932 in 1654, and 63,734 in 1692. The warrior population was registered at 30,000 early in the Meiji period, giving a population estimate of about 100,000.[10]

The lord of Kagoshima had an annual income of 770,000 *koku*, and the total population is put at 59,727 in 1764, and 72,350 in 1826[11]. The annual income for Hiroshima was less, 420,000 *koku*, and the number of townsmen households, both privately-owned and rented, was but 4,065, as reported for 1619, though there were also 700 warrior households excepting lower-class samurai. Again, in 1633 there were 3,504 townsmen households involving 36,142 townsmen, plus 1,350 warrior households, giving an estimated 70,000–80,000 population.[12] Other records show an income of 310,000 *koku* and a townsmen figure of 28,669 for Okayama in 1667,[13] and a 1764 population in Sendai of 23,098 townsmen and 44,000 warriors, plus an annual income of 600,000 *koku*.[14]

Tokushima, Fukui, and Akita had about 20,000 townsmen each, suggesting total populations of 40,000 each. Castle towns in the 20,000–30,000 class are thought to have included: Fukuoka, Kōfu, Hikone,

Tottori, Kōchi, Matsue, Yonezawa, Himeji, Takada, Takaoka, Yamagata, Hirosaki, and Wakamatsu of Aizu. Other castle centers on smaller fiefs are regarded as having possessed populations of 10,000 or less.

All these castle centers were connected, as indicated above, by the larger highways cutting across the many domains and leading to Edo and Ōsaka. The major routes, numbering five, spread out radially from the capital of Edo, namely, the Tōkaidō, Nakasendō, Ōshū-kaidō, Nikkō-kaidō, and Kōshū-kaidō. Interlacing the domains from these national highways were numerous branch roads, *wakikaidō*, and all were under the supervision of the commissioner in charge of finance, *kanjō bugyō*.

These roads served to accelerate cultural and economic interchange between the capital city and the many domains, expediting development in all towns. In addition to couriers of commodities and common people going about daily business, the highways were often crowded with leading families and their trains of subordinates making their way to or from a year's residence in Edo. Some 159 of the feudal lords passed along the Tōkaidō to reach Edo, while thirty-seven used the Ōshū-kaidō, thirty-four the Nakasendō, twenty-five the Mitokaidō, and three the Kōshū-kaidō.

Along the highways were constructed stations controlled by a travel license commissioner, *dōchū bugyō*. Placed some 1.5–2.5 *ri* (3.6–6.1 mi.) apart, the station centers were the *toiyaba* where station officers and town elders handled the business of horse and courier supply. This supply was regulated, so that 100 couriers and 100 horses were to be held in readiness at Tōkaidō stations. The numbers were fixed at fifty for Nakasendō stations, with only twenty-five of each at stations along the Nikkō, Kōshū, and Ōshū routes. Horses were for use of those on official trips and holding appropriate certificates (*tenma-shuin*).

Traffic increases caused shortages of couriers and horses. Station officials were authorized to get two laborers and two horses from the *gōson* village associations for every 100 *koku* of rice production, for which villagers received no compensation except exemption from other duties, a system called *sukegō*. As the traveling seasons of feudal lords fulfilling residence requirements in Edo coincided with the busiest seasons for the farmers, this system imposed heavy burdens on them. At times the peasants revolted against these impositions; these revolts were called *sukegō-ikki*.

To accommodate the daimyō and court nobles there were the main and sub-inns, *honjin* and *wakijin* respectively, for which the managers were appointed by the *bakufu* from among village leaders. The position became hereditary, and its holders were permitted to use surnames. For the commoners there were ordinary inns, merchants' inns, and other cheap lodgings. The station towns also housed express messengers of several types for use by the *bakufu*, the daimyō, and local leaders. These services were also supplied by local townsmen.

These stations expanded into towns where traffic was heaviest, as on the primary routes like Tōkaidō and Nakasendō, at points of travel difficulty such as river and mountain crossings, and at highway junctions.

They had a peculiar style, in that houses were strung out in long singular lines on either side of the road to which they owed their existence.

A few station towns evolved into castle towns, but most had only the travel function and rarely surpassed 10,000 in population, according to an 1843 census. Along the Tōkaidō, only fourteen towns exceeded 5,000 population: namely, Shinagawa—6,890; Kanagawa—5,793; Odawara (castle town)—5,404; Numazu (castle town)—5,346; Ejiri—6,498; Fuchū—14,071; Shimada—6,727; Hamamatsu (castle town)—5,964; Yoshida (castle town)—5,277; Okazaki (castle town)—6,194; Atsuta (port town)—10,342; Kuwana (castle town)—8,848; Yokkaichi—7,114; and Ōtsu (port town)—14,892.

Along the Nakasendō, no station town exceeded 5,000 population, the largest being Honjō with 4,554. Only Shirakawa, on the southern end of Ōshūkaidō, claimed a sizable population of 5,959, and it was also a castle town. Other large station towns were Yokoyamajuku on the Kōshū-kaidō with 6,026, and Senju with 9,956 and Utsunomiya (castle town) with 6,457 inhabitants on the Nikkō-kaidō.[15]

Despite remarkable highway development, transportation of bulky cargoes utilized waterways for the most part. This was due in part to vehicular limitation to ox and horse-drawn carts, and in part to other drawbacks on the roads, namely, the inconveniences of checking points, bandits, road deterioration and inadequate bridges at river crossings. Shipments of rice in payment of taxes to the Edo and Ōsaka warehouses constituted the major cargo, of special importance to the Kantō district, which supplied only a small portion of the extensive demands of a sharply expanded populace.

The bulk of Edo's supplies came from the Kinki district where the exchange economy had developed in former days. The Kinki district depended upon Ōsaka, the best port in the area, for both collection and redistribution of commodities. Trading contacts with foreign countries was, as we have noted, forbidden. This policy was backed up by a prohibition against construction of ships capable of carrying over 500 *koku*, restricting navigation to Japan's coastal regions. Regular marine services, such as the *higaki-bune* for miscellaneous goods and the *tarukaisen* for *sake*, were established between Edo and Ōsaka, while similar services were opened between Ōsaka and Nagasaki, Shimonoseki and Matsumae, and Edo and Ōshū in the northeast.

Lakes, rivers, and even marshes, provided a secondary means of transportation. Lake Biwa connected districts along the Japan Sea with the city of Ōtsu on the southern tip of the lake, making it an important center of traffic and economy serving the Kinki district. The Yodogawa river linked Ōsaka and Kyōto, the two focal points of commerce and culture in the same Kinki region.

Likewise, the Tonegawa river brought commodities from the north Kantō, Chūbu, and Hokuriku districts to Edo, stimulating the formation of riverside markets (*kashi*). Boat services developed along all major rivers of the country, although construction of larger vessels late in the Edo era favored downstream towns, forcing some to move from increasingly inaccessible locations upstream.[16]

The importance of water transportation was evident in the large warehouses built in port towns to receive, and often re-sell, large volumes of goods, as well as in the emergence of shipping agents, *kaisen-donya*, and the large number of laborers employed by them. Behind the waterfront warehouses were set up all sorts of shops to serve those engaged in the shipping trade.

Within the overall controls of the powerful administrative organs of a fully accomplished feudal system, the port towns developed their own structures for local self-government. The sheer volume of the shipping trade required extensive organizational networks, especially in Ōsaka where the administrative functions and mechanisms far outstripped all other port towns in size and complexity. Even in other important port towns, though, there were relatively few warriors, e.g., Sakai, Fushimi, Sakata, Tsuruga, Kohama, Mikuni, Niigata, and Aomori. The founding fathers and effective rulers of these towns were the rich merchants who controlled the large warehouse business. It was their local power, administered through the councils noted above, that was able to withstand, and often counteract, the controls of the *bakufu*.

The largest port town population, of course, centered in Ōsaka, which was administered through local commissioners over three burroughs, Tenma, Kita, and Minami. Population increases, including the priestly community of Honganji, were as follows:

| *Era* | *Population* |
|---|---|
| Kan-ei 2 (1625) | 279,610 |
| Genbun 1 (1736) | 389,866 |
| Kan-en 2 (1749) | 404,146 |
| Tenmei 3 (1783) | 499,777 |
| Ansei (1854–60) | 310,000–320,000 |

The decrease after the Tenmei era was caused by a severe famine. On the other hand, the population so exceeded manageable limits for a commercial city that, in the Tempō era (1830–44), the municipal government issued an order (*hitogaeshi-no-hō*) requiring many inhabitants to return to their native provinces.[17]

In contrast to the flourishing coastal maritime trade, foreign trade was meager, being limited to the Dutch and Chinese trade at the single port of Nagasaki. The population of this town was 64,523 in 1696, but dropped to 41,500 by 1715. The opening of routes from the Japan Sea district of Hokuriku brought goods shipments to the Inland Sea ports, in addition to the inflow from the northeastern Ōu region. Sakai had a population of 69,368 in 1665, which fell to roughly 50,000 by 1751. Hyōgo and Onomichi on the Inland Sea, though, rose to 20,000 in 1739 and 10,035 in 1789 respectively. The Yodogawa river town had a population of 30,655, and the Japan Sea ports of Sakata, Tsuruga, Kohama, Niigata, and Aomori generally expanded from 10,000 to 20,000 in the same period.[18]

Various reconstructions in Kyōto, following its devastation in the War of Ōnin, gradually transformed it from an ancient into a feudal city in ecological and social structure. Oda Nobunaga, coming in 1568, repaired the imperial residence and helped rehabilitate the court nobility. Later Toyotomi Hideyoshi erected his own mansion, Jurakudai, on the grounds formerly occupied by the main palace building, Daidairi, and fostered commercial and industrial prosperity. After Tokugawa Ieyasu rose to power, he repaired the Nijō Castle and established the *Shoshidai* office of the shogunate for liaison with the imperial court and nobility. There are no definite figures on record for Kyōto's population, but, according to a survey made by Honjō Eijiro, it was between 400,000 and 500,000 throughout the Tokugawa period.[19]

Urbanized residential patterns developed in temple towns as well, promoted not only by political and economic functions but also by religious pilgrimages, especially after peaceful conditions were restored. Adherents to specific shrines and temples were organized into groups for pilgrimages (*kō*), though these activities in time took on additional characteristics as pleasure excursions. During the Middle Ages most temple and shrine towns, with their priests and subordinates, tended to function as living units in themselves. In the Edo period a number of shrines and temples became centers of nationwide devotion, drawing large groups of visitors, though smaller than their medieval predecessors in terms of permanent residents.

Ise Jingū, Kotohiragū, Zenkōji, and Izumo-taisha attracted great throngs of worshippers from all over the country. Even the largest of their towns, Yamada, where Ise Jingū was located, had a population of only 10,000. Similar conditions prevailed in shrine towns catering to merchants, such as Narita-fudo and Toyokawa-inari, where streets lined with inns, tea houses, and gift shops were clearly oriented to the visiting crowds.

The communications network built up among the three major cities and the provincial castle towns in connection with political and economic integration of the nation naturally brought social and economic changes into isolated rural districts and the smaller towns at ports and along the highways. The ideas and values of the Tokugawa feudal order became more widely disseminated than would have been possible under the more insular circumstances of former days. Local cultures became fused with each other; an overall system of total national integration became a possibility through greater communications.

Yet it was not, of course, a fully modern system of transportation and communication. As the entire country existed in isolation from the world, so its integrative controls operated on the basis of relative isolation of the respective domains. Each domain maintained a more or less self-supporting economy, and strictly controlled all movements of people and goods to protect its own interests. Such controls were applied especially to rice and other staple products through transport restrictions (*tsudome*).

Neither were the people of one domain allowed free contact with those of another. Peasants were legally bound both to the land and to their status. If they wished to move, they had to acquire a domestic passport (*ōrai-tegata*) from the village head, head of the five-family group, or local temple where they were registered, though there was no guarantee it would be issued. Those who ran away to the cities illegitimately were often listed in the official registry (*ninbetsuchō*) as lacking an official residence (*mushukumono*).

Further controls were exercised at the highway checkpoints (*sekisho*) such as those at Hakone, Arai, Usui, Fukushima of Kiso, Nakata and Kobotoke. People and goods passing these points were allowed to pass only during the day. For military reasons no bridges were built over large rivers along the Tōkaidō. Besides these political hindrances, highway robbers and physical conditions added to the range of forces working against total integration in society.

All in all, during a 70–80 years' period from the latter part of the 16th century to the early part of the Tokugawa era in the 17th, the overall number of castle, port, highway, and temple towns reached enormous proportions. We have seen that the urban populations were composed chiefly of the warriors and the merchants and artisans who served them, clearly separated from the farmers. With over one million estimated in Edo alone, 300,000 and 400,000 in Ōsaka and Kyōto respectively, over 300 castle towns, and all the port, highway, and temple towns, the scope of the urban sector of the nation was quite sizable.

The enabling conditions of such urban development were substantial increase of agricultural productivity and expansion of the exchange economy. The town-ward pull of the latter factor was strong as more and more peasants left the land to become craftsmen, servants, and laborers in the towns, despite prohibitions against movements of the agrarian populace. In some isolated instances people were moved from one town to another for special reasons, but, as a rule, the emergence and expansion of cities and towns depended upon the flow of population from the rural districts, rather than upon natural increase.

There were various reasons for the peasants' leaving the land, but the commonest cause lay in the heritage system that passed land rights only to the eldest son. Population increases exceeded land availability, driving younger sons to the towns. Poor families also sent daughters to the towns under contracts of indentured service. Farmers themselves, bankrupted by taxes and debts, often moved to the towns. Such cases included farmers who had managed to become independent landowners but were vulnerable to the misfortunes of a bad year with their crops. Escapes to the towns were made either with or without one's family.

Although some of the peasants could find work as subordinates to more successful rural neighbors, opportunities were usually better in the cities and towns. With a little personal capital one could become a peddler, or an apprentice to acquire some skill for earning a living as an artisan. Otherwise, they might become day laborers or beggars. These circumstances led to large numbers of poor in the cities, giving rise to the expression, "Edo is the dumping ground of the domains."

The degree of influx into the cities from the rural districts is not statistically clear. Such a trend is clearly evident, however, in the increase both in the number of cities and in their populations. Some data on the growth of groups of day-laborers due to peasant migration is available. In Okayama peddlers selling cheap household goods (*nichiyō-zarufuri*) numbered 7,974 in 1707, constituting 28% of the total population of 28,299. Of 1,669 houses listed for the year 1801 in Okazaki, 304 (17%) were occupied by day-laborers. An even larger proportion (39%) is reported for Yamaguchi in 1844, or 641 out of a total 1,441 houses. In Edo cooperatives were formed to exercise controls over the many day-laborers. The local government of Hirosaki issued day-laborers' cards (*hiyatoi-fuda*) in 1792, while in Tsuyama the feudal government appointed a supervisor who also fixed official wages.[20]

A renowned scholar, Ogyū Sorai, wrote sometime shortly before his death in 1728, warning of the dangers of the "sharply increasing number of peasants leaving the land to become day-laborers or peddlers in the castle town, swarming into an area of not more than five *ri* compass."[21] Noting further that "Edo expands with every passing year, and dwellings have filled the area between Senju to the north and Shinagawa to the south," Sorai's concern was for the eventual decline of the rural districts, as well as for undue expansion in Edo.[22]

Kōda Shigetomo has classified the commoners' population of each town in Edo according to place of origin for the period beginning in 1843 and ending in 1867. Those with indeterminate origins were less than 1%. Those born in other provinces reached 29.5% in the Tempō era (1830–44), but this dropped to 21.7% by the end of the survey period. In general, then, about one-quarter of the Edo townsmen were of rural pedigree, although the rate of influx from outlying districts was greater early in the Edo period.[23]

A striking example of this tendency of migration to the cities can be seen in the case of the town of Minose Yukimachi in the Iida district. According to inspection records on rented houses for 1792, only 23% of the total population were native-born residents. Of the remaining 77%, some 62% were of agrarian origin.

An earlier (1698) record for the town of Okazaki shows that only 64 out of a total of 362 laborers in service to others in a total population of 780 were of local origin. The other 298, or 80% of the total, were of rural background. A similar report for Okayama gives a total of 1,223 men and 694 women working as servants or laborers in others' households. Of these only thirteen men and three women were born in Okayama. Of the total, 1079 men and 666 women came from nearby areas, and 131 men and 25 women came from other provinces.[24]

The sex composition of population movements to cities deserves special attention. As a rule the male-female ratio of a nation is usually equal. Sometimes the balance is upset by special relations between sex and occupation factors. Below is a list of the numbers of men and women in Edo, exclusive of warriors and priests:

| *Year* | *Total Edo Population* | *Men* | *Women* | *Ratio* |
|---|---|---|---|---|
| 1721 | 501,000 | 323,000 | 178,000 | 181/100 |
| 1832 | 545,000 | 297,000 | 248,000 | 119/100 |
| 1867 | 539,000 | 272,000 | 266,000 | 102/100 |

The inference to be drawn from this list is that the ratio of men to women becomes smaller as the city becomes older but is never less than one to one. Newcomers to Edo generally found employment as apprentices in merchants' or artisans' shops; hence, it is quite natural that men outnumbered women. Indeed, if warriors and their subordinates were included, the male component would become much larger.

A similar predominance of men can be seen in a brief listing of some castle towns:

| *Town* | *Year* | *Men* | *Women* | *Ratio* |
|---|---|---|---|---|
| Kurume | 1699 | 5,143 | 3,621 | 143/100 |
| | 1859 | 5,805 | 4,403 | 132/100[25] |
| Kōchi | 1829 | 8,370 | 6,072 | 137.8/100 |
| | 1843 | 8,692 | 6,600 | 131.7/100 |
| | 1853 | 8,971 | 6,924 | 129.5/100[26] |
| Matsumoto | 1725 | 4,317 | 3,889 | 114/100 |
| | 1864 | 4,925 | 4,515 | 104/100[27] |
| Himeji | 1771 | 8,290 | 8,039 | 103.1/100[28] |

Here again it appears that the male ratio declines as the city ages.

Contrary cases can be found where men not only exceeded women in numbers, but the male ratio grew gradually, or at least remained higher. The towns of Fukui and Ōgaki are cases in point:

| *Town* | *Year* | *Men* | *Women* | *Ratio* |
|---|---|---|---|---|
| Fukui | 1713 | 10,827 | 10,566 | 102.5/100 |
| | 1750 | 10,472 | 9,538 | 109.8/100 |
| | 1792 | 9,650 | 8,714 | 110.7/100[29] |
| Ōgaki | 1721 | 3,028 | 2,515 | 120/100 |
| | 1785 | 2,928 | 2,415 | 113.2/100 |
| | 1843 | 2,708 | 2,389 | 113.3/100[30] |

In some cases, of course, the male population became less than the female, as in the city of Takada, where many men left to seek jobs elsewhere:

| *Town* | *Year* | *Men* | *Women* | *Ratio* |
|---|---|---|---|---|
| Takada | 1680 | 11,157 | 11,010 | 101/100 |
| | 1840 | 7,875 | 8,971 | 88/100[31] |

In general, though, men outnumbered women in the cities. Even in Ōsaka, where there were few warriors, the male population superseded the female in later periods. In 1661, women had a slight edge, at 131,161 to 121,467 men. After 1665 the male component always exceeded the female in Ōsaka. No single pattern emerges with reference to sex vis-à-vis urban population; a number of factors influenced the composition of each city. As a matter of fact, though, men enjoyed both greater mobility and job opportunities than women, which helps explain the predominance of men in the feudal cities.

Examples of the relation of status and occupation to the population structure of castle towns have been given by Shimomura Fujio as follows:

| *Town* | *Year* | *Warriors* (%) | *Townsmen* (%) |
|---|---|---|---|
| Hirosaki | 1764 | 46 | 54 |
| Tsuruoka | 1770 | over 40 | over 50 |
| Wakayama | 1846 | over 40 | over 50[32] |
| Yoshida | late Edo | 38 | 62[33] |

In castle towns it appears that townsmen outnumbered warriors, as the following figures further indicate:

| *Town* | *Year* | *Warriors* | *Townsmen* |
|---|---|---|---|
| Akita | 1747 | 17,650 | 21,313 |
| Matsumoto | 1725 | 6,072 | 8,206[34] |
| Okayama | 1764 | *ca.* 26,000 | *ca.* 30,000* |
| Takatsuki (Settsu) | 1745 | over 2,000 | 2,448 max.** |

* Estimated on assumed five persons per household for 5,296 houses of warriors. Townsmen moved out into surrounding areas after the Kyōhō era (1716–36).[35]

** Maximum at beginning of the Kyōhō era; declined later as townsmen's flow reverted outward.[36]

Local circumstances in the castle towns and their domains caused considerable variation in the population structures of the castle towns. Thus, it would not be wise to assume that townsmen always outnumbered warriors. A couple of examples will suffice to show the opposite situation:

| *Town* | *Year* | *Total Population* | *Warriors* | *Townsmen* |
|---|---|---|---|---|
| Hikone | 1695 | 36,000 | 19,000 | 15,500[37] |
| Matsushiro (Shinshū) | 1671 | *ca.* 6,000 | *ca.* 4,000 | *ca.* 2,000[38] |

In Kagoshima, efforts of the feudal lord to bolster his military forces brought the warriors' ratio to three times that of townsmen, though this would be more like eight times if the retainers to the ranking warriors were included. Likewise, the warriors and craftsmen in their service in Sendai numbered 44,000 out of a total population of 58,000 in 1661.[39]

Notwithstanding the variety in population composition with reference to status and occupation, the general rule was that the number of townsmen in the castle towns was, at best, only slightly more than the number of warriors. In the latter half of the Edo period, however, the warrior population steadily declined as townsmen became both more numerous and more influential. This process is described in greater detail in Chapter VII, on "The Decline of Feudal Cities."

## 3. The Ecological Structure, Social Organization and Control of the Castle Town

New castle towns always drew together new concentrations of warriors, their vassals, foot soldiers and servants. They were transferred from former estates by the feudal lords who sought to muster all available forces, concentrating them in the new castle towns. Commoners usually followed the removals to new castle towns, hoping to find their own prosperity there.

A few examples from Ono Hitoshi's detailed studies will indicate the processes of concentration. When Toyotomi Hideyoshi transferred his main castle from Kotani to Nagahama in 1574, the people living in the former center moved with him. He gained control of Ōsaka after constructing Ōsaka Castle, begun in 1583, and proceeded to transfer the inhabitants of Sakai to Ōsaka. Through such wholesale removals Ōsaka was transformed from a collection of six small towns spread before the temple of Ishiyama Honganji into one of the major cities of the land.

Similarly, when Ukita Hideie built a new castle town in Okayama in 1593 two sections, Nishi-ōdera-chō and Katagami-chō, were formed of residents transferred from a temple town and a port town bearing these respective names. Again, when Gamō Ujisato was appointed to his new fief, Matsugashima, from Hino, he ordered all but the peasants to follow him there. They followed also in subsequent moves to Matsusaka and later to Wakamatsu of Aizu, where a township was named Hino-machi after their earlier home.

Additional examples of the movement of whole communities of people to new castle towns following reappointment of their lords can be seen in the cases of Toyotomi Hidetsugu's receiving Gōshu as his fief in 1583, and the removal of Hori Kyūtaro from Kasugayama to Fukushima in 1607, and later to Takada, where a new castle town was erected. When Date Masamune received the Sendai post, he took with him all commoners living in the town of Iwadeyama.

In the processes of formation of castle towns the daimyō not only forced population concentration but exercised their power to strengthen the economic functions of their base towns. In 1577 Oda Nobunaga, for instance, restricted all horse-trading in his domain to his castle town of Azuchi. Toyotomi Hidetsugu ordered market concentration in his own Hachiman-yamashita-chō, while Ukita Hideie, in the last decade of the 16th century, consolidated the breweries of his domain in his castle town of Okayama, prohibiting brewing elsewhere in his domain. Freedom in commercial transactions was denied other districts as well.[40]

The importance of transportation and other communicative facilities to political, economic, and military integration has been made clear, especially with reference to persistence in constructing and repairing suitable roads, ports, and such secondary systems as waterways. While these measures were intended to benefit the castle towns in general, some feudal lords took specific steps to assure such results. Oda Nobunaga required all merchants entering or leaving the inland road called Nakasendō to stay overnight in Azuchi. Toyotomi Hidetsugu exacted the same of merchants passing Hachiman, as well as requiring boats with commercial cargoes to lay anchor in the Hachiman port. Gamō Ujisato forced travelers to stop over in Hino.

All measures for fostering prosperity in the castle towns were not, of course, executed by forceful means. Profitable privileges were granted merchants to attract them voluntarily to the towns. Finance houses that had suffered from the medieval practice of debt cancellation were now omitted from this practice, especially in Azuchi, Hino, and Hakata. Another medieval policy, that of exemption from land taxes for a privileged few, was now often extended over the whole area of new castle towns. (Ono Hitoshi lists 24 examples.[41])

Another important factor in strengthening the economic basis of the castle towns was the policy of establishing free markets, begun by Oda Nobunaga and followed by other lords. The annoying market fees and the monopolistic *za* cooperatives were abolished, freeing merchants to come in from other districts and to trade freely in the town markets in any commodities. This trend received a great boost early in the Edo era when the principle of free transactions in commerce was implemented in the three major cities of Kyōto, Ōsaka, and Edo. From these centers the principle of free trade spread out to the lesser castle towns.

The castle towns, then, developed more rapidly in shorter periods than more gradual processes would have permitted. Accelerated growth was achieved by mobilizing various political, economic, and military forces, and was greatly aided by increased productivity in agriculture gained through new methods and by increased stability in society managed through the status system. The methods of forced acceleration included, as we have seen, enforced concentration of both population and commercial facilities, on the one hand, and persuasive measures such as free markets and tax exemption, on the other hand. With such positive encouragement there emerged many cities around the base castle towns.

Castle design underwent certain changes during the Age of Civil Wars and up to the end of the 16th century. It shifted, as mentioned above, from being a mountain-top fortress for defense alone to being a castle town on the plains. The name changes from *yamajiro*, "mountain castle," to *hirayamajiro*, "hilltop castle on the plain," indicate that castles were still constructed on top of some small hill to assure their defense at the center of the plain. In the plains castles, warriors' quarters and merchants' markets combined to form the towns. At this stage merchants operated in close connection with the feudal lords. As long as civil strife continued the residences of both warriors and merchants were thrown together within the town's walls and moats.

In the early half of the 17th century the scale of the castle towns was expanded, not spontaneously, but according to intentional plans of the daimyō. An example of one line this expansive activity took is Kuwana, where a new town was planned and constructed where an old one had been destroyed.[42] In other cases, new towns were built around older ones, or they simply annexed older towns. The overall pattern shifted from towns that consisted of several loosely-connected living centers, with only vague cultural distinctions and physical boundaries vis-à-vis rural areas, to castle towns much larger in size and more clearly distinct from rural areas, with residential areas for warriors and townsmen definitely separated.[43]

In some of the new castle towns the houses of townsmen were included within protective walls or moats, notably, Inuyama-jō, Okayama, Kōfu, Kanazawa, Himeji, Yatsushiro, Iida, Kuwana, and Iwatsuki. In most of them, however, defense facilities were provided only in the area of the daimyō's mansion and his warriors' residences.

Castle structures always made up the nucleus of a castle town, regardless of location. Taking advantage of natural terrain, they might be constructed by the sea (Takamatsu of Sanuki, Hagi of Nagato), on a lakeside (Takashima of Suwa, Zensho of Ōmi), or on a river bank (Okayama and Inuyama). Such locations made one or more sides of the castle less accessible to an enemy. The town areas developed in the open land space opposite the natural barriers, usually in front of the castle. Where waterways were used the town sometimes developed on both sides of a river, even though the castle faced the river on one side only (Kokura, Wakasa, and Kohama).

Some castle towns developed around their castles, as in Edo, Kanazawa, Ōgaki of Mino, Uwajima of Iyo, Mihara of Bingo, and Takayama of Hida. In these towns, major streets ran radially away from the central castle sites, and were intersected perpendicularly by secondary roads, thus forming large rectangles. In Uwajima the pentagon-shaped castle prevented rectangular patterns, yielding a network of roads resembling a spider's web.[44]

While topographical and military conditions contributed to a variety of road patterns, the most common was the checkerboard design stemming from the ancient cities under the *ritsuryō* system. Though most roads met rectangularly, additional defense devices were used, such as graded inclines, T-shaped intersections, all intended to restrict both visibility and penetration by arrows, bullets, or troops themselves. Moreover, the main gate was not connected directly with main roads inside, but removed and accessible only by indirect, crooked ways. Maximum width, even for main roads, was 3–4 *ken* (6–8 yds.), and they were laid out carefully with defense needs in mind, in contrast to the relatively spontaneous road patterns of medieval towns.

Organization of the castle towns, rather poor in the early stages, improved as the integrative functions within each domain progressed. In time distinct zones for warriors, townsmen, and religious groups appeared. In contrast to the one-story homes roofed with straw, miscanthus, cedar bark, or wooden shingles so typical of the Middle Ages, there appeared early in the Edo period many two-storied houses. By the middle of that period, the main streets of Edo were thickly lined on both sides with two-storied homes of uniform width and depth (5 × 15 *ken* = 10 × 30 yds.), roofed with tiles, and presenting a neat and orderly appearance.

Throughout the Edo period the policy of one castle per domain was strictly enforced. Located centrally with respect to transportation, the castle was constructed as a symbol of the magnitude of its lord's wealth and power. A distinct "plains-style" castle, *hirajiro*, was developed, although most castles continued to mix features of the older mountain-top structures and new trends of construction in the lowlands. These hybrid structures, *hirayamajiro*, appropriated both natural advantages as well as architectural advances being made in response to widespread demand. Typical of this mixed style were the castles of Edo, Ōsaka, Wakayama, Hikone, Himeji, Okayama, Sendai, and Hirosaki.

Many improvements in design and devices for defense were made during this era; so that, for instance, even if one section of a castle were occupied by an enemy, the rest of the castle might be safely defended. Innumerable factors were considered in securing the defense of the castles, such as shape, height, distribution and means of connecting the fortified parts, as well as the relation of the inner area to the outer defense areas surrounded by moats and embankments. The basic pattern comported with the three traditional defense lines, the *honmaru, ninomaru,* and *sannomaru,* that is, the primary, secondary, and tertiary fortifications. But as castle construction developed, the number of fortified structures tended to increase, or the defense area was expanded and divided into sections.

Medieval castles averaged eight *chō* (20 acres) in overall size. According to classifications common to studies of Edo military practices, there were three gradations of castle sizes.

The largest castles had the following measurements:

| | | | | |
|---|---|---|---|---|
| *Honmaru* | — | 4 *chō* | = | 10 acres |
| *Ninomaru* | — | 8 *chō* 20 *ken* | = | 20 acres 80 sq. yds. |
| *Sannomaru* | — | 14 *chō* 40 *ken* | = | 35 acres 160 sq. yds. |
| Total area (castle) | — | 27 *chō* | = | over 66 acres |
| Total defense area | | 36 *chō* | = | over 88 acres |

Medium-sized castle measurements were:

| | | | | |
|---|---|---|---|---|
| *Honmaru* | — | 2 *chō* 45 *ken* | = | 5 acres 180 sq. yds. |
| *Ninomaru* | — | 5 *chō* 40 *ken* | = | 12.5 acres 160 sq. yds. |
| *Sannomaru* | — | 10 *chō* 35 *ken* | = | 25 acres 140 sq. yds. |
| Total area (castle) | — | 19 *chō* | = | 46.5 acres |

The smaller castles were, proportionately:

| | | | | |
|---|---|---|---|---|
| *Honmaru* | — | 2 *chō* 10 *ken* | = | 5 acres 40 sq. yeds. |
| *Ninomaru* | — | 5 *chō* | = | 12.5 acres |
| *Sannomaru* | — | 8 *chō* 55 *ken* | = | 20 acres 220 sq. yds. |
| Total area (castle) | — | 16 *chō* 5 *ken* | = | 40 acres[45] |

Arising from the foundations of fortified sections were white-walled towers for lookout, counter-offensive, and storage of weapons and food supplies.

The main tower, *tenshukaku*, was usually five-storied with three of the stories visible from outside the castle area, or eight-storied with five visible. It was the command tower, a central storage base, and the final defense position, similar to the keep in European fortifications. Serving sometimes as the residence of the feudal lord, this central tower was constructed on as large and, often as ornate, a scale as possible to bespeak the dignity and power of the lord to his people.

The *honmaru* included earthen-walled fireproof storehouses for food and weapons. The lord's quarters were more generally in the *ninomaru* section. Administrative offices and quarters of senior warriors were found in the *ninomaru* and *sannomaru* structures. The latter were not built for purely military use, as in the Age of Civil Wars, but were more permanent buildings for governmental administration. In making use of the natural setting attention was given, in addition to defense advantages, to the aesthetic harmony of the entire castle structure with its natural background.

Divisions of the castle towns reflected the feudal status system of four classes: warriors, farmers, artisans, and merchants. Hence, residential areas for warriors (*samurai-machi* or *tono-machi*) were set apart from the townsmen's communities, and from temple precincts and townships. The exclusiveness of the warriors' quarters was evident, for example, in the prohibition against opening a shop in the *tono-machi* of Matsusaka issued in 1588. In Okayama a restriction against mixed residential areas was enforced after a revision of the city's divisions in the last decade of the 16th century.

Ground areas of the exclusive warrior dwellings varied according to wealth based on rice income in *koku* (one *koku* = 4.96 US bu.). Relative dimensions are indicated in the following record of samurai residences in Nagaoka in 1621:

| *Income* (*koku*) | *Area of residential grounds* |
|---|---|
| 200–300 | 25 *ken* square (49.6 sq. yds.) |
| 100–200 | 24 *ken* square (47.6 sq. yds.) |
| 50–90 | 20 × 17 *ken* (39.8 × 33.8 yds.) |

For *kachi-gumi,* unmounted officers, housing dimensions were:

| | |
|---|---|
| 40 *koku* | 15 × 20 *ken* (29.85 × 39.8 yds.) |

Warriors' grounds were allowed an additional 4.5 *shaku* (5.9 ft.) strip for walls and fences, plus a 5 *ken* (10 yds.) allowance for roads for mounted warriors and 3 *ken* (6 yds.) allowances for foot soldiers' paths. The total area of the warriors' quarters in Nagaoka was some 100 *chōbu* (245 acres).

The residential area of the foot soldiers had houses of 60 *tsubo* (240 sq. yds.) each, with 32 *tsubo* (128 sq. yds.) homes for servants. Roads were 2 *ken* (4 yds.) wide, the whole area being 25 *chōbu* (61 acres). By way of comparison, warrior and foot soldier residences in Sendai were slightly larger, being 30 *ken* and 25 *ken* respectively.[46]

Senior officers of the daimyō constructed spacious homes, the higher the rank, the closer to the castle. Their structures included accommodations for retainers and for storage, and if the town had protective moats, the ranking officers' homes were within the circle. Low ranking warriors, on the other hand, were quartered in a densely concentrated circle outside the castle town, even beyond the lowly merchants' dwellings, to assure the town's defense.

Hikone, a typical castle town of medium size, has been researched by Yamori Kazuhiko for the period 1532–1750. His report shows that over 74% of those residing within the castle grounds (*uchiguruwa*) were those with incomes over 1,000 *koku,* including some receiving more than 3,000 *koku* annually. Construction of townspeople's residences was completed by 1624. At that time the lord of Hikone was granted additional income, consequently swelling the ranks of his soldiers. For the latter new quarters were erected outside the existing town, where all warriors of less than 100 *koku* income lived.[47]

An interesting aspect of the residential areas for warriors was the sort of names given to communities within the areas. These names might derive from the occupations of those serving the warriors' needs, as in the following examples:

| *Community name:* | *Resident group:* |
|---|---|
| Okachi-machi | unmounted officers |
| Chūgen-chō | servants |
| Dōshin-chō | constables |
| Koshō-machi | pages |
| Kobito-chō | lesser servants |
| Yoriki-chō | policemen |
| Ozenbu-machi | cooks |
| Esashi-machi | bird keepers |
| Takasho-machi | specialists in breeding and training hawks used in hunting |
| Kinjū-machi | butlers |
| Yumi-no-machi | archers |
| Teppō-chō | firearms specialists |
| Wakatō-chō | servants |
| Omori-machi | guards |
| Hata-machi | standard-bearers |
| Shinobu-machi | spies |
| Sukiya-chō | teahouses |

There were other equally revealing systems of naming, such as by income levels (on *koku* basis) as in:

| *Community name:* | *Income level:* |
|---|---|
| Sengoku-chō | 1,000 *koku* community |
| Hyakkoku-chō | 100 *koku* community |
| Gojukkoku-chō | 50 *koku* community |

Sometimes township names were based on the numbers of residents, such as:

| *Community name* | *Resident indication* |
|---|---|
| Sanbyakunin-chō | 300-person township |
| Nihyakunin-chō | 200-person township |
| Rokujunin-chō | 60-person community |
| Gojunin-chō | 50-person community |
| Juhachininshu-chō | 18-member neighborhood |
| Kumi-machi | neighborhood of one group |

Again, the towns might simply be numbered according to relative proximity to the front gate, *Ote,* of the castle, giving:[48]

| | |
|---|---|
| Ichiban-chō | township no. 1 |
| Hachiban-chō | township no. 8 |

Although the warrior segment of each town's population was usually less than the townsmen, their spacious residential areas occupied far more than half of the total town area. In Edo the warriors' share was two-thirds; it was four-sevenths in Kagoshima, three-fourths in Kumamoto and Fukuyama, and in Kanazawa three times the area given the townspeople.[49]

The ecological structure of a typical castle town was neatly divided into separate residential zones for warriors and townsmen, and distinct shrine and temple grounds. In the early, formative stages, though, there often remained more typically medieval areas within the castle grounds for quartering warriors, called *uchiyamashita.* After stratification by status was fully established, the latter disappeared, except in the smaller castle towns. Conversely, the larger castle towns sometimes went beyond the clearly distinguished division into castle, warrior, and townsmen zones, and developed a number of nuclei on the outer circle of the town.[50]

Not only were the townsmen separated from the warriors and forbidden to engage in commerce in the *samurai-machi;* the warriors and their subordinates were not allowed to live in the townspeople's zone. Wooden gates were erected to keep out vagabonds and criminals, or to trap suspects. In Nagoya there were ten such gates; in Wakayama 150; in Matsumoto twenty-five. In Hiroshima there were 107 gates before 1759, seventy-three in 1759, and only sixty-nine by 1820. The gates were opened in the morning, closed in the evening, and permits had to be applied for when passing through at night. A 1723 regulation in Hiroshima stipulated that a gate pass was necessary even when going to fetch a doctor at night. In short, there was essentially no freedom of the streets after dark.[51]

In a central location in the townsmen's zone several blocks were given to the merchants for their shops. Commercial activity was dominated by those serving the local government and earning its special favor in the early history of the town. If the town was in an economically prosperous domain, the business community included powerful merchants who were originally warriors, but had sold their lands to invest in such profitable enterprises as financing offices, dry goods stores, and so on. Built often on a large scale, the stores together with the large inns presented an impressive scene, especially with the small colorful stalls gathered at corners and open lots.

In the formative days of a castle town many peddlers came to spark the new markets into activity. In time established stores and wholesale houses developed, and the peddlers' function vanished. The supply of horses and footmen was stabilized in *tenma-donya* near the main gate of the castle (*ōte-mae*), and the livery grounds, *tenma-cho,* were often tax-exempt. Salt dealers were located nearby to gain easy access to these facilities.

Merchants opened their stores on the main streets, or along the highways running through the towns. They gathered by occupations in the same areas for several reasons, such as facilitating tax collections, purchase and delivery of merchandise, and other forms of mutual benefit and safety. In most cases the occupational groups were granted monopoly rights in their specialities by the feudal lords

Merchant communities assumed names as descriptive as the trade names listed above for those serving warriors directly. Some examples are:

| *Community name* | *Trade reference* |
|---|---|
| Ryōgae-chō | Money exchange |
| Gofuku-chō | clothing supply |
| Tenma-chō | livery services |
| Shio-chō | salt dealers |
| Kome-chō, or Koku-chō | rice dealers |
| Aburaya-machi | oil supply |
| Kamiya-chō, or Kami-machi | paper shops |
| Yaoya-chō | green grocers |
| Cha-machi | tea merchants |

The first four of these were, as we noted, usually near the main castle gate.

The Zaimoku-chō township for lumber was located close to available waterways. The more odorous fish market, Sakana-machi, Sakanaya-chō, or Uo-chō, was generally put somewhere on the back streets of town. The Bakurō-chō market for horse trading was at the edge of town at major highway junctions.

Other town names simply referred to relative positions, such as Uchi-machi (inner township), Soto-machi (outer township), Kami-machi (Upper townships), Naka-machi (mid- or between-towns), and Shimo-machi (lower townships). Sometimes shape was the point of reference, as in Naga-machi (long town), Chōtō-chō (long sword-shaped town), and Yanagi-chō (willow-shaped town). Finally, names from native lands were sometimes revived as town names in new places, as in the case of Hino-machi alluded to above.

The power and status structures of the towns were reflected in their ecological make-up. Rich merchants living in the central Honchō or Ōmachi districts constituted the upper class of town merchants. Their ranks included also any who had prospered in the wider regional economy. Patronized by the feudal lords and senior officials, the merchants frequently responded to requests for funds with donations, and were often rewarded with official titles. Working closely with the military leaders, the merchants tended to control local city administration.

Below the upper class merchants there were, in descending order, minor merchants and craftsmen with their own houses, common people renting land or houses, and the lowest group, called *eta* (outcasts). Citizenship rights and duties were limited to homeowners. Those on rented premises and below had neither the rights nor the duties of citizenship. They were the objects not only of economic but legal and status discrimination as well.

Toyoda Takeshi has described in great detail the stratification of townsmen according to status. For the moment, though, it is sufficient to note that conditions varied in the daimyō-townsmen relations in different periods, especially as between the early times of town-building and later periods when status strata became solidified. Regional differences can also be found in relations between the feudal lords and non-warrior groups.

It is instructive at this point to draw on the comparative studies made by Kawai Masaharu on relationships between lords and merchants in two cities, Hiroshima on the Inland Sea, and Sendai on the northeastern Pacific shore.[52]

According to Kawai's account, Sendai was constructed on a plain with accommodations for only a few merchants. Commerce does not appear to have been strongly emphasized in the plans of the reigning lord. Lots of equal size, 6 *ken* (12 yds.) width, were allotted each merchant, giving each of them roughly equal status and power at first. Gradually, of course, some enlarged their economic position and social prestige.

In stark contrast to Sendai's history, Hiroshima was begun on the initiative of influential merchants who persuaded their lord to build his castle town around their existing commercial center. Differences in wealth and status already existing among the merchants were incorporated into the city from the start. The largest stores boasted 20–30 *ken* (40–60 yds.) fronts, while the smallest were no more than two *ken* (4 yds.) wide. Residences varied in size, likewise, according to personal wealth, and were not controlled by the lord of Hiroshima. The range of stratification extended from mansions of "millionaires" to peddlers in rented cottages. In 1619, when Lord Asano assumed control of Hiroshima, there were only 265 rented homes as against 2,000 personally-owned residences. Seven years later rentals had increased to 1,393 houses. Such a sharp increase in rented homes did not occur in the Tōhoku district. It was characteristic, rather, of the Kinki and Inland Sea districts.

In Sendai and Wakamatsu of the Tōhoku district the merchants, though relatively few, had been associated with government leaders even in medieval times. They cooperated in the programs of castle construction, and were given titles and other tokens of privileged positions. They retained their power and social prominence during the formative days of the castle towns and afterward.

In Hiroshima, however, former members of the warrior class, such as *nanushi*, who had no particular connection with the lord prior to the constructing of the castle town, came into the town-building process from the start and worked hard to gain places in its power structures. Taking advantage of the free markets, they were able to compete successfully with the original merchants' group that invited the daimyō to Hiroshima. This pattern of influx of a new type of merchant during the formative stages of castle towns was another distinctive feature of the Inland Sea region.

In taking the initiative for forming a city at Hiroshima, the powerful merchants organized a council of selected elders of the towns and communities in Hiroshima. Although the positions within this upper class group were not hereditary, this was the top stratum of Hiroshima merchant society.

Minor retailers of tea, salt, oil, soybean paste, sundries, fuel wood, and fish made up the middle class of merchants who owned their own homes. The lower class of commercial folk were the apprentices and workmen in crafts and retail shops, and peddlers who managed such trades as were not covered by the established stores. Homeowners were distinguished not only by fortune but by differences in status and legal rights as well, from those who depended on tenancy in rented quarters. If the latter desired to take any legal action, they first had to obtain a guarantee from some homeowner, who was called *ukenin* in this role. Most of those living in rented homes had come from the rural districts. Originally tenant farmers, they had acquired independent ownership of their lands by sheer hard work, only to discover that they could not meet the heavy and oppressive demands of the feudal governments enforced through strict land surveys. They had left their lands to seek better fortunes in the castle towns.

Here again, a distinction between the Tōhoku and western Honshū regions is possible. There were very few people in the Tōhoku area who could live in rented homes in the towns with only their physical labor to bargain with in supporting themselves. This phenomenon too was more common in the Kinki and Inland Sea districts. Such a phenomenon is a normal stage in the development of agrarian economies. But it would be unwise to press the distinction too far; both the northeastern and western Honshū patterns were part and parcel of the developmental processes of whole domains, and of the social controls exercised over the economy by the respective feudal lords.

In the process of building up their domains the daimyō abolished the binding, hereditary hold of established merchants over commerce and industry by opening up the markets and ports to free trade. The nuclear position of the castle towns was greatly strengthened by this stimulation of economic activity centered in them. Once the structural conversion was accomplished, however, policies were shifted to maintain relative isolation from other domains and to fix the *status quo* within each territory. Monopolistic cooperatives, the familiar *za* guilds or merchants' associations called *kabu-nakama*, were restored to sustain the prosperity of the castle centers by keeping commercial activity solely in the hands of a limited number of townsmen. With this isolation of the rural districts from all commercial enterprises, the differentiation between urban and rural districts was greatly intensified, further solidifying the place of the castle town as the nucleus of total integration throughout the whole domain.

In the early days of town-building, population concentration was not very heavy and demands were limited. Established shops were few, as needs were met by open markets, of which there were two types. One, *sai-ichi*, was not fixed as to place, but involved peddlers who circulated throughout the town every other day. Another, *toshi-ichi*, was opened once or several times a year at fixed places for several days (excepting shrine or temple festival days). The *sai-ichi* handled daily necessities; the *toshi-ichi* specialized in more durable wares. The *sai-ichi* type of mobile market tended to disappear as established shops dealing in daily necessities increased.

Wholesale firms handling basic items such as rice, fish, and vegetables in bulk quantities dominated the commodity economy throughout the entire country. Huge rice markets were developed in Ōsaka, Edo, and Kyōto. Even in the local provinces wholesalers were granted monopoly rights in collecting the products of the domains. In time the merchants operating fixed stores replaced the open marketeers, especially as the former were patronized by local governments which, in turn, had close connections with the lord of the domain. This line of relations led to privileges which gave established merchants a base of power from which they could overcome merchants from other regions, as well as completely outmaneuver any farmers attempting to market their own produce.

The integrative activity of the daimyō, from the times of civil wars on, greatly stimulated the overall demand for goods. It was those merchants who supported their lords in times of great need, whether battles or castle construction, who won privileges that lasted long after the lord died. Once the favored merchants had gained special privileges, other merchants had access to wholesale supplies and retail markets only through patronage of the senior merchant households. The latter's strength lay especially in the monopolization of rights to control production sources, and the feudal lords even utilized the wholesalers in tax collecting functions. Under the protection of their lords, the privileged wholesalers of the castle towns enjoyed a complete monopoly in commerce.[53]

Monopolies were not confined to the domain level. Local communities within the castle towns were sometimes granted monopoly privileges with respect to specific goods, either to serve a town just beginning, or to salvage the dwindling economy of an established community. In such cases, other towns were not permitted to deal in the commodity reserved for the authorized zone. According to a study made by Toyoda Takeshi, as many as fifty-nine townships were given such rights over more than 100 items in the following castle centers: Sendai, Fukushima of Echigo, Hirosaki, Aomori, Ajikazawa, Niigata, Kanazawa, Nagoya, Takada, Tanabe, Wakayama, Shingū, Okazaki, Okayama, Kōchi, Tokushima, Iida, Tsuruga, and Kubota of Akita.[54]

Called *za* in some towns, the area of application of monopoly rights varied greatly. The smallest covered only a single residential unit, *chō*; while some of the largest extended over entire castle towns. These rights were distributed quite evenly among merchants in the early days of the Tokugawa era, though they shifted into the hands of the wholesalers with the passage of time. Wealthy wholesalers displaced the zonal *za*, being more adaptable to the special needs of the feudal lords. On the other hand, merchants from other domains, though warmly welcomed when a city was being built, had less intimate ties with the daimyō and cared less for the prosperity of the castle towns as such. When they became barriers to progress, the daimyō took suppressive actions against them.

A variety of restrictions were laid down in each domain to protect native interests by limiting outsiders. One method was to limit the kinds and/or quantities of goods that could be transported in or out of a particular domain. Another measure involved outright rejection of merchants from other places. If allowed to enter the native markets, the outsiders were placed under a number of prohibitions. Inns permitted to accommodate them were fixed; they were required to report their arrival to officials; terms of stay were limited; and local guarantors were needed for periods over thirty days. Controls over merchants from other domains covered their wares as well, especially goods deemed harmful to the local economy. Special effort was made, of course, to protect the monopoly interests of the local wholesalers.[55]

These measures served the interests of the feudal lords in isolating their own domains so as to command all prosperity within their own boundaries. The functional differentiation of urban and rural districts, and the restriction of commerce and industry to the towns served further to guarantee the feudal lords' full command over the economic prosperity of their regions. In such an arrangement, the castle towns became the nuclei of economic as well as political activity in each domain.

In castle towns of the Edo period craftsmen were grouped into occupational neighborhoods just as the merchants had their own townships. Although theoretically above merchants in social standing, the economic power of the merchants gave them command of main street locations, leaving the back streets for the artisans' workshops. Transportation conveniences were not so important, of course, to craftsmen's daily work. Those artisans providing direct services to the local government, however, lived near the castle site.

The most common craft communities of all castle towns were those of blacksmiths (Kajiya-machi), dyers (Konya-machi), and carpenters (Daiku-cho), who were engaged mainly in supplying the military and other needs of the government. There were many other crafts communities, originally organized into residential areas according to specialities when towns were founded. As towns developed into larger urban units, the craftsmen were usually dispersed from their compact communities. Merchants moved into their communities to meet expanded needs of increased populations.[56]

Some of the more important crafts communities were:

| | |
|---|---|
| Saiku-chō | refined handicrafts |
| Himono-chō | wooden containers |
| Shokunin-chō | craftsmen in general |
| Kawara-machi | roofing tiles |
| Kanaya-chō | metal utensils |
| Migakiya-chō | polishers |
| Tsuchi-machi | earth dealers |
| Ōnoko-chō | large saws |
| Tatami-chō | straw mats for flooring |

Besides these more obvious trade communities, there were many, many more, such as:

| | |
|---|---|
| Teppō-chō | small firearms |
| Fukiya-machi | smelting |
| Kawaya-machi | leather goods |
| Imonoshi-machi | foundry |
| Funadaiku-chō | shipbuilding |
| Nabeya-chō | pots, pans, kettles |
| Nushi-machi | lacquer painting |
| Mageshi-machi | wooden containers |
| Sayashi-machi | sword sheaths |
| Sakan-machi | plastering |
| Okeya-machi | tubs and buckets |
| Sakuji-chō | architects |
| Kodōgu-chō | small utensils and tools |
| Kamaya-chō | rice cooking pots |
| Tsunaya-machi | rope making |
| Kasaya-machi | umbrellas |
| Kamisuki-chō | paper making |
| Shirokane-chō | silversmiths |

While craftsmen were under the control of the feudal lords, they did not enjoy the same privileged relations as did the upper class merchants. During the Middle Ages groups of artisans had been patronized by warrior cliques, shrines and temples for their own purposes. Their services were especially necessary to the warriors during the generations of domestic wars.

When the daimyō turned in earnest to construction of castle centers in the Edo period, they gathered groups of craftsmen specifically for that purpose, settling them into designated zones. A senior member, *tōryo*, of the crafts community was made responsible for their work in a semi-official status. Controls were exercised through several kinds of organizations, such as *nakama* (a kind of union), *za* (cooperative guilds), or *kō* (fraternal associations). Services were due the lords for definite periods of each year, and the craftsmen were exempted from various taxes and duties.

The agency of direct control was the official workshop of the castle itself, from which foremen (*kashira*) were appointed to supervise all work. Applications for jobs had to be made through these foremen. Wages decided by the lord's own workshops were made standard for all craftsmen, even those employed by warriors and townsmen. Employers and employees could not make private contracts on other terms. The same rules held for working hours, which were fixed at the official workshops.[57]

During the prolonged era of peace under Tokugawa supremacy, demands for weapons production declined drastically. Consequently, the daimyō altered the mode of their controls over the craftsmen toward other purposes.

Such a shift in the control system for artisans is demonstrated in Murai Masuo's comparative studies of the ironsmith communities (*kaji-chō*) of Ueda and Okayama. By granting sole production rights to the castle town ironsmith groups, controls were established not only over all other ironsmiths, but over farm production as well. In both localities the feudal government placed controls over the water systems so necessary to the ironsmiths' craft, in Ueda by levying duty on water consumption, and in Okayama by taking charge of sales of their products. In either case, the system of government controls over water constituted control over technical production of the tools used by farmers.

The controls deprived lesser lords of the ironsmiths' help in making new weapons by denying them access either to the techniques or to the products of weapons and ammunition production. The rulers' aims for strengthening each his own domain were well served; but, from the craftsmen's point of view, they were trapped in forms of government service and thereby denied access to industrial production where they might develop their skills and so improve their economic conditions.[58]

Temples were important to the castle towns and the daimyō either compelled temples to relocate in the base castle towns or simply to construct new temples. In Himeji there were sixty-eight temples, thirty in Takada, and more than twenty in Hirosaki. Because of spacious grounds and sturdy buildings, the temples had added value as defense positions in case of enemy attacks.

Temple sites were chosen to form a defense line, especially, says Orui Noboru, with reference to weak points in the castle defenses. In some cases the temples were located at some distance from the castle area, possibly as retreat havens, on a plateau (as in Kanazawa) or at the foot of a mountain (as in Morioka). The temples served sometimes as a buffer zone between the castle town and the castle proper (as in Sendai). They were sometimes lined up along points of entry into the castle towns as sentries standing guard over all traffic (as in Kumamoto and Aizu). Another utilization of the temples for defense ends was to disperse them in a circle around the town (as in Takada, Yonezawa, Akita, and Hirosaki).[59] Apart from importance to defense, the temples and shrines were, of course, places of genuine worship for both warriors and ordinary citizens; not to mention their special functions of providing the primary forms of public recreation in the many seasonal festivals.

The outcasts, called *hinin* or *eta*, were the victims of extreme discrimination, being actually "status-less" in that they were strictly isolated from the closed status system of warriors, farmers, artisans, and merchants. The existence of such a lowly class served, as in many societies, to strengthen the feudal lords' control over the other classes. The outcasts were located in semi-developed areas on the outskirts of town, often by a river or other waterway. They were used mainly in unpopular leathercraft work, for cultivation of lands. or for carrying out executions of those condemned to death—all jobs thoroughly disliked by ordinary citizens.

Separated as they were, ordinary people harbored feelings of fear and even horror with regard to the segregated *eta* communities. Such feelings were utilized by the rulers in the placing of the outcasts' block of dwellings near the town entrance, a psychological impediment to free entry and exit. In this position the *eta* could be used also as a first line of defense against rebellious peasants. At times they were even moved to battle fronts as supplementary troops (Fukuyama, 1786; Kishū, 1823; and Chōshū, 1831).

Special strongmen of unchallenged authority were needed to oversee the *eta* villages, like the lordless, free-lance samurai (*rōnin*) put in charge of an outcast village in the Matsushiro castle town. These strongmen actually assumed a variety of civic responsibilities: labor boss of farm lands and hands; public policing and secret detective work; service in military parades; and cleaning the castle inside and out. Roving entertainers had to apply to these bosses for permission to enter a town.[60]

The social order was founded on a high degree of mutual exclusiveness between classes and mutual isolation between town and rural districts, and between separate domains. To help maintain this kind of social order, the line of demarcation between the inside and the outside of the castle towns was strictly drawn. Checking stations were set up at all entry-exit points to scrutinize all people and commodities and to levy required passage fees. Stations were also placed along rivers, as on the River Ōta in Hiroshima. Toward the end of the Tokugawa *bakufu*'s reign society was increasingly in turmoil and the number of watchtower checkpoints increased, as did the strictness of surveillance.[61]

The castle town was not only an integrative organization of economic and ecological importance; it performed a significant administrative function through the rigid controls that enforced the status system affecting every group in society. The townsmen, who had enjoyed certain freedoms during the more fluid Age of Civil Wars, where brought increasingly under the integrative structures of the *bakufu* after the beginning of the Edo period. The castle towns were also cut off from remaining affinities with the rural tradition of perennially tilling the land, gradually expanding into cities oriented to the lavish consumption of warriors in season and out. The new cities differed from rural districts not only in outward appearances, then, but also in internal administrative structures designed to maintain a complex status system. That system kept the majority of the people in the various classes of townsmen subservient to the ruling military class at the top.

For each of the distinct areas of the castle town, warriors' residences, townsmen's residences, and townships formed around the grounds of temples and shrines, official commissioners were appointed. These commissioners were charged with responsibility for, and given full authority over, all affairs in their respective areas, whether warriors, townsmen, temples, or ports. Commissioners overseeing townspeople's activities generally delegated some responsibilities to elders among the townsmen for actual administrative work.

The titles of the elders' councils varied from city to city, though all of the terms used, *sōdoshiyori*, *sōmachidai*, *sōmachi-doshiyori-gashira*, and so on, indicate seniority and general responsibility. Some titles, like *funadoshiyori*, indicated special responsibilities; in this case, for collecting duty and controlling traffic on the waterways.[62]

The city elders occupied large houses in the central part of the townsmen's sector of the city, usually called Ōmachi or Honchō. They were selected by the commissioner of townspeople's affairs, the *machi-bugyō*, from a variety of groups: families traditionally associated with the castle towns, powerful gentry on old estate lands near the castle centers, successors to the laborer and horse suppliers of highway stations converted into castle towns, ex-warrior merchants, and others who had gained privileged positions under either the *bakufu* or the feudal lords. These elders exercised hereditary controls in the administration of the castle towns.

In each sector (also called *machi*, "town") of the castle towns, there were one or more officials with titles similar to the town elders. These men were in charge of local community affairs. Generally, these posts were held by certain families hereditarily, although some towns with highly developed commercial or transportation activity selected their leaders by general elections among houseowners, or even townsmen in general.[63]

The smallest administrative units in the castle towns were neighborhood groups of five (*gonin-gumi*) or ten (*junin-gumi*) households. Each unit had a head (*kumigashira*) who was the link between his unit and the town elders or town commissioner.

More important, the units constituted a system of surveillance, of mutually watching every neighbor's move. Strict, minute regulations stipulated, for example, that all members of a unit had to be present at events affecting any one of them, such as marriage rites, adoption proceedings, and other formalities involving two or more families. Matters internal to a single household, such as succession, wills, or disinheritance proceedings, required the presence of one's unit-members. The household seals of all unit members were needed for legal documents, and all were held responsible for any wrong behavior of any member of the neighborhood group. While the units generally consisted of five households, ten was not uncommon early in the Edo era.

Citizenship was limited to houseowners, and participation in the local administration of the towns was confined to citizens. In other words, administration of the townsmen's communities was exclusively by upper class townsmen.[64]

The daimyō were especially jealous of controls in their own castle centers. To secure order, status groups were held rigidly fixed, townsmen were prevented from forming private organizations of their own, and unquestioning obedience of government orders was expected. Through such measures, freedom and initiative were denied to the townsmen by their lords.

Restrictions extended not only to group activities but to individual behavior as well. In the early days of the feudal period, when castle towns were still in developmental stages, the townsmen enjoyed some liberty. Sometimes warriors were even punished for unreasonable treatment of townspeople. The liberties permitted townsmen, however, were few and narrowly confined to utilitarian purposes of building up the castle towns, especially commercial prosperity, and not derived from any convinctions about man and society.

The means of suppressing freedom among the townspeople were numerous and varied greatly in points of application. The regulations imposed on the five-households units in the town of Maebashi are indicative of such controls: (1) Sons and daughters must strive to be perfect in filial piety, propriety, and devotion; (2) Bear in mind always your social position, working diligently at your occupation; (3) Never steal another's property; (4) Do not accept applications for tenancy of houses or lands from those outside our town, unless information concerning the applicant's character can be obtained from the city elders or head of the household unit in his former residence; applications can be accepted if accompanied by a certificate of guarantee sealed by his relatives; (5) Residents are not to leave their own neighborhoods for viewing *sumo* matches or puppet shows. It is easy to see that the administrative units of households were bound by rules that virtually restricted all vertical or horizontal mobility in society, even for amusement.[65]

Some of the behavior-binding rules were designed primarily to elevate the status and authority of the warrior class. In Hiroshima, for instance, townspeople were to stand erect when warriors passed by, or dismount when on horseback. Impudence, even within their own shops, could bring townsfolk imprisonment, as part of these patterns of enforced obedience. Okayama regulations called for removal of all headgear upon encountering warriors, even the typical twisted towel tied around the head by artisans; a toothpick held in one's mouth was also held offensive.

To prevent display of wealth by townsmen, Ōsaka ruled in 1648 against their constructing three-storied houses. Dice games, backgammon, *sumo* matches, and performances on popular instruments such as the *shakuhachi* (a Chinese woodwind) and *samisen* (three-stringed banjo type instrument) were all restricted from open practice in the streets of Okayama.

Daimyō especially feared criticism by, and private concentrations of power among, their subjects. The lord of Kōfu threatened his people with official investigation if they publicly criticized his decrees. Orders issued in Matsuyama toward the middle of the 17th century forbade townsmen to organize their own groups, even if there were some special reason to do so.

While the rigid status system prevented vertical social movements, the five-family units, plus requirements for registering at designated temples (*shūmonchō*), imposed heavy impediments on horizontal mobility as well. The Kaga domain in 1604 and Takaoka city in 1621 issued orders against moving out of one's village, town, and domain. Nagoya restricted moving by property-owners in 1667. If residents were unsuccessful in making a living, or were invited by someone successfully established in another locale, movements were approved, though every movement of townsmen had to be reported to the appropriate commissioner.[66]

Strict control by the feudal lord applied to city and rural districts alike. Development of commodity markets in rural areas was suppressed so as to retain the traditional economy of agricultural production, from which taxes were excised. Merchants and artisans in the towns, on the other hand, were encouraged through privileges and tax exemptions to foster the prosperity of the towns. It must not be thought, however, that the townsmen's burdens were light, but simply that the peasants' burdens were heavier.

Rich townsmen often won tax exemptions by donating funds to their lords. Exemptions were usually granted only to established families in the older sections of the castle towns, called variously *furu-machi* (old town), *uchi-machi* (inner town), *gofudai-machi* (town of hereditary households), or *korai-chō* (town of antiquity). New sections of towns were rarely given such privileges. If they were, other official duties were required as a rule. Taxes imposed on households, *kakekin,* were generally paid even by residents of the upper class central districts, the Ōmachi or Honchō.

Investigation of the responsibilities borne by eight townships of Matsushiro town (Nagano district) has turned up details on some 2,000 townsmen around the year 1671. Obligations included provision of 600 horses per year for the highway relay system, in addition to 720–780 horses needed in cargo transport or official travel, a duty known as *tenma-yaku*. Supplying laborers for official needs (*buyaku*) such as support of warriors, palanquin-bearers, and so on, ran to 455 men per year in 1813, or an average of seven duty times per household in a year's time. Cash obligations, *chōnin-yō,* were demanded for any number of reasons: expenses covering all eight townships or any one of them, as well as helping meet needs of the domain itself, not to mention *bakufu* needs such as construction of roads and buildings at Nikkō. Crop failures or destruction of official domain buildings in the capital city of Edo could always add further burdens. The duties imposed on townspeople were quite sizable, then, yet still far less than those demanded of peasants.[67]

# 4. Relationships between Castle Towns and Surrounding Areas

4. *Relationships between Castle Towns and Surrounding Areas.* While the feudal order was founded economically upon agriculture, that is, rice production, the development of a money economy in the cities and towns and its penetration into surrounding districts complicated things considerably. A dual system of controls was needed, not only to distinguish clearly between town and rural areas, but to keep the status distinctions between peasants and their overseers as clear as that between townsmen and their warrior superiors. Restricted mobility was necessary to maintain fixed economic and social patterns throughout the total domain, urban and rural areas alike.

Crafts production in the rural districts was stimulated whenever a castle center was developed. After completion of a castle town, the tendency was to specialize in market sales of products. As a rule, rural production of handicrafts was suspended by the daimyō to confine peasant energies to agriculture, chief source of finances for the feudal regimes. The peasants were forced thereby to be content with only the lowest level of subsistence. All surplus was absorbed by the lords, keeping the farm districts tied to a natural economy of self-sufficiency and subject to treatment quite different from the towns.

Where farmers were forbidden to engage in crafts production and sales, merchants and artisans were mobilized in the towns, usually according to specialization. Privilege and protection made them parasites who not only enjoyed monopoly rights of production and marketing, but were spared competition by merchants from other domains. They held the upper hand in their special fields over both outside merchants and the rural folk of their own domain.

We have seen earlier how merchants were warmly received in the formative stages of castle towns, only to defend their acquired privileges against encroachments by latecomers after the towns were established. The measures used to block inroads by competitors from outside included: limitations or prohibitions on use of inns, or on permissible lengths of stay; restrictions on the numbers of merchants or goods, or both; forced sales within prescribed periods of time before compulsory exit; and harassment by inspection of baggage.

Controls were exercised also on the exporting of goods to other domains. All locally produced goods had to be forwarded first to authorized wholesalers. Operation of shops for direct sales of products in areas outside the castle towns was forbidden. In this way, then, peasant energies were kept in agricultural channels, the productivity of the lands was geared completely to purposes of the daimyō, and prosperity arising from handicrafts production and sales was confined to the towns and their control systems.

With large-scale restriction of production and sales of commodities to specific groups inside the towns, and overall controls held by leading merchants and wholesalers, the farmers were utterly dependent upon the wholesalers in disposing of their own farm products. The rural district was completely subordinate to the city as well as thoroughly isolated within the general economy.

Administrative zones were set up in the towns for handling all commercial transactions with rural areas, and the trend was to extend the administrative scope of these zones. Buyers from the outside were not permitted in these zones, as its goods were intended only for each town's own consumption. In non-castle towns only special agents could deal with castle town merchants, although non-castle towns were allowed wholesale transactions with each other. Cotton dealers in Sendai appealed for monopoly rights over a five *ri* square area (12 sq. mi.) in 1781. After reviewing the petition, the authorities granted instead a franchise covering thirty square *ri* (73 sq. mi.).[68]

Despite the fact that diffusion of the commodity economy into the rural districts worked against feudal policies, it remains true that those policies were effective in depriving the rural regions of commerce and industry as long as the feudal system survived. A 1781 decree of the Sendai lord cleared all roads, primary and secondary, of unwanted merchants. Another in Hirosaki in 1754 against silk, cotton, and miscellaneous goods threw such prosperous towns as Itabarai, Iizume, and Yukawa into temporary depressions.[69]

It was quite difficult absolutely to prevent any and all operations of small shops, and a few were always allowed in the rural areas to serve the minimum needs of peasants. Footgear for humans (*zōri* and *waraji*) and horses (*umagutsu*) were approved for sales in Sendai in 1861, as were sales of simple cakes. Earlier rulings in Okayama permitted teahouses to re-open (1782) and small shops serving travelers to open (1812), though luxuries were excluded from their shelves. As early as 1759 the town of Tokushima had approved sales of small quantities of tea, salt, tobacco, footwear, and farm tools; a 1762 ruling, however, hastened to fix the number of recognized merchants and hold the number of approved necessities down to forty-three items.

Approved sales lists were subject to fluctuation, of course. The Tosa domain permitted peddling of thirty-six items in 1692. Developments in the exchange economy led to the addition of twelve more items in 1734, and five more in 1746, raising the total to fifty-three items. Besides these, there were some forty items approved for sales in the rural areas. All in all, the sales list of approved items numbered ninety-three in this domain.

Controls were relaxed somewhat in the fishing villages, as it was recognized that special needs existed. An investigation made in 1782 in Okayama prompted approval of sales of lumber, fishing tackle, vinegar, soy sauce, oil, and other necessities. Special conditions also yielded *sake* (rice wine) allowances for fishermen in Sendai in 1757, for whom, an old saying claims, "*sake* is as essential as food itself."[70]

If non-castle towns were limited in commerce possibilities, the situation in the distinctly rural districts was severe. Studied efforts were made to keep peasants from improving their lot economically. In the Karatsu district during the Genna era (1615–23) no cakes, fish, or *sake* were put on sale. No merchants were allowed to operate in this rural district. Only low class peddlers carrying baskets full of goods relieved the austere isolation from town markets.

Peddlers were restricted from rural areas in Okayama domain in 1655, though given permission to go out in the next year with licenses from the rural commissioner. In 1668 a list of eleven goods was approved, being extended to eighteen items in 1683, and finally to thirty-one items in 1705.[71]

In addition to approving forty items for rural sales in 1820, the government of the Tosa domain also fixed price levels. In general, transportation costs drove prices up the farther one went from the town markets. In the Kōchi district prices within a fixed radius of the town were held to the town's level. Beyond that to a certain second circle, prices were 15% higher, and 20% higher beyond the outer circle. All prices in the town of Kōchi were based on price levels fixed originally by the local government.

Restrictions applied not only to items and prices but often to seasons. A 1696 ruling of the Okayama domain prohibited merchants from working in rural areas in the spring (mid-fourth to seventh months) and fall (mid-eighth to twelfth months) seasons. The local managers (*nanushi*) bought and distributed necessary supplies during these seasons. After 1782 and up to 1812 this domain eliminated all merchants from the rural districts except those living there.[72] Delivery of agricultural products to the cities was often done by merchants returning from sales trips to rural areas, when not done by the farmers themselves. As a rule, though, merchants were denied this function so as to strengthen controls against peddling to farmers.

Private purchases of products directly from the farmers was generally prohibited. Exceptions were made in the case of certain items that lost their value if not delivered soon, such as rape seed or fish. Even where merchants were allowed access to farm products, they were rarely permitted to purchase them directly at the production localities. The products were delivered first to a local economic center, before purchase and delivery to the wholesale houses in the castle towns. All those caught acting in violation of these regulations were severely punished.[73]

The feudal structure and its castle centers relied on effective implementation of three goals, namely, expanded agricultural production, development of the town-based commodity economy, and differentiation of handicrafts and commerce from agriculture. The feudal lords were largely able to achieve these goals through strict separation of town and rural districts, and by restricting commerce and industry to the towns. They could not always eliminate commodity production and exchange, however, from rural districts where relative regional isolation in economy had been established since the Middle Ages.

Minor castle, port, and highway station towns and small market centers were quite sensitive to the shifting fortunes of the warlords or religious groups to which they owed their existence. Advantageous locations made it possible for some towns to survive even after the sponsoring lord's or group's position declined, especially when such location advantages included traffic or port conditions that served the total domain's purposes. Such towns were marked usually by services performed for the provincial government in labor, transport, or military needs.

On the other hand, under the emerging feudal order of the Tokugawa regime there appeared many minor towns with commercial, crafts production, and agricultural functions, that served as the control centers of the agrarian economy of surrounding rural areas. Merchants and craftsmen were the chief organizing agents of these minor towns, and populations were drawn from among peasants with no special status, a kind of surplus population where intensification of status structures had left them without any particular place in society.

A cluster of four towns near Kumamoto that had performed harbor and other commercial functions since medieval times made up a complex which came to be known as the "Five Towns" (*Gokachō*). With a single commissioner for the total complex, the cluster was regarded as identical with Kumamoto.[74]

Similar groups of towns of varying distance from the castle centers were in other domains. In the Sendai domain nine such towns were recognized in the Bunsei era (1818–30). Kōchi domain had a union of nine small towns, Mori and Takada domains unions of five each. In unions of the Kaga domain there were over fifty villages which served as local markets run by minor merchants.

Thirteen population centers in Okayama domain revived their former functions as bases of powerful households, or as port, highway, and temple towns, and were officially recognized early in the Tokugawa period (Kan-ei era, 1624–44). Some ten of them developed further, four applying for their lord's approval as full-fledged commercial towns in 1783.[75]

The feudal lords could not wholly overlook the strong petitions from local merchants for official recognition of their commercial centers as legitimate towns. Nevertheless, the lords could, and did, put them under strict administrative controls. Usui-mura in Higashi-kazusa district, for instance, had once been a cattle-grazing area. In 1629 a pioneer farming village was opened up there, but the peasants were unable to make a living. Petitioning for approval to operate a market in 1661, they were able thereafter to sustain themselves and the number of households increased to ninety-five.[76]

Peddlers and markets were attracted to the Kameta district of Echigo (present Niigata Pref.) by progress made in agriculture and coastal trading. Shopowners sought recognition as a commercial town in 1694 which, being granted, further stimulated business. The official market area had 101 shops averaging 5 *ken* width by 20–30 *ken* length (10 × 40–60 yds.).[77]

Marketing privileges approached those enjoyed in castle towns, although they were not granted unconditionally. Restrictions were put on the range of operation and on trips into rural districts. Nor were outsiders permitted to come in and make use of local markets.[78]

Transactions were confined to approved market locations, as in Koarai-machi in Wakamatsu, a marketplace carried over from olden days. This was expanded to two market centers, Honchō and Haramachi, in the Keichō era (1596–1615), and here the same restrictions of transactions to designated locations and dates applied. Exchange activity could not exceed geographical limits of three *ri* (7.3 mi.), to keep the commodity economy from penetrating the countryside.[79]

While the feudal lords could not suppress the emergence of commercial centers other than castle towns, they did persist in strengthening measures to prevent the spread of commodity exchange into farming areas throughout the Edo period. Instead, they acted to direct gains from commerce into their own treasuries. Not only increased agricultural productivity, but the consumer needs fostered by the system of required residence in Edo in alternate years and the improved transportation system, gave an almost irresistible stimulus to the overall commodity economy.

In general, direct imports of goods by-passing wholesalers in the castle towns was prohibited. A directive issued in 1802 for Awa domain on Shikoku island made allowances for unions of at least four commercial centers to make collective transactions that needed not be handled through their castle town of Tokushima. Such freedom did not extend to local merchants in the rural areas, who were still bound to the castle town and were obliged to pay commissions on all purchases.

Similarly, the Iida domain made exceptions for direct imports in the case of twelve items in 1719, but basic staples such as fish, salt, and tea were kept under standard castle town controls. Sendai domain allowed only three of its nine approved commerce centers to engage in direct imports, as of 1862.[80]

Despite these examples of slight loosening of rigid controls in favor of the minor commercial towns in various domains, the castle towns remained, without exception, the major centers of all economic activity. Minor towns were wholly subordinate to the superior positions and privileges of the castle towns. Differentiation of the urban and rural districts was tightly maintained, preventing the diffusion into rural Japan of the commodity economy.

# Chapter VI | The Ecological and Social Structure of Edo

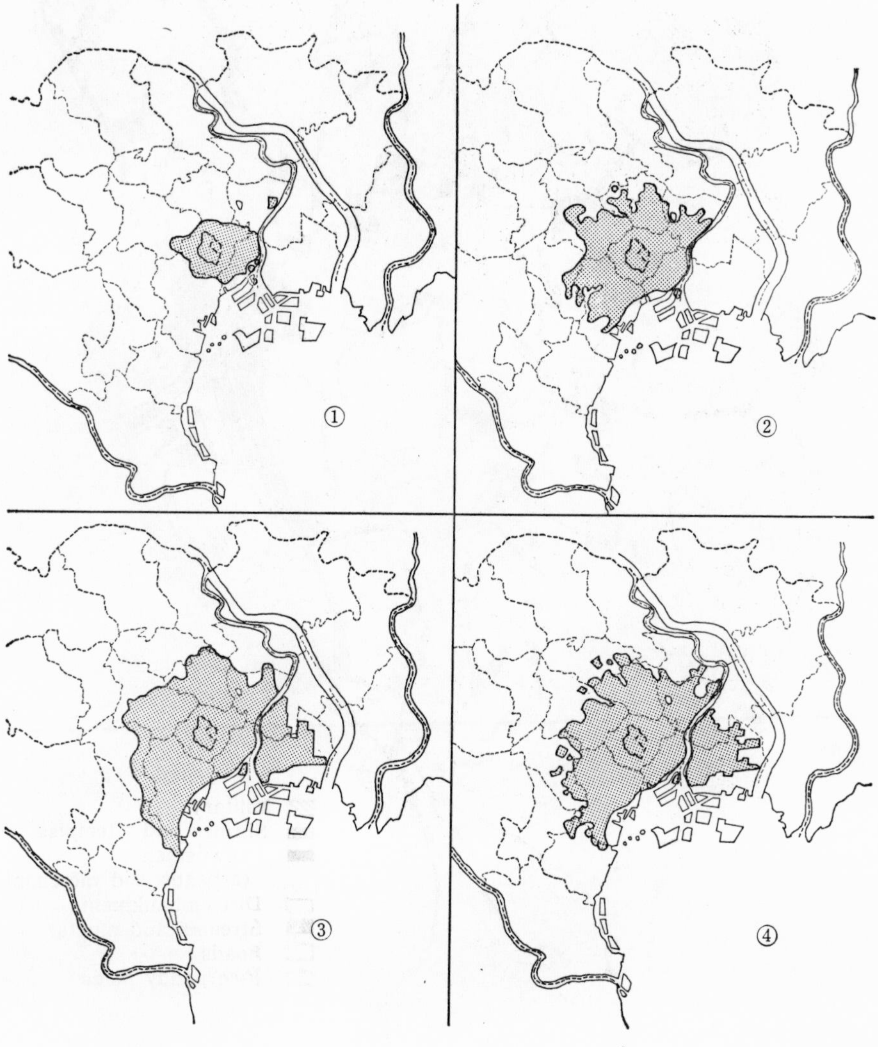


**Fig. 17 Expansion of Edo**
1 Built-up area, 1624–43
2 Built-up area, 1652–54
3 Built-up area, 1673–80
4 Built-up area, 1830–43

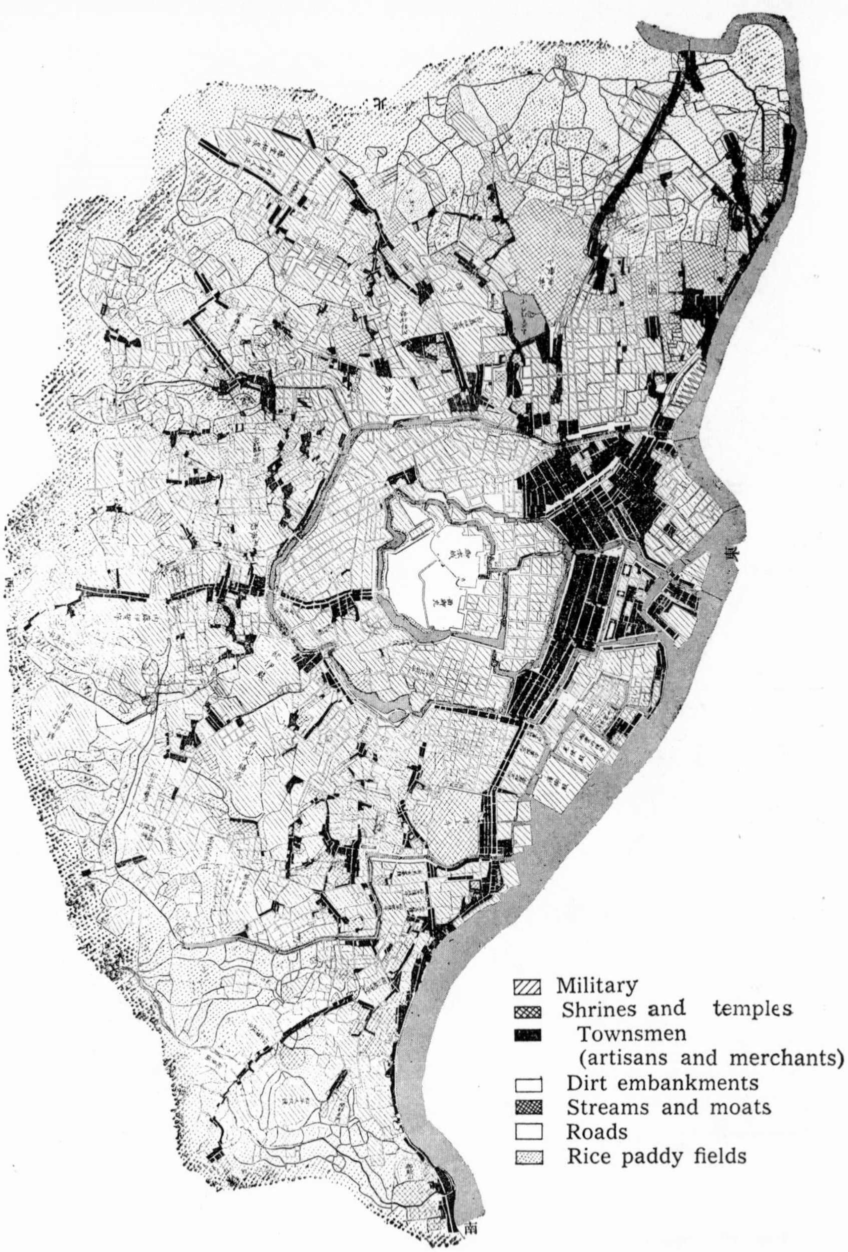


**Fig. 18 Spatial Pattern of Edo (Kyōho period, 1716–35)**

Like other castle towns, Edo's structure was determined by defense and status considerations, but, because of its large-scale military and political functions, plus the alternate year's residence system, the population was over 1,000,000. With increase in population and rise in the standard of living, the economic integrative function of the Nihonbashi section was enlarged as the center. The spatial structure took on a circular shape around Nihonbashi and the castle, with the streets extending radially from this center. As the size of the city was quite large it developed a multi-nuclear pattern, connected by ribbons of streets lined with stores, and this pattern served as the prototype for modern Tōkyō.

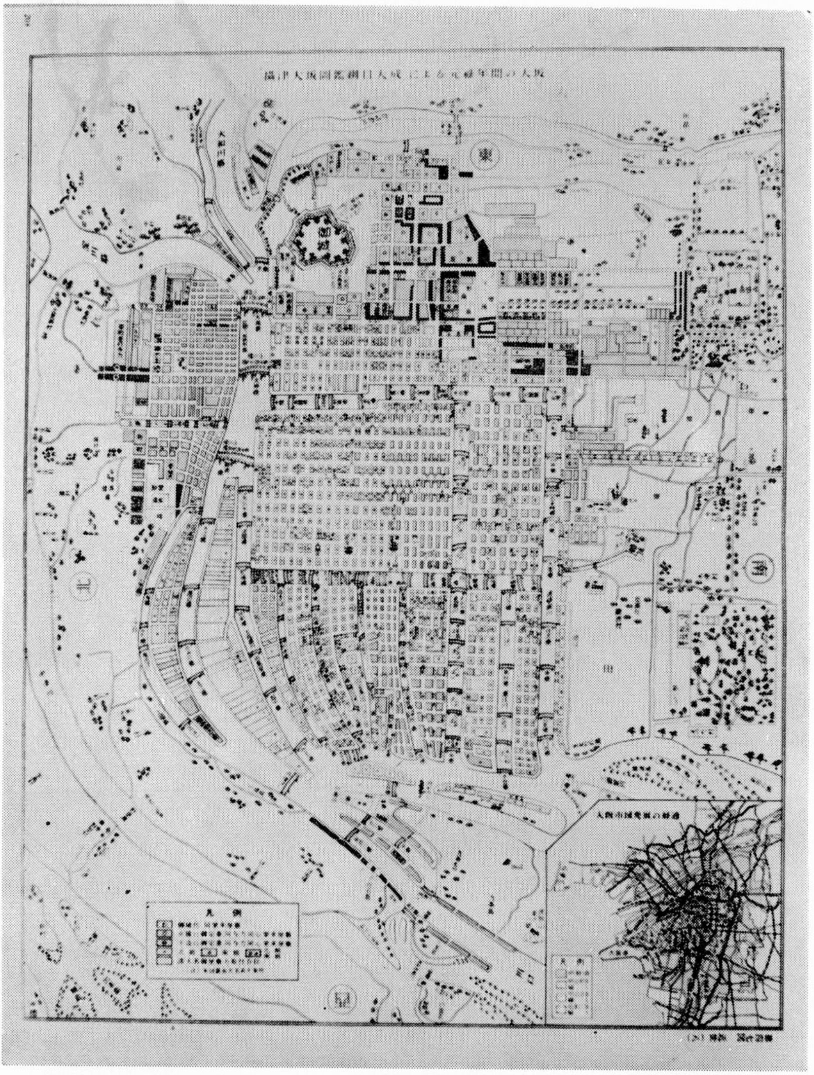

**Fig. 19 Spatial Pattern of Ōsaka**

Called the "kitchen of the world" as the supply center for Edo, Ōsaka developed into the national trade center. Most of the residents were townsmen, not warriors. On the central island in the river large warehouses, *kura-yashiki*, were constructed for the sale of the products of each domain; the money was sent to Edo for the support of the warriors there from the domain concerned. Wholesale houses concentrated near the harbor, and the streets were patterned according to the ancient Chinese chess board, in contrast with Edo's radial pattern, and there were no particular sections according to status.

# 1. THE ECOLOGICAL STRUCTURE OF EDO

1. *The ecological structure of Edo.*
This castle center of Tokugawa Ieyasu on the eastern coast of the great Kantō plain was quite distinct from all other castle towns. For here Ieyasu established the *bakufu* offices that were to stand secure as the nucleus of the total integrative structure for all Japan for two and a half centuries.

Quite naturally, then, the ecological structure of Edo differed greatly from the castle towns in the provinces, especially in terms of size and structure. For one thing, there were 80,000 standard-bearers, *hatamoto hachimanki*, directly subordinate to the *bakufu* in residence there. The more than three hundred daimyō were under *bakufu* orders to establish permanent residences in Edo, where their wives and children remained permanently, while the feudal lords had to spend every other year there. Retainers to the lords either stayed in Edo permanently or in shifts. This gave the city a great warrior population, pouring a huge amount of the total national wealth into the capital city to undergird their consumptive demands. Their vast purchasing power drew together a concentration of merchants, artisans, temples and shrines, forming a gigantic city on a scale never found before in the history of the world.

Although the immediate cause of this development lay in the unprecedented integrative power of the Tokugawa family over politics, economy, religion and the expanded communications system, the origins of the city of Edo can be traced to the Heian era. In that earlier period many powerful clans had founded their domains in the Kantō plain's district known as Musashi-no-kuni. One of the powerful cliques of warriors in this region was called Edoshi, a branch of the Chichibutō household, itself descended from the old Heishi clan. After Yoritomo of the Minamoto clan assumed control of the whole country Edo Shigenaga was appointed governor of the province of Musashi, and he located his base castle at a site near the present imperial palace. The Edo Castle center at that time consisted of two parts: Daikan-chō at its present location, and Hirakawa-mura, a mixed farming and fishing village. Even in its early stage this castle center occupied a very strategic position of command over land, river, and sea traffic. Called Edojuku, it maintained its strategic importance through the next several centuries, enjoying relative prosperity and a sizable population.

In 1456, or the middle of the Muromachi era, Ōta Dōkan rebuilt the Edo Castle. Around the main *Honmaru* section (later reconstructed by the

Tokugawa leaders) moats of about fifty *chō* (3.4 mi.) in length were constructed. Encompassed by twenty-five gates of stone construction, there were three lines of defense, the *kojiro*, *nakajiro*, and *sotojiro*, or central, middle, and outer forts. Around the castle were built such shrines as the Sannō, Hirakawa-tenjin, and Tsukudo-myōjin, plus other shrines and temples. The foundation of the future city of Edo was thus laid by Ōta Dōkan. Hirakawa was the name of a river that flowed through the town, along which there developed boating services bringing products from other regions to the town's merchants. City streets ran parallel to the larger national highways intersecting the town. In general, Edo was a thriving castle town of medieval proportions.[1]

At the same time, however, the city of Odawara, castle center of the powerful Hōjō family, competed for prominence in the Kantō plain. In 1486 the Kantō district was thrown into turmoil by the assassination of Ōta Dōkan at the hand of his lord Uesugi Sadamasa. The Hōjō family seized Edo Castle, making it a branch of its own domain. Thenceforth, Odawara prospered while Edo declined. When Tokugawa Ieyasu entered the castle of Edo a hundred years after the death of Ōta Dōkan, there remained only a greatly diminished Edojuku at the mouth of the Hirakawa river with only a handful of merchants and craftsmen. Only humble cottages with simple stone fences could be seen in the village called Hirakawa-mura surrounding the Edojuku nucleus. As yet there was no great concentration of warriors in Edo.[2]

The Odawara stronghold fell in 1591 and the Hōjō power was ruined. On Toyotomi Hideyoshi's advice, Tokugawa Ieyasu transferred his residence to Edo, where he strove to erect a great city according to carefully laid out plans. Prior to his entry the central, intermediary, and tertiary (*Honmaru*, *Ninomaru*, and *Sannomaru*) fortresses had fallen into decay; embankments were poor earth and wood structures, with bamboo growing wild all over them. Entrances consisted of four or five wooden gates, and castle roofs were thatched with miscanthus. At one place the floor of the castle was nothing more than planks salvaged from old boats. The little town of Edojuku itself contained only a hundred thatched-roof houses.[3]

The layout of the town area was relatively simple. Hibiya Inlet cut between the castle area on the Musashi tableland and peninsular Edo Sotojima (an extension of Mount Kanda), reaching up to Babasaki-mon. To the south was Hamachō and the sea beyond. Between lay the Shiba hill country with little flat land. To the east were the marshes of Ueno and Asakusa, and the Honjo, Fukagawa, and Shitaya areas were mostly sand dunes and banks. The Hirakawa river basin area and the Musashi tableland constituted the primary inhabitable lands.

Fishing villages lay along the seashores of Hibiya and Shiba. Other residential villages includes a list of names, many of them used today: Chiyoda, Takarada, Tokita, Hirata, Fukuda, Kamihirakawa, Shimo-hirakawa, Tsubonezawa, Shibasaki, Kaizuka, Hibiya, Kanda, Sakurada, Iigura, Azabu, Shiba, Mita, Hitotsugi, Aoyama, Ushigome, Ichigaya,

Koishikawa, Yushima, Hongo, Shitaya, Ueno, Torigoe, Asakusa, Hashiba, Imado, Ishiwara, and Yanagishima.

Recognizing that conditions were most unsuitable for assembling his warriors and the merchants and craftsmen needed there, Ieyasu sent his vassal Ōkubo Mondo ahead to remedy the situation prior to his own entry. Special attention was given to the inadequate water supply and poor traffic facilities. Soon after entering the castle Ieyasu ordered the construction of a special moat, Sanbori, to connect the castle area with Edo's port. More roads and bridges were also built in and around Edo-juku.

Vassals of the Tokugawa house based in the local provinces of Suruga, Mikawa, Tōtōmi, Kai, and Shinano were given fiefs near Edo and residential grounds inside Edo. Following their transfer to Edo, merchants and craftsmen came, on their own initiative or by invitation, to serve the warriors. They came mostly from Odawara, Ōmi, and Ise. The bridge at Tokiwa was an early gathering place for them, and it thrived as a trade and working center.

Although Ieyasu's initial efforts were directed also to improving Edo's streets, he succeeded only in repairing the castle, and that but inadequately. In 1593, though, construction was begun on moats starting from Wadakura-mon and extending by way of Sakurada-mon to Hanzō-mon. The earth obtained was used to fill in Hibiya Inlet to prevent damage to the streets from periodic overflowing.

Main streets prior to Ieyasu's coming were found in Kōji-machi, Akasaka, Hitotsugi, Ushigome, and Shiba, plus the temple area of Asakusa. A few merchants' houses were located in front of the castle (Ōte).[4] Residential areas for the warriors were in three sections: Daikan-chō north of the castle, where government officials lived; Ban-chō, where the castle guards lived; and the groups of warriors living in Ogawa-machi, Kōji-machi, Aoyama, Maruyama, Hongo, and Shitaya. Temples and shrines previously located near the castle were transferred chiefly to Kanda-dai and Yanokura.

An organization to control merchants was established as their influx increased. An administrative system for governing all townsmen other than warriors and priests was set up, with appointment of a commissioner, *machi-bugyō*, and town councilors, *machi-doshiyori*. These officials were authorized to assume surnames, bear swords, and occupy houses given them by the government officies in Hon-chō. Their titles became hereditary; for instance, Taruya Tōzaemon and Naraya Ichiemon were brought from established Tokugawa fiefs and made *machi-doshiyori* in 1590. Kitamura Yahei and others were added in 1592. These men controlled the *nanushi*, or managers of each town, which meant control, then, over Edo Sōmachi, all the towns of Edo.

The *nanushi* were chosen from among those who had served the Tokugawa family in its other domains, those who had ruled Edo prior to Tokugawa occupancy, and those lordless warriors (*rōnin*) who had assumed prominent positions among the townsmen. Some of the *nanushi* were clearly identified with the Tokugawa regime by having founded their towns at the time of reconstruction of Edo by the Tokugawa house. Called *sōsō-nanushi* or *kusawake-nanushi*, they enjoyed special privileges symbolized by the right to enter Edo Castle on New Year's Day to make presentations to the ruling shogun. They held the highest positions among all *nanushi*, and received favorable treatment from the government in the administration of their towns.[5]

Gradually Edo was transformed, from being just one among many average castle towns, into a city equipped with the many facilities needed to serve as a national capital with a large population. Successful accomplishment of this process must be marked after the time of Toyotomi Hideyoshi's death in 1598, and after Tokugawa Ieyasu rose to power after victory in the battle of Sekigahara in 1600. Ieyasu was appointed to the highest military post in the land, *Seii-tai-shogun* (generalissimo) by the emperor in 1603, making him the effective ruler of the country. With the relocation of the *bakufu* military government in Edo, this city came into its own as the center of the country's integrative organs.

The decision to make Edo the national nucleus was not an immediate one, however. Consideration was also given to Kyōto, traditional capital and cultural center, as well as to Ōsaka, growing economic center of the land. Ieyasu had some particular reasons for preferring Edo, which may be summarized as follows:

(1) The Heishi clan had grown effeminate and lost its power after taking up residence in Kyōto; and the Ashikaga family had not experienced good fortune in founding its *bakufu* in Kyōto.

(2) Ieyasu was impressed with the simplicity of warrior life in the Kamakura *bakufu*.

(3) Locating the goverment in the center of a wide, open plain afforded greater advantages for defense, as well as for land and sea transportation.

To expedite his policy for making Edo the national capital, Ieyasu ordered the major daimyō in western Japan to ship 1,120 pieces of large stone per 100,000 *koku* of rice collected in their domains. A single stone required 100 laborers to move it, costing 11,925 *ryō* in labor costs. Stone shipments were supervised by Tōdō Takatora, and it is said that 3,000 boats gathered in the ports of Izu alone to deliver shipments to Edo. Each vessel carried only two of the large stones per trip, and made two round-trip voyages each month.

Sustained shipment of large stones made it possible to complete the basic construction of the expanded castle by 1607, including stone walls for the *Honmaru*, *Ninomaru*, and *Sannomaru* sections. In 1639, when the third Tokugawa shogun, Iemitsu, was in office, the largest castle in the history of Japan was completed. Moats were added on the inland side from Akasaka to Ushigome via Yotsuya. The Kanda river on the north side was converted into a moat. Gates and fortifications were improved, especially at Koishikawa-bashi, Sujikai-bashi, and Asakusa-bashi, thus completing the farthest lines of defense for the castle.[6]

Within the *Honmaru* section were included the private mansion of the shogun, and the innermost keep, *Tenshukaku*, in the northwest corner. The latter was built of granite, in five stories, measuring 39 *ken* 1 *shaku* (77.8 yds) above the water level of the moat—a gigantic structure of grandeur. The main *Honmaru* buildings were in three sections, *Omote*, *Nakaoku*, and *Ō-oku* (front, middle, and innermost parts).

In the *Omote* section were the government offices and halls for ceremonial performances, such as the *Tōzamurai* (warriors agency) and *Ōhiroma* (grand hall). Annexed to the latter was *Matsu-no-rōka* (corridor of pine trees) in which there were pictures of pine trees painted by the artist Kano Tan-yu on wooden plates extending 72 *ken* (143 yds).

*Nakaoku* was used by the shogun for the official business of the *bakufu*, and in the *Ō-oku* section were the private accommodations of the shogun and his subordinates, guest rooms, kitchens, and rooms for ladies and their attendants. In a sub-section called *Nishinomaru* were built a retirement residence for the shogun and another for his heir on a terraced annex west of *Nishinomaru*. North of these structures was a shrine built in veneration of deceased shogun on the Hill of Maples (Momiji-yama). Adjacent to, and west of *Nishinomaru* was the Fukiagekuruwa residential area for the mansions of Tokugawa families from the Kii, Owari, and Mito domains, with a large garden area in the rear part.

These sections, along with the *Kitanomaru* of Daikan-chō, made up the central sector of the Edo castle grounds, covering a vast area of 222,182 *tsubo* (181.4 acres). This sector was enough to accommodate over 260 daimyō together with 50,000 standard-bearers if necessary.[7]

South of the *Nishinomaru* section were the houses of high-ranking retainers. Beyond their residences to the east were the homes of the daimyō of the larger domains, and this part of the city was called Daimyō-koji, or "lane of feudal lords." Surrounding all these residences of the daimyō and their retainers were high stone embankments planted with pine and Japanese cedar trees. The long line of embankments started at Kiji-bashi and extended all the way to Asakusa-gomon, passing by Kanda-bashi, Tokiwa-bashi, Kaji-bashi, Tameike, Akasaka-mitsuke, Yotsuya-mitsuke, and Ichigaya-mitsuke. This line of defense and lookout was referred to variously as the "thirty-six watches" (*mitsuke*), the "thirty-six gates," or the "sixty-six gates" of Edo Castle.

As indicated by the above, the castle facilities included a variety of gates for military and social control purposes, each guarded by a contingent of soldiers. The main gate in front of the castle, Ōtemon, was guarded by officers and troops belonging to the *fudai-daimyo* (hereditary vassals of Tokugawa) with over 100,000 *koku* annual revenue. Its guardhouse was equipped with twenty firearms, ten bows, twenty lances, two cannon; two teams of bowmen were always on duty. The gate at Soto-sakurada was manned by troops of the *tozama-daimyō* ("outside," i.e., not hereditary vassals) with 30,000–50,000 *koku* annual revenue. Their equipment included ten firearms, five bows, ten lances, a pair of cannon, with one team of bowmen on constant duty. The Akasaka gate drew on troops of daimyō with 3,000–10,000 *koku* annual revenue; had five firearms, three bows, five lances, a pair of cannon, and one team of bowmen. Men from the regiments of daimyō with only 5,000–10,000 *koku* annual revenue also kept the gate at Asakusa, equipped with five firearms, three bows, ten lances, a pair of cannon and a team of bowmen. The guards were all under orders to maintain the strictest vigilance.[8]

Ieyasu's plans for improving the layout of Edo included determining the divisions of the city to be used by the townspeople, which was done in 1603 when it was made the capital. At that time, though, only Banchō-honchō was established. Later civil engineering projects for opening up new divisions for townsmen were carried out by requiring some seventy daimyō to supply one laborer per one thousand *koku* of their revenue. The Yamate hillside west of the castle was utilized in its natural form, and in lower areas east of the castle on the north shore of Edo Bay some marshes, ponds, and bogs were filled in. River banks were reinforced and canals dug to make large tracts of land usable. In the process the port facilities of Edo were reconstructed, and a drainage system was installed for the city's streets. Bridges were constructed where rivers blocked the flow of traffic, and the city water supply was increased by channeling the water from Inogashira Lake to the west of the city.

The most important project in building up the ecological pattern of Edo was the reclamation work of filling in the shallow shore areas at Hamachō and Shinbashi. The earth needed was acquired by leveling Mount Kanda, which permitted the establishment of 300 new townships in the leveled area. This was accomplished in the first quarter-century of Tokugawa rule, so that these townships were later called "the old towns" (*furumachi*). Townsmen living in these older communities enjoyed certain privileges such as exemption from land taxes, access to official jobs in the towns or in the *bakufu*, and attendance at Noh performances in the castle on special occasions like shogunate succession.

The main street running through this district extended from Aoyama-kaizuka in the west to Asakusa-bashi in the east. There it connected with the Tōkaidō national highway which entered Edo at Shinagawa on the southside, passed between the sea and the castle area through the Shiba, Kyōbashi and central Nihonbashi sections before reaching Asakusa-bashi. Thus, the major national highway of the nation, the Tōkaidō, became also the chief thoroughfare of the capital city. A bridge built at Nihonbashi became at once the center of Edo city and the starting point for all the major highways leading out to all regions of the country, the Tōkaidō, Nakasendō, Kōshū-kaidō, Ōshū-kaidō and Nikkō-kaidō. These roads were repaired in 1604, and provided with distance markers (*ichirizuka*) one *ri* (2.4 mi.) apart. Each marker occupied a space five *ken* square (100 sq. yds.)

While Nihonbashi was the official base point of the highway system, the government set up terminal stations for four of the highways on the city's periphery. They were Shinagawa, Itabashi, Naitōshinjuku, and Senju. Called Edo Yon-shuku (four stations of Edo), they were administered by the commissioner for travel and highway stations, *dōchū-bugyō*. Each station had a gate for checking travelers and cargo, and they were usually crowded with people entering or leaving Edo.

Shinagawa, first station on the Tōkaidō, was operated locally under the town commissioner (*machi-bugyō*) and related offices. There were many suppliers of footmen and horses, plus lodging and trading facilities. As many as 180 inns and shops are reported early in the 18th century, though this is said to have dropped to half that number in the middle of the same century. There were ninety-three inns and shops in the Tenpō era (1830–43). Around 1772 the Shinagawa inns are said to have employed about 500 *meshimori* (maidservants, often prostitutes), indication of considerable traffic and prosperity.[9]

Originally, the terminal for the Kōshū-kaidō was not Naitōshinjuku, but Takaidojuku farther out. The latter was found to be too far from the center of Edo, so a more convenient site for the terminal was chosen in 1698.[10] This station began with inns employing girls but was closed in 1718 for lack of travelers. It was reopened in 1772. By 1796 there were three *honjin* (official inns for daimyō and their retainers), one *wakihonjin* (semi-official inn), and thirty-eight other inns. The station seems to have thrived, for in 1806 there were sixty-two *chaya* (teahouses).[11]

Itabashijuku on the Nakasendō possessed similar inns and suppliers of footmen and horses. As in other station sites, the town took shape along the course of the highway. Increasingly daimyō chose this alternate route between Kyōto and Edo for their biennial trips for required residence in Edo, in order to avoid excessive inconvenience in using the main Tōkaidō route. Indeed, their numbers rose year after year so that the *bakufu* instituted restrictions on use of the Nakasendō by daimyō.[12]

Senju was officially designated as the terminal station for the Nikkō-kaidō in 1594, when a bridge named Senju-ōhashi was built over the Arakawa river.[13] Shimojuku town south of the bridge was the center for travel facilities such as inns, shops, and horse and footmen agencies. It was a thriving town, 1,256 *ken* (1.3 mi.) in length, not much different from the central sections of Edo.[14]

In addition to supervising these many land transportation facilities, the *bakufu* also developed marine transportation as part of its overall integrative activity. Ieyasu designated the five ports of Shinagawa-guchi, Tayasu-guchi, Kanda-guchi, Asakusa-guchi, and Funa-guchi to serve Edo's needs, and these ports were usually congested with the many boats drawn by the capital city's importance.

To these were added three inner ports on the banks of the Nihonbashi, Kyōbashi, and Fukajikawa rivers, transferred there when Hibiya Inlet was filled for land reclamation. Of these three, the docks on the Nihonbashi river were the busiest, unloading goods shipped from the local provinces. Warehouses owned by wholesalers crowded its banks. The inner ports, though, were for use by the townsmen, separating them from ports built farther out on the bay and on the banks of Sumidagawa river for use by the feudal lords and warriors. Great warehouses, *kura-yashiki*, were built at the outer ports for storing the large amounts of goods shipped by the lords and their warriors for use when in Edo.

Whereas Tokiwa-bashi had been the commercial center of Edo in former days, the center shifted to Nihonbashi in accordance with changes occurring in land and sea traffic patterns. The Nihonbashi district lay directly in front of the castle, between it and the bay, so it was most natural that it should become the central locus of commerce. Thus, politics and commerce were welded together into a single integrative nucleus, from which and to which all roads led in a radial pattern. It was written in *Keichō Kenmonshu* (Collection of Observations on the Keichō Era), "When one surveys Nihonbashi he sees throngs of people coming and going, day and night, as if it were one vast market, never stopping to greet others on the bridge, whether they know each other or not. . . ."[15]

The key factor in the city's prosperity was undoubtedly the enforcement of the *sankin-kōtai* system requiring alternate years' residence of the daimyō, already referred to earlier. This kept the families of the lords in Edo permanently, and brought great numbers of retainers and warriors regularly to the capital. Each domain had its own splendid mansions and villas, called *kami-yashiki*, *naka-yashiki*, and *shimo-yashiki*. *Kami-yashiki* was the main mansion and office of a domain; *naka-yashiki* was the lord's residence. *Shimo-yashiki* referred to lesser residences for occasional use. Besides high-ranking officials there were over 50,000 standard-bearers and retainers in Edo, the total number of warriors reaching 500,000 or more. When the expanding numbers of townsmen and personnel attached to shrines and temples are taken into consideration, it becomes quite evident why the government was pressed to work out a thoroughgoing policy for the apportionment and utilization of the many sections of the city.

Primary attention went always to the city's defense. To fulfill this function troops directly under Tokugawa command were based close by the city's main gates as follows:

—Troops positioned in Surugadai, Hongo, and Shitaya in a defense line covering Kandabashi, Sujikaemon, Ueno, and Hongo gates;

—Placements in Banchō and Ushigome covering Tayasumon and Ushigomemon gates;

—Placements in Banchō, Yotsuya, and Naitoshinjuku to guard Hanzōmon and Yotsuya gates on the Kōshūkaidō highway;

—Placements in Aoyama and Azabu to cover the Akasakamon and Shibuya gates along the Oyama-kaidō route.

Lower areas of the city exclusive of reclaimed land, such as Kasumigaseki Daimyō-koji, were occupied mainly by residences of the daimyō. After the city expanded and streets were extended many of the daimyō built their residential mansions and villas (*naka-yashiki* and *shimo-yashiki*) farther out in suburban areas. Feudal lords in hereditary or blood relations to the Tokugawa family took over the central districts reserved for high-ranking officials. The *kami-yashiki* of the Mito domain was constructed at Koishikawa (present-day Korakuen), that of the Owari domain between Ichigayamon and Yotsuyamon (present-day Office of Defense), and the Kii domain's official building was between Yotsuyamon and Jikimon (Akasaka Detached Palace grounds).[16]

As each feudal lord shipped needed goods to Edo from his own domain or from the Kansai region, one of the domain's offical *yashiki* structures was usually located near one of the ports set aside for use of the warrior class. This is one reason why the *kami-*, *naka-*, and *shimo-yashiki* were not located in the same place. The presence of these structures at the warriors' ports greatly emphasized their separation from ports designated for the townsmen, clearly manifesting the system of controls through status differentiation.

The rising prominence of Edo was expressed also in the building of many new shrines and temples, about forty large ones being completed in the period from 1590 to 1626 in the Kōji-machi district alone. From this one can imagine how many more must have been erected throughout all Edo. It should be remembered that small towns generally formed around the temple gates. This city's central areas being occupied by ranking warriors, the shrines and temples were located on the outer circles of the city as a rule. Most of them were concentrated in Sujikaemon (present-day Kanda Shōheibashi) and Yagura. After the city's streets were expanded to link the many towns together, the temples and shrines tended to spring up along these streets.[17]

Pictures and maps published after the Kan-ei era (1624–44) witness to the vast areas claimed for warriors' residences. Since each daimyō maintained three or four *yashiki*, the total number ran to more than 600. There were also several thousands of houses for official retainers to the shogun. Records for the end of the Edo period show that 11,692,747 *tsubo* (9,548.8 acres) were occupied by the military class, and another 2,661,747 *tsubo* (2,173.6 acres) by temples and shrines. This left only 2,696,000 *tsubo* (2,201.5 acres), or 20% of the total area of the city, for the townsmen.[18] It may be assumed that the ratio was much larger for the warriors and, hence, much smaller for the townspeople in the earlier stages of rule by the Tokugawa *bakufu*.

By far the most important part of Edo was the central Nihonbashi district and the adjacent districts of Kyōbashi, Kanda, and part of Asakusa. From this central sector Edo's many towns were strung out along the major highways, generally as far as the terminal stations. The Kantō region was not equipped to supply the vastly expanded demands of the rapidly growing population of Edo. Great quantities of materials and finished products had to be imported from the economically more advanced Kansai area. Nihonbashi became the funnel for the large shipments from the Kansai, fixing it clearly as the center of commercial activity in Edo. The success of the Tokugawa *bakufu* in establishing Edo as the national capital prompted further population growth, increasing in turn the quantities of goods shipped from the Kansai region.

An Ōsaka agency for handling shipments of goods to Edo, named *Edo Kaisendonya*, was opened in 1624, and a shipping line between the two cities, named *Higaki Kaisen*, was begun in 1627. A shipping service specializing in transporting rice wine (*sake*) was opened in 1661. The quantity of goods exported to Edo by various provinces through the port of Ōsaka in 1716 was as follows:

| | |
|---|---|
| *Sake* | 180,000–200,000 kegs |
| Soybean oil | 110,000–160,000 kegs |
| Oil | 50,000– 80,000 kegs |
| Cotton cloth | 810,000–2,000,000 *tan** |
| Cotton fiber (ginned) | 70,000–140,000 bundles |
| Rice | indefinite |

(**Tan*=1.14 yd×1.1 ft.)

Even taking into account uncertainty regarding the above quantitative values, these figures still indicate the large bulk of shipments made from Ōsaka to Edo in those days.[19]

The west-bound route from Ōsaka was also developed further, as were routes on the Japan Sea side of the main island of Honshū. Although Edo continued growing in position and size as the nation's capital, Ōsaka became the national center for the concentration and redistribution of commodities for the whole country. Goods produced in the northwestern (Ōu) region were formerly shipped to the port towns of Tsuruga and Kohama just north of Lake Biwa, where they could be transshipped to Ōsaka by way of Kyōto. With improved shipping services along the west coast, these goods could now be sent directly by ship to Hyōgo or Ōsaka by way of Shimonoseki on the southwest tip of Honshū, avoiding added costs and labor in unloading and transshipment through Kohama and Tsuruga.[20]

Until late in the 17th century shipments from the northeastern (Dewa) region had usually been unloaded at the port of Naka (near Mito) and transferred to smaller boats that plied a long inland waterway to Chōshi at the mouth of the Tonegawa river. Up this river an inland canal provided access to the Edogawa and Arakawa rivers that entered Tokyo Bay just east of Edo. Again, improved shipping permitted sailing straight down the coast, past Naka port and around the Bōsō (Chiba) peninsula into Edo Bay. Even so, the waterways from Chōshi to Edo continued to be used.

From the middle of the 18th century on industry in the Kantō region developed remarkably. This can be seen from the number of boats arriving at Edo's ports from various Kantō districts and the large volume of commodities delivered, as listed below:

*No. of boats* (excluding those belonging to the warrior class): 7,424.

| *Goods shipped:* | *Quantities:* |
|---|---|
| Rice | 861,893 bales |
| Soybean paste | 2,828 kegs |
| *Sake* | 795,856 kegs |

| | |
|---|---|
| Firewood | 8,209,687 bundles |
| Charcoal | 89,790 bales |
| Salt | 1,670,880 bales |
| Vegetable oil | 90,811 kegs |
| Fish oil | 50,501 kegs |
| Soybean oil | 132,829 kegs |
| Cotton | 36,135 bales |
| (100 *tan* per bale; 1 *tan*=1.14 yds×1.1 ft.) | |
| Coins | 19,407 packages |

Shipping agents for receiving and forwarding these commodities numbered 163. Needless to say, a considerable quantity of products was hauled on horseback and by ox carts from surrounding areas to add to the overall concentration of goods for consumption in Edo.[21]

Cargo owners generally suffered losses en route through secret deals made by shipping agents with the ship captains. One step toward eliminating such losses was taken in 1694 by forming a cooperative of wholesalers dealing in ten major items, called Edo-jukkumi-tonya-nakama. This union of Edo and Ōsaka wholesalers served not only to protect cargoes during shipment, but to establish a monopoly over the shipping services (*kaisen*) between the two cities.

In an effort to extend similar controls to all commercial activities the *bakufu*, in 1721, ordered all merchants and craftsmen to form and adhere to cooperatives within their respective enterprises. The merchants took advantage of the straitened financial conditions of the *bakufu* whereby, in making required contributions (*myōgakin*) to the government, they bought "protection" sufficient to establish monopolies over the production and distribution of the commodities handled by their cooperatives (*nakama*). Some of them became, in contrast to their formally low status, very wealthy men.

A directory of wholesalers in Edo, compiled in 1813, lists 1,931 representatives belonging to sixty-two cooperatives, indicating the effectiveness of the *bakufu* order. Some 1,581 wholesalers, or more than 80% of the total, were located in the Nihonbashi district, evidence of the supremacy of this central area over all commercial activity in Edo.[22]

The fact that bulky cargo was more easily transported by boat did not, of course, eliminate the need for land transportation. The integrative activity of the central Nihonbashi area especially depended upon the relay system of the highway stations on the five major and other lesser highways. At the beginning of his rule in Edo Ieyasu had appointed several citizens in the Takarada and Chiyoda townships to posts responsible for providing horses and footmen, primarily for official use. The posts were called *tenma-yaku*, carried rice stipends called *kyūmai*, and went first to such men as Magome Kageyu, Takano Shinzaemon, and Komiya Zen-emon. Their descendants became village heads, *nanushi*, of Ōdenma-chō and Kodenma-chō of Nihonbashi, and Minami-tenma-chō of Kyōbashi. These posts became hereditary in the families of the *tenma-yaku*.

There were three different grades of livery and porter service, *shuin-tenma*, *chin-tenma*, and *daba*. Residents of the Ōdenma-cho and Minami-tenma-chō were alternately responsible for half a day to provide the *shuin* and *chin-tenma* services. The term *shuin-tenma* originated from the official vermilion seal (*shuin*) used on the orders calling for this grade of service for official use, for which no direct compensation was made (apart from the rice stipend). Two town elders (*machi-doshiyori*), Naraya Ichiemon and Taruya Sanshiro, were responsible for issuing the necessary papers, *tegata*, stamped with the red seal, for obtaining horses and porters at the various relay stations.[23] For *chin-tenma*, services, wages and expenses were provided at a fixed rate; this grade was also for official use. *Daba* was the lowest grade, offered only after official needs were met. Fees were worked out by the parties concerned, as this grade of service was for use by merchants and other commoners.

Inns in Edo were concentrated in the two townships of Bakuro-chō and Kodenma-chō. These thriving communities had two types of inns, *kuji-yado* and *ryonin-yado*. The former was for those coming to Edo in connection with legal affairs. In Bakuro-chō there was an office of the *bakufu* judicial system for handling provincial suits, which accounts for the concentration of such inns there.

In time the inns for normal travelers, the *ryonin-yado*, formed three cooperatives known as (1) Bakurochō Kodenmachō-gumi Ryonin-yado, (2) Sanjukkumi Hyakusho-yado, and (3) Hachijūniken Hyakusho-yado. The first was made up of the older inns in the Bakuro-chō and Kodenma-chō townships, existing since Ieyasu's time. They dispatched guides to the four terminal stations of Edo to solicit business among those making pilgrimages (*dōshamonomairi*), sight-seers, and those on legal business.

The other two cooperatives were unions of thirty and eighty-two inns respectively, that were set aside for use by farmers visiting Edo. They were not permitted to solicit business through guides sent to the highway terminals. The Sanjukkumi Hyakusho-yado (32 inns) were in Bakuro-chō, and were reserved strictly for farmers coming with proper introductions from provincial authorities. The Hachijūniken Hyakusho-yado were distributed in various parts of Edo, and they were for farmers on official business or involved in judicial affairs. Other facilities such as teahouses and noodle shops were not allowed by government regulations to entertain overnight guests.[24]

Express messenger services (*hikyaku*) were of three kinds: *tsugi-bikyaku* maintained by the *bakufu*, *daimyō-bikyaku* performed solely for the feudal lords, and *jō-bikyaku* for use by the townsmen. The *tsugi-bikyaku*, founded in 1590, provided for the transport of official communications and cargoes by porters and horses of the relay stations. Usually it took three and a half days from Edo to Kyōto, and four days to Ōsaka, although emergency service could be had in sixty hours. The special messenger services for daimyō ran only between Edo and the feudal centers. This express service vanished gradually after the *jō-bikyaku* system for townsmen was developed.

The *jō-bikyaku* express service was founded in 1615 by merchants in

Ōsaka. Prior to its formation warriors on duty at Ōsaka Castle had men on thrice monthly relays between Edo and Ōsaka. Merchants pressed into financial support of the Ōsaka Castle guard gradually assumed the express services as their own enterprise. In 1663 those operating express services in the three cities of Edo, Kyōto, and Ōsaka acquired independence from the warriors in the operation of their business. In the 1780's (Tenmei era) there were six groups of express messengers in Edo, named Nihonbashi-gumi, Kyōbashi-gumi, Shibaguchi-gumi, Honshiba-gumi, Akasaka-gumi, and Kanda-gumi. 114 operators of express businesses joined these groups. In time similar services were founded all over the country, completing this form of the communications network.[25]

Edo itself enjoyed a special inner-city service, which originated from minor messengers who operated initially within the limits of specific towns. The range of their operations was later extended to cover the entire territory of the city of Edo.

The prosperous commercial and traffic center of Nihonbashi has already been mentioned. The Jesuit priest, João Rodriguez, who visited the city of Edo in the Keichō era (1596–1615), described the commercial and industrial activities of this area as follows:

"All houses face the streets, and have gates. Residential areas are divided according to occupation and status. For instance, on one street there are carpenters' families and no others. With groups of professional workers occupying specific sections, then, one can find makers of footwear and iron tools, tailors and merchants. In other words, there are all sorts of people plying as many trades as one can imagine, including some scarcely found in Europe. Merchants also adhere to the rule of sectional separation. Silver, gold, and silk merchants all have their particular sections. Nowhere does one find shops handling different goods all mixed together. Here birds, there animals, and fish at one price in one place, and at lower prices in yet another. Vegetables and fruits each have their appointed places. We saw several streets full of inns with no shops among them [Hatago-chō], and there is also a township that specializes in horse trading. Prostitution houses are always grouped on the outskirts of town."[26]

Further details on the sub-divisions of Edo are given in a guide book to the city of that period entitled *Zoku Edo Ōrai:*

"Edo is a thriving city. The city streets are crowded with the various shops of both merchants and craftsmen in more than 1,700 townships. Throughout the city there are many centers of commercial activity, such as Ryōgae-chō handling gold and silver; Suruga-chō and Honchō dealing in dry goods and medicines; Muro-machi's nunneries and shops for lacquerware, tools, nails, and metal products; Nihonbashi-dōri for books; lumber and mortar in Nishigashi; fish and fowl in Odawara-chō and Anjin-chō; thread in Motobune-chō; fresh fish in Shinbashi, Dobashi, and the Kishi-dōri section of Motofune-chō; salted fish in Kobune-chō and Yokkaichi-machi; Ise-machi, Kamakuragashi, Shio-chō, and Hatago-chō for rice; Horie-chō for other grains, fish and vegetable oils, fans, and seasonal pastries. In Koku-chō there are rooms for rent by the hour, and leather stockings; dolls are sold in Jukkendana; cotton, paper, and tea in Ōdenma-chō; pictures and sundries in Tsūyu-chō; salt and soybean oil in Shiogashi; salted fish and dried vegetables in Setomono-chō; dyes in Setomono-chō Uragashi; floor mat covering in Horidome; decorated mats in Ukiyo-kōji. . . ." and so on.[27]

From this description the occupational divisions and concentration in set areas is quite clear. It is also evident that the character of commercial activity in the Edo era differed sharply from that of the preceding, as well as the present age.

We have already seen that the center for commerce originally in Honchō-dōri had shifted to Nihonbashi-dōri, where the major merchants operating shipping agencies, storage warehouses, the dry goods trade, and money-changing all gathered. Being near the harbor, there was a fish market as well as many forwarding agents. Similarly, craftsmen concentrated in the Kanda area, and other distinct occupational communities developed throughout the city.

While the vocational groups came from many parts of the country, most of them came from Ise, Ōmi, and Ōsaka. A common saying was that Edo was "too full of Iseya (shops operated by men from Ise), Inari (shrines), and dog dung." Many powerful Ōsaka merchants had branches in Edo. Many Edo-based merchants were supplied with operating capital by Kansai merchants. Large financiers such as the Kaiho and Nakagawa houses, along with the Mitsui house with its home in Kyōto and branches in Ōsaka, belonged to a special "Group of Ten" (Jūnin-gumi) which served the Tokugawa *bakufu* in exchange transactions. This group opened offices in the Suruga-chō area of Edo in the Genroku era (1688–1704).[28]

Dry goods dealers concentrated in Honchō (in the 1-chome and 2-chome; i.e., "blocks"). The largest among them was Echigoya, founded by an enterprising man from the province of that name. Beginning first in Kyōto, he opened a shop in Edo in 1673. During the 1680's he enjoyed remarkable success, limiting all sales to cash transactions. Eventually his Edo, Ise, Kyōto, and Ōsaka stores employed 1,000 persons, and daily sales were voluminous. Indeed, competitors suffered sharp decline due to the success of the Echigoya. Cash sales enabled this firm to lower commodity prices, since the disadvantages of slowly revolving capital funds involved in credit sales were avoided. Moreover, it opened up wider markets to eliminate the need for knowing one's buyers well enough to take the risks required in credit transactions. Trading was converted to pure commerce from more traditional patterns depending heavily on carefully cultivated human relations. The freer cash methods were far superor to the sluggish traditional ways so far as sales success was concerned.

A guide book to Edo (*Edo Zukan Kōmoku*) published in 1689 listed four dry goods dealers, Echigoya, Toyama Saemon, Yashiro Tarojiro, and Izukura, in the Honchō 1-chome and 2-chome area. The Echigoya establishment moved to Suruga-chō in 1683, opening also a money exchange office. Another famous dry goods store named Shirokiya was founded by the Kimura family of Nagahama in Ōmi in the year 1662.

A listing of shops of other well-known citizens of Edo might include:

Iwashiya—handling medicines; moved from Sakai in Senshu in the Tenshō era (1573–91);
Kiya—lacquerware, from Ōsaka;
Kuroeya—lacquerware, from Kishū;
Yamamotoya, Yamagataya, Ninben, and Yamamoto—sea foods;
Hanaya and Shimomura—stationery and sundries, from Kyōto;
Mikagedo—stationery and sundries, from Nara;
Kikyōya, Beniya, Shioze, and Eitaro—cakes and candies.[29]

Since olden times there had been a fish market in Shibaura, though it was small in scale. Fishermen connected with this market supplied high-quality products to the shogun, as well as to the local market. After Edo's consumer demands rose sharply a large market specializing in fish grew up in Nihonbashi. This market dates back to Edo's earliest days. It was opened by Magoemon, a village head from Settsu who came to Edo when Ieyasu made it his capital. The fishermen who accompanied him were more skillful than the local Edo fishermen. Highly esteemed by the *bakufu*, they were appointed the official suppliers of the government. A grandson named Kyūemon opened shops in Odawara-chō for selling the surplus left after supplying the *bakufu*.

As operations and techniques in fishery improved, the quantity of fish going into the open markets increased. The number of merchants handling fish increased due to population growth and elevation of the standard of living. A union of fish dealers was organized in 1628, grouped in four areas. These were Motofune-chō, Motofune-chō Yokodana, Anjin-chō, and Odawara-chō. In the early half of the 19th century the fish market prospered remarkably, drawing supplies from many areas, such as Musashi, Sagami, Ise, Tōtōmi, Awa, Shimōsa, and Jōban. Fish products were also brought into Edo from as far south as Settsu and Hizen, and from the northern regions of Hokuriku, Ōu, and Hokkaidō.

The *bakufu* officials depending upon the official fish supply included many different ranks and positions, and the official supply was rather limited in both quantity and variety, though delivered at advantageously low rates. The *bakufu* was forced to make purchases also at the markets, a purchasing office (*Kaisho*) being set up in Odawara-chō. Even so, prices for fish sold directly to the *bakufu* were ridiculously low compared to the going prices for townsmen, whose increased numbers and improved living standards drove prices up inexorably. Just the same, fish dealers could by no means reject *bakufu* demands, as they were rewarded with government protection for their markets. Such protection sometimes took the form of land or money grants to the union of fish dealers.[30]

Less concern for spoiling than in the case of fish made it possible to import wheat to satisfy Edo's needs from all provinces of the country. Vegetables, on the other hand, had to be obtained from the surrounding areas, for which Edo's plain was a distinct advantage. Certain districts became famous for quality production, such as Nerima, Senju and Ogu for radishes, Takinogawa and Sunakawa for carrots and burdock, Senju for stone-leeks, and Ebara for bamboo shoots.

In the early days farmers sold their agricultural products to the city's merchants on a consignment basis. In the early part of the 18th century a wholesale system was established. Vegetable markets for supplying the *bakufu* were set up in various parts of the city, notably three large ones in Kanda, Komagome, and Senju. In addition to these three, markets emerged also in Kyōbashi, Honjo, Yokkaichi and Hamachō to meet increased demands. A corps of peddlers made deliveries to consumer households.

These were the many integrative functions of the central sector of the city of Edo, indicating its ecological structure. Much of Edo was destroyed by a large fire in the Meireki era (1655–8), after which the residential areas of the warriors become more widely distributed throughout the city. Following their patrons to new locations, most of the townsmen, both merchants and craftsmen, became more widely dispersed. This gave rise to new communities of townsmen graced with the many agencies necessary to their daily lives—shops for *sake*, bean curds, and other foodstuffs, public bathhouses, barbers, doctors, private and temple schools for children, and places for entertainment (song and dance).

Turning to description of specific districts other than the central area, Asakusa was an especially thriving section in the Edo era. In pre-*bakufu* times it had existed as a town centered on the Sensōji temple, said to have been formed in the era of the Empress Suiko (593–628), and reconstructed later by Ōta Dōkan. In the Middle Ages there were carpenters and blacksmiths in the town who specialized in temple construction and repairs. Ieyasu lent his own patronage to the temple, and the town grew in response to the expansion of Edo. Following the Meireki conflagration (1657) the rebuilding of Edo on a large scale brought central city streets into connection with streets of the Asakusa district. In less than a century there were over fifty townships in the Asakusa area, and as many as 235 by the end of the Tokugawa period.

Inclusion in the street network of Edo brought a great increase in worshippers to the Sensōji temple, stimulating in turn commercial activity around the temple. Local gamblers were granted operational privileges within the temple precincts in reward for services offered in cleaning and repairing the temple.

Warehouses for storing warriors' rice stipends were erected along the road connecting the towns of Umayabashi and Sugabashi in this district. The *hatamoto* subordinates of the Tokugawa *bakufu* were official receivers for these warehouses early in the Edo period, although later operators of wayside teahouses (*koshikake-jaya*) were authorized to handle the receiving accounts. These men became quite wealthy, especially through money-lending operations with daimyō. It is said that there were over one hundred such agents.

Asakusa acquired also the character of being an important amusement center. After the big fire of Meireki a group of authorized prostitutes moved from Yoshichō in Nihonbashi to Asakusa's Shin-yoshiwara section. Also, three theaters were built in the Saruwaka section following an edict of the Tenpō Reform (see Chap. VII) that *kabuki* theaters were to be removed from the central part of Edo. Smaller show-booths, archery ranges, and teahouses serving *sake* were added, making Asakusa the sightseeing paradise for visitors to Edo. Here in one single district were found both the *Kanzeon* (Goddess of Mercy) statue of Sensōji temple—the most common object of worship in all Japan—and the thriving red-light district of Shin-yoshiwara. Such was the chief entertainment center of the long and peaceful Edo era.[31]

The network of Edo's city streets continued to expand in accordance with sovereignty over the entire land. The ecological structure was improved in accordance with progress in living patterns and with perfecting of the system of feudal controls. Still, as alluded to above, that structure suffered great damage in the fire occurring in the third year of the Meireki era (1657). Edo had gone a long time without rain, when a fire broke out in Honmyōji temple in Hongo Maruyama on the eighteenth day of the third month of that year. Caught up in a strong wind, the fire spread swiftly through the streets of the city. On the following day another fire erupted in Dentsūin temple in the Koishikawa section, which continued burning for two days till it reached the seashore.

The impressive structures of Edo castle were burned to the ground. All of the *Honmaru*, including the keep, the secondary *Ninomaru*, and the tertiary *Sannomaru* constructions were lost. Over 500 mansions of daimyō with revenue of 10,000 *koku* were destroyed. More than 770 residences of the *hatamoto* (standard-bearers) class were lost, plus over 350 temple and shrine structures. Over 400 of the towns were damaged, leaving more than 50,000 dead. The total length of burned out streets measured 22 *ri* 8 *chō* (54.3 mi.). The total loss was almost more than the city could sustain. Nevertheless, the *bakufu* began soon after the inferno to reconstruct the city, this time on a larger scale designed to prevent a similar recurrence. Efforts were directed also toward controlled expansion for the sake of a better city.

The *bakufu* began by commanding Hōjō Awanokami, an inspector-general, and Watanabe Han-emon, head of a detachment of guards, to draw up a map of the Edo territory. City divisions were fixed by this map. City road widths were standardized to facilitate repair and reconstruction work.

Old roads of only 6 *ken* (12 yds.) width were widened. The main street of Nihonbashi was widened to 10 *ken* (20 yds.) according to provincial measurements (*inaka-ken*), while the main street in the Honchō section was extended to 7 *ken* according to more generous Kyōto standards (1 *ken* equals 6 *shaku* 5 *sun*, as against 5 *shaku* 8 *sun* in the *inaka-ken*). Lanes of only 1 *ken* were called *ōroji*, though narrower paths were common in every section of the city.

Measures for preventing the spread of fires from one section to another included the digging of moats in the Shiba and Asakusa areas, and the width of the Kandagawa river was enlarged. Earthen walls were raised in Kyōbashi, Teppōzu, Akasaka, Koishikawa, and Kohinata. Open spaces to stop spreading fires were provided in two locations and eighteen wide streets (*hirokōji*) were interlaced throughout the city.[32]

Mansions of the three powerful lords of the Tokugawa domains of Owari, Kii, and Mito, which had been located within the castle grounds, were transferred to the outside. The *bakufu* granted these lords *shimo-yashiki* (villas) for use in case another large fire did occur. The keep (*tenshukaku*) of the castle was not rebuilt as there was little need of it in peaceful times, although another reason was that the high windows of the keep attracted leaping flames, from whence they advanced downward into the surrounding castle structures. Many temple and shrine buildings formerly in Hatchōbori, Yanokura, Bakuro-chō, and Kanda were removed to points farther from the center of the city, such as Fukagawa, Asakusa, Komagome, and Meguro. Religious structures tended to be too big and unsuited to successful fire prevention, or to control of a fire once started.

Following expansion of the city's streets through reconstruction, bridges were laid across the Sumidagawa river; e.g., Ryōgoku-bashi was completed in 1660, Shin-ōhashi in 1693, Eitai-bashi in 1696, and Azuma-bashi in 1774. Completion of these bridges opened up the Honjo-Fukagawa area for the daimyō and *hatamoto* who were given residential lots there. Merchants and craftsmen followed soon after, building up new townships east of Ōkawa ("Big river," i.e., Sumidagawa river), under supervision of Edo's town commissioner. The urban territory of Edo was fixed for the most part in this period, measuring five or six times larger than the previous scope of the city.

According to the book *Edo Suzume* (Sparrows of Edo), the following structures were found in Edo in 1677, just 20 years after the big fire:

| | |
|---|---|
| Mansions of daimyō (major lords) | — over 2,870 |
| Residences of *shōmyō* (minor lords) | — over 2,870 |
| Temples | — 850 |
| Shrines | — 120 |
| Bridges | — 270 |
| Total length of city streets | — over 80 *ri* (195 mi.)[33] |

Several fires occurred in 1682, one of them beginning on the twenty-eighth day of the twelfth month and continuing for six days. Lands in the Honjo section that were damaged by floods in 1668 were re-opened for residences of the *hatamoto*, 240 of which were transferred there. In 1677, without pretext of fire or flood, some of the warriors' residences were removed from the central to more remote parts of the city. Gradually the *bakufu* acquired open spaces here and there for fire prevention purposes. These lands around the castle, located variously near Kōji-machi, Kiji-bashi, Hitotsu-bashi and Kanda-bashi, covered 240,000*tsu bo* (196 acres), and the ground level in places was elevated. Newly opened tracts to which warriors' households were removed included Azabu, Akasaka, Aoyama, Sendagaya, Ōkubo, Yotsuya, Koishikawa, Komagome, Hongō, Asakusa, and Honjo.

In 1713 the smaller towns on the outskirts of Edo were absorbed into the city and the whole region was put under the town commissioner. Some 359 towns were amalgamated with the older city, including such better known towns as Fukagawa, Honjo, Asakusa, Koishikawa, Ushigome, Ichigaya, Yotsuya, Akasaka, and Azabu. The total township count swelled to 933 from the old number of 674. The consolidated townships were referred to as *machinamiji*, a term indicating that their place in the city corresponded to that of the original, older towns, *furumachi*.

Fires continued to break out in Edo from time to time, occasions that were utilized to expand the city in every direction. In the book *Gofunai Bikō* (Edo Directory) there appears some data on the structural scope of the city:

| | |
|---|---|
| Number of towns in the city in 1747 (including temple towns) | — about 1,678 |
| Same, for 1781—— | — over 1,650 |
| Those controlled by town commissioner | — over 1,200 |
| Those under temple controls | — over 400 |
| Primary residences of daimyō | — 265 |
| Secondary residences of daimyō | — 466 |
| Shrines | — about 2,000 |
| Temples | — about 1,000 |

Development of tracts of land for residential occupation by warriors and townsmen was continued, the number of towns finally reaching over 2,000.[34] The territory covered was about the same as the urban area of the city of Tōkyō, with fifteen wards, at the beginning of the Meiji era. Along the streets joining residential areas and temple towns, the townsmen built their houses, thus filling the open spaces.

Population pressures forced increasingly dense construction of dwellings. Four fire-fighting companies (*machi-hikeshi*) were formed in 1658, in Iida-machi, Sanaizaka of Ushigome, Ochanomizu, and Kōji-machi, all under direct administration of the *bakufu*. Auxiliary fire companies were ordered to be built by the daimyō to control spreading along vital routes (*hōkō-hikeshi*) or into otherwise unprotected places (*tokorodokoro-hikeshi*). The former were placed strategically in the northern, southern, eastern, and western parts of the city, while the latter were founded for specific protection of important government facilities.

The daimyō were ordered, further, to organize neighborhood fire-fighting teams (*kinjo-hikeshi*) that were responsible for outbreaks of fires within 3 *chō* (360 yds.) of each domain office. The *hatamoto* were also required to organize their own fire-fighting teams (*kumiai-hikeshi*).

Among common citizens there were 48 minor groups (*kogumi*) for fire control. One such group was organized, for instance, by some twenty towns in an area west of the Sumidagawa river. The *kogumi* was usually subdivided into small groups (*kumi*).

Fire-fighting corps for local townships (*machi-hikeshi*) were supervised by the town councils (*machi-gyōji*) or heads (*nanushi*), and other town officials performed various functions when fires actually occurred. Only construction laborers were really of much use in actual fire-fighting, so it was these men who formed the fire control groups.[35]

As in fire prevention, urban expansion placed greater demands upon transportation facilities for both goods and people. Bulky and heavy cargoes were transported by boat, and on land horses, oxen, and palanquins born by porters were used. Townsmen and porters were not themselves permitted to ride horses in the city, only the warriors. Others had to walk. Those coming to Edo to work as porters and pack-horse attendants were required to register at government offices, according to a 1660 regulation.

Broad-bottomed palanquins of top quality were called *norimono* (simply "conveyance"), and were restricted to the use of court nobles, senior priests, feudal lords, and ladies of the shogun's household. More common palanquins were for use by the leading retainers of the daimyō and others of equivalent rank over fifty years of age, according to regulations issued in 1661. The *bakufu* in 1665 issued public prohibitions on use of palanquins by ordinary citizens in the urban and suburban areas of Edo. Later, in 1700, the operators of palanquins were authorized by the *bakufu* to make 300 of these conveyances available for limited use by sick persons, women, and infants. This privilege was voided afterward because it was abused by wealthy merchants. In 1726, however, all restrictions on palanquins were lifted, and they became the most important means of personal transportation in the city.

In addition to pack-horses for land transport of cargo, there were also ox-drawn carts, called *jiguruma*. Another type of cart, invented after the big Meireki fire and called *daihachi-guruma* (lit., "No. 8 Cart"), was designed for pulling by a man. Such carts were officially registered for monthly taxation purposes. Horse-drawn carts were used for the first time in 1866, though they were for carrying baggage and not people.[36]

Thus far we have indicated only roughly how the living patterns of the people fitted into the ecological framework of the city. The citizens were quite mutually dependent upon each other throughout the total Edo territory, although Edo's boundaries were not clearly defined. That portion of the territory under the control of the town commissioner (*machi-bugyō*) was about the same as the municipal area of the City of Tōkyō (*Tōkyō-shi*) in the seventh year of the Shōwa era (1932), being the fifteen wards prior to expansion.

The operational areas of temples in authorized solicitation of donations for construction serves somewhat to indicate the former scope of Edo. Fund collections were authorized in the following areas: westward as far as Yoyogi-mura, Tsunohazu-mura, Totsuka-mura, and Kami-ochiai-mura; to the south as far as Kamiosaki-mura and Minami-

Shinagawa; northward it was Senju, Ogu-mura, Takinogawa-mura, and Itabashi-mura; and, finally, the eastern limits were Sunamura, Kameido, Kinoshita-gawa, and Suda-mura.

Those who were punished by expulsion from the city had to remain outside the line described by the terminal stations, i.e., the Yonjuku, Motojuku, and Fukagawa. Another clue to city size comes from public notices put up in Shibaguchi concerning any dead found in the streets, lost children, or those killed or drowned. These casualty lists utilized the following as city limits:

| | |
|---|---|
| East: | Kinoshita-gawa, Nakagawa-dori, and Hachiro-emon Shinden; |
| West: | Yoyogi-mura, Kamiochiai-mura, and Itabashi; |
| South: | Shinagawa and Nagamine-rokkenjaya; |
| North: | Shimoitabashi, the Ōji river, and the Ogu river. |

The warriors directly under the Tokugawa house, i.e., the *hatamoto* and *gokenin*, were obliged to report to the offices of the *bakufu* whenever they planned to travel more than four *ri* (9.8 mi.) beyond the outer limits of the castle grounds (hence, beyond Tokiwa-bashi, Hanzō-mon, Soto-sakurada-mon and Kanda).

Because of the confusion arising from these conflicting definitions of *funai* (i.e., "within Edo"), the top administrative council of elders (*rōjū*) under the shogun commanded the city inspectors (*metsuke*) to clarify the city limits with a red line on the official map. The decision defined an area roughly equivalent to the fund-collection areas authorized by the Commissioner of Temples and Shrines (*jisha-bugyō*) and to that indicated by the public casualty notices at Shibaguchi. The area thus recognized was more extensive than the territory administered by the Town Commissioner. In general, it covered the following wards of present-day Tokyo: Chiyoda-ku, Chuō-ku, Minato-ku, Shinjuku-ku, Bunkyō-ku, Taitō-ku, Sumida-ku, Kōto-ku, part of Shinagawa-ku, Shibuya-ku, Toshima-ku, parts of Kita-ku and Itabashi-ku, and Arakawa-ku. The boundaries were defined by the following waterways: the Nakagawa river in the east, Kanda Josui conduit in the west, the Arakawa river and the lower part of the Shakujiigawa river in the north, and from the Minami-Shinagawa district roughly to Megurogawa river in the south.[37]

The above provides the outlines of the ecological context within which the feudal social order of Edo was contained. We turn now to a consideration of some of the styles of dwellings reflecting the stratification of status within the total community structure.

The most impressive, and the most extensive, structures were those belonging to the 260-plus feudal lords gathered in Edo in allegiance to the *bakufu*. Each constructed suitable buildings for offical residence and offices of the domains (*kami-yashiki*), and family residences (*naka-yashiki*), and villas (*shimo-yashiki*). Apart from official functions, the multiple units provided retirement quarters as well as alternate locations in case of fire. Besides these, of course, each lord provided himself with warehouses (*kura-yashiki*) and houses purchased privately (*kakae-yashiki*).

A lord's holdings in Edo were called *Edo-yashiki*, and each had a minimum of three such structures. Powerful lords, of course, had more, such as the ten *yashiki* of the Ikeda family from Tottori, the nine *yashiki* belonging to the Mori house, and eight maintained by the Tokugawa family of Kishū. The *kami-yashiki* residential complex contained various units such as the official residence of the lord, houses of his vassals, offices of his domain and some storage buildings. This more complicated group of buildings was situated close to Edo Castle, and it was where the lord stayed while in Edo. The *naka-yashiki* was constructed for the sons and daughters of the lord and for his retainers who could not be accommodated in the more centrally located *kami-yashiki*. The simpler *shimo-yashiki* was a villa where the lord could seek rest or later retire. It was usually located in quiet surroundings and had beautiful, well-kept grounds.[38]

The *yashiki* of the daimyō were similar in structural design to the buildings of the *bakufu*. In front was the main gate, *ōmunemon*, a large two-storied affair, with a stable for two or three horses nearby. Immediately in front of the official residence was an entrance room (*genkan*) to which was attached a special room (*tomomachi*) for retainers. The entrance way included a wood-floored space (*shikidai*) for greeting guests. Proceeding from there one came to the offices of the elders and other followers serving the lord. Next came the *ōhiroma*, a ballroom equipped with a stage, for performing ceremonies, then a reception parlor, *omote-shoin*, and a waiting room, *gotaimensho*. Besides these official rooms, the lord also had private quarters within the same mansion, though strictly separated from the official rooms. In the private quarters were bed rooms for the lord and his family, guest rooms, kitchen, and rooms for maid-servants.

Encompassing the main *yashiki* structures there were *omote-nagaya* which were connected long-houses for warriors, two-storied buildings roofed with tiles. Within the compass of long-houses were built one-storied *kado-nagaya* in two or three concentric lines around the central mansion of the lord with its garden. The *kado-nagaya* were used for offices and storage. The Akasaka *naka-yashiki* of the Tokugawa family of Kishū occupied an area of 18,200 *tsubo* (14.8 acres), and the Kōji-machi mansion of the same lord covered an equal area. There were 670 of the one-storied *nagaya* around both the Akasaka and Kōji-machi residences for the retainers who stayed permanently in Edo. Adding the buildings used to accommodate the retainers coming for alternate year's residence, the total number of buildings at one site sometimes reached 1,000.

In the central mansion of a lord there lived his closest retainers, his stewards (*yōnin*), warriors endowed with their own estates (*kyūnin*), pages (*chūkoshō*), minor retainers (*wakatō*), and ranking soldiers (*chūgen*). The number of people living in the mansions of certain feudal lords has been estimated as follows:

| *Name of lord* | *No. of people* | *Period* |
|---|---|---|
| Tokugawa of Kishū | 5,000–6,000 | End of Tokugawa era |
| Maeda of Kaga | 7,000–8,000 | Genroku (while lord was in Edo) |
| Maeda of Kaga | 4,000 | Genroku (while lord was in domain) |
| Ii of Hikone | 5,000 | Genroku |
| Matsuyama domain of Bitchū | 1,000 | End of Tokugawa era |
| Mizuno domain, of Matsumoto in Shinshū | 1,300 | Kyōhō |

This list indicates, then, that more than 5,000 people resided in the Edo residential complexes of major lords, while only about 500–1,500 occupied the residences of minor lords, in Edo.[39] According to investigations made at the time of the Meiji Restoration (1868), the largest ground of any of the Edo mansions of the daimyō was that of the Tokugawa family of Owari, which covered 210,000 *tsubo* (171.5 acres). The Maeda, Tokugawa of Mito, and Tokugawa of Kishū mansion grounds were of similar sizes. The smallest was that of the Asō domain, measuring only 1,800 *tsubo* (1.5 acres).

Competing with each other in purchasing new land on which to demonstrate their wealth and power in lavishly built mansions, the daimyō were the central force in turning Edo into a vast city of spacious and splendid structures. As expressed in *Keichō Kenmonshū* (Keichō Era Review), "The mansions of the lords look themselves like a range of small mountains." With repeated fires, as in 1601 and the large fire in 1657, some of the more luxurious features disappeared, such as *Yagura-mon*, a large turreted gate decorated in lacquered colors. Afterward gates, though large, were of unpainted natural woods.

In the early days of Edo mansions tended toward luxurious two-storied structures, with gold foil decorations on conspicuous parts of the buildings like the entrance way. The *yagura-mon* of the Katō Kiyomasa mansion used gold foil on all pillars and even on the roof. Reliefs of rhinoceroses stood between pillars supporting the ceilings, and even the kitchen wall was adorned with a bamboo relief of a tiger. It is said that this relief measured eight *ken* (16 yds.). The Meireki fire in 1657 destroyed this and many other such extravagent structures. After the fire the *bakufu* ordered the daimyō to refrain from such expensive construction to save money. Houses were to be limited to a modest three *ken* (6 yds.) maximum, based on the standardized length of wooden beams. Two-storied structures were ruled out, even for major daimyō with their own domains (*kunimochi-daimyō*). From 1668 on, it was prohibited to add lacquered decoration to the shelved alcoves (*tokodana*) in rooms. The *bakufu*'s prohibition included as well both relief work and the complicated, multi-layer structure of stays, called *kumimono*, on top of supporting pillars. Hence, the elaborate features like the *yaguramon* of the Katō Kiyomasa residence were seen no more.[40]

In the Jōkyō era (1684–8) the *bakufu* set up regulatory standards for the residential structures of the daimyō that provided for graded demonstration of their relative rank and dignity yet, at the same time, achieved the necessary economizing in expenditures. The regulations issued in that age controlled the sizes of gates and *nagaya* built, being fixed as follows:

| *Rank/Revenue* | *Style of Structures* |
|---|---|
| *Kunimochi-daimyo* | Both sides of main gate widened, and with Chinese-style gables |
| 100,000 *koku* or more | *Nagaya-mon**, with stone walls, roofs with extended eaves |
| 50,000 *koku* or more | Same as above |
| *Tozama-daimyo* of more or less than 50,000 *koku* | *Nagaya-mon*, stone walls on one side, gabled roofs |
| 30,000 *koku* or less | *Nagaya-mon*, stone walls on one side, roofs with eaves |
| 10,000 *koku* or more | *Nagaya-mon*, with extended grilles on both sides[41] |

**Nagaya-mon* was a gate with *nagaya* (extended multi-unit dwellings) extending from each side.

Later, in the Kyōhō era (1716–36), fire-preventive finishings of plaster and other materials were used on residential walls. Grilled windows, called *mushamado* or *yorikimado*, were provided for the *nagaya*.

In contrast to the daimyō, the *hatamoto* and other warriors lived in rather simple houses in the early days of the Tokugawa era. When the mansions of the daimyō were rendered more modest, the warriors' structures were improved. The *hatamoto* gradually acquired residences comparable to those of minor lords, though smaller. Built in the *shoin-zukuri* style, a standard design with a reception parlor (*shoin*) as the main room, these residences also boasted main gates with a guard on duty at a small side door. To each side of the gate were elongated quarters (*munewari-nagaya*) for military and civilian subordinates. Walls surrounding the *hatamoto* residences were finished with fire-preventive plaster and tiles (*namako-kabe*).

At the entrance of these residences paper lanterns bearing the family crest were hung high on tall poles. Inside the entrance was the wooded reception platform (*shikidai*), and the residence itself was divided into the official (*omote*) and the private (*oku*) parts, as in other *yashiki*. Next to the entrance was the official waiting room (*yoritsuki*), and next to it the official guest room (*oku-zashiki*), all occupying the best part of the house. The kitchen and other rooms where the family of the master of the house lived and worked were dim, if not dark. Where the master's rank and revenue warranted it, there were gardens and fire-proofed warehouses (*dozō*). Retainers and common subordinates lived, of course, in smaller dwellings. At times there were cultivated areas within the residential grounds.

Regulations of the *bakufu* based on rank and revenue governed the permissible acreages of the residential grounds of the daimyō. The standards applied by the *bakufu* from 1738 on, were as follows:

| *Revenue (in koku)* | *Acreage allowed* |
|---|---|
| 10,000–20,000 | 2,500 *tsubo* (1,000 *tsubo*=0.8 acres) |
| 20,000–30,000 | 2,700 〃 |
| 30,000–40,000 | 3,500 〃 |
| 40,000–50,000 | 3,500 〃 |
| 50,000–60,000 | 5,000 〃 |
| 60,000–70,000 | 5,500 〃 |
| 80,000–90,000 | 6,500 〃 |
| 100,000–150,000 | 7,000 〃 |

Departures from this set standard were permitted from time to time in certain cases. The grounds of the Tokugawa families of Kii, Mito, and Owari, and of the Maeda family from Kaga, were far more extensive than allowed by the above standard.

Grounds acreage for the *hatamoto* were also fixed as follows:[42]

| *Revenue (in koku)* | *Acreage allowed* |
|---|---|
| 300– 900 | 500 *tsubo* (1,000 *tsubo*=0.8 acres) |
| 1,000–1,900 | 700 〃 |
| 2,000–2,900 | 700 〃 |
| 3,000–3,900 | 1,000 〃 |
| 4,000–4,900 | 1,500 〃 |
| 5,000–7,000 | 1,800 〃 |
| 8,000–9,000 | 2,300 〃 |

Although these limits were revised in the Genroku (1688–1704) and Kyōhō (1716–36) eras, there were no significant changes in the scale of lots granted the *hatamoto* by the *bakufu* throughout the entire Edo era.

Feudal lords of the Edo period were quite ashamed if their residences seemed shabby in comparison to those of other domains. Living standards were completely controlled by the idea that improving external appearances superceded all other elements of their livelihood. Official and private life were strictly separated, so that most of them suffered a great deal under so unrealistic a sense of propriety. Controls applied to the size and style of their structures helped them avoid, then, complete dissipation of the wealth they had accumulated earlier in the course of development of the commodity economy. This is, restrictions were aimed at enabling each to retain his dignity within the stratified status system of the feudal order, both with respect to others in the warrior class and in relation to the increasingly prosperous townsmen.

Prescribed distinctions between the houses of townsmen and those of the warrior class were even greater than those applied within the latter group. Here again the frame of reference was the clear stratification of status. Early in the Edo period the townsmen occupied houses built in the style of farmers and townsmen common to the Kamakura and Sengoku eras, with roofs of miscanthus straw or wooden shingles. Even among these houses, though, there appeared two and three-storied structures, distinguished by windows with black-lacquered frames. Sometimes there were carved wall reliefs and gold or silver foil decorations. After the big 1657 fire such decorations and three-storied houses were outlawed. Interior accessories were held to a modest level befitting the inferior status of townsmen. For example, decorative nails, oversized handles (*hikite*) on sliding panels, as well as glass or gold ornaments were prohibited.

Following the Meireki inferno the *bakufu* set up fire prevention schedules to be observed in all residential areas of the townsmen. To suppress extravagance among the townsmen they were forbidden the use of roofing tiles, but to diminish the danger of fires their straw or shingled roofs were plastered with mud. Nevertheless, fires continued to break out and, in the fifth month of 1720 (Kyōhō 5), the *bakufu* authorized all, warrior and townsmen alike, to utilize tile roofing. Thick mud-plastered walls and fire-proofed storage buildings were also permitted then. Indeed, the *bakufu* encouraged such methods of construction in order to prevent rapid spreading of fires, even to the point of making loans, refundable in ten years, to town residents whose homes were burned.

Under the control and aid of the *bakufu* Edo gradually became characterized by mud-plastered walls and storage buildings, in contrast to the traditional wood surfaces of Kyōto structures. The common style of houses for townspeople became a two-storied structure with gabled roofs, and extended eaves were confined to the front side over the ground floor only. The ground floor generally had an open front used for shop space. Second floor windows were provided with sliding storm windows of wood plastered with mud. Wall construction on all sides consisted of latticed framing heavily plastered with mud (called *nurigōshi*). Roofs were steeply inclined and tiled; the main and side ridges were thicker than before and often finished with mud-plaster (*shikkui-nuri*).[43]

As the economic position of the townsmen steadily improved their plaster-finished houses and warehouses in Edo became lovelier year after year. Those of exceptional wealth, such as Kibun-daijin of Hatchōbori and Naraya Mozaemon, a lumber dealer in Kuroe-chō, were quite plain and simple in external appearance. Interior decorations, however, were quite luxurious, with considerable funds expended on the construction of many small rooms done in exquisite taste. These exceptions, though, were made only by very rich merchants in defiance of the *bakufu*'s restrictions.

A great many of the townspeople's dwellings were very humble structures of only one story, with shingled roofs. They were built with roughly-hewn cedar boards secured by wooden pegs, the outer walls consisting of packed earth covered with wooden planks. Such dwellings had little resistance against fires. The houses were built up close to the city streets, and besides individual structures on separate lots there were many *munewari-nagaya*, extended oblong structures accommodating several families in separate sections. These multi-unit dwellings were usually occupied by renting tenants, and were located on vacant lots on back streets not suitable for ordinary townsmen's houses. The *nagaya* were, nonetheless, a great help to those who had great difficulty in securing housing in the latter days of the Edo era due to a greatly expanded population.

According to a book on "The Thriving City of Edo" (*Edo Hanjōki*), "Eight hundred and eight streets weave a complicated pattern throughout the city. Long-houses (*nagaya*) on the back streets contain as many as five, ten, or in the poorest areas, fifty different family sections in one building. Houses are lined up along both sides of every available lane (*roji*). All residents in a single block share a common well and a common toilet. Refuse is carried off to a fixed place, and a single gutter along each lane suffices for drainage."[44] The reference suggests not only the congested conditions of the scores of families in the *nagaya* but the quite unsavory living conditions that existed.

## 2. Social Stratification and Controls in Edo

*Social Stratification.*——The primary fact of social structure in Edo was the large concentration of warriors active in support of its integrative functions in military and political affairs. The warrior class in Edo, as we have already indicated, consisted of those under the direct command of the *bakufu* plus warriors coming from the various domains in connection with the requirement of alternate year's residence. The politics, economy, and culture of the city were subject to the intense influence of these military men, who in turn stood under the dominant sway of the shogun. The retainers and standard-bearers directly subordinate to the shogun alone numbered at least 200,000 or 300,000. Those under the daimyō are estimated to have been between 300,000 and 400,000. In any event, the warriors are considered to have outnumbered the 500,000 to 600,000 townsmen living in Edo.

Some further clarification is needed, however, with regard to the two categories of warriors mentioned previously, namely, the various daimyō, *hatamoto*, and *gokenin* directly responsible to the shogun, and the men serving under the daimyō, called *baishin*, who were themselves differentiated into many groups.

Gradations obtained, of course, within the ranks of warriors directly subordinate to the shogun, all of whom were authorized to receive annual incomes of 10,000 *koku* or more. The daimyō directly under the shogun numbered between 260 and 270, although the number was not fixed. At the top were the three households, *gosanke*, of the sons of Tokugawa Ieyasu. Next came the three households of the third and fourth sons of Tokugawa Yoshimune and the second son of Tokugawa Ieshige, called together the *gosankyo*. Branch families of the Tokugawa house bearing the name of Matsudaira (Ieyasu's former name) constituted the third grade of related daimyō, and were known as *gokamon*.

Other daimyō were classified according to hereditary relations, the *fudai-daimyō*, and those "outside" such relationships, or the *tozama-daimyō*. The former included all the daimyō who were subordinate to Ieyasu prior to War of Sekigahara (1600), numbering about 140. *Tozama-daimyō* consisted of about 90 daimyō who swore allegiance to the *bakufu* following the War of Sekigahara.

Both groups, the *fudai-daimyō* and the *tozama-daimyō*, were classified also according to the relative character of their domain holdings. This classification had five grades, as follow:

| *Grade* | *No.* | *Title* | *Explanation* |
|---|---|---|---|
| 1 | 18 | *kunimochi-daimyō* | Lords with their own domains |
| 2 | 516 | *kunimochi-nami-daimyō* | Those of equivalent rank to *kunimochi-daimyō* |
| 3 | 120–130 | *shiromochi-daimyō* | Lords with their own castles |
| 4 | 15–16 | *shiromochi-nami-daimyō* | Those of equivalent rank to *shiromochi-daimyō* |
| 5 | 110 | *mujo-daimyō* | Lords with no castle |

Such stratification governed all treatment of the daimyō by the *bakufu*, including appointments to offices and positions of authority. Rankings were represented also in the different rooms of the shogun's castle to which the daimyō were permitted entrance. The names of the rooms, indicating eight ranks, were:

| *Rank* | *Room* | *Explanation* | *Rank allowed entrance* |
|---|---|---|---|
| 1. | *Ōrōka-zume* | "grand corridor" | Only the *gosanke* |
| 2. | *Tamarima-zume* | "lounge" | High-ranking families among the *gokamon* and *fudai-daimyō*. |
| 3. | *Ōhiroma-zume* | "main hall" | *Gokamon*, *fudai-* and *tozama-daimyō* of over 100,000 *koku* annual income |

| | | | |
|---|---|---|---|
| 4. | *Teikannoma-zume* | "reception hall" | Most of the *gokamon* and *fudai-daimyō*; almost all of them had less than 100,000 *koku* incomes |
| 5. | *Yanaginoma-zume* | "willow room" | *Tozama-daimyō* with less than 50,000 *koku* incomes |
| 6. | *Karinoma-zume* | "wild goose room" | *Fudai-daimyō* with less than 50,000 *koku* incomes |
| 7. | *Kikunoma-zume* | "chrysanthemum room" | Lords without castles and incomes between 10,000 and 20,000 *koku* |
| 8. | No designated room for the lowest grade of daimyō. | | |

(Ranks 1 and 2 included most of the important members of those involved in the shogun's castle in Chiyoda.)

The daimyō occupied the most important posts in the administrative organization of the *bakufu*. They were subject to the dictatorial control of the shogun whose unequivocal authority was much like that of the "head" of a "family" of all the daimyō. His governance of all administrative work was exercised directly through those appointed to executive posts in the *bakufu* system. Executive posts went to those in the immediate kinship group of the shogun, even if they enjoyed lesser incomes than some powerful *tozama-daimyō* or other daimyō closely connected with the shogun, who were not included in the top ruling group. All major decisions were handled in meetings of the executive group. The members were on duty every other month. Such measures were taken by the shogun to prevent any concentration of power at lower levels of the administrative organs.

Although sometimes a "Grand Elder" (*tairo*) was appointed, there were usually four or five elders (*rōjū*), selected from among the *fudai-daimyō* of more than 25,000 *koku* income who had their own castles. These men controlled all the other daimyō. Three to five assistants (*waka-doshiyori*="younger elders") were chosen from among *fudai-daimyō* with no castles of their own. The younger elders were in command of the *jikisan* (*hatamoto* directly subordinate to the *bakufu*). The executives on alternate month's duty formed the administrative cabinet, *goyō-beya*, of the shogun in Chiyoda Castle. This cabinet formed the nucleus of the total administrative system throughout the country.

Another key administrative organ was the office of the commissioner of temples and shrines, the *jisha-bugyō*. This office, too, was controlled at the highest level by four or five persons directly related to the shogun. Their control over all religious affairs, including legal suits, extended to the remotest provinces. These officers also rotated on duty every other month.

Approximately one-half of the warriors living in Edo were under the direct command of the shogun. Among them there were two grades, the *hatamoto* who were permitted direct audiences with the shogun, and the *gokenin* who were not. Both groups were referred to as *bakushin* (retainers to the *bakufu*), or *jikisan* (retainers under direct command.) The *hatamoto* derived from several sources:

—*okunishū*, those who had served Ieyasu when he went under his family name of Matsudaira on his Mikawa domain;

—*kingokushū*, those who joined Ieyasu after he left his Mikawa domain but before he entered Edo;

—*kantōshū*, those who joined Ieyasu after he entered Edo;

—descendants of distinguished families; and,

—men of exceptional learning and skill.

The men from distinguished families (*kōke*) were given special treatment by the *bakufu*, ranking between the daimyō and *hatamoto*. The *sankin-kōtai* obligations for alternate year's residence in Edo fell also upon them, though, as a general rule, *hatamoto* were required to live in the city of Edo. They were organized into groups (*yoriai-gumi*) and subject to tax levies (*kuyaku-kin*).

Those serving in the offices of the *bakufu* were of two classes. One was *yakukata*, those functioning as officials, the other *bankata*, or castle guard. Among the *yakukata*, there were the following officers:

—*machi-bugyō*, the commissioners who administered the affairs of the town, and *kanjō-bugyō*, which handled the finances of the *bakufu* including claims and obligations of territories managed directly by the *bakufu;* both of these offices were supervised by the elders' cabinet.

—*ōmetsuke*, or inspector-general, who served the elders in overseeing the behavior of the daimyō and in transmitting orders of the *bakufu* to them.

—*metsuke*, inspector responsible for the behavior of, and relaying orders to the *hatamoto*.

—*hyōjōsho-tomariyaku*, officers serving under the three commissioners for finance, towns, and temples and shrines (*kanjo-*, *machi-*, and *jisha-bugyō*), as well as other important agencies of the *bakufu*.

The *bankata* class consisted of five groups who were in charge of many soldiers (*banshi*) in maintaining watches over the grounds and gates of Edo Castle.

The maximum income allowed the *hatamoto* was 10,000 *koku*. According to the *Hatamoto Bukan*, a directory of the *hatamoto*, there were only 676 with incomes over 1,000 *koku*, and only 626 receiving stipends over 500 *koku*. Some 3,097 had incomes over 100 *koku*, while 7,660 were paid less than 100 *koku* per year (only 4 had unknown incomes). Among the total of 5,167 *hatamoto* there were wide differences in income, though 60% were paid less than 500 *koku* annually.[45]

The *gokenin* also lived in Edo, and their individual wealth varied greatly. The richest were endowed with their own fiefs, while the poorest received only a mere pittance, barely enough for one man's livelihood (*ichinin-buchi*, 3 *ryō*). Between these extremes were such as the *yoriki*, assistants to senior officials, with stipends of 200 *koku*. Some of the *gokenin* were employed as *yakukata* officals, though most served in groups of ten or a hundred as *bankata* guards. One theory holds that there were 60,000 *gokenin* living in Edo,[46] but in the Kyōhō era (1716–36) there were only 17,309.

The *hatamoto* and *gokenin* together made up the rank and file of the *bakufu*'s own warriors and, though not paid high salaries, they often outranked the warriors of the daimyō and were certainly treated more favorably. They could win appointments into the ranks of govenment officials, and they were fiercely proud of the culture of the city of Edo, with which they imbued themselves.

The retainers to the daimyō were organized into administrative systems for the respective domains that were small-scale models of the *bakufu* government. Special groupings were needed, though, to accommodate the alternate year's residence requirement. *Jōfu* were those who remained in Edo permanently, in the offices of the various domains. *Kinmuban* were those who rotated every one, two, or three years. *Tachikaeri* were always with their lord, whether Edo or fief. A final group remained permanently in the lord's provincial territory. The largest domains kept several thousands of men in Edo, and even the smallest ones had several hundreds, or possibly over one thousand. It is easy to see that the total number of retainers reached several hundreds of thousands, as already mentioned. The *kinmuban* and *tachikaeri* did not take their families with them to Edo. The permanently resident *jōfu* kept their wives and children with them in Edo, all of them virtual hostages of the *bakufu*. A special group of officers of each domain (called *rusuiyaku*) performed liaison work with the other domain offices and the *bakufu*. Their duties took them frequently to the private quarters (*ō-oku*) of the shogun's castle on behalf of their lords. It will be remembered that these quarters housed the many female attendants to the shogun. These liaison operations consumed considerable funds of the daimyō, imposing heavy financial burdens upon them.

At the bottom of the warrior class were the foot-soldiers, or *ashigaru*. Following tactical changes since the Muromachi era, these troops were authorized to bear swords, as the mass movements of battle called them into regular duty. Some of them (*dōshin*) performed police services under the town commissioners, while others were assigned to guard duty at the 36 gates of Edo Castle. They also took part in the formal parades of entry into, or departure from Edo by the daimyō.

This did not exhaust the scale of subordinates, however. Below the *ashigaru* there were many kinds of servants. Some served in the mansions of the warriors themselves. There were, for example, servants to the *hatamoto* and the retainers to the daimyō, such as:

—*wakato*, young menservants;
—*chūgen*, ordinary servants;

—*kobito*, lower class servants;
—*arashigo*, servants of the lowest class engaged in various projects requiring heavy labor.

Similarly, there were many types of servants directly under the *bakufu*, such as the *dōshin* and *kobito* described above. Additional types included:

—*kurokuwamono*, laborers used by the *sakuji-bugyō*, agency for civil engineering projects, especially castle construction;
—*kagomono*, palanquin-bearers;
—*sōjimono*, sanitation workers;
—*kunin*, parade guards; and even
—*chōsekinin*, a valet who carried a small portable latrine for use by the shogun when he went out from his castle.

Most of the servants were employed by the warriors for six-month or one-year terms at a time.

The *chūgen* stood between the warrior-employer and lesser servants like *kobito*, hence the title means "intermediary." They were clearly separated from the lowest levels of the warrior class, the *ashigaru*. That is, they were not regular troops, but served rather as flag-, staff-, and armor-bearers, and attended the horses of mounted warriors. Their salaries were low (2 *ryō* 2 *bu* per year), although housing was provided within the compounds of the warriors.

The *kobito* were assigned more menial tasks, such as carrying boxes of miscellaneous gear for the warriors, or doing numerous household jobs when the master stayed home. They had no pride of military service and felt little loyalty toward their masters. They were easily given to vain and boisterous amusements and, taking advantage of their master's covering authority, often treated the townsmen quite harshly.

There remains a special class, the lordless warriors, or *rōnin*. Deprived of masters, they also were without official posts in the feudal system. Due to the dissolution of many fiefs through absorption by the *bakufu* in the process of establishing the Tokugawa regime, their number was quite large, an estimated 400,000 in all.[47] Nevertheless, they, too, were subject to the stratification so characteristic of the age.

The top class of *rōnin* was made up of those descended from famous warriors distinguished by kinship lines and meritorious service in former wars. They did not suffer financially as they were quite wealthy. Ill-treated by former masters who paid salaries much too low, considering their pedigree, they had resigned local government posts and left their masters.

The middle class of *rōnin* consisted of warriors who had served as middle or low class attendants (pages), but had been fired as a result of momentary discord between them and their master . These *rōnin* hoped to regain the favor of their masters and return to their posts. At the bottom of the *rōnin* group were those who had been dismissed for personal errors or greed, who could not reveal the names of their former masters. This meant that alternate posts in the feudal system were closed to them and they became increasingly poverty-stricken.[48]

A number of options were open to these disenfranchised warriors. Some were able to obtain new employment under the daimyō or *hatamoto*. Some chose to study hard and become specialists in some field of learning, technology, or military strategy. There were also possibilities of becoming priests, farmers, or townsmen. Because of the success of the *bakufu* in maintaining domestic peace and stability, there was little need for new warriors and very little likelihood that political changes would create such a need. It is understandable, then, that the *rōnin* were more inclined to harbor hopes for some changes in the political world. This rendered their chances of new military assignments even less.[49]

Inasmuch as the basis of the stratified feudal structure was the military and political authority of the daimyō, it was absolutely essential that the common people be completely obedient to their masters. Relations were reciprocal only in the sense that gaining the master's favor was utterly dependent upon the unswerving loyalty of all subordinates. Individuals were bound within a family-type social system of stratification based on the specific status of each person. In all interpersonal relationships it was imperative to have all lines of authority firmly fixed.

Warriors were differentiated from all other peoples both by titles and by the sword-bearing privilege which symbolized their right to govern all classes of farmers, artisans, and merchants. If their authority was questioned or their honor insulted by any non-warrior, they were free to kill them on the spot, a custom known as *kirisutegomen*. Martial arts, *budō*, were promoted as the primary expression of the warriors' morality. Each warrior family had its own special norms to observe, according to its relative place in the hierarchy. Their authority was protected against threats from other classes by manifest and strict adherence to their own specific norms, and behavior permissible among the warriors was thus highly restricted.

The family system of the warrior class had developed in conjunction with the evolution of the feudal order. Hence, the regulations and laws of the *bakufu* and domains had strong implications for that family system. The basic thrust was focused in the family as a whole as the norm for all human relations within it. Under the overarching authority of the head of the family, each member had his designated place, according to sex and age. Every member was expected to live each day in such a way as to guarantee the continued existence of the family.

In this system the head of the household held absolute authority over every single component member, in much the same formalized way that a feudal lord governed his domain. Predominance over other members by the head of the family was symbolized by the places of authority of the father, husband, and eldest son. The wife, other sons, and all daughters were to obey the family head, such obedience constituting the highest moral code for their lives. This morality was articulated for the wife's role by Kaibara Ekken in his work "Great Learning for Women" (*Onna Daigaku*, sometimes rendered "University for Women") as follows:

"Approach your husband as you would heaven itself; for it is certain that if you offend him, heaven's punishment will be yours." Not only was the eldest son heir to the family property, but men in general were treated more favorably than women throughout all society. According to the feudal code the propagation of the household always took precedence over the individual. Therefore, parental relations were accorded priority over marital ones, a priority reflected in the saying, "The womb is a thing borrowed [for begetting heirs]" (*hara wa karimono*).

Sons other than the eldest were regarded as impositions on the household. Some of them were offered for adoption to other families. A few were given employment by the master over the household if they possessed suitable talents. Given no such alternatives, lesser sons were forced to remain as life-long dependents (*heyazumi*) in the household of the eldest son, bothersome boarders who could not pay their own way.

Each household was a basic unit in the stratified social structure geared to status. Individuals as such were neglected. The character and worth of a particular household depended upon its relative place in the social stratification. Occupations were transmitted by inheritance just as faithfully as family property. Even a warrior's stipend, *karoku*, was a kind of household property for successive transmission to descendants. A family's honor was guarded with the same sort of concern for continuity. The tradition, precepts, and behavioral code of a family were nurtured for transmission to its heirs generation after generation. The ancestors of each family were enshrined in the household, serving to integrate all members into the larger family and giving final sanctification to the primacy of the total household over each individual member.

Marriage was not between individual persons but, rather, between households and, even then, within the limits defined by their status. There were official regulations fixing these limits. Marriages between warriors and non-warriors, whether farmers, artisans, or merchants, were prohibited. Marriages between residents of different domains were prohibited. Regulations forbade the formation of power cliques through marriage arrangements. Marriage proposals had to be cleared with the proper authorities, and marital negotiations between two households had to be conducted by officials whose own status was commensurate with that of the families concerned.

Marriage plans for daimyō or *hatamoto* with incomes over 10,000 *koku* required the approval of the shogun, even after all other conditions of family rank and such were duly met. Approval by the ruling elders (*rōjū*) or their assistants (*waka-doshiyori*) sufficed for warriors drawing less than 10,000 *koku*. Retainers to a daimyō of the middle grade and above had to get approval of their lord, and common warriors, *shibun*, and above needed approval from the elders in the local government. Other warriors were supervised in such affairs by the inspectors (*metsuke*). There was scarcely any individual freedom in the selection of marital mates. Top-ranking warriors and other upper class personages were allowed to keep mistresses in their households to compensate for the unreasonable conditions imposed by these restrictions concerning marriage. Interesting data on this particular form of regulatory controls over households can be found in some prescriptions written by Tokugawa Ieyasu before he died, designating the number of mistresses appropriate to each grade of the daimyō and their retainers.[50]

If sons or daughters exceeded the bounds of family precepts in love affairs, they were punished by the household head with scoldings or beatings. In extreme cases, they were disowned by the head of the family. Divorces resulted more often from dissatisfaction with a wife's deportment on the part of the husband's parents, than from initiatives taken by the husband himself. The wife's position in the home was exceedingly weak as she was forced to be subservient to her husband's entire household.

From youth the warriors were nurtured in the cultural forms and norms formalized in their special status and family system. They constituted the ruling elite of the feudal order and represented its power and authority before the common people. They were expected to lead exemplary lives. From the very beginning of the Tokugawa *bakufu*, Ieyasu sought always to educate the warrior class through public institutions.

As late as 1867 the *bakufu* issued instructions that the heads of all families of the *hatamoto* and *gokenin* groups must study at the official Shōheizaka Institute of Learning (Shōheizaka Gakumonjo). This top school established by the *bakufu* was attended also by the second and third sons who were eight years old and above. Prior to this the government had founded children's schools (*dōka*) in 1792. The curriculum consisted of nine basic books in classical Confucian studies (*Shishogokyō*). The first four (*Shisho*) were taught to youngsters 8–10 years of age and the remaining five books (*Gokyō*) to boys between 11–15 years old. There was no course for children 7 years and under.[51]

The neo-Confucianist philosophy known as *Shushigaku*, based on the ideas of a medieval Chinese Confucian scholar, Chu Hsi, was authorized as the basic content of education in the *bakufu* and no other schools of thought were presented. One of the principles of *Shushigaku* was that a person's fate and fortune were determined by the social conditions of his birth. No one could, nor should he try to, alter his inherited station in life, a notion uniquely tailored for the stabilization of authority in a feudal social order.

Maintaining offices and residences in Edo, each domain made provisions for the training of its men there as well as in the local domain. In addition to schools, the domains also operated a kind of gymnasium for cultivating martial arts. Towards the end of the Tokugawa era studies in these schools were expanded to include Western, and particularly scientific learning. Successful completion of courses of study came increasingly to constitute one of the criteria of qualification for succession to the hereditary titles and positions of the family. Upon clearance, the young men were introduced ceremoniously into adulthood at the age of fifteen. Thereafter they were qualified to assume positions as heads of their families and to enter into marriage.

Upper class girls were given instruction in certain martial skills, elementary reading and writing, and in cultural refinements appropriate to their status. They were trained in the formal handling of *naginata* (long swords) and *shinai* (bamboo fencing staffs). They also learned to play the *koto* (Japanese-style harp), to perform the tea ceremony, and to make stylized flower-arrangements. They, too, were deemed suitable for marriage at age fifteen, although most young men and women were married at about seventeen or eighteen.

Official efforts on the part of the central and provincial governments served to keep the level of education in Japan quite high during the feudal period. It is estimated that 40%–50% of the men, and about 15% of the women, were capable of reading books and writing letters in this era.

In the three centuries since the Kamakura era the relationship patterns of households had changed considerably. In the Kamakura period households were tightly bound into kinship groups under the control of the head of the main family (*sōryō*), though the scale of the kinship group was not so large. During the subsequent Muromachi era the family system based on kinship was loosened somewhat, although the formal mode of sucession of the eldest son remained intact. Kinship relations gave way gradually to regional relationships which bound the warriors to the masters (*Shugo-daimyō*) to whom they pledged allegiance.

In the Tokugawa era under discussion here, master-subordinate relations assumed precedence over pure kinship relations. Had kinship relations as such been allowed primary place, their extension across the regional boundaries of the feudal domains would have constituted a constant threat to the inner integrity of the authority and administrative systems within each domain. Consequently, the kinship relations among warriors could not be restored in society in general, although such relations were honored within individual families. In token of the kinship pattern all members within a larger family connection assumed the same surname as the ancestor of the family, yet this frequently included those without actual consanguineous relations. The inheritance rights of the eldest "son" were preserved, and the main family was called, therefore, *sōryō-honke*, or "main house in the line of succession." Branch families in the larger household bearing the same name were called simply *bunke* ("branch" family) or *makke* ("last" or "end" family).

According to Fukuo Takeichiro, the branch families did not owe any special allegiance to the main household but were, rather, independent—whether their land was received from the *bakufu*, feudal lord, or directly from the main household. Such allegiance belonged to the larger feudal order. But branch and main families did maintain relationships of formal courtesy with each other.[52] That is, they contacted each other more on the basis of being relatives for joint decisions on matters of mutual interest, such as submitting a petition to the local government.

The status strata motif of society resulted in many differences in living conditions of the warriors. This was evident in the style of houses, areas allowed for residential lots, and even the locations of residences, not to mention actual incomes and the different levels of culture enjoyed. If this was true within the warrior class, how much more pronounced were the differences between them and the lower classes of farmers, artisans, and merchants. Preservation of the varying social and cultural levels appropriate to each class, and to each grade within the classes, depended upon maintenance of the radical differences in political and economic power that existed between the warriors and their inferiors. Only when changes occurred in the economic structure did cracks appear in the stratified edifice of status that so clearly separated the rulers from the ruled.

This refers us once again to the system requiring alternate year's residence in Edo. The daimyō, top men in the status system, were obliged to maintain two complete residences, one in Edo and the other in their respective domains. Legal wives and heirs were left permanently in Edo, while the daimyō themselves resided alternately in the separate residences. The year spent in Edo was by far the more expensive of the two, especially with the competitive atmosphere requiring each lord to demonstrate, beyond his actual means, his power and wealth to his peers. The amount of funds expended in Edo grew steadily regardless of actual resources, particularly prior to the restrictions instituted after the great fire of 1657. Competitive spending only served to elevate prices in Edo. Overall expenditures in the last decade of the 17th, and the first decade of the 18th centuries were especially extravagant. Conspicuous consumption on the part of the military class markedly improved the economic lot of the townsmen and, eventually, their social positions.

As the financial resources of the warriors were drawn from the productive capacities of the farmers, the latter were placed over the merchants in the status scale of society. In connection with this it is instructive to introduce here an analysis by Takikawa Masajiro of two regulations issued by the *bakufu* for controlling farmers and merchants. One was a "notice," *ofuregaki*, for farmers issued in 1649; the other was a 1657 edict for townsmen called *Edojū-sadame*, or "regulations for all Edo."

Takikawa explains that, while the townsmen were forbidden certain exhibitive luxuries such as decorative lacquered furniture, interior decorations of gold or silver foil in their homes, and expensive silk clothing, they were free to enjoy rice wine, tea, and tobacco. Farmers were not permitted even these small luxuries. They were required to forego rice for other grains, and even to divorce wives too much given to tea-drinking. But townsmen enjoyed more than these minor privileges.[53]

Shortage of funds in the local governments became quite desperate late in the 17th century. For example, the Sakai domain (Shōnai district) spent 38,400 *ryō* yearly in Edo during the Hōei era (1704–11), as against a total revenue of only 35,900 *ryō*, producing an obvious deficit of 2,500 *ryō*. The income figure, however, includes 11,000 *ryō* acquired by *chigyō-kariage* (borrowing on the salaries of its warriors), so the Sakai domain was registering an actual shortage of 13,500 *ryō* annually. The revenue of the domain's government amounted to only 65% of the funds used in Edo. The local debt climbed to 90,000 *ryō*, as its unsound fiscal policy was marking up a 27,000 *ryō* excess of expenditures over income each year.

An even more blatant case of over-spending occurred in Nagaoka domain (Echigo district) during the fiscal year beginning with the tenth month of 1864 and ending the ninth month of 1865. During that twelve month period the local government expended 58,860 *ryō*, against a revenue of only 20,308 *ryō*, a ratio of roughly three to one. 24,000 *ryō*, or 40% of the total expenditure, went into interest payments on funds borrowed. Operating expenses of the domain for that year ran to 34,555 *ryō*, of which 79% was spent through the Edo office.

Other local governments spent similarly large proportions of their annual revenues in Edo, as the few examples below indicate:

| *Domain* | *Year* | *Percentage spent in Edo* |
|---|---|---|
| Kishiwada in Senshū | 1776 | 84 |
| Matsuyama in Bishū | 1850 | 77.8 |
| Shinjō in Dewa | 1855 | 77 |

In a word, every local domain suffered severe financial shortages due to heavy spending through its Edo offices.[54]

The growing funds shortage at the local level prompted the daimyō to issue orders providing for salary cuts for their retainers. Sometimes the salaries were simply cut in half; in other instances subordinates were forced to make loans of similar proportions to their lords. Borrowed amounts were never repaid, so that, in either case, the vassals were left much poorer. For a time the *bakufu* made loans to relieve the shortages in the domains, reducing its own warriors to straitened circumstances earlier than those serving the daimyō. From the beginning of the Genroku era (1688), the *bakufu* was not able to secure the finances needed in its own administration. This resulted in issuance of regulations to restrict the lives of the people to the lowest possible level, warriors and peasants alike, though the latter suffered most from this action of the government. It was not easy, of course, to enforce the regulations upon a people who had not so long ago seen a general rise in their standard of living.

The daimyō issued local bonds and opened new commercial enterprises to raise additional funds. They also borrowed money from local merchants under the guise of contributions (*goyōkin*). The funds obtained by these means revived their purchasing power. The *hatamoto*, for their part, enjoyed but poor credit standing and lacked even the minimum capital for commercial ventures. Their financial situation was considerably more strained than the daimyō. They were compelled to put their stipend rice on the market at a time when it was already glutted. Their conditon became increasingly bad.

About the time of the Kanbun era (1661–73) there appeared many rich merchants in Edo to meet the heavy demand for goods of the shogun and daimyō. These merchants also capitalized on many construction projects for temples and other structures. Kinokuniya Bunzaemon, a lumber dealer, became a contractor for civil engineering works of the *bakufu*, and Naraya Mozaemon, another contractor, won bids for construction work on the shrines of Nikkō. Both these men became millionaires through successful deals with *bakufu* officals, and lived quite extravagantly.

In contrast to the increasingly healthy economic progress among townsmen, the feudal lords' finances steadily worsened. Obligations to the *bakufu* had to be met, though, and operational expenses for official business and residential requirements in Edo swelled due to rising costs. There were no daimyō who had not turned to borrowing funds. Being confined to fixed revenues, they could hardly expect ever to liquidate their debts. Instead, the creditor merchants were offered warrior status in lieu of payment. Such promotions threw the status orientation of the social structure out of line.

The *hatamoto* and *gokenin*, who really felt the pinch of shortened finances, received their stipends in rice. Men assigned as their receiving agents, called *fudasashi*, went to the government warehouses in Asakusa, received their rice allotments, and immediately put them on the open market. The agents deducted their own commissions from the money gained for their masters.

A contemporary work, *Seji Kenbunroku* (Social Report), reports that there were some 96 offices of *fudasashi* agents in Edo. In due time they began lending money to the warriors at high rates of interests, holding the warriors' rice stipends as collateral.[55] Although the 25% *per annum* interests rates which they exacted were highly irritating to the financially desperate warriors, these 96 agents were able to pour huge sums into loans to the *hatamoto* and *gokenin.* Employing large clerical staffs to assist in accumulating great wealth, they managed to corner the money market of Edo. They evolved their own colorful style of life, known as *kuramae-fū* ("life down at the warehouses"), a style associated with townsmen of refined tastes. Their luxuries included entertainment both in the theaters and in the gay quarters of Yoshiwara.

Ihara Saikaku has classified Edo's "millionaires" on a silver coin standard, but if this were converted to gold it would yield the following rankings:

—*chōja*, up to 17,000 *ryo*, or the equivalent of daimyō with incomes over 25,000 *koku*;

—*bungensha*, up to 8,500 *ryō*, or the equivalent of daimyō with incomes over 12,000 *koku*;

—*kanemochi*, up to 3,300 *ryō*, or the equivalent of *hatamoto* with incomes over 5,000 *koku.*

If the comparison is made in terms of expenditures, though, the picture is quite different. The daimyō spent from one-half to two-thirds of their total revenue on salaries of their vassals and lesser warriors, while the merchants needed far less for salaries of the limited number of their employers, the *banto* and *tedai* (managers and clerks). The operating expenses of the daimyō ran to ten times as much as those of the merchants. Thus, the *chōja* was actually equivalent in real wealth to a daimyō commanding an income of 20,000 to 30,000 *koku.*[56]

The *hatamoto* and *gokenin* fell into desperate impoverishment, forcing the *bakufu* to come to their rescue in the interests of preserving the feudal order. A blow was struck at the wealthy *fudasashi* by the *bakufu*'s decision to establish an office for supplying them with funds, this office being called officially a "loan agency," or *kashitsuke-kaisho*. This was done because the *fudasashi* feigned shortage of funds as a pretense for charging high interest rates. But the disabling blow came in 1784 with the declaration of a kind of moratorium by the *bakufu*. By this action all debts incurred prior to that date were cancelled. Money borrowed from 1785 on could be repaid by small annual payments at low interest rates. This measure hit the lending agents very hard. It is said that the *fudasashi* suffered a collective loss of 1,187,808 *ryō*, 3 *bu* of gold, and 4 *monme*, 6 *pun*, 5 *rin*, 5 *mo* of silver.[57]

A similar action was taken in 1841, again lowering the boom on the *fudasashi*. But the *hatamoto* and *gokenin* actually suffered more from this measure, as they now experienced great difficulty in acquiring funds. Many were reduced to selling family treasures passed down through the generations. Some even turned to side jobs to earn extra money. The *Seji Kenbunroku*, quoted above, tells of "samurai and foot soldiers alike working at low-paid miscellaneous jobs, such as pasting paper on umbrella and lantern frames or making thongs for sandals and clogs. Wives and children worked alongside these humbled warriors. Eventually these men became more attached to the merchants who gave them jobs out of sympathy than to their military posts, and preferred to be townsmen themselves rather than warriors."[58] Dire poverty caused some to cast aside martial honor and became thieves. Others adopted sons of merchants as their heirs, in effect selling their family titles to townsmen. Such concourse with the townsmen enlarged the distortions already made in the stratified status system by diluting the privileged status of warriors.

The field of commerce was marked by an extensive development of the wholesaling mechanism. The impossibility of providing the immense quantity of goods needed in Edo from nearby areas has already been observed, as has the important place of the Kansai region in supplementing the necessary supply. The Kansai area was the center of Japan's commodity economy, from which expanded shipping and transportation services carried goods to all parts of the country. The *bakufu*'s free trade policy enhanced the operation of these services, such as the *Higaki-kaisen* and *Taru-kaisen* shipping lines opened in 1627 and 1661 respectively. Most of the wholesalers servicing Edo, it will be recalled, depended mainly upon products shipped from the Kansai area. The point to be made here is that the wholesalers found it difficult to function individually and established unions to counteract the overwhelming power of shipowners and shipping agents. Their concern was to protect their mutual interests as wholesalers in such concrete areas as marine casualties.

An example of such unions was the *Edo-jukkumi-donya,* a union of ten wholesalers, handling ten different kinds of wares: rice and oil, household goods, cotton, lacquerware, iron utensils and nails, sundries, *sake*, rapeseed, paper, ladies' accessories, and so on. In Ōsaka, on the other hand, there was founded a "union of Edo shipping brokers," *Edo-kaitsugi-donya*, later named *Nijūyonkumi-donya*, or "union of twenty-four wholesalers." These two unions in Edo and Ōsaka worked hand in hand to monopolize transactions between the two cities.

The *bakufu* made use of these unions of wholesalers to put newly-issued currency into circulation. In 1715 the *bakufu* helped various wholesaling cooperatives, *tonya-nakama*, to establish themselves, by giving them responsibility for circulating newly-coined gold and silver currencies. In the Kyōhō era (1716–36) the *bakufu* actively promoted the establishment of unions to strengthen price controls on goods. In 1721 official approval was granted existing unions, and where none existed the *bakufu* ordered their formation. All merchants proposing to open new businesses were forced to join a union.[59]

While union formations were encouraged within the context of a free trade policy, the intention of the *bakufu* was to increase its controls over commercial activity. Hence, two unions were allowed in the same occupational field so long as *bakufu* controls were not hampered. On the other hand, the merchants took advantage of the straitened circumstances of the *bakufu*, buying favors with large contributions (*myōgakin*) to the government's coffers, in order to secure monopolies in their respective fields. In the long run, it was the merchants who enjoyed the upper hand, amassing tremendous profits and vast economic power.[60]

The wealthier merchants and wholesalers depended heavily on close connections cultivated among feudal lords and warriors in charge of the executive offices of the *bakufu*. The primary mode of cultivating close relationships was to come to the aid of financially depressed warriors. In return, they were treated as equals by the warriors. This treatment was as precious to the merchants as commercial gain, for, in the framework of the feudal order, they respected the warriors very much and sought to emulate them. The merchants tried in their own lives to copy the style of the warriors. Even as the wealthiest and most powerful men of the merchant class they could not free themselves from the claims of feudal society, for they had attained to their positions of prominence by currying special favors from the military leaders. Prominence could not, however, conquer eminence. They were followers of the feudal order and not founders of a new society.

We have seen already, in the section on ecological structure, how most of the powerful merchants of Edo were concentrated in the Nihonbashi and Kyōbashi areas. The head households (*honke*) of these merchants maintained tight connections with their branch families (*bunke*). Relations among relatives were kept close not only for advantages in lending money and goods when needed, but also for pulling together in strengthening their social positions in general. Cooperation was a prime ingredient in their attaining to leading places in society.

Nakai Nobuhiko has pointed out that among merchants of the Edo period one's clients, in terms of both customers and connections with producers and sellers of goods, were passed on hereditarily. This sort of inheritance was as valuable as negotiable funds. The good name and reputation of a business firm, symbolized by the trade mark emblazoned on the short curtain (*noren*) generally hung over the door of a shop, store, or office, constituted as valuable a piece of "property" as any piece of land or consignment of commodities. Sharing the commercial rights to use of the cultivated name and mark, a practice known as *noren-wake* (sharing the *noren*), enabled branch "families" to capitalize on the prestige of a reputable trade name and mark regardless of whether the relations were actually based on kinship lines or not. The connection of main and branch households in this practice reflected clearly the master-subordinate motif of the age.

The well-known Mitsui firm's tradition of *noren-wake* dates back to around 1725. Those who were allowed to adopt the now famous name and trademark were called *katoku* ("household manager," implying a successor) and this title was transmitted hereditarily to each descendant. If a son other than the rightful heir sought to open a branch business, it was necessary to obtain first the approval of the main family. The same held true for any employee who proposed opening a branch under the Mitsui name.

Whenever a new *katoku* launched a new branch he paid an initiation fee called *makura-kake-gin* (lit., "price of laying one's head on the pillow") and subsequent monthly payments, *tsukizuki-kake-gin*, to the executive group of Mitsui family heads, *katoku-sōzoku-kō*. Such an arrangement made him a member of the executive fraternity of family heads. Twenty years after joining the management group he became eligible for a regular bonus paid at a fixed rate from the common holdings of the group. Also, if any number of the group got into financial difficulties, he could borrow from the group's joint holdings. Semi-annual executive meetings were held in the first and eighth months of each year. The success of any member was welcomed warmly by all, and they all worked together when conditions were not good. Mutual help and vigilance characterized the activities of all constituent families of the Mitsui union of households. All relationships, economic and social, were held to the norms necessary to accomplish total integration of all member families around the nuclear head family.[61]

The Mitsui pattern was but a large scale version of the lineage relationships existing among merchants in general. Intra-familial relations between a household head and his employees were formed along lines similar to those pertaining to households in large family unions.

Young employees entered firms as apprentices at age seven or eight by recommendation either of relatives of the head of that firm, or of merchants with whom the head did business. Their apprenticeship lasted for nearly ten years, during which time they underwent training that involved cleaning, messenger service, using the abacus, and learning to write letters. At ages fifteen or sixteen the apprentices were presented by the house master at the ceremony of *hangenbuku*, becoming semi-adults. From this time they were assigned to various jobs as assistants (*tedai*) to full clerks. When they became twenty-two or twenty-three years old they began serving as full-fledged clerks. This meant that they handled business directly, including negotiations with customers. Around age thirty they were regarded as having completed their apprenticeship and were promoted to management posts (*banto*). At this stage they were also permitted to marry.

Sons of the household head other than the eldest and employees of the *bantō* level were eligible to open new branches, although capital and market limitations often prevented them from doing so. Some established residences separate from the main household, called *uchibekke*, and were thus known themselves as *kayoi-bantō* (commuting managers). Young men still in apprenticeships received no wages; they were completely dependent upon their masters for food, clothing, living space, all necessary training, and even care when sick. All in all, compensation received was minimal.

Master-apprentice relationships were of exceedingly long-term duration. Even after a former apprentice became head of his own branch household and business, the same basic relationship of dependence and obligation toward the master persisted. Indeed, the relationship remained intact between the branch and the main households for generations after the persons originally involved were deceased. The pattern of mutual protection and obligation bound together the total complex of head and branch families and businesses into social entities very much like kinship groups.

This was a time of national isolation with no overseas markets. The limits of the domestic market left the craftsmen's position completely inferior to that of the merchants. One group of craftsmen, however, fared better than most. This group, called *goyōtashi-shokunin*, consisted of those who worked for the *bakufu* and daimyō. They enjoyed considerable influence in the city of Edo, and were provided houses similar to the regular warriors, had fixed salaries, and were even allowed to wear swords. A few were permitted audiences with the daimyō. Quite a number became wealthy, especially those who were directors (*kimoiri*) or elders (*toshiyori*) of the craftsmen's cooperatives. Such directors and elders represented the craftsmen in official contacts with the government.

The other main class of craftsmen were called *hira-shokunin*, or common craftsmen. Some worked outdoors at such jobs as carpentry, plastering, or mat-making; others plied indoor crafts such as tailoring, lantern-making, or making wooden clogs. Outdoor laborers worked for wages under contractors who were capitalistic enterprisers. The indoor artisans did piece work for wholesalers who placed orders with them. They, too, were subservient to capitalistic captains of commerce, and their standard of living was quite low. Most of them lived in rented houses on back streets (*uradana*).[62]

A craftsman boss' house was also his shop. Boys apprenticed to him came between ages eleven to thirteen. They lived in his house, received winter and summer clothes as well as their meals from him, plus small allowances of money. They were put to work at miscellaneous tasks as part of the training that was to prepare them for life-long roles in society as technicians. After living ten years as apprentices in the workshop of a particular boss they were acknowledged as adult craftsmen (*oyakata*) who were eligible to run their own shops, at around age twenty. If approved by their elders in the tradesmen's unions, they were admitted to membership (unions were established by order of the *bakufu* after the Kyōhō era (1716–36). They were then expected (in Edo) to work as roving craftsmen (*watari-shokunin*) to polish their technical skills and toughen their characters.

Capital funds, tools, and materials were limited, however, and many could not operate their own workshops as *oyakata*. Those who were not legal heirs of *oyakata* had to purchase, or succeed to another's, capital and title. Unable to do this, many were compelled to become wage earners sub-ordinate to some master and subject to the stringent obligations that went with such an inferior status. Many were reduced to being mere day-laborers, among whom were many dispossessed artisans from other provinces.

Conversion of craftsmen into wage earners loosened the bonds of the master-subordinate relationship. Even under the strictest surveillance of the craftsmen's cooperatives and of the workshop bosses, there were still some workers who left the shops. The unions sometimes organized religiously-oriented bodies to protect the interests of employers by thus strengthening the bonds of relationships through privately-controlled organizations. The system of apprenticeships was important to the *bakufu*, however, to turn out trained men to keep up industrial production. For this reason private organizations were outlawed by a notice of the *bakufu* circulated in 1795. From that time on, one could not find such mutual aid societies set up by the craftsmen themselves.[63]

Consumption levels in Edo reached a high peak during the last quarter of the 17th and the first quarter of the 18th centuries. The growth in economic power among merchants that resulted from supplying increased demands served to precipitate further differentiation in the status stratification of the townsmen. The following list of the groupings among townsmen is indicative of the differentiation:

1. The top group of townsmen included the wealthy merchants (*gōshō*), powerful wholesalers (*tonya*), and old established families (*monbatsu-chōnin*) concentrated in the central part of the city.
2. Next came leading merchants (*shōnin*) owning their own businesses and houses, located along the main streets on land

of their own, the *bakufu*'s and feudal lords' favored craftsmen (*goyōtashi-shokunin*) and leading contractors (*tōryō*) who also possessed their own properties.

3. Established landowners (*jinushi*) who were capable of supplying laborers and funds for public projects.
4. Tenants owning their own houses situated on rented property (*jikari*).
5. Tenants capable of renting front street shops and homes (*omotetanakari*).
6. Tenants who could afford only rented back street accommodations for living and working (*uratanakari*).

These categories indicate also the population distribution of townsmen in Edo. But this recalls our previous observation that the city had experienced quite an influx of lower class people who had deserted their native lands. The upper-middle layer of townsmen was composed mainly of merchants who had acquired their own shops after completing apprenticeships, those appointed as *kayoi-bantō*, and those craftsmen who had gained independent workshops as adult craftsmen with the assistance of contractors.

Development of the money economy accelerated the concentration of low class people in dirty back streets, producing an atmosphere of filth and degradation in striking contrast to the bright, prosperous shops of leading merchants on the main streets. Dwellers in the dark hovels jammed together on the back streets included the following types: low class servants of the warriors such as *kobito* and *wakatō*, low class artisans, low income laborers hired by merchants, peddlers of fish and vegetables in the markets, day laborers, palanquin bearers, porters, ox drivers, night stall operators, scrap paper dealers, and other low wage earners.[64]

The majority of Edo's population were men. This condition was pronounced in the back street districts, where the bachelor men were not, on the whole, strong-willed. The occasional woman on the back streets tended to be tough, ruling over private little petticoat kingdoms, contrary to the dominance accorded male members of the upper classes of warriors and townsmen.[65]

The most important thing in the lives of the common people of low status was the kind of relationships existing between landlords and tenants. Many landowners built cheap houses on secondary lots in their possession and put them under the supervision of rental agents, known variously as *yanushi*, *yamori*, or *ōya*. The *yanushi* managed all aspects of the business connected with his employer's lands and houses, including contacts with the municipal government. He looked upon all tenants on his lands or in houses, large or small, as his personal wards (*tanako*). He not only checked into their backgrounds and scrutinized their daily behavior, but also stood as guarantor when they bought or sold properties, acted as official witness for everything from birth, marriage, and death ceremonies to administering their wills, and attended the prosecution of legal suits involving them. At the same time he was responsible for seeing that government assessments made on his district for fire-fighting, bridge and drain construction, and local shrine festivities were all duly paid. The agent had a voice in local government affairs and membership in township associations. The tenants in his charge enjoyed none of these privileges, bore none of these obligations.

The *yanushi* received healthy incomes. Estimates based on the cost of rights to an agency indicate that *yanushi* were paid around 20 *ryō* per year by the landowners. Other miscellaneous income amounted to about 10 *ryō* annually. The sale of human waste collected in an agent's area for use as fertilizer brought in another 30 *ryō*–40 *ryō* a year, giving a total annual income of 60 *ryō*–70 *ryō*. Tenants on lands (*jikari*) or in houses (*tanakari*) presented the agent with "*sake* costs" (*tarudai*) in proportion to the size of the land or house rented when they first took up occupancy. The gifts varied from 2 *shu* 1 *bu* to as much as 3 *ryō*–10 *ryō*. Gifts of money were also offered the agent on five festival days (*gosetsu*) during the year. Such were the various sources of the miscellaneous income (*yotoku*) mentioned above.[66]

Among the many sorts of tenants, the lowest grade dwellers in humble shacks on the back streets had the greatest difficulty in paying the rents due daily. The rents often went unpaid for prolonged periods among these people, causing conflicts to erupt frequently between them and the agents. Some became vagabonds after being ousted by a landlord following some disagreement.

Below the lowest commoners were two types of outcasts, the *eta* and *hinin* (the "dirty" and "inhuman"). The *eta* and *hinin* were completely separated from all other classes of people. They could not become commoners, nor could the latter become *eta*. Marriages were permitted only within the *eta* groups, and they were forced to live within a fenced-in area, *kakoiuchi*, in Asakusa. Their isolated community had its own governing apparatus. The group's head, named Danzaemon, had his own assistants (*tedai*) and clerks (*shoki*). The *eta* were given monopoly rights for the rather distasteful work of tanning cowhides and producing leather goods. In return, they served as prison guards, guards for persons paraded publicly as punishment, and as executioners.[67] In 1800 there were 232 houses in the *kakoiuchi* community in Asakusa. Danzaemon, chief of the Asakusa community, also ruled over twelve *eta* communities in eight districts in the Kantō plain, Kai, Izu, Mutsu, and Suruga. The families under his control numbered 5,430.[68] His income is said to have been 597 *ryō* a year,[69] enabling him to live in the style of a daimyō with an annual income of 3,000 *koku*.[70]

Below even the *eta* were the *hinin*, essentially a criminal class. They were permitted to roam the country as beggars, and many earned a living watching patients in prison hospitals. The head of the *eta* community was also the overseer of the *hinin* people, and he arranged four residential places each in Asakusa and Shinagawa for their use. These residential sections were separated from other townships. Heads of the *hinin* shanty towns, such as Kuruma Zenhichi of Asakusa and Matsuzaemon of Shinagawa, were appointed to their posts. Kuruma Zenhichi is known to have been granted 900 *tsubo* (0.7 acre) by the *bakufu*, and he managed to live as comfortably as Danzaemon of Asakusa.

The *hinin* consisted of the following types of people:

1. Those born in *hinin* homes.
2. Those guilty of abnormal sexual behavior.
3. Those guilty of adultery and failure at attempted suicide.
4. Household heads who had attempted double suicides with maids but failed.
5. Men who had seriously injured their divorced wives.
6. Criminals convicted of a special form of gambling called *torinoki-mujin*.
7. Unregistered youths guilty of theft at less than fifteen years of age.
8. Those who, for personal reasons, sought entry into the *hinin* community of their own accord.

It was possible for a man who had come originally from the commoners' community to return to his previous status, on two conditions. One of the conditions was that in ten years or less of marital relations with a *hinin* woman there had been no children born of the relationship. The other provision was that his application for reversion to commoner's status be guaranteed by his relatives or some other party. Too, his application had to be processed according to procedures fixed by the *bakufu* office.[71]

*Hinin* had to shave their beards, bind their hair, and could wear no headgear. Clothes had to be cut at the knees. Women could not shave their eyebrows or blacken their teeth, as was common among ordinary married women. Clothes similar to those worn by common people were prohibited, and intermarriage with commoners was strictly forbidden.[72]

In addition to these two groups of outcasts, there were a few miscellaneous types, such as monkey-trainers (*sarumawashi*), and other low class showmen (*misemonoshi*), attendants at crematories (*onbo*), lowly shrine servants (*inujinin*) and certain gardeners (*mon-home* and *niwa-home*). They came under the control of the Asakusa *eta* village head, or some chief in their respective groups.

These are the outlines, then, of the status stratification that shaped life in the city of Edo. Not surprisingly, the status structure also influenced educational and entertainment possibilities, and the social functions varied in response to changes in the expression of feudal authority in the basic structure.

The educational policy of the *bakufu* with respect to cultivation of warriors contained much that was valuable. Its advantages, however, were not open to townsmen. Early in the Edo era education for children of commoners was, at best, minimal. Boys attended small schools in temples or shrines until they were eleven or twelve years old, before leaving home to enter some apprenticeship. Girls went to the same schools until they were fourteen or fifteen, when they too left home to work as maidservants in the homes of warriors and other citizens. There was a gradual increase in the number of these schools operated by temples (*terakoya*), by Shinto priests (*kannushi*), or in some cases, by lordless warriors (*rōnin*). The Kyōhō era (1716–36) marks the time generally when education among common people expanded. It is reported that in Edo there were 498 teachers (*tenaraishi*) in such private schools in the year 1821. This averages about two or three teachers for each township.

There was no prescribed curriculum in the private schools for commoners. Each teacher selected materials he considered appropriate. Educational aims cohered, however, in the preparation of youngsters for work in trades and commerce. Letter-writing and skill with the abacus formed a kind of "core curriculum" for all. Various travel guides (*ōraimono*) were used as texts for teaching history and geography. Laws and regulations for the conduct of the warrior class (*bukeshikimoku*), as well as copies of public notices posted by the government (*kōsatsu*) were utilized for civic instruction. Tales were told of the exemplary loyalty and constancy of persons who had lived in former eras. Such stories made up a kind of moral education for the pupils.

In the latter half of the Tokugawa period when the social position of the merchant class had improved greatly, upper class townsmen were permitted (1793) to attend lectures held in the Confucian temple (*Seidō*) in Yushima. Prior to that time this institute for the dissemination of the officially-adopted ideology had been exclusively for warriors. It was the growing capability of powerful merchants to influence the *bakufu* that opened the doors of this educational mecca to leaders among the townspeople. Thus, the monopoly of the warriors over education at its highest level was broken.[73]

The entertainment features of the city of Edo were shaped by the pre-eminence and wealth of the warrior class in the early half of the Edo period. Facilities for townsmen were greatly different and inferior. Noh drama, for instance, was shown to townsmen only on rare occasions for special celebrations when some of them were admitted to the castle or other places of performance. Otherwise, performances were restricted to enjoyment by the warriors.

The Yoshiwara quarter was founded by Shōji Jin-emon, a *rōnin* from Odawara, at Yoshi-chō in Nihonbashi soon after Ieyasu entered Edo. The land was given by Ieyasu to this entreprenuer. The ladies of the quarter, called *shōgi* (licensed prostitutes), were tutored in writing letters, composing Japanese verse (*waka*), playing musical instruments, performing the tea ceremony, and in the use of fine perfumes. They were all-round entertainers skilled in the fine arts of the day. They were classified into several different grades appropriate to serving the many ranks of daimyō and warriors. Yoshi-chō was the socializing center of Edo.

Following the conflagration of the Meireki era, Yoshi-chō was incorporated into the city's central area in the restoration and reconstruction that was part of the urban expansion programs already described. The entertainment quarter of Yoshiwara was transferred to a new district near Sanya in Asakusa, and was now called Shin-yoshiwara, or "New Yoshiwara." By this time the warriors were poorer and the merchants richer. Shin-yoshiwara thrived from patronage by affluent townsmen. Classified standings among the courtesans became confused, and the cultured tone of the old quarter gave way to an atmosphere of debauchery and decadence. It was converted from a place of exclusive entertainment to a common amusement center.[74]

The prosperity of Shin-yoshiwara derived partly from a shortage in the supply of girls available in Edo, where the male population constituted an overwhelming majority. Not only were the prostitutes in the officially recognized Shin-yoshiwara district licensed by the *bakufu*, but engaging in prostitution was prohibited in other places. Groups of girls trained as geisha did appear in certain sections of the city, however, where the economic standing of the resident community had developed to a rather high level. In the Tenmei (1781–89) and Kansei (1789–1801) eras geisha groups were found in the following places: Naka-chō in Fukagawa, Takanawa in Shiba, Nigai-chō, Yagenbori in Ryōgoku, Yanagibashi, Shinmichi in Hon-chō and Koku-chō, Naka-chō in Asakusa, Hirokōji in Shitaya, around Tenjin Shrine in Yushima, and in front of Shinmei Shrine in Shiba.[75]

Kabuki drama shared with Yoshiwara the place of first importance in amusement in Edo. No established theaters appeared in the early construction stages of the city. For performances there were only simple tents of straw matting supported with bamboo poles. In 1624 Saruwaka Kanzaburo erected a small theater for temporary use, the first of its kind. In 1632 it was transferred to Negi-chō. Yamamura-za theater (later called Ichimura-za) was built in Fukiya-chō in 1634. The Saruwaka-za theater (later called Nakamura-za) was moved to Sakai-chō in 1651. Another Yamamura-za was built in Kobiki-chō in 1642. The three theaters in Fukiya-chō, Sakai-chō, and Kobiki-chō enjoyed prosperous patronage.

After the Meireki fire theaters were concentrated in Sakai-chō and Kobiki-chō, including new ones such as Morita-za and the Edo-shiza ("four theaters of Edo"). Yamamura-za was ordered destroyed afterward because of an illicit affair between a leading actor named Ikushima Shingoro and a court lady named Eshima from Ō-oku. Concern for public morals had other, far-reaching effects on Kabuki customs. Female actreses were employed at the theaters initially. Aroused about immorality the government took steps to replace them with young boys (*wakashū*). Then homosexual practices became a problem, and the authorities prohibited the employment of youths. Thereafter, until the present, female parts were played by men, called *oyama*.[76]

Much of the public entertainment in the Edo era derived from religious celebrations. The festival of the Sannō Shrine drew on the assistance of all citizens of Edo, and was regarded as one of the three major festivals of Japan. The shogun was always present to review the grand parade through the city's streets, in which portable shrines (*mikoshi*) and decorated mobile stages (*dashi*) were central attractions. Each township in Edo competed with the others for prestige in decorations and costumes. Prominent citizens invited friends and relatives to receptions in their homes on this occasion.

The citizens all participated in the festivals of Hachiman and Kanda Shrines. Particular pride was exhibited in these festivals by those who were native born or long-established in Edo. Such persons were known as *Edokko* (children of Edo). "*Edokko*" was defined by Ashinoya Sanjin in his book *Edo-funai Ehon Fūzoku Ōrai* (Pictorial Guide to the Manners and Customs of Old Edo) as a person who was a parishioner (*ujiko*) of the Kanda Myōjin or Sanno Daigongen (shrines) and was born in the parishes of these shrines. In addition to these festivals, there were such common leisure activities as petitionary prayers for prosperity in business (*ebisu-kō*), the annual fireworks display near the Sumidagawa river celebrating the opening of the summer season (*kawabiraki*), and viewing cherry blossoms at their peak in springtime. These were the most widespread public recreational outlets among the common people.

*Social Controls.*——Edo's citizens enjoyed limited freedom in certain areas of life. On the whole, though, they were tightly bound within the status system that affected every stratum of society. In the feudal order informed by an isolationist nationalism there were mechanisms of control for every structural level of culture and society. These mechanisms were either tied to, or embodied within, the administrative system of Edo which maintained and strengthened them.

The administrative network was based upon the major constituent entities, namely, the warrior and townsmen classes, and the temple and shrine institutions. We have already seen that the warriors' communities were under the vigilant supervision of a corps of inspectors, *ōmetsuke* and *metsuke*, which, in turn, was controlled by the ruling elders and their assistants, *rōjū* and *waka-doshiyori*. Civic obedience was further enforced by patrolmen, *mawarikata*, who functioned under orders from groups of ranking *hatamoto* under command of the *waka-doshiyori*. Areas under the immediate administration of temples and shrines were subsumed under the official bureau of religious institutions, *jisha-bugyō*. Likewise, communities of townspeople were governed in all administrative and judicial affairs by the town commissioner's office, *machi-bugyō*. Authority over all townsmen was implemented in terms of numerous laws and regulations reaching into every sector of life.

Division of authority into three primary bureaus for the military, religious, and commoners' communities rendered the overall system much too complex. Incidents occurring within the official scope of more than one bureau often caused delays in administrative action while documents were exchanged to determine proper procedure. Under such conditions municipal administration could not be integrated adequately. Officials in the top bureaus for finance, military affairs, and religious institutions were responsible for administration of the widespread territories not within particular feudal domains but controlled directly by the *bakufu*. They also had executive duties within the city of Edo. In general, national business took precedence and the concerns of Edo comprised but a minor part of their official business. Consequently, officials in the *machi-bugyō* became the effective rulers of Edo. They were the contemporary specialists in complicated metropolitan administration.

Prior to the Kan-ei era (1624–44) appointments to the office of town commissioner were restricted to warriors with incomes over 10,000 *koku*. Because the *bakufu* needed men of ability in this important office, men were later appointed from among high-ranking *hatamoto*. In some cases the position went to warriors receiving only 500 *hyō* (bales). Remuneration for the town commissioner's job was originally 1,000 *hyō* of rice, as in 1666. This was revised in 1723 so that, if a warrior was drawing only 500 *koku* before being appointed to the *machi-bugyō* position, his salary was increased by an additional 2,500 *koku* for a total of 3,000 *koku*.[77]

The town commissioners were increased to three in number temporarily in the Genroku era (1688–1704). As a rule, though, there were only two, one each for the southern (*minami-machi-bugyō*) and northern (*kita-machi-bugyō*) halves of the city. These two officers were in charge of overall administration in alternate months, the commissioner-in-charge being *tsukiban* (monthly duty), the other *hiban* (off-duty). Locations of the town commissioners' offices changed often, until 1804 when *minami-machi-bugyō* was situated in Sukiyabashi, and *kita-machi-bugyō* was put in Gofukubashi.

Boundaries of the territory controlled by the town commissioners tended to fluctuate irregularly, some areas being actually separated from the main city of Edo. The boundary line may be indicated in general as follows: from Takanawa of Minami-chō on the Tōkaidō route, it passed through Meguro-fudō of Nakahara of Sōshū, to Dōgenzaka of Shibuya on the road to Atsugi, to Ōkido of Yotsuya on the Kōshū-kaidō highway, to Okago-machi of Sugamo on the Nakasendō route, to Hichiken-chō of Somei on the highway to Iwatsuki and, finally, across the big bridge of Senju to the front gate of Genchōji temple in Kamonjuku on the Ōshūdō highway. Honjo and Fukagawa on the far east side of the Sumidagawa river were included in the territory of Edo, as were also Shinagawa and Shin-yoshiwara.[78]

Townships in Edo were classified into three categories: old towns, ordinary towns, and temple towns (*furumachi*, *machinamiji*, and *monzen-chō* respectively). Old towns were those registered with the *machi-bugyō* before 1624. This category included 300 townships, later subdivided into 387 townships. Residents in the old towns were exempted from taxes, but were liable for duties (*kuyaku* and *kuniyaku*) levied to meet national needs for riparian works and other civil engineering projects. Other towns registered with the commissioners' office by the Genroku (began 1688) or Hōei (began 1704) eras were treated much the same as *furumachi*.

Residents of the ordinary towns were registered with the *machi-bugyō*, although the lands were administered by local magistrates (*daikan*). These towns were originally farming communities. As Edo expanded, registrations were changed to the Edo administration, most of them during the Shōtoku era (1711–6). Taxes were paid through the *daikan*.

Temple towns were built up on a portion of the lands owned by, and surrounding, some shrine or temple. During the Enkyō era (1744–8) residents of most religious communities came under the control of Edo's *machi-bugyō*, although lands remained under temples' and shrines' registration. Rents for use of land were paid to the shrines and temples, rightful owners of the land.[79]

The increase in the number of townships under the control of the *machi-bugyō* in the latter half of the Tokugawa period is shown in the following list:

| *No. of townships* | *Era dates* | | |
|---|---|---|---|
| *Ca.* 300 | Kan-ei | | (1624–44) |
| 933 | Shōtoku | 4 | (1714) |
| 1,483 | Kan-en | 2 | (1749) |
| 1,668 | Kansei | 4 | (1792) |
| 1,685 | Kōka | 4 | (1847) |

Sizes of the towns varied greatly, from very large to very small. On the average, a township had some 350–360 residents, belonging to about 90 households.

Guards (*yoriki*) and policemen (*dōshin*) were employed by the Edo administration to maintain law and order throughout the extensive territory of the city. In the early stages there were only 25 *yoriki* and 50 *dōshin* each under the southern and northern offices of the *machi-bugyō*. The number increased until there were 140 each of the guards and policemen under the two commissioners' command by 1859. *Yoriki* received payment of 200 *koku* annually, though the method of payment made it equivalent to 800 *koku*. Base pay for the *dōshin* was 30 bales of rice, but payment was made in double allotments as a single allotment amounted to only about five *go* (less than one quart) per day. They were, however, provided with house lots in the Hatchōbori section of Kyōbashi district and were known as *Hatchōbori-no-danna* (bosses), a name that struck fear in the hearts of ordinary citizens.[80] While the town commissioners were often replaced, the *yoriki* and *dōshin* usually passed on their jobs to their sons. Hereditary tenure in office afforded them considerable access to vital information. This accumulated knowledge aided greatly in their effectiveness in securing public order even with limited forces, and they could usually count on support from the citizens' self-government organizations.

Guards and policemen were divided into five companies of men, with the head of the *yoriki* guards being also in charge of supervising duties and status of the *dōshin* patrolmen. In the formative days of the *machi-bugyō* responsibilities were not clearly defined. When the police force became quite busy the ranks and duties came to be more specifically determined. The list below indicates the extent of the division of responsibilities developed:

*nenban-kata*—officer on alternate year's duty
*ginmi-kata*—criminal investigator
*shichū-torishimari-kakari*—street patrolman
*yurushichō-kata* and *senchō-kata*—bookkeepers
*reikuri-kata*—recorder
*yōbeya-kata*—assistants to executive officers
*tōban-kata*—officers-in-charge
*Honjo-mimawari*—patrolmen in Honjo area
*yōjōsho-mimawari*—hospital patrolman
*jōbashi-kakari*—supervisor of bridges
*machikaisho-kakari*—supervisor of township offices
*machikaikeisho-kakari*—supervisor of township accounting offices
*Saruya-chō-kaisho-mimawari*—patrolmen on duty at office of Saruya-chō township
*kodōbukisho-mimawari*—patrolman for waste copper smelting office
*takatsumi-aratame*—guards for large stocks of supplies
*Hakozaki-kaisho-torishimari-kakari*—supervisor of Hakozaki township office
*shōseki-kaisho-torishimari-kakari*—supervisor of office for gunpowder
*machihikeshi-ninsoku-aratame*—chief of fire brigade of a township

As a rule, the *yoriki* and *dōshin* worked together on a ratio of one to two in the above duties. *Dōshin* worked alone at certain tasks, such as:

*onmitsu-mawari*—secret patrols
*jō-mawari*—regular patrol duty
*rinji-mawari*—temporary duty
*ninsokuyoseba-kakari*—inspector of detention camps for minor criminals.

In addition a special section for fire prevention, apprehending thieves, and being on lookout for gamblers was established in 1666. *Hatamoto* were in command of this section, assisted by *yoriki* and *dōshin*.

A lower rank of men were called *okkappiki*, the guards and regular patrolmen making the daily patrols of the towns. They were paid very low wages yet, even so, hired assistants called *tesaki*, who were dependents living in their houses. Relationships between these low-ranked deputies were strictly of the boss-subordinate type. These men often arrested innocent citizens on false charges to collect fines as supplementary income. The citizens were constantly annoyed by this misuse of connections with the powers of government.

Territorial expansion and the proliferation of types of people in the city of Edo precipitated a wide range of civic disorder such as quarrels, fights, vandalism, riots, injuries, abandoned children, dead left in the streets, and fires. Lookout posts were erected in the streets as an additional measure for securing public safety. In the residential communities of the warriors, 871 of these watch points (*tsujiban*) were built in the Genbun era (1736–41). In 1853 similar lookouts (*jishinban*) for townsmen districts are reported to have numbered 1,016.

Of the *tsujiban* there were three types. *Kōgi-tsujiban* were built and maintained by the central government; *daimyō-tsujiban* by the feudal lords. Another type, *kumiai-tsujiban* (or, *yoriai-tsujiban*), maintained by the *hatamoto*, were the most numerous, reaching 669. Guards working in these street lookouts were placed under the strict control of the *bakufu*, and any one of them caught concealing money or goods valued at over one *ryō* was punished by death after being paraded through the city.[81]

The *jishinban* lookouts were built in every township, with towers erected for detecting fires. Landlords and other watchmen took turns at lookout duty night and day. These local leaders of the townships gathered in the *jishinban* whenever some incident occurred in their precinct to discuss corrective measures. The guards and patrolmen (*yoriki* and *dōshin*) of the *machi-bugyō* often attended the local meetings to check on arrests being made. Notices issued by the town commissioner were posted at the town lookouts, which were situated on the boundaries of the local townships. Watchmen (*bantarō*) of the lookouts lived close by, tending the town's gates opposite the lookout. Such a watchman often carried on a side-business selling cakes for children, paper supplies, candles, and straw sandals (*waraji*). The town gates were closed at 10:00 p.m., after which entrance was possible only by a small side gate (*kuguri*). When anyone passed through the *kuguri*, the *bantarō* announced the fact by striking wood clappers (*hyōshigi*). Doctors or midwives on emergency calls could gain immediate entry.[82] If a crime occurred, the town gates were closed to help in catching the offender.

Legal codes for controlling society through implementation by the judicial organs of the government bear looking into. Regulations for control over the warrior class, *shoshi-hatto*, were issued in 1632 along with similar laws governing farmers, *gōson-hatto*. Regulations applicable to ordinary citizens, *Edo-machijū-sadame*, followed in 1655. Many additional laws and regulations were added. Capital punishment was decided by judges; their decisions were rendered according to the body of laws.

In 1742 the *bakufu* published its legal codes in two volumes titled *Kujikata Osadamegaki*. The first volume covered police administration, the second the penal code and judicial procedures. The contents were not publicized and they consisted of brief abstracts to which judges appended their own opinions in rendering decisions. Consequently, the range of application of the police and criminal laws was very wide indeed.

Major punishments provided for in the *Osadamegaki* were as follows:

*kashaku* —formal admonishment;
*oshikome* —brief confinement;
*tataki* —beating with a rod;

*tsuiho* —expulsion from a limited residential area;
*entō* —expatriation to some island far from the main island of Japan;
*shikei* —death penalty.

Secondary punishments included:

*sarashi* —pilloried in public, at Nihonbashi or other places;
*irezumi* —tattooed on the left arm;
*kessho* —confiscation of family land, with other lands taken in heavier punishments;
*hinin-teshita*—degrading to *hinin* status.

Particular penalties were prescribed for persons within a specific status group. For example, the following punishments could be dealt to warriors:

*hissoku* —limited confinement;
*heimon* —moderate confinement, with the gate of one's house closed officially;
*chikkyo* —strict confinement to one room;
*inkyo* —extended strict confinement;
*naga-inkyo* —confinement for life, with relinquishing of all official posts;
*kaieki* —removal from the official registry as a warrior, including confiscation of all lands;
*azuke* —placement of a warrior in another's custody;
*seppuku* —condemned to commit "suicide," though actually involving decapitation when the condemned took his sword in hand;
*zanzai* —death by decapitation.

Examples of punishment meted out to townsmen included:

*karyō* —light fines;
*keimon* —house confinement with the house gate closed for 50 to 100 days;
*tegusari* —hands of the punished were chained.

Special punishments for priests found guilty were:

*sarashi* —pillory
*tsui-in* —expulsion from the temple to which the priest belonged;
*ippa-kamae* —expulsion from the particular branch of his sect;
*isshu-kamae*—expulsion from his sect.

In meting out punishments the central criterion was that the heaviest penalties were given those who violated the master-subordinate relationships so essential to maintaining the feudal system. Examples taken from the *Osadamegaki* will bear this out.

Those who killed their masters were sentenced to multiple punishment, beginning with two days in the pillory, one day of being paraded publicly in the streets, infliction of wounds with a handsaw, and finally crucifixion. Persons guilty of injuring their masters were punished only by pillorying and crucifixion. The same applied to anyone killing a former master. If a man and woman were guilty of attempted double-suicide, they were subject to three days in the pillory and degrading to *hinin* status. Priests engaging in illicit relations with women were punished in the pillory and turned over to the chief abbot of their sect for further punishment according to the sect's own regulations. Theft involving more than 10 *ryō* was punishable by death, as was accidental homicide and even serious injury caused by negligence. Certainly from a modern viewpoint, most of these punishments were far too cruel and harsh.

Not only were the punitive measures severe, but the exercise of justice, that is, the judicial system itself, was subject to strong pressures from those in top positions of authority. The mass of people were quite powerless in the face of the overpowering pressures of government and were, therefore, timid and fearful. While it is true that the values of the feudal system were indeed internalized to a great extent, the preservation of the solidified social order based on stratification by status, where there was no equality before the law or fundamental respect for the individual, was possible only through the exercise of such stringent external controls.

Social control measures were not limited, however, to negative, punitive provisions, but also included more positive means of guiding public behavior. In an age of no mass communication instruments like newspapers, radio and television, the official boards for posting public notices (*kōsatsu*) were of special importance. There were six main notice boards at the following places: Tokiwabashi gate, Sujikaebashi gate, Asakusabashi gate, Kōjimachi Hanzomon, Fudanotsuji and Nihonbashi. In addition to these, there were 35 *kōsatsu* boards at various places in the city such as crossing points of rivers, port entrances, and the Ōmon (large gate) of Yoshiwara. The *kōsatsu* posting places commanded great respect from the people, for here they learned of the laws and regulations effecting their lives. Posting boards were surrounded by low stone walls with fences on top, and were covered by roofs. The sign boards were made of selected plum, pine, or Japanese cedar wood. While many examples of *kōsatsu* notices might be given, we have chosen for an example a notice put up by the *machi-bugyō* in the fifth month of the year 1711 (Shōtoku 1), concerning public morals.

1. All persons are to exhibit courtesy in all relationships, toward parents, children, sons and daughters, brothers and sisters, husbands and wives, and even servants. Everyone must be diligent in serving his or her master. Each must do his utmost in his appointed work, and no one must exceed the bounds of his status.
2. Do not lie, or otherwise impose senseless harm or duties upon others.

3. All gambling is prohibited.
4. Do not quarrel or fight with others. If you encounter such disputes, do not take sides or join in. Do not conceal injured persons in your houses.
5. Use of firearms is prohibited. If you know of such use, inform the proper authorities. If you fail to do so and the information is reported by others, you will be subject to severe punishment.
6. The government must be informed of any thieves or vandals. Prompt reporting will be rewarded.
7. Citizens are forbidden to gather at places where criminals are being punished by death.
8. All purchasing and selling of human beings are strictly prohibited. However, male or female servants who have served traditionally or for a long time may be traded legitimately through decisions made by the parties concerned. Once established in another place with their families they may not be recalled or received in your house again, except as implementation of a penalty imposed upon them for criminal action. This notice must be strictly obeyed. Anyone acting contrary to this notice will be punished severely.[83]

The *kōsatsu* continued in use up to the time the *bakufu* was dissolved. The importance of this instrument of public communication was not only in making known the behavioral norms expected of the common people, but also in strengthening the parent-child, master-subordinate morality that undergirded the feudal order.

Certain notices were left up and in effect permanently. The intent of such notices can be surmised from these issued in the Shōtoku era (1711–16):

—A prohibition against use of poisons, against counterfeit gold and silver coins, and against starting fires;
—A prohibition against Christianity;
—A notice concerning rates for pack-horses.

Similar examples from the next era, Kyōhō (1716–36), included prohibitions on possessing firearms, and horse and porter rates. In other words, most of the *kōsatsu* were directed toward achieving public safety and order. For this purpose it was necessary to restrict individual freedom. The most significant of the notices, in terms of cultural history, was the ban on the Christian faith.

When Japan was closed to foreign intercourse, the edicts against Christianity were an integral part of this move. But the embryonic Christian movement could not be entirely suppressed, and certain groups survived underground. Three groups of Christians of about fifty each were punished at Shibaguchi in Edo in 1623, 1638, and 1640 respectively. They were either burned at the stake, or crucified upside-down at the seashore with their heads in the water. In 1654 it was announced that the reward for reporting those suspected of Christian affiliations was to be increased. Likewise, those found guilty of concealing Christians were subject to severe punishment along with fellow members of their neighborhood group (*gonin-gumi*). The reward for informing on Christians was increased again in 1711.[84] The continued concern of the *bakufu* in apprehending Christians is evidence, then, of their persistent clandestine existence.

The foregoing paragraphs have indicated (1) the organization of the central government as it effected municipal administration in Edo, (2) the social control system, and (3) the social norms informing the city's administration. It is important to realize that such policies and programs were executed for a vast population by a relatively small class of ruling elite. Hence, it is necessary to explore further the reasons for the effective rule by so small a corps of leaders.

First of all, the thorough penetration of the feudalistic morality into all layers of society must be underscored. Through its application to family life, to life in the neighborhoods and townships, and to occupational structures, the people were domesticated so as to follow the lead of the feudal authority. In Edo society one could not observe any emerging freedom of the individual based on the rising power of people from the bottom. There was lacking among the people any strong critical spirit or thought pattern based on respect for individual worth. The norms imposed by the ruling class were accepted passively. Parallel to such conformity, and as if to assist the process voluntarily, organizations were formed by and among the citizens which facilitated the governing processes imposed from above.

Under the overall supervision of the *machi-bugyō* of the central government, the ranking townsmen were three elders (*machi-doshiyori*) operating under the inherited family names of Taruya, Naraya, and Kitamura. These men were superior to the elders of particular towns. Their function was to connect the *machi-bugyō* of the *bakufu* with the local township organizations, and they controlled the township unions (*sōmachi*). These three officials took turns at monthly duty (*tsukiban*). Duties included distribution of notices (*ofure*) issued by the *machi-bugyō*, investigating matters at the request of the *machi-bugyō*, allocating lands during expansion programs, collecting rents and taxes on land and forwarding them to the *bakufu*, and appointing and dismissing the heads of townships (*machi-nanushi*). Operative at the most important levels of the city's administrative business, the three elders were general managers of the townsmen.

The elders were descended from former vassals of Tokugawa Ieyasu who had good records of service and had been appointed to office when Ieyasu set up his government in Edo. Endowed with their own lands, their residences served also as their offices. Their incomes ran from 550 *ryō* to 600 *ryō* per year, coming from rents due on their lands but going into expenses incurred in the fulfilment of their positions. Though townsmen, their status was highly esteemed and they were permitted to wear swords. The fact that they were granted audiences with the shogun suggests the character of their roles as semi-officials of the *bakufu.*

Just below the elders were the heads of towns, *nanushi.* Some were heads of unions of smaller townships (*sōsō-nanushi*) ranging from three or four to more than twenty. There were heads of the old towns, the ordinary towns, and the temple towns. Some of these, of course, had responsibility for only one township. Toward the end of the Tokugawa period there were nearly 1,700 townships in Edo, but as early as 1790 there were 252 *nanushi.* On the average a single head managed six townships with 550 households. In the unions of several towns, the individual towns had a chief clerk (*tsuki-gyōji*) who was responsible to the *nanushi* of the union.[85]

Official notices relayed through the top three elders were posted at the police lookouts in townspeople's communities. It was the town head's responsibility to see that due attention was given the notices. To restrict influx from rural areas the town heads investigated any unfamiliar persons in their communities. To support the national government's intensified campaign to control public morality, the *nanushi* also checked on observance of obligations for loyalty and filial piety.

Routine work included fire prevention, town finances, and submitting petitions to offices of the *bakufu* on behalf of his town. Influence of the heads in their townships was quite strong. Their business was conducted largely in the entrance halls (*genkan*) of their homes, so the homes of the heads of towns were referred to as *genkan.*[86] Residents of a township could appeal to the *bakufu* if dissatisfied with decisions of the *nanushi,* but the appeal document had to have the official seal of the town head. Actually it was impossible for townsmen to avail themselves of this legal right. The *nanushi* became petty dictators among the citizens.

The *nanushi*'s office usually passed to his heirs by hereditary rights, though formal procedures of "recommendation" were enacted. The formula of recommendation remained through later ages. Whenever an heir was to succeed to office, and especially when a new town head was to be appointed, he was formally recommended by joint action of the landowners, *yanushi,* of the town, who were the effective bosses of local communities. Formal appointment was made by the *machi-bugyō* after receiving the recommendation of the *yanushi.* The *machi-bugyō* could also dismiss a *nanushi.* The town heads were supposed to confine themselves to official business, refraining from commercial transactions. Exceptions were made in the case of townsmen with the title of *yōtashi,* that is, merchants operating with the special favor of the *bakufu.* Salaries for the town heads were paid by the *bakufu,* and differed greatly in individual cases. The lowest was paid 1 *ryō,* 2 *bu* a year. The highest, paid to Magome Kageyu, *nanushi* of Kodenma-chō, was 301 *ryō,* 2 *bu* of gold and 12 *fun* of silver. Salary levels depended upon the circumstances under which the towns heads were appointed. The most common income of the *nanushi* was less than 100 *ryō* of gold. Supplementary income was obtained, however, in the form of commissions received for mediating contracts on lands and houses.[87]

Hereditary succession to the office of town head inevitably meant that some came into power only to abuse it. In such cases the *bakufu* often failed to appoint a successor and closed the office, thereby reducing the number of *nanushi*. The elder Naraya petitioned the government not to decrease the number of *nanushi* in 1722, and the *bakufu* responded by reorganizing the offices so as to hold them mutually responsible for each other.

At that time there were 263 *nanushi* organized into seven sub-groups (*bangumi*). As temple towns were added the groupings were upset, causing reformation into twenty-one groups plus two special groups for Shinagawa and Shin-yoshiwara. In 1790 there were elected two or three *nanushi* from each of the groups (*bangumi*) who were called *kimoiri-nanushi*, or managers. There were forty-seven of them, and they were responsible for the other *nanushi* in each of their groups. Abuse of power continued to breed trouble, and in 1831 the system of *kimoiri-nanushi* was revised. In the new arrangement thirty-two stewards (*sewagakari*) were nominated to represent each group, one or two from each group. In the process of supervision there emerged a degree of differentiation of functions, necessitated by expansion in the volume of their administrative work.[88]

The smallest organizational units of citizens' self-government were teams of five landlords, called *yanushi-gonin-gumi*. The *yanushi* numbered 20,115 in 1791, although political measures reduced this figure to 15,192 by 1853. Normally about ten of these local landowner politicians were in one township, forming two five-member teams. They worked collectively to solve local problems.

The five-man teams determined the managers (*tsuki-gyōji*) who handled the town's routine work, using the town lookouts as offices. Their duties included: investigation of reported Christians and vagabonds; witnessing official inspection of dead persons; maintaining custody of prisoners; supervising fire brigades and winter fire watches; and overseeing road repairs. Their seal was required on contracts of house or land tenancy, and the *tsuki-gyōji* accompanied the party concerned to the *machi-bugyō* office to petition for approval of the transaction.

The *yanushi* were landowners of both lands and houses for rent in their towns but, as we mentioned earlier, hired bosses (*ōya*) to handle concrete business details. The hired agents represented their employers in public rights and duties, which were neither few nor light. For instance, the landowner could be held liable if a criminal was found among residents in his houses. Therefore, the *yanushi* took extreme care in checking the background and behavior of their tenants, or *tanako*. The latter could do virtually nothing without first consulting the landlords. The relationship was a paternalistic one that was almost absolute. If a tenant had the misfortune to be under a tyrannical landlord, legally he had the right to petition the town head for dismissal of the landlord. But, as town heads (*machi-nanushi*) and *yanushi* worked hand in hand to maintain stability and security in their town, the tenants were quite helpless.

The organs of local government in Edo were designed to strengthen and sustain the hierarchical structures of complete obligation on the part of inferiors by organizations of mutual responsibity at every level. Controls over the warriors were strict. Even more so were the townsmen prevented from taking individual or group initiatives among themselves, as is common in modern times. The organizations of government tied the behavior of every class of citizens to the sufferance of immediate superiors, all the way to the very top of the warrior-dominated feudal order.

## 3. Relations between Edo and Ōsaka

To see the relations, and the contrasts, between Edo and Ōsaka, one the political and the other the commercial center of the nation, it is necessary to recapitulate some of the broad outlines of the national situation.

Political administration of the country was a combination of the *bakufu* structures and the provincial governments of the domains. The national economy had its foundation in the many domain economies. There was no foreign trade feeding into, and thus stimulating the overall economy. Despite this, there developed a number of very large cities in Japan, the largest being Edo. This development was accelerated, on the one hand, by the concentration of consuming populations in the cities that were centers for the large warrior class, with many priests and military subordinates to swell the total number. On the other hand, there was the equally important concentration of those engaging in intensified commercial activity to supply the extensive demands of the large consumer population drawn together by political power. The total process depended upon an increased surplus provided by the rural communities. The process evolved its own regulatory instruments in the form of the free markets (*rakuichi* and *rakuza*), traffic and transportation means, a money system, and standardized weights and measures. The concentration of expanded commercial communities in the urban areas was a most significant enabling factor in the development of huge cities in Japan.

Increased consumption of goods and funds followed soon upon completion of the castle in Edo and in conjunction with carrying out the plans for constructing a suitable castle city. After the system of alternate year's required residence was established under Tokugawa Iemitsu, the third shogun of the Tokugawa regime, there was a sharp increase in population and, hence, demands for goods. The population and consumption levels were sustained at a high peak because of the vast numbers of subordinates kept in permanent residence in Edo by the feudal lords.

Their competitive efforts to exhibit their relative power through extravagance in residential construction and luxurious living were not incidental factors in stimulating commercial activity.

Already we have shown the extent of the concentration of merchants and craftsmen to supply the warrior groups, and how the population of Edo was pushed over the one million mark in the Edo period. We have seen, too, how the sustained impulse toward even better living conditions helped to push the level of consumer demand far beyond the productive capacities of the Kantō district surrounding the city of Edo. Thus it was that Ōsaka attained so important a place as the chief supply center to the national capital of Edo.

Ōsaka had been the center of the commodity economy even in ancient times. The insatiable market of Edo served to enlarge this function many times over, enabled primarily by the effective development of marine transport, as we shall see shortly. Whereas Edo was a warriors' city, Ōsaka was a city of townsmen, with a population of 350,000 in the Genroku era (1688–1704).

The expansion of Ōsaka was closely connected with the achievement of greater mobility in the transportation of goods, not just between it and Edo, but all over the country. Transport mobility was not easily gained over land routes due to mountainous terrain and relatively poor roads, and to dependence upon horses and oxen. Bulky cargo could best be shipped by sea.

The natural and technical conditions of Edo did not lend themselves to receiving heavy cargoes. Boats from the northeastern (Tōhoku) region stopped first at the ports of Shimoda and Uraga just south of Edo before proceeding to Edo port itself. This was because of difficulties encountered in navigating a direct course into Edo bay. Under such circumstances Edo was not able to establish a priority for itself in marine transport. Instead, all kinds of products were gathered first in Ōsaka and then redistributed to various parts of the country. A series of primary sea routes spread out from Ōsaka to each of the major regions of the country. They were referred to according to general directions, in the following manner:

Southern route (*minami-kairo*): Edo-Ōsaka-Iyo
Western route (*nishi-kairo*): Ōsaka-Nagasaki
Northern route (*kita-kairo*): Shimonoseki-Matsumae
Eastern route (*higashi-kairo*): Ōshū-Edo

A number of marine services were available along the southern route, but the most important ones have been mentioned earlier, the *higaki-kaisen* and *taru-kaisen*. The former was managed by wholesalers (*Edo-jukkumi-donya* and *Ōsaka-nijuyonkumi-donya*) for shipping general cargoes, while the latter was a special line for transporting *sake* from Itami port to Edo.

The western route had existed from ancient times. Connecting the Kyōto, Nara, and Ōsaka centers with the fertile lands of western Japan, its chief terminal port westward was Nagasaki, the sole port for foreign trade during the period of isolation.

The northern course ran from Ōshū and Hokuriku in the far north and west of the main island, halfway down the Japan Sea side of the island to the small ports of Tsuruga, Wakasa, and Kohama where goods were carried by land to the northern end of Lake Biwa for shipment to Kyōto or Ōsaka. The intermediate unloading and reloading, as well as the short land transport to Lake Biwa, were troublesome and expensive. The sea route was later extended to connect with the western route at Shimonoseki, permitting direct passage to Ōsaka without the troublesome transshipment en route. Even from the Tōhoku district, most goods were sent around the combination northern-western course, than by the shorter but more difficult eastern route. Navigational conditions, then, also contributed greatly to the establishment of the city of Ōsaka as the center for handling raw materials and finished products from all over the country.[89]

To make full use of the opportunities afforded by the Ōsaka situation, local governments of all districts built their own warehouses in the port area. When the domains needed more funds than came from normal selling of products, extra large shipments of rice and other products were poured into Ōsaka for marketing. The upper hand was held, however, by the Ōsaka merchants who served as brokers, and they became very powerful. They made use of special devices of communication such as flags, carrier-pigeons, or signal fires to relay information on the going market prices to points as far away as Ōtsu city on the southern end of Lake Biwa. By such enterprising efforts they gained control of the entire national rice market.

As demands in Edo rose, the commercial functions of Ōsaka expanded. Total rice production in Japan is estimated to have been 26,000,000 *koku* (133,120,000 US bu.) in the Genroku era (1688–1704), and 30,000,000 *koku* (153,600,000 US bu.) in the Genna era (1615–24). Ten per cent of the total, or about 3,000,000 *koku*, is thought to have been handled by the Ōsaka merchants. Eighty-five per cent of payments made in Ōsaka for goods shipments were for rice.[90] Provincial governments authorized wholesalers and brokers among Ōsaka townsmen to handle their products on a consignment basis. Monies received from sales were received by moneylenders and exchange brokers (*ginkakeya* and *kakeya*) on behalf of the provincial governments. In most cases, though, the wholesalers and the exchange brokers were the same persons. Funds were forwarded, not back to a provincial government, but to its Edo office to support its warriors and subordinates there.

Edo's currency was gold coins, Ōsaka's silver coins. There was a fixed rate of exchange between the two cities which necessitated acceptable bills of exchange. By the Kanbun era (1661–73) the economic structures were sufficiently developed to accommodate a professional exchange business. The merchants specializing in gold and silver exchange transactions were called *hongaeya*, though there were also brokers dealing in copper coins.

The most powerful group of merchants dealing in bills of exchange was a clique of ten top brokers united under the name *honryōgae*. They operated as both wholesalers and money brokers, and became the core group in the financing business in Ōsaka. Kōnoike Zen-emon, leading member of the group, served as broker for five domains, namely, Kaga, Yanagawa, Hiroshima, Awa, and Okayama. At the same time he was an authorized "favored merchant" (*yōtashi*) for the Kishū and Bishū districts. His position carried the privilege of sword-bearing, and his income reached 10,000 *koku* merely in salaries (*fuchimai*) paid by his daimyō patrons alone. Other members of the core group, such as Tennōji Gohei and Hiranoya Gohei, were also men of wealth comparable to the daimyō themselves.[91]

Finance firms were also founded in Edo, but the Ōsaka financiers continued to hold a powerful upper hand. That primacy was manifest in their monopoly over the rice market and their ability to control its prices. Ōsaka wholesalers, for their part, continued to dominate the shipment of vast quantities of goods into the city for redistribution to other regions. In the process of redistribution the Ōsaka brokers managed to boost prices enough to yield handsome profits for themselves. Their supremacy in the world of commerce was evident too in the fact that many of the Ōsaka firms opened branches in Edo.

The intimate connections of Edo's demands and Ōsaka as the source of supply can be seen in other dimensions. Provincial governments that overspent their budgets in Edo often sought the remedy in loans from wealthy merchants in both Ōsaka and in Edo. Again, the supply was far greater in Ōsaka. The great city of warriors came, in time, to be indebted for huge amounts to the city of merchants.

Enterprising merchants did not restrict themselves to money-lending ventures. Vast sums were invested in reclamation projects for creating new farm lands. Eventually the expansion of commercial activity reached the limits of the domestic market, diminishing the values of competitive efforts. The merchants sought, then, to eliminate competition in favor of secure monopolies to guarantee the sustained inflow of profits. Startled by the inherent threat of independently formed power groups, the *bakufu* countered with its own policy of government-authorized merchant unions, in which certain government controls were preserved.

New members of the merchants' unions paid initiation fees at a predetermined rate for their market rights (*kabu*), and the bonds of the unions were embellished with religious overtones. In short, they were prevented from acting as individuals and were forced to submit to group controls. One condition of membership was sticking to one's own specific business and refraining from invasion into another's territory. The merchants were also obliged to make "contributions" (*unjō* or *myōgakin*) to the central government. These special levies were not merely for balancing the *bakufu* budget in bad times. It was also in the interest of the merchants to protect and cultivate the relations with feudal authority that enabled them to retain their monopolizing power over the national economy.

While the expanding network of commerce favored an increase in the economic power of the Ōsaka merchants, the warriors became proportionately poorer. Nonetheless, the merchants could not assume a stance opposing the warriors as their advantages in business always depended upon the continued favor and support of the feudal authorities. The positive and negative elements of the process which gave economic ascendancy to the Ōsaka merchants inevitably produced different characteristics in the ecological, political, and social structure of Ōsaka city, as compared to the warrior city of Edo.

Geographically Ōsaka's position was advantageous, with the Yamato river to the east and the Yodogawa river to the north. The city was linked to much of Japan by its access to the Inland Sea, that is, via the western and northern sea lanes. The city was called Naniwa in the ancient period. It was a metropolis already during reigns of the Emperors Nintoku, Kōtoku, and Shomu. In the later Heian period the city's position suffered because the Yodogawa river shifted its course into the Mikunigawa river. In the late Middle Ages it prospered once again when the priest Rennyo the VIII founded an important branch of Ishiyama Temple there in 1496. (Its site was later to accommodate construction of Ōsaka Castle.)

The branch temple was erected during the Age of Civil Wars, a fact reflected in the moats and walls included in its structure. Several thousands of households comprised the town that grew up around it. It was connected with the powerful Honganji temple, and became involved in more than ten years of armed resistance against Oda Nobunaga. It had joined forces with the Miyoshi clan of Awa in refusing to pay a war tax (*yasen*) imposed by Nobunaga. When Nobunaga finally defeated the Ōsaka rebels, the city was granted as a fief to Ikeda Nobuteru.

In 1583 Toyotomi Hideyoshi assumed control over Ōsaka by transferring the Ikeda family to Mino. Hideyoshi embarked on an ambitious program of reconstructing both the castle and the city. Between 70,000 and 80,000, and at times 100,000, laborers gathered from over thirty domains were poured into the construction plan. The castle measured 3 *ri*, 8 *chō* (7.3 mi.) in its circumference. Inside were the *Honmaru*, *Ninomaru*, and *Sannomaru*, a five-storied keep, and gorgeous residential mansions gilded with gold foil. It was the grandest castle of its time. All daimyō who had their own castles built mansions in the city. The city grew to an expanse of more than seven miles across, encompassing Tennōji, Sumiyoshi, Sakai, and Tsu. Houses of townsmen filled its wide stretches of land.[92]

Tokugawa Ieyasu destroyed Ōsaka Castle in two battles known as Fuyu-no-Jin (1614) and Natsu-no-Jin (1615). Besides the castle, the Tennōji temple structures and citizens' houses were completely demolished. Thousands of citizens fled the city. Ieyasu ordered Matsudaira Shimōsano-kami Tadaaki, a grandson who held a fief as a *fudai-daimyō*, to restore the city with an eye to its importance as the primary trade base serving the entire country. The merchants were encouraged to return. Merchants in more than eighty towns in Fushimi were asked to rebuild the streets of Ōsaka. Within fifteen years after its ruin, that is, by the Kan-ei era

(1624–44), the city was almost completely rebuilt on a scale twice its size in the time of Hideyoshi (d. 1598).

The reconstructed city contained 601 townships in 1703. There were 351,708 residents belonging to 17,279 households—a very large city in its time. The maximum population of Ōsaka in the premodern period was reached in 1738, numbering 526,812. Although the population fluctuated from time to time, it never fell below 300,000 during the Tokugawa era.[93]

As regards ecological structure, there was a concentration of temples in the Kami-honchō and Tenmaji-machi districts. The temple town of Tenma Tenjin was highly prosperous. Within the residential communities of warriors around the castle there were built the residences of the governor (*iōdai*), ranking officers (*shirodachi-yoriki*), assistants to the governor (*ryōjōban*), and low-ranking warriors (*dōshin*). Here also were found the buildings of government offices (*bugyōsho*) and local magistrates (*daikansho*). Near Tenma there were some houses of guards and police (*yoriki* and *dōshin*) who worked under the town commissioner (*machi-bugyō*). Senior retainers to the daimyō, standard-bearers (*hatamoto*), and local governments built their respective offices and warehouses in Nakanoshima and neighboring areas to store and sell goods shipped from the domains of their lords. The number of such offices reached 95 in 1703, and 125 in 1843.[94] The actual business of storage and marketing was handled by merchants serving the domain officials. Consequently, there lived only a small number of warriors in the city and the ratio of townsmen was overwhelmingly large. The ratio of warriors' homes to the total number of houses was exceedingly low in comparison with the situation in Edo.

Ōsaka was definitely a city of merchants. Wholesalers were concentrated in and around an area called Senba. But there was no definite separation of residential areas according to status stratification as was clearly seen in Edo and other castle towns.

The system of political controls was somewhat unique in that the *bakufu* brought the city of Ōsaka under its direct control after placing Matsudaira Shimōsanokami Tadaaki there in 1619. To implement its direct governance a governor was appointed for the city, the first being Naito Nobumasa, protector (*jōban*) of Fushimi Castle. Until the end of the Tokugawa *bakufu*, governors of Ōsaka were selected from the *fudai-daimyō*.

Immediately under the governor there were two town commissioners, *machi-bugyō*, similar to the Edo officials. Organizations of the townsmen centered in three unions (*gō*) of towns controlled by ten, seven, and five elders' councils. Toward the end of the Edo era, the elders' groups decreased slightly to six, seven, and four, or five less than before. Official business was conducted by the elders in public buildings in Ōsaka, not in their own homes as in Edo.[95]

Elders were chosen from among families established in Ōsaka since the Genna era (1615–24). Referred to originally as *motojimeshu* ("chief of the people"), their title was changed to *sō-doshiyori* (elders) when the *bakufu* established the town commissioners' posts in Ōsaka. Formally the elders' positions passed hereditarily to their heirs, although in actual practice that was not always the case as the fortunes of the merchants rose and fell radically. In reality the title was an honorary one, with no monetary compensation except exemption from household taxes (*ikken-yaku*). On the other hand, they possessed a fleet of harbor vessels (for unloading larger ships) totalling 500 freight loaders, and 299 special tea haulers of 20 *koku* and 10 *koku* capacity respectively. Supplementary income came in from chartering these vessels. They also charged fees for the carts used in Ōsaka, called *beka-guruma* (cart pulled by two or three men, slightly smaller than the Edo *daihachi-guruma*).[96] Four of the elders served also as executives (*itowappu-doshiyori*) of a silk importers' union, one of them visiting Nagasaki each year as the silk arrived there from China.

In contrast to the town elders (lower than city elders) of Edo, their counterparts in Ōsaka received no salaries. They were exempted from taxes, though, and received some compensation in the form of reimbursement of expenses involved in providing themselves with a kind of formal costume trousers called *hakama*; hence, the name for the reimbursement, *hakamazureryō*. Seasonal gifts were received in the New Year's season and at other times.[97] The Ōsaka townsmen generally preferred to earn money than to receive honors, and they had little interest in being chosen as a town elder. Even if chosen, they tended to turn the official duties over to clerks (*machidai*) who functioned in their stead. Economic, rather than political, power was their goal, and many became very wealthy indeed, such as the wholesalers, financiers lending money to daimyō, and the exchange brokers. Their wealth and social positions rose especially in the latter half of the Tokugawa period, while the influence of town elders seriously declined.[98]

Nor could Ōsaka follow strictly the Edo pattern of hereditary transmission of the office of town head (*nanushi*). The more rapidly changing socio-economic conditions of the commercial center of the nation made it imperative that town governments be put in the hands of men of known talents. Only townsmen who owned their own houses had a voice in the selection of the town elders. Records of the balloting listed the candidates in a descending order of votes received. Successful candidates were then subjected to character examinations (*hitogarami*) by the city elders above them. Those passing this test were reported as qualified to the town commissioner. It is not surprising that, with this degree of local efficiency, the Ōsaka organizations of local government were permitted a relatively higher degree of local autonomy.[99]

The Ōsaka townsmen worked hard to settle local affairs by themselves, houseowners enjoyed a degree of participation in local government, and the dominance of the warrior class was relatively less than in Edo and other castle centers. Yet these differences should not be overestimated. The morality of the feudal order penetrated every facet of this commercially-oriented city. There is no evidence that its citizens ever seriously attempted to overcome that morality, or could have had they tried. They never wavered from loyalty to the basic ideals undergirding the hierarchical status system, for in it they saw the protective advantages of feudal authority for themselves. They did not see themselves, even potentially, as townsmen in an open society with individual freedom and independence, but always as townsmen whose lives were firmly structured into a fixed feudal society.

# Chapter VII | Decline of the Feudal Cities

Thus far our attention has centered on the rise of the feudal cities as the necessary centers of the integrative apparatus of feudal domains, and in the cases of Edo and Ōsaka, of the integrative organizations for national politics and economy. The main focus has been on the ways in which the cities of the feudal age fulfilled their functions. Now we turn to a consideration of the principal factors that led to the breakdown of the feudal patterns of these cities, preparing the way for the emergence of modern characteristics in these cities in terms of ecological and social structures. When the modern style and shape of Japan's cities are dealt with later on, it will be seen that a heavy residue of feudal patterns survived well into the modern era.

The principal factors in the decline of the feudal cities that are germane to the present chapter include the following: (1) changes in the rural social structure upon which the cities depended; (2) demographic changes in the cities; (3) widespread resistance of the people against feudal authority as such; (4) collapse of the monopolistic mechanisms of urban trade and industry; (5) development of new industrial and foreign trade cities under the stimulus of ports opened to foreign ships; and, finally, (6) dissolution of effective political power of the Tokugawa government discerned in the transformation of the capital city of Edo into a modern city with residual feudal elements.

## 1. The Process of Disintegration of Rural Society

The feudal order was maintained through the exercise of integrated controls over the farming communities by the castle towns. All military, political, economic, and cultural powers were centered in the castle towns to facilitate the control function. The towns enjoyed a very superior position of privilege and power over all rural communities.

The farmers formed the major segment of the population, roughly 85% of the total. The taxes they paid constituted the foundation of the urban existence of both warriors and townsmen. Administrative control by city authorities and strict obedience by the farmers to the status system were imperative. The rural communities were held, as much as was possible, in a static state of isolation from the cities and from each other. The heavy demand for consumer goods in the cities stimulated both local specialization and provincial differentiation of work and production. This was true both in areas close to the cities and in outlying districts. The more remote areas were forced increasingly to rely upon each other, breaking down their isolation and altering the self-supporting economies of each local community. The whole country was drawn into an economic circle centering on the cities of Ōsaka and Edo.

In the process collective family ties were weakened, while the independence of individual families was strengthened. A number of factors were operative in this shift. Areas surrounding the large cities, castle towns, and highway station towns turned increasingly to production of agricultural products for direct sales to these cities and towns. Families functioned more and more as separate units instead of larger local collectives, altering status relations between landowners and tenant farmers. Local industry developed in the rural districts, producing new groups of capital holders and employing laborers no longer bound to the land according to traditional patterns. On the other hand, the financial burdens faced by the *bakufu* and provincial governments were transferred to the hard-pressed farmers remaining on the land.

Some farmers sought relief through leaving the villages to find work in the cities, while others sought redress through rebellion against feudal authority. Rebellion led to cooperative action across the boundary lines of village and domain. The fixed and isolated character of rural communities in the feudal order was gradually dissolved under the two pressures of progressive differentiation in social functions and inclusion in a wider range of social processes. The structural relationships between the organs and power of the integrative system and between urban and rural society were gradually transformed.

Some of the villages of the Edo period were simply those left over from the late Middle Ages, communities originally managed by warriors. The warriors had moved away to live in the castle towns. But most of the villages resulted from programs of the central and provincial governments to open up new lands through reclamation projects. There were also many villages pioneered by wealthy merchants through reclamation work at their own expense. Such ventures were approved in the latter half of the Tokugawa period, on the condition that the merchants took responsibility for guaranteeing tax payments by the villages.

Villages had, then, different origins as well as varying ecological structures and sizes. The village people included former warriors who had chosen to remain when other warriors moved to the castle towns, or families released from their warrior-masters who did not relocate in castle towns. Both types of people were combined into collective organizations marked by master-subordinate relations. They made collective use of available forests, fields, and water resources. Villages were not always organized on the basis of a shared geographical location, but in the Tokugawa system they were always organized as administrative units with clearly defined responsibilities under the domain and national governments. Primary functions of the local units were for tax collection and social control.

In the villages there was no resident official of the central government. Local administration was in the hands of three officers (*sanyaku*), namely, the village head (*nanushi; shōya* in the Kansai district), the head of neighborhood groups (*kumigashira*), and the representative of the farmers (*hyakushōdai*). These three men were responsible to a local magistrate (*daikan*) in governing the village. The *sanyaku* pattern was a traditional one from earlier periods, and the officers governed according to long established customs, although the influence of the laws and regulations of the *bakufu* was felt increasingly with the passage of time. The *sanyaku* were chosen by various methods, such as election, mutual discussion, or direct appointment by the feudal lord. Most often they were former warriors who had remained in the villages, and their position was comparable to that of a tribal chieftain. Succession to office was generally confined to hereditary transmission among families with deep roots in the villages. The *nanushi* was responsible for full payment of taxes, for supervising the use of water and other resources in agricultural production, and for maintaining good social order. The *kumigashira* assisted him in these duties, and the *hyakushōdai* organized the activities of the farmers. In addition to tax payments, the *sanyaku* also saw to the proper apportionment of expenses among the villagers.

In addition to local systems administered autonomously, the *bakufu* required the establishment of five-member household units, called *gonin-gumi*. Full tax payments, crime prevention, and general mutual aid and surveillance were responsibilities shared by the *gonin-gumi* with the village officers. Peace and order were strictly enforced publicly and privately.[1]

There were also independent farmers (*honbyakushō*) in the villages who were grouped with the *gonin-gumi* only for tax purposes. Working for the independent farmers were some very poor peasants whose poverty was indicated by their name *mizunomi-hōkōnin* ("water-drinking serfs," i.e., no tea, etc.). These peasants took no part in village administration. The independent farmers formed larger households along kinship-type lines. They were bound together tightly by bonds of status and loyalty to a common deity (*ujigami*). They formed a kind of lineage group with head (*honke*) and branch (*bunke*) families, including their servants (the *hōkōnin*).

The main family (*honke*) was recognized by the daimyō as a legitimate tax-paying landowner, called *naukenin*. The branch families cultivated the lands allocated them under the head family. These people acquired partial independence by producing raw materials for crafts industries, and selling them to purchase farm tools and fertilizer. Complete independence was not possible because they were dependent upon the larger family organization and its patterns of mutual aid and cooperative work, not to mention the obligations accruing from status relations within the lineage-type arrangement.

In many ways this particular family structure was not so strictly differentiated by the status hierarchy found among warriors. There was more relative equality. Nonetheless, the laws of land division made it most difficult for second and third sons to set up branch families. In mountainous regions the paucity of arable land virtually precluded establishing an independent family. Sometimes younger brothers were compelled to live as lifelong subordinates to the eldest brother, whose position as the eldest son was most powerful.[2]

Inasmuch as the financial foundation of the city life of the warriors came from the taxes exacted from farmers, effective tax collection had top priority in administration of the rural districts. Early in the Edo period the tax claims were for 40% of the crops, leaving 60% for the farmers. By the beginning of the 18th century this was adjusted to a fifty-fifty basis. Later financial strains prompted the government to reverse the earlier ratio, claiming 60% for itself, leaving only 40% for the farmers. On top of this burden were imposed additional taxes on fruits and wood, and levies to cover public works projects; and villagers living near national highways were forced to supply carrier service for goods and ranking travelers.

In order to secure income from tax sources the feudal lords endeavored to fix the status quo of the farm villages; that is, to forestall the changes provoked by development of the commodity economy which were causing distintegration of the village structure. A government registry (*kenchichō*) was instituted to ascertain existing relations between specific lands and those cultivating them. Land was registered as *naukechi* and cultivators as *naukenin*. Laws restricting land divisions (*bunchi-seigen-rei*) were issued, freezing permanently all sales and purchases of arable lands. The objectives of such laws were not only to fix the farmers in their locations, but also to prevent their further impoverishment through infinitesimal division of all land. Restrictions were also placed on living standards with regard to clothing, foods, and houses permitted farmers, as well as on the products to be cultivated. Their lives were held to the lowest levels, with little hope of improvement.

The ruling class kept the farmers in a state of virtual confinement by prohibiting any transfer of residence or free choice of occupation. Tax rates were imposed arbitrarily and made heavier time and again. The farmers were deprived of both freedom and surplus, making it extremely difficult for them to improve either their standard of living or the material means of their agriculture.

The narrow tracts of land of the small farms afforded common farmers only the poorest level of living. Personal necessities of food, clothing, and dwellings they had to produce by themselves, as also many of their own tools and much of the fertilizer needed. Theirs was a self-supporting economy, except for items they could not provide such as metal, medicines, and seafoods. Those items were available only in limited areas of the country.

Mutual assistance societies (*yui*) were formed among the villagers themselves to add the strength of numbers to the major functions of the village: rice-planting, cropping barley, road-building, and thatching roofs. The societies provided the context too of major social functions: weddings, funerals, and informal socializing. But the basis of the societies was the traditional family pattern, formed around a head family (*honke*). The *yui* were a defense against, and conversely, further entrenched the isolation and self-sufficiency and the status structures of the village.

The *yui* community organizations possessed powerful controls over village life. Behavior completely contrary to local customs and taboos could be punished by ostracism (*mura-hachibu*). Adherence to traditional formulae in all behavior was nowhere more forcefully required than in the villages. The idea of individual freedom was totally absent in such communities. There was no apparent escape from the stifling combination of low living standards, fixed status, and lack of surplus production that might afford viable options. Moreover, the warrior class was relentless in pressing its demands for expanded production to fill its own financial gap.

The way out of the binding trap was slow in coming. But the initial opening was made by the *bakufu* itself, unwittingly. It promoted increased acreage through reclamation and technical improvements in the utilization of water resources. Reclaimed fields were made tax-exempt for a set period, or only lightly taxed. Such measures attracted merchants with capital to invest in new lands, and the total acreage of workable land increased sharply.

Following the Tenmei era (1781–9) new fields were opened up by draining the Inba marshes and areas along the Kiso and Shinano rivers. Paddy-fields were reclaimed in the Tsuruga district. Whereas arable lands in the Keichō era (1596–1615) had been only 1,635,000 *chōbu* (4,005,750 acres), they totalled about 3,050,000 *chōbu* (7,472,500 acres) by the Kyōhō era (1716–36). Reclamation of lands for rice cultivation, though, reduced available space for growing fertilizer grasses. Districts that cultivated vegetables for commercial sales suffered especially from a shortage of naturally-produced fertilizers. It was necessary, then, to purchase other fertilizers made from dried sardines, soybeans, and, in later periods, lime and whale fat. Although demands for these fertilizers expanded, cut-grass fertilizer remained the major supply.[3] The rate at which the commodity economy penetrated the rural regions was very slow, yet it gradually changed the socio-economic structure of rural society.

The *bakufu* did not allow merchants to exploit the rural districts, and the urban and rural sectors were kept separated. Penetration of the commodity economy proceeded more rapidly in districts close to consuming centers, such as large cities, highway station towns, and especially Ōsaka and Edo where there were large markets for vegetables.

Other districts responding to specific demands were the Kishū district, producing mandarin oranges, and the Kōshū district that specialized in grapes. Cotton and rape seed used as raw materials for cloth and fuel were produced in the Kinai district and in areas around the Inland Sea of Seto. These products had a ready market in the Ōsaka area. Sericulture and weaving developed to the east of the Kinki district, supplying makes of high grade silk in the Nishijin sector of Kyōto, an industry of renown since the Middle Ages. During the medieval period techniques of the weaving industry in the Nishijin district had been diffused to outlying districts, enabling people in the northern provinces of Ōshū, Fukushima, and Jōban to master these skills.

Agricultural products introduced from abroad had found a place in the production not only of suburban but provincial areas as well. Accelerated commercial cultivation was promoted for these products, which included wax trees, potatoes, sweet potatoes, watermelons, pumpkins, corn, carrots, peanuts, and tobacco.

After the Meireki era (1655–8), the warriors began in earnest to solve their financial problems by pushing reclamation work with funds supplied by the townsmen. They encouraged the farmers to cultivate vegetables on a commercial basis, which gradually strengthened the role of commerce in the rural districts. The isolation of each domain and village was broken down further, as the whole community was drawn progressively into a larger national economy.

Forced into a larger economic circle, each locality sought to protect itself by converting from general production of many kinds of products to specialization in some specific crop or industry. Certain provinces became known for quality production of certain items, such as salt in Himeji, paper in Okayama and Uwajima, and sugar in Satsuma. Concentration in particular localities of specialized industries resulted in greater interdependence among the provinces. This, along with increased currency payments, precipitated further growth in the money economy.

Developments in the commodity economy combined with specialization of production to activate exchange patterns all across the country. Farmers gradually produced more products for sale than were required for subsistence. With marginal funds they purchased more tools and fertilizers. By farming on a commercial basis minor families belonging to larger lineage groups were able to strengthen their own independence without severing ties with the larger households. This new independence broke down the traditional isolation and self-sufficiency of the villages and provinces. In return each family had to accept a new level of dependence upon the larger communities which bought its products. The end result was a transformation of family-community structures.[4]

The progress made toward greater independence by individual families was undercut all too often by the imposition of heavier taxes. Natural calamities, occuring frequently, could easily tip the scales toward bankruptcy. To salvage themselves from desperate situations, or to add needed equipment, the newly-independent farmers fell deeper into debt; and the poorer the farmer, the deeper the debt. Repeatedly they were forced to sell or mortgage their lands to richer farmers or merchants, in order to meet the heavier tax claims.

Many rich farmers became large landowners, absorbing lands sold by bankrupt farmers. Some of the rich ones ventured into new fields such as money-lending, *sake* breweries, or granaries, becoming primarily merchants and only absentee landlords. Others expanded their farming into large-scale operations. The majority of the farming population were reduced to subordinate roles as tenants of the rich farmers. Differentiation of status distinctions in the rural communities was thereby intensified.

The same tendency was even more pronounced in the suburban areas of the cities, and it became worse as the Edo era wore on. In the book

*Keizai Yōroku* (Economic Digest), published in the Bunka era (1804–18), it was reported that "30% or 40% of the peasants have already lost their lands to the rich farmers in the provinces."[5] Just how many tenant farmers there were is unknown. Hirano Gitaro estimates that about one-third of the total acreage of arable land was in tenancy in the sixth year of the Meiji era (1873).[6] The proportion might have been slightly less than one-third in the Edo period.

The degree of status differentiation was not the same in every part of the country. In the Chūgoku and Kinki districts independent farmers vanished on a large scale, becoming hired servants to rich landowners who were mainly merchants and financiers. In the Kantō and northern sections of Japan most of the peasants were poor subordinates of wealthier farmers. They bore the double burdens of rent paid in labor and taxes paid in farm products.

Opportunities provided by a hungry commodity market drew the farmers into various secondary occupations to earn extra money. Parasitic landowners and venturesome merchants developed monopolies for wholesale marketing of goods produced in the rural cottage industries. Sidestepping the controls of the merchants' unions, these enterprisers supplied raw materials and tools to the farmers in return for exclusive rights over their products. Moreover, they built workshops of their own to employ dispossessed farmers. Some manufacture based on division of labor, employing wage laborers, emerged in the textile, brewing, and mining industries, though on a minor scale.

The peasants were prevented by law from leaving the land, yet the relative isolation of the rural districts severely limited their access to both raw materials and markets. Cottage industries could operate only through the intermediary wholesalers. In the pattern of manufacturing that developed there was, then, a distinct differentiation between the laborers producing goods and the owners of the means of production. The control of capital owners over production was introduced, transforming the peasants from land-based men paying taxes to a feudal lord into laborers being paid wages for their work by a workshop owner. The initial stage of human relations in production under capitalism had been formed, a kind of relations quite different from the status relations of a feudal system with its foundations in cultivated lands.

Another factor effecting serious changes in the rural structure was the relation of population to agricultural productivity. Yoshida Tōgo estimates the population of Japan in the Tenshō era (1573–92) at about 18,000,000. His calculation is based on annual rice crops of 18,000,000 *koku* for the entire country in the same era.[7] During the century from the beginning of the Tokugawa period to the Genroku era (1688–1704) the increase in productivity was considerable as peaceful conditions enabled people to work in safety.

The national population also expanded considerably. By the Kyōhō era (1716–36) it reached 26,000,000 or more. This figure must be adjusted to over 30,000,000 if one includes classes not registered officially, such as warriors, persons connected with the Imperial Household, and groups of outcasts.[8] Sekiyama Naotarō puts the population figure at 30,000,000 for a period of 120–130 years after the Kyōhō era. Nomura Kentarō judges the population to have been 35,000,000 in the latter part of the Tokugawa period, computing this from the figure of 33,010,000 given for 1872. A higher figure for the late part of the Tokugawa era is quite plausible as there were very likely some citizens not registered even in the 1872 census, five years after the modern period began.[9]

Early in the Tokugawa period the expansion of agricultural production made it possible for some people to accumulate wealth, but the majority were held to low standards of living to accommodate an increase in population. By the middle of the Tokugawa era the central and provincial treasuries were under strain, and the burden was transferred to the farmers through increased tax claims. Damages by wind and floods, and invasion of the rural economy by commercial interests and greedy money-lenders, compounded the farmers' plight. But agricultural productivity had reached its limits. Farmers simply could not meet the obligations put upon them.

Some fell back on the mutual aid societies formed by extended families. But these resources were quickly exhausted. It became prevalent among poor peasants to practice forced abortion. This was done openly by poverty-stricken people, except in cases involving a potential heir. Informed people warned them that such practices went against human morality. Government authorities, national and provincial, imposed the heaviest punishment on those guilty of feticide or infanticide. Official concern was focused only on a large labor force as a means to increased revenue. Rewards were even offered by the *bakufu* and the domains to those having many children.[10]

Some of the peasants sold their lands and left, taking their families. Boys and girls not in line to inherit land also evacuated the rural areas. Jobs were sought in Kyōto, Ōsaka, Edo, and the castle towns. They became everything from servants, peddlers, craftsmen and day laborers, to beggars and prostitutes. Cities and towns became filled with them. Lesser numbers went to work as miners, porters in transportation services, or as hired hands on reclaimed lands.

As a result of the rapid concentration of population in large cities and castle towns, one-fourth of the total population in Edo alone consisted of persons born in other places.[11] In the cities the swollen ranks of low class people and beggars were easily excited into rioting when the price of rice rose sharply due to poor crops. On the rural scene the sudden loss of a large portion of the adult population put the remaining farmers in an impossible position. Taxes were heavier than ever, and techniques for achieving higher yields were inadequate. Bad weather conditions could ruin a farm family in a single season. The condition of the land itself deteriorated rapidly.

The exodus from the rural areas left them in desolation. Tax payments declined to dangerous levels. The *bakufu* could not permit so serious a decline in its revenue and survive. To reverse the depletion of the rural labor force, in 1777 it issued orders restricting the number of employees that could be hired from other provinces. Again, in 1873 it was decreed that laborers were prohibited from leaving the provinces of Mutsu, Hitachi, and Shimoda. Persons working in localities other than where they were born were ordered to return to their native domains.

The *bakufu* took steps as early as 1790 to return workers in Edo to their rural origins by offering to pay travel expenses and to provide tools to work with once they were back on the farms. Those without lands to which they could return were even offered land grants in other provinces, plus permission to resettle their families.

In addition to this policy aimed at relocating peasants in the rural areas, the *bakufu* took additional steps to prevent possible newcomers from transferring into Edo. Those found living in Edo on a temporary basis were sent back to their native lands, except for those already engaged in some business of their own, with their families, for a fairly long time. Peasants who made it to Edo and found work were forced to return home after a definitely fixed period.[12] Provincial governments adopted similar policies for reversing the flow of peasants back to the farms. The rural exodus decreased temporarily, but could not be stopped permanently.

These contradictions inherent in the structure of rural society were the main causes of the peasant revolts against feudal controls that erupted in various parts of the country. During the 268 years from 1599 to the end of the Edo era in 1867 there were about 1,240 such uprisings (*ikki*).[13] Rebellious activity was at its lowest in the Genroku era (1688–1704) when Tokugawa power was at its peak. Revolts occurred with ascending frequency in the Kyōhō (1716–36), Tenmei (1781–9), and Tenpō (1830–44) eras, reaching a high pitch toward the end of the Tokugawa reign when its power was about to collapse.

In the early stages revolts were led by powerful local landowners, backed by the peasants, against repressive measures such as increased taxes, land inspection, and abuses of authority by local magistrates. From the middle of the Tokugawa period on, the uprisings were directed against a wider range of abuses. These included (1) official land inspection by the feudal lords designed to acquire extra funds to cover financial shortages; (2) rises in the price of rice due to recoinage of currency; and (3) institution of local government monopolies in the commodity market at the expense of the producers of commodities. Riots occurred also against suppression of the peasants planned by rich farmers who operated in conspiracy with village officials to forestall the trend toward independence based on specialization and division of labor. These revolts were mounted by tenant-farmers against landowners.

In any event, the uprisings were aimed at the feudal system itself. They were not always against the feudal lords but equally against officials and rich farmers acting in their own selfish interests. Late in the Edo era the revolts erupted on a scale that crossed over village and provincial boundaries. They spread, finally, on such a scale as to include the lower classes in the cities. So wide a range of unified action among people without ready means of communication bespeaks not only the shaky condition of the feudal order and its stringent status system, but also a violent rejection of local life based on intended isolation of the villages.

Actually, even the warriors were prohibited from acting in groups under the feudal system. Naturally, then, the instigators of the peasant revolts had to be rooted out and punished. In later stages, however, the number of people punished for rebellious activity diminished and the peasants' requests were often accepted by the authorities. Even large-scale revolts lasted only a short time. Local isolation rendered interregional communication extremely difficult, and there was, therefore, little chance of mobilizing people of the same status groups into a larger, unified national movement.

Just the same, the uprisings must be recognized as one of the effective forces causing the ultimate disintegration of the feudal system. Nor should it be overlooked that the feudal system itself produced the resistance movements against its own dominant power groups: the ruling elite, the capital owners and money-lenders who commanded the world of commerce, the absentee landowners, and the local officials who too frequently accommodated all of these power groups. The peasants and low-class city folk provided the telltale signs of creeping disintegration in an age otherwise marked by unprecedented national integration in Japan.

## 2. Disorganization of the Feudal City System

Here we must look into the processes of change provoked by a relative degree of breakdown in the feudal order of the cities. The disintegrating processes were closely connected, of course, with the diminishing isolation and self-sufficiency of rural society, and with the shifts occurring in the structure of ruling authority. The fact that the governments, national and provincial, were increasingly short of funds left the warriors less and less able to patronize the markets developed to supply their demands. Markets in the castle towns, that were so prosperous in earlier eras such as the Genroku (1688–1704) and Kyōhō (1716–36), declined seriously, although they were sustained in some cases by the new economic power of townsmen.

Status differences were intensified by the great influx of poor peasants into the cities. Sharp rises in rice prices touched off riots in the cities that often developed into large-scale rebellions. The ruling class was forced increasingly to retreat from its former positions of uncontested administrative authority.

In the rural districts, source of the cities' economic life-blood, local markets (*gōchō*) were promoted. Merchants at the local level in the rural areas strengthened their role in economic affairs. They resented, and some rebelled against, the privileges reserved to the cities and to the monopoly-holding wholesalers. Sometimes rural merchants made inroads on the city wholesalers' exclusive markets. Monopolization of trade rights by a limited few choked off the free and mutual exchange of goods unreasonably. Development of the national economy was virtually suspended by city privileges. It was at this point that the structure had to be transformed.

While the feudal cities were drifting, on the whole, toward disintegration, some of the castle towns and other provincial cities were able to move forward. Whenever a castle town could develop an industry geared to the emerging social patterns of its own territory, it was able to make some progress. Local cities that could develop industries free from the stifling pressures of feudal lords and from the crippling controls of monopolizing wholesalers could likewise advance.

Certain cities were awakened to new life by the opening of the country's ports to foreign trade. A few emerged as special foreign trade cities to serve as the bases for international contacts and for the importation of Western culture. The cities that managed to restructure along modern lines of free trade and industry, along with those open to new stimulus from abroad, replaced the feudal cities as the driving force toward a modern society.

*Changes in the structure of urban populations.*——Changes in social structure are accompanied by changes in status stratification, changes in population composition and numbers, and changes in ecological structure. Populations in the castle towns increased generally in the early part of the Edo era. Reaching a peak in the first quarter of the 18th century, populations then leveled off. The ecological structure of castle towns began to change, due to creeping bankruptcy of the warrior class whose incomes were stationary, though the commodity economy continued to advance.

Lower class warriors developed side jobs in home industries in their residences. Many did sub-contract work for wholesalers. Some of them were adopted by townsmen families. Some even returned to their native places to work at farming. The stratified status structures of the cities began to disintegrate as the warrior population atrophied, or even decreased where there was no industry to sustain it.

While some townsmen were able to increase their wealth, most found themselves in greater difficulty. The ratio of people living in rented houses grew as rising commodity prices intensified differences among the townsmen. Local governments panicked as finances dropped drastically, and imposed heavier taxes on the already hard pressed townspeople.

Taxes and special assessments were laid not only on the wealthy; the poor were hit hard too. Heavy tax burdens combined with the diminished purchasing power of the warrior class to depress the markets, forcing the citizens into greater poverty. The feudal system itself had forced the castle towns into stagnation.

Reference has already been made to the fact that the townsmen population of Edo exceeded 500,000 by 1721. This figure climbs to 600,000 when the people of shrines and temples are included. Then, when the unregistered warrior population is added, the count rises above 1,000,000. After the Kyōhō era (1716–36), the population of Edo fluctuated some, but held fairly close to the 1,000,000 level.

Castle towns experiencing population declines after the peak Kyōhō era included the following:

| *Okayama*[14] | *Fukui (townsmen only)*[15] | *Ōgaki*[16] |
|---|---|---|
| 28,699 (1667) | 21,393 (1712) | 5,757 (1721) |
| 27,950 (1717) | 20,010 (1743) | 5,343 (1785) |
| 23,579 (1773) | 18,364 (1792) | 5,096 (1843) |
| 20,173 (1838) | | |

| *Kanazawa*[17] | *Hamamatsu*[18] | *Wakamatsu (houses)*[19] |
|---|---|---|
| 68,636 (1697) | 1,698 (1759) | 3,515 (1669) |
| 64,987 (1710) | 1,686 (1866) | 3,380 (1735) |
| | | 3,028 (1807) |

The castle town populations did not always show a straight line of decline, though the general trend was downward as the end of the Tokugawa era approached. Some examples of such cases are:

| *Takada*[20] | *Tottori*[21] | *Himeji*[22] |
|---|---|---|
| 21,567 (1680) | 13,125 (1748–50) | 18,769 (1749) |
| 17,303 (1698) | 10,228 (1810) | 22,390 (1751–63) |
| 18,434 (1840) | 11,440 (1846) | 16,329 (1771) |
| | | 13,872 (1845) |

| *Ueda*[23] | *Kōfu*[24] | *Imabari*[25] |
|---|---|---|
| 2,610 (1663) | 14,334 (1689) | 5,260 (1718) |
| 2,427 (1710) | 9,290 (1724) | 4,551 (1742) |
| 2,609 (1755) | 11,071 (1864) | 5,046 (1843) |
| 2,520 (1858) | | |

Not all castle towns suffered population decreases in the latter part of the Edo era. Where some sort of industrial venture succeeded there was considerable population growth. Others enjoyed gradual growth, while still others were able to grow after once having decreased. In any case, the rate of population increase was very modest. Some examples follow:

| *Kagoshima*[26] (total pop.) | *Kurume*[27] | *Toyama*[28] (total pop.) |
|---|---|---|
| 59,727 (1772) | 8,764 (1699) | 23,093 (1676) |
| 72,350 (1826) | 11,208 (1858) | 26,936 (1841) |

| *Nagaoka*[29] (est. pop.) | | *Takasaki*[30] | | *Matsumoto*[31] | |
|---|---|---|---|---|---|
| 12,450 | (1694) | 6,458 | (1784) | 8,206 | (1725) |
| 13,190 | (1712) | 6,516 | (1801) | 8,709 | (1795) |
| 14,735 | (1818) | | | 10,047 | (1817) |

The ratio between warriors and townsmen was never stable. The warrior population was ever decreasing, while the townsmen were always on the increase. The following list indicates this inverse relationship for three cities:

*Matsumoto*[32]

| *Year* | *townsmen pop.* | *warrior pop.* |
|---|---|---|
| 1725 | 8,206 | 6,072 |
| 1864 | 9,440 | 5,284 |

*Kōchi*[33]

| *Year* | *townsmen households* | *warrior households* |
|---|---|---|
| 1929 | 3,701 | 1,119 |
| 1843 | 3,951 | 1,114 |
| 1853 | 4,069 | 1,102 |

*Kanazawa*[34]

| *Year* | *townsmen households* | *warrior households* |
|---|---|---|
| 1755 | 13,443 | 1,365 |
| 1789–1801 | 14,909 | 1,086 |

The indication is that castle towns without industry could not adequately feed many unproductive warriors. Townsmen moved into residential areas set up originally for warriors, upsetting ecological patterns designed to preserve the status system. Expansion of both the population and the city structures became suspended after the early 18th century peak. The primary causative factors were two: infanticide or abortion among the poor, and general decline of the nation's markets.

Even in the city of Ōsaka, where commerce was most prosperous, feudal decay led to population decline, as follows:

| *Year* | *Ōsaka Population*[35] |
|---|---|
| 1738 | 520,000 |
| 1801 | 376,117 |
| 1854 | 317,436 |

Similar trends appeared in the port cities of Sakai and Nagasaki, which thrived in the Edo period. Sakai escaped the ravages of the immediate pre-Edo Age of Civil Wars through local resistance of its residents. Merchants in Sakai had taken advantage of pre-Edo era opportunities in foreign trade, and the economic power gained reinforced the powers of local government. Establishment of the Tokugawa *bakufu* brought Sakai under the control of the Ōsaka *bugyō*, depriving Sakai of its independence. Advances in shipbuilding techniques rendered the port of

Sakai obsolete. Unable to accommodate larger ships, vessels from abroad went, rather, to Nagasaki. The latter's subsequent prosperity was further aided by improvements in the means of land transportation. Sakai's fortunes dwindled, as indicated in its population losses: 62,860 (1688); 52,446 (1731); 44,769 (1813); 40,977 (1848).[36]

The port of Nagasaki developed from the year 1600, when Chinese vessels commenced trading ventures there. It handled trading with the Chinese and Portuguese, and served as a base for the "Red Seal Ships" (authorized for foreign trade by documents bearing the vermilion seal of the *bakufu*). The "Red Seal Ships" plied between Japan and Southeast Asian lands such as Annam and Taiwan, enriching the Nagasaki merchants' accounts. In 1635 the shogunate called off the "Red Seal" trade as one means of protecting the country from the dangers of foreign encroachment it sensed in overseas trade, and especially in the activities of the Portuguese traders and the Catholic missions. Foreign trade was restricted to the one port of Nagasaki, and the Portuguese were not allowed to leave an artificial island provided in the bay, called Dejima, while in port. Shortly after, even the Portuguese traders were excluded from Japan and only the Dutch, who had arrived for the first time in 1600, and the Chinese were permitted use of Nagasaki port. Under such conditions, the population of Nagasaki decreased, as follows: 64,523 (1696); 31,893 (1789); 40,019 (1833); 27,343 (1853).[37]

Not all urban populations ceased growing. Niigata, Shimonoseki, Onomichi, and Hyōgo experienced population growth due to the acquisition of new economic functions related to certain upgrading movements in the domestic economy. One source of domestic economic improvement was the *bakufu*'s order to Kamakura shipbuilders to improve on maritime facilities. Another was establishment of a workable system of currency exchange.

Niigata had 2,500 houses in 1680. Development in this port town had begun in 1616 under the governance of Hori Naoyori. When the sea route for western Japan was opened in 1672 many ships began to put in at Niigata. Receiving, distributing, and shipping goods brought prosperity to the town. The number of houses jumped to 3,000 by 1818, and reached 5,754 in 1843.[38]

When the flow of goods from the north country began going around the western tip of the main island, instead of bothering with transshipment halfway, the port of Shimonoseki emerged as an important intermediate port. Its population rose to about 20,000, with over 400 wholesaling agents working in the city. Boats from Kyūshū, and even from overseas, made calls at this port.[39]

The port of Onomichi had a history of serving Inland Sea traffic dating back to the Nara period. When the westbound sea route was connected with the route up the Japan Sea to northern regions, goods destined for the north were gathered at Onomichi for shipment. Return trips brought rice and fertilizers. Merchants in this port town acquired primacy in the trade of the surrounding region. The number of houses almost doubled between 1692 and 1789, from 1,680 to 2,690. A currency devaluation in the Tenpō era (1830–44) caused a temporary recession. Wholesalers' unions were organized to offset insecurities in commerce, and the town regained its prosperity, restoring the town in 1816 to a level of 2,926 houses.[40]

Hyōgo was also an old port town with its own important place in Inland Sea service. But its fortunes, like Onomichi, were favored by the westward sea route. Shipping agents prospered in handling *sake* shipments from breweries in Nada bound for Edo. Ōsaka's port was unsuited to larger ships. Incoming cargo was reloaded to smaller craft in the Hyōgo harbor before reshipment to Ōsaka. Of the rice shipped out of Japan's northern region, 80% was handled by wholesalers in Hyōgo. Its population of 19,700 in the Kyōhō era (1716–36) rose to over 21,900 by 1796.[41]

Quantitative changes in population were followed by changes in population composition. We have already seen that the relative ratio of townsmen to warriors increased regardless of growth or decline in the total population of castle towns. In the latter half of the Tokugawa era urban population growth consisted chiefly of increases in the number of lower class citizens. Back in the earlier phases of the period, feudal lords were inclined to provide residences for those from other districts so as to build up their towns. As the towns became older, they became ordered more and more in accordance with the interests of established citizens, principally wealthy merchants and money-lenders. Local governments granted privileges, not to attract new citizens, but to entrench the lives of its own solid citizens.

Differences among city dwellers became accentuated. Townsmen whose businesses failed put their houses up for sale; these properties were absorbed by merchants already rich. Castle towns had drawn their early populations from the rural areas too; but they were merchants and artisans forming a middle class and sustained by expanding consumptive activity. Cities in the later stage were confronted by a great influx of peasants of the lowest class seeking alternatives to the disorganization and poverty of village life. Their coming vastly increased the number of poor residents living in rented houses, greatly enlarging the social gap between landlords and tenants.

According to a survey made by Harada Tomohiko on the ratio of rented dwellings to the total number of houses in over forty cities for the period beginning at the end of the 17th century and ending with the close of the Edo era, rentals ran 50% to 70% in most cases. The maximum was 81% for the town of Imai in the Yamato district, followed by 80% for both Nagasaki and Sakai. The same trend was found in Edo. The rental percentage ran higher in cities of larger size and more developed commodity economies. Examples among castle towns include Hiroshima, Kōriyama, Yonago, Tsuyama, Himeji, Fukuyama, Tanabe, and Ōgaki; among port towns Nagasaki, Sakai, Hyōgo, Tomo, and Niigata; plus the temple town example of Imai mentioned above. The percentage of rented houses in these cities had climbed rather rapidly.[42]

Houses for rent were called *shimotaya.* A class of wealthy landlords making their living solely on rental incomes emerged. But renters were not all of one single status. Notable differences developed between those renting front street dwellings, mostly minor merchants and craftsmen, and tenants in back street dwellings such as day-laborers, gamblers, and entertainers. Differences between renters and landlords were not just economic; there were legal discriminations as well. Tenants had no civic rights or duties; they could neither vote nor be elected to office. The pattern of landlord-tenant relations was a thoroughly feudal one of masters and subordinates.

The swollen ranks of poverty-stricken peasants in the cities presented little prospect of increased revenue for local governments. Rather, they became financial and administrative burdens, and were a constant threat to public peace and order. Complicated procedures were introduced, therefore, to stop the rural influx. Persons seeking to rent houses were required to pay fees exacted for a variety of reasons and to secure guarantors for their petitions. From the Genroku era (1688–1704) on, local governments were prone to add special assessments to periodic taxes. These were applied initially to wealthier citizens, but were imposed gradually upon the tenant populace. Tax drains upon the meager resources of those already desperately poor drove them into even greater poverty and desperation. Conditions were more than ripe for the riots that began to erupt in the urban centers.

*Riots in the Cities.*——The discontent caused by poverty and social discrimination smoldered until it finally came to a head. Antagonism focused primarily on the constantly increasing tax burdens. Action on the part of the poor was precipitated, though, when rice prices skyrocketed because of poor crops. Riots broke out in which the poor attacked the homes of rich merchants favored by *bakufu* officials. Houses of the wealthy were destroyed and their possessions, rice and other goods, were stolen. The rioters had at last chosen to press their political demands upon the officials by force. In the beginning there existed some antagonism between farmers and townsmen. These differences were later resolved and they were able to stand together in organized resistance against the government and upper class citizens. A few riots provoked others on a larger scale, and they became increasingly political in character. The ruling class was forced to retreat and make concessions to the enraged citizens. The influence of the general populace gained strength and signalled the approaching downfall of feudal power and authority.

According to Harada Tomohiko, there occurred over two hundred riots in the cities between the end of the 18th century and the fall of the Tokugawa *bakufu.* There were only ten riots in the first half of the 18th century, concentrated in the Kyōhō era (1716–36). When a famine in the Tenmei era (1781–9) drove the price of rice sky-high, more than sixty riots erupted throughout the country. Similar conditions provoked a similar number of riots in the first half of the 19th century. During the

Tenpō era (1830–44) over forty-five urban uprisings followed sharp rises in rice prices due to successive years of crop failures. Some thirty-five riots were mounted in the last twenty years of the *bakufu*'s existence, half of them occurring in a single three-year period of desperation over tax and rice price advances.[43]

In the following paragraphs are presented examples of some of the riots which are most important to an understanding of the changes that took place in the power structure of the feudal cities, especially with respect to social and ecological organization.

In the second month of 1761 (Hōreki 11) a riot broke out in the city of Ueda in the northwest corner of the Kantō plain. Farmers already oppressed by heavy taxes suffered a severed drought which virtually ruined their crops for that year. They arose, with the support of village officials, and marched on the castle town of Ueda. There they were joined by two hundred townsmen who answered their call to action, bringing their numbers to 5,000–6,000. Fifty houses of privileged merchants were promptly destroyed. Operators of the town's shops suspended business to serve meals and *sake* to the rioting crowd. Rice and fuel shortages led the townsmen to sympathetic support of the petition put before the government officials. The government complied, instructing wholesalers to release 100 bales of rice. Compliance, however, was reluctant, and the government officials admonished the townsmen, denouncing their willingness to take advantage of the rioting. The Ueda riot was a clear case of combined resistance of farmers and townsmen against the ruling class of their community.[44]

In Fukui domain rice prices soared once when the local government sold 25,000 bales of rice to the Kaga domain to compensate for heavy expenditures by its own Edo office. On top of this came announcement of a special assessment (*goyōkin*) by the *bakufu* in 1768 of 15,000 *ryō*, of which a 7,000 *ryō* burden was allocated to the castle town of Fukui. Unable to provide so large an amount, the farmers of Hatamae rose up in resistance, with other towns and villages joining them. They forced the rich to provide them with meals and *sake*, or tore down their houses. The riotous situation took a sudden turn for the worse when the town's leaders were thrown into jail abruptly. The riot thenceforth assumed greater force, and the government was pressured into accepting the demands of the people to release those put into prison, to cancel unpaid taxes, and to release sufficient rice to rescue the people from starvation. Subsequently, local laws and regulations were revised to ease the people's situation. The riot had attracted 20,000 people from various districts for demonstrations in the castle town, and had continued for two months.[45]

The immediate cause of an uprising in Uji-yamada was the corrupt administration of a notorious town commissioner named Matsuda Kawachi-no-kami Sadaori. Townsmen in this famous shrine town several times had petitioned the elders and assistant elders, as well as the government bureau of temples and shrines, for corrective action during the year 1773. In the following year two priests (*sanbōnin*) and four representatives of the town's council of elders left secretly for Edo to petition the bureau of temples and shrines to dismiss the notorious commissioner. They succeeded in seeing the religious institutions commissioner, Toki Mino-no-kami, who granted their petition. The corrupt Matsuda was removed from office, punished with house confinement (*heimon*), and transferred to a bureaucratic position having little to do with actual administration. The success of these townsmen in non-violent measures against governmental excesses was possible because of their taking unified action, backed by local consensus.[46]

A 1782 incident in the highway station town of Fushimi on the Tōkai-dō route provides another example of successful political action by townsmen. This town was under direct administration of the *bakufu*. The local commissioner, a man named Kobori, decided to levy special duties on ships entering the town's port. When this decision was announced, the townsmen rebelled against him, led by officials of the town. The town commissioner of the *bakufu* punished those townsmen who were responsible for the rebellion, but acceded to their demands that duties on ships be paid directly to them to compensate for the labor provided. Resistance broke out once again, however, when Kobori granted wholesalers a monopoly over the local fish trade. Townsmen put pressure on the shogun in Edo to dismiss him, and were successful. Kobori was fired and exiled to Odawara.[47]

After a big fire in Aomori on the the tenth day of the seventh month of the third year of Tenmei era (1783), the price of rice climbed steadily day by day. The townspeople sank further and further into poverty. On the twentieth day of the same month, 700–800 townsmen, representing many grades of rich and poor alike, swarmed around the town office demanding that the price of rice be restored to the springtime level of the previous year. Several thousands more townsmen congregated at the port authority office demanding that ships loaded with rice for shipment to other domains be held up, so that the rice could be used locally.[48]

Rioting erupted, destroying thirty houses belonging to the town head, rich merchants, and other wealthy persons. The town commissioner tried to stop the rioting, but in vain. Port authorities also moved to restrain raiding of rice storehouses, but 8,000–9,000 bales were carried off. The number of rioters rose to 7,000–8,000. Finally, on the twenty-first day, representatives of the townspeople gathered and submitted an official written petition to the town commissioner's office. It included the following points:

1. A one-year's supply of rice for the townsmen is to be held in reserve in government warehouses. Rice from this supply is to be sold at the rate of one *monme* of money for one *shō* four *gō* of rice.
2. Rice grown in the Aomori and Hirosaki districts must be sold free of existing controls. Unlawful exports of rice are to be eliminated under supervision of the townsmen.
3. Travel expenses for the many officials who come to Aomori, here-

tofore borne by townsmen, must be borne by the government.

4. Taxes imposed on sales of houses and for town administration are to be held at present levels, or lowered.

5. The secret police (*meakashi*) must be abolished.

In response to these demands, the town commissioner rejected outright the article calling for rice reserves as involving a direct insult to the authority of the feudal lord. The real significance of this incident lay in the organized attack of the general public on the policies of the local government, and not merely with regard to economic problems.

The most remarkable case of a riot engaging a whole town was that which occurred in Niigata in 1767. The townsmen had been suffering for some time from a conflux of bad fortune: repeated natural disasters, declining markets, illegal deals by shrewd merchants, and the ubiquitous rise in rice prices. When an assessemnt of 1,500 *ryō* on the townsmen was announced by the domain (Nagaoka), half of the townsmen pleaded for a postponement. The government rejected this appeal. The townsmen gathered at Saiyūji temple to discuss the situation, under the leadership of one Wakui Tōshiro, on the thirteenth day of the ninth month. The town commissioner was quite irritated with this, and tossed Wakui in jail while placing thirty others under house confinement. The townsmen were infuriated by this action and resolved to free Wakui themselves. Fifteen hundred rebels gathered at Mt. Hiyori and then marched on the town, destroying about twenty houses and other property. The houses belonged to town elders who had bought up rice reserves, or to minor officials who arrested those engaged in rioting.

The crowd was planning to attack the town commissioner's office on the evening of the twenty-seventh day with a task force of 2,000 men. The commissioner had little choice but to release Wakui in an effort to pacify the people's tempers. Wakui was freed and persuaded the townsmen to cease rioting. He possessed a fine talent for controlling the people; he became also the town's administrator thereafter. Commodity prices were stabilized. Taxes on buying and selling were spread out over every other year. Funds were made available for loans to poor people. Wakui introduced genuinely democratic administration into the tense situation until suddenly, two months later, he was arrested again. Investigations dragged along for over two years before he was paraded in public and punished with death.[49]

The Fushimi, Aomori and Niigata incidents occurred in commercial cities where the townsmen were, relatively speaking, less under the heavy hand of the feudal powers. Riots were raised in every district of the country, not just in commercial centers, as attacks on the feudal system. The commercial city riots were most important as the origin of movements among the common people to resist the feudal order and as tokens of the movements to come later that would overthrow that order and build a new one.

There were other crucial uprisings, though, notably in Ōsaka and Edo where the nation's key organs for integration of political and economic life were concentrated. Riots in these two major cities were directed mainly at destroying the homes and prosperity of wealthy citizens.

A scourge of locusts created famine conditions that drove the price of rice in Edo sky-high in 1732. Rioting broke out in the first month of the following year. From the first year of the Tenmei era (1781) similar natural disasters occurred repeatedly. Large-scale famines continued for a number of years, and it is said that several hundreds of thousand of peasants died from starvation. Countless beggars roamed all parts of the country. The government was incapable of coping with the situation.

From 1783 to 1785 famine conditions became unbearable. Then in 1786, a great flood devastated the Kantō district, catapulting rice prices to a new peak the following year. Shrewd merchants moved quickly to corner the rice market, accelerating the price rise even further. One *koku* of rice (5.1 US bu.) in 1781 had cost sixty *monme* of silver; the same measure cost six times that much in 1787. The *bakufu* decided to release 60,000 bales of rice together with 20,000 *ryō* of money for relief of the desperate lower classes in Edo. Before distribution could be carried out, however, a riot erupted on that same evening.

About 5,000 people gathered here and there in the city and commenced destroying the stores of rice wholesalers, beginning with some shops just outside the gate of Asakusa. These shops were located as follows:

*20th day*—Kōji-machi, 5–6 shops,
—Fukagawa, 6–7 shops,
—Honjo, 13 shops,
—Minami-denma-chō, 5–6 shops;
*21st day*—Kamakura-gashi, all shops,
—Kobune-cho, Isecho, Koami-chō, Kayaba-chō, Kameshima-chō, Teppōzu, Kuramae, Asakusa, Shitaya, Sakamoto, Minowa, Senju, Hongō, and Ichigaya,—— 150 shops in all.

The whole urban area of Edo was affected. Rioters consisted mainly of townsmen, most of whom were shop apprentices, with assistance from gamblers, vagrants, and *rōnin*. It is said that they were led by a young boy and a tall priest!

Destruction was not limited to the shops of merchants, but spread to the shops of *fudasashi* and homes of the wealthy. However, nothing was stolen. This riot ended at dawn on the twenty-second of the month. The *bakufu* immediately closed the big gates of the thirty-six major lookout posts (*mitsuke*). Ten warriors under the command of a military officer (*sentegashira*) named Hasegawa were assigned to lead ten patrols through the city to quiet the rioters. At the same time the *bakufu* ordered local governments to deliver emergency shipments of rice to Edo's port, allocating relief funds of 200,000 *ryō* to finance the collective operation. This action proved sufficient to pacify the people.[50]

Social unrest and rioting occurred frequently in Ōsaka. Considerable confusion in 1755, and riots in 1782, 1787, and 1789, followed upon the heels of sudden rises in rice prices. Poor crops precipitated further rioting in 1833, 1834, and 1836. The most serious uprising in Ōsaka was one in 1837 centering in the leadership of a former police guard named Ōshio Heihachirō. Its significance lay in exposing clearly the defects in the administrative system of the Tokugawa *bakufu*.

Ōshio had served in the east office of the Ōsaka town commissioner. He was learned in literature and skilled in martial arts, as well as a recognized scholar of the Wang Yang-ming (*Ōyōmei* in Japanese) school of Confucian philosophy. The commissioner and police often sought his opinion on many things concerning Ōsaka affairs, both public and private. Ōshio became quite sensitive to the poverty that increasingly plagued the lives of the poorer classes in Ōsaka and submitted a recommendation to the commissioner's office that the rice reserves of the government be used to alleviate the people's sufferings. The commissioner turned down this plea.

The wealthy merchants could not be persuaded to give succor; their concern for huge profits for themselves was their reason for buying up rice, thereby aggravating price increases. Ōshio took things in his own hands and sold his own books, distributing the proceeds to 10,000 people. He then penned and distributed among the people a declaration accusing the town commissioner of irresponsible, selfish deeds against the people. The declaration also decried the guilt of rich men who looked only to their own interests at the expense and sacrifice of countless poor people. After proclaiming publicly the guilt of social and governmental elite alike, he laid a plan to instigate a rebellion and set about rounding up firearms and ammunition.

Before Ōshio could get his uprising under way, one of his comrades lost heart and informed the town commissioner. Ōshio was forced to begin his attack on the troops of the *bakufu* without adequate preparation. His forces included three hundred low class warriors and farmers of means from Ōsaka's suburban areas. They attacked Tōshōgu and Tenma Shrines with guns. Kōnoikeya, Tennōjiya, Hiranoya, and Masuya were set aflame with *hiyahō* (guns shooting flaming arrows) and *rokudama* (primitive hand-grenades). Gold and silver coins were looted from the merchants' shops for distribution among poor people. Fires were set in many places throughout Ōsaka. The rebellious troops drew close to the castle of Ōsaka.

The troops of the *bakufu,* under the town commissioner's command, were poorly trained for actual fighting. It took them quite some time to put down the rioters. When defeat finally came, Ōshio committed suicide together with his own son. All those who had participated in the rebellion were severely punished.[51]

How broad Oshio's actual base of support among the citizens was, is not altogether clear. It is certain, though, that he represented a wide feeling of complaint and unrest. The attempted revolt lasted only for a day. But it pinpointed accurately the injustices of administration and the greedy extravagance of the wealthy. It also dealt a heavy blow to the *bakufu* by demonstrating the weakness of the government for all to see in the major commercial city of the age.[52]

Ōshio was called "Sir Heihachirō" (*Heihachirō-sama*) by the common people after his death. Nor did rioting cease; Settsu, Echigo, Suhō, and other domains had their own uprisings. The collective effect of riots throughout the country was to impress upon the warrior class a sense of crisis with respect to the feudal system for which they were responsible. This consciousness of a serious malady in their system was one of the causes leading to the Tenpō Reform. It was the last attempt of the pre-modern period to restore and secure the feudal order in the hands of the warrior class.

*Collapse of city privileges, and of the wholesalers' monopolies.*——Merchants enjoying the patronage of the feudal lords could hold on to their monopoly privileges only as long as the Tokugawa rulers were powerful enough to maintain the socio-economic system through their administrative organization. The merchants' favored positions became unstable when the common people's resistance threatened the *bakufu*'s power and, as a consequence, the patronage of its administration. Governmental power had weakened, as we have seen, because of changing social conditions resulting from the growing poverty of the masses staggering under the burden of increasingly heavy taxes. Price rises following repeated famines accelerated the processes producing ever greater differentiation between the expanding low class population and the ruling groups struggling to hold on to privileged positions.

It was not just privileged people who were threatened. The feudal cities which were the foundation of the socio-economic system were equally endangered. The dominance of the cities over the rural districts was challenged, the most serious threat being focused on the wholesalers' monopolization of the market. An expanding nationwide commodity economy strengthened the development of local markets, giving more economic power to local merchants, and thereby intensifying pressures for reform of the socio-economic system centering in the cities. Local merchants opposed the monopoly rights of a limited number of upper class merchants precisely because of the strangling effects of such rights on the expansion of the national economy along lines which permitted their own businesses to grow.

The transformation of the mechanisms of monopolized trade has been described by Toyota Takeshi in relation to changes in ecological structure, up to the reforms introduced in the Tenpō era (1830–44).[53] The major outlines of that transformation, based on his study, are traced in the following paragraphs.

Most castle towns did not emerge spontaneously but were constructed to meet specific political and military requirements. In the process, the feudal lords divided their towns into distinct sections that were given specific functions. With the assigned functions went the necessary privileges for the service provided or the goods produced. The prosperity of each section was able to proceed without violating the controls of the lords. As the commodity economy expanded on a national scale, the privileges granted originally to a limited few prevented the free participation of others in the growing trade of the country. Common merchants (as distinguished from the few privileged ones) in both castle town and rural district began agitating for the withdrawal of merchants' privileges. Increasingly the system of assigned sections with special concessions was disregarded. Merchants from other towns were sometimes allowed to set up shops, in castle towns already possessing similar shops, if the newcomers made adequate contributions to official treasuries. Monopoly privileges in some trades in some castle towns were thoroughly wiped out in this manner. Structural changes naturally followed in these towns.

Developments in the economy brought changes not only in the structures of the castle town itself, but also in the relation of the towns to rural districts. Farmers increased production to meet the demands of an economy shifting from local and regional to national dimensions. The isolation and self-sufficiency of rural society were shattered. Rural production expanded to include handicrafts as well as agricultural products, and the number of rural people engaged in commerce and industry swelled. Not only were they able to provide more products for sale in the periodic markets of the towns, but gradually they were able to sell directly to consumers, by-passing market channels entirely.

Wherever merchants maintained monopolies over trade, the rural producers were compelled to sell to wholesalers, being themselves deprived of free access to consumers. The number of merchants who went out into the rural districts to buy up goods gradually increased. Consequently, small shops in suburban areas could now buy goods from these merchants in castle towns, without dealing through wholesalers. The monopoly mechanisms of wholesalers were thus undercut by the growth of the suburban trade. Expansion of cultivation of agricultural products for sale stimulated the growth of commercial centers at important traffic junctions which had ready access to wider markets. At first the feudal lords sought to prevent the establishment of such centers of commerce by laws. The laws could not be successfully enforced, though, and the lords were forced to grant trading rights to a limited number of the trade centers. Compensation for the lords came from taxes imposed on the new centers; but the rural districts had acquired strategic points of entry into the commodity economy. Hence, they were able to overcome the repressive barriers to trading, and the ruin of the castle town wholesalers' privileged positions was assured.

As the castle towns lost their exclusive roles in the commodity economy by sharing trade with the rural districts, so the wholesalers lost exclusive control over trade channels within the city. Opposition of townsmen against guilds of wholesalers weakened the latters' positions but, more important, retailing merchants developed new lines of direct transaction with rural producers, especially those in adjacent suburban areas. In a word, the retailers themselves took over some of the monopolizing prerogatives formerly possessed by the wholesalers.

The tendency to do away with wholesale monopolies was especially strong in areas where commercial agriculture was highly developed and local merchants were very active. Wholesalers in the city of Sakai had monopolized all cotton produced in the villages of four counties (*gun*) in the Izumi district. When prices offered for their products fell too low, the heads of the villages in the district joined in sending a petition to the government for permission to sell to merchants in districts other than Sakai.[54] During the Bunsei era (1818–30) more than one thousand merchants and well-to-do farmers in the three provinces of Settsu, Kawachi, and Izumi fought against the exclusive controls of wholesalers over cotton and oil products. Struggles against wholesalers occurred also in Edo and Kyōto. In the weaving industry of Tango, wholesalers dealing in thread bought raw silk from merchants in Itoya-machi in Kyōto and sold it to weaving farmers. Fabrics produced by these farmers were sold back to the Kyōto wholesalers on a consignment basis. When the westward sea route became operational, merchants in Iwataki started importing raw silk directly from the Tōhoku district, and put it into the looms of local weavers. The products were then sold in Kyōto, but not through wholesalers.

In the town of Kiryū local merchants successfully opposed an effort made in 1689 by wealthy merchants in Edo to acquire a monopoly over sales of their silk products. The Edo merchants were seeking compensation for duties exacted from silk sales by the government. Resolute opposition by the Kiryū producers against the design of the Edo capitalists forced cancellation of the plan.

Sales of silk crepe produced in Ojiya, center of Echigo district's silk industry, had long been controlled by a union of merchants selling dry goods in Edo. In the Kansei era (1789–1801) the producers increasingly sold directly to retailers in Edo. The wholesalers in Edo filed suits against the Echigo producers.[55] Similar cases occurred in Hachiōji and Yonezawa. Local merchants gradually exercised greater freedom in marketing, presenting a growing menace to wholesaling monopolies and eventually forcing their retreat from the market.

Development of industries in many parts of the country intensified the efforts to set up direct channels between producers and retailing firms. More and more suits were filed to ward off this trend. Merchants belonging to the established unions of Ōsaka (*Nijūyon-kumi-donya*) and Edo (*Jukkumi-donya*) strengthened their cooperative efforts to protect their monopolies over the supply of goods for Edo. When threatened they raised the price of goods, bought up supplies when shortages occurred, or even held up the unloading of ships in the harbor to create shortages. Both warriors and commoners were antagonized and hurt by such measures.

The *bakufu* was advised by certain scholars that the flow of goods into Edo would improve and prices would come down if trade was freed from all forms of monopolization, including the artificial devices for raising prices. This advice was accepted and, in the last month of the twelfth year of the Tenpō era (1841), the *bakufu* called a meeting with the *Jukkumi-*

*donya* union of Edo to advise them that they were released from the obligations of providing 12,000 *ryō* in annual "contributions" (*myōgakin*). The price of this concession, the merchants learned, was liquidation of their collective monopoly rights (*tonyakabu-nakama*). Liberation of the market from control by the wholesalers meant that any and all goods could now be purchased directly from producers and sold directly to retailers. Sellers and buyers could bargain directly for all ships' cargoes. No controls would be applied to any commercial transactions.

Similar regulations were put into effect on the twenty-third day of the same month and year (1841). The Ōsaka wholesalers' union (*Nijūyon-kumi-donya*) had always supplied the Edo union, and held a very favorable credit balance. During a period beginning with the Bunka era (1804–18) and ending with the Tenpō era (1830–44), the amount of credit supplied by Ōsaka to Edo merchants reached 16,000 *ryō* or more. Such a large volume of unpaid loans seriously hampered the Ōsaka groups; increasingly they were incapable of purchasing enough goods to supply the undiminished demands of Edo. Prices in Edo climbed considerably. This was the situation that provoked the liquidation of Edo's monopolies.

In Ōsaka, the name of the cooperative union, *kumiai-nakama*, was first eliminated, as the very existence of such an organization fostered price rises. Merchants were prohibited from buying up goods that were scarce, and from keeping hoarded supplies secretly stored. Regulations were put on wholesaler-retailer relations. That is, wholesalers were instructed to sell not only to brokers but to retailers directly. If shortages occurred, wholesalers were not to limit the supply of goods to retailers, even if brokers could not be supplied adequately. Wholesalers were forbidden to sell at higher rates to retailers than to brokers, in collusion with the latter.

Entrenched customs in commerce could not, however, be eradicated simply by issuing regulations, although some merchants assisted the government in arresting lawbreakers among money-lenders, used-furniture dealers, and dealers in waste materials and equipment. But what was needed were regulations requiring the dissolution of the merchant unions one by one. This was done, except that some one official (*nen-gyōji*) was left in each union as a point of control, and the unions were kept alive just enough to receive from them annual "contributions" under new names (*jidaikin* and *yakukin*, = taxes) instead of the old *myōgakin*. Even after restrictions were placed on monopoly action, prices did not recede as the *bakufu* had expected. Moreover, the *bakufu* had looked only at the defects of the union system and had overlooked its merits, such as the exercise of discipline by the unions over its own members, the advantages they provided the government for controlling merchants by groups, and the security in transactions afforded by the unions, thus promoting trade in general.[56]

Orders to abolish merchants' organizations (*kabu-nakama*) in Kyōto and Ōtsu were also issued in the third month of the thirteenth year of the Tenpō era (1842). Enforcement of restrictions in the monopolization of markets was rather thorough in Edo, Ōsaka, and Kyōto, especially as compared to Hyōgo where only the name was changed and the old practices continued as always. No change was evident in Sakai. Monopoly activity could not be easily erased in the provincial towns either. The market-freeing actions of the Tenpō Reforms were effective in only a few provincial towns such as Okayama, Nagoya, and Tsuruga where there were strong pressures from merchants in the rural districts. On the whole, though, the anti-monopoly measures could not be enforced. There were many kinds of merchants to whom the restrictions did not readily apply. Even if they did not use the names *kabu-nakama* or *tonya*, many merchants were bound together by private organizations affording the same advantages as organized unions. The managers (*nen-gyōji*) left in office to facilitate government controls gathered into groups (*kumi*) or fraternities (*kō*) which found ways to subvert or evade the anti-monopoly regulations.

Under such conditions, the *bakufu* could not achieve the goals of the Tenpō Reforms, namely, abolition of monopoly unions. Overall production began to decline, and the distributive system fell into disorder. The exchange of goods became bogged down, while the credit system was suspended completely. Market prices experienced a sharp rise.[57] The government was forced to reinstate the merchant unions in 1851, in order to regain even indirect controls over production and prices.

When the unions were restored, it was done along lines similar to times prior to the establishment of the *jukkumi-kabunakama*, before the Bunka era (1804–18). The *myōgakin* duties were not imposed this time, nor were restrictions placed on the number of market privileges (*kabu*). That is, membership in the unions was open. Shipping services between Ōsaka and Edo (*higaki-bune*) were prohibited from restricting ships to one-way cargoes. These were the conditions the *bakufu* exacted in return for reinstating the unions. Wholesalers who went into business after the liberation of trade in the Tenpō Reforms were officially recognized, in addition to the wholesalers whom the *bakufu* had sought to abolish but had now reinstated.[58]

There were now 12,469 wholesalers in Edo, handling 95 kinds of goods. This number included both the older group with restored privileges and the newcomers, comprising the influential merchants in the rural districts and city merchants connected with the rural merchants who had emerged in the interim. It was the rising influence of the newcomers which had forced a retreat by the older, established wholesalers, leading to the attempt at completely liquidating the older group. With the restoration of the older unions, the newcomers were gathered into provisional organizations.[59] These were abolished in 1857, and the *myōgakin* payments reinstituted in 1864, as the *bakufu* sought, in its final days, to reinforce its crumbling foundations.

The Ōsaka unions were rehabilitated in 1857. Merchants in Sangō, Settsu, and Kawachi reestablished their unions. Again, the price of reinstatement was acceptance of direct controls by the *bakufu* office. Wholesalers were not allowed to deal with unauthorized persons. All imports from the provinces and shipments made to Edo were confined to the recognized unions. Once again the merchant groups were obliged to offer certain goods and labor free of charge to the government. However, whereas it had been necessary to limit membership in the unions under the old system, members could now be added or reduced according to their own needs and wishes. The Ōsaka wholesalers were also required to make *myōgakin* payments again.[60]

We observed earlier that the Tenpō Reforms were not executed successfully in most of the provinces, due to the private adherence of wholesalers to the old system. Inasmuch as the reform program had proved ineffective, it was rescinded in the provinces as well, and the unions were officially recognized. On the other hand, the newly-emerged merchants of the rural districts mobilized their own opposition to the power of the old monopolies, and many local governments took steps on their own initiative to liquidate the old *kabu-nakama* in their districts.

*Changes in the structure of industry in the castle towns, and the beginnings of modern cities.*——Both the monopolistic powers of the privileged wholesalers and the castle towns that authorized and patronized them were forced to give way in the face of a developing national economy that favored a new kind of city. The power base of the warrior class and the thrust of the expanding commodity economy were fundamentally in contradiction to each other. In the difficulties that developed, it was the warriors' style of life that changed and, with it, the internal structure of the castle towns.

As the warriors became financially distressed, local governments encouraged them to engage in household industry. Low ranking warriors came under the control of merchants possessing great capital assets, working as mere wage-laborers. Special products processed by low grade warriors turned craftsmen are indicated in the book *Kinoene Yawa* (Tales of the Year of the Rat): "The lower samurai are all busy making things; writing brushes in Yonezawa, paper umbrellas in Nagato, bamboo hats in Nabeshima, medicine kits in Akitsuki, and rain coats in Kokura."[61] Without renouncing their warrior status, these workers earned supplementary income by filling orders made by either merchants or well-established craftsmen. Industry of this kind was a phenomenon peculiar to a dying age, to a time of transition, and not an emergent industry of a new era.

An example of such an industry comes from Sendai where the national economic malady of high rice prices had depleted the resources of many warriors. The local government supplied them with certain necessities, such as fuel, soybean paste, and salt; yet more than this was needed. They began to take on side jobs, which varied according to different areas. Foot-soldiers on a salary level of *sanninbuchi* or *yoninbuchi* (average annual rice consumption of three or four men) were given jobs by the wholesalers. They produced paper lanterns in quantities reaching 300,000 pieces per year, which were exported to Fukushima, Morioka, and Yamagata.

Production of a kind of hair-band called *motoyui* was recommended by the government for warriors' work, to suppress imports of the bands from other regions. The Sendai government also sponsored work on fossil-wood (*umoregi-zaiku*), dyed paper, heavy cord for sewing mats, and tobacco cultivation. The warrior-workmen were not permitted to retail their wares openly, but brought them to the wholesalers at night with their faces covered by cloth masks. The wholesalers bought and marketed their products. Warriors with no capital became wage-laborers, while rich merchants bought their way into the warrior's ranks through substantial payments to the government. There were about 150 such merchants with warrior rankings in 1868. Minor merchants also purchased rights (*kabu*) to low grade warrior standing (*ashigaru*).[62]

In the process of deterioration of the warrior class and structural changes in the castle towns, some of the latter developed new industries geared to the emerging forms of a new social order. For example, the castle towns of Fukui, Hamamatsu, Yonezawa, and Maebashi became centers of local industries benefiting from expanding markets. When Japan was opened to foreign trade in a later period, these local industries were transformed into factories operating on larger scales of manufacture. These industries then led Japanese society into a new phase of history.

After the Kyōhō era (1716–36), the warriors in Fukui, including those of upper ranks, cultivated mulberry trees in the rear areas of their grounds for use in sericulture. Cotton spinning was also developed as a source of income to supplement their inadequate government stipends. Women of the households were proud of their work in weaving fabrics, in that they earned money by themselves. But they were not allowed to negotiate directly with the merchants as it might belittle the dignity of the warrior class, still the ruling group in society. Fabrics produced in the warriors' households were collected by stewards (*karō*) of the elders, who delivered them to wholesalers for sale on consignment and received new supplies of raw silk in exchange.

In 1858, Yokoi Konan advised the Fukui government to establish an agency in Nagasaki to promote its products and enrich the domain. Such an office (*bussan-sōkaisho*) was opened in the following year. Fukui's silk sales to the Dutch traders in Nagasaki for that year (1859) amounted to $200,000 (US), or about 1,000,000 *ryō* in Japanese gold currency. These sales constituted Japan's maiden venture in silk exports. The Fukui silk industry's export sales reached 2,000 000 *ryō* by 1861, only two years later. Even after the Meiji Restoration production of high grade silk fabrics continued, promoted by the families of warrior pedigree who had developed technical expertise in sericulture and weaving. As weaving became the main industry of Fukui, production reached a level so high that, even after the Meiji transformation of society, this province was able to sustain itself economically without making radical changes in its traditional ways. It was the skilled men of the warriors' households who took the lead in introducing machines for weaving heavy twilled fabrics (*hattan*) and furthering the sericulture and weaving industry in their province.[63]

The city of Hamamatsu changed hands from the Mizuno to the Inoue domain in 1845. The latter sought relief from a severe shortage of funds by encouraging a number of industries, including mulberry tree cultivation in warriors' gardens to develop sericulture. Some warriors were relocated on reclaimed waste lands to grow tea, mandarin oranges, and persimmon crops. Raw materials (mulberry and *edgeworthia chrysantha*) for paper production were also promoted. Before transferring to Hamamatsu the Inoue fief had its center in Tatebayashi, where its warriors had learned the technique of striped textiles (*yūkijima*). They discovered that they could adapt the cotton cloth industry of Hamamatsu to the same technique and, in time, improved the quality of their fabrics. The high quality of the cloth won for it a good market, first among the people of the city, but eventually in Edo and Ōsaka, between which Hamamatsu was situated. Production of the *yūkijima* fabric grew year after year, converting to large-scale manufacture in the new age under the name *enshūjima*, which became well known abroad.[64]

A larger national market than ever propelled industry in castle towns like the one described above to unprecedented production peaks. In general, though, most castle towns hung on to traditions supported only by privileges granted by the dying feudal order, and failed to develop industries to sustain them in the coming social order. Certain commercial centers with fewer ties to the feudal order were able to develop as industrial centers; such as Kiryū, Ashikaga, and Isesaki in weaving; Ōmihachiman, production center for mosquito netting; and Takaoka and Miki (Banshū district), centers for metal casting and forging. These centers expanded production gradually, from the middle of the Tokugawa period, within the limits of regional economies and relatively free from intrusive feudal controls.

Takaoka was a town constructed by Maeda Toshinaga in imitation of Kyōto's checkerboard street plan. It contained 630 houses and a population of nearly 3,000. After Maeda's death, his warriors returned to Kanazawa in compliance with the law permitting only one castle town in each domain. The merchants and craftsmen gathered in Takaoka to supply warriors' needs were left high and dry, and many left town. Maeda's heir, Toshitsune, ruled in 1620 that no townsmen were to leave the town, an act that saved the town's casting, lacquerware, dyeing and leather industries. Protected by the Kanazawa government, these industries were able to attract a greater number of townsmen. Toward the end of the Edo period an outport was developed at Fushiki that accommodated large boats of more than fifty *koku* capacity, and many wholesalers helped build Takaoka into the center of the nation's copper utensil casting industry. Some eighty dye plants were also operating in the city. It was nicknamed the "Ōsaka of the Hokuriku region," a name well known even in Kyōto and Ōsaka.[65]

Kiryū was a small town under the direct administration of the *bakufu*. It had been built between 1591 and 1596 by a local magistrate and consisted of a few townships of townsmen and government offices. Until the

Kanpō era (1741–4) it remained essentially a rural community, with little commerce or industry. There was little fertile land, and the people were obliged to subsidize themselves through weaving. Tax payments were made in silk goods every year after 1600, until taxes became payable in money in 1647. Commercial production was promoted thereafter and markets were cultivated. Production expanded remarkably in the Kanbun era (1661–73), with sales extending to Edo and Ōsaka in the Genroku era (1688–1704). Around 1738 the Kiryū weavers were able to introduce techniques heretofore monopolized by the Nishijin masters in Kyōto. By the end of the Tokugawa period they managed to provide a serious threat to the Nishijin weaving industry which had for centuries enjoyed a privileged and unchallenged prominence.

Progress in production methods enabled the silk merchants to introduce production controls and the scale of production was enlarged to a manufacturing level. As capacity expanded, there followed an accelerated division of the processes of producing raw silk, spinning, and weaving. A corps of wage-laborers emerged. The basic processes of weaving were expedited in weaver's workshops owned by the merchants, but other production processes were carried out in household industries under supervision of the wholesalers. A unit workshop for weaving in the Tenpō era (1830–44) consisted of about ten looms engaging fifteen or sixteen workers. The number of apprentice weavers increased annually.

In the Shin-machi district of Kiryū there were 331 weavers in 1757, and this doubled to 651 by 1812.[66] The town had 141 houses in 1657, but this figure expanded rapidly, as the following list shows:[67]

| *No. of houses* | *Date* |
|---|---|
| 141 | 1657 |
| 278 | 1742 |
| 324 | 1757 |
| 774 | 1819 |
| 989 | 1855 |

As a city Kiryū was a combination of feudal and modern components. Its modern thrust consisted of its establishment of industry as a secondary occupation for agrarian people which developed without the restrictions of the unions and guilds of the feudal city. On the other hand, it was not free from feudal controls since its industry was run by rich farmers who were also the wholesalers of its products; in both roles they kept the farmers in virtual serfdom.

Many centers of the weaving industry emerged all over the country at the end of the Tokugawa period. To these were added the cities that expanded rapidly after Japan's ports were opened to foreign trade, such as Kanagawa, Hyōgo, and Niigata. These cities for international trade became important bases for the importation of Western culture. By making an early breakthrough in the restrictive walls erected by wholesalers in the feudal system, these cities, then, were the forerunners of the modern cities appropriate to the emerging social order.

In 1858 Kanagawa opened its port, now known around the world as Yokohama, to foreign trade. It was previously only a small port for use by local fishermen. A section on the east side of town was provided as a residential area for foreign traders, who soon exported large quantities of silk, tea, and seafood. The healthy development of the town is evident in the export-import figures for a five-year period beginning five years after the port opened.

| *Year* | *Exports* (US$) | *Imports* (US$) (*mainly cotton and woolen fabrics*) |
|---|---|---|
| 1863 | 6,000,000 | 2,960,000 |
| 1864 | 9,350,000 | 5,530,000 |
| 1865 | 16,860,000 | 13,030,000 |
| 1866 | 8,980,000 | 14,240,000 |
| 1867 | 9,700,000 | 13,000,000 |

Overseas trade transacted through Yokohama amounted to 80% of all foreign trade at the end of the Edo period, being handled predominantly by Yokohama merchants.[68]

In 1859, the year after the port opened, the *bakufu* took steps to encourage its use by granting freedom to domestic wholesalers to transfer residences to the city and operate their businesses there under supervision of the Commissioner of Foreign Affairs (*gaikoku-bugyō*) In the seventh month of 1859 there were only ninety-nine trading firms in Yokohama.[69] By the next year the number increased to 198, twice the original count. In 1863 the figure reached 390, as the small village of fishermen and farmers rapidly expanded into a city of traders. Yokohama assumed a significant place as the country's primary link with the economy and civilization of the Western world.

Merchants in the rural districts, as we have seen, had long been confined to local markets, with no direct channels even to markets in Edo. The rapid expansion of international trade through Yokohama's port soon changed all this. Commodity prices climbed swiftly as merchants discovered that quick profits were easily gained due to the lucrative margin between domestic and export prices. Merchants in Yokohama purchased goods directly from rural merchants or from producers in more industrialized areas such as Kiryū, Ashikaga, Chichibu, and Fukushima. The old rights of trade monopolization reserved by the merchants of Edo, in silk, oil, and other goods, were completely overthrown. The effective power for deciding price levels passed from the hands of domestic wholesalers to those of foreign buyers, whose competitive bids increasingly controlled the overseas trade market.

In a final move to protect the wholesalers' position, the *bakufu* published a notice in 1864 requiring that five kinds of commodities, (cereal grains, vegetable oils, wax, dry goods, and thread), were to be channeled through Edo's dealers. This notice, called *gohin-Edomawashi*, was opposed by the Yokohama merchants dealing in exports and it also drew protests from the foreign countries engaged in the booming Yokohama trade. The effort to retain traditional controls was in vain.

From a small village of farmers and fishermen, Yokohama was transformed into a foreign trade city, breaking the bonds of national isolation and presaging the modern city. Culturally it became an international city, the country's chief receptacle for the goods and ideas of other cultures that had been purposely shut out for more than two centuries. In terms of social structures too, Yokohama became a place for pioneering in the new forms of a modern city.

## 3. Breakdown of the Feudal Order and the Transformation of Edo

The disintegration of the feudal cities derived from many sources, and some of the disorganizing elements were stronger in certain regions than others. But the combined, destructive force of all these elements came into focus on the capital city of Edo: the progressive poverty of the warriors; their dependence upon loans from rich merchants; the swelling influx of an impoverished peasantry into the city; advanced differentiation among merchants; commoner's growing resistance to authority; compromise and concessions by the authorities, as the people pressed claims for power; emerging economic power of rural merchants, disrupting the dominant position of the cities; and the wholesalers' failing grasp on monopolistic mechanisms in trading. On top of all this, the final blow was administered when the ruling regime in the capital city of Edo, under increasing pressures applied by foreign countries, was toppled from its place of national power by strong, domestic anti-government forces.

Tokugawa Ieyasu had bequeathed a considerable accumulation of gold and silver to the government treasuries, but these reserves were almost exhausted by the time of Tsunayoshi (ruled 1680–1709), fifth of the Tokugawa shoguns. Beginning with the eighth shogun, Yoshimune (ruled 1716–45), the *bakufu* attempted by various means to refurbish its depleted finances, culminating in the reforms of the Tenpō era (1830–44). The reforms, of course, were aimed not only at restoring government finances, but also at remedying the very unstable social conditions precipitated by a bad famine in the northern Ōu district in 1833, a nationwide famine in 1836, and the peasant uprisings, especially that led by Ōshio Heihachirō.

The Tenpō Reforms undertaken to alleviate social disturbances included, it will be recalled, liquidation of wholesaling monopolies (*kabunakama*), and consolidation of all lands within 10 *ri* (24.4 mi.) of Edo and Ōsaka under direct control of the *bakufu*. These measures were inadequate to the needs of the times, however, being essentially a reversion to practices of the Kyōhō (1716–36) and Kanpō (1741–4) eras when fiscal frugality and austere limitations were imposed on the living patterns of the common people. The reform measures were not designed to relieve the government of its excessive dependence upon farm productivity and turn it to a more progressive accommodation of the expanding commodity economy. This contradiction between government structures and economic trends was left unresolved, and social conditions only worsened.

The feudal lords shared in the sufferings, overburdened by extravagant spending in the required residence programs in Edo and by obligations to support *bakufu* civil engineering projects. Emergency budgets were devised, incorporating loans from the agents handling the rice business of each domain, though with little hope or intention of repaying the loans. Interest on the loans alone gave the money-lenders vast capital accumulations.

The burdens were passed on increasingly to the peasants, who were forced to give up first 40%, then 50%, and later 60% of their crops in tax payments. Far from understanding or seeking to remedy the plight of the peasants, the provincial goverments met failure to pay taxes in full with severe punishment. With farm productivity pushed already to its possible limits, and no further technical improvements in sight, peasants either fled from the farms or rose up in rebellion.

From the Kyōhō era (1716–36) on, the whole country was brought into the framework of the commodity economy, depriving local domains of simple self-sufficiency and independence. In contrast to the *bakufu*, local leaders moved away somewhat from total dependence upon agricultural revenue to promotion of crafts production as secondary occupations for warriors and peasants. Local industries received assistance from local administrations not only in production means, but also in marketing goods through the special offices set up to handle sales, called *kokusan-kaisho* or *bussan-kaisho*. Currency issued by the local governments was loaned to producers for operating capital and products were bought by the local governments.

While such policies promoted trade, they stifled individual enterprise. In Ōsaka trading was handled in a zone centering around the warehouses managing products from the various domains, this zone constituting the primary place and portion of Ōsaka's commodity business. Centralization of business expedited expansion of the money economy, although local governments often were forced to "borrow" on their warriors' salaries by cutting them by one-half, gradually reducing the latter to poverty.

Warriors, in turn, turned to the merchants for high-interest loans, putting up their diminished stipends as collateral, and just as often took on secondary jobs to salvage their positions with the wages earned. The secondary jobs were organized, as described above, by the wholesalers, thus introducing a conflict in their status. Socially, the warriors belonged to the governing organs of the provinces, while their actual lives depended on their working outside the administrative organizations. The combined disabilities of reduced government stipends plus actual dependence upon merchants rendered the relationship of the warriors with their lords progressively unstable. The monopolistic means through which local governments sought to secure for themselves the profits realized in commodity sales prevented free sales of products by the farmers, who became increasingly resentful of government domination. This resentment erupted in rebellious rioting with growing frequency toward the end of the Tokugawa period, in attempts to deny the local governments exclusive controls over all commodities.

Once the feudal foundations were impaired, upper class warriors could no longer hold strictly to conservative policies and methods in local governments. Lower ranking warriors, who had first-hand knowledge of the unstable conditions and had been influenced by cooperation with merchants and landowners, acquired positions within the central offices of local government. They then introduced administrative reforms, while holding down the rebellious farmers. Large domains in southwestern Japan used the profits from government monopolies of the commodity market to manufacture firearms and ammunition. The relative distance from the watchful eye of the *bakufu* enabled them to build up regional strength through special contacts with foreign powers. In time they were strong enough to stand against the weakened political and military power of the *bakufu*.

This ominous situation eventually reached the point where transformation of the system of controls under the *bakuku*, daimyō and warriors was inescapable. The structural changes that occurred were sweeping, involving (1) the basic relationships of the *bakufu* to local governments, (2) internal shake-up in the community of warriors itself, and (3) a revamping of the power of the ruling warrior class over the people ruled. The situation had not ripened sufficiently, however, for the common citizenry to assume a central role in overcoming the contradictions of feudal society or in giving birth to a new social system.

Japan had been too long isolated from the international market. Her farmers were poor, bound to small farms and to a strict feudal code. Economic gains in the commodity market were tied down to a capital base controlled by money-lenders. Acquisition of land wealth through reclamation ventures gave the merchants a dual role as parasitic landowners; they benefited too much from the status quo to take any initiative in reforming rural society. They also controlled much of the crafts industries in the rural sectors by supplying the operating capital. But they assumed very little role in the technical aspects of management and production; again their posture was parasitic.

Even where local industries were controlled by wealthy farmers, development could not exceed certain limits prescribed by prohibitions against movement outside one's domain, limitations of available raw materials, and limited access to markets. The most important avenue to accumulating wealth for the merchants was that of lending money to the warriors at high interest rates, for the warriors' claims to farm surplus was backed by the entire feudal system. So, the expansion of commercial activity was a denial of the feudal order, although this counterforce was allowed to operate only in the field of commodity exchange. On the other hand, the merchants would have undercut their own best source of profits by opposing the warriors. For this reason they were incapable of forging a rival concentration of power for evolving a new system of government and society.

While Japan struggled with her own internal problems in almost total isolation from the rest of the world, the countries of Western Europe and North America were making vast strides forward through the appropriation of modern science and technology in the industrial revolution. They had already achieved modern economies and armed forces long before Japan came to the end of its feudal era and to its own threshhold of modern statehood. The modern states of the West were seeking new markets for their goods and raw materials for their factories. It was only a matter of time before they looked to Japan and pressed her to open her ports.

Reinforcing economic weakness by strengthening her military prowess, pre-revolutionary Russia had extended her territorial frontiers far into the Orient. A Russian envoy made visits to the cities of Nemuro in 1792, and Nagasaki in 1804. In both instances, requests were made for opening up trade relations.

Great Britain arose as the manufacturing mecca of the world after her industrial revolution in the latter half of the 18th century, and in the following century occupied colonies pioneered by other European powers in the East. In 1808 a British delegation put in a bid for open ports in a visit to Nagasaki.

The United States of America had made remarkable progress as a world power after winning independence, and also turned her attention to the Far East. In 1853 a small U.S. squadron entered the port of Uraga, the most strategic point in Edo's bay. This mission pressed the insistence of the Western powers for open ports with new force.

Although the Tokugawa government had had sufficient fire-power to drive foreign ships from her shores more than two centuries earlier, she now found that her military strength was far inferior to that with which she was confronted. She was forced to agree to enter into negotiations concerning opening her doors to trade. The *bakufu* reported the matter to the imperial court and solicited opinions from the daimyō. Before these internal procedures reached a conclusion, the Tokugawa leaders signed a treaty, in the sixth month of 1858, opening the country fully to trading with the United States. It was followed by similar treaties with other Western countries, all prior to having the final approval of the imperial court. The ports of Hakodate, Nagasaki, and Yokohama were opened to international trade after more than 200 years of almost total global seculsion.

Drastic changes in the domestic economy followed soon. Large quantities of silk, tea, silkworm eggs, copper, and marine products were exported from this land that was as yet not industrialized. Equally large volumes of imports included such finished products as woolen fabrics, mixed cotton and wool cloth, merchant vessels and warships, and modern weapons. In a four-year period soon after trading began, exports doubled while imports multiplied five times, as shown below:[70]

| *Year* | *Exports* (US$) | *Imports* (US$) |
|---|---|---|
| 1863 | 6,859,000 | 3,580,000 |
| 1867 | 12,123,000 | 18,476,000 |

Long removed from the international market, Japanese merchants discovered there was a great difference between domestic and world prices. Prices available for exports exceeded domestic prices by five to ten times. Those taking early advantage of export opportunities earned large sums of money. They were traders, local shippers, brokers, and wholesalers who already had command of the domestic commodity exchange. The export business was quickly activated, driving internal prices up just as rapidly because inadequate industrial capacity simply could not meet the new demands. Speculative activity soon emerged to complicate the already unsettled social situation.

Gold coins were bought up avidly by foreign traders as the rates in Japan were lower than on the international market. The *bakufu* reminted in an effort to block the flow of gold out of the country and succeeded to some extent. This move, however, devalued the domestic market, causing a sudden rise in commodity prices. Between the years 1859 and 1867 the prices of goods rose as follows:

| *Export item* | *Rate of increase*(%)[71] | *Domestic item* | *Rate of increase*(%)[72] |
|---|---|---|---|
| silk (Suwa) | 400 | rice | 340 |
| 〃 (Maebashi) | 450 | veg. oil | 400 |
| 〃 (Iwashiro) | 140 | spun cotton | 430 |
| silkworm eggs | | roof tiles | 250 |
| (Shinshū) | 1,000 | wax | 240 |
| kelp | 600 | | |
| tea | 200 | | |

The rapid rise in prices spread all over the country, affecting all commodities.

A limited group of merchants profited from the new export trade, but low grade warriors and commoners only became poorer, hard-pressed even to make a living. The *bakufu* could hardly help them; it was faced now with pressing financial claims in national defense and diplomatic relations. Emergency budgets to meet these claims meant new taxes for the common people and a moratorium on the salaries of warriors. Insurrections among the peasantry and riots among low class urban people increased, while resentment of added poverty after the ports were opened drove the low grade warriors to notions of expelling foreigners from the country. When four Britishers encountered a procession of the lord of Satsuma in a village near Yokohama named Namamugi, one of them was killed by a warrior for what was considered a lack of due respect. Other incidents involving the killing of foreigners near Edo and Yokohama occurred.

The warriors who were convinced that foreigners should be expelled expected the imperial court to support them against the *bakufu* and its policy of reducing them to poverty in favor of recognizing foreign trade without obtaining a national consensus. There arose a movement to restore the authority of the imperial court as the traditional seat and center of a unified country. This movement was fostered by the court nobles who had been shunted aside by the Tokugawa regime, and by feudal lords ignored by the Tokugawa leaders in matters concerning succession to the office of shogun. Together they began pushing for abolition of the Tokugawa *bakufu*.

In this time of crisis, the *bakufu* appointed Tokugawa Yoshinobu (or Keiki) as guardian of the shogun in 1862 to reform the administration. The *sankin-kōtai* system was revised so as to require residence in Edo only once every three years, releasing funds for new coastal defenses. Residence in Edo was reduced to a one hundred-day limit, except for the three main households of the Tokugawa household and those registered for the *Tamarinoma* group of the castle, who still had to put in a full year in Edo. Families of the feudal lords were allowed to remain in their fiefs instead of moving to Edo, and the number of retainers staying in Edo dropped off considerably.

As the revised requirements went into effect, the warrior population in Edo diminished, and many houses of the provincial governments stood vacant. They fell into disrepair and some were dismantled for relocation in native provinces, causing the city of Edo to dwindle. A far more important aspect deriving from revision of the administration was a shift of the center of political integration to the city of Kyōto, still the seat of the imperial court.

This shift was promoted by the anti-government forces, which drew upon the changes taking place in the economic and power structures for their strength. Feudal lords of the domains that were building up their own power often visited Kyōto, and low ranking warriors of the Chōshū and Tosa domains took the initiative in organizing the anti-government movement all over the country. They infiltrated local governments where daimyō were having trouble maintaining controls. They won support from warriors denied positions in local governments, or even from those in office who were against the policies of the *bakufu*. Before long they were able to exercise leadership in national politics.

The lord of Chōshū pushed forward a program for expelling foreigners in cooperation with radical warriors and the disgruntled court nobility. But the Satsuma and Aizu domains decided to oppose the movement, and succeeded in persuading those in court circles who favored the plan to change their minds. The Chōshū forces sought to force the program through by a large display of armed might in Kyōto, but were defeated and compelled to retreat to their own province. Back home in Shimonoseki they opened an attack on some ships of the U.S.A., France, and the Netherlands, closing the strait of Shimonoseki on the day scheduled for attacking all foreigners in Japan. A joint fleet of the three countries together with British ships entered the port of Shimonoseki and subdued it, forcing the Chōshū leaders to surrender. This defeat seriously weakened the hand of the party in the Chōshū domain which favored the anti-foreigner policy.

The Satsuma domain refused to pay the indemnity demanded by the British after the killing of one of their countrymen in the Namamugi incident, and fired on seven British ships sent to Kagoshima, the domain's capital, to enforce the demand. The superior cannon of the British vessels were turned on the city, leveling much of it to the ground. The Satsuma military leaders realized that it was nonsense to try expelling the foreign powers by force. Instead, they requested British help in acquiring modern weapons, and were able to arrange imports of some. Leaders in Chōshū also made an about-face, and began focusing efforts on building both economic and military power sufficient to defend their land against invasion by foreign powers.

Both the Satsuma and Chōshū groups dropped the idea of expelling foreigners in favor of reconstructing the administrative system of the national government. They forged a league to overthrow the *bakufu*, which stood, they felt, in the way of social reforms needed to make the country less vulnerable to foreign pressures.

The *bakufu* reinforced its military posture and financial position through French aid, and in 1865 sent a punitive expedition against the Chōshū rebels for their designs and deeds against the central government. The Satsuma government had previously concluded a secret mutual assistance pact with Chōshū, and hence did not answer the rallying call of the *bakufu* against Chōshū. Other fiefs also failed to obey orders to send troops into the expedition. More crucial, the Chōshū forces had acquired modern weapons and were well trained in their use. Troops of the *bakufu*, on the contrary, had only antiquated arms and suffered as well from poor morale. The spiritless atmosphere among the *bakufu* forces stemmed from the resistance to recruiting efforts in the various domains, due to sudden rises in rice prices caused by the prospects of civil war. The *bakufu* was unable to achieve a clear victory, and finally sued for peace. The political prestige of the *bakufu* was completely destroyed by the failure of this punitive expedition, suffering an embarrassing defeat by a single domain.

Struggles over political power heightened social confusion, and rioting broke out in 1866 on the largest scale yet. Over forty peasant revolts and urban rampages occurred in the latter half of that year, all the way from the northern Ōshū region to Kyūshū in the southwest. The presence of the shogun in Ōsaka was greeted with widespread destruction of houses on the eighth and ninth days of the fifth month of 1866. Rioting followed in the nearby cities of Hyōgo, Nishinomiya, Nada, Ikeda, and Itami on the fourteenth of that month, as the entire Ōsaka district was swamped with violence and the destruction of residences numbering 885 houses in 366 townships. To pacify the people the government provided boiled rice soup for the poor, and wealthy citizens distributed rice and money, after which rioting finally subsided.[73]

Not long afterward, though, the rioting spread to Edo, erupting on the twenty-eighth day of the same month. It began with demolition of houses in the station town of Shinagawa, with warriors, townsmen, and servants participating. The rioters moved on to Shiba, Azabu, Yotsuya, Ushigome, Waseda, Akasaka, Honjo, Kayaba-chō, and Midori-chō, attacking shops and homes of rice dealers, soybean paste dealers, fuel merchants, warriors and rich men, and demanding of them rice and money. Merchants closed their shops and remained quietly in their homes.[74] In the sixth month of 1866 a vicious revolt was mounted in western Edo and Musashi, just at the time when the shogunate was negotiating an armistice with the Chōshū leaders in Edo. Again, in the ninth month, groups of poor people arose and demanded rice and monetary relief from the rich while carrying out widespread house destruction in Fukagawa, Asakusa, Kanda, and Hongō.[75]

The fighting with Chōshū domain ceased in 1867, commodity prices went down, and the people relaxed as social unrest eased off. A mysterious mood arose first in Nagoya, then spread quickly to Kyōto, Ōsaka, and throughout the Tōkai coastal district, in which people, regardless of sex or age, danced feverishly in the streets, exclaiming, "*Ējanaika*!" ("Everything's alright!"). The pro-imperial forces capitalized on this sudden burst of relief and naive optimism to promote the idea that things would work out fine, indeed, if power and authority were restored to the Emperor himself. Such skillful maneuvering further compounded the mounting difficulties of the *bakufu*.

The shogunate's base of operations for the Chōshū campaign fell into confusion, and Edo itself was subjected to continued rioting. Confidence in the ability of the *bakufu* to withstand the anti-government movement was damaged irreparably. On their side, the Satsuma-Chōshū league was ready to force the demise of the Tokugawa regime. It became clear to the latter that the reins of government would have to be returned to the imperial court, though it was expected that the shogunate system would be retained in some compromise form as even its opponents derived their own power from the feudal system. So, without serious fighting between the parties concerned, the powers of government were turned over to the Emperor on the fourteenth day of the tenth month of the third year of the Keiō era (1867).[76]

This act of submission by the Tokugawa shogun gave vent to the worst elements in the confused social conditions of Edo. The Satsuma-Chōshū league decided to destroy the shogunate's organization, and their forces advanced secretly to Edo. Gathering in the Edo office of the Satsuma domain, they perpetrated disturbance throughout Edo through violence, robbery, and obtaining "loans" from Edo's merchants by force. It is estimated that over 200,000 *ryō* were taken in this manner. They conspired to burn the *Ninomaru* section of Edo Castle in the tenth month of 1867.

Lookout posts of the Shōnai domain were fired upon by someone and the *bakufu*, presuming the culprits to be *rōnin* serving the Satsuma leadership, attacked the Satsuma office in Edo, ordering troops of domains loyal to the shogunate to open fire.[77]

The existing police system was inadequate for maintaining peace and order in the city. An auxiliary police force had been organized in 1862, called *shinchō-gumi*, drawing on men of proven ability of pro-shogunate domains, as well as unappointed *rōnin*. Warriors from sections of the Tokugawa domain, such as *Ōban*, *Shoinban*, and *Koshōban*, were organized into auxiliary patrols in 1863. Many warrior parties patrolled the city streets, and gates were erected on minor lanes and roads in addition to the old gates (*tsujiban*) already in the residential areas of warriors.

When authority was returned to the Emperor, four larger domains were instructed to form additional patrols for use in the main part of the city, while fifty-two lesser domains received orders to do extra guard duties in areas far removed from their own Edo offices. The whole city was put under strict surveillance day and night.[78]

When the edict of restoration of imperial authority was announced in the twelfth month of 1867, the shogun was ordered by the Emperor to return all his fiefs and resign from office. This ran counter to the expectations of the warriors under the *bakufu*. When the information reached Ōsaka where the shogun was staying at the time, the Tokugawa standard-bearers and pro-shogun troops of Aizu and Kuwana domains became infuriated and decided to march from Osaka on Kyōto where the imperialist forces were based. They were roundly defeated at Toba and Fushimi south of Kyōto and had to retreat to Edo, having earned the onerous reputation of being "enemies of the imperial court." Kyōto was securely in the hands of the rebellious imperialist forces, and all daimyō in the Kansai region became loyal to the imperial court.

In the second month of 1868, troops of the imperialist camp left Kyōto for Edo on a punitive campaign of their own, under the leadership of Satsuma officers. They came from over twenty domains. In the third month they reached the outskirts of Edo, where they took up positions for a general attack on the city. The shogun fled Edo Castle, taking refuge in Daiji-in temple in Ueno, and surrendered without resistance. Edo Castle was turned over safely to the imperial court without further damage, having served for 278 years as the center and symbol of political integration, since Ieyasu first established himself there in 1590.

Some warriors could not accept either the decision to give up the castle of Edo to the imperial court, or the conditions imposed on the Tokugawa household reducing its revenue to only 700,000 *koku* from the three provinces of Suruga, Tōtōmi, and Mutsu. Three thousand warriors assembled in Ueno to defend their rights, but were crushed. The Aizu domain continued the flagging resistance in the Tōhoku area, retreating to Hokkaidō where they were overcome in a last-ditch stand in May, 1869. The battle in Ueno was the first fought in Edo since its establishment by Ieyasu and, although it did not last very long, many houses were burned down in the precincts of Kaneiji temple, with the fires spreading to the neighboring district of Ueno Yamashita.

The military power of the feudal regime collapsed after the defeat at Ueno. Feudal lords who had acquired houses since 1862 left their residences, returning to their native provinces with families and retainers. Many large mansions stood empty, each one of which had once accommodated several hundreds, or even several thousands, of warriors in its grounds. Residential areas of the warriors fell into decay, with dense weeds parted only by narrow paths covering the grounds. These desolate areas were avoided by persons going about alone at night as they had become lawless and dangerous.[79]

Standard-bearers of the Tokugawa household lost their government stipends and had to turn their lands over to the new government. They faced the unhappy choice of following the Tokugawa family to its vastly reduced domain, with no hope of payment, or of remaining in Edo with hopes of engaging in some kind of business. Among them were 6,572 heads of families, which meant that the total number of persons involved was more than 30,000. They released their vassels and servants, and put their houses up for sale, though there were few prospective buyers in those uncertain and disordered times.

Some warriors opened small teahouses with their wives and daughters serving customers; others set up antique shops peddling valuable furniture and articles inherited from generations of ancestors at ridiculously low prices. Still others became vendors of sweet potatoes roasted over ovens built in their own homes. In front of many once-glorious warriors' homes appeared incongruous little shops handling various and sundry items.

The fighting in Ueno had also caused the townsmen to scatter in all directions, only to return and find the warriors' ranks so depleted that they could no longer maintain their businesses. Some returned, then, to farms in their native places, and Edo became vacated and quiet. A population that had gone over 1,000,000 late in the Tokugawa era dwindled to 597,905 (in 149,383 houses) by 1873. The social and ecological structures, so characteristic of Edo in its heyday as the nucleus of the centralized feudal system, became disorganized as the whole system disintegrated.

Edo had to change its characteristic features from those of a mecca of the military class to something more befitting the new structure of authority being put together. But it was not clear yet just where the new government's capital would be located, though the primary contenders were Edo and Ōsaka. Ōkubo Toshimichi submitted written recommendations in favor of Ōsaka to the Emperor in 1868. His reasoning was that a policy for accumulating greater national wealth with which to build up the military might of the nation could best be carried out in the city already functioning as the nation's center of commerce and industry. Such reasoning was adapted to the most important task of the new government, namely, to work out suitable policies and practices with the foreign countries insisting upon relations with Japan. The Meiji Restoration itself was, at least to some extent, a reformation from the claims of warriors toward those of the citizenry, adding strength to the proposal of putting the capital in a city of commerce and industry rather than leave it in a center based upon control of agriculture, even though commerce and industrialization were only potentially the basis of the new social order. This, then, was the case for Ōsaka as the capital of the new government.

The Ōsaka proposal proved rather weak, though, agains the bid to keep the capital in Edo. Maejima Mitsu and others insisted on retention of Edo as the capital, advancing the following reasons:

1. Edo was in an advantageous position for dealing with troops that had fought against the imperialist movement.
2. The Russian threat made it mandatory for Japan to secure its territories to the north, and Edo offered a better vantage point for this task.
3. While Ōsaka was a convenient site with respect to domestic traffic and transportation, its port could not accommodate large ships. The Bay of Edo was large enough to construct port accommodations for large merchant vessels and warships, and already had a good maintenance and repair base at Yokosuka, just south of Edo.
4. Overall territory around Ōsaka was too limited for future capital expansion, while Edo was surrounded by a vast plain.
5. The streets of Ōsaka were too narrow, and large sums of money and labor would be needed to reconstruct them. Edo's streets would require no such reconstruction immediately.
6. Edo Castle had not been destroyed, and many office, residential, and even educational structures were available for immediate use, thus saving the new government considerable expense.
7. Ōsaka could be expected to continue its prosperous activity, even if it were not made the capital. Edo, however, would almost cease to exist if its political functions were not quickly restored. Many citizens had already departed, and if the trend persisted it would become a deserted city.[80]

In addition to these reasons, it was low ranking warriors who had fought for the restoration movement, not townsmen, and they took it for granted that Edo was a proper base for themselves. The new government had no ready reserves for constructing a new political center and, accordingly, the Maejima recommendation was accepted.

The Imperial Edict proclaiming Edo the capital was issued on July 10, 1868, stating: "Edo is the largest city in eastern Japan, an important center of traffic and transportation. We shall govern the state ourselves in this capital. Henceforth it shall be called Tōkyō, instead of Edo. This name derives from our belief that all citizens throughout the land are as members of the same family, and East shall be treated the same as West. We trust that we have the people's full understanding in these matters." With this Edict, Edo became Tōkyō, "Miyako of the East," and the Emperor's move there wedded the tradition of ancient "West" to the restored authority of government in the new "East" capital.

The Emperor Meiji arrived in the city of Tōkyō on October 13, 1868. Edo Castle was renamed Tōkyō Castle and chosen as the Emperor's palace. Returning briefly to Kyōto, he came back to Tōkyō on February 28, 1869. This time the transfer to Tōkyō was complete, vacating the imperial seat in Kyōto where successive emperors had resided for more than a full millennium since the time of the Emperor Kanmu (781–806). The city of Tōkyō underwent a gradual transformation thereafter, in which the social and ecological structures of the feudal city were dismantled and replaced by facilities and patterns appropriate to the requirements of the new politics and economy of a rapidly emerging modern state.

# Chapter VIII | Formation of Modern Cities in Meiji Japan (A. D. 1868-1897)

## 1. New Social System

Disintegration of the feudal system as a whole could not, and did not, wipe out all residual forms of feudal life overnight. That the processes of modernization of the political and economic structures would eventually effect the total society was evident, however, in the appearance of new shapes and styles in old familiar cities.

Modernization in Japan did not occur so much from within the private and local units of society as it was pushed forward from the top by the new Meiji government. Far-reaching modifications were promoted in the crucial fields of politics, defense, economy, education and social system. Pioneering steps designed to remake the basic political and economic structures of the total society included the following:

1. Displacement of the feudal domains by establishing a system of prefectures as the major administrative units, completely destroying the isolationism of the feudal states.
2. Creation of bureaucratic controls over the entire administrative organization, with the sanction of imperial authority for the bureaucracy.
3. Formation of a class society following reforms carried out in the feudal status system and implementation of a revised taxation program.
4. Establishment of a firm basis of government finances, especially through tax reforms.
5. Promotion of capital investments in industrial development as the best means for achieving the espoused goal of "a rich country and a strong military."
6. Adjustments made in monetary and banking systems to stabilize and standardize financial affairs.
7. Special emphasis placed upon export and munitions industries.
8. Monopolization of business by financial cliques (*zaibatsu*) which enjoyed government support.

The creation of new organs of government, defense, education, and economy, as well as transportation and communications, greatly strengthened the mutual relationships between the cities themselves, between the cities and rural districts, and between the cities and international society. These interdependent relationships formed an overall network with its centers remaining in the political capital of Tōkyō and the commercial center of Ōsaka. The total network served, in turn, to expand the new organs of state. Immediate necessities directed financial aid, however, to central areas of the country, so that modernization was expedited mainly in the major cities, new culture and civilization were extended to upper class citizens, and government protection went to the big enterprises capable of capitalizing on the radical changes taking place.

Leadership in the introduction of social changes geared to modernization was provided by bureaucrats drawn from the former warrior class and from among merchants already skilled in utilization of government connections. An advanced standard of living for the common people in smaller enterprises or in the agricultural communities was not made a part of the initial program for modernization. Social development progressed on an uneven keel.

*Changes in the System of Administrative Controls.*——Problems inherent in Tokugawa society, far from being eliminated by exposure to the advanced capitalist economies of the West, were intensified and it became even more difficult to maintain an isolated political stance. The core of leaders in the new government of the Meiji period came from the ranks of low grade samurai, together with some of the court nobility. They had been reared in a style of life that was itself one of the inner causes of the self-defeating character of the very feudal society they sought to reform. By all counts, the times seemed premature for the kinds of changes needed to bridge the gap between feudal and modern societies.

The new leadership was surprisingly capable of recognizing the necessity for introducing certain democratic political reforms,and for appropriating some of the Western capitalist mechanisms, as they set about restructuring the political and economic framework of the nation. Just the same, they exhibited an innate wisdom in performing the adaptations in ways suitable to their own country. Bit by bit, the feudal political system was dismantled—not demolished in a single thoughtless attack—and a bureaucratic system was assembled from certain elements retained, and others imported and modified. Imperial authority acted as a kind of magnetic force pulling the whole together, eventually in the direction of absolutism. The lodestone of the bureaucratic structure was the capital city of Tōkyō, location of the headquarters of the new administrative organs of national integration. In ways reminiscent of Tokugawa days, its network of controls extended out to the former castle towns, nuclei of local administration under the old regime.

During the first year of the new government civil wars continued, particularly in battles at Toba and Fushimi, south of Kyōto, as some of the vassals of the shogunate sought to forestall the demise being forced upon it. The new power was able to stand firm, calling upon the combined help of provincial powers relatively independent of the shogunate. The reform leadership had to make it unmistakably clear that it represented more than just the private interests of the two leading domains of Satsuma and Chōshū. It sought out the opinions of other domain leaders in an effort to instill a sense of equality in those who elected to recognize the emerging political authority.

In a concrete action to assure representatives of other domains that they could secure satisfactory roles in the new order, the young government issued a "Covenant of Five Articles" (*Gokajō no Seimon*), sometimes called the "Charter Oath," in March, 1868. While an immediate aim was to rally support for its position, the five points were unique in terms of the attempt to proclaim publicly the significance of the reformation movement. The "Covenant" consisted of the following articles:

1. Deliberative assemblies shall be widely established and all matters decided by public discussion.
2. All classes, high and low, shall unite in vigorously carrying out the administration of affairs of state.
3. The common people, no less than the civil and military officials, shall each be allowed to pursue his own calling so that there may be no discontent.
4. Evil customs of the past shall be broken off and everything based upon the just laws of Nature.
5. Knowledge shall be sought throughout the world so as to strengthen the foundations of imperial rule. [Translator's note: this rendering of "The Five Articles Oath of 1868" comes from *Sources of the Japanese Tradition*, by Tsunoda, de Bary, and Keene, p. 644.]

The articles did not articulate the principles of modern democracy so much as they sought to give encouragement to feudal leaders not yet committed to the formation of a new centralized government. The articles endeavored to relieve the apprehensions of nobility, daimyō, and samurai whom the reform leadership was trying to draw into its new administration. Certainly it would be a mistake to regard the "Covenant" as an expression of a common national sentiment.[1]

The initial efforts at establishing actual mechanisms of administration included issuance of a constitution that embodied the ideas of the "Covenant of Five Articles," as well as an apparent imitation of the American pattern of separating the executive, legislative, and judicial branches of government. At the same time, governing power was declared to derive from the sovereignty of the Emperor and, furthermore, religion and state were held together in unity. That unity was instituted in an Office of Shintō Worship (*Jingikan*) which was responsible for administration of shrines and religious ceremonies. Its position was made superior to the Council of State (*Dajōkan*), the supreme administrative organ. This latter organ consisted of a legislative body (*Giseikan*), a judicial body (*Shihōkan*), and five other administrative departments. The centralized bureaucratic organization was thus provided, for the time being.

In the local provinces, life for the peasantry continued without any marked differences. Instead, tax burdens were made even heavier by the new government's needs in putting down the last resistance of shogunal forces on the one hand, and the demands of remodeling the political system, on the other. No more capable now than before of bearing such heavy tax claims, the peasants rose up in revolt here and there. The new political power no longer enjoyed a position of leadership for united local resistance against entrenched rule, but had itself to forge a centralized structure of national integration. It had now to overcome the insularity and recalcitrance of localized power.

A major step in bringing all territories under the direct administration of the new government was that of persuading the daimyō to turn over their domains, a measure called "the return of the domain registers." This policy was greatly facilitated by the increased difficulties faced in actually controlling the domains after new knowledge of the world at large seeped into the local provinces. The order to return all domains was issued in 1869, although 262 of the daimyō essentially retained their positions through appointment as governors of the newly-designated prefectures. Further conflict was avoided also by appointing the former junior officers of the daimyō as consultants to the new governors.

Another move was directed toward the breakup of traditional power groups without totally eradicating all position and prestige. The complicated system of rankings among samurai was revised so as to allow them to remain military officers (*shizoku*) or soldiers (*sotsuzoku*). Local governments of the domains were transposed into local units of the national administration, responsible for reporting all information concerning political, economic, and military affairs to the central government. The new organs of centralized control gradually took charge of affairs throughout the whole country.[2]

People and lands came under the national government officially, but leaving the daimyō in operative posts as governors caused trouble. Lord-vassal relationships and regional relationships among those accustomed to ruling kept much of the old feudal system functioning. In 1871 the government concentrated the military forces of the Satsuma, Chōshū, and Tosa powers in Tōkyō and proceeded to dismiss the daimyō, ordering them to live in Tōkyō.

Government-appointed officials took over the local governorships and all military forces of the domains were demobilized. Castles in the provincial capitals were taken over from 1871 by the central command of the Ministry of Military Affairs (*Hyōbushō*). Administrative divisions were established, with three urban prefectures (*fu*) and seventy-two other prefectures (*ken*). These divisions were revised in 1890 to the three *fu*, Tōkyō, Ōsaka, and Kyōto, and forty-three prefectures, after all vestiges of the former domain divisions had been thoroughly eliminated.

The new political system assumed a sturdier basis after the 1871 order abolishing the old domain system, and a drastic revision of the central administrative organs was carried out. The ancient imperial pattern of unity of religion and state was rescinded, and three executive departments were formed. That is, the Council of State (*Dajōkan*) was replaced with three executive chambers, namely, *Sei-in*, *Sa-in*, and *U-in*. The *Sei-in*, or Central Chamber, assumed authority over legislative and administrative functions, including the Office of Shintō Worship which was reduced from its superordinate to a subordinate status as an ordinary ministry. The *Sa-in*, or Left Chamber, functioned as a legislative council; while the *U-in*, or Right Chamber, consisted of ministers and vice-ministers in the government ministries.

The character of the new government began to emerge clearly after dissolution of the domains. Gone was that aspect of national power produced formerly by forging together the many domains into a shogun-led structure. The top group of government officials was made up of lower grade samurai from the four domains of Satsuma, Chōshū, Tosa, and Hizen. The conciliatory deliberative assemblies were abrogated, emasculating the interim channels for eliciting consensus with respect to policies. A new degree of autocracy increasingly characterized the bureaucracy that had successfully displaced the feudal lords and their retainers.

To back up the new political posture it was necessary to organize a national standing army, as well as a centralized police force, to repel the double dangers of colonization from without and the constant threat of domestic rebellion from within the country. National development could be programmed only if the vacuum left by the demise of domain battalions was filled, and the possibility of rebellious regrouping precluded.

A conscription law requiring military service of all adult men was announced in 1872. Local headquarters for recruitment (*chindai*) were set up in the main cities (former castle towns) of powerful domains, such as Tōkyō, Sendai, Nagoya, Ōsaka, Hiroshima, and Kumamoto. Men were inducted for three years, followed by four years of reserve duty. Large budgetary allocations were made to support this policy of strengthening the military arm of the government year by year.

The central police organization was founded in 1874. Supervised by the Ministry of Home Affiairs, this organization had a head office, *Keishichō* (Metropolitan Police Board), which controlled the prefectural offices. The police network combined with the army to give the new government effective control over the entire country.

Controls alone, though, were not enough to create a new style of national life. Attention had to be given also to the cultivation of new ideas that would liberate the people from the feudal tradition. Reformation of the political system could provide only the opportunity for innovation.

Educational provisions of the feudal order had varied widely according to status, whether warrior, townsman, or peasant, and there was no unifying principle for the different levels. Elimination of status considerations and equalization of educational opportunity were the intent of educational reforms that discarded the different kinds of education and instituted a system of compulsory education for all classes modeled after French and, soon afterward, American patterns of public schooling. Guidance of the people's thinking, however, was no less a concern of the government than the modernizing intent of the educational laws drawn up in 1872 and enacted in 1879. From 1886 four years of elementary education became compulsory for all school age children and, by 1888, 63% of the boys and 32% of the girls in the country were enrolled.

In the initial stage the content of the curriculum was selected from educational materials of advanced Western countries. The feeling was strong, though, that these materials were lacking in the kind of moral training necessary for preserving the essential tradition of the Japanese people. An imperial directive concerning moral guidance in public education (*Kyōgaku Taikei*) was issued, emphasizing the traditional values of benevolence, justice, loyalty, and filial piety (*jin*, *gi*, *chū*, and *kō* respectively).

In 1890 the educational system was revised so as to provide at least one middle school in each prefecture, beyond compulsory elementary schooling. One or more normal schools were founded in each prefecture following regulations instituted in 1897. These schools were to be financed through prefectural governments, though this proved a heavy burden on the limited resources of the prefectures.

The ambitious program for catching up with the Western powers through rapid industrialization made it imperative, in addition to elementary and secondary schools, to develop higher education as well. The first "university" (Daigakukō) was formed in 1869 by combining the Confucian "higher learning institute" (Shōheikō) in Edo, the Institute of Medicine (Igakusho) of the shogunate, and the Institute for the Study of Foreign Books (Kaiseiko). This institution was renamed Tōkyō University in 1877, with the term "Imperial" inserted in 1886.

A number of private schools for higher education were also established, such as Keiō Gijuku Univerity founded by Fukuzawa Yukichi, Dōshisha University founded by Niijima Jō, and Tokyo College (Senmon Gakkō) founded by Ōkuma Shigenobu and later named Waseda University. Each of these schools had its own distinctive features, different from that of the government's Imperial University. The private universities deserve considerable credit for the many men of talent produced, who exercised much influence in the development of modern Japan.

The early Meiji leaders consciously sought to mobilize the spiritual forces of the nation into a unity under the emperor system. Allied with emphasis on Confucian morals was the warm support of Shintō shrines, which were organized in a hierarchical system with the Grand Shrine of Ise at the top. We have already noted that the Office of Shintō Worship was subsumed under the Central Chamber in 1871, actually a step down from its earlier status, and this office was replaced by a more general Board of Religious Instruction (*Kyōbushō*) in the following year. This latter board was abolished in 1878, and in 1886 the formal separation of religion and education was proclaimed in an unveiled attempt to conform to patterns in the democracies of the West. Any changes, though, were hardly more than formal ones and the effect of governmental promotion of spiritual unity under imperial authority through Shintō shrine worship can hardly be overlooked.

Although devoted individuals found great value in Buddhism, as an institution it had been largely domesticated during the long period of Tokugawa supremacy. It was the victim of a harsh attack shortly after the Meiji Restoration, though in time certain sects made positive responses of their own to the influx of stimuli from abroad, notably the coming of Christian missions.

Christian activity in the initial decades of the Meiji era enjoyed relative success, though the way was not easy by any means. The government withdrew the ban on propagation of the Christian faith in 1873, the first year, coincidentally, of its acceptance of the Gregorian calendar. Abrogation of the anti-Christian prohibition resulted chiefly from protests by Western nations, a situation that was disadvantageous for the Japanese statesmen whose most fervent desire was revision of the unequal treaties imposed upon them in opening up the country. A few missionaries came even before the Meiji Restoration, but many mission boards began work in Japan after 1873. Their programs included considerable engagement in educational fields, and quite a member of Christian schools were founded. One of the most significant initiatives in Christian education by a Japanese was the energetic efforts of Niijima Jō in establishing Dōshisha University in Kyōto. He had ventured abroad secretly before the Tokugawa *bakufu* fell, and returned, a Christian convert, to work strenuously and effectively for his country's new age.

Although the Christian movement was not spared attacks by ultranationalists, its emphasis upon internationalism and charitable work gave to the Japanese people fresh insights into the world currents into which they were stepping for the first time. These currents included, of course, humanism, socialism, and communism. Besides affording an important perspective on the Western culture being introduced, the Christian movement also fed the broader movement among intellectuals striving for a long-delayed realization of people's rights and freedoms. In 1889, the year of promulgation of the new constitution, Christianity was officially approved as a viable religious option, even though its actual position was clearly below that of Shintō, which was regarded much as the national faith. The important thing, for our purposes, is that the Christian schools were accepted widely by the people themselves and, along with more tradition-oriented schools, were fully utilized in the social processes of forming a modernized country.

Reformation of local administration was accomplished at two levels: first, by completely revising the organizational units, and secondly, by setting up the system whereby the units were thoroughly controlled by the central government. Feudal society had exercised a system of local controls through unions of villages (*gōson*) directly responsible to the provincial domains. Residents of the villages were closely connected with, and responsible for, each other, in naturally formed associations. Officials controlling the villages were responsible in turn to the feudal lords for tax collection and for acceptable conduct in the villages, the smallest administrative units in the feudal order.

The political reshaping of the Meiji government reached down to the smallest village. A census law was enacted in 1871 to clarify the actual movements of the people during the confusion surrounding the restoration. The offices of village heads, *nanushi* or *shōya*, and elders, *toshiyori*, were canceled. Old township and village lines were nullified and a new district unit, *ku*, introduced. The area of a *ku* was determined by the number of residents needed to support financially the schools and police offices founded anew in the Meiji era. Hence, there were various sizes of *ku*, large and small. In a large *ku*, a chief officer and assistant, *kochō* and *fuku-kochō* respectively, were appointed, and in the smaller *ku* a single head, *shōchō*. The *ku* served as the basic units of local administration under the control of the central government.

Actual day-to-day management of the villages remained in the hands of the local village head even after the *ku* districts were established. The *ku* units, even the smaller ones, proved ineffective and only nominal as a means of unifying the old villages. The villages, after all, had evolved as associations of households which shared elemental functions and facilities, such as utilization of water and wood resources, cooperative work schemes, communal worship of local deities, and common relations with the Buddhist temples that handled the registration previously required by the shogunate. Administrative units functioned realistically only in the limited areas where groups of people actually gathered.

In 1878 the government experimented with a new consolidation of the local administrative system, proclaiming an organizational law for counties, districts, towns, and villages (*gun*, *ku*, *machi*, and *mura* respectively) called *Gunku-chōson Hennyū-hō*.[3] This law was one of three new directives concerning local administration, the other two having to do with the urban and provincial prefectures regulations (*Fukenkai Kisoku*), and with tax regulations for local areas (*Chihōzei Kisoku*).

Under the new law the *gun* were intermediary units, and some of the smaller *ku* were abolished. Within each *gun* the old towns and villages were restored as administrative units. While the top official of the *gun* had authority over the town and village heads, the *kochō* (official head of the *ku*) worked solely as an administrative functionary of the central government without any operative role in the management of the towns and villages. This was because the reinstated village officials performed a dual function as administrative servants of the central government and as managers of the corporate life of the villages.

Local elections for towns and villages were approved by the government in August, 1878, though suffrage was limited to those paying land taxes, thus favoring the landowners. Moreover, the finances for *ku*, towns, and villages were supplied largely by prefectural governments; consequently local autonomy was rather restricted. The law provided only nominal autonomy for these smaller administrative units, where traditional systems remained quite operative. In fact, little that could be legitimately designated local autonomy actually existed in the *ku*, towns, and villages.

In 1888 the local administrative system was again revised to provide some substantive local autonomy based on the rights and duties of residents in the cities, towns, and villages. To qualify as a city, there had to be a population of 25,000 or over, with adequate streets. A group of streets was treated as a unit, and there were no township or village units in a city. The cities were released from the control of the *gun* office and were made to constitute a basic administrative unit in themselves.

City administration differed in several respects from that of towns and villages. The chief organ was a Board of Councillors (*Shisanji-kai*), of which the mayor was chairman. Electoral procedures also differed, in that heads of towns and villages were nominated by town or village assemblies for formal approval by the prefectural governors. Candidates for mayor were recommended by city councils to the central government's Ministry of Home Affairs, which submitted candidates' names to the Emperor for final decision.

The immediate superiors over town and village affairs were the heads of the local county, *gun*, while the supervisors of city mayors were the prefectural governors. For a time the three major cities of Tōkyō, Kyōto, and Ōsaka were put under the direct control of the governors of the urban prefectures (*fu*) embracing these large cities, eliminating the mayoral posts. This move was dictated by the convenience of the central government which saw these urban centers as quite different from other smaller cities. But the government reverted to the previous system in 1898, because of dissatisfaction among the citizens who preferred the relative advantages of administration under their own mayor to the inconveniences involved when the chief administrative officials of the nation's largest cities were responsible also for even larger prefectural areas.

The administrative systems of the prefectures, urban and provincial, were gradually transformed into more suitable forms as the experience of the Meiji leadership was extended. A key factor in the process stemmed from a series of local peoples' meetings in the provinces, especially in 1873. In the following year a cry for parliamentary government was raised, which was forged into a "movement for freedom and people's rights" (*jiyū minken undō*). This occurred under the leadership of more democratically disposed men like Itagaki Taisuke, Goto Shōjiro, Nakae Chōmin, and others. Independent political associations supporting the movement sprang up all over the country.

Among other responses made by the central government to this challenge, revision of the prefectural and county systems was carried out in 1890. Prefectural boundaries were redrawn, abolishing, combining, or even subdividing some prefectures. Prefectural assemblies were established, and certain administrative rights were granted to the prefectural governments, such as ownership of property, and the right to levy taxes and issue bonds to carry on local government work. This did not mean, however, that the prefectural governments became autonomous bodies. The prefectural assemblies could not, for example, enact separate laws and ordinances, nor was there any articulation of the rights and duties of citizens as prefectural residents.

The governors of the prefectures continued as central government appointees, and their budgets included expenses incurred in performing national administrative tasks as well as in running the local administration. A governor could, if his prefectural assembly rejected his budget proposals, present them to the Ministry of Home Affairs for approval.

Representatives to the prefectural assemblies were elected by the city and county (*shi* and *gun*) councils for four-year terms. Half of the total number of assemblymen faced re-election every two years. Since the electorate was limited to city and county councils, it cannot be said that the opinions of the wider general public were well represented. Ex-samurai, wealthy farmers, merchants, and landowners appear to have exercised the effective power in the councils and assemblies. Voting rights were held only by adult men paying government taxes of ten yen or more, which meant, on the average, citizens with landholdings of one *chō* six *tan* (3.9 acres) or more.

The intermediary county (*gun*) administrative unit was only a very feeble instrument of local self-government. Nothing in the administrative laws provided it with any legal functions, nor was the relationship between the *gun* and the people resident within it made clear. Its head was a central government appointee, while its own councils drew on two groups of people. One group consisted of those elected by town and village councils; another was composed of big landowners whose holdings had assessed values of 20,000 yen or above. The *gun* was intended as a system for preserving the traditional power of large landowners over local citizens and, as such, as a means of strengthening the central government's controlling powers over towns and villages.[4]

These systems of prefectural, county, city, town, and village government had the appearance of carrying national politics closer to modern forms of democratic government, by overcoming the isolation of local regions and providing for representation at each level. Actually, all of the organizations were easily controlled by the central government. Prefectural governors and county heads were all appointed by the central government, and assemblies could be dissolved by imperial order, just as city, town, and village councils could be dissolved by order of the Ministry of Home Affairs. Although assemblymen and councillors did represent limited segments of society, even their representative rights could be overturned easily by central government action.

Regional and local self-government in this period was not genuine democratic autonomy guaranteed by the national political system. On the contrary, it amounted to a system devised to strengthen central powers, backed ultimately by the authority of the imperial office. The routine work of public administration was parceled out to the regional and local bodies without a commensurate division of real authority that would make possible effective sharing in the decision-making processes of government.

While moving swiftly toward modernization in many sectors of national life, Japan retained a centralized political system revised only in terms of territorial units of administration, the prefectures, counties, cities, towns, and villages. That is, the system of political controls had been restructured in such a way as to replace the former ruling class of daimyō and warriors with a newly-organized administrative bureaucracy. The system remained a hierarchical structure with Tōkyō, now the site of the Emperor's residence, continuing as the nucleus of the entire country.

*Changes in Social Stratification Structures.*——The external form of the feudal political system was reshaped by dismantling the domains and reorganizing them into the prefectures and other units described above. But it was also necessary to reform the complicated status system, the most important foundation of feudal society, in order to make the transition to a more modernized social structure. The first reforms were the initial step toward transformation from a status to a class system within a capitalist structure. In the cities especially there emerged new groupings such as capitalists, bureaucrats, members of the armed forces, businessmen, shopowners, and laborers.

Social discrimination based on status, a legacy of the Tokugawa era, was reduced to some extent through the vigorous initiative of low ranking samurai and their townsmen colleagues who assumed leadership positions in the new government. The stricter features of status gradations were removed after 1869. In the revised system of stratification the Emperor and members of the Imperial Household were given top place. Below them were the nobility, called *kazoku*, consisting of courtiers and former daimyō. Men of samurai pedigree were next and now called *shizoku*. Farmers, artisans, and merchants continued to rank as commoners (*heimin*). In 1871 the outcast groups, *eta* and *hinin*, were formally recognized as commoners.

Simplification of the status system was accompanied by certain important new freedoms, and by removal of demeaning restrictions. The people were released from restrictions on the selection of occupation and residence. The samurai were forbidden to wear swords. Regulations governing dress, dwellings, and other matters of daily life were canceled and new freedoms in business and marriage were acquired. Monopolization of trading by the former *za* or *kabu-nakama* was prohibited. These reforms were essentially formal revisions of feudal privileges and restrictions, a tenuous process of compromise between the passing feudal, and the coming new society. They were engineered by men of samurai status in conjunction with the wealthier citizens, and it could hardly be expected that drastic changes would occur in actual practice under such leadership.

The warrior cliques lost their basis of power when the domains were broken up into prefectures and, as effective power groups, were liquidated. Involved were 1.9 million warriors in 400,000 households, including daimyō, roughly one-sixteenth of the total population, as against 31 million commoners. Deprived of territorial rights, the four hundred year old pattern of relationships between lords and retainers began to crumble. The government instituted a series of revisions in the system of stipend payments to warriors aimed at eventual abolition of the system altogether.

In the interim when daimyō were appointed governors of the old domain territories with the title *han-chiji*, they received one-tenth of their former incomes and lived in their old residences. Revised rates in stipend payments to warriors in the domains lessened the differences based on rankings, an action called *narashizura*, or "leveling-off." The adjustments in stipends were begun in 1873 and were paid by the new government. In 1876, though, all stipends were canceled, and the warriors were issued government bonds in compensation. With the bonds received, the warriors began life anew in the new social system as capital owners and cash consumers.

The total amount of bonds issued by the government reached 174 million yen, although regular revenue amounted to between 60–70 million yen. Eighty-five per cent of the annual income of the government came from land taxes, and the new bonds burden was to be borne by the farmers. While it is true that the warriors were deprived of enormous hereditary wealth, that wealth was restored in generous portions by further sacrificing the farm population. The daimyō and upper class warriors were able to recapture important positions in society through skillful use of the bonds issued them, becoming landowners, stockholders, and captains of industry.[5]

However, only a few nobles and warriors were able to live comfortably on interest earned from their bonds. Some 133,000 warriors who had served as subordinates to the lords and high ranking samurai received only an average 548 yen per head.[6] Clearly, this was insufficient for earning a living through investments. Not a few samurai capitalized on their educational backgrounds and social prestige to assume important roles in the emerging society as government officials, businessmen, military officers, railroad executives, police officials, newspaper men, teachers in public schools, and even interpreters in the crucial relations with foreign concerns. Such roles enabled them to retain suitable dignity in social life.

In the directory of government officials (*Hyakkan Rireki Mokuroku*) for the interim when the *Dajōkan* (Council of State) system was in effect (1868–71), the distribution of officials according to status pedigree occurred as follows: of a total of 458, 78.9% had been warriors, 18.1% former daimyō, with only 1.8% from the ranks of the nobility (including members of the Imperial Household), and a mere 0.7% were commoners. (Five per cent were of unknown origin.) These percentages indicate that status distinctions had been eradicated primarily within the warrior ranks, and not yet between them and the farmers, artisans, and merchants, despite the emphasis put upon finding and promoting men on the basis of ability.

In fact, the traditional attitude of according greater respect to officials than to common people persisted. All the higher posts in the new government were held by men of the warrior class, though they came, it is true, from the lower ranks. They included Itō Hirobumi, Kido Kōin, Ōkubo Toshimichi, Saigō Takamori, Kuroda Kiyotaka, Gotō Shōjirō, Yuri Kimimasa, Hirosawa Hyōsuke, and others, who were honored with promotion to the peerage in 1884.

Development of modern industries also depended heavily on the leadership abilities of men from the lower samurai ranks, men such as Iwasaki Koyata, Yasuda Zenjirō, Shibusawa Eiichi, Nakagamigawa Hikojirō, Godai Tomoatsu, Wada Toyoji, and others. Their efforts were particularly valuable in persuading the merchants, who were often reluctant to depart from accustomed ways, to invest boldly in modern industries. As a result, private enterprise became the effective handmaid of the government's own programs of industrialization.[7]

Here again it is instructive to look into the leadership distribution in commerce and industry according to status backgrounds. Of the presidents of two hundred of the largest firms in a number of fields, one-quarter were ex-samurai even though their old status groups now made up only 5.6% of the total population. One-half of the company presidents came from merchant households. The remaining quarter were from the farmer population which made up 87% of the overall national population.

While previous political experience, cultural grooming and educational training, as well as their household traditions gave the former samurai definite advantages for rising quickly to power in commerce and industry, their leadership position was not as strong in the latter as in the government offices. Other ex-samurai turned the same gifts of cultural background into valuable contributions of intellectual leadership. In many of the schools and publishing firms, for instance, the core groups of staff leaders were men of warrior background. Nishi Amane and Fukuzawa Yukichi were notable for their courage in casting aside feudal traditions to promote the appropriation of Western knowledge and culture so necessary to the modernizing process. Ex-samurai pioneered the large majority of the more than one hundred Japanese newspapers and journals that appeared by 1875, of which some of the more famous ones were the Tōkyō Nichinichi, Yūbin Hōchi, Chōya Shinbun, Tōkyō Akebono, and the Tōkyō-Yokohama Mainichi.

In 1882 some 72% of the total number of teachers in the schools established by prefectures or cities were former warriors. Students enrolled in institutions of higher education were mostly from samurai households, although stress was put increasingly on achievement records rather than on previous status. The percentage of graduates receiving degrees from Tōkyō Imperial University who were from warrior families was remarkable:

| *Year* | *Percentage* |
|---|---|
| 1878 | 73.9 |
| 1879 | 77.7 |
| 1880 | 77.6 |
| 1881 | 51.8 |

Although the percentage dropped to only slightly over half by 1881, even this was an overwhelmingly large proportion in terms of the ratio of warriors to the total population.[8]

The power of samurai-bred leaders in society was the central reason for the relative ease with which social reforms were expedited. Yet, there were only a limited number of leadership positions in the new systems. Following loss of privileged status, the bulk of the warrior class found lesser roles as operators of small enterprises, or in agriculture, industry, and trade. Many of them experienced great difficulty in overcoming the feudal predilection against the profit motive. Not a few lost their government bonds to enterprising loan agents and commercial capitalists, many falling into abject poverty. Some moved to wastelands to reclaim tillable lands and, thereby, their own livelihoods. Others entered industry as laborers, and still others became day-laborers in construction and other work. Many women of former warrior families went to work in factories, especially those of export industries.

Apart from direct reform action, another factor seriously undermined the traditional system, namely, revision of the land tax system. The reasons for, as well as effects of, the tax revision form a somewhat complicated story. Fundamentally, it rooted in the need for a stabilized source of greater revenue to support the new political and economic programs. The actual money expenses of the government increased annually to finance the new bureaucratic system and the standing army, and to promote industrialization. As these, and other organs, were inescapably necessary to complete the new integrative system, the government simply had to find revenues equivalent to expenditures.

Temporary relief was found in loans from wealthy merchant households such as the Mitsui, Ono, and Shimada families. Some loans were floated with foreign countries, and domestic bonds and notes were issued.[9] The long-range problem lay, however, in the fact that agricultural taxes were based on crop and commodity yields, and these fluctuated too much annually to permit dependable advance budgeting. The government already claimed, as we have seen, between 40%–50% of agricultural yields, and this revenue provided 85% of the yearly budgets. The need was not only to regularize annual income, but to increase it.[10]

Under Tokugawa controls farmers were neither free to cultivate and market as they chose, nor could they buy or sell land freely. Restrictions on cultivation and sale of agricultural products were lifted in 1871, and on land sales in 1872. Even then it took seven years to implement the tax revisions. Whereas taxes were formerly imposed on available crops, the shift was made to taxation based on assessed land values, the rate being set at 3%. Furthermore, while the actual farmers (*honbyakushō*) were formerly responsible for tax payments, the responsibility was now shifted to the owners of the land.

With rate and responsibility for taxes clearly fixed, the government was able to budget on a firmer foundation. Ownership of land was confirmed on a modern basis that permitted conversion of property into cash. But the heavy tax burdens of the people were not decreased, as the government's aim was, not to reduce, but to increase its revenue. This had the effect, in time, of greatly increasing tenancy among farmers and, eventually, of driving them into bankruptcy.

The relationship between the farmers responsible for tax payments (*nauke-hyakushō*) and tenant farmers had been rather ambiguous under the feudal regime. The Meiji government clearly designated the ownership of land as belonging to the *nauke-hyakushō*, thus causing tenants to lose land and everything belonging to the land. Differentiation between landowning and tenant farmers intensified as the money economy penetrated the rural districts. Farmers operating small-scale farms were unaccustomed to marketing their products, so they turned to big farmers to sell them. In the transactions the profits always went to the buyers, and small farmers were reduced to tenancy and eventual landless poverty.

Land tenancy amounted to 30% of the total arable land before the revised tax system went into effect, but increased to 40% ten years afterward.[11] Few of the great landowners farmed their own lands. They turned these functions over to tenants, while investing surplus funds in city industries. Some of them became quite wealthy through capital investments.

While social differentiation in rural society advanced beyond that of feudal times, the traditional cooperative relations between households and villages remained the same. Some of the farmers on small farms or tenant farms did not leave their villages, supplementing insufficient incomes by working at secondary jobs, or by taking on off-season work in other places. Young daughters of tenant farmers streamed into the textile factories developed in the cities, where the techniques of production may have been quite modern but the labor conditions were not. Their wages were usually sent home to their families, whose financial desperation made it easy to hire the girls at very low rates.

*Industrial Changes and the Cities.*——Three factors shaped the administrative organization of the cities early in the Meiji period. One of them, of course, was the consolidation of administrative powers in the centralized bureaucracy, breaking up the insularity of the former domain-oriented society. Even greater fluidity and mobility were precipitated by the other two factors, namely, rescission of the old status system and revision of the land tax system, as described above. The organs of urban administration were but one phase of the broader foundation laid in politics, economy, and population structure to promote full industrialization through a combination of private and government enterprises.

Banking firms, armaments and export industries, and commercial monopolies were developed—many of them by the government, only to be sold later to financial cliques—all under the government's slogan for creating a "rich country and strong military." The concentration of tremendous resources of men and women in these many economic ventures is generally regarded as having provided the major impetus to the formation of new cities and their expansion.

The demise of the political system of feudal society was followed by a collapse of its meager means of production. The ability of foreign traders to supply commodities in quantity at prices below domestic levels made it doubly difficult for the new government to accomplish its dual goals of formation of a new administration, and development of industries capable of competing on the international market. The problem faced was how to overcome serious handicaps to effective entry into the capitalistic economy without paying the excessive price of colonization.

The necessary condition for productive development in a capitalist system is free activity over a wide territorial range that forms and expands its markets. In compliance with this necessity the highway checking stations and other barriers to free movement in transportation were abolished during 1868–69. Holding up cargoes in harbors, a practice employed to protect domain interests, was prohibited. Bridges or ferry boats were provided at large rivers to facilitate travel. The *za* and *kabu-nakama* privileges that favored a limited number of merchants and restricted free activity among others were taken away. Monopolization of goods by the central or local governments was prohibited as the domestic market was opened up to free transactions. In addition to liberalizing the market, the government actively promoted importation of new production systems from foreign countries, including many experts for guidance in operating the systems. All energies were directed toward expanding capital assets and production means.

We saw in the last chapter that Japan had developed an elementary level of manufacturing late in the Tokugawa period, operating with capital provided mainly by large money-lenders. Resources of the latter were insufficient for the installation of imported factories, however, and the *bakufu* and daimyō negotiated contracts for certain imported systems. By like token, the new Meiji government was forced to raise capital on its own to expand the domestic market and cultivate international trade.

Modernizing the economy also necessitated revamping the currency system. Currency controls under the shogunate were rather poor, and too many local currencies—more than 1,500 varieties—were issued by different domains in addition to a variety of gold, silver, brass, and iron coins minted by the shogunate. In 1868 the government issued a paper currency, called *Dajōkan-kansatsu*, for meeting emergency expenditures and making loans to local governments, merchants, and farmers for commercial and industrial ventures. Again, in 1871 laws for issuance of new currency were enacted. They provided a standarized paper currency backed by gold reserves, with auxiliary coins of silver. All other currency was voided. Public bonds were floated in both the domestic and overseas markets. Thus, the government raised the capital needed to make up for the inadequate resources of private firms.

Banking reforms were just as imperative as capital-raising campaigns to consolidate the legacy of brokerage and exchange practices of the Tokugawa period. Larger brokers with agencies in Kyōto, Edo, and Ōsaka had made loans to the shogunate and domain governments, and local governments had sometimes issued currencies or marketed goods backed by these semi-independent brokers. While the Tokugawa financiers were not official agencies of government, they profited only through cooperation with, and protection from the feudal system. Most of them suffered heavy losses when the shogunate fell as they could not collect on loans made to the daimyō who were stripped of their lands. On the other hand, merchant households who had served the domains which took the lead in toppling the Tokugawa regime, such as Mitsui, Sumitomo, Kōnoike, and others, were able to expand rapidly under the protection of the new government.

Indeed, the government encouraged the wealthy merchants of the Mitsui, Ono, Shimada, and Nagata families to form a joint-stock corporation to handle bills of exchange, with capital to be loaned by the government. Such a corporation was founded in 1868, with branch offices in the port cities of Tōkyō, Ōsaka, Kōbe, Yokohama, Tsuruga, and Niigata, as well as the lakeside cities of Kyōto and Ōstu. The plan did not work very well as the corporation executives were not familiar with the complexities of this sort of business, but it did afford them an important lesson about the process of modernization. They realized, that is, how important it was for businessmen to establish such corporations themselves with government backing, rather than leave such functions entirely to the government. In short, this venture was a significant initial phase in the course of economic modernization in Japan.

A government bank was established by law in 1872, which issued notes for payments on public bonds and reserved gold specie for conversions of currency. Four offices were opened, which did not keep large sums on deposit as the people did not yet fully understand the bank's function. Gold prices in Japan were less than in the international market, causing a rapid depletion of specie reserves and a run on the bank that sent the Ono and Shimada households into bankruptcy.

Conversion of paper currency was suspended in 1876, after which banking business became more profitable, and the number of government-approved banks increased to 153 by 1879. Considerable amounts of capital funds were deposited by commercial firms, landowners, and warriors with substantial bond holdings. Public funds were also handled by the banks, and earnings rose as confidence was built up on the basis of government banking. The capital held by money-lenders was transformed into banking capital, providing the financial basis upon which Japanese commerce and industry were nurtured.

The nation's dual goals of fostering wealth and avoiding colonization naturally favored expansion in the export and munitions industries. The late Tokugawa era developments in home industries and limited manufacturing were useful beginnings, but there were no industries engaged in mass production capable of competing successfully with the advanced techniques and large-scale operations of Western industries. The feudal entrepenuers simply did not have the necessary capital to move into production on a scale commensurate with international competition. Silk was the top export commodity, and cotton thread and cloth the major import items. Japanese industry needed to move as quickly as possible into mass production of these items.

The government installed a spinning mill of standard scale at Tomioka in Gunma Prefecture in 1872, employing and training daughters of depressed samurai families. The Ono and Kankōryō spinning mills along with others in various prefectures were opened through funds loaned by the government to local cities. These mills also had the additional purpose of providing jobs for warriors' families. Rural home industries for silk production also increased, producing more than the spinning mills even as late as 1897.

Sharp increases in cotton imports had spurred the flow of gold out of the country. Early in the Meiji period spinning and weaving mills for cotton goods were set up in Kagoshima, Sakai, and the Takinogawa township of Tōkyō. More machines were imported to equip other mills established by private firms through government loans requiring no interest payments. Two large-scale mills were founded in 1883, the Ōsaka Spinning Company and the Mie Spinning Company, the first to operate free of government backing. Although these light industries were developed in the cities, woven goods were produced mainly by minor factories and farmers' home industries. The government supported only large enterprises, and as yet no equipment loans were made available to the minor enterprises.

In any event, the accumulation of greater national wealth had its underlying purpose in national defense, and rapid development of a substantial munitions industry was of utmost importance in government policy. Armaments plants built by the shogunate and powerful daimyō were taken over and new factories were added to form the nucleus of heavy industries geared to production of weapons and ships. An illustrious group of factories were developed, including the National Armory (Hōhei-kōsho), the Ishikawajima Shipbuilding Yard, and the Itabashi and Meguro Gunpowder Plants in Tōkyō. There was also an armory built in Ōsaka, and shipbuilding yards in Yokosuka, Hyōgo, and Nagasaki, plus other factories in a number of cities. Most of the entire machine industry of this period was integrated into the armaments program of the government.

All mining rights were reserved by the Meiji government. It took over coal mines in Miike and Takashima, and operated its own mines in Ikuno and Sado. Mining equipment, techniques, and technical advisors were brought in from Europe to promote the mining of coal, iron, gold and silver. By monopolizing the mining industry the government added a crucial support to its armaments program and also aided in reducing the unfavorable balance in foreign trade.

Whereas government initiative through public bonds, loans, and equipment imports proved rather successful in getting various industries started, maintenance of large factories became a heavy drain on the national treasury. Growing inflation had precipitated a financial crisis and the Meiji leaders, rather than seek foreign loans, opted for retrenchment. Except for defense, communication, and public service facilities, the government industries were sold to private firms with which the government had close connections and upon whom it could depend to guard the national interest. Content that the industries would be ably maintained, the government let most of them go at prices far below the original investments—some for as little as 11% of cost.

Private enterprise developed in the Meiji era, not simply because of government loans and moral support. The private firms had also their own traditions and expertise carried over from the feudal age. The Mitsui "business clan" is often taken as a representative example of the human relations and practices of such private businesses. The head of the main household became the master of the executive group (*ōmotokata*) which included the heads of each of the branch households. The executive group supervised a pool of Mitsui capital which was loaned to branch offices, and profits were divided among the Mitsui firms after a fixed portion was deposited in the *ōmotokata* pool. Capital accumulations were the joint property of the entire Mitsui group, and were administered under strict controls by the executive body.[12]

Dominance of industry by a number of such corporate households, or financial cliques (*zaibatsu*) as they are frequently termed, is one characteristic feature of modern Japanese socio-economic life. These financial houses developed as aggregates of branch families centered in a main household that preserved many feudal patterns and values. On a larger scale these patterns and values marked the combining of politics with militarism that emerged as a characteristic feature of Japan's modern statehood itself.

The Mitsui group was closely connected with the financial department of the government from the start, a relationship growing out of its contacts with the Satsuma and Chōshū leaders, and later leading to substantial donations to the new government. The cooperation of leaders from the Tosa domain with the new government brought another financial group into the foreground, namely, the Mitsubishi group, whose early developer of samurai background was Iwasaki Yatarō. This group expanded the Tosa commercial and shipping activities into a virtual monopoly of marine services in the coastal regions. With repeated government support the Mitsubishi concern expanded further into overseas shipping and occasional naval assistance to the government. Another major merchant group, the Sumitomo firm, built up its business initially through effective modernization of its copper mines, which it was allowed to operate despite government rights to all mining. On this foundation the Sumitomo concern became the third largest financial clique, after the Mitsui and Mitsubishi groups.

After the national parliament, or Diet, was established in 1890, the power of the bureaucracy waned as political parties gained prominence. The financial cliques were forced, in addition to maintaining relations with the provincial powers rooted in the old domains, to cultivate contacts with the now influential political parties. The Mitsui group fostered connections with the Liberal Party (Jiyū-tō) formed in 1881, later with the Friends of Constitutional Government (Rikken Seiyū-kai) founded in 1900. Likewise, the Mitsubishi firm formed connections with the Constitutional Progressive Party (Rikken Kaishin-tō) founded in 1882, and later with the Constitutional Party (Kensei-tō), a coalition formed by

Itagaki and Ōkuma in 1898. The decline of old domain powers gave the financial interests opportunities for stronger leadership in the political parties. Indeed, they seemed to hold decisive power in both the economic and the political arenas.[13]

Thus, in the formation of capitalism in Japan, there developed large monopolistic enterprises with government protection. Keen competition did not characterize the development so much as the continued influence of the feudal system, built upon capital drawn originally from the agricultural sector of the economy. On the other hand, small enterprises had to struggle without any special government aid. Modernization of society was hampered by the persistent retention of many feudal elements. The cities, then, became the nuclei for the total integration of society, both in terms of the expansion of bureaucratic organs of the government, and of the large business organizations that were equally active and influential in politics and the economy.

As the integrative functions of the cities enlarged to implement the growth of both the capitalistic and bureaucratic systems, the force of city controls over activities in the whole of society was greatly strengthened. Life in the rural districts was caught up in the sweep of expanded urban controls, precipitating marked differentiations in the political, economic, educational and military movements in rural society.

Reorganization of the local integrative centers followed the lead of new national movements. Shifting priorities brought new life to older cities and rapid growth to certain new cities. Some of the old castle towns became centers of political activity within the new government system, while new cities expanded around international trade ports, military bases, and export industries. As expected, and already indicated, Tōkyō continued as the primary center of political integration, and Ōsaka remained the integrative nucleus of economic activity. From these two focal points transportation and communications lines were improved technically to extend integrative controls to other cities and the rural districts, all within the overall thrust toward greater economic wealth and military might. The legacy of interregional insularity maintained by the Tokugawa shogunate through highway barriers and checkpoints was overcome by the new policies allowing free interchange of both people and goods. International isolation was reversed by opening the ports to overseas trade. Mutual relationships between regional populations was strengthened in conjunction with greater intercourse with other countries.

First on the government's schedule were plans for improving connections between the major centers of political, military, economic and cultural life, that is, between Tōkyō, Ōsaka, Kyōto, and the larger trading cities. In 1872 the first railway was built, connecting Shinagawa (in Tōkyō) with Yokohama. There followed successively rail lines between Ōsaka and Kōbe (1874), and Ōsaka and Kyōto (1877). The 375-mile rail artery from Tōkyo to Kōbe was completed in 1889, binding politics and economy closer together than ever.

Railroads could not be easily financed out of the government's regular budget; therefore, to speed up construction, the Japan Railway Company, Ltd. (Nihon Tetsudō Kabushiki-kaisha) was established with capital investments of members of the nobility (*kazoku*), in 1891. A line between Tōkyō and Aomori was constructed, bringing the entire northern region into greater accessibility to the capital region. This line, with the Tōkyō-Kōbe line, provided a continuous link across most of the main island of Honshū.

When it became clear that the railways were very profitable ventures, many railway companies were established. By 1891 there were twelve private railway companies with a combined total of more than 1,100 miles of railroads, twice the mileage owned by the government.

The railways afforded drastic reductions in the time needed to move people and goods. For example, foot travel from Kyōto to Edo late in the Tokugawa era took 13–14 days, or a day less on the average by palanquin, thanks to the endurance of the porters. Travel on the new railroad took only 30–36 hours over the same course. Costs for palanquin service between Edo and Ōsaka was 95 *kan* 777 *mon*, equivalent to 9 *yen* 57 *sen* in Meiji currency. A third class ticket on the railway was priced at only 3 *yen* 55 *sen*.[14]

Postal service was instituted between Tōkyō and Ōsaka in 1871, and the express messenger service (*hikyaku*) was discontinued the following year. The government retained control over the postal system, extending it each year. There were only 180 post offices in 1871 but the number climbed to 3,245 in the next three years. These offices handled ordinary mail, parcels, government bureau gazettes, newspapers, assorted documents and commodity samples. Not only did the postal network gradually spread over most of the nation, but the costs were kept lower than express rates during the Tokugawa period. Telephone service between Tōkyō and Nagasaki began in 1873, and by 1880 most of the main domestic lines were completed.

Rapid progress in transportation and communications greatly facilitated the process of political integration of the entire land around its Tōkyō nerve center. Likewise, economic activity was greatly served, assuring the final demolition of the insularity in which rural districts had been trapped. Farm villages were drawn inexorably into the dominant urban culture, creating greater interdependence in politics, economy, and culture.

## 2. STRUCTUAL CHANGE IN THE CITIES OF THE MEIJI ERA

*Urban Population and the Process of Change in Ecological Structures.*—— Population statistics for the Edo era are incomplete and not always reliable. More accurate data on population are available from 1872 on, due to enactment of census registration laws.

| *Year* | *Population* | *Rate of increase(%)*[15] |
|---|---|---|
| 1872 | 34,806,000 | 4.8 |
| 1877 | 35,780,000 | 8.2 |
| 1882 | 37,529,000 | 8.3 |
| 1887 | 38,703,000 | 8.4 |
| 1892 | 40,508,000 | 8.7 |
| 1897 | 42,400,000 | 11.5 |

The rate of population increase shown for 1872 was relatively low due to enactment of the census laws at that time. A subsequent elevation in the economic standard of living accounts for the higher rate of increase in the following five-year periods. Population did not increase so sharply in the twenty-five year span covered in the above table, though, as it did during the period of industrial revolution in Japan after 1897.

Population increase has a direct effect on population density, and this effect was visible in Japan during the same twenty-five years as indicated in the figures below.

| *Year* | *Population density (1 sq. ri = 13.3 sq.mi.)* |
|---|---|
| 1872 | 1,335 persons per square *ri* |
| 1877 | 1,396 〃 〃 〃 〃 |
| 1882 | 1,480 〃 〃 〃 〃 |
| 1887 | 1,575 〃 〃 〃 〃 |
| 1892 | 1,657 〃 〃 〃 〃 |
| 1897 | 1,743 〃 〃 〃 〃 |

Population density by regions was as follows:

| *Region* | *Pop. density per square ri*[16] |
|---|---|
| Kinki | 3,113.8 |
| Kantō | 3,085.1 |
| Tōkai | 2,483.6 |
| Shikoku | 2,310.4 |
| Hokuriki | 2,227.4 |
| Chūgoku | 2,147.4 |

| | |
|---|---|
| Kyūshū | 2,040.8 |
| Tōsan | 1,443.0 |
| Tōhoku | 936.8 |
| Hokkaidō | 44.8 |

From the above table it is clear that there were regions such as Kinki and Kantō with high population density of urban proportions, as well as regions—other than the pioneer territory of Hokkaidō—with relatively low density, such as the Tōsan and Tōhoku areas.

Below is a table showing the number of cities in each region according to population size, at the beginning of the Meiji period.

| *Region* | *10,000–30,000* | *30,000–50,000* | *50,000–100,000* | *100,000 and over* | *Regional*[17] *Total* |
|---|---|---|---|---|---|
| Hokkaidō | 2 | 0 | 0 | 0 | 2 |
| Tōhoku | 8 | 2 | 1 | 0 | 11 |
| Kantō | 11 | 0 | 1 | 1 | 13 |
| Chūbu | 23 | 2 | 1 | 2 | 28 |
| Kinki | 17 | 2 | 1 | 2 | 22 |
| Chūgoku | 4 | 3 | 1 | 0 | 8 |
| Shikoku | 6 | 1 | 0 | 0 | 7 |
| Kyūshū | 4 | 4 | 0 | 0 | 8 |
| National Total | 75 | 14 | 5 | 5 | 99 |

Of the total number of ninety-nine cities with populations of 10,000 or more, sixty-three were former castle towns or cities. The five cities with 100,000 or more population were:

| | | | |
|---|---|---|---|
| Tōkyō | 670,000 | Nagoya | 110,000 |
| Ōsaka | 290,000 | Kanazawa | 100,000 |
| Kyōto | 230,000 | | |

Both Nagoya and Kanazawa had been castle cities of exceptionally powerful daimyō with large domains.

The five cities in the next class of 50,000–100,000 were:

| | | | |
|---|---|---|---|
| Hiroshima | 76,000 | Toyama | 58,000 |
| Wakayama | 62,000 | Sendai | 55,000 |
| Yokohama | 61,000 | | |

All, except the port city of Yokohama, were former castle centers.

The 30,000–50,000 group of fourteen cities included:

| | | | |
|---|---|---|---|
| Sakai | 45,000 | Hirosaki | 33,000 |
| Fukuoka | 45,000 | Hyōgo | 32,000 |
| Kumamoto | 44,000 | Nagasaki | 32,000 |
| Fukui | 41,000 | Kagoshima | 32,000 |
| Matsue | 36,000 | Hakodate | 31,000 |
| Niigata | 35,000 | Akita | 30,000 |
| Tottori | 34,000 | Takamatsu | 30,000 |

Nine of these cities were castle towns, and the remaining five were developed as foreign trade ports. Hence, it is evident that all cities with large populations at the beginning of the Meiji period were either previous castle towns or port towns opened to foreign trade.

Another distinctive feature of urban populations early in the Meiji period is that the cities were fairly evenly distributed throughout the country. This was due to the Tokugawa policy of dividing the whole country up into small domains with local governments roughly equidistant from each other. The domains endeavored, on their part, to become self-sufficient, integrating the districts surrounding the castle centers into self-contained units of politics, economy, and defense. Even after the domains were broken up by the Meiji government, organs of local administration were placed in the castle towns and industries were developed, compensating for loss of some of the warrior population. The castle structures themselves were often converted into local military headquarters. In these ways, then, many of the castle towns retained fairly large populations, keeping the distribution of large cities fairly even.

Turning to changes occurring in city populations during the twenty years from 1878 to 1897, let us look first at the seven cities with populations of 100,000 or more. The rates of increase in those cities were as follows:

| *City* | *Pop. in 1897* | *Rate of Increase, 1878–1897 (1878 pop. = 100)* |
|---|---|---|
| Tōkyō | 1,330,000 | 188.60 |
| Ōsaka | 750,000 | 258.39 |
| Kyōto | 320,000 | 142.84 |
| Nagoya | 250,000 | 222.52 |
| Kōbe | 190,000 | 1,628.98 |
| Yokohama | 180,000 | 306.57 |
| Hiroshima | 110,000 | 148.52 |

Kanazawa, an old castle town with a population of 100,000 in 1878, lost most of its samurai population and failed to develop industry or other means of compensating for losses. Its population decreased to 82,000 by 1897. Kōbe and Yokohama show remarkable growth rates due to foreign trade developments. The other five listed above comprised the three main cities of the feudal age, and two other major castle cities, all of which retained important functions in the new age.

Cities with populations between 50,000 and 100,000 that show population changes, with the 1878 populations taken as a base of 100, were;

| *City* | *Pop. in 1897* | *Rate of Increase/Decrease, 1878–98 (1878 = 100)* |
|---|---|---|
| Kanazawa | 82,000 | 76.36 |
| Sendai | 82,000 | 152.50 |
| Nagasaki | 74,000 | 228.61 |
| Hakodate | 73,000 | 237.24 |

| | | |
|---|---|---|
| Fukuoka | 63,000 | 139.67 |
| Tokushima | 61,000 | 336.42 |
| Toyama | 58,000 | 100.67 |
| Kumamoto | 58.000 | 130.87 |
| Wakayama | 57,000 | 92.59 |
| Okayama | 56,000 | 168.40 |
| Kagoshima | 54,000 | 168.50 |
| Niigata | 51,000 | 144.44 |
| Sakai | 50,000 | 109.80 |

Among these thirteen cities, nine were old castle towns, and the remaining four, —Nagasaki, Hakodate, Niigata, and Sakai—had been developed as port towns in the Edo period.

There were twenty-one cities with populations between 30,000 and 50,000 in 1897, as follows:

| *City* | *Population* | *City* | *Population* |
|---|---|---|---|
| Fukui | 43,000 | Mito | 33,000 |
| Shizuoka | 40,000 | Maebashi | 33,000 |
| Amagasaki | 37,000 | Ōtsu | 33,000 |
| Kōchi | 36,000 | Yamagata | 33,000 |
| Uwajima | 36,000 | Morioka | 31,000 |
| Utsunomiya | 36,000 | Gifu | 31,000 |
| Kōfu | 36,000 | Tsu | 31,000 |
| Matsue | 34,000 | Hirosaki | 31,000 |
| Matsuyama | 34,000 | Takaoka | 30,000 |
| Himeji | 34,000 | Matsumoto | 30,000 |
| Takamatsu | 34,000 | | |

Of the above, sixteen had been castle towns, while only five were not former castle centers. Nine of the fourteen cities registering 30,000–50,000 populations in 1878 had expanded enough for inclusion in the 50,000–100,000 class by 1897. Tottori lost part of its earlier 34,000 population, dropping out of the 30,000 minimum class. Eleven of the above cities were new to this group.

Throughout the two or three centuries of the feudal age, society was rather stable, without significant population changes. During the twenty years from 1878 to 1897, there were, as shown in the preceding lists, considerable changes in urban populations with attendant shifts in social and ecological structures. It is noteworthy that the top three cities of feudal society, Tōkyō, Kyōto, and Ōsaka, did not lose their positions of prominence, that the old and new ages cohered, as it were, in the persistence of many castle towns and the emergence of new overseas trading cities.

The remarkable expansion of the port cities of Yokohama and Kōbe due to international trade has already been noted. But it should be clear that other port towns, castle towns, and especially the three major cities continued to function as the nuclei of national life in the many fields of domestic politics, defense, education, commerce, and industry. More than feudal background, though, it was the modernization of socio-economic structures that made possible the continued importance of these cities and caused the population changes within them.

The privileged position of the feudal cities had been undercut partly by the growing activity of merchants in the rural districts as feudal powers waned from the middle of the Tokugawa era on. But it was the reform program of the Meiji government that struck the telling blows on the social structures of the cities. The commerce laws (*Shōhō Tai-i*) of 1868 destroyed the old trade monopolies, and restrictions that bound status groups to occupations were removed. Citizens became free to engage in businesses of their own choosing. Land tax exemption privileges were canceled by an 1871 law governing land and streets in the cities (*Shigaichi-hō*), eliminating the advantages enjoyed by cities over farming areas.

The castle towns, which constituted the majority of pre-Meiji cities, suffered most under the Meiji transformation. Feudal lords left their castle centers for Tōkyō under government orders, and most of the castles were destroyed when the domain system was abolished and the prefectures were established in 1817. The warrior groups, consistently more than half of castle town populations, were left without stipends or status. Bankrupted by such sudden and drastic measures, some managed to enter bureaucratic service, though many turned to operating shops of their own and many more returned to the farms. Losing their best customers, the merchants faced severe depression, and the castle towns dwindled in size, structure, and prestige as their former integrative place and function came to an end.

The terms for determining the location of cities in the age of modernization were found essentially in the geographical conditions that had dictated placement of the old castle towns. Most of them had been positioned in the center of wide plains or near waterways such as rivers or sea lanes. They were usually situated, that is, at convenient traffic junctions. Travel and communications networks had built up around the castle centers, and they were the effective control points of surrounding local economies.

Therefore, it was quite natural that newly established prefectural offices, as well as military and other facilities, should be located in the old castle center sites, even after dissolution of the castle town functions. The military and political functions of the castle towns were restored in many cases. Banks and business firms were constructued in central areas of the old castle towns to manage the local economies, and schools and factories were also built in suitable places. Residential areas formerly occupied by warriors were transformed into housing areas for employees of prefectural offices and manufacturing plants. New life was introduced into the otherwise doomed centers of local politics, economy, and culture.[18]

The structure of commerce and industry underwent radical changes in accordance with the new formations of the old towns. Wholesaling privileges (*kabu*) were gone; anyone could now become a wholesale dealer if he had sufficient capital to get started. Commodity producers in local areas could sell their goods directly to urban consumers, by-passing wholesalers if they wished. In fact, wholesalers became far less influential in controlling trade than they had once been.

Prior to 1897 urban producers did not command a particularly strong position as they were limited to the scale of home industries. Wholesalers exercised powerful influence over them through zonal marketing of their goods, as did also the money-lenders who subsidized their production through advance or special loans, or by negotiating contracts covering long periods of time. Traditional, premodern forms of dependent relationships could be maintained easily when the odds were so clearly on one side.[19] This pattern was distrupted mainly by the Sino-Japanese War (1894–5). The dominant strength of commercial capital diminished as large-scale modern industries displaced the ineffectual home industries.

Heretofore, urban expansion could not proceed beyond the limits of home industry and its low demand for laborers. When machines were introduced and factories went into large-scale production, the demand for workers shot up, as did also the manpower requirements of the distributive and retailing systems. Activation of large-scale industry necessarily caused growth in the urban populations.

Previously the provincial governments had sought to supply all of their own needs and thereby avoid undue dependence upon other domains. There was almost no specialization in production, and the industrial structure of the castle towns was uncommonly uniform.

One of the most important factors in the process of bringing local economies out of self-sufficient insularity into nationwide interdependence was the introduction of mass production techniques. Productive efficiency was raised by simplifying working methods, shortening work hours, and standardizing production processes. This permitted the manufacture of standard products in large quantities in a few locations, to be shipped to any markets, near or far.

Concomitant with the introduction of machines in factories, the utilization of the steam engine on the railroads and at sea revolutionized transportation. Large quantities of goods could be delivered further at lower costs than ever before, and with this development the basic conditions for differentiation of city functions were completed. Increasingly the cities of Japan turned to specialized functions as political, commercial, industrial, educational, military, or foreign trade cities. These roles were not mutually exclusive, of course, and many cities combined several of them. Specialization of one sort or another made each of the cities, however, that much more dependent upon the different services of other cities, hastening the processes of total national integration.

The transportation revolution lifted the industrial capacities of the cities out of dependence upon the limited resources of nearby regions. Raw materials in increased quantity and kind could be drawn from more distant sources, as, conversely, goods could be sold in larger and more distant markets, especially with new access to international trade following opening of the nation's ports. Mass production and large-scale transport led to absorption of mass populations by the cities.

Hence, it is clear that the cities were subject to vast changes in community structure equally as much as in population composition. Structural change within the city, along with changes in organizational relationships between the cities, followed the lead of the transformation of industrial patterns.

The three truly national cities, Tōkyō, Kyōto, and Ōsaka, despite certain distinctive features, had once all shared in the whole spectrum of integrative relationships encompassing the country. In the sweep of the industrial revolution, with its unprecedented impact on domestic insularity and international isolation, the distinctiveness and particularity of the three national cities were strengthened. Tōkyō steadily developed as the nucleus of national political and cultural integration, in addition to being the focal point of all life in northeastern Japan. Ōsaka emerged more positively than ever as the nation's center of economic integration, plus performing a central role in life of the southwestern section of the land. Kyōto's traditional character remained, though addition of certain new organs contributed to its distinctive development.

Life in the old castle towns diverged sharply from the long-time legacy of uniformity, as specialization was promoted. Some became primarily political centers, others military or educational centers, although they maintained many of the interrelationships with other large cities, especially the top three, that derived from the peculiarities of geography and the necessities of politics, economy, and culture. Distinctive characteristics resulting from entrance into international relations was particularly outstanding in the trade and port cities.

The cities of the modern era were characterized, then, in contrast to their feudal predecessors, by the wide range of interdependence, remarkable growth in population, and enlarged integrative mechanisms. Not all cities, to be sure, shared fully in these characteristics. A few fell into serious decline, while others managed merely to hold on to their inherited positions. As such they were unsuitable as centers for the new social order. The limiting conditions that prevented them from growth in terms of integrative organs and population, and from overcoming once self-sufficient but now self-defeating insularity, included disadvantageous geographical locations, and inadequate ability to adjust to the new dynamics of politics, economy, and production techniques.

*Fluctuations of Growth and Decay in the Various Types of Cities.*——

THE THREE LARGEST CITIES. Although there was some contention over the location of the capital of the Meiji government, the decision went, it will be recalled, to Edo. It was renamed Tōkyō, and the Emperor Meiji took up residence in Edo Castle in 1869, changing its designation to Tōkyō Castle. Tōkyō embarked upon a new career as nucleus of the bureaucracy forged under the sanction of imperial authority.

The transition was not a smooth one, by any means. Tōkyō suffered serious decline after the shogunate fell, and depletion of the warrior sector of the population virtually ruined its markets. Deprived of their primary customers, many merchants and craftsmen returned to their native areas to engage in farming. The government attempted to rescue the fortunes of its dwindled population by putting lands up for sale at low rates and promoting cultivation of mulberry trees and tea plants. Had this proved successful, the once great feudal capital would have been transformed into a complex of farm villages. But there were no buyers, and Edo hung on the edge of even further desolation.

We have seen that Edo at the height of its power in the Tokugawa era boasted a population over one million, largest in the world at that time. By 1872 its urban area contained but half that number, a mere 520,000. It managed to recuperate to 670,000 by 1878, though this was still far short of its earlier size. The remedy came primarily from the program to increase national wealth and might which brought, among other heavily centralized bureaucratic and economic organizations, the main lines of the railroads running northeast and southwest into its own center by 1891. The rail artery put Tōkyō in much closer connection with the major regions of the country, as it also gave it ready access to the new life-blood flowing into the major international ports of Yokohama and Kōbe. The integrative organs centered in Tōkyō began to expand accordingly.

Moreover, the new organs of government and economy developed along modern lines, rapidly increasing Tōkyō's population, as can be seen in the following figures:

| *Year* | *Population* |
|---|---|
| 1878 | 670,000 |
| 1887 | 1,060,000 |
| 1892 | 1,180,000 |
| 1897 | 1,330,000 |

In a word, Tōkyō doubled in population size in two decades. (Social and ecological structures in Tōkyō during this period will be treated in detail in the latter half of this chapter.)

In contrast to the political and highly consumptive character of Edo, Ōsaka in feudal times flourished in its typical role as chief supplier of goods for the nation. Its Edo era zenith in population was 500,000, but disintegration of the feudal system reduced this to 290,000 by 1878.

In 1868 the government suspended the traditional silver standard of Ōsaka's currency. Bills of exchange and all other credit notes issued by Ōsaka brokers on the old standard were no longer honored, throwing the city's economy into utter confusion. The financially pressed government, like the shogunate before it, raised part of the budget through forced loans (*goyōkin*), and Ōsaka was a prime target of this tactic due to the large concentration of wealthy merchants there. Many of the latter group closed their stores for lack of business. Moreover, much of Ōsaka's prosperity had derived from the storehouses (*kura-yashiki*) operated on behalf of the old feudal domains, which were discarded in favor of the prefectural system (1871), thus undermining part of Ōsaka's economic foundation. When the wholesalers' associations (*kabu-nakama*) were abolished in 1872, disruption of the distributive system gravely compounded the economic confusion in Ōsaka.

The year 1875 brought yet another severe blow to the Ōsaka merchants. Bonds issued by the domain governments were either rendered void, or the payment periods were extended and interest rates reduced. Many of these bonds were on the credit sheets of Ōsaka merchants. The prosperity they had enjoyed through serving as financiers for the entire nation vanished overnight.

Ōsaka rose again from the ashes of economic ruin, beginning around 1884–5. The transformation was wrought by industrialization and revived commercial activity. Factories were erected for diversified production of many commodities, such as textiles, knit goods, paper, cement, brushes, motors and engines, spinning machines, and ships. The city recaptured its primacy in commerce, transportation, and finance. The population low of 290,000 in 1878 soon swelled to a healthy 340,000 in 1887, and to a new peak for Ōsaka of 750,000 by 1897.

The Sino-Japanese War brought prosperity to Japan, and construction of railways and banks increased, aiding the Ōsaka situation. Of woven fabrics produced in the whole country, 40% were turned out by the spinning mills in Ōsaka. Houses and factories filled its communities, intensifying demands for space. In April, 1897, the Ōsaka municipal government scheduled its first expansion plan, in which the urban area was extended to 550,000 sq. km. (212,300 sq. mi.), almost four times the original of 150,000 sq. km. (57,900 sq. mi.).

Port facilities for the city were also improved, and its population swelled to 990,000 by 1905. It was no longer just a distributive center as in Edo times but was now a production center as well, with convenient access to raw materials and foreign products. From intensified production came increased accumulation of commercial capital that helped stimulate further development.[20]

Kyōto's heritage, of course, was unique among the top three cities. Ancient seat of the Emperor and the Imperial Household, as well as of the court nobility, it also boasted possession of many of Japan's most honored shrines and temples. A special crafts tradition had been developed that expressed a long cherished cultural tradition in woven fabrics, dyeing, embroidery, lacquerware, ceramics, and carvings. Sixty-eight domains had maintained mansions in Kyōto, and many feudal lords stopped over on their way to and from Edo. The city had close connections with many sections of the country, and the financial houses of Mitsui, Ono, and Shimada won influential places in Kyōto society. Beyond commerce and culture, Kyōto was also the focus of deep spiritual sentiments that served as the rallying ground for the anti-shogunate forces that toppled the Tokugawa regime.

This special spiritual function was lost when the Emperor Meiji moved to Tōkyō in 1869, as was much of Kyōto's political importance. Though for different reasons, it too suffered serious decline for a time. Succor came to Kyōto, however, in the form of a 100,000 yen industrial fund provided by the Imperial Household. With this fund new financial and overseas trading organs were established, transportation was improved, and export business got under way. Kyōto was handicapped by lack of access to the sea and its topography was unsuited to industrial development on a large scale. Its crafts industries were unexcelled in quality and refined taste, but it was not a city that could adapt to modern machine industry. Consequently, its population increase was very modest, from 230,000 in 1878 to only 330,000 in 1897.

OLD CASTLE TOWNS. The social disruption that ensued upon collapse of the feudal order forced a decline in the populations of these towns ranking next in importance to the triumvirate of Tōkyō, Ōsaka, and Kyōto. Most of them, however, were transformed into modern cities through acquisition of new functions as centers for prefectural offices, military bases, schools, banks, business firms, and factories. Others were poorly situated for adaptation as modern cities and decreased rapidly in size and importance.

A few of the more fortunate castle towns quickly doubled their populations. We have seen that Nagoya was in the population class of 100,000 or above; Tokushima was in the 50,000–100,000 class; and in the 30,000–50,000 class were Tsu, Shizuoka, Ōtsu, Matsumoto, Maebashi, Fukui, and Mito.

Another group of former castle towns experienced moderate population growth, six of them entering the 50,000–100,000 class, namely, Okayama, Fukuoka, Saga, Kumamoto, Sendai, and Toyama. Ten castle centers of moderate growth were found in the 30,000–50,000 class: Kōfu, Utsunomiya, Morioka, Hirosaki, Yamagata, Takaoka, Himeji, Takamatsu, Matsuyama, and Kōchi.

Castle town of the Tokugawa family of Owari, Nagoya claimed a revenue in 1645 of 620,000 *koku*, this figure rising to 650,000 toward the end of the 18th century. It was one of the largest castle towns along with those of the Maeda family of Kanazawa and of the Shimazu family of Kagoshima. Its townsmen alone numbered 55,000 in the middle of the 17th century, and its early Meiji population stood at 100,000 (including warriors). It went on, in the Meiji period, to become Japan's fourth largest city after the renowned trio—Tōkyō, Ōsaka and Kyōto. Its geographical location in the center of the Nōbi plain, a fertile area midway between Tōkyō and Ōsaka, was a distinct advantage to its development.

Nagoya's development was due to conveniences in transportation and communications, on the one hand, but due also to the forward-looking policies of Lord Muneharu of the Owari Tokugawa family, on the other hand. This daimyō disregarded shogunate policy by promoting commerce and industry in his own way, buying less goods from the Kansai and promoting production in his own domain.

Though the city dwindled after abrogation of the feudal system, a prefectural office was located there in 1871. Pottery-making industries had existed there in feudal days, and a joint-stock corporation for spinning was introduced in 1880. A Chamber of Commerce was founded in 1881 for promoting industry. The Nagoya Spinning Company appeared in 1884, followed in 1887 by the Owari Spinning Company and others for producing cotton fabrics, silk goods, and blankets. Around 1901 watch and clock factories were built which turned out 180,000 pieces in the following year, some of which were exported to China and India.

Progress was furthered when the Tōkaidō trunk line was completed in 1890, passing through Nagoya. Other rail lines serving the city followed, such as the Kansai Railway in 1897, and Nagoya Electric Railway in 1901. Provided with access to a wider area, industry expanded remarkably. Starting from 110,000 in 1878, the population rose to 150,000 in a single decade (1888), and swelled to 250,000 by the end of the next decade (1898).[21]

Most of the cities which developed rapidly in the early half of the Meiji era had some connection with the expansion of export industries and markets, usually with roots in late Edo era activities. Fukui, castle town of the Matsudaira family, was a case in point. Its revenue ran to 350,000 *koku* annually and townsmen numbered 18,000 (1792). Reference has been made earlier to the activities of its warriors in silk spinning and production of cotton yarns, and to the formation of a merchandizing agency (Bussan Sōkaisho) in 1859 to promote exports soon after the ports were opened to overseas trade in 1858. The Fukui domain agency in Nagasaki was called Echizen-Kurayashiki, and in 1859, one million *ryō* ($200,000) worth of silk was sold to Dutch traders—the first time silk was exported from Japan. By 1861 silk exports reached three million *ryō*.

Because the warrior families in Fukui had developed skills in silk producing and spinning, they were able to ride out the confusions surrounding the changeover in government with relative ease. Machines were introduced under the leadership of a warrior named Yuri Kimimasa to step up production of high grade silk fabrics, and new organizational needs were met by forming companies to handle both sericulture and spinning. In 1889 a cooperative (Dōmeisha) was established to manage sales. The Silk Exchange of Fukui was formed in 1894, the first one of its kind for handling term contracts in silk transactions in Japan.

In terms of Japanese currency, silk production in Fukui amounted to 200,000 yen in 1877. This expanded to 1,264,500 yen by 1891, with 1,188 factories employing 6,364 men and women to work at 5,158 machines. By the following year, 1892, Fukui silk production jumped to 2,780,000 yen worth.[22] The population of the city almost doubled from 1878 to 1897, rising from 27,000 to 43,000.

The castle town of Tsu was built by Tōdō Takatora during the Keichō era (1596–1614). There were 3,000 houses in the town in the Tenpō and Kōka eras (1830–47 inclusive). Expansion of industry was stifled in the feudal period by the shogunate's closed-port policy. In 1872 the city became the site for construction of a district court, a local administrative office, a post office, and the Anōtsu school. These were followed by a prefectural office in 1873, a normal school in 1874, and newspaper and bank offices in 1877. Expanded commerce and transport soon brought added life to the city.

The municipal administration of Tsu city sought energetically to develop industry from the outset. Kansai Manufacturing Company began operations in 1896, followed by the Mie Spinning Company in 1898. The latter was, in its day, unexcelled in top grade production. In 1899 a railway to the city was completed, rapidly accelerating its commerce, a development especially visible in the construction of streets and stores around the Tsu Railroad Station, and around the nearby station of Akogi.[23] Population rose remarkably under the stimulus of high-speed modernization, as shown below:

| *Year* | *Pop. of Tsu* |
|---|---|
| 1878 | 10,617 |
| 1887 | 15,597 |
| 1897 | 31,421 |

Horses and local commodities from the Shinano region, plus an annual revenue of 70,000 *koku*, were the substance of economic life of Matsumoto, castle town of the Mizuno domain, in feudal times before it evolved into a city of commerce and industry in the Meiji period. Its industries handled hard and bast fibers, tobacco, *sake*, and white-spotted cotton fabrics. In 1864 Matsumoto had a population of 9,440 townsmen and 5,284 samurai. During the transition years from 1865–7 (Keiō era), poor crops and heavy taxes combined with confusion in its currency system to thwart local commerce and industry, causing the city to decline seriously. A financial corporation (Kaisansha) for subsidizing industry was established in 1875, followed by the Fourteenth Bank (Jūshi Ginkō) in 1877, and the Matsumoto Bank in 1881. These banks also channeled funds into local industry, bolstering the foundations of municipal government.

Tracts were loaned to former samurai who developed forestation projects, and farmers embarked on sericulture ventures in response to foreign trade demands. Certain wood fibres were utilized in production of silkworm-egg paper and other woods were used for doll-making (*oshiebina*). Dyeing of cotton fabrics declined, so production of materials used as soles in Japanese socks (*tabi*) was substituted. Around 1879–80 the city of Matsumoto regained its previous level of prosperity. Sericulture developed notably during 1885 and 1886, and many mechanized silk spinning mills were set up in various parts of the prefecture. Establishment of the Katakura Silk Mill in 1890 marked a special turning point for a process of great expansion in the future. Sericultural production reached an all-time peak in 1894, leading into a period when "silk is money" was the prevailing mood.[24] Matsumoto's population more than doubled, from 14,549 in 1878 to 30,588 in 1897.

Rapid growth cannot be seen in the case of old castle towns that were unable to provide themselves with industrial foundations. Nonetheless, some of the former castle centers managed more moderate rates of expansion as centers for politics, education, or military bases.

The largest feudal city in the Tōhoku region was Sendai, castle town of the Date house. Its large revenue of 600,000 *koku* reflected its somewhat one-sided population composition of 44,000 warriors and only 2,385 townsmen (1772). This city practically vanished when the warrior class lost its basis in society. In 1872, however, a district military headquarters was placed there, later to be called the Second Division Headquarters of the Imperial Army. In the city there were quartered a reserve regiment, an artillery regiment, a special services battalion, and the Military Training School of Sendai.

In addition to these military installations, a prefectural office and various agencies of the central government were located in the city. To these were added a normal school (1873), the Miyagi School of Foreign Languages (1874), and Tōhoku Imperial University (1907). The city of Sendai became well known for its military installations and educational institutions, an impressive city with wooded areas and many reminders of its days as a castle town.

After 1877 a variety of business firms were established for silk spinning, horse breeding, wood and lumber, along with transportation facilities and banks. The lines of privilege among established merchants were effectively disrupted by the laying of the northern trunk line from Ueno (in Tōkyō) to Sendai in 1887. There appeared a new corps of merchants on the scene, and Sendai became the distribution center of the northeast region. Its population did not increase so rapidly as those reviewed above. The 1878 population of 55,000 had risen to only 82,000 by 1897.[25]

The city of Kumamoto, on Kyūshū island, was another example of moderate though steady growth. Castle town of the Hosokawa family, it had a feudal age revenue of only 55,000 *koku*. It too received a local headquarters office of the army, in 1871, and had a population of 44,866 in 9,499 households. The city was damaged twice by fires during civil wars; one was the Gishin-tō revolt of 1876, another a rebellion led by Saigō Takamori in 1877. The revolts served to liberate the lives of the people, though, and two banks were formed to rescue the warriors' plight, the Fifteenth Bank (Daijūgo Ginkō) and the Ninth Bank (Daiku Ginkō). Loans from these banks were used to found the Kumamoto Spinning Company and the Tōhi Paper Company around 1897. Plagued with poor management, these companies did not do well and the banks came very near to bankruptcy, until the Hosokawa family and another powerful family, Yasuda, stepped in to help.

In the early stages of its development commerce and industry were not key factors. A prefectural office was built in 1876, and a municipal office in 1889. In the latter year, the Sixth Division Army Headquarters was located in the city. As for schools, there were a normal school, a medical college, and a pharmaceutical college that grew out of the traditions of the old Kumamoto domain school (*hankō*) that had been named Jishūkan ("Contemporary Training Institute").[26] A city with multiple functions in politics, education, and defense, its population increased by a modest 30% from 44,607 in 1878 to 58,376 in 1897.

Kōfu can be taken as an example of castle towns with populations of 30,000 or more that experienced modest expansion. Situated at the center of a narrow basin with relatively low productivity, commerce covered products gathered from only a limited area and was marked by rather non-aggressive wholesalers who depended heavily upon protection and privilege from their lords. No notable development was realized in the Tokugawa era, and the market declined quickly when the feudal order was overturned by the new government. Recovery began in 1873 when Wakao Ippei established a silk processing firm, following transportation improvements in the prefecture. In 1874 the prefectural lieutenant-governor, named Fujimura, founded a financial agency (Kōekisha), and the Kangyō Silk Spinning Mill was built soon afterward. The market was reactivated rather easily due to readily available raw materias, sericulture being the prefecture's major productive activity.

Commercial cultivation of grapes was begun in 1903 and this enterprise was greatly stimulated by the completion, in the same year, of the Central Railway (Chūo-sen) connecting Kōfu with Hachiōji in the western suburbs of Tōkyō. This line was extended south to Nagoya in 1911. Prior to these developments, Kōfu's growth was limited by the natural conditions of its immediate vicinity. Even so, its population increased 70% between 1878 and 1897, from 21,325 to 36,159.[27]

The populations of some castle towns decreased, chiefly because of failure to acquire some industry to replace lost political functions. Larger towns in this category included Kanazawa and Wakayama—the former losing 34% of its people since 1878—and smaller towns showing population decreases included such examples as Matsue, Takata, and Hagi.

Turning first to Kanazawa, its population decline was the greatest among the larger cities. Once it had flourished as capital of the Kaga domain, ruling over the three provinces of Kaga, Echizen, and Noto, from which it extracted an annual income of one million *koku*. Nucleus of political, military, and cultural integration throughout the three centuries of Tokugawa rule, its combined townsmen-samurai population in 1778 of 64,987 climbed to 123,363 by 1871.

The Meiji transition hit Kanazawa hard. The prefectural office was first put in Mikawa town in 1872 and moved the following year to Kanazawa. This slight deviation from usual procedure, however, was enough to ruin the city. When it became clear that the prefectural office was not destined for Kanazawa, the residents were thrown into confusion, and the market fell to pieces. Warriors left for their native villages after destroying their homes. Merchants could not make a living and closed their shops. In the main section of the city wide open spaces appeared where houses had once stood, and local farmers cultivated some of the vacant lots.[28]

The remaining populace then turned to rebuilding their lost prosperity. Traditional crafts for producing silk fabrics, ceramics and porcelains were applied in new factories; and metal foil plants and silk spinning mills were opened, the former employing 1,500 girls, the latter 200 girls, in 1880.

Industrial development in Kanazawa was frustrated, though, because of limited demands for art and crafts products and due to lack of rail access to the large urban markets on the eastern coast. This thwarted condition showed up in Kanazawa's population changes, as below:

| *Year* | *Population* |
|---|---|
| 1871 | 123,363 |
| 1878 | 107,878 |
| 1888 | 96,639 |
| 1892 | 92,239 |
| 1897 | 83,378 |

Population also dropped in Wakayama. Castle town of one of the three major Tokugawa families (*gosanke*) with an annual revenue of 550,000 *koku*, it was once the most prosperous city in the western coastal plain of the large peninsula south of Ōsaka. Warriors' residences there had splendid gates and lovely tiled walls. The entire town was similar to the residential areas of daimyō and *hatamoto* in Edo itself.

True to form, the Meiji programs removing warriors' privileges and wholesalers' monopolies left Wakayama desolate. Former samurai grounds became fields of mulberry trees and barley. The markets were sluggish. But the Meiji government's positive programs were felt in the city too. Banks were founded in 1872, spinning companies in 1880, and a chamber of commerce in 1881. The industries were beginning to show some movement by 1882, with production of 1,032,000 yards of fabrics, only to have the economy hard hit by a bad drought in 1883 and a heavy flood in 1887. The population decreased to 55,955 in 1887 from the 1878 level of 62,009.

It was after 1897 that Wakayama's industries experienced healthy growth as suppliers of the expansive markets of nearby Kyōto, Ōsaka, and Kōbe, supplying cotton flannel, thread and printed goods, as well as knit goods, furniture and other woodwork, lumber, leather, *sake*, and machines.[29] So, the population decline appears to have been caused chiefly by natural calamities rather than by failure in the functions or organs of the city itself.

The castle town of Takada (revenue: 260,000 *koku*) was essentially a case of simply standing still, as the following figures indicate:

| *Year* | *Population* |
|---|---|
| 1698 | 17,303 (townsmen) |
| 1840 | 18,434 |
| 1878 | 20,115 |
| 1897 | 20,009 |

Industry in Takada manifested little growth in the Edo period and was cast into disorder by the advent of the Meiji government. To revive the damaged market situation, some warriors tried to operate various industries but were not very successful. Various attempts included a cotton spinning mill (1872), a bank (1876), and a cotton mill operated especially to provide work for unemployed samurai (1879). The last venture was reorganized as a joint-stock corporation in 1900. At any rate, Takada made little progress prior to 1897, and afterward made some headway only by exploiting silk producing and processing techniques already known in the Edo era.[30]

Castle towns lacking adequate capital resources and transportation facilities could not easily make the transition into modern cities. Some dwindled, instead, into poor local towns, as did Hagi and Matsushiro. These towns were formed under the power of feudal lords to concentrate a population for political and military ends. When these functions were withdrawn, lack of industry and transport facilities reduced the town to the small scale required only by the immediate local area.

For example, Hagi had once commanded an annual intake of 360,000 *koku* of rice, supporting the ruling Mori family and 5,300 townsmen (1667). Its population had grown to 25,600 by 1878, but fell off 30% by 1897. Moreover, while industrialized cities grew considerably during the years of the industrial revolution up to the beginning years of the Taishō era (1912–26), Hagi slipped further to a population of 17,159.

PORT TOWNS AND TRADING CITIES. During the period beginning with the Meiji Restoration and running up to the start of the 19th century, there were a number of crucial changes wrought in the port towns by the general social reformation carried out in that period. Recalling the Edo era conditions against which these changes must be measured, the waterways were the primary means of transporting heavy and bulky cargo. The major sea lane was that developed between Ōsaka and Edo for shipments to the capital of rice tribute and various goods produced throughout the country. The sea routes along the nation's coasts were no less important, however, for collecting goods destined for the capital and for expediting interdomain trade. Port towns were distributed rather evenly along the coastal routes as gateways to the domains, where prosperity was centered in the semi-official warehouses of the port town wholesalers. The wholesalers served as agents under government protection for gathering and shipping goods, virtually controlling the rural producers and the smaller merchants and transportation workers in the port towns.

Needless to say, the port town markets were also controlled by the wholesalers and financially powerful merchants, and they held on to their controlling powers even after their feudal privileges were taken away. They continued exercising controls in the ports along customary lines until their traditional hold on the market was disrupted not so much by political action as by the diffusion of rail and steamship services.

Where harbors could not accommodate steamers, old port towns lost their place as commercial ports, either becoming fishing centers or handling local transport needs on a small scale. Where possible, freight agents and passengers alike took advantage of the railroads being rapidly extended to all parts of the country, and offering savings in both time and money. An entirely new pattern of movement of men and goods emerged that simply erased many former port towns from the national transportation map.

Yokohama and Kōbe were blessed, on the one hand, with good harbors and, on the other, with ready access to large urban centers surrounded by wide, productive rural areas, not to mention the emerging industries of the Kantō and Kinki districts. Under the added stimulus of the new international trade arrangements, these two ports developed in a short time into large port cities with modern facilities and socio-economic structures.

Nagasaki, the only authorized port for foreign trade in the Tokugawa period, lost that important function to Yokohama and Kōbe, but altered its stance to that of heavy industry, especially shipbuilding. Other port towns such as Hakodate, Niigata, Amagasaki, and Aomori possessed the natural and social conditions, that is, harbors large and deep enough for steamships and wide regional connections, to adapt to the new society. They became regional equivalents to Yokohama and Kōbe.

As for population changes in the port towns, Yokohama, Kōbe, Nagasaki, and Hakodate rose to more than 50,000, over twice their feudal size, whereas Sakai failed to double its size. Port towns in the 30,000–50,000 class that also increased though less than twice were Akamagaseki and Niigata; Ōtsu more than doubled. In the 10,000–30,000 class Aomori exceeded twice its former size; Sakata, Noshiro, Uotsu, Kanagawa, Funabashi, and Onomichi failed to double in population. The port town of Niiminato, with less than 10,000, decreased in size.

Yokohama had been a village of only 101 houses before the ports were opened in 1859. After free trade was approved and merchants were encouraged to come in, export-import trade climbed swiftly to a 190 million yen volume by 1898, having reached only 35.4 million yen in 1873. Goods flowed in mainly from the western and northern regions. The 1878 population of 60,000 more than tripled to a 188,000 count for 1897.

Expansion in Yokohama began with the establishment of a silk processing company in 1873 that gained control of Japanese silk exports, handling 60%–80% of total shipments abroad. Warehouses for silk were built in 1881 to help Japanese merchants achieve independence in international competition. In 1882 port facilities were improved to insure safe anchorage of sea-going vessels, followed by modernization of the municipal water supply, electric service, police and fire-fighting systems. A Silk Inspection Office and Chamber of Commerce were founded in 1895 to fill out the list of organizations necessary in a modern port city.[31]

Kōbe had been a good port, known as Hyōgo, as early as the Nara period. Its functions expanded in the Tokugawa era through activities of wholesalers handling *sake* and other cargoes in behalf of nearby Ōsaka. In 1769 it had a population of 21,000. Its relations with productive areas in the Kinki district were conducive to its development as a modern port city as was Yokohama's accessibility to the Kantō plain and the Tōhoku region.

Many factors contributed to the rapid and remarkable development of this ancient port town. An abundant labor supply was available in surrounding districts for operating the many industries that sprouted up in the Hanshin (Ōsaka-Kōbe) urban complex. Construction of several railroads servicing the region gave it a helpful mobility. Its port was subjected to repeated construction and improvement programs, making it well-known around the world as a well-equipped international harbor. The number of foreigners resident in the city gradually increased as business expanded, and many of them were active, along with Japanese entrepeneurs, in founding and expanding many firms and factories.

In 1869 a foreign firm built a steel mill at Kawasakihama in Kōbe, and the Kanazawa feudal domain started a weapons factory. The government bought up these factories to push its program in steel and machine tool production, renaming the whole as the Hyōgo Shipbuilding Yard. Heavy industry developed further as transportation services improved. Around 1877 more steel mills were built, and there were new factories for making matches and processing camphor. Toward the end of the Meiji period a number of factories manufacturing rubber products were constructed in Kōbe, including one of the Dunlop firm. The new Kōbe, with modern structures, expanded from a 1878 population of 119,999 to 194,000 in 1897.[32]

Nagasaki's course ran differently. Whereas it had enjoyed a monopoly on foreign trade and relations with China and Holland during the Edo era, its political and economic functions shifted to Tōkyō and Ōsaka in the modern period while the overseas trade went to Yokohama and Kōbe. Responsive to these changes, foreign firms also transferred one by one to Yokohama and Kōbe. Consequently, the number of vessels using Nagasaki's port decreased. Part of the business went to other Kyūshū ports opened to handle coal exports, such as Moji, Kuchinotsu, and Misumi (in Fukuoka, Nagasaki, and Kumamoto Prefectures respectively). Exports exceeded imports in all three of these ports, while the reverse was true for Nagasaki.

Small-scale home industries had produced goods of superior quality in various arts and crafts in premodern days in Nagasaki. Things changed abruptly when the government founded a shipbuilding industry there in 1871. Operations were turned over to the Mitsubishi firm in 1884, which expanded the industry. Another shipbuilding facility named Matsuo Tekkōsho was established by private interests, which began manufacturing engines in 1883. Though forced to retreat from overseas trade, the city of Nagasaki rebuilt its prosperity around heavy industry. Light industry included a government-built spinning mill. Population increased more than twice the 1878 count of 32,000 to 74,000 in 1897.[33]

The northernmost port town of Hakodate on the southern tip of Hokkaidō island emerged around 1793 as a base for the Tokugawa shogunate's diplomatic negotiations with Russia. Successful exploitation of rich resources for marine products promoted the concentration of people coming from the northern Ōu region of the main island of Honshū. The port of Hakodate was opened to foreign trade in 1858, by which time improvements in fishing techniques permitted greater progress in marine industry. Hakodate developed, then, as a distribution center, mainly for the fishing industry. From 31,000 in 1878, its population rose to 73,000 in 1897.[34]

NAVAL BASES. Meiji era development of port towns such as Yokosuka, Sasebo, and Kure derived from location of new naval bases in these towns, fitting them for important roles in the national movements toward heightened military prowess. Placement of the naval bases was made according to the overall defense and expansion policies of the government. That is, Yokosuka was chosen in 1872 for the defense of Tōkyō, Kure in 1890 for the defense of industrial areas in the Kansai district, and Sasebo in 1884 as the base of operations for advancing state interests in East Asia. Each of these cities enjoyed topographical advantages for natural protection, and the many buildings erected for naval purposes occupied the main sections of the cities. They were specialized cities full of naval personnel and skilled workers.

The development of Yokosuka began with construction of an iron foundry by the Tokugawa government in 1865 with the help of French engineers. Ship maintenance facilities there were taken over by the Meiji government and enlarged into a shipbuilding complex. In 1868 there were some 400 craftsmen employed in the Yokosuka shipyards; their numbers jumped to 1,000 by 1871, and again to 1,500 by 1876. Location of Naval Headquarters in Yokosuka triggered further development. By 1879 there were 2,256 houses in the city. In 1894 naval training facilities such as the Gunnery School, Torpedo School, and Engineering School were enlarged. In 1907 about one-third of a total population of 42,725, including 13,452 skilled laborers, were employed directly in the naval yards.[35]

Kure was a conglomeration of fourteen villages centered around the small port prior to the designation of this site as a naval base in 1883. Three years later a navy ordinance authorized construction of an official Navy Yard in Kure. Most of the following structures were completed by 1889: office of the shipbuilding department; a wood-working shop; a machine shop for making ship's fittings; a ship engine manufacturing plant; a steel processing plant; a casting works; a wrought iron works; subsidiary machine shops; a boiler making plant; a torpedo boat plant; and the main dock. Sons of farming and fishing families were drawn into employment in the dockyards as the whole establishment expanded after the opening of the Navy Yard in 1890. Newly-laid streets were lined with banks, such as Sumitomo, and business firms, such as Takada Company and Okura-gumi, which supplied the Navy's needs. Kure's population increased from 11,000 in 1873 to 39,000 in 1898, and yet again to 60,000 in 1903.[36]

Sasebo was a poor farming-fishing village of only 3,000 residents prior to its designation as a naval base in 1883. A Marine Corps Headquarters was completed in 1889, followed by naval offices and warehouses. These buildings accommodated several thousands of navy personnel. Supply firms and a fish market prospered through services to the defense installations, and a soy sauce plant and *sake* brewery were developed in the city. Regulations governing Navy Yards were put into force in 1897, controlling also the 4,155 skilled civilians employed in the yards by 1898. A sizable number of steel foundries and machine plants were established to supply necessary parts to the large dockyards operations. The 1902 population of 50,000 marked a remarkable transformation from the humble village of only twenty years earlier.[37]

HIGHWAY STATION TOWNS. Changes in these towns also deserve attention because of the important functions they performed during the feudal period, and not because they expanded to city proportions. The highways were important links in the relationships of mutual dependency of the separate districts in the Edo era, especially in connecting the three cities of Edo, Ōsaka, and Kyōto with each other and with the castle and port towns. The location and size of cities cannot be said to have changed markedly, in every case, even after entering the Meiji period. Railway construction generally followed the old highway routes, and the fates of the highway station towns were affected drastically by the relative promixity of the new rail lines. Some of the station towns were close enough to the railroads to enjoy development as railroad station towns, while others were condemned to ruin by being by-passed.

Many of the highway towns possessed other functions, as they were combination castle, port, or temple towns. A relatively large group were combined castle-highway towns, such as Odawara, Numazu, Fuchū, Hamamatsu, Yoshida, Okazaki, Takasaki, Iwamurota, Koza, Utsunomiya, Shirakawa, Wakamatsu, Fukushima, Shiraishi, Sendai, Inchinoseki, Morioka, and Mito. Combination highway-port towns included Tsuchiura, Miya (Nagoya), Kuwana, Ōtsu, and Ōsaka. The third group of highway-temple towns included Miya, Nagano, Nikkō, and Uji-yamada. Railroad stations were placed in these towns, as terminal points or junctions, because of their importance in other areas, such as political, economic, and religious life. They too acquired large populations.

Towns with only the highway station function, though, did not have very large populations. According to a 1843 survey, the highway towns of more than 4,000 people were Fujisawa, Fujieda, Mishima, and Kanaya. Five towns had populations of over 3,000 namely, Ōiso, Kakegawa, Mitsuke, Arai, and Narumi. Twelve towns had over 2,000: Kawasaki, Hodogaya, Totsuka, Hiratsuka, Yoshiwara (Shizuoka Pref.), Kanbara, Okabe, Maisaka, Shirasuka, Minaguchi, Kusatsu, and Yodo. All of them lay along the primary Tōkaidō route. Another twenty highway towns had small populations ranging from 100 to 1,000.[38]

Many of these towns benefited from the construction of railroads in their immediate vicinities. But in all cases the railroads could not be made to coincide with highways designed for passage on foot or horseback. Foot travel can, as a rule, take a more direct route than railways, as the latter need more gradually graded courses. The railroads completely by-passed certain mountainous districts, such as the Hakone and Suzuka (west of Nagoya) Passes that the Tōkaidō route transversed. Even on open plains, the railroads made long detours around such towns as Goyu, Akasaka, Fujikawa, Okazaki, Chirifu, and Narumi on the Tōkaidō, and Kitsuregawa, Sakuyama, Ōtawara, and Ashino on the Ōshū highway.

Sometimes the reason for the detours was opposition by local residents, whether they were afraid visitors to the highway stations would decrease due to the noisy, dirty railroad stations, or whether they complained that the vibrations of passing trains would damage flowers and rice plants, or the poisonous smoke would hurt their crops. In any event, by-passed towns dropped radically in size and importance. Indeed, a few became extinct, with only the foundation stones remaining as reminders of their former existence. Such was the fate, for example, of Oiwake of Shinano district (west of Karuizawa on the Nakasendō route) and Sumo-modaira at Itaya Pass (in Yamagata district).[39]

Summarizing the main points of this section, we have seen that radical changes were forced inescapably upon the cities of Japan, and that to understand the nature and causes of those changes, the cities must be seen as integral parts of the total society. The changes came about in the process of carrying out sweeping reforms in politics, defense, economy, and education during the thirty years' period from 1868 to 1897.

In most cities the dominant warrior class was ruined. The cities lost their function as integrative centers of political, economic, and military activity within the feudal system, and likewise lost their privileged positions with respect to rural districts. Populations had been forged together by political power, and life was sustained by traditional techniques and political privilege. When the feudal powers and privileges were swept away, the city that did not replace its antiquated techniques with modern ones—whether port or castle town—did not grow. Some became veritable ghost towns.

Some of the castle and port towns were propitiously situated for assuming important functions in the new society, and this they did by performing one or more of the necessary political, economic, defense, or educational functions. Concretely, this meant construction of prefectural and municipal offices, business firms, banks, factories, schools, and military installations, backed by government and private capital.

Changes in such cities occurred at a rapid pace. Accustomed to relatively little change during the long Edo era, they were suddenly confronted with an accelerated rate of change, a pace that transformed their character overnight, as it were, from feudal political cities to modern industrial cities.

Population increase depended primarily on the rate at which a city could appropriate large-scale modern industry. Cities which experienced only modest population growth were those which developed some other character, as a political, educational, military, or cultural center.

Industrial development could proceed, though, only upon the premise of freedom in commercial activity. Because of the pervasive Tokugawa policies of insularity and self-sufficiency within each domain, and almost total national isolation from the rest of the world, there were no marked differences in the industrial structures of the feudal cities. Such structures were rigid, limited, and seldom specialized. Cities that developed rapidly after the Meiji Restoration were no longer merely integrative centers for their immediate districts, but grew in response to larger regional and national movements. The most effective form of response for urban expansion lay along the course of differentiated functions oriented to specialized industries connected with large urban or attractive foreign markets.

Among the rapidly developed cities of the early Meiji period, there were two types of special significance—the cities for international trade, and those with naval bases. There were no precedents in Japanese history for rapid expansion of a city through initiating contacts with foreign countries, certainly not in the centuries of seclusion under the Tokugawa regime. When the sails of the ship of state were shifted suddenly to accept trade relations with other countries, cities handling the new trade developed with exceeding rapidity. The naval base cities, designed as a complementary program for protecting and promoting the nation's new international position, also shared in the accelerated rate of expansion.

Hence, our definition of a modern city must include more than the integrative functions related to immediate surroundings; it must involve, rather, development of one or more specialized functions within larger national and international systems.

## 3. Changes in the Ecological and Social Structures of Tokyo

*Development of New Integrative Organs and Ecological Changes.*——In analyzing the passing of the feudal order and the emergence of the new social system, one must observe especially the effects of this process on the capital city of Tōkyō. By looking carefully into the transformation experienced by Tōkyō, one sees the character and extent of changes effected eventually in the whole of society, and in its relations to the larger international community. For this purpose, attention is focused upon the formation of various systems required in a modern state, and the ways in which contradictions between the old and new were overcome, or adjustments and compromises made.

The division and utilization of land according to status was one of the first of the feudal systems to be subjected to drastic alteration by the new government. The population of the city was rearranged into new ecological patterns as it once again began to expand. The expansion of the population stemmed from the introduction of new life into the capital through construction of new organs of politics, economy, and education. Such organs concentrated in Tōkyō at a rapid pace following the decision fixing the Edo capital as the integrative center for the new modern state.

Confusion reigned during the final days of resistance by the pro-shogunate forces against the take-over by the imperialist movement. To restore peace and order as quickly as possible, a provisional army headquarters (*Edo Chindai*) was set up in Edo Castle in May, 1868. Its commander had control over thirteen provinces in the eastern portion of the Kantō plain around Tōkyō. Immediate changes in municipal administration involved replacing the two town commissioners' offices (*machi-bugyō*) with a North and South Municipal Court that functioned much the same as the former commissioners' offices in maintaining public security.

When Edo was renamed Tōkyō in July, 1868, a more permanent Tōkyō Prefectural Army Headquarters (*Chinjufu*) was established, and the Tōkyō Prefectural Office was opened in September of the same year at the official quarters of the former Yanagisawa domain in Uchisaiwai-chō. The imperial residence was transferred to Tōkyō in October. In the following year (1869), when the feudal lords "returned their lands to the Emperor," the organs of government were moved from Kyōto and concentrated in the city. But this was not simply a matter of restoring the capital to Tōkyō and recalling the apparatus of government. The city gradually assumed both the appearance and structure of a modern capital city.

As Tōkyō adjusted to an urban prefectural system, the form and substance of municipal administration underwent drastic changes. The old system of township heads, which had administered the unit organs under the town commissioners, was abolished in March, 1869. In their stead a system of elders and assistant elders (*naka-doshiyori* and *soe-doshiyori*) were appointed, from among whom were selected certain managers and stewards (*sewagakari* and *kimoiri*). The five-household neighborhood units (*gonin-gumi*), and local township affairs were taken over by town elders (*machi-doshiyori*) who assumed the various functions previously performed by the neighborhood "bosses" (*yanushi*). The overall urban territory was subdivided into fifty wards (*ku*), in each of which one of the *naka-doshiyori* and an assistant *soe-doshiyori* handled administrative details. Over each of ten five-ward sections was placed one steward, or *sewagakari*.

The changes effected were external ones of offices and procedures, though, and not necessarily in the character and mentality of the personnel occupying the new posts. For instance, ward offices were constructed instead of using official residences, and elders were appointed by the prefectural government rather than succeeding to office by right of inheritance. Officials were no longer a privileged ruling group but, rather, duly appointed bureaucrats. Nonetheless, even though the people appointed were not particularly different from their predecessors, the revisions introduced into the control systems were in principle very important ones.

In April, 1871, the Family Registration Law was enacted by which the citizenry was registered on the basis of actual residence in specific wards, without regard to the defunct area classifications that had previously defined warrior, townsman, temple, or shrine districts. The registration was designed to overcome the social confusion resulting from dissolution of the domains, leaving thousands of people, warriors and commoners alike, without any distinct place in society. It was aimed at opening the way for normal employment for everyone by eliminating the status criterion from every citizen's residential position.

The government decided on a revision of the city ward system in 1871, establishing six larger wards (*daiku*), which were each subdivided into sixteen sections, or smaller wards (*shōku*). For each larger ward there was appointed a head called *sōchō*, with similar heads (*kochō*) and assistants for the smaller wards.

A further reorganization was implemented in September, 1878, through three new laws concerning administrative divisions of the prefectures and other smaller units. One of the laws stipulated the reorganization of counties, wards, townships, and villages (*Gunkuchōson Henseihō*) while the other two set up regulations to control urban and regional prefectural assemblies (*Fukenkai Kisoku*) and local taxation (*Chihōzei Kisoku*). These laws provided the new political authority with a good foundation for domestic controls. The regulations governing prefectural assemblies and local taxes embodied important steps in the direction of modernized government in that they provided for election of assembly members and for establishing tax collection methods that permitted dependable budget-planning.

The law on administrative units gave Tōkyō fifteen urban wards and six suburban counties. The fifteen wards were: Kōji-machi, Nihonbashi, Kyōbashi, Kanda, Shitaya, Asakusa, Shiba, Azabu, Akasaka, Yotsuya, Ushigome, Koishikawa, Hongō, Honjo, and Fukagawa. They extended over a slightly broader area than the urban area (*Shubikichi*) of old Edo. The six counties included the following: Higashi-Tama, Minami-Toshima, Kita-Toshima, Minami-Adachi, Minami-Katsushika, and Ebara. Both counties and wards had government-appointed officers who constituted the basic bureaucratic corps for local administration under the new government. The ward boundaries were fixed mainly on the basis of topographical criteria, though some consideration was given to the legacy of historical connections in particular areas, such as former warrior and townsmen districts.[40]

The number of members in each ward assembly was fixed according to the number of houses per ward as of July, 1878. Citizens were eligible for election to the assemblies if they were men over twenty-five years of age, had lived in a particular ward for three years or more, and paid land taxes of ten yen or above. Voting rights went to men twenty years of age or above, paying five yen or more in land taxes. These stipulations restricted the electorate and potential candidates to a narrow group paying relatively high taxes.

The assembly regulations introducing elections for wards, townships, and villages were issued in December, 1879. The old systems of public management began to crumble as the new systems of administration began to function.

The three new laws for self-government were epochal in themselves, but also a signs of things to come. As social conditions were stabilized after the confusion of governmental changeover, there arose strong demands among the people for more democratic rights, especially in terms of local administrative reforms. The government recognized the necessity for some degree of reform and, thus, instituted a new framework of local government for cities, towns, and villages (*Shichōsonsei*) in April, 1888, that went into effect in April of the following year. The Meiji leaders saw the importance of cultivating in the people the modern ideas of public participation in processes of self-government, and government concessions to demands for parliamentary rule created precedents through which the citizens could gain experience and understanding of basic forms of representative government.

In the new administrative system cities, towns, and villages were acknowledged as legally incorporated bodies with the right to enact laws and ordinances effective within their own administrative boundaries. The central administrative organ of a city was a council consisting of the mayor, his assistants, and elected members of the council, plus honorary members. Appointment of the mayor of Tōkyō was made by the Emperor from a list of three candidates submitted by the Ministry of Home Affairs, recommendations for these candidates having been made earlier by the City Council. Honorary members could be selected by the Council from among citizens twenty years of age or older who otherwise qualified as voters, though their selection had to be approved by the Governor of Tōkyō Prefecture (*Tōkyō-fu*).

Qualifications for candidacy to the Council itself required that a man be of Japanese nationality, twenty-five or older, resident in the city with citizen's rights for two years or more, and paying at least two yen in direct national or city land taxes. The basis was laid for shifting suffrage from land tax to direct national tax provisions, a significant step in the direction of modernization.

Even with these improvements, though, women were not granted suffrage, nor were tenant farmers. In fact, the two yen tax condition largely limited the franchise to higher ranking officials and operators of large enterprises. There were only 41,000 persons qualified to vote in the election of Council members out of a total population of 512,500 in the city of Tokyo in 1905. Voters themselves were classified according to taxes paid. Class A voters paid about one-third of the total submitted by the entire electorate, with one-third of the remainder paid by Class B voters. All other taxes came from Class C voters. According to Abe Isō, though, the relative strength of the Class A vote was about 1,012 times the elective power of the Class C vote.[41]

The metropolitan trio of Tōkyō, Ōsaka, and Kyōto were considered much too important for inclusion in the regular administrative system, and they were provided for in a Special Municipal System Law. This was done even though the general administrative framework was contained entirely within the centralized order of the Meiji government.

Tōkyō was granted incorporation rights as a city, but had no mayor or deputy mayors, nor even any offices or administrative personnel of its own. The mayoral duties were assumed by the Governor of Tōkyō, and his deputies and clerks performed the various tasks of municipal administration. These officials were under central government appointment, leaving Tōkyō with little in the way of organs of self-government, either in nature or in function. In the 1888 law for municipal systems, the wards (*ku*) were designated as units within a city structure but the heads of Tōkyō's wards worked directly under the Governor, a rather unreasonable arrangement that worked poorly. Public dissatisfaction was expressed at all levels in a vigorous campaign to have the "special cities" system rescinded. Finally, the City Council was dissolved and the government conceded to the opposition by canceling the "special cities" law in 1898.

A municipal office was set up within the prefectural administration, and a mayor and deputy-mayor were appointed. Administrative organs were established that gave Tōkyō the formal equipment of a self-governing modern city. The majority of the citizens, however, still could not vote or be elected to public office at any level, whether prefecture, city, or ward. Only a small minority of wealthier citizens exercised an electoral monopoly at each level.

The Meiji Restoration was not a thoroughgoing modern revolution but, rather, a movement to integrate the state through a centralized system with the sanction of traditional imperial authority. It was a reformation, of which the integrative organs were the major instruments; the driving force of the reformation operated through the functions of these organs which, along with the controlling groups of bureaucrats and military officers, were organized into a hierarchical structure of which the formal head was the Emperor. On the other hand, the total integrative system of society and state was oriented to the central roles of the nation's cities which, in turn, constituted an urban hierarchy of which Tōkyō was the summit and nucleus. Tōkyō's community structure, centering around the Emperor's residence in Tōkyō Castle, was the ecological counterpart of the integrative structure of the nation.

The Emperor Meiji established his residence in the Nishinomaru structure of Tōkyō Castle after his arrival in Tōkyō in March of 1869, and the Yamasato section of the castle was designated as the Imperial Sanctuary. The castle was renamed the Imperial Castle at that time. The grounds, locus of three centuries of military government, covered 108,398 *tsubo* (358,342 sq. m., or 88.5 acres).[42] Double moats surrounded the Honmaru and Nishinomaru structures, and the thirty-six guardhouses (*mitsuke*) of Edo days remained to seclude the emperor from the general public. The imperial residence gave a mystic aura to the capital, revealing the semi-modernized character of Meiji Japan.

The Imperial Castle was burned to the ground on May 5, 1873 by a fire originating in a court lady's room. It was reconstructed by 1888 with a 4.9 million yen budget (7.35 billion yen at current rates).[43] The old Nishinomaru residence was rebuilt in European style, but the Yamasato Sanctuary was restored in traditional Japanese style. At this juncture the name was changed to Imperial Palace (*Kyūjō*).

The ecological structure of feudal Edo derived from considerations of defense and residential areas based on status stratification. The ecological pattern of Tōkyō was reformed in accordance with a number of crucial social movements: (1) abrogation of feudal restrictions and prohibitions; (2) dissolution of the status system; (3) enforcement of laws providing for new city, town, and village organization; (4) introduction of European cultural forms; (5) progressive completion of large-scale political and economic organs of integration; and (6) emergence of new social classes. The official residences (i.e., domain offices) of the daimyō in the Kōji-machi section south and west of the Palace were converted into government offices, while in the Marunouchi section in front of the Palace wide streets were constructed that soon became filled with European-style company offices.

In the traditional commercial districts of Nihonbashi and Kyōbashi there arose many office buildings for companies and banks, interspersed with department stores, all done in European architectural modes. The Kanda section to the north of the Palace was transformed into an academic community, its streets lined with university buildings and book stalls. These areas with differentiated functions made up the inner core of the city, the enlarged integrative systems being connected with each other by modernized means of transportation and communication.

The factories built by the government or by private firms at the beginning of the Meiji period were located somewhat more distant from the Palace in Honjo, Asakusa, and Shiba. They were neither numerous nor large in scale. At this stage, most of the citizens earned their living in home industries operated at a crafts level, or in retail businesses no different from those of the Edo era. The industrial structure of Edo continued without any marked modification in the initial phase of the Meiji period. Likewise, the Edo merchants continued to control Tōkyō's markets in Nihonbashi, Kanda, and Asakusa quite as if the Meiji Restoration had never occurred.

Reformation came, as we indicated above, through the functioning of organs designed to replace feudal patterns and procedures with modern ones. The social and ecological reformation was accomplished, though, entirely through the political power of those who ruled and not of those being ruled. Even so, remarkable changes swept over the central part of the city, followed by gradual changes in the other parts of the city as new cultural forms and forces penetrated out from the inner core to equalize old disparities and reshape the entire city.

One important event that precipitated a more rapid rate of change in the central area of the city of Tokyo was a fire that broke out on the twenty-sixth of February, 1872, in the headquarters of the Army Department (Hyōbusho), which had once been the office of the Aizu fief. This fire enveloped 288,000 *tsubo* (235.2 acres) in forty-one townships in the Marunouchi, Kyōbashi, and Tsukiji districts. Some 19,872 residents lost their homes. Most of the old daimyō residences, government offices, and houses of officials were destroyed, not to be rebuilt for some time. The heart of the city lay devastated.

A new element was introduced into the city's layout at this point. The government felt it necessary to concentrate an Army contingent near the Imperial Palace in some of the space opened up by the great fire, as the country was not entirely peaceful. Barracks were built and a large parade ground was provided. Other portions of open area were used to build the Metropolitan Police Office at Kajibashi in 1882, followed by construction on the same site of the headquarters of the Fire Department and the Central Prison in 1884.

The First Division Army Headquarters and a Tōkyō garrison were erected near the moats around the Wadakura-mon and Babasaki-mon gates of the Palace. The Army in this period served chiefly as an imperial guard and to quell riots erupting in various places. Some 36,000 troops were stationed in the Tōkyō garrison, nearly half the total of armed men in the whole country.

Equipped to maintain peace and order, the government moved next to construction of the administrative offices needed to keep the nation moving. These new government structures were also clustered around the Palace, symbol of their undergirding authority.

A cabinet system was adopted in 1885, and many of its branch offices were erected in the Kasumigaseki section south of the Palace. Some were modeled after European styles, while others were located in former domain offices still standing. The following organs were transferred from Marunouchi to the Kasumigaseki area: the Ministry of Justice, the Supreme Court, the Court of Review for Misdemeanors, the Court of Appeals, and the Felony Court. Newly-constructed buildings were occupied by the Ministry of the Navy, the Ministry of Justice, the Tōkyō District Court, and an official residence was built for the Minister of Justice. Kasumigaseki became an auspicious center of government activity.

On a nearby hill the Diet Building was erected in 1890. Extensively connected with the many organs of civil, judicial, and defense administration throughout the whole country, the Diet location, combined with the Courts and Ministries, gave to the Kasumigaseki site a distinctive character as the nucleus of the national integrative framework, clearly distinguishing it from the castle centers of feudal society.

Auspicious as the government center was, the most important factor in overcoming regional isolation and welding the country together was the extended range of intensive integrative activity of economic and, especially, commercial organs.

The development of commerce and industry in the Edo period was characterized by the dominance of monopolistic wholesalers, parasitic profiteers spawned by the protection and patronage of feudal lords and supported by the productive labors of the vast majority of the people. The Meiji government aimed at involving much larger numbers of the people in modern systems of production in the form of joint-stock corporations, by which they hoped to catch up quickly with the advanced countries of Europe and North America. This program was helped in part by the active participation of ex-samurai who brought to it some of the capital resources accumulated in the previous period. Their contribution included also leadership in the semi-official enterprises organized or encouraged by the government.

Following issuance of the new Commercial Code (*Shōhō-tai-i*) in 1868, an official government organ was established to control international trade and transportation, finance, and commerce (Tsushōshi). Its purpose was to strengthen the competitive position of Japanese merchants in international trade, which was largely commanded by the foreign traders. Mitsui Hachiroemon was appointed general director, and the main office was established in Tōkyō with branch offices in port towns and cities handling overseas trading. The primary function of this organ was to focus the total resources of the nation into support for founding trading and exchange companies capable of competing successfully in the international market.

Exchange companies were established in the larger cities in May, 1869, modeled after foreign banks. The Tōkyō Exchange was founded at Nihonbashi, taking the lead in both domestic and overseas trading and drawing on the support of many wealthy people. A shipping firm under semi-government management was formed about the same time at Reiganjima in Tōkyō, in conjunction with the establishment of a foreign trade company. The shipping firm purchased some steamships, made in Europe, to operate a line between Tōkyō and Ōsaka. Commodities handled on the Edo era *Higaki-kaisen* were transported by this shipping company and new items, such as rice bran and straw mats, were added.

Of central concern to the government was formation of a concrete system of financing to promote industrial development, through the incorporation of joint-stock companies as provided for in the banking laws. The Mitsui and Ono interests, which were in charge of handling credit notes, were asked by the government to form modern banks. In 1873 the First National Bank (Dai-ichi Kokuritsu Ginkō) was established in Nihonbashi, housed in a European style building.[44] Following revision of the banking laws in 1876, many private banks were opened by the Mitsui group and others.

Enactment of the Stock Exchange Law in 1874 prompted establishment of rice exchanges throughout the country. The central exchanges were at Kakigara-chō and Kabuto-chō on opposite sides of the Sotobori canal in Nihonbashi.

Development of the banking business engendered greater understanding of the business functions of joint-stock enterprises among the people. Many firms were founded in the Nihonbashi and Kyōbashi districts, such as Rikuun-moto-gaisha, Mitsui Bussan Kaisha, Kōgyōsha, Eiransha, Kōtsūsha, Ōkura-gumi, and Kiritsu-Kōshōsha. It is hardly necessary here to comment on the success of the Mitsui firm in developing an extensive volume of foreign trading business. Special government support was given the Kōgyōsha firm to advance commercial activities on the Chinese mainland. A branch office of this firm was opened in Shanghai to pioneer in business relations with China under protection of the Japanese government. Similar privileged treatment from the government enabled the Land Transportation Company to gain a monopoly in the transport and communications business.[45]

Social forces were realigned to build up the foundation for an industrial revolution in Japan. Transportation improvements were deemed especially important to activate free interchange of commodities, thereby strengthening the domestic market and broadening its capital base. This emphasis got under way seriously around 1877.

In 1881 the Japan Railway Company was founded with a capital base drawn mainly from the public bonds issued to warriors, a gigantic capital for its day of 20 million yen. The highly profitable record of this government-owned company prompted the formation of many private rail companies in various parts of Japan. Inevitably, the railroads intensified the integrative movements in politics and the economy, focused centrally on Tōkyō.

Government policies, revised banking systems, and expanded rail facilities worked together to create a context in which corporation ventures flourished. There were only twenty such firms in Kyōbashi by 1886. Fourteen new companies were formed in the following year, and thirty-one more in 1888. The corporation count for both Nihonbashi and Kyōbashi reached 174 by 1897.[46]

Capital investments in the Kyōbashi district totalled more than 30 million yen in 1903, 80% of which went into joint-stock corporations. Classified according to the nature of the business done, the corporation investments ran as follows:

| | |
|---|---|
| Transportation and industrial firms | 70% |
| Mining companies | 20% |
| Commercial firms | 5% |

Just as leadership in the new government had been taken by former warriors of the old Satsuma, Chōshū, Tosa, and Hizen domains, so merchant households from these provinces seized leadership in the new economy by capitalizing on favors extended by fellow leaders in government. Tightly organized into giant financial cliques (*zaibatsu*), these households provided the motive power in Japanese industrial development.

The stock formation procedures of these firms served to differentiate the functions of management from the ownership of capital stock. Most of the managerial staffs of the firms came from two groups, namely, ex-warriors with experience as governing officials, and merchants accustomed to dealing with political authorities. They were distinguished from ordinary merchants by the appellation "gentlemen merchants" and constituted a distinctly new social class.[47]

The government organs and business firms concentrated in Marunouchi, Nihonbashi, and Kyōbashi played a central role in connecting Tōkyō with both national regions and international society. This role precipitated the reshaping of the structure and functions of the central area of the city of Tōkyō. This transforming process was greatly aided by still another development, namely, establishment of commodity-display markets (*kankōba*) and department stores closely geared to the consumer needs of Tōkyō's citizenry. In short, there was added to the international and national roles of the city a strong municipal function.

The 1878 Industrial Exhibition of Japan opened at Ueno had several objectives: one was the introduction of modern technology and its dissemination in society; another was expansion of the domestic market; and a third was attraction of new customers. After the Exhibition closed, the exhibitive method was appropriated in a new style of market in Nagatachō (Kōji-machi ward) called *kankōba*. There were a number of these bazaar-type shops which made a point of effective display of various kinds of goods for sale.

Consumers in Tokyo were stimulated by this approach to merchandizing which met so well their heightened desires to improve their standards of living and to adapt to the style of the new era. The *kankōba* spread rapidly throughout the city, numbering as many as 297 in 1902. Eleven of them in the Nihonbashi-Kyōbashi district drew large crowds. As roads improved and streetcars were installed, bringing even larger crowds, the *kankōba* style of retailing evolved into large-scale department stores. Incidentally, the man-drawn rickshaw added to the low cost transportation mobility that fed into this new development.

In describing retailers of the Edo era, we made reference to the famous dry goods store called Echigoya Gofukuten and its success with specialized retail methods such as no credit sales, no discounts even in cash sales, and willingness to sell woven goods by the piece instead of by the entire roll. The master of this shop, by virtue of having supported the anti-shogunate forces with financial contributions, enjoyed intimate political affiliations that were of great benefit in the expansion of his business.

Echigoya was renamed Mitsukoshi in 1872 when its retail accounts were separated from its parent-group, the Mitsui household, to form an independent company. It was reorganized as an unlimited partnership in 1895 under the new commercial code. Fresh executive talent was sought among young men who had studied abroad in the United States, and a new managerial system was set up in the store. Old-fashioned account books were abandoned in favor of Western-style bookkeeping. The overall management of the department store was put under a general manager who then supervised the various departments and sections that had charge of highly specialized sales.

The traditional system of having clerks seated about the floor to greet customers and later show them various goods was replaced by effective exhibition of a wide variety of goods to attract the customers' attention. Trucks were acquired to make deliveries. Through a series of such reform measures, Mitsukoshi laid the foundation for the modern operation of a department store. The old store was replaced by a three-storied building done in Renaissance styling, giving the firm a modernized external appearance in addition to its updated internal operations.[48]

Shirokiya, an old sundries shop, founded a department store for ladies' apparel in 1886. It sought to capitalize on the almost fanatic fad for Western dress among upper class ladies and students provoked by activities at an extravagant hall, called Rokumeikan, established by the government to dine and dance foreign guests. These days were the "Gay Nineties" in Japan, and Shirokiya imported a certain Miss Curtis from Great Britain to supervise displays in the new department store. This store also moved into a three-storied structure in 1903, and adopted the method of exhibiting wares instead of keeping them in storerooms for clerks stationed on the sales floor to bring out after arousing customer interest. Clerks were still needed, though, and this store had 150, many of them girls.[49]

Other department stores soon appeared, such as Takashimaya, Matsuya, and Matsuzakaya, which were joint-stock companies formed by absorbing the capital of many smaller shops. The department stores evolved into the dominant powers in the retail field, by operating on a scale larger than ever before imagined, and by revolutionizing the retail function. That is, small local shops would never have shared the department stores' keen interest in promoting so constant and complete a flow of customers in and out of the city's central area.

The overall geographical range of customers served by these stores extended over vast areas, due to progress made in low-rate transportation facilities, especially among upper and middle class citizens. But the customers actually utilized two sources in obtaining goods: one, of course, were the large-scale, centrally-located department stores; the other the small-scale shops in local neighborhoods. The means of transportation were not developed so highly as to make the central department stores always convenient sources. To cope with this, the stores instituted a messenger service called *goyōkiki*, a corps of young men who visited individual households to take orders for goods.

Shirokiya cultivated a clientele of good customers first in the Nihonbashi area, then extended its customer service to Fukagawa and Honjo eastward, and to Kyōbashi, then to Shiba and Shinagawa in the southern section of the city. It also acquired a clientele among cultured families living in the hill sections of Hongō, Koishikawa, Kōji-machi, Azabu, and Takanawa. Customers were also cultivated among the old feudal families, such as Date, Sōma, Mōri, Abe, Matsudaira, and Hotta.

Salesmen making their rounds carried a bundle of dry goods on their shoulders, and offered special services such as helping housewives and maids with the proper airing and other maintenance of clothes. They developed special relations with loyal customers who reciprocated by refusing to patronize salesmen from other stores, a form and spirit in patron-merchant relations not unknown in premodern Japan.[50] Indeed, the cultivation of middle and upper class customers by the dominant retail merchants in Nihonbashi to assure steady prosperity reminds one very much of the feudal era.

The changing forms and functions of commercial enterprises in the Nihonbashi district had certain effects on other commodities. The fish markets that had flourished in the Edo period in Motofune-chō, Honda-wara-chō, and Anjin-chō began to experience various changes stemming from the new economic situation.

The government offered special protection to the fishing industry in both fishing techniques and sales operations, and the quantity of fish delivered to the market rose. In 1881 and 1882 the government ran off new issues of currency to finance suppression of the last major effort by feudal forces to oppose the Meiji government, led by Saigō Tsugumichi and called the Battle of Seinan (or the Satsuma Rebellion). At the same time restrictions on fish sales were lifted. Ready money and an open market combined to break the control of boss-dealer collusions over the fish market.

Fish deliveries direct to neighborhood markets were begun, and as the sardine catch fell off fishers competed fiercely to bring in catches as large as possible. The wholesaling and distributing mechanisms began to disintegrate, forcing the Nihonbashi fish markets to undertake drastic changes. Official responsibility for the fishing trade rested in the prefectural office of Tōkyō, which moved to establish a new order in the productive and distributive systems of the fish market. A central collection and distribution agency was established at Uogashi, bringing a degree of order to the fish business, including stabler prices.

Similar action was taken with respect to other commodities. The Rice Exchange in Kakigara-chō and the Stock Exchange in Kabuto-cho were the nerve centers of the entire economic system, reflecting shifts occurring anywhere in the country's economy.

The new government had, since the time of its establishment in 1868, met with repeated difficulties in its attempts at controlling the rice market. In August of 1876 it promulgated a law concerning the Rice Exchange, at first founding two offices in Kabuto-chō and Kakigara-chō, and providing for an open market with fixed price quotations. Later these two offices were amalgamated into a single Rice Exchange in Kakigara-chō in order to eliminate certain disadvantages stemming from competition between two separate exchange offices. The exchange systems of all other commodities were later absorbed into the Kakigara-chō office, now renamed the Tōkyō Rice and Commodity Exchange (Tokyo Beikoku Shōhin Torihikisho). Quotations for various commodities produced all over the nation were available, including rice, salt, cereals, fertilizers, sugar, oil, metals, and cotton, both raw and yarns.[51]

An exchange law concerning securities enacted in 1878 established the Tōkyō Stock Exchange (Tōkyō Kabushiki Torihikisho), which was located in Kabuto-chō. Public bonds were issued at that time by the Japanese and foreign governments, although the majority were bonds issued in compensation of stipend losses by the warriors (*Kinroku Kōsai*). Around 1887 shares of industrial companies appeared on the Exchange. Joint-stock companies flourished in the spinning, marine and rail transportation industries.[52]

The Ōsaka Stock Exchange was founded in Kitahama in 1878. It served, with the Tōkyō Exchange, as a barometer of the development of Japanese capitalism, the two being highly sensitive nerve centers of all economic organs in the land.

In addition to these political and economic organs of national integration centered in Tōkyō, there were important organs of cultural integration. In 1869 the government university, Daigakukō, was formed by consolidating the school of Chinese classics (Shōheikō), the medical school of the shogunate (Igakusho), and the shogunate's agency for studying imported foreign documents (Bansho-shirabesho, or later, Kaiseisho). Reorganized later (1877) as Tōkyō University (Tōkyō Daigaku) and renamed Tōkyō Imperial University (Tōkyō Teikoku Daigaku) by a 1886 decree, it was located in Hongō on the grounds of the old feudal office of the Maeda household of Kaga domain. The first university in modern Japan, it was soon followed by the establishment of a number of private universities such as Keiō Gijuku (first founded as a private academy in 1858); Meiji, Hōsei, and Senshū (1880); Waseda (1882); and Nihon (1888). These universites all developed their own distinctive school characters, and attracted students from all parts of the country.

Demands for educated men far outstripped supply in those days, so that graduates of the universities were guaranteed good positions and rapid promotion in nearly every field of society. Ambitious young men were easily attracted to the institutions of higher education in Tōkyō. Most of them desired appointment in government offices and, accordingly, enrollment in the law courses of the schools swelled. During the two years of 1878 and 1879 there were fifteen graduates of Tōkyō Imperial University receiving the Bachelor of Laws degree. Four of them were born in Tōkyō, and the others were from the following prefectures: two from Kōchi, and one each from Ishikawa, Chiba, Okayama, Saitama, Shiga, Gunma, Yamaguchi, Ehime, and Aomori. Only one of them came from a commoner's household. Most of them were related to high-ranking bureaucrats who were originally warriors of the various domains, and they were able students. Only later could there be found among university graduates those who were sons of upper class landowners and merchants.[53]

Keiō Gijuku was founded by Fukuzawa Yukichi, who stressed the ideas of the common rights of man in harmony with individual freedom, and that every man should discipline himself by exercising diligence and frugality so that his own success would benefit others as well. This school bred many men of ability who became business leaders. Popularly referred to as Keiō University, most of its students up to 1871 came from families of samurai pedigree. After that time sons of commoners increased. In 1883 only 42% of the 396 students in the university were of warrior background, clearly outnumbered by the 57% from common families.[54]

The Tōkyō School of Fine Arts and the Tōkyō Academy of Music were founded in the Ueno section. Research institutes founded in these early years were the Central Meteorological Observatory, Tokyo Astronomical Observatory, and the Institute for Research in Infectious Diseases.

The Tōkyō Library (now Ueno Library) was built in Ueno Park in 1872, followed in 1882 by the National Museum and Zoo in the same public park.

Although there remained considerable feudal residue in the many social structures being transformed into modernized systems, the most influential ingredient for positive realization of the modernization process was the flow of ideas into the nation from the West. Whereas university education was limited to a select few, the founding of news agencies opened up a much broader channel for the flow of new ideas to a wider public. Newspapers had been published on a limited scale in Nagasaki and Yokohama prior to the Restoration. The first newspaper issued daily in Tōkyō appeared in 1872, the *Tōkyō Nichinichi* (Tokyo Daily). It was followed by *Yūbin Hōchi* (Mail Report), *Yomiuri Chūgai* (Yomiuri Domestic and Foreign News), and others. Newspaper offices centered in the Ginza around 1884–5. They took great, and justifiable, pride in their roles as pioneers in introducing the ideas of modern civilization into their own society. The newspapers fought a vigorous and, ultimately, successful battle to defend editorial rights against government pressures. Since 1888, when the *Asahi Shimbun* (Asahi News) was founded, the affairs of government and society in general have been reported daily.

In addition to newspapers, there were many publishing companies that gathered in the Ginza area, such as Hakubunkan, Tōyōsha, Sekibunsha, Saishōsha, Sanbokudō, and Kokubunsha. Ginza became the center of mass media for Tōkyō, and Tōkyō itself the nation's mecca of the printed word.

The cultivation of international relations received visible manifestation in the diplomatic and consular offices erected in the capital city. Hotels, private residences, and shops catering to the new foreign community were built in the Tsukiji area between Ginza and Tōkyō bay. Mention has already been made of the grand social hall constructed for entertaining foreign envoys and holding various international social gatherings, the famous Rokumeikan. This hall had its own special cultural role as a center for transmitting the manners and customs of Western society through visual presentation before the Japanese high society crowd who frequented the hall.

The seeds of a truly modern city were planted in the central districts of Tōkyō, in Kōji-machi, Marunouchi, Nihonbashi, Kyōbashi, and Ginza. The institutions operative in these districts proceeded to expand in dimension and functions, gradually penetrating not only surrounding areas in Tōkyō but, through improved communications and extension of the differentiated political, economic, educational, and military agencies, into other cities and regions of the country. Even while these seeds of modernization sank roots in central Tōkyō and sprouted new branches in suburban areas and other cities, there remained, even in central Tōkyō, many species of traditional culture. The older systems and organs were only gradually transformed by the modernizing forces. The conversion process had two directional thrusts, one geographically defined from central Tōkyō to outlying districts, the other moving vertically from the upper class to the lower strata of society.

In the commercial communities of Nihonbashi, Kyōbashi, Kanda, and Asakusa, most of the wholesalers and merchants held firmly to traditional reins of influence, even after institution of the Meiji reforms and the partial modernization of Tōkyō. Drastic changes were least to be expected among the wholesalers and merchants who had managed well enough in the old society. In time, though, they were compelled to adapt their own businesses and behavior to the new conditions of government and economy.

According to a statistical report on Tōkyō Prefecture for that period (*Tōkyō-fu Tōkeisho*), there were 4,401 wholesalers in all Tōkyō in 1882, distributed as follows:

| *Ward* | *Number* | *Ward* | *Number* |
|---|---|---|---|
| Nihonbashi | 1,536 | Asakusa | 270 |
| Kanda | 1,128 | Honjo | 267 |
| Kyōbashi | 398 | Shiba | 180 |
| | | Fukagawa | 146 |

It is quite evident that the three wards on the left above, in central Tōkyō, contained an overwhelming majority of the wholesalers. A similar concentration of brokers in the central part of the city is clear from the following figures:[55]

| *Ward* | *Number* | *Ward* | *Number* |
|---|---|---|---|
| Nihonbashi | 555 | Ebara | 338 |
| Kanda | 470 | Fukagawa | 124 |
| Kyōbashi | 295 | Higashi-Tama-gun and Minami-Toshima-gun | 119 |

In Edo times, the wholesale organizations in the capital handled all goods coming into the city for distribution to retailers, as they also collected commodities from local producers for shipment to other provinces. Their monopolization of the distributive system and consequent influence in the total economy was due not only to entrepenuerial expertise but derived largely from political privileges that strictly differentiated their own function from the retailing function.

The wholesale associations fell apart after their privileges were canceled and a moratorium was declared on debts incurred by the shogunate in borrowing from the wholesalers. The economic and social confusion that followed these blows to the crucial wholesaling agencies was not resolved easily or soon.

The Meiji leaders took early steps, however, toward revising the country's economic mechanisms, beginning with announcement of the commercial code (*Shōhō-tai-i*) in 1868. The code aimed not merely at stripping the wholesalers of exclusive rights, but more positively at liberating the citizenry from status restrictions, giving them freedom to select their own occupations. With this new stance the government hoped to increase gross national production.

Conversion to a free economy, however, brought unexpected confusion in the market, and prices began to rise sharply. Reluctantly, the government approved a temporary reinstatement of the wholesale associations in 1871. As transportation facilities developed sufficiently to permit freer movement of people and goods, the government decided once again, in 1873, to liquidate the wholesale associations. In time they were completely eliminated. Shipping agents in local districts could now consign shipments to anyone they chose, and liberalization of commercial activity was promoted throughout the land. Brokers were free to transact business with producers and retailers directly, disregarding the customary wholesale channels.

Faced with the possibility of complete dissolution, the wholesalers altered the character of their operations to buying and selling with their own capital instead of dealing on a consignment basis. The distinction between the wholesaling and brokerage business faded. Or, they became wholesalers more in the modern sense of large-scale merchandizing of goods to local retailers. The outcome was that the pervasive power of groups of wholesalers over large areas of private enterprise was greatly diminished.[56]

As long as many products continued to be made at small-scale home industries, the wholesalers could stay in business, supplying raw materials to the home industry operators and collecting their products for marketing. It was only after the emergence of large-scale industries from 1897 on, that they lost their distinctive function and ability to compete.

A secondary function of the wholesalers served to sustain them for some time, namely, the inns they operated in the wholesale districts to accommodate customers. Yokoyama-chō had the largest concentration of big wholesalers in a district ranging from Nihonbashi to Asakusa, a fact reflected in the large concentration of inns in nearby Bakuro-chō.

Travel in the early part of the Meiji period was much improved over Edo times, though nothing like the rapid transit system of today. There was a limit to the distances that could be covered in a day by the new railways. The extent of the accommodations provided in the commercial and wholesale districts, out of a total number of 269 inns in Tōkyō in 1896, can be seen in the following list:

| *Ward* | *No. of inns* | *Ward* | *No. of inns* |
|---|---|---|---|
| Nihonbashi | 60 | Hongō | 28 |
| Kanda | 39 | Asakusa | 18 |
| Kyōbashi | 37 | | |

Inns in Nihonbashi and Kyōbashi alone constituted 38% of all the inns in Tōkyō's fifteen wards.

There were two types of inns in Bakuro-chō, a more general sort for sightseers (*dōsha-yado*), and inns reserved for those coming on legal business (*kuji-yado*). But the inns were not just for overnight lodging; they were virtual trade centers. Merchants stopping at the inns were treated to exhibitions (*yado-zeri*) of commodity samples by wholesalers competing for customers in the Bakuro-chō inns. The inns were marketplaces as much as the more officially designated places.

Rail facilities made it possible for more people than ever before to visit Tōkyō for sightseeing, and curiosity about the new modern structures drew great crowds into the capital. Such travelers preferred accommodations nearer the railroad stations. Bakuro-chō was too removed from the stations, and its trade dwindled.[57]

Local retail shops, in contrast to the business firms and the wholesale and brokerage houses concentrated in the city's center, were fairly evenly distributed throughout the various wards. These shops were the intermediary channels between consumers, on the one hand, and producers and wholesalers, on the other. Of a total of 41,382 retailers in Tokyo in 1882, ward distribution was as follows:[58]

| *Ward* | *No. of shops* | *Ward* | *No. of shops* |
|---|---|---|---|
| Kanda | 7,546 | Shiba | 2,607 |
| Kyōbashi | 3,444 | Ebara | 2,554 |
| Asakusa | 3,071 | Fukagawa | 2,168 |
| Nihonbashi | 2,564 | Hongō | 1,907 |
| Honjo | 2,562 | Koishikawa | 1,278 |
| Shitaya | 2,787 | | |

While the numbers of shops were well distributed, the volume of trade and the merchandizing patterns were not uniform. Nihonbashi and Kyōbashi each had its grand old houses of high quality traditional goods, to which were added the latest items imported from Western countries. Merchants in the heart of the city were proud of their tradition as the nation's best stores, and were careful to cultivate their reputations among the people. Special attention was given to groups of loyal customers in and outside the city.

The character of the retail shops was altered noticeably by the improved transportation facilities that activated the internal flow of population within the city. Shops in the central portion of the city, other than department stores and other large establishments, switched from supplying daily necessities for local residents to specialized merchandizing that catered to pedestrian crowds coming into the central area. Handling of a wide range of items was replaced by specialization in goods of guaranteed quality on a large scale. Moreover, retailers who had once produced their own goods dropped their own production as the same items gradually came to be manufactured at lower costs by large-scale industries which realized profits primarily through commissions earned on retail sales.

Introduction of foreign products led to the development of a new retailing zone in the Ginza, in addition to the traditional center of Nihonbashi, Kanda, and Kyōbashi. Actually the main street of the Ginza area was a rather poor, dirty street at the beginning of the Meiji period, even though it was a part of the major Tōkaidō highway leading into the better Nihonbashi district. Along the section between Owari-chō and

Shinbashi there were many humble dwellings of low ranking samurai and craftsmen. Most of these houses were roofed with wooden shingles, only a few having the more expensive roofing tiles or being equipped with private storehouses (*dozō*). Even in Shinbashi, the *sake* shops were no better than simple tea stalls.

The Meiji government was anxious to improve the appearance of the city in accordance with Western standards and, after the big fire of 1872, notified all parties concerned that all buildings constructed in central Tōkyō were required to make use of brick or stone architecture. Reconstruction plans aimed as much at fire prevention as at appearance. Styles in Paris became the model for rebuilt city streets, while London's architectural designs were the guide for reconstructed buildings.

Yuri Kimimasa, Governor of Tōkyō Prefecture at that time, engaged a British engineer, Thomas Waters, as superintendent for the reconstruction of the main street between Kyōbashi and Shinbashi. A terminal was built for the new Tōkyō-Yokohama railway at Shinbashi. Buildings along the street were rebuilt as two-storied imitations of Victorian structures, with balconies. The street itself was widened from the former width of 10 *ken* (19.8 yds.) to 15 *ken* (29.8 yds.), and was paved with bricks. It was also divided into pedestrian and vehicular lanes, with trees planted along the walks. The reconstruction work was completed in 1876.[59]

Eighty-five gas lights were provided along both sides of the street in 1873, causing great astonishment among the citizens who, on first seeing the strange new illumination, remarked that night had been converted into day. Horse-drawn streetcars were installed between Shinbashi and Nihonbashi in 1882, and were extended to Asakusa in 1897. The novel *jinrikisha* was invented in 1870, and was widely utilized for inner city travel. For a people denied even the use of palanquins since 1665, the new means of urban transportation were nothing short of marvelous.

Between Shinbashi, new gateway to Tokyo, and the prosperous Nihonbashi center, a new style of shopping street emerged along the Ginza. Specialized shops for tailoring, printing, watches, as well as restaurants, fruit stores, and shops featuring Western furniture and footwear attracted a new clientele of business executives and salaried men that emerged in the process of modernization. Catering to particular customers by means of specialized services, these shops did not seek to draw the passing pedestrians so much as did the many clothing, notions, and *sake* shops along the main street. All of them, however, were more interested in the daily transient population than in local residents.

Capitalizing on the surge of interest in Western goods and fashions, Ginza gradually captured Nihonbashi's place. The Ginza merchants were greatly helped by the government's efforts in creating a modern, Western façade in the Ginza area. That façade covered only the main street, however, as the side lanes and back streets remained unchanged. Even when residents rebuilt their houses on off-Ginza streets, they were finished with the old style plastered walls and shingles.[60]

Although central Tōkyō developed as the modernized nucleus of a larger metropolitan area, the fact that the surrounding areas were part of a metropolis meant that large community centers for commerce were needed to supply the daily needs of the vast population. In the broad flats nearer the bay there were such centers in Ueno-hirokōji, Asakusa-hirokōji, Kanda, Ogawamachi-dōri, Ningyō-chō, and Monzennaka-chō in Fukagawa. In the rambling hills west of the Palace, there were Kōjimachi-dōrisuji, Yotsuya-ōyokochō, Ushigome-kagurazaka, and Azabu-jūban.

In these centers there were dozens of small shops selling sweet cakes, rice, *sake*, notions, medicines, accessories, Japanese-style footwear, as well as traditional restaurants.[61] The community centers also included the *kankōba* shops for displaying goods, and certain amusement stalls such as *yose* (a story-teller's parlor), billiard parlors, and archery ranges.

Asakusa had been the chief amusement center since the Edo era, with wholesalers and the Kannon Temple of the goddess of mercy sharing its precincts. Beyond the Sensō-ji temple stood Okuyama, a remote hill, adding beauty to its busy life. In 1884 an amusement center called Rokku was built on the site of a reclaimed pond. Soon the original atmosphere provided by the religious structures was thoroughly engulfed by new recreation facilities. An amusement hall called Panorama Hall was built, plus a zoo and a large flower exhibition hall. A tower of twelve stories called *Ryō-un-kaku*, "tower over the clouds," with an elevator, was completed in 1899—the first high tower constructed in Japan. It stood as a symbol of the fad for modernity among the common people. Around it gathered theaters, movie houses, and other showplaces. The local neighborhoods lacked such amusement facilities, and Asakusa soon became the most popular place in all Tokyo.[62]

There was also an amusement center with many specialty shops in front of the Yushima Tenjin Shrine in Ueno. A Buddhist temple with extensive grounds, called Kan-ei-ji, was burned down during the battle in 1868 between the imperialist forces and the die-hard troops loyal to the shogunate. The grounds of Kan-ei-ji were converted into Ueno Park in 1873, though it was without any particular park facilities at first. An exhibition hall was built in 1877, and in 1882 a museum and zoo, combining educational and recreational facilities for the people's enjoyment. Most of the lowland area (Shitaya) around Ueno had been occupied by samurai residences and temples in the Edo period, except for the lone commercial center in Ueno-hirokōji, which thrived between 1764 and 1843. In that location there were many shops, restaurants, tea houses, and story-tellers' parlors, as well as the prosperous dry goods store of the Matsuzakaya house.[63] In 1882 a horse-drawn streetcar was installed that connected Shinbashi and Ueno. In the following year a railway between Ueno and Kumagaya was completed by the Japan Railway Company, and this line was extended far north to Aomori in 1891. Ueno supplanted Senju as the city's main northern entrance, with many travelers gathering in its shops and inns, making it the major sub-center of the metropolis.

According to the descriptions given by Okui Fukutarō, the urban area of Tōkyō toward the end of the Meiji period could be encompassed by a circle with a four-kilometer radius, taking the present site of Tōkyō Station as the center. The eastern sector reached to Honjo and Fukagawa, the northern boundary to Ueno Park. The western area of the circle extended to present-day Yotsuya, Shinano-machi, and the Meiji Outer Gardens (*Gaien*). The southern side of the circle passed through Mita and the present Yamate Line station of Tamachi. Beyond the imaginary circle lay what was, at that time, the suburban areas.

The present-day Outer Gardens of Meiji Shrine was formerly the official Aoyama Parade Ground. The area alongside the Chūo Line of the National Railway from Sendagaya (by the Outer Gardens) to Ōkubo (west of present-day Shinjuku) developed early in the Meiji era as a suburban residential area. Areas near Ueno Park developed similarly. The flatlands beyond Honjo and Fukagawa were not densely settled. The Mita area was rather well developed, since the main road to Shinagawa ran through it, although just beyond was a hilltop section called Takanawa that was an upper class residential area.

These residential sections contained few people who were born there originally. Many of the houses belonged to townspeople with permanent residences that were more centrally located, that is, they were villas used as retirement homes. The owners also used the villas for entertaining guests, or for sheer enjoyment of the changing seasons. At any rate, they had little need for modern travel conveniences connected with the central urban area, and little was developed.[64]

As the Meiji period progressed, the expanded organs of government and commerce, that brought so many radical changes to central Tōkyō, prompted similarly extensive changes in the suburban areas. These changes can be grasped by reviewing conditions in the four highway stations towns of Shinagawa, Naito-Shinjuku, Senju, and Itabashi that were just outside the imaginary circle described above.

The inns of Shinagawa had usually been so crowded in Edo times by warriors on official business, that it was difficult for them to accommodate ordinary travelers. But the social confusion surrounding the fall of the shogunate discouraged most people from making trips. Added difficulties for the owners of the inns in maintaining operations were caused by big fires in 1866 and 1867.

In 1872 the government issued an anti-prostitution law, but the Shinagawa inns simply changed their names to "rooming houses" (*kashizashiki*) to cover up the system of secondary services by room maids, in a covert effort to stay in business. The highway station system was suspended in the same year, as the new rail service between Tōkyō and Yokohama was opened, making stopovers in Shinagawa unnecessary. The inns thus fell further into financial depression as the number of visitors decreased sharply.[65]

Although cultivation of edible seaweed (*nori*) had been developed in former generations along the seashore near Shinagawa, the number of applicants wishing to enlarge or develop *nori* cultivation areas increased around 1885–6. An association of seaweed and oyster growers was founded about this time. Construction of factories along the coastal region between Tōkyō and Yokohama was begun in 1897. Factories appeared one after the other, leading later to the extended Keihin (Tōkyō-Yokohama) industrial belt along the seashore.[66]

There were many brothels in the Naito-Shinjuku station town up to the very end of the Tokugawa era, but this activity declined after the Meiji reforms were instituted. Later, some ten of them reopened as "rooming houses," but the Naito-Shinjuku district did not share in the prosperity of the early Meiji period.

The nearest center of commercial importance was Ōyoko-chō in the Yotsuya area, with a number of shops handling charcoal shipped from the Kōshū and Tōhoku districts. A station on the Yamate loop line was located in Shinjuku in 1885, which became also a terminal station for the Kōfu Line in 1889. Both cargo and passenger traffic to this station increased thereafter.[67]

Although Senju on the Nikkō highway forfeited to Ueno the claim to being the major entrance for traffic coming from the northern regions, its own strategic location near Ueno and the northbound traffic gave it a share in the prosperity of the Meiji era. The town developed from a highway station town into a suburban area of Tōkyō city, eventually annexed to the growing urban area. Paddy-fields were transformed into vegetable farms to supply the urban districts, and open fields were utilized as residential or factory sites.

Senju Spinning Mill was built in 1879, employing as many as 25,000 workers within a few years. Along the Arakawa river running through the Senju district, the following large factories were built:

| *Construction year* | *Factory name* |
|---|---|
| 1886 | Tōkyō Cardboard Co., Ltd. |
| 1888 | Senju Mill, Ōji Paper Co., Ltd. |
| 1893 | Senju Plant, Tōkyō Gas Co., Ltd. |

In the latter part of the Meiji period many medium and small industries were built along the road from Senju to Nippori, in the neighborhood of Ueno. The overall area expanded into an industrial zone in the Taishō era (1912–26)[68]

A freight station called Sumidagawa Station was built in the Senju area in 1895, and a connecting link to Tabata Station on the northeast trunk line near Ueno in 1896. Two stations, Kita-Senju and Minami-Senju (north and south Senju) were completed in the same year to service traffic in the area. The Tōbu Railroad connecting Kita-Senju with the town of Kuki (in present Saitama Pref.) was completed in 1899. Thus, industries and rail services gave Senju a commanding position as a suburban area, utterly different from its highway station days.[69]

The terminal station on the Nakasendō route, Itabashi, was not seriously effected by the Meiji transformation. Merchants coming from the Echigo, Jōshū, and Shinshū provinces with silks and other commodities stopped over there, and the number of inns for this customary clientele actually grew. Completion of the railroad between Ueno and Kumagaya in 1883 rendered the stopover unnecessary. A large fire in the next year seemed the fatal blow, as the old station town's inns approached bankruptcy, and the number of houses in the town decreased. The latter condition, however, opened up land space into which, in 1884, moved large defense plants, such as the Army Arsenal and the Itabashi Gunpowder Plant, along Arakawa river. The new rail line made this area, with its low density of residences, an ideal location as a manufacturing zone for munitions.[70]

We have seen thus far how the process of modernization differentiated the traditional warriors' and townsmen's zones of Edo into the many functional zones for government, business, educational, wholesaling and retailing activities. Attention was turned then to the development of residential communities in the westward hill sections, and of industrial districts in the flats eastward nearer Tōkyō Bay, especially around traffic junctions. Such differentiation into functional zones was a basic requirement in the modernization of the social structure of the capital city. It remains now for us to look at the way large-scale manufacture replaced manual crafts and home industries as the driving power of modernization. In concluding this section on renovation of the ecological structure of Tokyo, we will make some final observations on markets, consumption patterns, and public works projects.

The only large industry inherited from the preceding Edo era by Tōkyō was the Ishikawajima Shipbuilding Yard, built by the Mito domain in 1849. Importing both equipment and technical advisors from Europe and America, the government itself built a number of standard factories in Tōkyō in the Meiji period, such as a paper processing plant in Ōji, a cement factory in Fukagawa, a glass plant in Shinagawa, the Senju Spinning Mill, the Government Printing Bureau in Takinogawa, and a sulphuric acid plant.

At the same time, the government imported factory equipment which was loaned to private interests affiliated with political authority. In some cases the machines were sold to the private companies at prices representing only a fraction of the original costs, to be paid back in small annual payments. By these measures, the government aimed at converting the large capital funds of the money-lending trade from parasitic to productive purposes, to shift the merchants from dealing only in goods produced by peasants and craftsmen on a minor scale to large-scale production of their own. Among such semi-private industrial companies, there were two of relatively large scale for the times. One was the Ōji Paper Mill, founded by Asano Sōichirō, equipped with a 50-horsepower engine, and affiliated with the Inaba-Nishimura combine.

Most of the factories built around 1877 were equipped with water wheels or had only manual power, though a few had small steam engines of less than 15 hp. These factories were for light industries such as printing, silk spinning, and other products. There were 54,639 households engaged in industrial production in the urban area of Tōkyō in 1877, and

19,204 households connected with industry in the outskirts. These constituted 25 % of the total number of 282,554 households in all Tōkyō Prefecture. Most of the households, of course, were occupied in various kinds of home industry at that stage.

As a retrenchment policy in relation to government finances, as well as to promote involvement of private capital in productive industry, the government decided to sell its own industries. For example, a machine shop in Fukagawa owned by the Ministry of Industry (Kōbushō) and a glass plant in Shinagawa under bureaucratic supervision were sold to private concerns in 1880.

The second and more expansive stage in industrial development in Japan came only after currency reforms enabled the government to stabilize its financial condition. From this time on, a broad range of industrial ventures were begun. Factories producing the following items were built in Tōkyō: railroad locomotives and cars, ships, machines, cotton yarns and fabrics, linen cloth, processed seafoods, electrical supplies and machines, cement, bricks, artificial fertilizers, processed leather, soap, glass, beer, sulphuric acid, and the city's gas supply. Most of these industries involved manual labor, and were not equipped with steam engines or electric motors. They employed, on the average, thirty or forty workers in each factory. In short, large-scale industries were not developed in Japan until after the Sino-Japanese War (1894–5).[71]

Manufacture on a scale sufficient to depress the home industries did appear, however, in the early half of the Meiji era. The major portion of the home industries had roots in the preceding era, and depended upon use of the traditional skills of carpenters, plasterers, barrel-makers, wood cutters, and spinners. The next largest group also involved traditional trades: stonemasons, metalworkers, mat makers, woodworkers, blacksmiths, tailors and seamstresses for kimono, split-toe socks (*tabi*) makers, furniture craftsmen, dyers, paper makers, roof thatchers, and gardeners. Still, another group, however, worked at trades that developed after the beginning of the Meiji period: shoemakers, clogmakers, cart makers, roofing tile and brick makers, rickshaw producers, photographers, tailors for Western-style clothing, goldsmiths, silversmiths, printers, makers of electric motors and other machines, and glassmakers.

With monopolies abolished, anyone could, if he had capital, become a wholesaler; that is, he could deal directly with the many craftsmen listed above. On the other hand, some craftsmen opened their own shops to market their products. Most craftsmen, however, depended upon wholesalers with sufficient capital to supply them with raw materials or to set up merchandizing channels. The wholesalers generally put conditions on funds loaned, namely, that products were to be released exclusively through them. In effect, then, the wholesalers tended to control the production and distribution of goods much as they had in the previous Edo period.[72]

Expansion of the labor population employed in the enlarged integrative organs caused a commensurate expansion of the residential areas of the city, as we have seen. Furthermore, it was liberation from the static restrictions of the feudal order that allowed a freer flow of people and goods, supported by greatly improved means of transportation, which in turn not only increased the size of the city but led to the differentiation of geographical areas and social classes. New groups of people emerged who were aligned with the multiplied functions of society, binding the city of Tōkyō into a larger and greatly strengthened integrative whole.

Functional differentiation within larger integrative unity was not the whole story. The process of modernization that brought about the functional and integrative transformation also ushered in modern styles and improved social conditions in the lives of the citizens. But this latter development did not occur without special efforts on the part of the municipal government to form the organizational systems necessary to improved living conditions. Hence, an account of social and ecological change in Tōkyō in the early part of the Meiji period is not complete without some concluding remarks on public projects concerning markets, roads, and electric and water supply.

Hasty liquidation of the wholesalers associations backfired, as indicated earlier, in the rapid decline of the market system and sharp price increases. Remedial measures taken by the government began with the reinstitution of protective privileges for wholesalers and brokers in specific markets, such as fish, poultry, vegetables, and fruits. For example, sixteen fruit and vegetable markets were authorized. Wholesalers and brokers operating in these markets were permitted to re-establish their cooperative associations and to set up an association office, and they were issued official operating licenses.

The Kanda market was designated as the Central Market of Tōkyō. In the years 1892 and 1893 there were 240 vegetable dealers, thirty-seven dried foods dealers, twenty-three shops handling miscellaneous household utensils and toys, forty-seven shops operating wholesalers' carts, and twelve eating establishments. It is said that 50,000 people gathered each day in this huge market.

There were also many other markets serving quite large areas, as shown in the following examples:

| *Market location* | *Area served* |
|---|---|
| Daikongashi | Shiba, Akasaka, Kyōbashi and Nihonbashi |
| Mikawashima | Honjo and Fukagawa |
| Meguro | Shiba and Azabu |
| Komagome and Yanaka | Koishikawa, Hongō and Shitaya |
| Shinjuku, Kotsukahara, and Honjo | Asakusa, Honjo, and Kasai |

Merchants handling vegetables and fruits hauled their products to market early in the morning by carts, to get ready for the day's customers.

There was a rather famous market in Toshima-chō in the Kanda area that featured bargains in used utensils and used clothing. Similar markets could be found in Nihonbashi, Asakusa, and other places. The need for low cost markets arose mainly from the loss of local neighborhood shops that supplied all one's basic needs due to the emergence of the large-scale markets serving extended regions as described above. Added handling costs made for higher prices which some simply could not afford. Hence, they obtained what they needed at the second-hand markets at lower prices.[73]

In the second decade of the Meiji era there arose serious discussion of reformation of the city's outmoded layout, especially with reference to rearranging the street patterns. These ideas were endorsed in a proclamation by the Emperor Meiji in August of 1888 stating, "We authorize the government to promulgate the Tōkyō Urban Reconstruction Law for rearrangement of the city streets in view of the permanent advantages to be gained in the municipal administration of commerce, public health, fire prevention, and transportion throughout the entire urban area." Although formally enacted, insufficient finances in both national and municipal treasuries prevented its implementation. By 1890 the financial situation was better, and a number of public works projects were begun. Old roads were widened and new roads constructed. Drainage systems were improved and riparian projects initiated. Ten streets over 20 *ken* (39.7 yds.) wide were laid out around the Imperial Palace, constituting a basic network of main streets connecting the central area of the city with the major areas around it.

After the Army's installation near the Palace was moved to Azabu, the land was sold by the government to the Mitsubishi firm. The land lay vacant for some time afterward, with weeds growing up among abandoned barracks, and it was referred to as "Mitsubishi Field" (*Mitsubishi-ga-hara*). It covered the area including present-day Sukiyabashi and Tatsunokuchi, in the Marunouchi district. Capping the process of formation of Tōkyō's municipal administration, the Tōkyō Prefectural Office was erected in Marunouchi, patterned after German styles. The Mitsubishi constructed its buildings, unimaginatively labeled Nos. One, Two, and Three, adopting British architectural styling, in the Marunouchi area.

The head offices of many large Japanese enterprises were built in the same area as capitalism developed in the country. Some of them were the Mitsubishi Bank, the Meiji Mutual Life Insurance Company, Japan Mail Steamship Co., and Takada & Company. In 1899 the office of the Tōkyō Chamber of Commerce was also built in this district. "Mitsubishi Field" was converted into a modern business center.[74] Even so, there were still many vacant lots in Marunouchi before the Tōkyō Railroad Station was erected there in 1914. Prior to that it was not a convenient location with respect to transportation facilities, and lacked the full functional requirements of an urban center. Moreover, the centripetal forces drawing buildings and groups of people into greater central concentrations had not come fully into play at this stage.

There were other factors that seriously effected the lives of the citizenry, especially in terms of modern consumption patterns. One of these factors was the installation of gas, electric, water, and sewage systems. In 1874 the Chamber of Commerce employed some French engineers to construct a city gas supply plant, which made possible the placing of gas lights along the city streets. Founded in 1885, the Tōkyō Gas Company expanded very rapidly within the next decade, virtually monopolizing the gas supply business for the entire city. Its services were gradually diffused, making gas available to households in almost every part of the urban area. The gas was used chiefly for lighting the rooms of homes (in addition to street lamps), the use of gas burners for heating appearing mostly after the Sino-Japanese War.[75]

Electric lighting came to Tōkyō with the founding of Tōkyō Electric Light Company in 1887, which operated five steam power plants near the Nihonbashi area. The unit cost rate of electricity was higher than for kerosene, making utilization of electric lighting prohibitive for the ordinary citizen. Moreover, the gas supply was much better distributed, and many common people used kerosene for lighting. Demands for electric power were limited largely to government offices, army installations, and business firms. Utilization of electricity did not penetrate into private households of middle class folk and below until hydro-electric power plants were built after the Russo-Japanese War (1904–5).[76]

The Tōkyō water supply, like Edo's before it, was drawn from the Tamagawa river. This system had no facilities for sedimentation or filtration of solid matter. The conduits were constructed largely of wood. From a sanitary point of view it was unsatisfactory, and could be rendered unpleasantly muddy by a strong wind. The watershed was much too narrow to supply adequately Tōkyō's expanding population. In modernization plans for the city, a thorough renovation of the water system was a project of utmost urgency. In 1891 the government launched a public works program to improve the water works. Bureaucratic efficiency seems to have been quite low in this field, as substantial improvements were very slow in coming. Even in 1903 only 10% of the city's households were supplied by the municipal water works, the rest of the populace obtaining water from private or community wells.

*Social Strata.*——Inasmuch as the social organs and functions of Tōkyō were consciously, vigorously and, at times, radically altered, it is to be expected that important structural changes occurred also in the social strata of the city. Such was, indeed, the case. Yet, the extent and significance of changes in social strata must be seen in terms of the total population and the degree to which residual feudalism limited certain changes to particular groups.

The population of Tōkyō in 1896 was 1,365,068, permanent residents being classified into the following three status groups;

| | |
|---|---|
| Peers (*Kazoku*) | 2,745 |
| Ex-warriors (*Shizoku*) | 114,512 |
| Commoners (*Heimin*) | 756,828 |

In preceding sections we have described the formation of the centralized bureaucratic administration that replaced the feudal domains which "returned all lands and people to the Emperor." Leadership in government changed hands from the Tokugawa household and its high ranking retainers to a composite group of lower grade warriors from the Satsuma, Chōshū, Tosa, and Hizen domains, and various court nobility and a few daimyō who supported the imperial restoration. But Tōkyō retained its dominant position in all fields, whether government, economy, education, or transportation, while acquiring a new prominence as the major center for introduction of Western cultural and technological forms. It is now necessary to take note of what happened to the various classes of people in the city in the process of transition from Edo to Tōkyō, from a feudal to a modern city.

The wealth and power of the feudal lords in the Tokugawa era varied considerably, ranging from a minimum index of 10,000 *koku* to a maximum of 1,000,000 *koku*. While they lost their political powers and administrative positions in the Meiji transition, as a class they retained the high esteem of their former vassals and subjects. Moreover, they were allowed to keep substantial portions of their residential properties in Tōkyō, and were granted peerage (*kazoku*) by the new government.

Financially, their social standing was salvaged by two measures. That is, heavy debts owed to wealthy merchants were automatically canceled by government order, and they were also awarded generous issues of government bonds. Added to the properties retained, they entered the new age as persons of wealth and honor. Some of them became high ranking bureaucrats, even ministers of government, while others became important stockholders in the newly-formed companies and banks. Others became major landowners, profiting from lands rented to others.[77]

Such successful examples, however, involved only a small proportion of the former daimyō. An essay on the prosperity issuing from the introduction of modern culture into Tōkyō (*Tōkyō Kaika Hanjōshi*)[78] reports that most of them had to dismiss their many retainers, employing only a few household servants. Some managed to open shops of their own, or to put their limited capital to work as investments. Even then, the majority did not handle their own business interests but turned such responsibilities over to trusted stewards. Older men, forty and above, suffered from having too much time on their hands and turned to spending freely both time and money at amusement centers or on sightseeing trips, taking either wives or mistresses along. Under such circumstances, their resources were quickly depleted, and many of the ex-lords lost their money and property.

Feudal society had been premised on the stratification of households according to status, and this was shifted gradually in the Meiji period to a determination of social position on the basis of individual ability and wealth. In the process the rich became richer and the poor even poorer, as the power of feudal privilege was combined with, and absorbed into, the development of Japanese capitalism. In the cities could be found both the lavishly rich and the desperately poor in extremes not found in the rural districts. The gap between extravagant wealth and demeaning poverty widened more than ever.

An "Official Viewpoint on Industrial Development" (*Kōgyō Iken*) was issued by the Ministry of Agriculture and Commerce (Nōshōmushō) in December of 1884. In this document the entire population was classified into three classes of economic standing, based on per capita cost of living, as follows:

| *Class* | *Living Costs* | *Explanation* |
|---|---|---|
| A | 110 *yen* 82 *sen* 5 *rin* | Expenses require for food, clothing, and dwellings; equivalent to ten times the contemporary price of rice. |
| B | 60 *yen* 45 *sen* | Same expenses as A; equivalent to five times the rice price. |
| C | 20 *yen* 15 *sen* | Same expenses as A; double the rice price.[79] |

An important breakdown by occupational groups as distributed in the three classes is given in the same report, given in percentages.

| *Occupation* | *A Class* | *B Class* | *C Class* |
|---|---|---|---|
| Government officials and Shintō priests | 50 | 50 | — |
| Buddhist priests and nuns | 20 | 80 | — |
| Merchants | 60 | 30 | 10 |
| Farmers | 10 | 30 | 60 |
| Miscellaneous professions | 10 | 30 | 60 |
| Industries | 5 | 15 | 80 |
| Fishing | 5 | — | 95 |

Government officials and Shintō priests, followed by Buddhist priests and nuns, clearly enjoyed the highest standards of living, with none in the lowest C class—except for merchants who had the largest percentage in the top A class!

The above data reflects not only the structure of society early in the Meiji period, but indicates as well the character of the mentality of the leadership groups consisting primarily of ex-samurai. The locus of their positions had changed from feudal warriors to government officials, but the basic ideas persisted that persons in positions of authority were superior to civilians and were due greater respect and compensation. Former samurai occupied 87% of the positions in the nine ministries of the central government and 74% of the offices in Tōkyō and other local administrations.[80] They performed their governing roles as extensions of feudal administration, clearly assuming that political power endowed them with the right to receive greater wealth.

To be sure, it was the bureaucrats who were most active in introducing new systems from abroad through the acquisition of new knowledge, in business, industry, and society as well as in government. There were genuine and prominent differences between the ruling group and the common people, with respect to general knowledge and social prestige. And the common people paid them the respect they felt due themselves, addressing them as "Sir Official" (*Kan-in-sama*).

Among the ministers of the new government there were a number of former daimyō, and their salaries reflected their prestige. The Prime Minister (*Dajō Daijin*) and other Ministers (*Sangi*) were paid from 800 to 900 yen per month, a very high salary scale in those days. Even officials of the lowest rank of the ninth class (*hannin-kan kyūtō*) were paid fifty yen a month.[81]

Government officials took up residence in homes owned previously by daimyō, *hatamoto*, or *gokenin*, either by directly purchasing the houses, or by making claims on vacated residences. Although such houses were distributed throughout Tōkyō, most of them were located in the hills west of the palace. In their new homes the officials managed to adjust with relative ease to a semi-warrior, semi-Western style of living. Enjoying both the prestige and the relative wealth of the upper class of society, the officials worked with a certain enthusiasm to introduce Western ways into their own homes.

Applying their own ideas of what constituted "Western styles," they set about redecorating their old daimyō or samurai residences. Modes adopted from different European countries were utilized in a variety of, sometimes ingenious, combinations. In general, though, there was a certain uniformity in the alterations made. A second floor was usually added, carpets put down, and standard furniture such as stuffed chairs, dining tables and chairs, and other items installed. Paper on windows was replaced by plate glass, and stoves were provided in rooms where small braziers had been standard for generations. The basic framework and design of the houses, of course, remained unchanged.

Money was spent lavishly in other areas to acquire Western appearances. Fashionable clothes filled wardrobes, and meats were added to their diets. They took every occasion to speak English, and took carriages when leaving home. Banquets were graced by the best *sake* and had many geisha in attendance. Not a few kept mistresses in Yanagibashi and other sections.[82]

Officials of middle class or lower standing were also ex-samurai, though their living patterns did not change so much from the previous age. Most of them also lived in former residences of the warrior group, but not usually of the daimyō, *hatamoto*, or *gokenin* level. When at work in their offices they wore Western clothes and sat at desks. For convenience in receiving guests in Western clothes, the entrances to their homes and a single parlor room were converted to foreign style. Privately, they preferred sitting on cushions on the *tatami*-mat floors of Japanese style rooms. Thus, their homes were separated into two distinct parts, namely, private quarters (*oku*, or "rear") and formal rooms (*omote*, or "front"). This kind of combination home, with one section rooted in the samurai tradition and the other an adapted Western mode, became the standard pattern for the intellectuals of Japan.[83]

Just what the family life patterns in the converted warrior dwellings were, is not entirely clear. Some insight can be gained from the first three sections of the Civil Law issued in 1896, and from the fourth and fifth sections of the Law of Succession of 1898. These laws were drawn up by referring to the standards of households with warrior backgrounds, having little in common with the lives of ordinary people, who were sometimes spoken of as "stupid beasts" by the ruling class. Conditions varied according to the social stratum or province concerned, but these laws are still valuable references for information on family life in the Meiji era.

Enacted first in 1890, the Civil Law was patterned, in many respects, after French laws, which articulated the basic concept of social equality among people. Consequently, the thoroughgoing discrimination against wives that was customary in the Edo era was modified. The wife's position in the household was made second only to the husband's, displacing male lineage priorities. The head of a household was made responsible for younger members within relatively narrow limits. His chief obligation was for their home training and for expenses required in compulsory education. The household head's authority was revised radically. He was not permitted to punish adult children who married without his consent, nor could he punish those who accepted adoption by another family without his consent.

Not only were such ideals unacceptable to many in positions of authority, but in actuality the existing households could not readily absorb such radical reforms. Moreover, the mobilization of all the people required in the programs for increasing national wealth and military strength demanded the cultivation of a populace that readily obeyed authority. A revised Civil Law was put into effect in 1898, standardizing the family system according to traditional feudal values.

The short-lived attempt to base family life on conjugal (i.e., marriage) relationships, giving the wives better positions, was abandoned. Lineage relationships were reinstated, and family ties were stressed as the basic structure of Japanese society. The centrality of the head of the household was reaffirmed as the one who bears the ancestral spirit of the family. Once again the right of eldest sons to inherit all family properties, and duties, was reinstated.

In the revised Civil Law the authority of the family head was obviously strengthened. Specifically, his will was determinative in deciding the residential location of all family members. Marriage and adoption plans could be made only with his consent. As conjugal relationships were rejected in favor of lineage relationships, the rights of wives were no longer recognized. While a household was not recognized in the Civil Law as a legal entity and, hence, family property was not legally recognized, family property rights could be established in some cases. For example, when ownership of property was not clearly established—that is, whether it belonged to the head or to family members—ownership was granted to the head.

Permanent continuation of the family was a strong emphasis of the law. Succession to the headship of the family was limited to males, to the legitimate, eldest son, and he was not permitted to desert his household and proper duty. He was required to venerate his ancestors, performing traditional ceremonies in manifestation of his sincerity. He was the duly authorized guardian of his family's genealogical register, of the ritual equipment of ancestral veneration, and of the family graves.

Family headship and parental authority were formally separated. The father assumed the primary role in parental authority, but the mother's role as next in line was acknowledged. This recognition of the maternal role was a significant step forward in a civil code otherwise reflecting conservative reaction. The law clearly defines the position of men as superior to that of women. A wife was regarded as incompetent to manage her own affairs and any property she might own was to be managed by her husband on her behalf.

The order of succession strongly favored male heirs. When a family head died, sons and grandsons took precedence over the wife. Only if there were no rightful male heirs could a wife come into ownership of the family property. Such regulations were expressive of the traditional feudal idea that lineage values and relationships took precedence over conjugal ones.[84]

The authority of the head over all members of the family was broadened to cover a wide range of affairs, so as to restore the more familiar elements of feudal society. The actual conditions of family life in the different social classes were not taken into consideration. Rather, the Civil Law was enacted to mold attitudes and behavior along lines of compliant obedience to authority. The more cooperative patterns of family life and organization among the common people began to disintegrate, especially in the rural districts. In the cities, though, the number of citizens living in small, independent family units increased. These were families formed by marriage that lived on the income earned by the husband, or by the couple jointly. Such families even included some of the former samurai who had gone to work in industry, transportation, or other modernized organs. It is doubtful whether their lives were in complete harmony with the conservative scheme of the family system outlined in the Civil Law.

Among the merchants, whose social positions ranked just below officials, priests, and nuns, the wholesalers were most prominent. Their operations had been modified by the shift from consignments to stocks as the basis of their business, after the loss of their monopoly privileges. Their role in processing products for retail sales diminished even further after large-scale industry developed. But these changes did not occur all at once. Mass production did not emerge on a broad scale until after the Sino-Japanese War (1894–5), and until that time the wholesalers maintained their influence in commerce through the traditional methods inherited from their ancestors, helping to keep alive strict feudal customs well into the Meiji era.

The position of head of a merchant household was absolute, and family members were bound together under his authority by sacred bonds. Equally as binding as the harsh demands of business on the family head was the obligation to worship the family deities each morning and evening. Within the context of unquestioned authority he treated his employees and servants with benevolence. Those connected with his business were treated as members of the family, were subject to his authority, were recipients of his benevolence, and were bound by the same sacred bonds.

Powerful merchants were extremely proud of the clipped curtains (*noren*) that hung over their entrances, bearing the household name or trademark. They bent every effort to make it a symbol of their own success in accumulating capital and in increasing their reputation among customers. Oriented to the practical goals of business, they were little interested in seeing their sons go off to the newly-established schools, least of all to the universities. Their concern was to educate their own sons in successful business practices.

Succession and continuity were the primary values of merchant households, and finding a suitable successor was a prime necessity. If there was an especially able man among the relatives or employees of a household in search of a successor, the household did not hesitate to adopt him as its heir, even if there were available sons in the household. Business took precedence over lineage.

The wife of the master of a merchant house (*okamisan*) filled a very important role in managing the household economy, so the daughters were trained very carefully. In addition to training in household chores, the girls acquired certain cultural skills after graduating from public school. Having received the cultural polish expected of women in merchant houses, they were married off to other merchant households, or a suitable suitor was found for adoption into her family.

Salaries received by employees in merchant shops were not thought so important to them as the business training they received. The head of a shop took a personal pride in the development of his apprentices. The wishes of master and employee coincided nicely. Employers addressed apprentices by adding the suffix *-don* ("boy") to their names when they first entered a shop at the age of fourteen or fifteen. At age seventeen they were addressed as *chūzō* (clerk), after a kind of initiation ceremony performed on New Year's Day, or possibly on the twentieth day of the first month of the year when special prayers (called *ebisu-kō*) were made for prosperity in the coming year. Central to the ceremony was *genpuku*, the celebration of his coming of age, symbolized by his changing to an adult hair style, receiving a half-coat called *haori* and a tobacco case. From this time on they were called *Kichi* (lucky) or *Hichi* (seven), and were given charge over a younger boy.

Sometime between the ages twenty-one and twenty-five the apprentice-graduates could be promoted to the status of managers (*banto*), and the suffix *be-e* was added to their names, e.g., *Hichibe-e* or *Kichibe-e*. After completing ten to thirteen years of internship as a manager they were permitted to marry suitable girls and live outside the shop residence. They were outfitted with silk robes and, as responsible managers, could act on behalf of their masters in business matters.

Symbolic of the careful attention given to continuity and succession was the system of "sharing the trademark curtain" (*noren-wake*). As indicated above, employees did not leave their masters after finishing their apprenticeship. They continued working for him until they were about thirty years old, a service known as *orei-bōkō*, or service rendered in appreciation for having been trained in business. After this period of repayment, they could then establish their own independent shops, using the funds deposited in their names by the master during the years of repayment service. The accumulated savings were rarely sufficient, however; the new ventures were backed by the credit standing of the master whose guarantee enabled the younger man to get started. This covering arrangement was given the added blessing of "sharing the trademark," which also helped with sales.

In the case of wholesalers, the total household, including the main and branch houses, in *noren-wake* arrangements was called so-and-so-*ikka* (one family). If any of the branch houses met severe difficulties, they were always rescued by the main household. Occasions of joy or grief—weddings, funerals, or even ancestral worship ceremonies—were shared by all, head and branch households together.[85]

Wholesale shops in the Meiji period were generally two-storied structures with black plastered walls, tiled roofs, and the dark blue *noren* half-curtain with name or trademark in white hung over the entrance. The front room of the shop had an open earthen floor near the entrance, beyond which was an elevated mat-covered floor where goods were displayed on a counter along the back wall. In the Meiji era (as in many places today), the shop building also included the living quarters of the shopowner and his family. The living quarters were in the rear part of the house. Employees lived on the second floor, or in the shop area itself. Sometimes the shops were three-storied structures, the third floor being used for storing goods. Annexed to the shop building was a warehouse (*tanagura*) for goods storage, and over it a private storeroom (*okugura*) for keeping the master's family treasures.[86]

The modernization and Westernization of the major organizations of government, business, education, and upper class residences in various key districts of Japan's major city were truly striking. But the benefits of these changes were enjoyed by only a small proportion of the total population of Tōkyō. The majority of the people belonged to a lower stratum of society that experienced little change in their daily lives, despite the remarkable changes taking place at higher levels. These were people engaged in minor businesses, artisans working in and out of doors, laborers in factories, day laborers, rickshaw men, and ragpickers. Such people could be found in nearly every township throughout Tōkyō, though the largest concentration of people in the lower classes lived in the Honjo and Fukagawa areas—inherently unattractive because of the frequent danger of flooding.

Apart from the major commercial centers, the main streets of Tōkyō were lined with minor shops dealing in various items such as rice, household necessities, *sake*, dried foods, wooden sandals, vegetables, soybean curd, roasted sweet potatoes, dry goods, pickles, and dishes. There were also many small pawn shops. The methods of merchandizing were essentially unchanged from those of similar shops supplying neighborhood communities during the Edo period.

The buildings of these shops varied according to the kind and volume of goods sold, although most of them were two-storied structures. Medium and small size shops ranged between two and four *ken* (4–8 yds.) in width. Lengthwise, they were divided into three sections. The shop was in the front section, facing the street, and the second section served as the residence of the master and his family. The living room measured 9 × 12 feet (six *tatami*-mats), with a closet to one side for bedding and miscellaneous articles. A ladder for ascending to the second floor stood in one corner of this room. The second floor room was arranged for guests, and was provided with an alcove (*tokonoma*) for flowers or a painting.

On the ground floor, the third section at the rear was the kitchen, which was equipped very simply with a cupboard for food and utensils, an open hearth for cooking, a wooden sink, and earthern urns for water. A vent in the roof allowed smoke from the hearth to escape. The floor of the kitchen was made of wooden planks, under which firewood and buckets of pickles were stored. The toilet room was next to the kitchen area.[87]

Wages did not improve much after the Meiji Restoration for the craftsmen living in rented homes on back streets, and their social standing actually declined. Of the three classes cited in the Agriculture and Commerce Ministry's report on economic conditions (*Kōgyō Iken*), craftsmen belonged in the lowest (C) class.

Craftsmen who plied their trades indoors (*ishokunin*) were distinguished from those who worked outdoors (*deshokunin*). The former group included, for example, goldsmiths and silversmiths, makers of clog straps and cloth bags, gold lacquerware artisans, bookbinders, dressmakers, tailors, as well as those who produced metal foil goods, other lacquerware, tobacco pipes, and paper lanterns. Outdoor laborers included men such as carpenters, plasterers, stonemasons, painters, and roofers.

Indoor artisans were merchants, in a sense. That is, they took some initiative in selling their products and had to have some capital funds for procuring raw materials. In a larger sense, though, they were dependent upon wholesalers who maintained the channels for marketing goods, and who had better contacts with a wider range of customers.

Craftsmen engaged in outdoor work were pure laborers. Whereas indoor workers wore the customary half-coat (*haori*) of ordinary townsmen, the outdoor workers had a distinctive costume of tight-fitting trousers (*momohiki*) and loose-fitting half-coat (*hanten*, or sometimes *happi* coat) of coarser material than the *haori*. Footgear worn by these laborers was a heavy hemp fibre sandal. They cared but for the day at hand, disdaining to be caught with one day's wage on the following morning. They scorned the prudential depositing of money as contrary to the proud spirit of a craftsman. Though free to sell their labors to anyone, the outdoor craftsmen maintained rather fixed relations with specific patrons who, in turn, treated them the same as their own contracted employees. These craftsmen made seasonal visits, bearing presents to their patrons to keep the established relationships in good order.

After the Meiji Restoration, jobs were often contracted through bidding. Men who were not craftsmen themselves could win contracts if they had some working capital. The relationship between the boss of a work crew (*tōryō*) and the crew itself changed from the traditional master-subordinate relationship based on pride in the quality of work done to one based on the wage offered. Of necessity, then, the emphasis shifted also from the craftsman's skill in his technique alone, to overall efficiency and speed.

Institution of a national conscription law, requiring young men to undergo examination at age twenty and possible enlistment in military service, shortened the term of apprenticeship from the traditional seven or eight years to five or, at most, six years. Under these new circumstances, the apprentices tended more and more not to live in the master's house where they were subject to his direction in all personal matters, as in former times. They lived elsewhere, commuting to the shops, and the close connection between master and apprentices was gradually lost.

The cities offered many job opportunities and increasingly young craftsmen chose not to stay with their apprentice-term masters to offer *orei-bōkō* gratitude-repayment services. They struck out on their own, seeking better wages and new experiences. Craftsmen had been prevented for generations, however, from competing for better wages by the trades associations established to protect, and control, specific occupations. The associations had provided the advantages of mutual aid and friendship but, at the same time, fixed the wage scales of the workers. They were assigned to jobs contracted by the associations with a set group of patrons, and there was virtually no possibility of personal bargaining or mobility on the part of the craftsmen themselves in Edo era patterns. Cancellation of occupational restrictions and promotion of new industries and public works projects undermined the position of the trades associations, and they rapidly declined.[88]

The number of poor people in the cities increased sharply in the latter half of the second decade of the Meiji period. Peasants who had lost their lands flowed into the cities seeking relief from the distresses of dire poverty. While the poor were ubiquitous throughout all Tōkyō, the poorest were concentrated in three places, Shitaya-mannen-chō, Yotsuya-samegahashi, and Shiba-shin'ami-chō. There were ordinary shops on the main streets of these communities, but there were many more stalls handling used articles and waste products than could be found in normal neighborhoods.

Second-hand household utensils, used clogs, edible leftovers from better homes, waste paper, and used furniture were typical items in the shops for the poor. Among the shops were offices of contractors who employed day laborers on public works projects. Dwellings were humble shacks jammed together along narrow lanes.

Daily incomes for these people averaged about ten *sen* per person. Their incomes came from such sources as: jobs as day laborers in construction and riparian projects under government supervision; public work jobs contracted by private bosses; jobs in commodity transportation firms; work as *tachinbō* stationed at steep grades to help push heavy carts up the inclines; rickshaw coolies, of whom it is reported that there were some 50,000 in Tōkyō in 1897; ragpicking; work as tumblers in shows; storytelling; and engagements as musical entertainers.

The poor were rarely solvent and frequently borrowed from pawnbrokers. Loan terms were for three days, after which collateral goods were claimed by the pawnshops. Constantly borrowing and ever working to repay the loans, the poor seldom escaped from the miserable trap of poverty.[89]

Tenement buildings housing many of the poor were single-story elongated *nagaya*, with a different family occupying each small room of four and a half or six mats (9 × 9, or 9 × 12 ft. respectively). In the corner of each there was a ground-level earth floor space (*doma*) about the size of one *tatami*-mat which served as an entrance where clogs were left upon entering. Part of the space was covered with a raised wooden landing for stepping up to the elevated mat floor, on which was placed a small wooden basin that served as a sink. Each tenement house had only one toilet for the common use of all the families in that building.[90]

Although the Edo system of rental agents was eliminated by the Meiji administration in 1869, the old custom of making these agents neighborhood bosses remained in effect in the social strata not readily influenced by the changes carried out on higher levels. According to a historical account of manners and customs in Tōkyō (*Tōkyō Fūzokushi*) in the Meiji era, each household was under special reciprocal obligations to the two households on either side of it and to the three households directly across the street from it. Whenever a family moved into a community, it gave goodwill presents to the other five households in its neighborhood group. On another level, the landowners exercised considerable public and private power through appointment of rental managers who had great influence over the local tenants and their five-household groupings.

The managers' operations were not limited simply to collecting rents. Residential registration papers had to be signed by the group of rental agents covering the area involved. They received additional income as commission on night soil collected in the neighborhoods for use as fertilizer. Newcomers to a neighborhood presented gifts of money (*tarudai*) for *sake*, and subsequent seasonal gifts, to the managers in recognition of their authority.

Investigations made by Takeuchi Toshimi have turned up a number of jointly-signed documents relating to the neighborhood of Shiba Tamura-chō 7-chōme (seventh block) for the period 1872–7. These documents clarify further the relationships between landowners, managers, and tenants. Assessments of local ward taxes, made according to the front footage of house lots and called *koma-wari* or *yashiki-wari*, were collected by the rental agents and paid in the landowner's name, just as in the Edo period. Local taxes were the responsibility of the landowners, and it was the latter who controlled local government in the townships. Customs remained unaltered from Edo days, still forming the foundation of cooperation among citizens on a local level in many instances.[91] Thus, we can see that the reforms implemented in the capital city by the bureaucrats of samurai pedigree and their merchant associates, while remarkable in themselves, were far from thorough. Feudal elements remained in effect in many places and in many ways.

The very fact that Tōkyō remained the nation's capital indicated the intention of the samurai-bred government leaders to continue and cultivate the essence of the military tradition. Selection of the shogun's castle as the Imperial Palace was determinative for the ecological structure of the capital city, in retaining the traditional shape of a feudal castle town. The ancient mystique of the emperor system gave added sanction to the Palace as the heart of the capital, and to the capital as the nucleus of the integrative system of the whole country.

Naturally enough, then, the major organs of integration were concentrated around the Palace, and the population of the capital city expanded to staff these organs. In the process, department stores, neighborhood retail shops, and improved transportation and public service facilities were added in rapid succession. Too, the influx of Western cultural forms added a dimension not experienced before. Men were freer to move about and they improved their financial and social positions in ways undreamed of a generation earlier.

The matters discussed in this section remind us, however, that the changes and advantages of the Meiji period were not experienced uniformly by all social strata. People in the middle and lower classes saw no substantial improvement in their standards of living, and they remained largely subject to the controls of feudal values and customs. The gains of added prosperity went mainly to the already rich, while the very poor sank deeper into depressing poverty. The pleasures of imported Western civilization were for the upper class citizens living and working in the central areas of the city. Three decades were not enough time to distribute evenly the benefits of modernization among all the common people. That possibility needed for its realization not only a longer period of time but also the liberating effects of the following decades of industrial revolution.

# Chapter IX

# Industrial Revolution and the Development of Modern Cities (A.D. 1897–1920)

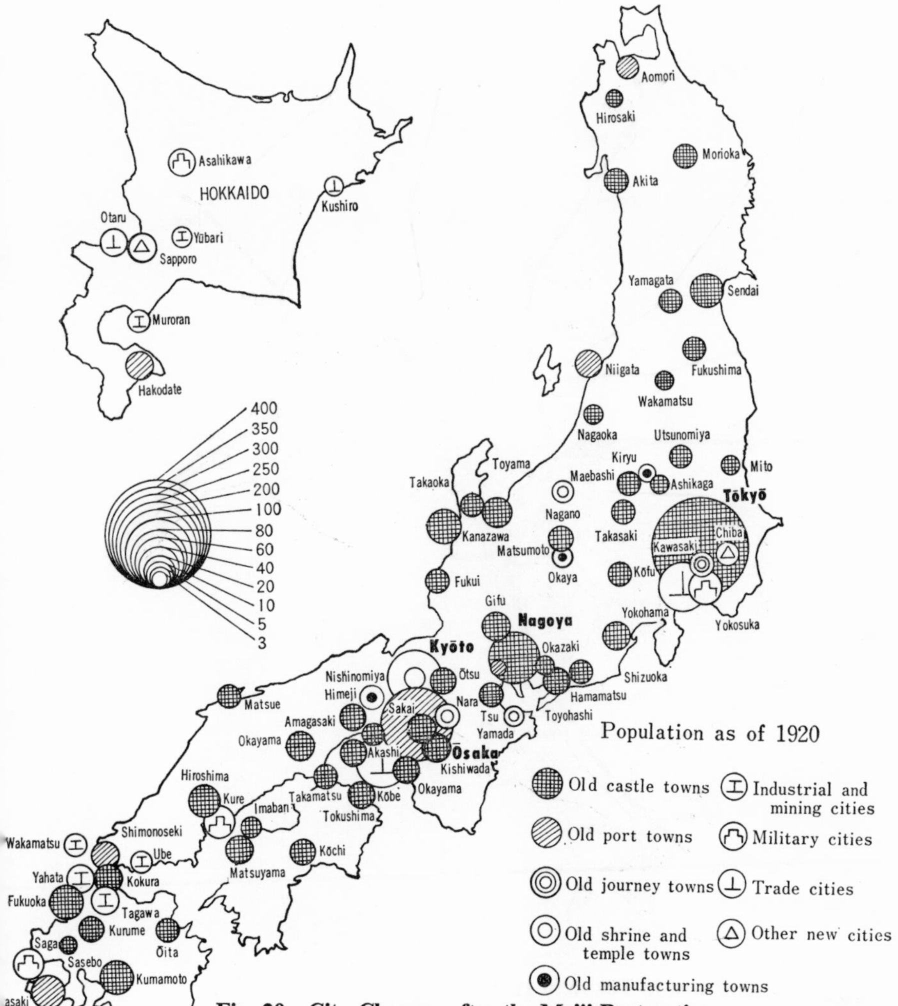


**Fig. 20 City Changes after the Meiji Restoration**

During the process of change following the Meiji Restoration and the industrial revolution (1897—) in Japan, most castle towns changed from consuming to producing centers. As the transportation system was built up, interrelations between the cities intensified, and many cities assumed specialized functions and expanded greatly in scale. The modern system of political and economic functions was enlarged and increased, capital was concentrated as capitalism developed, and the number of establishments increased and expanded in scale. Tōkyō and Ōsaka became the political and economic centers of all Japan, forming large metropolitan communities with clusters of satellite cities around them. As modern industry developed and international relations assumed importance, cities for foreign trade, military purposes, industrial needs and frontier projects (Hokkaidō) were developed free from any feudal tradition. The castle towns of the Tōhoku (northeast) and Hokuriku (northern) districts, though, were without industry and trade, so they remained as local centers without any significant change. (prepared by the author)

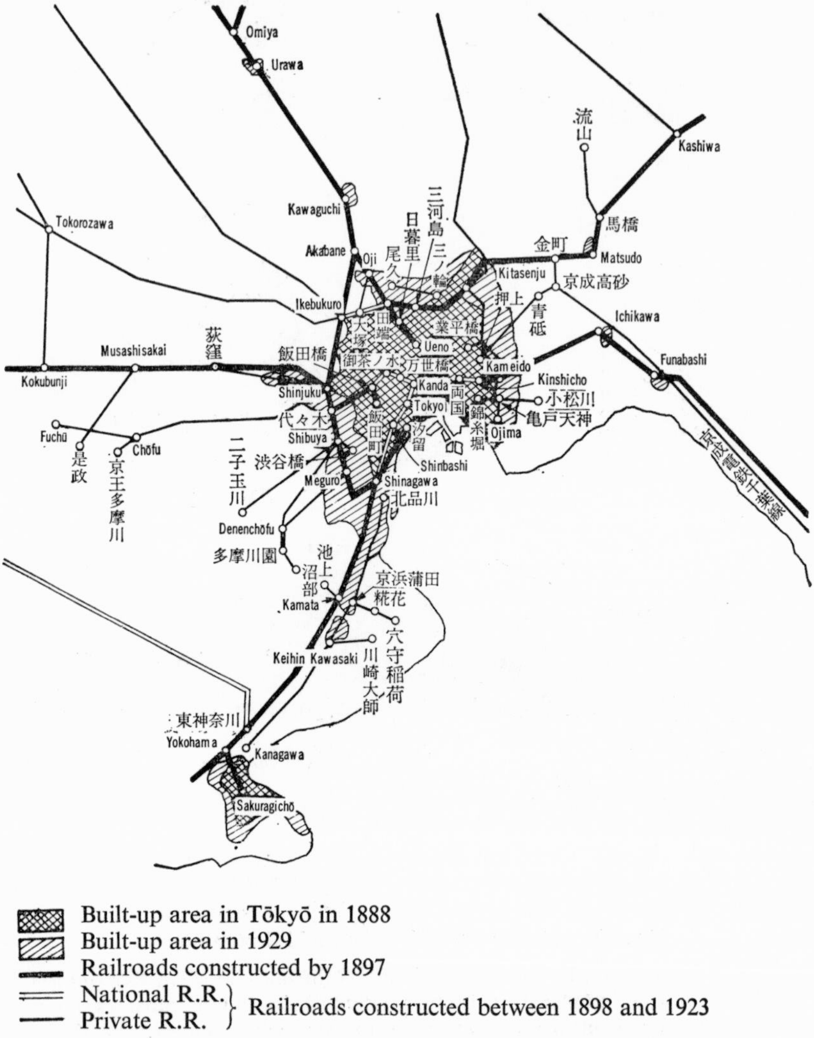


**Fig. 21 Progress of Tōkyō in Japan's Industrial Revolution**

With the remarkable development of Tōkyō in Japan's industrial revolution, government agencies and companies increased and expanded. Industries developed along rivers and by the sea. As the population increased, the spatial structure retained the status patterns of feudal times, though it gradually reflected the developing class system. Commuters' lines were constructed, and the rate of population increase on the periphery was much higher than in the center. Functions were dispersed, giving rise to satellite cities, and forming a metropolitan community. The same tendency can be seen in Ōsaka and its environs. (prepared by the author)

## 1. Changes in Social Stratification and Administrative Systems

The alterations that appeared in urban structures in Japan, ranging from slight to radical, issued from three key processes that marked the transition from feudal to modern society. One of these processes was the abolition of feudal systems in the fields of politics and economy, and particularly revision of the land tax system and cancellation of rigid status laws. The second principal process was the replacement of feudal systems with a new system of centralized controls exercised by bureaucrats. Finally, urban change in Meiji Japan must be seen in terms of the introduction of modern capitalism as related to, and supported by, government encouragement of upper class merchants, the development of modern military forces, the sudden stimulus of foreign trading ventures, and the modernization of transportation and educational institutions.

The old castle towns were transformed into modern cities, and new cities arose around military bases and international trade centers. These cities developed, however, not so much by eliminating all traces of the feudal age but, rather, by conscious building upon traditional social and ecological foundations. The more gradual progress toward modernization that marked the first three decades of the Meiji period was greatly accelerated by the advent of the industrial revolution in the second half of the Meiji period. Opening up new possibilities for social and occupational mobility, the conversion to large-scale industrial production added the necessary context and dynamic for cleaning out the residual status structures, permitting the formation of social classes based on the capitalist system adopted and adapted by the Meiji leaders.

Japan came late into the world of capitalism. Its entrance was neither spontaneous nor haphazard, but scheduled and programmed by government leaders through the cultivation of favored financial cliques. Both capitalist structures and techniques were appropriated in domestic and international policies. Victorious in two wars of her own, the Sino-Japanese War (1894–5) and the Russo-Japanese War (1904–5), and aligned with the victors in another, World War I, the Japanese economy was able to export not only commodities but capital funds as well. Moreover, Japan's sphere of influence expanded rapidly with the acquisition of overseas colonies following these wars.

The financial cliques concentrated in the urban centers moved into the center of the expanding sphere of influence, forming the nuclei of the industrialization process. They established effective monopolies over the business end of large industries, while absorbing many of the thousands of home industries through control of both raw materials supply and products sales, as well as of financial sources. Operating from a secure base in business and industry, the financial cliques moved into politics to gain major controls over the political parties. Notwithstanding the important roles of government leaders, it was the financiers who stood at the top of society.

The development of capitalism precipitated changes in the total power structure of society, and within this context the cities expanded further. The structures of the urban centers changed too, as can be seen from a listing of the major components of the population: politicians; financiers; military officers and troops; bureaucrats; salaried men and laborers that had flowed in from the rural districts seeking employment in large industries, as well as employees of medium and small industries; merchants filling consumer demands were not a particularly new class, but the new intellectual elite in the universities were.

Human relations in general underwent significant alterations as the cities were modernized, but the fundamental transformation of traditional master-subordinate relations of workers was particularly important. Many laborers became, no longer members of small groups of workers with close connections with their masters, but individual units in large masses of workers serving under a professional management class. There emerged an antagonism common to industrial capitalism, between labor and management, that began to find expression in labor union organizations.

Under the impact of the industrial revolution the cities not only increased in number; the dimensions of the cities were enlarged. The larger the city, the heavier the concentration of large-scale organs within its bounds; consequently, the larger cities expanded faster. The ecological conditions of the city were determined not merely by the centralization of people and integrative organs, however; intensified differentiation and decentralization of urban functions within the city were equally determinative of its ecological shape and structure.

Acquisition of overseas colonies provided greater access to natural resources, which accelerated the rate of transition of former industrial towns into industrial centers equipped with the facilities and conveniences of modern cities. Urban centers fulfilling only provincial functions could not keep pace with the accelerated pace of modernization.

On the other hand, the commodity economy penetrated more deeply into the rural areas than ever before, dissolving once and for all the insularity and self-sufficiency of the rural economy. All farm life became thoroughly oriented to supplying industry with raw materials and urban populations with foodstuffs. Thousands of farmers found it increasingly impossible to eke out their own living and, in desperation, turned themselves to the cities, providing industry with a large supply of cheap labor. Although industrial development benefited financially from the influx of cheap manpower, it suffered technologically in the sense that rationalization of industry was thereby delayed.

Against this background we propose to describe the development of large cities as the nuclei of national development, and the ecological changes within these cities in terms of the interrelationships between the cities and the overall processes of change. More specifically, we must look into the revolution that occurred in the structure of industry in the latter half of the Meiji period, and the subsequent realignment of population structures. These were the necessary conditions for the emergence of modern cities in Japan, as well as the context for the extensive revision of social strata and local government throughout the whole of society. Hence, we must also take note of the structural interaction between the cities and the total society.

*Changes in Industry and Population Structure.*——As shown in the preceding chapter, Japan became unified through the establishment of modern organs of government and ventured boldly into international relations and competition for markets. It soon became evident, however, that her merchants could not bear the financial burdens of the government's program of conversion to modern capitalism so long as they continued operating along traditional lines. It was necessary, therefore, for the government itself to assist them by forming trading companies and exchange firms under semi-official management, by investing funds drawn from land taxes imposed on farmers.

Similarly, the government offered protection to the shipping companies, while taking over industries begun by the Tokugawa shogunate, such as the Yokosuka Iron Foundry, to build up a modern industrial base. Standard factories such as the Tomioka Silk Reeling Mill, Shinmachi Spinning Mill (using waste yarns), Aichi Spinning Mill, and Hiroshima Spinning Mill were built and operated by the government to supply domestic needs, as well as to cultivate export markets.

Encouraged by government support and protection, private interests also embarked around 1877 upon construction of factories for production of cotton and silk threads and fabrics, paper, cement, sugar, sulphuric acid, glass, copper, and naval and merchant ships. Stabilization of the currency by laws standardizing conversion rates in 1886 served to expedite the rise of industries backed by private capital.

Of all industries developed during the early half of the Meiji period, the cotton spinning companies expanded to assume a primary position. Importing raw cotton from India, they were able to produce threads of superior quality capable of competing sucessfully with imported threads. In time, the cotton firms began exporting to China. The number of spindles increased remarkably, marking the beginnings of light industry in Japan.

On the other hand, success for the cotton factories inflicted heavy injuries on the small-scale domestic home industries producing cotton locally and making hand-woven cotton fabrics. The cottage industries were almost wiped out during the Sino-Japanese War (1894–5), as the industrial revolution spread through the cotton spinning industry of Japan.

Machines for weaving cotton fabrics had been installed in large-scale factories as early as 1887, followed by large-scale production of silk, linen, and woolen goods. Production far outstripped that possible in the manual operations of home industries. Paper mills began producing pulp for their own use as raw materials, while other industries were developed to produce machine tools, fertilizers, oil, beer, and for supplying electricity and gas to towns and cities.

Capital funds for the importation of machines and techniques were supplied by the newly-developed banks, and production was gradually shifted from small-scale manual operations to large-scale mechanized production. The foundation of a capitalist economy was laid in this beginning stage of modernization of industry during the first three decades of the Meiji period.

The increase in the number of factories during the second half of that period was as follows:

| *Year* | *Number of factories* |
|---|---|
| 1885 | 661 |
| 1892 | 2,767 |
| 1897 | 7,327 |

The concentration of capital to construct factories did not simply yield more factories, though; there was a considerable increase in the number of factories equipped with steam engines or electric motors to drive machines. The role of the worker was transformed from that of the craftsman manufacturing goods with his own hands to that of the technician operating the various machines now installed.

| *Year* | *Total number of factories* | *Factories equipped with engines or motors:*[1] *Number* | *Percentage of total* |
|---|---|---|---|
| 1894 | 5,985 | 2,409 | 37 |
| 1897 | 7,327 | 2,950 | 40 |

Even so, the gross production of home industries continued to outweigh that of factories, even after modern industries were established, as shown by the following figures:

| *Period* | *Gross production in home industries (yen)* | *Gross production in factories (yen)* |
|---|---|---|
| 1875–7 | 42,000,000 | 21,000,000 |
| 1893–7 | 380,000,000 | 318,000,000 |

While total production increased sharply during the two decades indicated above, the proportion accounted for by home industries was more than half in each period.

The relative weight of agricultural production with respect to total production changed during the same interval:

| *Period* | *Gross agricultural production (yen)* | *Percentage of total production* |
|---|---|---|
| 1875–7 | 276,000,000 | 81.5 |
| 1892–3 | 657,000,000 | 48.5 |

Although the actual amount of agricultural production more than doubled by the second period, its share of the gross national product dropped off considerably.[2]

Improved economic conditions based on increased production permitted a sizable population increase in the country:

| *Year* | *Population in Japan* | *Rate of increase (%)* |
|---|---|---|
| 1872 | 34,810,000 | —— |
| 1897 | 42,400,000 | 21.8 |

The population structure of Japan up to the end of the 19th century makes it clear that the basis of national life was still in agriculture. Of all those engaged in some occupation, a large majority were occupied with agricultural work, even after establishment of modern industries, as the following figures show:

| *Period* | *Agricultural workers* | *Percentage of total workers*[3] |
|---|---|---|
| 1875–7 | 14,000,000 | 81 |
| 1893–7 | 16,000,000 | 70 |

The combined effect of decreased agricultural production and industrial expansion in the cities was to stimulate population growth in the cities. Not only did the cities expand in size, but the number of cities increased.

| *Year* | *No. of cities with 10,000–50,000 pop.* | *No. of cities with 50,000–100,000 pop.* | *No. of cities with over 100,000 pop.* |
|---|---|---|---|
| 1868 | 87 | 5 | 5 |
| 1898 | 213 | 12 | 8 |

Although agriculture continued to constitute the larger portion of the Japanese economy up to the Sino-Japanese War (1894–5), the foundation for the development of capitalism was laid by that time. During the following period, beginning with the Sino-Japanese War and ending with World War I (1914–7), Japan underwent an industrial revolution accomplished by enlarging her world markets and her range of available natural resources in colonies acquired in those wars, and in the Russo-Japanese War occurring in the interim. Rapid expansion of industry in urban areas was accompanied by a series of important developments: penetration of the commodity economy throughout rural society, differentiation of the social strata, and a massive influx of peasants into the cities. These processes provided industry with a large force of cheap labor, enabling the country to convert from an agricultural state into a modern industrial nation.

Industrial enterprises expanded internally, but also through amalgamation with other firms. Smaller enterprises were absorbed within the structures of larger ones, setting the stage for monopolistic capitalism. Capital ownership had been made the key to social position, and monopolistic controls of large capital the major force in politics. Japanese society began shifting from a status-oriented to a class society.

While industrial development and expansion of foreign trade made new products available to the upper classes, the domestic market did not develop throughout the country as a whole because the farmers, still a majority of the total population, were too poor, even to purchase basic necessities in many cases. The government leaders felt increasingly the need for securing markets on the Chinese mainland, in order to establish a greater degree of independence over against the Western countries moving rapidly into Asian territories.

The bureaucratic and capitalist elite began promotion of an exaggerated nationalism and militarism as a rationale for expansion onto the mainland. Under such circumstances, the Sino-Japanese War broke out in 1894. Japan surprised the world with its victory in this war which gave her the overseas territories of Taiwan, Liaotung Peninsula, and the Pescadores. Korea was taken out from under the control of the Ch'ing dynasty in China. Japan, along with countries in Europe and America, assumed a superiority over the Ch'ing government, opening up markets for herself in the Far East.

With 360 million yen paid in reparations by the Ch'ing government Japan moved onto a gold standard, giving it an advantage over the Chinese nation which remained on a silver standard. The gold standard secured by Japan enabled her to deal more on equal terms with the Western powers, facilitating importation of armaments, precision machinery, and large shipments of raw cotton. Japan also secured export markets for tea and silk in the U.S.A.

The Ch'ing reparations payments resolved Japan's shortage of funds, which had held up purchases of machines for equipping her factories. It also strengthened the feeble position of the joint-stock corporations, which so far could not match the strong bargaining positions of Western powers in international trade. The number of factories built in Japan increased sharply. The cotton spinning industry benefited especially from the cancellation of export duties on cotton yarns and import duties on raw cotton in 1896. Production rose sharply, expelling imported yarns from the domestic market almost entirely, and facilitating acquisition of export markets.

Significant progress was made in other lines of production such as, for instance, the linen industry which was monopolized by four large companies formed by consolidation of many smaller enterprises. Paper mills soon supplied most of the carboards demanded by the domestic market. Mechanized factory production supplanted the less efficient hand-reeling processes in silk production and, by 1909, Japan's silk reeling industry gained top place in the world, outstripping China and Italy.[4]

Heavy industry, which had been unable to compete with the developed factories of the West, received a great boost from acquisition of overseas resources. Operations of the Yawata Steel Mill were begun by the government in 1901, importing iron ore from the Tayeh Mine in China; coal came from the mines in northern Kyūshū. The foundation was laid thereby for further expansion of the munitions industry, using iron and steel products of the Yawata Steel Mill.

There was no particularly remarkable development in the production of machines and tools in general. Shipbuilding was pushed, however, by the Navy. The combined efforts of government and private enterprise brought the construction of large vessels up to the highest world standards by the end of the Meiji period. Production of locomotives and equipment for telephone and telegraph services was also promoted. Directly and indirectly the Army sought to expedite development of all communication facilities, to gain greater efficiency in maintaining national security.

The installation of machines in both light and heavy industries was fostered so that, by 1903, the number of factories mechnically equipped reached 3,741, or 45% of the 8,274 factories employing ten or more laborers. Most of the machine-equipped factories were light industries, especially the textile industry, as is indicated in the large proportion of female workers.

| *Year* | *Total no. of workers* | *Female workers*[5] |
|---|---|---|
| 1897 | 439,549 | —— |
| 1903 | 483,839 | 301,435 (65%) |

The Sino-Japanese War gave Japan her first great leap forward in industrial development. The second was provided by the Russo-Japanese War of 1904–5. Russia had been on guard against Japanese advances on the mainland, and pressed her to return the Liaotung Peninsula to the Ch'ing government, backed by Germany and France in this demand. Japan's international position was not yet strong, and had been won only through hardship and privation imposed on her populace. Nevertheless, the government decided to assess even larger taxes on the people in order to enlarge the military budget. By 1898 the military budget already accounted for 51.79% of the total national budget. Germany's military expenditures were a little less, while Great Britain allowed only 31% of her national budget for military expenses. Japan arose as the most militarily committed nation of that age.[6]

As soon as the impotence of the Ch'ing government was demonstrated by the Japanese victory in the Sino-Japanese War, the Western powers entered into a vigorous competition for control over the Chinese territories. Anti-foreign movements promoted by the Chinese against these advances were taken by the Western powers as sufficient justification, that is, rationalization, for their encroachments upon Chinese provinces. Russia sent a large contingent of troops into Manchuria, occupying important positions. Japan countered by concluding the Anglo-Japanese Alliance Treaty, to check the Russian move. The next step in the struggle for control over continental colonies was war between Japan and Russia.

Prior to taking that step Japan had virtually accomplished the light industry phase of her industrial revolution, and the resources of rural society had been organized to support urban demands. Japanese success in the Russo-Japanese War raised the curtain on the second phase of her industrial revolution. Her victory gave her protectorate rights over Korea and the Russian lease of the Liaotung (Kwantung) Peninsula. She acquired railway and coal mine concessions in Manchuria and control of the southern half of Sakhalin Island just offshore from the Russian-held territories of the Asian continent, as well as fishing rights in the Siberian waters. The possibilities for exploitation of resources in Manchuria and China were vastly increased over expectations held at the time of the Sino-Japanese War.

The South Manchurian Railroad was developed by the Japanese government with capital investments amounting to 200 million yen, providing a trunk line for utilization of Manchurian resources through military protection and state capital. Rail gauges in Manchuria and Korea were standardized. Substantial support for Japanese industrialization was obtained by construction of the Penchihu and Anshan Steel Mills on the mainland, and Japanese capital was poured into the development of spinning companies in China.

Foreign trade ventures begun before and after the Sino-Japanese War received a tremendous stimulus now that Japan controlled extended markets in East Asia. The remarkable increases in annual exports are indicated in the following figures covering, roughly, the two decades between the Sino-Japanese War and World War I:

| *Year* | *Annual exports (yen)* | *Total amount of foreign trade (yen)* |
|---|---|---|
| 1897 | 163,130,000 | 382,430,000 |
| 1908 | 378,240,000 | 814,500,000 |
| 1914 | 591,100,000 | 1,186,840,000 |

Exports more than tripled during this period, while overall foreign trade increased slightly less than three times the 1897 amount. These figures reveal the notable development of the Japanese economy after the Russo-Japanese War, as well as Japan's ascension as a major military, political, and economic power in the East Asian sphere.[7]

Extensive development of modern industries accompanied the remarkable expansion of foreign trade, the chief course of industrial growth being expanded capital investments. There were several sources of new capital, such as government loans floated in the international bonds market to meet war expenses, introduction of foreign capital into Japan, progress made in the insurance business, monopolization of tobacco production by the government, and further construction of national railways.

Japanese products found their way into markets throughout the Orient, the textile industry acquiring particular stability through increased exports. Production in heavy industries such as shipbuilding, rolling stock, machines and tools, as well as gas plants and various kinds of mines, was fostered through government protection that imposed high duties on foreign imports competing with these heavy industries. There occurred, concomitantly, a kind of revolution in energy utilization around 1912, as electric power was diffused throughout the country. Even small and medium-sized industries could equip themselves with electric motors, and electric power was made available to many people regardless of quantity, time, or location.

Even though industrial capacities were boosted and political powers extended, Japan was limited in securing world markets by the favored positions already established by the more advanced countries. Limitations could be overcome partly by appropriation of advanced techniques, and the general technical level of production was raised considerably. But the primary means of catching up with developed countries lay in the direction of promoting highly competitive economic mechanisms. The Japanese authorities had fostered the formation of large-scale enterprises from the beginning of the Meiji period, but the demand for even larger corporations intensified after the Russo-Japanese War. New capital resources were channeled into expansion programs of existing companies and into amalgamated corporations, resulting in monopolistic combines.

Modern industry in Japan did not develop through open competition, but through government nurture to prevent colonization as witnessed in neighboring Asian lands. Organizational forms included both large joint-stock corporations or individually operated capital firms. On the other hand, a large rural population with little purchasing power could not begin to absorb the products of expanded industry, leaving always a surplus of goods. Business firms looked hopefully for overseas markets, but could not compete easily with larger, more efficient foreign firms. Monopolization and amalgamation presented the most viable options available.

Enlarged corporations appeared initially in the banking business. The government did not favor formation of small banks because of their inherent weakness and inefficiency and set, therefore, a minimum capital limit on the establishment of banks. Industry's need for large concentrations of capital added weight to the official policies of the government.

Following a recession after the Sino-Japanese War the cry for enlarged commercial and industrial corporations was stronger than ever. The movement toward consolidation of smaller enterprises into large combines was accelerated from late in the Meiji period on into the Taishō era (1912–26). The effects of this movement are indicated in the figures below showing a decrease in factories employing only a few workers, and a trend toward larger labor forces in the factories.

| *No. of employees* | *No. of Factories* | | *Percentage of total* | | *Rate of increase(%)* |
|---|---|---|---|---|---|
| | (1909) | (1914) | (1909) | (1914) | |
| 5–9 | 16,802 | 14,655 | 52.4 | 46.2 | −6.8 |
| 10–29 | 10,812 | 11,553 | 33.3 | 36.4 | 6.8 |
| 30–99 | 3,494 | 4,145 | 10.8 | 13.1 | 18.9 |
| 100–499 | 980 | 1,155 | 3.0 | 3.6 | 17.86 |
| 500—— | 140 | 209 | 0.5 | 0.7 | 49.3 |
| Total: | 32,228 | 31,717 | | | |

Thus, by 1914 the total number of factories decreased, as did the number of factories with five to nine workers. Not only did the number of larger factories increase; the rate of increase was much higher among large-scale factories.

Capital concentration in terms of paid-up capital in joint-stock companies was distributed as follows:[8]

| *Year* | *Less than ¥100,000* | *Less than ¥500,000* | *Less than ¥1,000,000* | *Less than ¥5,000,000* | *More than ¥5,000,000* |
|---|---|---|---|---|---|
| 1910 | 11.53% | 18.11% | 10.95% | 21.42% | 37.99% |
| 1913 | 10.43% | 16.74% | 9.88% | 24.88% | 38.07% |

The tendency toward enlargement of corporations was sustained at a fairly high level after the Russo-Japanese War but it did not keep pace with the trend toward capital concentration. This was because the bulk of industry was in textiles, which tended toward small-scale operations and enjoyed only limited domestic and overseas markets.

The above list excludes small workshops with four employees or less, though there was a considerable number of them in this period. Even in 1914 some 95.8% of the total number of factories employed between five and ninety-nine workers. Of the total number of workers, 51% were employed in these small factories. On the one hand, factories with large capital bases employed thousands of employees using modern facilities of production, while thousands of factories with only a few employees and poor equipment labored under conditions not far removed from the primitive industrial forms of cottage industry.

Ceramics and breweries comprised only local industries of small scale, as did match making and sundries. Small and medium-sized enterprises prospered among spinning, weaving, and dyeing industries. In the machine making industry especially there were many small and medium-sized plants that filled subcontracts for large enterprises with which they were connected. The interdependence of many smaller firms working under the protective umbrella of large enterprises was a characteristic feature of Japanese industrialization, and one that persists even today.

The concentration of capital in expanded corporations hastened the development of monopolistic controls over particular industries. The Kanegafuchi Spinning Company absorbed fourteen companies in twenty-five years between 1899 and 1923. Mie Spinning Company and Ōsaka Spinning Company merged to form Tōyō Spinning Company in 1914 Prior to merger the Mie firm absorbed eight smaller companies, and the Ōsaka firm three others.[9] Eight firms at the pinnacle of an association of spinning companies, embracing fifty-one different companies, owned 51.6% of the spindles in operation by 1903; the seven leading firms in that same association commanded 58% of the total number of spindles at work in 1913.

In 1913 five companies and the Navy produced 54% of all coal mined, and five companies (including Sumitomo) accounted for 69% of all copper. Dainihon Refining Company in sugar refining, Nihon Oil and Hōden Oil

Companies in the petroleum industry, and Dainihon Fertilizer Company all made strenuous efforts to command controlling positions in their respective fields.

The tendency toward monopolization took on added dimensions with the establishment of cartel arrangements to reach mutual agreements fixing prices and setting controls over sales and production. Industry-wide cartels appeared early in the industrial processes of Japan, as in the Great Japan Federation (*Dainihon Rengōkai*) founded in 1880 to limit the collective production of vellum and printing paper. The Great Japan Association of Spinning Companies was formed two years later to hold down production and realize cooperative arrangements in the transport of raw cotton. Similar cartels multiplied rapidly after the Russo-Japanese War.

The recession that followed in the aftermath of that war intensified the exercise of controls by the spinning association and other cartels. Paper mills introduced mutual trusts to control sales of their products, and other cartels followed in rapid succession: in the flour making industry in 1914, in silk reeling in 1915, and in wool spinning and bleach production in 1920. Monopoly formation became even more intense as panic over surpluses pervaded many fields after World War I.

New territories and markets won in the Russo-Japanese War, then, stimulated the development of heavy industry and led to strengthened capitalistic controls. The next stage of economic expansion began with the advent of World War I. In this stage the industrial revolution and capitalistic monopolies reached a peak, based on territorial expansion overseas.

The powerful nation states of Europe had pressed their policies of territorial expansion supported by substantial military preparations late in the 19th century. World peace was kept among them only through a precariously maintained balance of power. When the balance broke down, World War I ensued. Japan took advantage of her position as the only non-Western industrialized state to supply neglected Western markets and soon enjoyed the highest peak of prosperity in her history.

After the war began normal economic activity was utterly disrupted. Exchange systems were suspended, marine transportation came to a standstill, and foreign trade followed suit. The Japanese economy itself was thrown temporarily into confusion as prices on the international market fell off. This condition did not continue for long before Japan began receiving orders from European and other countries, and business took a swing upward.

Japan allied herself with Britain, attacking Tsingtao and occupying German holdings in the Shangtung Peninsula, as well as German possessions in the North Pacific islands. Far removed from the scene of battle, Japan suffered no damages from this war, enjoying rather heavy demands for ammunitions from Russia and other participant countries. Munitions plants under civilian ownership enlarged their production facilities to peak capacity.

Orders for large amounts of knitwear came from Britain and Italy, and the African and Asian markets formerly supplied by European manufacturers, especially British, switched their orders to Japanese producers. Japan was able to assume a monopoly position in exports to India and China. Her goods became a major source of supply to South Sea island countries as well. The total volume of Japanese foreign trade reached a record world peak.

During the four war years Japan exported about 5.4 billion yen worth of goods, while importing only four billion yen worth. A sharp decrease in available merchant vessels throughout the world presented Japanese shippers with an unprecedented opportunity for expansion in ocean freight transport. Accounts receivable, above and beyond the booming foreign trade business, amounted to 1.4 billion yen. This prosperity derived from three sources, namely, increased tonnage, sharp rises in ocean freight rates, and an expanded volume of receipts for marine insurance.

Gold reserves in Japan in 1914 at the beginning of the war totaled 218 million yen; by 1920 the total climbed to 1,247 million yen. Again, in 1914 Japan owed debts of some 1.1 billion yen, but in 1920 registered receipts totaling 2.77 billion yen, establishing a healthy credit balance.[10]

Expanded exports and marine transport created a boom in Japanese industry. Both agricultural and industrial production experienced phenomenal increases, as shown below:

| *Year* | *Agricultural production (yen)* | *Industrial production (yen)*[11] |
|---|---|---|
| 1914 | 1,400,000,000 | 1,370,000,000 |
| 1919 | 4,100,000,000 | 6,730,000,000 |

When industrial production finally exceeded agricultural production values, Japan crossed the line from being a semi-agricultural state to become a modern industrial nation.

Factory development between the years 1909 and 1919 reflects this transition:

| *Year* | *No. of factories with five or more workers* | *No. of workers* | *No. of unskilled laborers* |
|---|---|---|---|
| 1909 | 15,426 | 692,221 | 30,400 |
| 1919 | 43,949 | 1,520,466 | 92,729 |
| Rate of expansion: | 280% | 210% | 270% |

Moreover, an increase in the percentage of male workers in mechanized industries was indicative of the fact that heavy industry was beginning to replace light industry as the major portion of overall industrial capacity.

| *Year* | *Percentage of mechanized industries with five or more workers* | *Year* | *Percentage of male workers*[12] |
|---|---|---|---|
| 1909 | 43 | 1909 | 34 |
| 1919 | 59 | 1918 | 46 |

The relative place of light industry within overall Japanese industry diminished somewhat during and after World War I, though it retained its dominant role.

*Light Industry's share of total production:*[13]

| *Year* | *No. of factories* | *Mechanized factories* | *No. of Workers* | *Share of total production* |
|---|---|---|---|---|
| 1915 | 79.5% | 78.6% | 76.7% | 69.3% |
| 1922 | 73.3% | 72.4% | 69.5% | 70.7% |

At the top of the Japanese industrial pyramid in this period sat the big cotton yarn and silk industries. During the war imports of British cotton yarns were ceased and Japan took over the China market as well as expanding into Southeast Asian markets. Cotton yarn exports jumped from a prewar figure of 80 million yen (1912) to a postwar amount of 160 million yen (1920).

China began developing her own spinning mills, making it less profitable to export cotton yarns as such. Japanese firms responded by converting to cotton cloth production and experienced a sudden leap in cotton exports from 43 million yen to 350 million yen. Conversion to woven cotton goods served to strengthen five companies in particular: Kanegafuchi Spinning Company, Tōyō Spinning Company, Dainihon Spinning Company, Fuji Spinning Company, and Nisshin Spinning Company. Known as the "Five Spinning Giants" (*Godaibōseki*), these companies established a powerful monopoly over the spinning industry through massive capital accumulation and productive capacity.

Depressed by the general confusion caused by the beginning of World War I, the silk reeling industry recovered quickly in 1916–7 by cultivating a large market in the prosperous economy of the United States. Both sharp price rises and the increased U.S. trade drove silk exports up to a peak of 620 million yen. Large factories took advantage of expanded receipts to install production machinery during this period. The Katakura Silk Reeling Company and the Gunze Silk Reeling Company extended their controls over the entire silk industry all the way from silkworm egg cultivation to final sales.[14]

Turning out over 10,000 tons even before the war in Europe erupted, shipbuilding constituted the bulk of Japanese heavy industry. The only major industrial nation not caught up in the immediate throes of battle, Japanese shipbuilders began receiving orders for steamers to relieve the critical shortage already evident by the outbreak of the war. The tremendous expansion of this industry during the war years is seen in the figures below:

| *Year* | *No. of shipyards* | *No. of ships built* | *Gross tonnage* |
|---|---|---|---|
| 1913 | 5 | 79 | 82,800 |
| 1918 | 53 | 443 | 545,000 |

Before the war Japanese imports of foreign-made ships exceeded her own exports; by the end of the war this was reversed. Japanese shipping rose to third place behind Great Britian and the United States.

While many shipyards were built, most of them were only small-scale operations. Six major companies monopolized this industry, claiming about 80% of all shipbuilding, in terms of capital stock, the number of workmen, and production capacity. They were Kawasaki Shipbuilding Company, Mitsubishi Shipbuilding Company, Ōsaka Shipbuilding Company, Asano Shipbuilding Company, Ishikawajima Shipbuilding Company, Uraga Dock Company, and Imperial Steamship Company.[15]

Prior to the war the Japanese machine industry was not highly developed, and many industries depended upon imported machines. Again, the situation was reversed during the wary ears. Ōsaka Shipbuilding Company and Kawasaki Shipbuilding Company had monopolized locomotive production in Japan under government subsidies, and they were able now to eliminate all locomotive imports from the country in addition to initiating overseas exports themselves. As machine tools could not be imported easily during the war, the Japanese makers went into mass production in this field too. Engine and motor production were vastly improved under the same conditions, relieving Japanese producers from relying on imported products.

As for basic industry, steel manufacture was concentrated in the two mills in Yawata and Kamaishi before the war. The iron and steel works in Europe were destroyed, forcing them to abandon their overseas markets. Export orders gave new life to the Japanese companies, and a large proportion of increased profits were plowed back into factory expansion. The Yawata and Kamaishi Steel Mills were greatly enlarged and, in addition to these two, other iron foundries and steel mills were built. By 1918 Japan was able to supply 78% of her pig iron needs, and 48% of the demands for rolled steel.

Improvements had been made in coal mining since the Russo-Japanese War in both mining facilities and transportation means. Machines were installed and electric power supplied to the mines. Overall production increased under wartime demands, and the Chikuho coal fields of northern Kyūshū alone accounted for 79% of domestic production. Coal mines in Pyongyang in Korea, and Fushun and Penchihu in China were operated under joint arrangements between the Japanese government and the favored financial cliques.

We have already noted the rapid development of the electric power industry along with heavy industry after the Russo-Japanese War. An epochal success was made in 1914 when Japanese technicians succeeded in transmitting a high voltage current of 110,000 volts along the 150-mile distance between Inawashiro and Tōkyō. After World War I, electricity was utilized in most of Japan. Only 14% of the total horsepower used in industry in 1909 was consumed by electric motors; by 1919 the ratio climbed to 62%. When profits in the electric power supply business declined after the war, the larger companies quickly absorbed the many minor companies that had mushroomed all over the country, forming five major electric power companies.

A number of key Japanese industries thus achieved remarkable progress after World War I, and the total economy gained a stronger position with respect to the more advanced capitalist states. The trend toward greater accumulation and concentration of capital was strengthened, as evidenced, for example, in the decrease of small companies with less than one million yen in capital stock and in paid-up capital.

*Percentage of companies of less than ¥1,000,000 in relation to all companies:*

| *Year* | *No. of companies* | *Paid-up capital* |
|---|---|---|
| 1914 | 97.8 | 37.1 |
| 1920 | 90.9 | 18.6 |

*Percentage of companies with over ¥5,000,000 in capital:*

| *Year* | *No. of companies* | *Paid-up capital* |
|---|---|---|
| 1914 | 0.4 | 38.6 |
| 1920 | 1.8 | 57.0 |

From this it is clear that capital concentration in a few large companies was a characteristic feature of post-World War I economy in Japan.[16]

With expansion in both foreign trade and industry, the demand for capital funds also expanded. The banks increased their capital often, especially through amalgamation, as per the following:

*Number of banks absorbed by mergers:*[17]

1916——5 1919——54 1920——43

Five large banks emerged as the controlling giants of the whole banking business: Mitsui, Mitsubishi, Yasuda, Sumitomo, and Daiichi. An interlocking of banking capital and industrial capital was promoted during the years of World War I which led later to the establishment of firm monopolistic controls over commerce and industry by the great financial houses of Mitsui, Mitsubishi, Yasuda, Sumitomo, and Okura.

After acquiring concessions in Manchuria and Korea in the wars with China and Russia, Japan exported some capital as well as merchandise into the territories under her control. Imperialistic expansion by Japan was determined as much, if not more, by developments in her internal economy, and especially by the formation of monopolistic controls over her capitalist structures by the large financial firms, as by the strategic concerns of the military. Indeed, her aggressive diplomatic policies derived from a wedding of economic and military power and interests.

Concluding treaties governing loans and leases with the five major powers vying for "spheres of influence" in China, namely, Great Britain, France, Germany, Russia, and the United States, in 1907, Japan took advantage of the political confusion of the last decade of the failing Ch'ing dynasty to advance her own economic interests through railway loans in 1908 and again in 1911. A plan for "joint construction" by the governments of China and Japan of five rail lines in Manchuria and Mongolia was agreed upon in 1913.

World War I forced the European powers to revise their Far East policies, retarding their advances into China. A series of antiforeign, anti-Manchu, and antidynastic rebellions provided Japan with new opportunities to extend her interests and rights in China. Capital exports to the mainland were activated, especially in the textile industry. Spinning mills were constructed with Japanese capital in Shanghai, Tsingtao, and Tientsin, taking advantage of low wages and poor labor conditions.

The interests of the Japanese capitalists were reinforced by the Twenty-One Demands pressed on the Chinese government early in 1915, and backed by Japanese troops stationed in various parts of China. While not all of the demands were conceded, the effect was to confirm Japan's dominant position in the political, economic, and military affairs of Manchuria, Inner Mongolia, and North China.

In support of the short-lived efforts of the Peking premier Tuan Ch'i-jui's domestic struggles with the revolutionary forces of Sun Yat-sen in South China, Japan negotiated enormous loans, called the "Nishihara Loans," extending its controls over textile production even further and giving it inroads into other areas of economic activity such as railroads, electric power supply, financing, sea transport, and foreign trade. Extending capital aid to a less developed country such as China, Japan continued, all the while, to import foreign capital from more advanced countries in the form of public bonds, debentures, and stocks being sold in overseas markets of Great Britain and America. At this stage, Japan occupied an intermediary position between advanced and underdeveloped countries.

Industrial revolution was accompanied by rapid exploitation of overseas markets, and Japan was able to acquire a large share of these markets in Asia. Production capacity and capital accumulation rose sharply but, at the same time, agricultural production also expanded through utilization of improved techniques. Consequently, the population of Japan showed proportionate increases, as shown below:

| *Year* | *Population* | *Year* | *Population* |
|---|---|---|---|
| 1872 | 34,800,000 | 1907 | 47,410,000 |
| 1887 | 38,700,000 | 1917 | 54,130,000 |
| 1897 | 42,400,000 | 1921 | 56,780,000 |

In the fifty-year period covered above, the population swelled some 21,980,000, or 63.8%. This was an absolute increase, as there was very little movement in or out of the country, indicating a significant gap between the national birth and death rates.

The birth rate in Japan was kept quite low prior to the Sino-Japanese War, exceeding 30 (in 1,000) only once in 1889. With the development of industries in cities after that war, the birth rate climbed to 30 by 1896, staying above that line until, in 1930, a peak of 36 was reached in the heyday of industrialization and urbanization following World War I.

The death rate was as low as 12.2 (in 1,000) in 1872, and remained low so long as most of the population lived in less accident-prone rural communities. The death rate rose sharply to 20 by 1897, and reached a peak 26.8 in 1919, during years of rapid industrial expansion without adequate safety precautions for workers.

During this period of notable population changes there occurred also prominent changes in the distribution of national income by occupational groups. Whereas agriculture had been the income base for the Japanese people before the Meiji period, the radical changes in income sources that appeared in the half century after the beginning of the Meiji era were remarkable. These changes are indicated below:

*National income percentages according to occupations:*

| *Period* | *Agriculture & Foresty* | *Industry* | *Others* |
|---|---|---|---|
| 1875–7 | 39 | 6 | 55 |
| 1893–7 | 34 | 21 | 45 |
| 1918–21 | 29 | 28 | 43 |

The 1893–7 period marked the formation of the base of capitalism in Japan and the 1918–21 period the accomplishment of the industrial revolution, accounting for the decline in the relative weight of agricultural production in the structure of national income.[18]

Taking the early years of the Shōwa period (1928–32) as a standard (base = 100 yen), the per capita incomes according to occupations in the Meiji and Taishō eras were as follows:

*Per capita income according to occupation:*
*(base = 100 yen)*

| *Period* | *National average* | *Agriculture & Forestry* | *Industry* | *Other* | *Commerce* |
|---|---|---|---|---|---|
| 1875–7 | 101 | 48 | 139 | 398 | — |
| 1893–7 | 170 | 83 | 316 | — | — |
| 1918–22 | 220 | 163 | 444 | 401 | 448 |

Agricultural production in the 1893–7 period increased 77% over the 1875–7 period, although income increased by only 73% during the same two decades. Income increased in industry by 127% from the first to the second period, starting from a higher figure to begin with. Both agriculture and industry increased by 41% from the 1893–7 period to the 1918–22 period, but the disparity was still very much in favor of the strong position of industry in the economy.[19]

Changes in national and per capita income reflected the structure of population but, of course, the attraction of increased incomes in both industry and commerce worked to alter the population structure. This can be seen in the following percentages according to occupation groups:

*Population percentages according to occupations:*

| *Year* | *Agriculture & Forestry* | *Industry* | *Commerce* | *Others* |
|---|---|---|---|---|
| 1877 | 80.7 | 5.1 | 5.3 | 8.9 |
| 1897 | 68.5 | 12.1 | 8.2 | 11.2 |
| 1921 | 51.6 | 19.4 | 11.6 | 17.4 |

Thus, agriculture and forestry registered losses in average national income and per capita income, as well as in population, while commerce and industry recorded gains in all three areas. However, the population increase in industry and commerce are not to be accounted for solely in terms of the migration of the agricultural population to the cities, as there was an overall 63.8% increase in population in the nation between 1877 and 1921 (see above, p. 388).[20]

Moreover, urban population increases were not uniform, as there were limitations on the industrial and commercial potential of different cities, depending on geographical access to natural resources and markets. Most of the raw materials for industry had to be imported from abroad, and proximity to large domestic markets and foreign export outlets, as well as access to labor and capital supply centers, were conditioning factors. That the concentration of industries and commercial organs in the cities did account for the movement of large numbers of the agricultural population into the cities is indeniable.

Though somewhat removed from the Meiji period, data is available for tracing the increase-decrease ratios of various city populations in the Taishō period between 1920 and 1925. These figures indicate the rate of increase due to social movement, exclusive of natural increase, in relation to absolute population increase. These growth rates are given below for for cities classified according to population size:

| *Population size of cities* | *Percentage of population increase due to social movement* |
|---|---|
| Six major cities, with over 400,000 pop. | 73.4 |
| Over 100,000 pop. | 69.0 |
| Over 50,000 pop. | 61.6 |
| Over 40,000 pop. | 58.8 |
| Over 30,000 pop. | 56.1 |
| Over 20,000 pop. | 40.2 |
| Towns and villages, with more than 10,000 pop. | No social increase; aggregate 340,000 population decrease |
| Towns and villages, with less than 10,000 pop. | No social increase; aggregate 2,650,000 population decrease |

From this it is clear that there was a clear relationship between the population size of a city and its rate of social increase; the larger the city, the higher the rate. In other words, the expansion of the larger cities depended on population influx from the rural districts, smaller towns and cities. Even with the natural increase in population due to an elevated standard of living, the chief cause of population growth in the larger cities was migration of rural folk to urban centers.

The table above gives only percentages of increase due to social movements for a brief five-year period after industrial revolution was carried out. Overall urban expansion from early in the Meiji period up to 1920 was as follows:

| *Year* | *Percentage of total population in cities of more than 10,000:* |
|---|---|
| 1879 | 11 |
| 1887 | 12 |
| 1898 | 18 |
| 1908 | 25 |
| 1920 | 32 |

*Number of cities by population size:*

| *Year* | *10,000–50,000* | *50,000–100,000* | *more than 100,000* |
|---|---|---|---|
| 1891 | 196 | 12 | 6 |
| 1920 | 537 | 31 | 16 |

Up to 1887 it is manifestly clear that most of the people were yet resident in rural areas, including towns and villages with less than 10,000 population. Urban population advanced by great strides with each new stimulus afterward; six per cent after the Sino-Japanese War, and seven per cent after the Russo-Japanese War, and another seven per cent after World War I.

Specific figures for population growth in each of the six major cities from the foundation of capitalism to completion of the industrial revolution were:

| *Year* | *Tōkyō* | *Ōsaka* | *Kyōto* | *Kōbe* | *Yokohama* | *Nagoya* |
|---|---|---|---|---|---|---|
| 1897 | 1,330,000 | 750,000 | 330,000 | 190,000 | 190,000 | 250,000 |
| 1920 | 3,350,000 | 1,760,000 | 700,000 | 640,000 | 570,000 | 610,000 |

That Tōkyō was the national nucleus of integrative organs, and Ōsaka its chief partner, is attested to in these population figures. We shall describe later the role played by monopolistic capital in the expansion of integrative organs and social scale of these cities.

For the moment it is enough to remark that Ōsaka was not only the traditional center of finance for the Kansai district of economic activity extending all over the country, but that it developed also as the center of the expanded textile industry. Kōbe, Yokohama, and Nagoya benefited from the expansion of foreign trade through their ports. Population growth in all these cities was accompanied by extension of their integrative functions over wide regions of the nation. Yokohama, smallest of the big six, experienced an overall population increase in excess of 200,000 more than that of the other major cities.[21]

Functional and population expansion of these cities involved important relations not only with total society and with other cities, but embodied crucial ecological relations with small towns and farm villages. No population center, large or small, could escape the pervasive impact of the government's policy of pushing forward the development of industry and commerce to strengthen the power of the state.

However, the government did not take commensurately positive steps to modernize agricultural production, and the farming areas were far more subject to the limitations of natural resources and traditional social patterns. Hence, modernization of rural society was seriously delayed by these inherited conditions and by being subjected also to conditions imposed by the expansion of industry and capitalism. The initiative in social change was taken over by city-oriented commerce and industry, which were developed at the expense of the farmers.

One of the many reasons for the delay of modernization on the farms was simply that there was not enough land to go around, and individual farms were much too small to make significant improvements. Most of the farms were less than two and a half acres, as the following percentages of farms classified by size makes clear:

*Percentages of farms by size:*

| *Year* | *Less than 5 tan* | *More than 5 tan* | *More than 1 chō* | *More than 2 chō* | *More than 3 chō* | *More than 5 chō* |
|---|---|---|---|---|---|---|
| 1908 | 37.28 | 32.61 | 19.51 | 6.44 | 3.01 | 1.15 |
| 1921 | 35.13 | 33.40 | 20.95 | 6.13 | 2.76 | 1.63 |

(5 *tan* = 1.225 acres; 1 *chō* = 2.45 acres)

In 1908, 89.4% of total farm area was in small farms of less than two *chō*; 89.48% in 1921.[22]

Even a single farm unit did not usually have all its fields located together in a single location, but was divided into smaller sections distributed about in different places. The topographical levels of the fields varied, and they were rarely rectangular in shape. Most of the land was cultivated as rice paddy fields with time-honored techniques, which did not lend themselves to large-scale or mechanized operation. They were tilled by family units as small-scale enterprises.

After the Meiji Restoration lands which had been jointly-owned and cooperatively cultivated for fertilizers, fodder, and fuels were taken over by the government. After revision of the tax systems obligated owners of the land to pay taxes, rents for tenant farmers jumped to about 50% of crop yields. Far from being able to make progress in keeping with the rest of society, the farmers were ground down into greater poverty.

Although the rate of change was painfully slow, the rural districts did benefit some from advances made in the whole of society. New facilities for river control and irrigation were introduced, adding to the overall acreage of arable land.

| *Year* | *Total area of arable land*[23] |
|---|---|
| 1880 | 4,450,000 *chōbu* |
| 1897 | 5,030,000 *chōbu* |
| 1910 | 5,650,000 *chōbu* |
| 1919 | 6,070,000 *chōbu* |
| | (1 *chōbu* = 2.45 acres) |

Production of phosphate fertilizers was begun in 1877, and utilization of chemical fertilizers penetrated rather swiftly into farm areas, making intensive cultivation and, hence, larger crop yields per unit area of land possible.

| *Year* | *Rice yield per tan* | *Total rice production*[24] |
|---|---|---|
| 1877 | —— | 25,000,000 *koku* |
| 1878 | 1.015 *koku* | —— |
| 1897 | 1.185 *koku* | 33,000,000 *koku* |
| 1920 | 2.022 *koku* | 63,000,000 *koku* |
| | (1 *tan* = 0.245 acres; | 1 *koku* = 5.12 US bu.) |

The gradual increase in rice yields was essential to the population growth experienced during the Meiji era and afterward.

Development of agriculture for commercial purposes was accelerated by foreign trade and industrial growth. The social repercussions were far-reaching, as the rural communities were drawn more and more into the commanding web of urban society. For example, cotton production fell off drastically as a result of increased foreign trade relations. Initially cotton fabrics were imported from Great Britain, though later raw cotton was brought in from India and the United States for domestic weaving. After the Sino-Japanese War manual weaving and spinning in home industries, substantial sources of income as secondary occupations of the farm areas, were abolished. Following the Russo-Japanese War silk reeling in rural shops was completely replaced by reeling factories in the cities. Likewise, paper production in rural localities was overcome by the expansion of paper mills. The side jobs related to the cotton industry, that enabled the farmers to maintain even a degree of self-sufficiency, were eliminated.

On the other hand, farmers engaged in secondary production of raw silk and tea were favored by expansion of export trading in silk threads and cloth and packaged tea. Silk production had long depended upon world markets, especially the American trade. But it required considerable fertilizer, equipment, and labor to be effective. Such conditions made sericulture particularly susceptible to the penetration of capitalistic mechanisms. Vast improvements in transportation facilities made it possible, and more profitable, for farmers to specialize in the cultivation of one or, at most, a few agricultural products for shipment and sale in the urban markets. Prior to and a little after World War I specialization in sericulture appeared in some of the rural districts. Specialization in fruits and vegetables, of course, was another example of accommodation to the emerging capitalist urban society.

More and more the rural communities became integral parts of the organic structures of the city, and an important segment of the commodity market was occupied with receiving and distributing agricultural products. Just the same, commercialization and specialization were adopted by only a minority of the farmers; most of them still concentrated on growing rice, other staples and raw materials for their own use.

The most important of all changes wrought in the rural communities by pervasive penetration of the commodity economy was the tendency toward the centralization of ownership of lands. One of the reform measures of the Meiji leaders was the liberalization of land transactions, but in time it tended to become a distorted form of commodity exchange. The disparity between prices for farm products and goods on the market widened. Burdened already by national and local taxes the farmers were increasingly unable to purchase fertilizers and tools at prices that edged higher and higher. Consequently, many peasants feel even further into poverty.

Although held legally responsible for tax payments, landowners could claim, as we noted above, some 50% of crop yields. Inasmuch as the prices of farm products tended always to move upward, landowners could easily handle tax assessments and have sufficient marginal funds left over to buy up lands from impoverished farmers. With each purchase of new land, the landowners stood to gain, while the proportion of lands worked under tenant arrangements increased, as follows:

| *Year* | *Percentage of land area in tenancy*[25] |
|---|---|
| 1887 | 39.3 |
| 1903 | 44.6 |
| 1919 | 45.9 |

The increase shown above in the number of tenant farmers included some increasingly concentrated in the hands of merchants handling fertilizers, usurers, and established landowners. Their tactics were simple. Funds and goods were loaned to peasants with lands as security; lands were taken when the debts were not paid, as they frequently were not.

The process of land ownership concentration did not include concentration of agricultural production as such, only the lands. The landowners were not interested in the agricultural productivity of their lands; their concern was for the profits realized, the capital productivity. Their unproductive relationship to the land was parasitic, and the plight of their tenants became depressed. In time the farmers found a kind of release from their roles of supplying foodstuffs and raw materials to the cities for so little recompense; they supplied the cities with a fresh labor supply by leaving the farms and heading for the cities themselves, or at least sending members of their families in search of additional incomes to supplement the meager finances of tenant farming.

Poor families tended to be large, and girls especially could easily be spared, now that secondary occupations were scarce in the rural areas. Thousands upon thousands of young girls flocked to the cities to take their places on the production lines of silk reeling and other textile industries. Many of these girls, working for extremely low wages and under poor labor conditions, were less than twenty years of age. Undoubtedly, the low wage scales constituted one of the advantageous conditions that enabled textile firms to compete successfully with other domestic industries and foreign companies.

Sons other than heirs, who had no prospects of receiving lands of their own, also flowed into the cities to find jobs in industry. Industry could not always absorb all, male and female, who came from the rural districts, and they wound up in a variety of city jobs: minor merchants, servants, craftsmen, day laborers, maids, barmaids, and prostitutes. In any event, the urban population rose rapidly as the rural population shrank proportionately.

*Monopolistic Developments and Changes in Social Strata.*——

(1) CONCENTRATION OF MONOPOLIES IN LARGE CITIES——The stage of monopolization of Japanese capitalism was sired by a variety of forces, including large-scale industrial production, aggressive domestic and overseas policies of the government, and the legacy of traditional business ethics. The total integration achieved by monopolistic capitalism engulfed not only the cities but the rural districts and, indeed, the whole of society. The central agents of the monopolization process were the giant financial clans or cliques, known as *zaibatsu*, concentrated in the larger cities. Their controls covered industry and finance, and extended beyond to political life as well. Their operations were determinative in converting the total society from a status society to a class society.

The tendency toward cartelization appeared soon after the Sino-Japanese War and progressed rapidly after the Russo-Japanese War. Producers in the same industry formed cartels with more neutral sounding names like "association" (*rengōkai*) or "trust" (*kyōtei*), which might also be rendered "convention" or "pact." The objectives of these associations were (1) mutually determined production limits or quotas, (2) joint purchases of raw materials, (3) agreements fixing prices, and (4) cooperative sales arrangements. Collective efforts involving a majority or a sizable portion of the goods in a single industry not only tempered competition among themselves, but gave them virtual monopolies over the specific industry with respect to both production and sales.

Leadership in a particular cartel arrangement was not shared equally by all parties to the arrangement, but fell to one, or just a few, of the more powerful members of the cartel. Several examples of the more prominent of the leader-companies in their respective fields are:

| *Zaibatsu companies* | *Kind of cartel* |
|---|---|
| Mitsui and Mitsubishi | Banking and finance |
| Asano and Mitsui | Cement industry |
| Ōji Paper and Fuji Paper (both Mitsui affiliates) | Paper industry |

| | |
|---|---|
| Dainihon Jinken (Shibusawa affiliate) | Chemicals (bleaches and fertilizers) |
| Mitsui, Mitsubishi, and Fujiyama | Sugar (60%) |
| Mitsui, Mitsubishi, Sumitomo, and Kuhara | Mining |
| Furukawa and Kuhara | Copper industry |
| Mitsui, Asano, and Shibusawa | Steel products |

Most of the *zaibatsu* groups got a head start in business early in the Meiji period by buying up the government factories and firms put up for sale in the second and third decades of that period. By expanding within a particular industry or branching into various industries, they moved steadily toward monopolistic controls. The central organ of the *zaibatsu* was a holding company which held controlling shares in affiliate enterprises in a *Konzern*-type structure. Sometimes the controlling shares in a particular company consisted of the aggregate of all shares held by several of the *zaibatsu* affiliates in addition to only a relatively small percentage of shares held by the central holding company. It was the total complex of controls over many industries and over a massive capital concentration that provided the *zaibatsu* with the powers it exercised over politics.

The framework of a *zaibatsu* had its nucleus in a holding company (*gōmei kaisha*) founded with the capital of the original *zaibatsu* household. This central organ held controlling interest (often assisted by shares held by the founding household) in a number of affiliated industries and banks which, in turn, held controlling interests (not always a majority of shares) in sub-affiliate companies in an outer circle. The sub-affiliates constituted

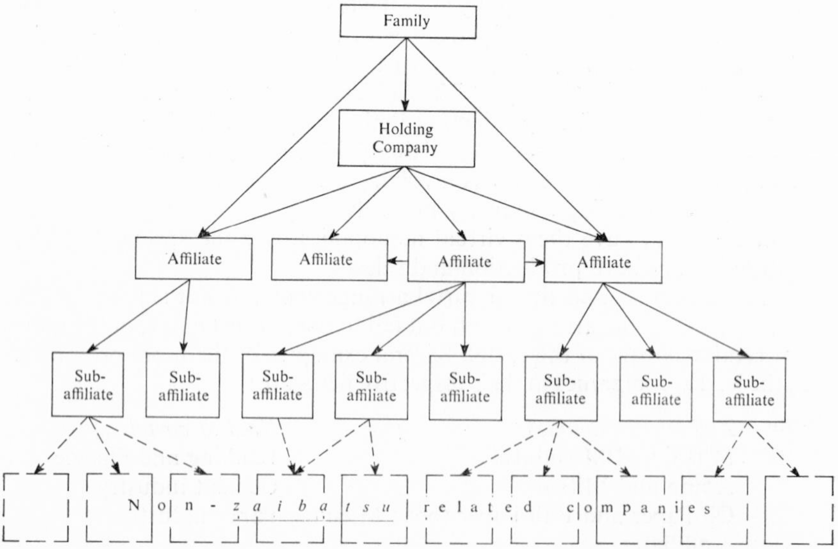

the major portion of the total capital holdings of the total *zaibatsu.* Under the sub-affiliates there were many companies with connections with the *zaibatsu* that were not actual members of the *zaibatsu* group. The top holding company, affiliates, and sub-affiliates constituted the stratified *zaibatsu* formation.

Among the *zaibatsu* there were three types, which may be differentiated as follows:

(a) The most comprehensive were those constituted basically with banking capital but owning large amounts of industrial capital. They included the gigantic bank-industry combines such as Mitsui, Mitusbishi, and Sumitomo.

(b) The second type of *zaibatsu* had its foundation in banking capital, which it used to participate in various industries through financing arrangements. Typical of this category was the Yasuda *zaibatsu.*

(c) The third type of *zaibatsu* was formed with industrial capital, and no banking capital. Examples of this type were the Furukawa and Okura *zaibatsu.*

In contrast to the large firms of the Western world, these giant combines did not build up their capital holdings through free competition, but with direct government favor and protection. Human relationships in the *zaibatsu* were heavily colored by the feudalistic traditions of the old commercial households.

Capitalism in Japan was greatly strengthened economically and politically by the concentration of capital in a few large firms. Originally the stocks of corporations connected to the *zaibatsu* were reserved only for others in *zaibatsu* relationships; outsiders were not permitted to hold shares in any *zaibatsu* companies. After World War I this exclusiveness underwent revision. Riding the wave of postwar prosperity in search of new profits and new investment opportunities, stocks were distributed beyond the confines of the *zaibatsu* clan. Large capital funds were gathered without taking great risks, as the *zaibatsu* continued to hold controlling interests in all its companies through one or more of the member companies. Controls were extended over wider ranges of finance and industry.[26]

The major *zaibatsu* were Mitsui, Mitsubishi, and Yasuda in Tōkyō; and in Ōsaka, Sumitomo, a comprehensive organization almost equivalent to Mitsui and Mitsubishi. A little smaller than Sumitomo was the Okura *zaibatsu,* in Tōkyō, which played an important role in investments and military financing in China. Joining Okura in the middle range was the Furukawa *zaibatsu,* specializing in the mining industry. Smaller *zaibatsu* included Kawasaki and Shibusawa, financing types, and Nezu, with industrial capital, in Tōkyō; and in Ōsaka, Nomura and Yamaguchi in financing, and Okazaki and Yamashita in the shipping business. Smaller *zaibatsu* under the the control of giant comprehensive *zaibatsu* included Shimazu (Mitsubishi) in Kyōto and Toyota (Mitsui) in Nagoya.

In addition to these *zaibatsu* concentrated in the major cities, there were a number of provincial *zaibatsu*: Katakura in Shinshū controlling silk reeling; North Kyūshū mining *zaibatsu* such as Yasukawa, Matsumoto, Asō, and Kaishima; and in Niigata there were a number of powerful landowners who invested in modern enterprises through *zaibatsu*-type organizations, as well as the Yamaguchi firm of Nagaoka and the Shirase firm in Niigata which acquired considerable *zaibatsu*-like controls over financing.[27]

Through their manifold connections in industry and commerce the great *zaibatsu* exercised controls over a vast range of enterprises five to fifty times their own range of capital and personnel. They stood clearly at the top of the framework of the entire national economy in a system of stratified levels reminiscent of the preceding Edo era.

As a result of rapid industrialization the capital accumulation of the large combines, controlling a majority of mass production means, soon put them in an entirely different class from smaller firms and individual capital holders. Genuine competition by the latter was out of the question. Instead, they were forced to seek new capital from many sources, most of which, whether bank deposits, stock and bonds systems, were eventually controlled by the *zaibatsu* giants. Commercial capital was gradually absorbed by financing capital.

Entering late into the capitalist economy of the world, Japan could compete effectively with the more advance countries of American and Europe only by rapid accumulation and concentration of large amounts of capital. The initiative was not left entirely to private enterprises; the government lent its support to the promotion of banking and joint stock ventures.

One of the measures the government took was to convert annual stipends into public bonds issued to the former noble and samurai classes. Many of the bondholders consolidated their new wealth into financing capital before commercial capital could develop a strong competitive position. In a word, feudal privilege was transformed into financing capital. The majority of production capacities were as yet organized into small-scale operations, and the creation of new capital concentrated in the hands of a few financial organs meant little for the overall development of capitalism at the levels of commerce and industry as such.

Joint-stock corporations, banks, and bonding companies developed remarkably in the second decade of the Meiji era, that is, after 1877, but the bulk of their capital came from the financiers whose controls over commerce and industry were quite strong from the outset. As the industries expanded, the financial interests were strengthened all the more. This is evident from the following data on the growth of financial capital:

| *Year* | *Amount of financial capital* (*yen*) |
|---|---|
| 1873 | 265,000,000 |
| 1887 | *ca.* 500,000,000 |
| 1897 | 1,300,000,000 |
| 1907 | 5,500,000,000 |
| 1916 | *ca.* 10,200,000,000 |
| 1925 | 32,200,000,000 |

Great strides were made after industry began expanding from 1897 on.[28]

The amount of capital in the banking business was rather small before World War I. The total face value of bank capital in 1913 was only about 560,000 or 570,000 yen, with paid-up capital of 392,000 yen. After the war, amalgamation and capital enlargement were promoted. The number of ordinary banks decreased by more than one-third between 1913 and 1928; other types of banks decreased about one-half in the same period. On the other hand, the number of branch offices of surviving ordinary banks more than doubled, and the amount of paid-up capital rose to 1,418,000,000 yen, three or four times that prior to the war. Thus, it is evident that enlargement and concentration of banking capital characterized the period between 1913 and 1928.[29]

Financial institutions for the promotion of industry, such as the Industrial Bank of Japan (Nihon Kōgyō Ginkō), The Hypothec Bank of Japan (Nihon Kangyō Ginkō), and The Agricultural and Industrial Bank of Japan (Nōkō Ginkō) had not functioned very well due to poor management, so these banks were reorganized and enlarged to fulfill better their functions of supporting industry. In order to build up capital, these banks, like other large banks, absorbed many small banks.

By 1923 there were only a few really large banks. The largest was the Yokohama Specie Bank, capitalized at 100,000,000 yen. Other large banks were:

| *Bank* | *Capital in 1913 (yen)* | *Capital in 1923 (yen)* |
|---|---|---|
| Yasuda Bank | 10,000,000 | 92,000,000 |
| Mitsui Bank | 20,000,000 | 60,000,000 |
| Sumitomo Bank | 7,500,000 | 50,000,000 |
| Jūgo (Fifteenth) Bank | 23,000,000 | 49,000,000 |
| Dai-ichi Bank | 13,000,000 | 43,000,000 |

Jūgo Bank, with the lowest growth rate, more than doubled its capital during the period 1913–23; the others increased three-, seven-, and ninefold.

The phenomenal increase of deposits in Mitsui Bank is shown below:

| *Year* | *Amount of deposits (yen)* |
|---|---|
| 1893 | 16,700,000 |
| 1914 | 99,600,000 |
| 1928 | 656,000,000 |

Enlarging the scope a little, we can see that the three big banks, Mitsui, Mitsubishi, and Sumitomo, captured an increasingly larger share of the total deposits and paid-up capital in all ordinary banks, as in the following percentages:

| *Year* | *Percentage of paid-up capital in all banks held by the big three* | *Percentage of deposits in all banks held by the big three* |
|---|---|---|
| 1903 | 2.76 | 13.5 |
| 1914 | 7.10 | 14.69 |
| 1928 | 10.14 | 19.65 |

If the scope is extended even further to include the five large banks of the major financial *zaibatsu*, Mitsui, Mitsubishi, Sumitomo, Yasuda, and Kawasaki, the total amount of deposits of these banks constituted 39.34% of the total deposits in all ordinary banks. And, if Dai-ichi Bank is added to this group, the six-member group made up 48%, or nearly half of all deposits in all ordinary banks in Japan.[30]

Turning to government enterprises, the Japan Industrial Bank was established after promulgation of the industrial banking law in 1900. It was the first organ for handling securities in Japan. In 1905 a law concerning trust firms for handling mortgages was enacted by the government. After that, many trust companies were established, some 226 being in business by 1913. Following World War I many of them went bankrupt, prompting a revision of the trust law in January 1923. Enforcement of the revised trust law forced the closing of over 500 trust companies, notably excluding those established by the *zaibatsu* or operating under their protection. By 1926 the trust companies under the protective umbrellas of the *zaibatsu* were in an overwhelmingly superior position, owning 72.34% of all properties held by trust firms.

*Zaibatsu* power was not so extensive in the insurance business, as many small companies had succeeded in establishing themselves securely outside *zaibatsu* circles. The giant combines attempted to buy up small companies but managed to capture only 26.8% of the total reserves of all insurance companies.

Capital holdings of the *zaibatsu* were most frequently invested in industries. In most cases, debentures issued by industrial companies were purchased by the larger banks. Hence, the prosperity of the latter depended heavily upon the success of the industries whose bonds they had bought. The *zaibatsu* saw it as imperative to bring these industries under their own supervision to protect their own interests. This they did by heavy loans that bound the industries to the *zaibatsu*, or by direct purchases of stock in the industrial companies. In many cases, stocks in a particular industrial company were owned by more than one member company of the *zaibatsu*. By hemming industries in with multiple ownership of stock, the *zaibatsu* could easily exercise controls over them, without having an absolute majority of any particular company's stocks. Needless to say, the *zaibatsu* controls were reinforced in such cases by simultaneous controls over other sources of finance and raw materials, not to mention markets. The overall controls system of the *zaibatsu* over subordinate firms increased by geometrical progression.

Executive decisions for management of subordinate companies did not always issue solely from within these companies. At times the *zaibatsu* arranged for one of its companies, in which it had invested an unusually large amount of capital, to sell goods at abnormally high prices to increase *zaibatsu* shares in the extra profits. Concern was for overall profits of the *zaibatsu* organization, rather than for a particular company. In other words, the *zaibatsu* exercised final decisions over the entire network of sales, including exclusive sales rights through affiliated companies such as

Mitsui Trading and Mitsubishi Trading Companies. At the same time they commanded supply lines for raw materials so as to strengthen their controlling powers over industrial companies.

In addition to such advantages accruing from the *zaibatsu* organizations, there were other factors that served their prosperity. Connected with every step from production to final sales and capable of relying on ready reserves at any point in the process, their operations involved exceedingly low risks. They were able to attract men of high ability, who were neither immature nor inexperienced. Nor were their executives irresponsible in carrying out their duties. Once attracted, the *zaibatsu* were able to hold and further develop capable executives, who were not allowed, then, to handle *zaibatsu* affairs in loose or temporizing ways. Sound business practices sustained over long periods were the objectives of *zaibatsu* leaders, and they were able to build up a tremendous backlog of trust and respect.

Taking a look at the organizational groupings of the Mitsui *zaibatsu*, we find a number of levels of relative subordination, with large capital holdings at each level. In the early days of the Shōwa era (1926——) it was the largest and most comprehensive of the *zaibatsu*. Its various groups were:

(1) The holding company, Mitsui & Company (Mitsui Gōmei Kaisha), founded by the Mitsui household with family capital.

(2) Six companies directly subordinate to Mitsui & Company, which provided 90% of the total capital of the six companies. The amount of paid-up capital of the six-member group was 242,000,000 yen.

(3) Thirty-seven companies were subordinate to the six companies of group 2. About 48% of the capital of each company in this group was paid by their parent companies; hence, these thirty-seven firms were securely under Mitsui controls.

(4) There were fifteen more companies subordinate to group 2, but not so perfectly controlled by Mitsui & Company. The total amount of paid-up capital of groups 3 and 4 was 202,700,000 yen.

(5) There were eleven branch companies of which about 50% of the capital was paid up by one or more of the companies belonging to groups 2, 3 or 4. The total amount of paid-up capital of companies in this group reached 640,000,000 yen.

(6) There were twenty-seven companies under group 5 companies, with paid-up capital amounting to 199,000,000 yen.

(7) There were fifteen companies with somewhat looser connections with the Mitsui organization, in which Mitsui held directorships or owned large amounts of stock. Total paid-up capital amounted to 284,000,000 yen

(8) Finally, there were thirteen more companies with some kind of connection with the Mitsui network, claiming 71,950,000 yen in paid-up capital.

All of these companies, 120 of them, made up the entire Mitsui combine, with a gigantic paid capital aggregate of 1.6 billion yen, which was 15% of the total capital of all business companies in Japan at that time. Moreover, all of the companies were top class companies in their respective fields; the real value of the Mitsui giant was much greater than its overall face value.[31]

The second most comprehensive *zaibatsu*, next to Mitsui, was Mitsubishi, with the following groups of companies subordinate to its central holding company:

(1) Ten direct affiliates with paid-up capital of 225,000,000 yen.

(2) Twelve sub-affiliates with paid-up capital of 211,000,000 yen.

(3) Twenty subsidiary companies with paid-up capital of 117,000,000 yen.

(4) Twenty-two collateral subsidiaries with paid-up capital of 61,000,000 yen.

(5) Fifty-four companies connected with one or more of the companies of groups 1,2,3 and 4 with paid-up capital of 1,319,000,000 yen. The total amount of paid-up capital of all companies in all groups of the Mitsubishi *zaibatsu* was 1,925,665,000 yen. But the real value of these companies was only 50%–60% of the Mitsui *zaibatsu*.[32]

These two giants, and their fellow *zaibatsu* with similar though smaller organizations, stood at the top of the Japanese business and industrial economy. They were able to exercise controls far beyond the scope of their own organizations through their power over financing, raw materials supply, and sales markets on which other manufacturers, minor enterprises, and even home industries all depended.

(2) TRANSFORMATION FROM STATUS SOCIETY TO CLASS SOCIETY.—— We have seen how, even in the short time it took to introduce capitalism and large-scale industry into Japanese society, a few very large *zaibatsu* won control over the economy of the nation. It is not surprising, then, that their economic power soon yielded them a degree of autonomy and, hence, a special place in national politics. That special position also precipitated a transition from a society based on status stratification to one divided into social classes, at times removing, at times reviving the legacy of feudal patterns.

The fact that the bureaucratic leadership of the Meiji government consisted of former feudal leaders had a direct bearing on the set of the sails of the new government. When the Diet was convened for the first time in 1890, after promulgation of the Constitution in 1889, Prime Minister Yamagata Aritomo proclaimed that the Diet was to exercise public authority under the sanction of the Emperor. The intention was that government was to be exclusively in the hands of the bureaucracy, with no political powers reserved to leaders in business. The Prime Minister's address proposed no legislation for the Diet to consider, but spoke only of the national budget, designed chiefly for strengthening the Army and Navy as the nation's bulwarks of defense, and of government policies for promoting agriculture, industry, commerce and foreign trade.[33]

As the industrial revolution progressed, the capitalist elite became increasingly conscious of its own power; dissatisfied with being forever subordinate to bureaucrats, they moved steadily into positions of influence in national politics and economy. The very success of the capitalists, of course, had come through cultivation of political connections from the beginning of the Meiji government as seen especially in the Mitsui relationships with the Chōshū leaders and Mitsubishi connections with men of the Satsuma group. The growing influence of business leaders in politics became quite apparent in March of 1895 when Matsukata Masayoshi entered the cabinet. He had nurtured friendly relations with the captains of business when he had served formerly as Minister of Finance. Now he was being brought back into that office to replace Finance Minister Watanabe who had failed in an attempt to win the business leaders' support of a 10 million yen bond issue after the Sino-Japanese War, due chiefly to the recession that followed the war.

Begun, then, after the Sino-Japanese War, political activity on the part of the major financiers was further activated following the Russo-Japanese War. Except for Mitsui and Mitsubishi whose empires ranged over industry and commerce as well as finance, the politically active group was composed of big bankers primarily, and not industrial or commercial capitalists, as it was financial capital that had established positions free of dependence upon the government by mobilizing the wealth and capital in public bonds of the noble and ex-samurai ranks. The government could not easily neglect the financiers, however, because of urgent needs for funds, and taxes were already about as high as they could be pushed. Public bonds were deemed preferable to large foreign loans, and the government had to accept proposals made by the big bankers. The more government officials leaned on the expanding economic power of the business elite, the more the latter pressed their political ideas upon government leaders.

In 1908 the financial bloc launched a campaign against government financial plans, in the name of 365 commercial and industrial associations. The Saionji Cabinet was forced to dissolve, defeated in its contest with the capitalist forces. Prime Minister Katsura, who replaced Saionji, invited the bankers in Ōsaka to a meeting in December 1909, prior to opening of the Diet. Outlining the government's financial policies in that meeting, he concluded by saying: "In short, I have made up my mind to carry out certain financial reforms, keeping in mind the conditions of the economy in general, to formulate the best possible policy for all, and I entreat your cooperation."[34]

It was a realistic posture, for without the support of the financiers, the government could not do much. The power of the capitalists had made great strides, even though they had no formal place in the government. From that time on it became customary for the prime minister and his cabinet to meet annually with top business leaders, explaining the government's financial policies and seeking their support. That is, policies were formed through a process of mutual compromises between political and business leaders.

The political power of the capitalists could not always be exercised directly or even singularly. Compromise movements were made with the military, the political parties, the Diet, and even the bureaucracy, all elements which contended for control of the cabinet. Between 1901 and 1913 Katsura and Saionji alternated in the office of prime minister, subject to pressures from these various groups. In 1912 Saionji was forced to resign for the second time under pressure of a combined intrigue of bureaucrats and military men. A strong advocate of parliamentary government, he did not welcome bureaucratic influence, and the military faction, disgruntled by failure to meet their demands for increased allocations for expansion, withdrew the army minister from the cabinet.

Katsura took over the premiership again, and the Diet matched the military's intransigence by forcing his resignation. Public demands for cleaning out residual powers of the old feudal cliques from government and more faithful adherence to constitutional government helped weaken the despotic powers of the bureaucracy, and the stage was set for greater participation in political affairs by influential men in the field of private enterprise.

Political parties gradually assumed relatively greater strength when the bureaucrats were tamed somewhat, and the parties offered the best channel of political participation by business interests. Connections with the parties had been nurtured in the periods following both the Sino-Japanese and the Russo-Japanese Wars. The parties took on new strength, facilitated by greater backing from the financial houses.

Party strength in the Diet was determined by the number of elected representatives, which placed great importance on successful elections and the heavy contributions needed to assure election victories. The capitalists, for their part, had better chances of seeing their interests represented by political parties than by professional bureaucrats, or the more independent military establishment. On the shady side, there occurred an incident in 1908 when the Japan Sugar Company (Dainihon Seitō) tried to bribe some twenty members of the Diet.

When wealth became crucial to political careers, the capitalists were able to outdistance the bureaucrats. Compelled to seek means for catching up with the more advanced capitalist systems of the West, the Japanese business circles could not depend upon their own economic skills alone; they needed the positive support of government policies. They were not so much interested in the raging controversy over democratic versus authoritarian forms of government, as in upgrading profits and extending their own economic power. Hence, they were not concerned to overthrow feudal traditions remaining in government, preferring rather to compromise with existing positions in order to gain substantial government protection.

In the prosperous days following World War I, the capitalists were able to spend even larger sums to mend their political fences, through huge donations to the parties. Bureaucrats were forced to yield power into the hands of party politicians. In 1920 Hara Kei, head of the Seiyūkai (Constitutional Party), came to power; he was neither a peer nor an ex-samurai, but a commoner. His appointment was designed to achieve a balance between the contending military, bureaucratic, and business factions, as well as to calm the troubled waters stirring among the populace as a whole.

Yet the parties looked more and more as if they were instruments of big capital, inasmuch as massive financial capital had established itself as the controlling force in the Japanese economy. The state seemed to prosper when the capitalists prospered, and decline when they declined. Political policies were ill-disguised economic programs.

Major support from the business firms went either to the Seiyūkai (Constitutional Party) or the Minseitō (Democratic Party). The former was supported by the Mitsui, Yasuda, and Sumitomo *zaibatsu*; the latter by the Mitsubishi, Yamaguchi, and Nezu combines. Selected personnel were sent from the *zaibatsu* into political life, and their influential participation in the parties strengthened the character of the parties as instruments of big business interests.

The process of modernizing Japanese industries had already introduced many characteristic features of a class society, though there were numerous compromises with feudal patterns of status stratification internal to the process. When World War I prosperity offered the capitalist elite added opportunities of extending their power over wider ranges of industry and finance and, beyond, to the world of politics, these features of a class society were intensified.

Leaders in society in the four decades beginning in 1880 were required to avail themselves of training in the new institutions of higher education as the technical qualifications rose in every field. Technical proficiency was increasingly valued over inherited status, and the whole tradition based on status was impaired. In the initial phase of the Meiji era leaders in the economic sphere averaged 39.8 years of age; but by 1920 the average age rose to 52.1 years. Graduates of universities and colleges comprised 63% of the leaders in industry, 83% in politics, and 86% of the cultural leaders.

Members of the warrior class in Tokugawa society had been educationally prepared for the special positions they were expected to assume in national and provincial governments; learning and refinement belonged to their station in life. They possessed the necessary value orientation and, often, the skills necessary for successful adjustment to the new society of the Meiji era. Many of them advanced rapidly in business when capitalism and industry formed the new centers of gravity in society. Ex-warriors made up 23% of the industrial leaders in the Meiji era, increasing their strength to 37% by 1920.[35]

The progress made by industrial revolution from the Sino-Japanese War onward stemmed from modernization of techniques, capital concentration, and expansion of business organizations, with the resultant elevation of capitalist influence in political activity. But industry involved labor as well, and there was a concomitant increase in the urban concentration of workers who, in turn, became increasingly organized as a distinct class. Within this context, labor problems emerged in the modern sense of the term.

Labor conditions had assumed problematic proportions even before the Russo-Japanese War, both at the practical level in the factories and at the academic level in the universities. However, industry was still in a rather underdeveloped stage before that war, and the objective conditions for dealing with labor problems on a broad social basis were not yet ripe. Since the end of the prior Sino-Japanese conflict, though, rapid progress had been made in industry, notably in replacement of cottage industries by factories. The employer-employee relationships in factories were different from the old master-subordinate relations, and the country was confronted increasingly with problems arising from the new situation.

When the factory production system first got under way, there was a definite labor shortage, with employers vying with each other for workers, and workers moving about to gain new experiences and better working conditions. The poverty crisis on the farms and resultant migrations into the cities gradually alleviated the labor shortage, seriously weakening the individual worker's bargaining position. Meantime, the felt need was to control the tense struggle between employers.

When conflicts between employers and workers added to the tension, the government stepped in with a new series of laws and orders. A 1900 police law for public peace and order (*Chian Keisatsuhō*) aimed at suppressing the labor movement. In 1901 the government ordered dissolution of the Social Democratic Party (Shakai Minshutō), hoping to quell its emphases on social equality, abolition of all armaments, cancellation of the class system, and establishment of state ownership of capital and land.

Meanwhile, the standard of living had risen generally as production and markets were advanced under capitalist leadership. Suppression of the Socialist movement and general improvement of the people's livelihood served to dissipate labor conflicts. Strikes were rare in the Meiji era; in the worst year, 1907, there were only fifty-seven instances involving but 9,855 laborers.

Industry in Japan can be said to have developed through the sacrifices of the common people, though benefiting capital owners considerably. Workers were poorly organized, lacking in leadership and a strong consciousness of human rights ideals. Governing groups were not strongly committed to ideas of social equality and individual freedom. And the inferior international position of Japan made it difficult to focus attention on internal needs.

Industrial progress was made through policies that subordinated the wages of laborers to promotion of efficiency by installing machines. It was necessary to compensate somewhere along the line for the high costs of the new machinery, and to cover interest due on capital loans—conditions that had not hit the Western nations so heavily or suddenly, in so short a time.

At a time when machines were kept in operation for eight or nine hours in England, or even ten in the U.S.A., Japan's factories were working an average of twenty-two hours per day. In the Japanese textile industry, investors could realize two or three times the earnings on investments made than was true for England and America in the same industry. Intensive utilization of labor was made the basis for expansion of overseas exports and the modernization of industry.

Intensive use of human energies was not limited to the factories, however; preparation for skilled jobs through compulsory education introduced the discipline of industrious effort far in advance of formal employment. Emphasizing the need to acquire new knowledge and skills as a national duty, Japanese society made a most successful appropriation of its established tradition of a deep respect for knowledge and competence, channeling this spirit into forms of training aptly integrated into both industry and business. The percentage of young people enrolled in primary schools early in the Meiji and Taishō periods is shown below, classified according to sex:

| *Year* | *Number of boys* | *Number of girls* |
|---|---|---|
| 1873 | 40% | 16% |
| 1918 | 98% | 97% |

By 1918 Japan had reached the level of advanced countries in Europe and America.[36]

Diffusion of education among all classes did not necessarily change the actual living conditions of all classes. Day laborers, for instance, lived as usual in miserable conditions, as has been amply described by a number of scholars.[37] According to a report of the Ministry of Agriculture and Commerce describing the situation of industrial workers in minute detail (*Shokkō Jijō*), it is clear that women and children were allowed to work under inhumane conditions for many years. In private enterprises there were half again as many women as men workers; in the textile industry, most of the workers were women and young girls.

In 1901 the female workers in textile industries constituted half of the total number of workers in all factories, and 11.4% of these were less than fourteen years of age. One-quarter of all laborers in twenty-one factories of various industries in Ōsaka were under fourteen. Match making factories especially were full of young girls from poor families, the majority being between ten and fifteen years old. In extreme cases, there were children only six or seven years of age in the match factories.[38]

Intensive exploitation of labor was evident in the lodging systems and all-night operations of industrial plants. According to an official survey made by the Ministry of Agriculture and Commerce in 1901 (*Menshibōseki Shokkō Jijō*) on the conditions of workers in the cotton spinning industry, oppressive conditions prevailed. Pointing out that laws in Western countries prohibited using women and youth in night operations, and that only men over twenty years of age could be so used, the survey recorded that there was no spinning mill in Japan which did not employ women and child laborers in all-night operations. Pointing out further that a certain mill had operated only twelve hours per day when established in 1883, it was stated in the report that the same mill had introduced night shifts in the following year due to large orders for its products. Since then that mill, as a rule, had been open day and night.[39]

The health of many workers suffered from long hours, unsanitary facilities, and poor meals furnished on the job. Malnutrition, loss in weight, tuberculosis, eye diseases, and health problems among women workers were frequent occurrences. Moreover, the workers came to realize the devious ways used by employment agencies to attract them to the mills, and that the empty promises of the agencies had no connections with the employers' intentions. Even if, after taking jobs, the young girls wished to return to their homes, they did not have sufficient money for the trip home. Mill owners would not permit them to leave the plant's residential area on holidays, fearing their escape. At some mills there were watchmen who patrolled the dormitory areas to prevent their running away.[40]

"Free lodging" in dormitories was essentially a system of placing restraints on working girls. Though a few commuted from their own homes or rented rooms, most of the girls were brought in from distant prefectures to factories in Tōkyō, Ōsaka, and Nagoya, or surrounding districts. In 1910 the big three of Japanese industry—spinning, reeling, and weaving—had between 60% and 83% of their workers in factory-owned dormitories.

While workers were sacrificed to industrial development in the early stage of industrialization in Japan, this situation was modified partly by the difficulty employers experienced in holding workers when treatment was worse than other factories to which employees might be attracted. So the employers were sometimes forced to improve working conditions and increase wages. Another ameliorating factor was the gradual technological refinement of production processes. When crude industries were begun in China during the Taishō era (1912–26), some of the Japanese industrialists were forced to convert to more precision machinery to maintain their advantage, diminishing the value of child labor, non-stop all-night operations, and large numbers of dormitory-confined but unskilled girl laborers. Labor conditions were altered not through social processes but, to some extent, through technical improvements introduced into production methods.

The labor movement and movements in society did play an important role, however, in bringing about changes in working conditions after the Russo-Japanese War. Since passage of the police law for public peace and order of 1900, the labor movement had been weakened. But developments in industry itself gradually altered the ratio of men to women workers, with greater numbers of male laborers concentrated in large urban centers. The majority of women workers had been working to supplement inadequate family incomes back home and, as their numbers decreased, the character of the labor movement and the social forces supporting it were changed. Activity was increasingly based on mass organization instead of individual action, whether escapes of girls or job switching of individual men aided by a shortage of workers, as in the early phase of industrialization.

Large-scale labor disputes arose in 1906 after the Russo-Japanese War at the Ishikawajima Shipyards and Army munitions plant in Tokyo, and at the Ōsaka arsenal. Demands were pressed for better wages and protests were made against the dismissal of workers. Laborers' rights came to be recognized among wider segments of society, beyond the boundaries of the immediate disputes, especially among urban citizens. The Japan Socialist Party (Nihon Shakaitō) was founded in 1906 under the leadership of Sakai Toshihiko.

World War I brought Japan a level of prosperity never experienced before or after. But it was realized not so much through expansion of production facilities as through maximum utilization of labor at low wages; that is, by the fullest utilization of equipment already installed. Increased profit earnings went, however, to the owners and operators of industry.

The cost of living and wage indices for 1915 and 1919 ran as follows:

| *Year* | *Cost of living index (1914 = 100)* | *Net wage index (1914 = 100)* |
|---|---|---|
| 1915 | 92.5 | 108.2 |
| 1919 | 216.9 | 102.3 |

The number of employees increased during the war but working hours were extended, lowering actual wages, and imposing added difficulties on working people in this age of prosperity.[41]

Some of the laborers had been organized before World War I, but increased conflict spurred further organization efforts during and after the war.

| *Year* | *No. of labor unions* | *No. of labor disputes* |
|---|---|---|
| 1913 | 6 | —— |
| 1915 | —— | 64 |
| 1916 | —— | 108 |
| 1917 | —— | 398 |
| 1919 | 71 | 497 |

A total of 63,000 workers participated in the disputes listed above.

A walkout at the Kawasaki Shipbuilding Yard in Kōbe by over 10,000 workers under organized leadership succeeded in getting an eight-hour work day for the first time in Japan. An aggregate of 27,000 workers employed in a munitions plant in Tōkyō and elsewhere went on strike for wage increases, the dispute lasting for twenty days.[42]

A labor union called *Yūaikai* (Friendship Society) established in 1912 was reorganized in 1919 as the Japan Federation of Labor (*Sōdōmei*), the largest labor organization in Japan eventually, embracing 70% of all organized labor. After reorganization in 1919 local branches were set up along trade union and industrial union lines. In May of 1920 it sponsored the first May Day rally in Japan at Ueno Park in the capital city of Tōkyō, adopting as its slogans abolition of the special peace police, minimum wage levels, and prevention of unemployment. The Federation became at once a nucleus of political and economic action, as well as the major force in labor organization.[43]

In this stage the labor movement changed substantially. The function of the labor unions was clarified as giving leadership in labor conflicts, drawing on the strength of collective action with definite strategies. Joint industry-wide strikes were promoted, emphasizing the solidarity of laborers as a class over against the propertied capitalists. Nurturing class-consciousness among the laborers ran parallel to the treatment of all labor disputes as involving, not particular localized interests, but the interests of all workers as a class.[44]

Subsuming the individual laborer under the labor union organization placed him in a quite different position from the age-old master-subordinate relationship. The growing strength of the labor movement had consequences for the government too, which realized that it must make some effort to improve the general standard of living of the people. As far back as 1910 a new law concerning factories had been drawn up, and it was put into force in 1916.

The factory law (*Kōjōhō*) prohibited the employment of youth below twelve years of age. Workers under sixteen as well as women could not be made to work over twelve hours per day. Workers were to have at least two days leave per month, and work beyond midnight was outlawed. A number of exceptions allowed by the law rendered its otherwise good effects often quite useless. The factory law placed requirements on employers to strengthen safety precautions and improve workers' facilities. But it left details of enforcement of the law to the separate prefectures. This was a fatal loophole, and it is doubtful if the law had any substantial effect in favor of the workers. The most important observation to be made is that this law covered only a small portion of the factory workers in Japan. That is, it was applicable only to factories equipped with power-driven machinery, factories employing more than ten workers, and factories deemed dangerous due to use of poisonous materials or other materials injurious to human health.[45]

There were far too many factories which were too small to fall within the stipulations of this law, the thousands of small enterprises and home industries. Statistics on factories in this period include only those with at least five workers yet, even so, the percentages of factories to which the factory law applied decreased as industrial revolution advanced:

| *Year* | *Percentage of factories to which the factory law applied:* |
|---|---|
| 1919 | *ca.* 70 |
| 1921 | slightly over 50 |
| 1925 | 〃 〃 〃 |

The total number of factories, including workshops employing less than five workers, is reported to have reached 1,551,000 in 1919, in which case the factory law would have applied to a mere 1.6% of all factories.[46]

In any event, most of the laborers in Japan were excluded from the benefits of this law. In factories outside its scope workers were still bound by the master-subordinate relations of feudal heritage, and the small factories themselves were in feudalistic subordinate relationships to larger companies. The irritations of low wages, long hours, and unsanitary working conditions remained to plague workers in these enterprises. Their standard of living and working could not be improved until old norms and systems were broken and replaced by new social structures and modernized norms, which awaited a general economic elevation in the total society.

*Local Administration during the Industrial Revolution.*——Under the successive impacts of the Sino-Japanese War, the Russo-Japanese War, and World War I, the socio-economic structures of Japan went through a series of extensive changes, expanding in size and scope. Accordingly, administrative systems on the local level were subjected to various pressures.

Our interest has focused thus far on the remarkable development of industry after victory in successive military campaigns, and upon expanded programs of national finance geared to the following processes: armaments build-up; colonization of Taiwan and Korea; construction of basic industries, especially steel mills; extension of rail facilities, electric, telephone and telegraph services; reorganization of financial organs; public works projects; and expansion of educational institutions.

Many of the specific tasks of the central government's policies regarding these processes were passed down to prefectural offices for implementation. Laws and regulations issued by the central government placing responsibilities on the prefectural offices for development of industrial and educational facilities, and for public health and services, put unprecedented demands on local finances. The local administrative systems could not bear the new burdens, and the central government was compelled to carry out reorganization of these local systems.

Governments in the provinces had been accustomed to levying taxes on business transactions as a source of local revenue. In 1896 the national government converted business taxes into national taxes, standardizing the rates to facilitate interregional commerce. Local governments were faced with greatly increased financial obligations, but with far less revenue coming in. The dilemma was resolved by subsidies from the central government, which vastly strengthened its role in provincial politics.

A number of revisions were carried out in prefectural and country systems in 1897. While the legal authority of the urban and provincial prefectures (*fu* and *ken*) was clearly recognized, these two administrative units were not allowed to enact laws of their own, or even make amendments to laws and regulations concerning them.

Election laws governing prefectural and county assemblies were revised from an indirect system in which representatives were elected by members of city and town councils, to a direct system of election by popular vote. Voting rights were granted, in prefectural elections, to citizens paying three or more yen in national taxes for a year or more; in county elections, the same franchise depended upon payment of two yen or more in national taxes. The general effect of the revision, then, was to restrict the electorate, because of the tax payment provisions, to large landowners, well-to-do businessmen, and industrial enterprisers.

Some progress toward democratization of local government was made, of course, in acknowledging the legal authority of the prefectural and county units, and to some extent in changing to direct elections of assemblymen. On the other hand, the prefectural governors remained under central government controls, and the governor's role in local government was strengthened. He alone could draft legislative proposals for consideration by the central government, and he could render decisions on his own authority in many areas, subject to approval of the national ministries concerned. Strengthening the lines of central control through the prefectural governors made for greater efficiency in administrative affairs, but the powers of the assemblies were proportionately weakened.

Again, the county's legal standing was recognized but it could not, for instance, impose taxes of its own accord. Direct elections gave more scope to representation of the will of the electorate, but here too, only in terms of wealthier citizens. Prefectural governors were authorized to take disciplinary action against county officials, thus assuring a strong controlling hand of the central government in administrative affairs at this level.

The Japanese government spent 1.98 billion yen on the Russo-Japanese War between February 1904 and September 1905. It was a total war effort requiring funds on a scale not experienced previously in the Sino-Japanese War. Strains on national finances naturally had serious repercussions on the resources of local administrative units. Soon after the war began the central government passed an Emergency Tax Law to raise 62 million yen through additional taxes on land and consumer goods. Prices on tobacco, a government monopoly enterprise, were increased sharply. To minimize the tax burdens on the people, prefectural offices were required to reduce expenses and limit their own tax revenues.

The Emergency Tax Law was revised in January 1905, introducing new direct and indirect taxes for the second time during the war. Taxes were imposed on inheritances, transportation, salt sales, and other items. The new tax schedule aimed at an additional revenue of 74 million yen. Local expenditures and taxes were decreased as follows:

| *Fiscal year* | *Local Expenditures* (*yen*) | *Local taxes* (*yen*) |
|---|---|---|
| 1903 | 166,000,000 | 110,000,000 |
| 1905 | 137,000,000 | 94,000,000 |

Compression of local administrative resources and added tax burdens were accepted by the people without resistance, under the thoroughgoing controls of militarism in that critical period.

Victory in the Russo-Japanese War brought new responsibilities as well as advantages, domestically and overseas. Activity in government organs and private enterprise expanded, changing the structure of national life. It was imperative to carry out the revisions and enlargement of local administrative facilities that had been postponed because of wartime demands. Budgetary reinforcement of administrative reoganization on the local level resulted in a doubling of local expenditures in the five-year period from 1904 to 1909, from 134 million yen to 272 million yen.

Some of the increased expenditures were due to natural expansion of prefectural, municipal, and town administrations as such; but most of the expenses arose from expanded public services. An Infections Diseases Prevention Law was issued in 1905, and in 1907 the term of compulsory primary education was extended from four to six years, in response to the rising technological demands prompted by industrial growth. The salaries of public school teachers were raised, and new technical schools were opened.

Legislative steps to promote industry were also forthcoming, such as a law to aid in the prevention of diseased silkworms, so important to Japan's major export industry at that time. In 1906 a law providing for state subsidies to industrial experiments was enacted; in 1909 regulations to promote mulberry cultivation, as well as the quantity and quality of arable lands. Relief funds following natural calamities and subsidies for land reclamation projects were provided by a 1911 law.

The Immunization Law of 1909 made a great contribution to public health, and new regulations for public water systems were issued in 1913. Steps had been taken right after the war, in 1906, to increase salaries of policemen and attract new recruits, to aid in maintaining public security in view of increased social unrest following the war.

Considerable progress was made in local administration in the years following the Russo-Japanese War, not only in terms of the new legislative measures, but in carrying out many of the social reforms projected earlier in the Meiji Restoration. The reform measures were undertaken, however, not in response to demands of the populace expressed through official channels. All measures deemed necessary to increase national income, develop industry, and improve public services derived solely from initiatives taken by the central authorities.

Territorial possessions acquired in Korea, the southern half of Sakhalin Island, and Manchuria imposed new defense responsibilities on the Japanese government, and capital was needed for the colonization of Taiwan and Korea. Expanded military operations required commensurate enlargement of supportive systems such as state-owned railways, telephone and telegraph networks, river conservation projects, expansion of production capacities in the Yawata Steel Mill, and establishment of new technical and commercial colleges. The budget of the government increased as follows:

| *Fiscal year* | *Military expenditures (yen)* | *National finances (yen)* |
|---|---|---|
| 1903 | —— | 249,000,000 |
| 1907 | 525,000,000 | —— |
| 1908 | —— | 636,000,000 |
| 1911 | 620,000,000 | —— |

Confronted with an enormous jump in national finances, the government could not afford to suspend the taxes added during wartime under the Emergency Tax Law. It acted, on the contrary, to prohibit any institution of new taxes by local governments, to prevent any decrease in national revenues caused by the intrusion of local taxes into the taxpayers' pockets. The wartime restrictions on local taxes remained in effect.

In 1908 the restrictions on additional taxes were loosened somewhat to permit the prefectural offices to increase their revenues, so as to enable them to fulfill the many functions required of them by the national government. The restrictions against additional taxes on incomes and business transactions remained in force, however. Local finance needs were kept subordinate to national programs of military expansion and development of the newly-acquired colonies.

Even under financial limitations, though, necessary reforms in local administrative systems had to be expedited. Steps were taken in 1911 to revise municipal systems. Whereas mayors had been selected by the city councils, they were now to be appointed from above. The mayors could convene the city council at will, decide certain matters on their own authority, and hire and fire administrative personnel. The mayoral authority was greatly strengthened, but only at the price of increasing their responsibilities under the central government. Tax collections were added to their office under strictly regulated procedures, and the range of taxpayers in their charge was extended.

Meanwhile, the outbreak of war in Europe brought Japan an unforseen economic boom; the Japanese stock market rose sharply, and the commodity exchange went into high gear. By 1918 commodity prices rose 130% over the 1914 level, and investors realized profits of 63% on investments in the latter half of 1918. The real income of workers, as we have observed, did not keep pace with rising prices but, indeed, fell downward. National expenditures before and after the war were:

| *Fiscal Year* | *National expenditures (yen)* |
|---|---|
| 1914 | 648,000,000 |
| 1919 | 1,172,000,000 |

Local administrative costs rose at a higher rate than that indicated above for the national government, due to extension of compulsory education from four to six years, and normal increases in routine administrative costs.

Increases in routine costs resulted from greatly expanded urban populations. As industry and commerce advanced, and municipal organs expanded, additional human resources were amassed in the cities. Urban problems were compounded, and more organized programs were needed to deal with the more serious of these problems. A City Planning Law was issued in 1919, followed by a Law for Construction in Urban Areas. The City Planning Law stipulated that all decisions concerning urban areas and planning schedules were to be handled by a city planning board which must include officials of the government ministries concerned. City, town, and village assemblies had little voice in the formulation of plans for their own administrative units, even though the cities, towns, and villages were obligated to bear most of the expenses required in the implementation of a wide range of projects: road construction; parks and plazas; river, moat, and port facilities; railways; water works and sewage systems; housing developments; schools; markets; and cemeteries.

A special city planning tax, plus additional charges for those benefiting immediately from improvement of facilities, were introduced to raise necessary funds for these many projects. The revenues accruing from the special tax and beneficiary fee were inadequate, however, and most of the financial burden had to be borne by municipal bonds issues, the bonds debts falling, of course, on local residents.

The urban development programs intensified city-to-city relationships, as well as connections between cities and farm villages. A roads-system law (*Dōrohō*) was issued in 1919, classifying all roads and delegating responsibilities for their upkeep. Six categories were stipulated: national and prefectural highways, and county, city, town, and village roads. The first two, national and prefectural highways, were under the supervision of prefectural governors; the others were maintained by the respective administrative units.

Although governors and mayors, and county, town, and village heads were responsible for road maintenance in their areas, ultimate powers of decision were placed in the central Ministry of Home Affairs. Local assemblies could do nothing more than express opinions, and await decisions from above. All standards regarding construction, maintenance, and repairs, including methods and employment practices, were determined by regulations issuing from the Home Affairs Ministry, where authority was consolidated.

A large share of road construction expenses was borne locally, except in the case of roads for military use and other special purposes. The government subsidized half the costs of national highways, and one-third the costs of other roads. While local citizens benefited from standardization of, and development of, the system of roads, their public finance burden was made heavier.

Two more examples of mixed blessings, benefits carrying tax burdens, were a Tuberculosis Prevention Law (*Kekkaku-yobōhō*) and a law providing for mental hospitals (*Seishin-byōinhō*). Enactment of these laws reflected growing concern for evils typical of large urban centers; yet they as also added weight to the overall tax load.

Local administration expanded considerably, then, during the post-World War I period of prosperity, though the bulk of expansion consisted of the official duties delegated by the central government to municipal governments. Financial obligations were progressively heavier, and without the sanction of wartime urgency. The benefits accruing from public projects have to be weighed against the involuntary commitment to near-poverty on the part of most citizens in support of national policies of industrialization, expanded overseas trade, colonization and militarization.

Local administration in this period is not to be equated with self-government. Each administrative unit was regarded as only an inferior level of central organs, an attitude amply reflected in the top bureaucracy, which had no intention of soliciting opinions from local leaders. Moreover, local officials were submissively obedient to national directives. There was no local self-government in the modern sense of the term in these days.[46]

Japan's concern was to cultivate imperial authority to prevent colonization or even subordination by foreign powers. The remarkable development of a capitalist economy was achieved through compromise with, and not a break away from, the legacy of feudalism. The capitalists worked hand in glove with the bureaucrats, who granted them the transposed forms of feudal privilege, and the lineage-type structures of the *zaibatsu* reflected the fundamental commitment of leading capitalists to feudal values. Businessmen capitalized on Japan's military ventures and the government's programs to build national strength through industrialization. By nurturing lines of political influence through affiliations with political parties, national strength became increasingly the strength of big business, the primary integrative force of the entire nation. The overall economy as such had no independent position outside the integrative command of the major business combines, even though the actual number of small and medium-sized firms, in the various textile, match making, and other industries, far outnumbered the large enterprises. Small enterprises were dependent on contracts with the dominant *zaibatsu* at every level of the economy, whether raw materials, machinery, production capital and techniques, or sales. The large laboring force operated under the multiple handicap of low wages, poor working conditions, and inferior social standings. They simply constituted the chief advantage of business and industry in competing successfully with advanced foreign enterprises.

As we have seen, the laborers' situation improved somewhat as the scope of industrial production widened to include technological improvements, alleviating the traditional master-subordinate relationships in factories; and union organizations began to win concessions from industrial management. The government even added succor to the laborers' cause by enacting the Factory Law. But the range of application of the law was narrowly restricted, and labor unions covered only a minority of the workers. The feudal character of employer-employee relationships could not be erased under such circumstances. Penetration of the money economy into rural society put the farmers into the stream of an expanded commodity economy; but, as it turned out, the farmers did not get enough of the money to buy the commodities. They tended to sink rather than swim in that stream. The farm units were too small to permit agriculture a position capable of balancing industry's new place in society. As a social stratum, the farming population began to disintegrate, unable to sustain itself. Individual farmers could survive only by changing their roles, either doing farm work for landlords who took over ownership of their lands, or migrating to the cities as fresh labor supplies.

Thus, industrialization in Japan was achieved with astonishing rapidity without drastically reforming feudal society. It was propelled partly by a growing desire for empire, shared equally by bureaucrats and capitalists. The modern democratic principles of elevating the social welfare of the majority of the people was not a central motivation in Japanese industrialization. The result was an grave imbalance between the lives of people connected with large urban industries, and those working in small and medium-sized industries, on farms, or as low-paid laborers in large enterprises. The standard of living of the latter groups had not been modernized at all; they remained within the structures of feudal patterns, including inferior social status.

In terms of industry and commerce the cities embraced increasingly modern structures; in terms of government and social life it should be clear from the preceding pages that the cities of Japan were not ready to serve as cradles for the birth of modern democracy and society.

Industrialization could not be achieved, of course, without all-out appropriation of modern science and technology. The acquisition of new knowledge, as we have also observed, did have far-reaching effects on the nature of human relationships; increasingly actual ability was honored in a transition from relations based on ascribed status to those relying on achieved status. This was true, however, only within the bounds of the more technical processes of business and production. Even managerial relations retained a great deal of traditional emphasis on ascribed status, and patterns in politics, government and society in general remained deeply embued with status features. Japanese society was yet seriously lacking in liberalized social mobility, respect for the individual personality, and natural orientation to a rationalistic, scientific spirit.

No level of government in this period better portrayed the wide disparity between the outward forms of modernization achieved and the inner persistence of feudalism than did local administration. The changes sweeping the Japanese nation were far broader in scope—regional, national, and international—than the local scene could comprehend. Yet no organs of government were so submissively obedient in paying the price of modernization while realizing so few of its benefits than local administration.

In fact, the emergence of modern structures in the cities of Japan cannot be seen until after World War II. Despite some progress made during the short-lived period of "Taishō democracy" following World War I, the full-fledged organs of a modern democratic society were not accomplished until the reform movements that appeared immediately after World War II, in which, with the help of measures instituted by the occupation forces, the dominant controls of a small ruling class were diminished. Other crucial factors in the democratizing processes following that major conflict also included: a widespread critical rejection of the ideology undergirding militaristic nationalism; the release of the common people from traditional authority by the introduction of democratic thought and systems in politics, law, economy, and education, and the diffusion of those ideas and systems among the people; and the emergence of voluntary organizations of the populace based on a revised constitution, educational reforms, land reforms, and a free labor movement.

## 2. SOCIAL CHANGES AND THE MODERNIZATION OF JAPANESE CITIES

The process of industrial revolution involves simultaneous changes in the structures of industry and the quantity and composition of population. Rural communities are drawn out of self-sustaining, closed economies into commercial production to support larger communities centered in the cities. Urban society, in turn, feeds back into rural communities the improved techniques that expand the productive capacities of rural lands. Agriculture becomes capable of supporting larger numbers of people, creating a surplus of human resources in the rural districts which, then, supply a fresh labor supply to the expanding organs of commerce and industry in the cities. The supporting conditions for a larger population throughout the entire country are thus enlarged, while the heavy losses in human life due to famines and epidemics are decreased by the introduction of modern medicine and hygiene. Improvements in transportation and communication systems strengthens the interdependence of rural and urban society, enhancing the possibilities of larger population maintenance.

The population of Japan remained fairly stable throughout the Tokugawa era, only to rise sharply in the succeeding Meiji period. By the time the industrial revolution was accomplished, it grew nearly 60%.

| *Year* | *Population* | *Rate of increase/period* |
|---|---|---|
| 1872 | 34,800,000 | —— |
| 1897 | 42,400,000 | 21.8% in 25 yrs. |
| 1920 | 56,960,000 | 34.3% in 26 yrs. |

Discounting the colonies acquired (whose peoples do not appear in these population figures), the total land area remained the same during this era of remarkable population increase. In the half-century when population swelled nearly two-thirds, population density jumped 77.9%.

| *Year* | *Population density* | |
|---|---|---|
| 1872 | 86 per sq. km. | (33.1 per sq. mi.) |
| 1902 | 120 per sq. km. | (46.2 per sq. mi.) |
| 1921 | 153 per sq. km. | (58.9 per sq. mi.) |

Given the mountainous terrain of Japan, population density was not uniform even in the Tokugawa period; population was most dense in the fertile plains. The development of industrial centers in areas with dual access to the food supply of fertile districts and to ports and highways further accentuated the disparities in population density.

Although every region in Japan experienced an increase in population amount and density, the rates of increase varied considerably. Between 1885 and 1913 the order of the regions according to density was altered significantly, as shown below:

| *Order* | *1885* | *1913* |
|---|---|---|
| 1 | Kinki | Kantō |
| 2 | Kantō | Kinki |
| 3 | Tōkai | Tōkai |
| 4 | Shikoku | Kyūshū |
| 5 | Hokuriku | Shikoku |
| 6 | Chūgoku | Chūgoku |
| 7 | Kyūshū | Hokuriku |
| 8 | Tōsan | Tōsan |
| 9 | Tōhoku | Tōhoku |
| 10 | Hokkaidō | Hokkaidō |

The Kinki district was and remained a large center of industry and commerce, and therefore retained a high place. But it was easily replaced in top place by the Kantō district where Tōkyō was developed into the national nucleus of all major functions of society. Industrial development in Kyūshū raised its position in the regional order four places, while failure to promote industry in the Hokuriku district brought it lower down in the scale by 1913. The more mountainous, remote, and poorer disticts of Tōsan, Tōhoku, and Hokkaidō stayed at the bottom, without notable development of industry.

The most important reason for the high rate of increased population density in various districts was the concentration of large urban populations where commerce and industry were developed the most. In these cities there were new jobs to attract depressed rural folk. In addition to population growth in the cities due to social mobility, there were also differences in the rate of natural increase in the various districts.

The number of cities, towns, and villages changed as Japan entered into the 20th century, as per the following:

| *Year* | *Total no.* | *Number of villages, towns, and cities acc. to population: under 10,000* | *under 50,000* | *under 100,000* | *over 100,000* |
|---|---|---|---|---|---|
| 1898 | 14,027 | 13,794 | 213 | 12 | 8 |
| 1918 | 12,243 | 11,686 | 510 | 31 | 16 |

While the total population of Japan increased during this period, the percentage of urban population with respect to the total population nearly doubled:

| *Year* | *Total population* | *Population in urban areas* | *Percentage of total* |
|---|---|---|---|
| 1898 | 45,403,041 | 5,391,424 | 11.9 |
| 1918 | 55,963,053 | 10,096,758 | 18.0 |

As we noted in the first half of this chapter, the rate of social increase of large city populations between 1920 and 1925 was much greater than the rate of natural increase. While towns and villages of less than 20,000 populations had no social increase, they did experience natural increase while losing large numbers to the cities.

| *Towns & Villages by pop. size* | *Natural increase in pop.* | *Social decrease* |
|---|---|---|
| 10,000–20,000 | 340,000 | 30,000 |
| less than 10,000 | 2,650,000 | 1,530,000 |

These figures amply demonstrate that urban expansion was due largely to absorption of a large portion of the rural population. The following figures indicate the degree of population expansion in the six major cities, by two or three times in each case:

| *Year* | *Tōkyō* | *Ōsaka* | *Kyōto* | *Kōbe* | *Nagoya* | *Yokohama* |
|---|---|---|---|---|---|---|
| 1898 | 1,440,000 | 820,000 | 350,000 | 210,000 | 240,000 | 190,000 |
| 1920 | 3,350,000 | 1,760,000 | 700,000 | 640,000 | 610,000 | 570,000 |
| *Increase:* | 1,910,000 | 940,000 | 350,000 | 430,000 | 370,000 | 380,000 |

A detailed discussion of metropolitan Tōkyō follows later, but its massive concentration of population was due, of course, to its comprehensive array of national functions. In addition to being the center of national government and politics, it had captured the major financing systems of a rapidly expanding capitalist economy, not to mention its place as the hub of cultural activity.

Ōsaka and other major cities are also treated in subsequent sections; here it is enough to observe that Ōsaka revamped its position as a modern industrial center, with expanding functional service to the Kinki district as well as to the entire nation. Kyōto and Nagoya added to their importance as centers of feudal political life by adopting new functions, while Kōbe and Yokohama evolved as the key foreign trade centers. The remarkable population growth in these six metropolitan communities was indicative of their roles as the nerve centers of total integration in the whole of society.

In 1898 these six, along with Hiroshima and Nagasaki, were the only cities with populations of more than 100,000 population. By 1920 the big six had moved into a special class of cities with over 500,000 population, while the group with more than 100,000 population swelled to include a total of ten cities, which were:

| City | Population | City | Population |
|---|---|---|---|
| Nagasaki | 180,000 | Sendai | 120,000 |
| Hiroshima | 160,000 | Otaru | 110,000 |
| Hakodate | 140,000 | Kagoshima | 100,000 |
| Kure | 130,000 | Sapporo | 100,000 |
| Kanazawa | 130,000 | Yawata | 100,000 |

These ten cities did not share a common starting point, however, as is seen from the following percentages showing the rates of increase from 1898 to 1920:

| City | Rate of increase(%) | City | Rate of increase(%) |
|---|---|---|---|
| Nagasaki | 64 | Sendai | 42 |
| Hiroshima | 31 | Otaru | 89 |
| Hakodate | 85 | Kagoshima | 92 |
| Kure | 150 | Sapporo | 173 |
| Kanazawa | 54 | Yawata | over 1,200 |

Old castle towns such as Hiroshima, Sendai, and Kanazawa showed relatively low increase rates, as compared to the phenomenal expansion of the pioneer city of Sapporo in Hokkaidō, the naval base of Kure, and the new industrial center of Yawata, national base for iron and steel production.

Of the fourteen cities with more than 50,000 population in 1898, six of them had risen to the 100,000-plus class by 1920, namely, Hakodate, Otaru, Sendai, Kanazawa, Kure, and Kagoshima. The remaining eight were Sakai, Niigata, Toyama, Wakayama, Tokushima, Okayama, Fukuoka, and Kumamoto; they held on to their populations of 50,000 or more. They were joined in the 50,000-plus class by sixteen other cities, giving a total in this category of twenty-four by 1920.

Cities which entered the 50,000-plus class by doubling their populations by 1920 included the following:

| City | Characteristic function |
|---|---|
| Moji | foreign trade |
| Toyohashi | military base |
| Hamamatsu | textile industry |
| Sasebo | naval base |
| Yokosuka | naval base |
| Ōmuta | coal mining (Kyūshū) |
| Asahigawa | pioneer city in Hokkaidō |
| Muroran | 〃 〃 〃 〃 |
| Yūbari | 〃 〃 〃 〃 |

A sizable number of cities failed to double their populations, and the right hand column of cities in the list of these enjoyed less than 50% increase in population:

| *Less than double:* | *Less than 50% increase:* |
|---|---|
| Sakai | Kōfu |
| Utsunomiya | Wakayama |
| Maebashi | Tokushima |
| Niigata | Matsuyama |
| Gifu | Kumamoto |
| Shizuoka | Toyama |
| Okayama | Fukui |
| Shimonoseki | |
| Fukuoka | |

All of the above cities were provincial urban centers, former castle towns which now served mainly as the sites of prefectural offices.

Cities with more than 30,000 population showed a modest gain in number, from twenty-five in 1898 to thirty-four in 1920. Two cities in northern Kyūshū, Ube and Wakamatsu, had expanded by more than 200% to enter this class, however, and Aomori, on the northern tip of the main island, had increased more than 100% to join this group. Cities in this class expanding by more than 50% in population were: Fukushima, Ashikaga, Kiryū, Matsumoto, Amagasaki, Hachiōji, and Kurume. All of these cities experiencing population expansion were industrial centers.

On the other hand, there were cities where population decreased, such as Hirosaki. Also, there were cities with only very low rates of population increase. Cities with less than 30% increase in population included Morioka, Akita, Wakamatsu, Mito, Chiba, Takaoka, Nagano, Himeji, Matsue, and Saga. Most of these cities were former castle towns.

By way of summary, we can say that the changes that occurred in both the extent and distribution of urban populations, between 1898 and 1920, were due chiefly to the transformation of feudal cities from centers of consumption to production centers employing modern techniques in large-scale enterprises, and absorbing large numbers of the rural populace.

The six major cities were able to expand on the basis of several factors: by establishing close connections with domestic and international activity; by making use of improved transportation and communications systems; and by embracing multiple functions in politics, economy, and culture.

Expansion proceeded, however, not just by absorbing people one by one; larger cities also absorbed local communities in their immediate vicinity. Moreover, differentiated functions were promoted in the local communities within the larger urban centers, each community having its specialized task as one functioning unit within the complex national and international roles of the larger cities.

Local communities in the vicinity of larger cities lost their relative independence as they became component parts, that is, satellite cities and suburban towns, of emerging metropolitan communities. Intensified interdependence and highly specialized functions characterized each of the metropolitan areas, and especially Tōkyō and Ōsaka.

The closer the geographical proximity of cities and surrounding satellite towns, the greater the degree of interdependence and specialization tended to be. We must note particularly the development of large industrial zones around Tōkyō and Nagoya along the Tōkaidō route, around Ōsaka and Kōbe in the center of the main land on its Pacific coast side, and in the North Kyūshū area centered in Fukuoka. Areas near the old castle towns along the Japan Sea coast of the main island and in the northeastern districts did not possess the proper combination of advantages, such as access to natural resources, convenience to transportation routes, and multiple functions, to expand rapidly or on a large scale. They survived as cities, but mainly as provincial urban centers performing localized functions.[47]

*Development of Metropolitan Communities.*——

(1) TŌKYŌ METROPOLITAN COMMUNITY. We have emphasized the importance of a multiplicity of functions in the large-scale expansion of cities, especially when these included both integrative activity within the whole country and on an international level. Key organs of every facet of national life were concentrated in Tōkyō, such as:

Political organs: the Imperial Palace, the National Diet, the Supreme Court, and central offices of the entire national administration;

International organs: foreign embassies and legations, and firms of foreign enterprises;

Economic organs: head offices of major financial houses and many large business firms, production industries and export firms, and a vast array of large, medium and small companies necessary to the consumptive needs of the metropolitan community such as markets, transportation offices, and retail stores;

Cultural organs: leading universities and colleges, and head offices of newspapers and publishers.

Under the successive impact of three wars, every level of national and international activity experienced enlargement in the various integrative organs concerned. Expansion in size and scope of integrative organs in Tōkyō not only strengthened the role of Tōkyō as nucleus of all national life; the number of people employed in these integrative organs increased threefold, resulting in significant changes in the ecological structure of the capital city.

While Tōkyō's ecological patterns changed in response to sweeping changes in the socio-economic structures of the total society, its characteristic feature as the seat of imperial authority remained unchanged. The emerging metropolis continued to be centered on the imperial palace, symbol of traditional authority, and the administrative and military organs immediately subordinate to that authority remained clustered around the palace. Just as "central" in another sense were the Marunouchi, Nihonbashi, Kyōbashi, and Kanda districts stretched out in front of the imperial palace. Locus of numerous foreign embassies and legations, business and finance organs, and major wholesale and retail enterprises, this sprawling center of economic activity was indicative of the fact that economic power was increasingly the center of actual domestic and international life. In the heart of the Marunouchi district was Tōkyō Railway Station, to which all trains are said to go "up" and all departing trains "down," reflecting the pre-eminence of the nearby imperial palace and the political and economic organs that controlled the nation.

In the process of industrial development throughout the entire nation, Tōkyō evolved the characteristic features of a large city as a center of both production and consumption. Within its ever-widening scope there were extensive resources of capital, labor, and raw materials for productive needs; its markets, distributive systems, and retail network were unsurpassed by any city in the country. Heavy and light industries were constructed along river banks and in coastal areas. People employed in all of the integrative organs were forced to extend their residential districts beyond the boundaries of the former urban area into the low hills west and southwest of the earlier urban core. As the population distribution spilled over the lines of previously developed urban facilities, new transit systems were required which brought surrounding towns and villages into the circle of the rapidly growing metropolitan community.

a. Development of Functions and Organs in Central Tōkyō. As the Emperor remained the symbol of total national integration in Japan's modern century, so Tōkyō, as the seat of the Imperial Household, retained its special place as the ecological nucleus of the nation, as also the imperial palace continued as the hub of the capital city. Within the precincts of the imperial palace were located the offices of the Cabinet, the Privy Council, the Lord Keeper of the Privy Seal, and the Imperial Household Agency. Just outside the main gate of the palace to the north was the Ōtemachi district, containing three important organs of government. These were the Ministry of Home Affairs, base of the expanding bureaucratic system and of related government and non-government offices; the Ministry of Finance, which expanded several times over in compliance with expansion of national finance and the prosperous government monopoly of the tobacco business; and the Bureau of Printing, employing thousands of workers in numerous printing shops.

In the Nishi-Hibiya district on the south side of the palace moats were found the Ministry of Justice, the Supreme Court, the Court of Appeals, Tōkyō District Court, and related courts. Across the boulevard leading away from Sakuradamon gate of the palace was the Kasumigaseki block containing the offices of the Ministry of the Navy, the Navy's General Staff, and the Ministry of Foreign Affairs. Just beyond, on the southwest corner of the palace grounds, was Nagata-chō where the Ministry of the Army, its General Staff, the Office of Mines Inspection, the National Diet, and other agencies were housed.

These government buildings lined an impressive group of wide streets in a limited zone around the imperial palace, commensurate with its importance as the nucleus of political administration throughout the nation. The modern styles of architecture employed in many of these structures were indicative of the modernization taking place in all society.

The modernization of Japan was not the realization of a broad citizens' movement, however; it was from the outset an undertaking led by government officials of former warrior pedigree. Expansion of the social structures feeding on the industrial revolution meant, at the same time, the expansion of the bureaucratic system that had its own tradition, its own criteria quite apart from modernizing factors. The bureaucrats ruled over a massive and mighty system that possessed an endowment of privilege and power proceeding from imperial authority.

The expansion of the bureaucracy is manifest in the following figures:

| *Year* | *Total number of government officials* |
|---|---|
| 1886 | 40,700 |
| 1897 | 65,700 |
| 1907 | 52,200 |
| 1920 | 308,200 |

These figures represent an increase of almost 750% in only thirty-five years.[48]

The rationale of the bureaucracy was that it functioned as a kind of holy order under the supreme imperial authority (*Shison no Taimei*). The offices to which they were appointed, all salaries, and appointments and dismissals as well were made with ultimate appeal to the sanction of the supreme authority of the Emperor. It was an absolutistic system, heavily feudal in its assumption of privilege and its demand for unswerving loyalty. Positions within the bureaucracy were consolidated in themselves, free from controls by the National Diet.

The execution of administrative authority was completely beyond the reach of criticism by the citizenry. Administrative procedures were carried out in secrecy, wedded to precedent, and weighted down with red tape. The inner dynamic of the whole bureaucratic organization was thoroughly informed by the elite consciousness of a privileged class that drew its norms from favored cliques, schools of thought, and human relations nurtured on pedigree and obligation. The notion that officials, even the lowest, were quite superior to any and every citizen was an unquestioned attitude, indeed, the ideology of every bureaucrat.

Formally the extensive administrative system was organized on the basis of highly differentiated functions necessary to the many tasks of government, with an appropriate stratification of official duties and authority. Technically speaking, such a rationalized framework was quite in order, indeed mandatory, for a modern state. But the norms and procedures were made amenable, in actual operations, to the inherited traditions of status stratification of feudal society, wherein there was little place for the efficient execution of business in terms of the freedom and equality accorded individual personality in modern societies.

The salaries of officials were regulated by two government ordinances, the Law for Salaries of Higher Civil Service Ranks (*Kōtōkan Kantō*

*Hōkyūrei*) and the Law for Salaries of Clerical Personnel (*Hanninkan Hōkyūrei*), enacted in 1910. The salary schedules provided for in these laws were as follows:

| *Offices* | *Explanation* | *Annual Salary* |
|---|---|---|
| *Chokuninkan* | Civil servants appointed by the Emperor (eight ranks) | ¥4,050–¥6,200 |
| | *Chokuninkan* appointed to central offices | ¥5,800 |
| *Sōninkan* | Civil servants appointed with the Emporer's approval | ¥1,050–¥5,050 |
| | | *Monthly salary* |
| *Hanninkan* | Clerical personnel | ¥40–¥145 |

Annual salaries of ¥5,800 were received by vice-ministers or directors of main bureaus in the various ministries, about 3.3 times the salaries of the highest ranking *Hanninkan.* The highest ranking *Sōninkan* even received 2.3 times the top *Hanninkan.* The highest ranking officials in the schedule were awarded salaries twelve times more than the lowest in office. Yet, the figures above represent only base salaries. The disparity between top and bottom becomes much greater when the various allowances paid are added.[49]

There was nothing strange in the fact that the bureaucratic system functioned in terms of seniority and privilege; the same was true of the whole society. There had been no popular democratic movement sufficiently strong to erase from the people the attitudes of submissive acceptance of bureaucratic discrimination which did as much to maintain the system as did official presumption of privilege.

The original idea behind the system of court ranks and the order of merit was to recognize meritorious services by outstanding persons, but the distribution of rank and merit had long since been granted automatically to all officials according to bureaucratic standing. Senior officials expected unconditional obedience from subordinates, who servilely flattered their superiors irrespective of the propriety of their thought and actions. The oppressive relationships prevailing among seniors and juniors in the bureaucracy were extended to all relationships between government officials and the public, who managed to do no more than offer up the obsequious obeisance demanded.

Working always to consolidate the powers of government within the circle of the bureaucratic mechanism, the political system of Japan was not designed to foster the welfare and freedom of the people; where public welfare was not oppressed it was, at best, neglected. While the authoritative posture of the bureaucracy characterized every government office in every town and village throughout the land, it was especially severe in the centralized organs in Tōkyō.

Thus, the capital city was certainly as feudal as it was modern. The chief cause of the push toward modernization of Tōkyō was the development of big business and finance firms. These were dominated, however, by the *zaibatsu* which sought technical modernity within the context of cultivating political favor in government organs along age-old feudal lines. Although the vehicles of business were increasingly modern, the operating mentality and controls remained strictly feudalistic.

The accomplishment of industrial revolution which we have traced favored the concentration and enlargement of financial organs especially in Tōkyō. Firms enjoying government protection were able to win control over huge capital accumulations before ordinary merchants could gain much strength in the finance world, and it was these large enterprises that appropriated the modern banking systems introduced from abroad by the government. A cumulative, reciprocal process was set in motion in which expansion of production through technological innovations permitted greater capital growth, which in turn fostered increased production, technical improvements, and further accumulation and concentration of capital. The accelerated pace of this process precipitated intensive use of credit systems.

The Bank of Japan was established in 1882 on a capital base, half of which was provided by the government, the other half being invested by the *zaibatsu.* Prior to its establishment bank notes had been issued by a number of agencies. Multiple currencies were abolished and a single currency system set up based on Bank of Japan notes. This move secured Tōkyō's position as the hub of all financing business in Japan.

The government supplied one-third of the capital to fund Yokohama Specie Bank in 1879 as a special organ for financing foreign exports. Its Tōkyō branch was opened at Nihonbashi in 1899, actually functioning as the main office of the bank. Raising its capital to 100 million yen in 1919, this bank invested capital in Manchuria and China and also sold bonds in overseas markets. In time it became one of the first class exchange banks of the world.

The selling of government industries to large private enterprises helped to increase the overall number of companies and the capital owned by them. To support the government policies of low-interest, long-term financing of both agriculture and industry, the government founded the Hypothec Bank of Japan in 1897 with a capital base of 10 million yen. The Agricultural and Industrial Bank of Tōkyō Prefecture (*Tōkyō-fu*) was founded just before that in 1896, and the Industrial Bank of Japan soon after in 1900.

Finance and credit systems had been stimulated by both the Sino-Japanese and Russo-Japanese Wars, but the World War I boom greatly accelerated the accumulation and concentration of capital, firmly establishing the position of Japanese industry in the world economy. This meant the establishment of the place of Japanese capitalism in the world, inasmuch as industry was modernized and developed in dependence upon banking capital.

The dominant strength of banking capital is reflected in the following account of deposits and capital in Tōkyō for years covering Japan's involvement in international conflicts:

| *Year* | *Amount of banking capital (yen)* | *Amount of deposits (yen)* |
|---|---|---|
| 1904 | 138,850,000 | —— |
| 1913 | 276,540,000 | 611,280,000 |
| 1919 | 562,470,000 | 3,239,840,000 |

Main offices of large banks built in central Tōkyō included Mitsui, Mitsubishi, Yasuda, Dai-ichi, Kawasaki Daihyaku, Jūgo, Furukawa, and Nihon Chūya. Branch offices of major banks based in the Kansai district, such as Sumitomo and Nomura, were erected in the same zone. These large banks all had smaller branches all over the country, implementing their networks of financial controls over Japanese industry.

The multiplicity of small trust companies that mushroomed once, were consolidated into larger firms with *zaibatsu* connections, principally Mitsui, Mitsubishi, and Yasuda. Out of 159 trust companies operating in 1913, 54 were in the Nihonbashi-Kyōbashi area alone, or 39.9% of the total number. They commanded 90.5% of all trust funds.

We saw in the first half of this chapter how the great *zaibatsu* emerged through a process of amalgamation, absorption, and merger under top holding companies to dominate the entire economy and also how cartel agreements on everything from raw materials to prices strengthened their monopolization of Japanese business. Primacy in international as well as domestic economic activity afforded the capitalist giants major influence in political and military policies. In the process Tōkyō was converted from the national nucleus of a bureaucracy rooted in feudalism to the home base of class rule by the capitalist elite.

One quantitative measure of the dominant role of business in Tōkyō is the enormous expansion, in sheer numbers and in capital investments, during the twenty-four year period from 1897 to 1920:

| *Year* | *Number of companies:* | | *Amount of paid-up and subscribed capital:*[50] | |
|---|---|---|---|---|
| | *In Japan:* | *In Tokyo:* | *In Japan: (yen)* | *In Tokyo: (yen)* |
| 1897 | 6,077 | —— | 532,500,000 | —— |
| 1920 | 20,917 | 2,691 | 8,238,100,000 | 2,756,000,000 |
| *Rate of increase:* | 344% | | 1,547% | |

Tōkyō's primacy in national finance and business is clearly revealed in that, with slightly over one-sixth of the total number of companies, its concentration of capital was nearly one-third of all capital investments in the nation.

Economic expansion increased the number and accelerated the pace of commercial transactions. The inconvenience of cash payments and bothersome details in such deals led to the formation of more complicated exchange procedures. The Tōkyō Clearing House was established in 1891, though it did not begin to operate effectively until 1900. The dimensional expansion of commercial transactions through bill clearances in the period under review is shown below:

| *Year* | *Clearances in Japan (yen)* | *Clearances in Tōkyō (yen)* |
|---|---|---|
| 1897 | 747,900,000 | 552,890,000 |
| 1920 | 73,713,950,000 | 32,691,450,000 |
| *Rate of increase:* | 9,736% | 5,913% |

Even at a time when the entire national economy was developing rapidly, the volume of cleared bills in Tōkyō amounted to over 50% of the total.[51]

A rather remarkable phenomenon in the development of Japanese capitalism was the conversion of private property into securities and the Tōkyō Stock Exchange in Kabuto-chō became, perhaps more than any other agency, the symbol of capitalism in Japan. State banks had been established as early as 1876 to issue bond certificates for public loan bonds; the Stock Exchange was established to assure smooth operations in bonds issuance in 1878 with a capital of 200,000 yen. The Stock Exchange really flourished after the Sino-Japanese War, as indicated in these capital amounts:

| *Year* | *Capital volume on the Stock Exchange (yen)* |
|---|---|
| 1878 | 200,000 |
| 1897 | 1,200,000 |
| 1905 | 4,000,000 |
| 1917 | 20,000,000 |

Spot trading activity arose during the war and a union of brokers specializing in ready cash transactions was formed in 1918. Cross trading on the spot market was activated, and a system of bonded brokers was established in 1920. A healthy market for public bonds was added to the already brisk business in bank securities.

Speculation was regarded as a kind of gambling at the time of the Meiji Restoration and it was outlawed. In 1876 the Tōkyō Rice Exchange was founded under government regulations. Renamed simply the Rice Exchange in 1895, it developed rapidly and was merged with the Commodity Exchange in 1908 and renamed again the Tōkyō Rice Exchange, with a capital of 1.5 million yen, handling rice, barley, wheat, silk, cotton yarns, and soy paste. Commodities other than rice were eliminated from the Exchange temporarily, although cotton yarns were put back on the Exchange in 1917. Cotton was set up in a separate location at Suginomori in Nihonbashi and called the Second Department of the Exchange; a Third Department for soy and wheat was formed in 1920 at Saga-chō in Fukagawa. The overall Tōkyō Rice Exchange, including these other departments, served as the key to all commodity quotations in Japan.[52]

The movement from formation of joint-stock corporations to emergence of the *zaibatsu* brought changes in the internal structures of large enterprises, due to the tendency toward functional specialization in the component units of the giant combines. To assure themselves of an upper hand in competition the *zaibatsu* distributed their own personnel throughout their network of companies. This placed a high premium on trained personnel with university backgrounds. Traditional business skills were no longer any more adequate in modern enterprises than were the crafts suitable in modern industries.

Positions in the large companies attracted increasing numbers of the graduates of colleges and universities. The Mitsui firms cultivated channels for acquiring personnel with the new knowledge needed in modern business among the graduates of Keiō University. Graduates of Tōkyō Commercial College (later Hitotsubashi University) also began seeking careers in the business world. Even though Tōkyō Imperial and Kyōto Imperial Universities were founded originally to train future government officials, an increasing number of graduates from these national universities also turned to business careers after the conditions of white collar employment improved considerably during the prosperous days of World War I.

The relative weight of status values in the structures of society was lessened as the companies were forced to seek out talented men, enhancing a greater degree of social mobility among the people. The importance of educational backgrounds to future job possibilities became clear to more and more families. Young people from the families of merchants and landowners whose incomes exceeded minimum daily needs assumed a larger place in college and university enrollments. Whereas most of the government officials and company employees in the first half of the Meiji period were from families of samurai pedigree, the sons of common people constituted the majority from World War I on.

Structural changes in society were promoted by the sharp increase in the number of salaried employees in companies, banks, and government offices. The percentage of salaried workers in Tōkyō quadrupled in a quarter-century:

| *Year* | *Percentage of salaried workers in Tōkyō (vs. total number in nation)* |
|---|---|
| 1908 | 5.6% |
| 1920 | 21.4% |

Feudal Edo had once been a clearly proportioned castle town with definite residential areas for warriors, merchants, and craftsmen. Establishment of a new government bureaucracy had introduced modifications in the feudal patterns of residence. But the suddenly swollen ranks of salaried men, business operators, and blue collar laborers transformed the residential patterns of modern Tōkyō.

The top positions in business and government, of course, were limited and far less influenced by the expansion and specialization in industry and business. They were filled with persons who tended to preserve the traditions of family lineage, status values, and cliques stemming from academic and privileged groups. Respect for individual ability and worth in a modern sense remained outside their scope, and they stood firmly entrenched at the pinnacle of society, while the lower strata spread out horizontally beneath them.

The percentage of senior officials in relation to the total number of government officials steadily declined:

| *Year* | *Percentage of senior officials* |
|---|---|
| 1887 | 0.76 |
| 1897 | 0.69 |
| 1907 | 0.46 |
| 1917 | 0.42 |

Obviously promotion possiblilties were lessened through the passing years, despite overall expansion in every field.[53]

A similar situation existed in companies and banks. The family lineage structures of the *zaibatsu* particularly tended toward concentration of managerial powers in the hands of a relatively small executive staff, which was increasingly differentiated from the working forces in the *zaibatsu* enterprises. Salaries of employees were ordered according to a wide range of classifications based on minutely divided duties.

There was no social security system, and salaries were based on minimum living costs rather than on proficiency in work. Employment itself was a kind of security system, in that companies "took care of its employees" even to the extent of providing housing in addition to living expenses. The companies became stabilized as they enlarged and, as cheap labor was increasingly plentiful, employment tended to be secured on a lifelong basis. Salary criteria in lifelong employment were scaled according to educational background, family size, and efficiency in work.

As specialization of jobs and division of labor became intensified, there were fewer personnel who acquired the necessary knowledge and experience to supervise an entire enterprise. Executive orders became increasingly one-way communications from top management down to the many divisions and sections of each company. The relative size of the managerial group as against salaried workers grew smaller, as its organizational powers expanded.

The relationship of the employer to his employees was understood as similar to that of a family head to the family. Compensation for work was but the bestowal of the master's favor upon good and faithful servants. Loyalty among employees was nurtured by frequent appeals to familial, religious, and other ethical values. Under such circumstances, control of employees was relatively easy; mobility among workers was at a minimum. It was rather rare for responsibility to be delegated to employees, nor did they share in the decision-making processes of the company. Managerial staff concentrated on flawless execution of the particular duties to which they were assigned, taking no initiative in matters above their office. Top management unhesitatingly assumed authority in decision-making, even after the actual dimensions of their enterprises expanded far beyond the competence of only a handful of executives. While efficiency in a technical sense might have suffered, organizational efficiency in terms of tight controls was well maintained.

The efficiency of Japanese capitalism cannot be seriously questioned, though, if one measures it by the rapid expansion of the number of companies, banks, and supportive government offices, including enormous dimensional expansion. Inevitable changes were effected, however, in interpersonal relationships, and in the ecological and social structure of Tōkyō.

Any assessment of ecological trends must begin with the unchallenged occupation of central Tōkyō by business firms. Industries settled for the less desirable areas of Honjo and Fukagawa which, with Koishikawa, constituted the poorest residential areas. Farming could hardly find the open spaces needed in view of the increasing population density of the capital city.

A look at the distribution of business companies in greater Tōkyō in 1919 will serve to demonstrate the dominant place of these firms in Tōkyō's central area:

| *Order* | *Ward or County (gun)* | *No. of companies* | *Order* | *Ward or County (gun)* | *No. of companies*[54] |
|---|---|---|---|---|---|
| 1 | Kyōbashi | 595 | 12 | Ebara-gun | 86 |
| 2 | Nihonbashi | 534 | 13 | Toyotama-gun | 82 |
| 3 | Kanda | 335 | 14 | Koishikawa | 49 |
| 4 | Honjo | 257 | 15 | Azabu | 46 |
| 5 | Fukagawa | 190 | 16 | Ushigome | 25 |
| 6 | Kōji-machi | 146 | 17 | Nishitama-gun | 24 |
| 7 | Minami-katsushika-gun | 127 | 18 | Akasaka | 14 |
| 8 | Hongō | 121 | 19 | Hachiōji | 14 |
| 9 | Shiba | 121 | 20 | Kitatama-gun- | 13 |
| 10 | Asakusa | 118 | 21 | Minami-tama-gun | 13 |
| 11 | Kita-toshima-gun | 111 | 22 | Yotsuya | 4 |

The distribution of capital investments yields an entirely different order among the wards and counties of Tōkyō. Of the top nine areas, the capital paid into any one of the top three, Nihonbashi, Kōji-machi, or Kyōbashi, was more than the sum total of the remaining six areas. Just below these three districts were the industrial zones in suburban areas, followed by industrial districts in the urban area, consisting mostly of small-sized factories. Capital investments in residential zones ranked lowest of all.

| *Order* | *Ward or County* (*gun*) | *Amount of paid capital in companies* (*yen*) |
|---|---|---|
| 1 | Nihonbashi | 752,000,000 |
| 2 | Kōji-machi | 614,000,000 |
| 3 | Kyōbashi | 352,000,000 |
| 4 | Minami-katsushika-gun | 92,000,000 |
| 5 | Kanda | 74,000,000 |
| 6 | Kita-toshima-gun | 63,000,000 |
| 7 | Fukagawa | 40,000,000 |
| 8 | Honjo | 39,000,000 |
| 9 | Ebara-gun | 32,000,000 |

It will be recalled that the old Army grounds in front of the imperial palace were bought up by Mitsubishi interests in 1890. Iwasaki Yanosuke paid 1.5 million yen for this area, which laid undeveloped so long it was overrun with weeds and referred to as "Mitsubishi field." Construction work for office buildings was begun in 1892, with streets laid out for future buildings. Streetcars were installed connecting Hibiya and Ōtemachi on a north-south run, and Hibiya and Sukiyabashi on an east-west run, the only available means of transit in the area at the time. Even after the Russo-Japanese War the only buildings in the "Mitsubishi field" area belonged to Mitsubishi interests. The Metropolitan Police Office was built there in 1911, as was the Imperial Theater. Done in Renaissance style with white tiled walls, the Imperial Theater was a kind of cultural showpiece which was built to foster international relations by engaging first class performers from all over the world. It quickly became a central gathering place for upper class citizens of Tōkyō.

By the end of the Meiji era quite a few office buildings had been erected in the Marunouchi area around "Mitsubishi field," though they numbered only forty-seven in 1911. The district got the needed stimulus for completion as a business center when Tōkyō Station was constructed in 1914, as the terminal of the Tōkaidō line. The boom days of World War I precipitated further construction by business firms. Matching Kōji-machi's concentration of administrative offices, the Marunouchi area blossomed as a truly impressive business center, symbolized by the construction of Tōkyō Kaijō Building, the first structure to discard familiar brick construction for the reinforced concrete architecture popular in the United States at that time. From that time brick structures were built no longer as large buildings. The Tōkyō Kaijō Building had a total floor space of 5,000 *tsubo* (4 acres), and its modern features later became distinctive of the Marunouchi district.[55]

In the Marunouchi and Kōji-machi areas there were many banks handling both domestic and foreign capital, such as the Hypothec Bank of Japan, the Industrial Bank of Japan, Mitsubishi Bank, and others. Major firms in the area included Japan Mail Steamship Line (Nihon Yūsen Kaisha), Tōkyō Railway Company, Tōkyō Electric Power Company, the Japan Times and Hōchi newspaper companies, and others. The number of companies in this area reached 146, with paid-up capital of more than 616 million yen, by 1919.

The number of companies in the Marunouchi district made it only fifth-ranked among Tōkyō's fifteen wards, behind Nihonbashi, Kyōbashi, Kanda, and Honjo, although it was second only to Nihonbashi in capital investments. Nihonbashi held first place in capital claims with more than 725 million yen. Kyōbashi district came third with 352 million yen; there was no other ward which even reached 100 million yen in capital investments.

While the streets of Marunouchi were relatively free of feudal traditions, those traditions were well preserved in the old commercial houses[56] of the Nihonbashi-Kyōbashi area, where wholesalers and retailers flourished. Firmly established in the Meiji era, the Kyōbashi and Nihonbashi merchants assumed a new importance in industry and commerce of the Taishō era.

In 1919 Kyōbashi had the largest number of companies, though Nihonbashi topped it in capital claims. The heavy concentration of large enterprises in the combined Kyōbashi-Nihonbashi area is indicated in the following figures for companies classified by capital amounts:

| *Ward* | *No. of companies with over 5,000,000 yen* | *No. of companies with capital between 1,000,000 and 5,000,000 yen*[57] |
|---|---|---|
| Nihonbashi | 48 | 105 |
| Kyōbashi | 34 | 141 |
| Kōji-machi | 39 | 44 |
| Kanda | 3 | 25 |
| Shiba | 3 | 18 |
| Honjo | 3 | 17 |
| Fukagawa | 3 | 15 |

In 1913 there were some thirty companies with more than 600,000 yen in capital investments in Tōkyō, covering a wide range of businesses, such as finance, trading, mining, shipping, insurance, electric power, textiles, cameras, securities, construction, petroleum, publications, and so on.[58]

In addition to the locating of the Bank of Japan (1883) and the Tōkyō branch of Yokohama Specie Bank (1899) in the Nihonbashi area, there were many other major banks in the area, such as Mitsui, Dai-ichi, Kawasaki, and many more. Reduction in the number of banks early in the Taishō era (1912–26) through absorption and mergers accentuated the concentration of financing capital in these large banks. The presence of Tōkyō Stock Exchange in Kabuto-chō and the Rice Exchange in Kakigara-chō of Nihonbashi proved an irresistible attraction to other securities firms. The congregation of large companies, banks, and the stock and securities establishments in the Hongoku-chō, Muromachi, Hon-chō, Edobashi, and Kabuto-chō subdistricts of Nihonbashi lent it a special atmosphere as the center of finance and business of Tōkyō and the nation.

The unprecedented expansion of integrative organs overseeing the political and economic life of the capital city and of the nation inevitably caused an equally and heretofore unknown increase in the population of Tōkyō. It was necessary, therefore, to develop more extensive and, often, new sets of integrative organs to manage the massive supply and demand in the consumptive activity of the swollen population. Hence, we must investigate some of the more salient features of the distributive and retailing systems that evolved in conjunction with the growth of political and economic organs as outlined above. These systems were quite complex, inasmuch as the consumer demands of the capital city were not only voluminous, but ranged over a wide variety of goods and services.

First of all we shall look into the wholesaling end of commodity distribution, especially as regards such staple items as fish, rice, vegetables, fruits, oils, fertilizers, and sugar. The central markets handling these goods were concentrated close by the major businesses in the Nihonbashi, Kyōbashi, and Kanda districts.

In preceding chapters we have described the existence of markets in old Edo and Tōkyō of the Meiji period, as we also mentioned the government's action in deactivating the wholesalers and brokers after the Meiji Restoration. Concerned about the market recession that set in, the Meiji government then reactivated the markets to restore and promote vigorous trading activity, in 1877. Four markets were established at Nihonbashi, Shinbashi, Shiba Kanasugi, and Senju that were controlled, and protected, through licensed operations. The collection, distribution, and marketing of goods was put into good order by 1888.

The Tōkyō Prefectural Office supervised operation of the fish market which had been open since that date, as it did other markets. The fish and poultry market of Nihonbashi embraced 341 wholesale shops and 141 brokers, with average daily sales of 2.28 million yen—the largest market in all Tōkyō. The next largest was that for salt and dried fish in Nihonbashi Yokkaichi, with daily sales averaging 910,000 yen, followed by the fish market in Fukagawa (70,000 yen), fish and poultry markets in Shiba Kanasugi (60,000 yen) and Senju (50,000 yen).[59]

One half of the total quantity of shellfish and other kinds of fish delivered to Tōkyō's markets came from Awa, Kazusa, and Shimōsa in Chiba Prefecture, on fishing boats flocking into the Nihonbashi port in the same great numbers as in Edo days.[60] Other products were shipped by rail from local agents in various provinces to the many dealers in the market.

There were also many dealers in the central markets for fruits and vegetables in Kyōbashi and Kanda. Dispersed throughout the urban area were the intermediary markets of Komagome, Hama-chō, Honjo, Chitose-machi, and Honjo Yotsume. In suburban areas were located the intermediary markets of Senju, Shinagawa, Aoyama, and Shinjuku. Some of the markets had only wholesale agents, others included brokers. In any event, the price of goods rose anywhere from 50% to 200% in passing through the hands of the many intermediary channels, on the way from producers to consumers.

Many minor markets were opened privately in numerous localities of Tōkyō, but these were gradually eclipsed by the central markets in Kyōbashi and Kanda where higher prices were offered, after better roads and carts for haulings products made it possible for producers to reach them. On the other hand, farmers sometimes sold directly to the local minor markets to avoid transport bother. The overall effect was to reduce the number of the intermediary markets.[61]

Whereas rice had been received traditionally at the wholesaling market of Fukagawa, a convenient dock for incoming shipments by boat from provincial sources with warehouses (*kura-yashiki*) standing from Edo times, this market declined with the development of more direct transport facilities by overland railways. Freight depots at many stations along the rail lines were built, lessening the degree of commodity concentration in the central markets. Wholesalers were also forced to adapt their operations to a number of changes precipitated by the development of capitalism in Japan.

In the preceding chapter it was shown that the number of wholesalers in the Nihonbashi and Kanda areas was overwhelmingly large, and that they had a style of life and work all their own in the Hongoku-chō and Asakusabashi sections of these areas based on traditional methods of working. The goods they handled comprised mainly agricultural and home industry products, collected and sold under government privileges. When large enterprises developed under capitalism, brokers were still needed in procuring foodstuffs and products manufactured in cottage industries; but they were no longer needed in procurement of large quantities of raw materials for large-scale factory production. Direct supply lines from raw material producers to factories were established for the large-scale industries.

Likewise, to market mass-produced commodities the intermediary channels of wholesalers, retail brokers and sales agents were sometimes utilized. Quite as often, though, more direct connections with retailing houses were employed. Once established, the more direct channels to retailers soon eclipsed the roundabout wholesalers' distributive system.

The wholesalers eventually lost their exclusive controls of home industry products also. Formerly they had maintained these controls chiefly by making loans or advance payments to brokers who gathered the products of cottage industries for them. With the legal annulment of wholesaling privileges, allowing anyone with some capital to enter into distributive supply business, the distinctions between wholesalers and brokers was eradicated, and the wholesalers could no longer monopolize supply and market routes between home industries and retail stores.

There were three different modes of operation among wholesalers: those who paid cash for goods to be sold as quickly as possible at some margin of profit; those who bought up unfinished goods to process themselves for final marketing; and those who handled goods on a consignment basis, making payments later. The wholesalers who received goods on consignment dwindled rather rapidly as producers found they could get immediate, or earlier, payments from other types of wholesalers and that, in such transactions, they were less subject to unfair treatment. Wholesalers processing goods for final sales were also in a weak position, due partly to the time lag in processing and the sales risks on goods already paid for, but mainly because they simply could not compete with the more efficient large-scale production methods of factories. Consequently, most of the wholesalers converted to the role of middlemen purchasing goods directly from suppliers for quick sales to local merchants and retail shops. As such, these dealers were classified further into those handling miscellaneous items, those handling foodstuffs, those supplying raw materials to manufacturers, and those dealing in all these supplies. Of these several types, those handling a comprehensive line of goods tended to prosper.

In the Taishō period wholesalers operating as private enterprisers were completely eliminated by sales agencies developed by the large corporations, called "commodity companies" (*bussan-gaisha*) or "trading companies" (*shōji-gaisha*).[62] At first the corporation-connected distributing firms sold goods through their own stores, but later developed corps of sales agents who made the rounds of customers for whose business other sales offices were keenly competing.

Whenever money became tight wholesalers could no longer afford the traditional long-term settlements, but were compelled to require monthly payments. Corporation trading firms relied on larger resources and could easily out-bargain them, especially as the trading companies dealt in large volumes of goods. Moreover, as the sole agents for large enterprises, the trading companies enjoyed commercial privileges not unlike the old government privileges that independent wholesalers once enjoyed but had lost. The trading firms under protection of the large corporations completely replaced the private wholesalers.

Employment practices were altered significantly as changes were made in the modes of distribution and retailing in the transition from the Meiji to the Taishō period. In the old apprenticeship system the master of a merchant house suffered heavy financial losses when it came time to share his trademark in helping an apprentice-graduate to set up his own shop; yet, some of the merchants continued operations according to this system.

Most of them turned, though, to one of two modes of wage employment. One was a live-in system with lower wages; the other, a live-out system, paid higher wages. The live-in arrangement permitted retention of certain advantages of the old apprentice system, without its heavy liabilities. That is, by having young employees resident on their premises, they could be trained in the details of business as one of the family, and traditional master-subordinate values were more easily preserved. Salaries, in whole or part, could be deposited in a fund that enabled the employees to set up their own shops later, eliminating the heavy expenses of establishing branch shops on the part of the employer.

The live-out system was a more purely wage-employment arrangement. Employees took responsibility for their own residences and commuted to and from work. Business hours and holidays were definitely fixed. They were paid monthly salaries plus annual or semi-annual bonuses, and salary increases came with job promotions. Whereas minor merchants tended to stick to the semi-apprentice live-in system, the live-out arrangement was more common in business companies, department stores, and larger retail shops. Since minor merchants and private wholesalers, who preferred the live-in system, decreased in the Taishō era, the live-out system of companies and larger stores became more widely prevalent.[63]

Progress made in urban transit facilities vastly increased the daily movement of more people with better incomes into the central retailing districts. Only the severest restrictions of time and money could now keep people interested in shopping "downtown" confined in isolated villages and towns in urban or suburban sections of the city.

Accordingly, the retail stores and shops responded quickly to the expanded opportunities presented by huge daytime populations gathering in the central areas. Originally, the leading retail shops had catered to people resident in the central districts, or, at best, to a special upper class clientele. Attraction of the pedestrian daytime population became a major concern, setting a premium on locations along main streets or near transit junctions. Retail merchants endeavored to improve or open up new streets in the shopping districts, quite apart from the wholesale sectors.

As retail stores concentrated along the main streets, there occurred greater differentiation of merchandizing functions; many of the old general stores (*yorozuya*) handling nearly everything converted to speciality shops featuring comprehensive coverage of a single, or several related, items. Most of the shops had produced finished goods of their own, and many continued to do so. Not a few, however, shifted to purely retail functions, obtaining goods produced more cheaply by mass-production plants. But the shift was neither widespread nor swift. Many of the shops had long-established reputations which they sought to preserve through personal services to customers. Also, apart from the very few really wealthy people, there was relatively little difference in the individual incomes of the various social strata in this period, and relative purchasing power was not high among most people. Close attention to customers' tastes and needs remained common in the retail business.

The most notable changes in retailing occurred in the department stores, to be discussed below, but the latter did not eclipse specialty shops by any means. These shops held their own against the department stores by maintaining their reputation for goods of superior quality personally produced. Examples of specialty shops lining the main streets and housed in convenient accommodations in large buildings include:

| *Shop* | *Specialty* | *Shop* | *Specialty* |
|---|---|---|---|
| Shioze | Cakes | Tsumura-juntendo | Medicines |
| Eitarō | Candies | Kokubu-shōten | Foodstuffs |

| | | | |
|---|---|---|---|
| Kiya | Lacquerware | Yama-motoyama | Dried foods |
| Kuroeya | 〃 | Yamamoto | 〃 〃 |
| Ninben | Dried foods | Banden | Mats & mosquito nets |
| Haibara | Paper products | Nishikawa | 〃 〃 〃 〃 |

In the merchandizing methods of early Meiji days goods were stored in stockrooms, clerks seated formally around the sales floor made initial contacts with customers, and brought out wares priced according to signals made by managers. These practices began changing from the middle of the Meiji period, and in the Taishō era stores increasingly utilized show windows and showcases, with clerks stationed conveniently by to serve interested customers. Bargaining for discounts was eliminated as prices were now marked on price tags. Except for shops handling daily necessities, credit accounts were abolished in favor of cash sales.[64]

An exception to the trend toward specialization by retail shops were the *kankōba,* or neighborhood bazaars built in many communities between 1887 and 1907. The bazaars were eclipsed by the department stores in the Taishō era, when public transit improvements enabled the department stores to attract large numbers of customers from widely dispersed communities. They appealed more to the emerging modern sensitivities of the people who appreciated the wider selection of goods, the freedom to make their own choices, and the speedier service in concluding a purchase in the department stores. Cash sales, discounts, amusement facilities and stage shows featuring traditional song and dance also appealed to the department store clientele. The *kankōba* virtually disappeared.

Most of the department stores originated from large dry goods stores; and dry goods were not only in heavy demand, their quality was not altered by keeping large supplies in stock, as in foodstuffs. Capital was more easily accumulated, and management practices were quite similar, and therefore easily adapted to department store methods. Large dry goods stores operating in Tōkyō around the middle of the Meiji period (1890's) were:

| *Store* | *Location* | *Store* | *Location* |
|---|---|---|---|
| Mitsukoshi Gofukuten | Nihonbashi | Shirokiya | Tori 1-chome |
| Daimaru | Hatago-cho | Matsuzakaya | Ueno-hirokōji |
| Echigoya | Ginza | Matsuya | Imagawabashi |

Of these dry goods stores, Mitsukoshi and Shirokiya led the way in the introduction of Western methods of department store management.

Mitsui & Company sent a number of executives to the United States around the turn of the century to learn the latest methods of department store operation, including conversion from accustomed methods of daily bookkeeping to Western-style accounting systems. In 1904 the retailing function of Mitsui & Company was put under separate management and renamed Mitsukoshi. Showcases helped to overcome the low efficiency and inconvenience of bringing each item out of the stockroom for each customer—a method introduced already by Shirokiya in 1902.

In addition to stylish Japanese-style apparel, such as the *azuma* coat worn by ladies over kimono, the Mitsukoshi store featured shawls, overcoats, and accessories imported from abroad in keeping with the "high collar," that is, high class styles so fashionable among upper class citizens. Steamer trunks were another typical feature of the Mitsukoshi store, as round-the-world trips were also quite popular among wealthier people. Quality goods were increasingly designed by Mitsukoshi personnel and an ever wider selection of items graced its shelves and showcases. Limousine service was provided for special customers, and deliveries made free of charge by trucks. The entire operation was a serious threat to the other retail shops in Nihonbashi, as it was a remarkable thing to have motored services when there were only about one hundred automobiles in all Tōkyō. It was an epoch-making venture in urban trade for the times.

Shirokiya abolished old patterns of employment in 1897, and Mitsukoshi followed suit in 1903. The positions of managers, clerks, and messengers (*bantō*, *tedai*, and *kozō* respectively) reflecting feudal status structures were replaced by a system of general managers overseeing department managers who, in turn, supervised specialized activities such as accounting, sales, cashiering, stockroom supplies, purchasing, and deliveries. Employees were on set salaries and lived out, commuting to work. Academically trained personnel were sought for executive positions. Such measures were required if the department stores were to keep up with the developing trends in the capitalist economy. All traces of feudal values were not eradicated from interpersonal relationships, however, and employees were hardly encouraged to cultivate free and open association with employers.

Having replaced its early Meiji quarters with a three-storied wooden frame structure in Renaissance styling in 1908, Mitsukoshi moved into a modern building of reinforced concrete in 1914. At the time it was called the most modern building east of the Suez Canal, and was equipped with elevators, cash conveyors, and heating and ventilating facilities. Shirokiya had completed and occupied a similarly modernized building in 1911.[65]

Not all commercial enterprises conformed to the modernization trend, and a considerable number of the more traditionally oriented shops were adversely affected by increased transit mobility and specialization in merchandizing methods. Most of the shops seriously affected were just off the main course dominated by the department stores, in Tōrisuji, Hon-chō, Ōdenma-chō, Tōri-hatago-chō, Yokoyama-chō, and Ryōgoku. Their wares included woolen fabrics, liquors, umbrellas, and ladies' accessories, and their practices remained old-fashioned. Sugar wholesalers in Ise-machi almost completely vanished in the early part of the Taishō period. Fabrics and mat dealers in Koami-chō and Shin-norimono-chō declined as did Horie-chō dealers in fans, tobacco cases and pipes, bags, brushes, and ink supplies. Traditional restaurants and noodle shops also decreased in number.[66]

Nihonbashi was converted from a special localized center of markets, wholesalers, and retail merchants to a modernized retail business center filled with the capitalist structures of big companies, banks, and department stores. Yet, its modernization was achieved with a degree of compromise with styles and values of former times.

The Ginza area, however, was developed somewhat artificially as the consciously decorated entrance to Tōkyō, with the new international relations in mind. It was also intended to serve as a medium for the introduction of Western culture. This function was expedited by the completion of the Shinbashi terminal on the Tōkyō-Yokohama railway in 1892. Before planned development, the Ginza had been no more than an humble road on the outskirts of Edo.

The following list of stores developed along the Ginza indicates its function as a receptacle of Western commodities, as each of the specialties of the particular stores were largely imported items or Western in style.

| *Name of store* | *Kind of goods handled*[67] |
|---|---|
| Aoki Kutsu-kaban-ten | Shoes and brief cases |
| Itōya Bunbōguten | Stationery and office supplies |
| Jūjiya Gakkiten | Musical instruments |
| Tamaya Tokeiten | Watches and clocks |
| Kintarō Ganguten | Toys |
| Satō Hōshokuten | Jewelry |
| Kondō Shoten | Books |
| Panya Kimura Sōhonten | Bread and cakes |
| Kyōbunkan Shosekiten | Books (including Christian literature) |
| Mikimoto Shinjuten | Cultured pearls |
| Yamano Gakkiten | Musical instruments |
| Kurimoto Undōguten | Sporting goods |
| Cafe Lion | Coffee house and restaurant |
| Taishōdō Tokeiten | Watches and clocks |
| Sekiguchi Yōhinten | Haberdashery |
| Sano Tabiten | Japanese socks |
| Kyūkyodo | Stationery and perfumes |
| Daimaruya Gofukuten | Dry goods |
| Shōgetsu Yōshokuten | Western-style restaurant |
| Daikokuya Shokuryōhinten | Foodstuffs |
| Cafe Tiger | Coffee house and restaurant |
| Mazuda Lamp Ginzaten | Electric lighting equipment |
| Morinaga Candy Store | Confections |
| Tenshōdō Honten | Watches and jewelry |
| Fujiya Kashiten | Confections |
| Kikusui Nagai Tabakoten | Pipe and tobacco supplies |
| Takahashi Stekkiten | Walking sticks |
| Miuraya Yōshu Shokuryō-ten | Foodstuffs and liquors |

These stores were located between Ginza 3-chome and Owaricho 2-chome in 1910, and represented the latest in Western goods. There were only a few older style shops in the area.

Ginza was by far the most modernized street in Tōkyō, with stylish shops displaying fashionable goods in broad store-front show windows. Although located near the heart of the city, its customers lived in the residential areas in the low hills west of the business center. They were government officials, business executives and employees of large companies who were attracted to imported goods, and took pleasure in dining out in Western style. The common people preferred the more moderately modernized department stores such as Mitsukoshi and Shirokiya in the Nihonbashi distirct, where new styles were featured in ways appealing to general tastes among common people.

The boom days of World War I increased the marginal funds of larger numbers of average people, who then changed their habits and tastes. The Ginza became more familiar to them, and "strolling along the Ginza" (*Gin-bura*) became a favorite pastime. Crowds of curious strollers could be seen until late in the evening (9–10 p.m.), and night booths were put up to cater to those engaged in leisurely meandering along the famous street. It became also an evening amusement center, with many cafes and other facilities catering to the evening crowds, including red light districts on side streets.[68]

In nearby Kobiki-chō the grand theater of Kabuki plays was erected, as was the Shintomi-za theater. The Ginza became the mecca of Kabuki. Beyond Kobiki-chō toward Tōkyō Bay was Tsukiji, settlement for foreigners for thirty years from 1867 to 1899, though most of the foreigners' residences had been moved to other areas by the Taishō era. There remained here, though, St. Luke's (Episcopal) Hospital and a Roman Catholic Church as reminders of the old foreigners' settlement.

When newspapers were first founded they congregated along the Ginza, though these gradually relocated in the Marunouchi area as Ginza expanded as a major retail center. A considerable number of publishers and book dealers moved to the Kanda district, closer to the educational institutions built there. In Kanda one could find row upon row of second-hand book stores, some 70% of all to be found in Tōkyō.

The central area of the capital city, then, embraced everything from government offices, large companies, banks, markets, and stores for retailing and wholesaling business. Many were new, some grew out of older enterprises. Many prospered, though not a few declined.

With all of these changes in the integrative activity of central Tōkyō, the ecological structure of the central area was transformed from a limited orientation to local townships structured according to status stratification, to a functional centrality connected with the entire metropolitan community, with the nation as a whole, and with international society. The basic enabling condition of that transformation was the accomplishment of complex systems of transportation and communications that permitted ready access to each of the three larger zones: metropolitan community, nation, and international society. Only through progress in the network of communication and transportation systems was it possible for the integrative organs to expand in size and number on such a scale requiring the movement of people and goods and the transmission of ideas and information over wider and wider ranges.

The accomplishment of extensive communicative and transport systems to serve total integration comprised many different components, and we cannot investigate all of them. A particularly revealing example of the overall transport system is found in figures on the tremendous movement of cargoes into and out of Tōkyō in 1926 (although this represents the culmination of Taishō period trends). The total volume of cargoes leaving Tōkyō in that year was 2,964,932 tons. An indication of the provincial destinations of this total, by percentages, follows:

| *Destination* | *Percentage* |
|---|---|
| Greater Tōkyō and six prefectures in immediate Kantō district | 56 |
| Tōhoku district | 23 |
| Yamanashi, Nagano, Gifu, and other points on Chūō Line | 7 |
| Shizuoka, Aichi, and Mie along Tōkaidō Line | 6 |
| Kinki district | 4 |
| Hokuriku district | 3 |

The remaining one percent was distributed, in descending order, among the following: Kyūshū, Hokkaidō, Chūgoku, Shikoku, Korea, Sakhalin, and Manchuria.

Tōkyō was organically connected with the provinces and overseas markets, of course, in terms of its intake of cargoes. What is important is that the distances between the metropolis and the surrounding area, the provinces, and the overseas sources—distances more ecologically than geographically determined—were overcome in ways that enabled the city to function as a huge city and as the integrative nucleus of the nation in all spheres.

Another key element in the ecological knitting-together of the vast city was development of modern means of transit. Completion of a series of rail lines, using steam and electricity, provided the necessary transportation facilities for yearly expansion of Tōkyō, as per the following:

| *Year of completion* | *Terminals at each end of line*[69] |
|---|---|
| 1872 | Shinbashi–Yokohama |
| 1883 | Ueno–Kumagaya |
| 1889 | Shinjuku–Tachikawa |
| 〃 | Shinbashi–Kōbe |
| 1891 | Ueno–Aomori (Tōhoku Line) |
| 1896 | Tabata–Tsuchiura |
| 1897 | Honjo–Chōshi |

| | |
|---|---|
| 1898 | Ueno–Sendai (Jōban Line) |
| 1901 | Shinbashi–Shimonoseki (Tōkaidō and Sanyō Lines) |
| 1904 | Electric cars began to run between Iidabashi and Nakano |
| 1905 | Ueno–Niigata |
| 1909 | Electric car services from Karasumori (present Shinbashi)—Shinagawa–Ueno; and Ikebukuro–Akabane |
| 1911 | Iidabashi–Nagoya (Chūō Line completed) |
| 1912 | Chūō Line extended to Manseibashi (present Akihabara) |
| 1914 | Tōkyō Station completed as terminal of Tōkaidō Line |
| 1919 | Electric car service, Tōkyō–Kichijōji |

As the rail extensions closed the geographical distances between Tōkyō and the rest of the nation, the ecological framework of integration was constructed. With completion of electric car services into and around the central part of the capital, exercise of its integrative functions was vastly implemented. Now the performance of various functions of political, economic, and cultural importance could reach out easily and quickly to suburban and provincial places, greatly conserving both time and energy.

New relationships between Tōkyō's population and integrative activity emerged as the improved transit facilities permitted a wider distribution of urban and suburban residential areas of those employed in the centrally located organs of integration, with essentially no more time consumed in reaching offices and stores and schools. Managerial executives took early advantage of the opportunity to separate their residences from companies and office buildings. The live-in system of employment declined. The citizens were motivated to move out into dispersed residential areas not only by rapidly rising land prices in the central districts of the city; increased noise, dust, and dirty streets common to large cities made the inner city less suitable for daily living. Finally, the central urban areas became so saturated with people that there was increasingly little choice other than locating at some distance from the downtown areas.

The rates of population increase in four concentric circles, including the nuclear central area, illustrate the gradual movement away from the inner to the outer districts of the larger metropolitan community:

| *Area* | *Rate of population increase* (*1897–1920*) |
|---|---|
| Central | Less than 30% |
| Inner urban | Over 50% |
| Total urban | 94% |
| Suburban | 183% |

As most of the populace of greater Tōkyō made their living in jobs either directly or indirectly connected with the central integrative organs, each day called forth a massive movement of people from residential areas widely separated from places of business. Development of a complex system of low cost transit was absolutely essential to the smooth functioning of the capital city.

Horse-drawn streetcars served a limited area in the central portion of the city from 1882, running between Shinbashi and Nihonbashi, Muromachi 3-chome and Asakusa, Manseibashi and Asakusa, and Shinbashi and Shinagawa. Just before the Sino-Japanese War electric streetcar services were installed along these routes (1903). In 1902 there were 47,085 rickshaws and 536 horse-drawn carriages operating in Tōkyō, the major forms of rolling transportation. After electric streetcar lines were installed, the number of rickshaws fell off to 18,183, and carriages dropped to 108 in number, by 1917.

Plans drawn up in 1919 projecting new urban developments in the areas of Ebara, Toyotama, Kita-toshima, Minami-adachi, Katsushika, and Kita-tama estimated overall transit volume in Tōkyō at 496.9 million passengers per year. The utilization of different means of travel was projected as per the following percentages:

| *Type of facilities* | *Anticipated passenger traffic* (%) |
|---|---|
| Streetcars (elec.) | 79 |
| Electric trains (urban area) | 12 |
| Electric trains (suburban areas) | 9 |
| Buses | less than 1 |

Since most citizens depended on the streetcar system, a high degree of interdependence between local communities could be realized only within the range of that system.[70]

Three companies were active in the installation and operation of streetcar lines in the central area of the city around 1903–4. One was Tōkyō Electric Car Company; another Tōkyō Streetcar Company, and the third Tōkyō Electric Railway Company. Each serviced a particular section of the inner city. They were merged in 1905 to avoid unnecessary competition, forming the Tōkyō Railway Company.

This company was put under municipal authority and administration in 1911. Passenger transportation was almost completely monopolized by the city from that time on; and most of the present network of streetcar lines were actually laid out in the Meiji period. The accomplishment of a modernized transit system resulted in a high mobility rate for Tōkyō's inhabitants. The average number of passengers per day in 1908 was 446,000; by 1917 it had almost doubled to 812,000. The annual rate of population increase in Tōkyō during the Taishō era averaged 4.6%; the annual rate of increase in streetcar passengers during the same period averaged 7.4%.

Added mobility accentuated the trend toward separation of home and office and, as students, clerks in shops and banks, workers in offices of business and government hurried to reach their appointed places at roughly the same time each morning, Tōkyō was introduced to its maiden experiences—though not its last—of the rush hour phenomenon. Late afternoon and evening hours reversed the flow of passengers, adding another rush hour to each day.

Each individual carefully calculated the amount of time and the daily expense involved in commuting to and from work; this calculative element became a major determinative factor in the formation of ecological patterns of Tōkyō. Another crucial factor in determining ecological conditions, however, was the traditional mode of land utilization in Tōkyō, and it is to this we direct our attention in the next section.

b. Residential Areas. Given a greatly increased population with improved transit mobility that was less and less responsive to status values, the ecological and social structures of the city were bound to change. Topographical conditions could be altered to some extent, and they were; inherited land use patterns resisted change stubbornly, though these too gave way to a considerable degree to the cumulative pressures of urbanizing and modernizing forces. But the basic determinative factors in the lives of Tōkyō's citizenry were the relative degrees of proximity to, or remoteness from, the centrally grouped integrative organs or the more widely dispersed industrial zones.

The laws and regulations of Edo society that relegated particular status groups to, and effectively kept them isolated within individual townships, were formally abolished by the Meiji government; yet the inbred customs and habits of mind of the feudal order remained in effect long after the Meiji reform programs became legally valid. In the long run, it was the progressively powerful economic conditions of the new capitalist society that served to intensify mobility among the people, loosening the neighborhood and status group ties that had bound them so tightly for so long.

Recalling the Edo situation for a moment, it will be remembered that there existed distinctive differences in ecological and social structures within the topographical context of the low lying areas near Edo Bay and the residentially desirable hills that rambled west of the Edo Castle grounds. In between, in front of the Castle precincts, were the thriving commercial districts of Kanda, Kyōbashi, and Nihonbashi, receiving goods from local cottage industries and from the provinces through the nearby rivers and ports. The warrior class, main customers of the old commercial center, resided for the most part in splendid mansions in the low western hills section, where the only commercial activity consisted of small shops providing daily necessities required by the warrior households.

When Edo became Tōkyō it became also the principal scene of remarkable expansion and change catapulted forward by the stimulus of three successive wars from which the internal developments of business and industry benefited enormously. The expanding energies of national life were increasingly caught up in the centripetal forces of political, economic, and cultural integration of functions and organs in central Tōkyō, as the preceding section described. The successful operation of the central integrative organs created concomitantly centrifugal forces that determined the development of industrial zones along major rivers, such as Sumidagawa, Arakawa, Furukawa, and Megurogawa, as well as in coastal districts. The centrifugal impetus was so strong that industrial districts within the urban area of Tōkyō were gradually converted into residential sections for workers, large factories finding sites rather in suburban areas farther from the center of the city.

The hill sections west and southwest of the central area became, no longer privileged zones for ranking warriors, but densely populated residential communities of ordinary salaried workers whose economic orientation was in the organs of business, government, and education in the central part of the city. When the hill sections became saturated, new residential districts had to be developed farther out in suburban and satellite towns. Thus, the ecological structure of Tōkyō was made to conform to the social, economic, and technical requirements of a capitalist society.

In order to gain some perspective on the ecological changes that occurred during the period under review (1897–1920), it is helpful first to observe the relative population density in the various wards of the city in 1897, given in descending order:

| *Order* | *Ward* | *Population density:* (*persons per sq. ri*). | (*per sq. mi.*) |
|---|---|---|---|
| 1 | Nihonbashi | 918,751 | (153,127) |
| 2 | Kanda | 693,320 | (115,553) |
| 3 | Kyōbashi | 675,627 | (112,604) |
| 4 | Shiba | 579,110 | ( 98,185) |
| 5 | Asakusa | 452,699 | ( 75,450) |
| 6 | Shitaya | 356,716 | ( 59,786) |
| 7 | Honjo | 341,663 | ( 56,944) |
| 8 | Yotsuya | 333,924 | ( 55,654) |
| 9 | Fukagawa | 273,349 | ( 45,558) |
| 10 | Hongō | 262,108 | ( 43,685) |
| 11 | Akasaka | 166,487 | ( 27,748) |
| 12 | Ushigome | 160,659 | ( 26,743) |
| 13 | Kōji-machi | 140,634 | ( 23,439) |
| 14 | Koishikawa | 136,083 | ( 22,680) |
| 15 | Azabu | 108,093 | ( 18,015) |

Population density was much higher in the central wards. The rates of population increase between 1897 and 1920, however, varied considerably. In general, the rate of increase was quite low in the central portion of the city, as compared to the very high rates of increase in the residential and industrial zones surrounding the city, as is evident from the following:

| *Order* | *Ward* | *Rate of population increase* (%) (1897–1920)[71] |
|---|---|---|
| 1 | Koishikawa | 219 |
| 2 | Ushigome | 158 |
| 3 | Yotsuya | 107 |
| 4 | Asakusa | 99 |
| 5 | Honjo | 97 |
| 6 | Shitaya | 94 |
| 7 | Fukagawa | 92 |
| 8 | Hongō | 79 |
| 9 | Azabu | 75 |
| 10 | Shiba | 67 |
| 11 | Akasaka | 58 |
| 12 | Kanda | 24 |
| 13 | Kyōbashi | 21 |
| 14 | Nihonbashi | 11 |
| 15 | Kōji-machi | −16 |

Koishikawa experienced the highest rate of increase; even so, its population density in 1920 of 433,403 persons per square *ri* (72,234 per sq. mi.) was the lowest of all fifteen wards in that year. This means that the city wards of Tōkyō had almost reached the saturation point, excluding Akasaka where large tracts of land were reserved for official use. All other wards had population densities above 440,000 persons per square *ri* (73,333 per sq. mi.) in 1920. Population density had leveled off at a high level in all wards, drawing near the saturation line in all sections.

The residential sections reserved for warriors in the low lying hills immediately west of the imperial palace grounds gave way only very slowly to the city's demands for more space for expansion of its integrative organs and for housing the people employed in these organs. Family lands inherited by succession rights continued to constitute a sizable proportion of the hills section (*Yama-no-te*). Even so, foreign embassies and legations moved into locations in the Banchō and Azabu districts, as did industries into the Shiba lowlands. The areas were mixed in community composition, however, with many residences of ex-warriors' families remaining.

Government officials, military officers, company employees and independent merchants found places for new residences in some of the old warriors' sections, such as Yotsuya, Akasaka, Azabu, Ushigome, Koishikawa, and Hongō. The increased demands for goods consumed in daily living prompted development of retail shops along streets in these areas, such as Kagurazaka, Yotsuya-dōri, and Aoyama-dōri. On the whole, though, these old sections remained essentially the same, with few significant changes.

Official residences of members and relatives of the Imperial Household were the least amenable to change. Such residences as those of Fushimi-no-miya, Kan'in-no-miya, Yamashina-no-miya, and Arisugawa-no-miya remained in the Kōji-machi district. In Shiba there was the palace of the Crown Prince on the former grounds of the Hosokawa domain, and the Asaka-no-miya, Kitashirakawa-no-miya, Takeda-no-miya, and Kachō-no-miya mansions. In Azabu lived Higashikuni-no-miya and the Korean Prince of the Li Dynasty. In Akasaka there were the Akasaka Detached Palace and the residence of Higashifushimi-no-miya. In the vicinities of the residential quarters of members of the Imperial Household there were still found many grand residences of families of warrior pedigree who retained various privileges in society, as well as new homes of top-ranking government officials, military officers, and business executives.[72]

Hongō had been the locus of institutes of advanced learning in the Edo era, with such agencies as the shogunate's school for Confucian studies (*Shōheikō*) and the institute for the study of foreign literature (*Bansho-shirabesho*). The academic atmosphere of the district was strengthened when these scholastic agencies were combined to found Tōkyō Imperial University in the Meiji period. Houses for salaried employees appeared in the district where warriors residences once stood; but otherwise the Hongō district manifested little significant change.

The mansions built by the nobility and wealthy in the Meiji era were usually quite elaborate, but not always done in Western styles. The Asano mansion built in 1898 and called "Mansion of the Purple Cloud" (*Shiunkaku*) was an example of the finest techniques of refined Japanese architecture, with gold-lacquered interior decorations in its best rooms. Its structural lines followed the style of mansions of high-ranking court nobility of the Middle Ages (*gotenzukuri*).

Other residences of the nobility often appropriated European architectural designs, such as that of Count Watanabe, Minister of the Imperial Household. Construction of this mansion commenced in 1905 in Shiba Takanawa-minami-chō, blending the external lines of English country homes with interior designs reminiscent of the era of Louis XIV in France. All exposed wood surfaces inside were exquisitely carved, and windows were fitted with stained glass.

In stark contrast to the demonstratively elaborate homes of the wealthy, the dwellings of commoners were built in the old style of the Edo period, although windows were often provided with imported plate glass. Even in the Shiba, Azabu, and Akasaka districts one could see many humble tenement houses of unadorned wood construction. Shops serving the common people's neighborhoods often were finished in the fire-preventive mudwalled style called *dozō*, with overall floor spaces of only 5–6 *tsubo* (19.7–23.7 sq. yds.).[73]

While the development of Japanese capitalism enabled a few to attain great wealth, there were many poor people with incomes of 50 yen–60 yen, representing the earnings of all members of a family unit. The poor were called *saimin*, meaning "people of slender, i.e., scanty means." They were mostly laborers, unskilled workers, rickshaw and cart handlers, and their communities could be found in every section of the city.

An investigation into their situation made by the Bureau of Social

Affairs of Tōkyō Municipal Office in 1920 reveals that there were some 74,493 persons belonging to the *saimin* class, grouped in 18,351 families. These indigents were distributed in the following seven wards as follows:

| *Ward* | *Number of saimin* | *Number of families* |
|---|---|---|
| Fukagawa | 19,303 | 4,818 |
| Honjo | 11,704 | 2,681 |
| Asakusa | 9,849 | 2,443 |
| Koishikawa | 7,719 | 1,871 |
| Kyōbashi | 4,255 | 1,150 |
| Yotsuya | 4,181 | 1,004 |
| Ushigome | 2,858 | 749 |

Of all the indigent communities, the following were the most notorious:

Kanda-misaki-chō
Shiba-shin'ami-chō
Shinjuku-asahi-buraku
Asakusa-tamahime-chō
Kyōbashi-hatchōbori
Yotsuya-samegahashi
Fukagawa-tomioka-chō
Tanaka-chō

Their dwellings were shanties joined together, for which rents were usually about 2.8 yen per month. One family occupied a single room of four and a half *tatami* mats (9×9 ft.); and a single toilet facility served fifteen or twenty family units. The Bureau of Social Affairs' report lists 41% of the *saimin* as born in Tōkyō; many came from Chiba, Saitama, and other prefectures close to Tōkyō. Most of them had been pressed into poverty by company failures, loss of jobs, or simple inability to make ends meet as prices climbed far out of reach of the low wages common among laborers, especially unskilled ones. The report indicates, further, that few of the *saimin* class were poverty-stricken because of personal or moral reasons, such as alcoholism or sheer laziness. The overriding cause of poverty among them was one or more defects in the social system.

In addition to settled communities of the poor, there was also a fluid substratum of roving poor people, lodging in flophouses (11,140 persons), living on river and harbor crafts (10,712 persons), and an indeterminate number of vagabonds.[74]

Both arable and waste lands decreased as the population of Tōkyō expanded. The following list shows the changes in various types of non-residential areas over the second decade of the 20th century, the basic measure given in *tan* (1 *tan*=0.245 acre):

| *Year* | *Paddy-fields* | *Meadows* | *Woodlands* | *Wastelands* | *Ponds & Swamps* | *Other* |
|---|---|---|---|---|---|---|
| 1912 | 937 | 13,582 | 18,577 | 178 | 372 | 5 |
| 1920 | 199 | 3,496 | 225 | 42 | 430 | — |

Even in 1920 when population density had reached the saturation point, there was still a considerable amount of arable land in cultivation. Distribution of cultivated lands according to wards was as follows:

| *Ward* | *Paddy-fields* | *Meadows* | *Woodlands*[75] |
|---|---|---|---|
| Fukagawa | 110 *tan* | —— | —— |
| Honjo | 55 *tan* | 52 *tan* | —— |
| Koishikawa | 21 *tan* | 120 *tan* | 34 *tan* |
| Hongō | 3 *tan* | 59 *tan* | —— |
| Shiba | —— | 58 *tan* | 54 *tan* |
| Azabu | —— | —— | 55 *tan* |

(1 *tan*=0.245 acre)

In Shiba, Akasaka, and Azabu there lived 37 families of farmers, with an average of eight members per unit in 1901. They cultivated 72 *chō* (176.4 acres) of arable land, independently owned or sharecropped. Farming in these areas was suspended around 1917 due to increased population in these wards.

World War I days saw a tremendous increase in the flow of population into Tōkyō, creating a critical housing shortage which reached an all-time low around 1919–20. Illegal activity became so rampant among real estate agents that the Bureau of Social Affairs of the municipal government set up a special office for directing home-seekers to houses and rooms for rent, a function assumed by each ward office later.[76]

The most characteristic feature of residential development from the turn of the century to the 1920's, however, was the expansion of residential sections in suburban areas to the west, where land prices ran increasingly high as demands intensified. The westward movement was made possible, of course, by the installation of rail services, especially low-cost electric lines, beyond the population-saturated urban zones of Tōkyō.

While the street system in the urban zones had been improved by rezoning of administrative divisions and construction improvements, the areas opened up for new residential sections developed without definite planning for streets and roads.

The movement of residential areas away from the center of the city to suburban areas is reflected in the following figures on relative population increases in the urban and suburban sectors:

| *Year* | *Urban population* | *Suburban population* |
|---|---|---|
| 1901 | 1,630,894 | 387,233 |
| 1920 | 2,173,201 | 1,184,985 |
| *Rate of increase* | 94% | 183% |

The suburban sector was later consolidated within metropolitan Tōkyō.

The extension of government and private rail services and the movement into suburban areas were accelerated to a high pitch following the disastrous earthquake of 1923 when it became painfully clear how dreadful the super-saturation of residential zones could be. Even before that holocaust, though, the expansion of rail facilities to new residential areas was remarkable. The Chūō Line running due west to the suburbs was accomplished first, followed by the Yamate Line which crossed it at Shinjuku running a north-south course that encircled the outer edges of the established urban area. These two lines were completed according to the time schedule below:

| | |
|---|---|
| *Chūō Line:* | 1889—Shinjuku-Tachikawa section completed |
| | 1911—Shinjuku-Iidamachi section; same year that Chūō Line was extended overland to Nagoya |
| | 1912—Iidamachi-Manseibashi (present Iidabashi-Akihabara) electric train service installed |
| | 1919—Electric train service extended from Tōkyō Station to Kichijōji on this line |
| *Yamate Line:* | 1905—Great arc from Akabane north of Ueno to Shinagawa completed, passing through Ikebukuro, Shinjuku, and Shibuya: length =21 km. (13 mi.) |
| | 1903—East-west section from Tabata, between Ueno and Akabane, to Ikebukuro completed |
| | 1919—Tōkyō-Manseibashi (present Akihabara) section completed |

Private railway companies began construction of auxiliary lines soon after completion of the above government lines, beginning at some station on the Yamate Line and running radially outward to residential and industrial zones. In chronological order they were:

| *Year* | *Line* |
|---|---|
| 1901 | Section from Kita-Shinagawa to industrial zone in Minamibanba to the south on the coast |
| 1913 | Shinjuku-Chōfu (present Keiō Line) |
| 1913 | Shibuya-Tamagawa (present Tōkyū Tamagawa Line) |
| 1914 | Ikebukuro-Kawagoe (present Tōbu Line) |
| 1915 | Ikubukuro-Hannō (present Seibu Line) |
| 1917 | Shinjuku-Kita-tamagawa (present Odakyū Line) |

The number of passengers boarding and leaving electric trains at stations on the Yamate Line are compared for the years 1907 and 1917 in the list below, according to the numbers served:[77]

| *Station* | *Passenger traffic (1907)* | *Order* | *Station* | *Passenger traffic (1917)* |
|---|---|---|---|---|
| Ueno | 2,685,411 | 1 | Ueno | 4,757,834 |
| Shinjuku | 1,271,392 | 2 | Shinjuku | 2,592,365 |
| Shinagawa | 656,692 | 3 | Shinagawa | 2,778,838 |
| Nippori | 269,722 | 4 | Nippori | 1,213,409 |
| Tabata | 235,208 | 5 | Shibuya | 1,204,874 |
| Meguro | 181,707 | 6 | Ōtsuka | 1,145,071 |
| Shibuya | 171,602 | 7 | Mejiro | 852,411 |
| Mejiro | 135,683 | 8 | Ōsaki | 842,469 |

| | | | | |
|---|---|---|---|---|
| Sugamo | 119,565 | 9 | Gotanda | 830,058 |
| Ōsaki | 73,915 | 10 | Ikebukuro | 814,268 |
| Ōtsuka | 58,332 | 11 | Ebisu | 766,571 |
| Ikebukuro | 49,050 | 12 | Meguro | 724,198 |

A prosperous town even in Edo days, Ueno district developed into the major sub-central area of Tōkyō, as it was the terminal point for all traffic coming in from the northeast regions. If a sub-central district is understood in terms of the dispersion of functions of the central integrative organs, though, or even as the second major center of consumptive activity, Shinjuku is more appropriately defined as the major sub-central district of Tōkyō. Ueno's place had primary reference to Tōkyō's role as the national capital; Shinjuku's importance was oriented to the metropolitan community, as the mid-point between urban and suburban sectors.

Shinjuku was, as we have seen, the principal junction of the Chūō and Yamate transit lines, with streetcars added, and terminal of the radial lines to Chōfu and Kita-tamagawa. People moved quickly from the crowded urban areas into this district, causing a sharp increase in population in the decade between 1907 and 1919. Data for its integral communities are given below:

| *Townships* | *Population in 1920* | *Rate of increase(%) (over 1907)* | *Percentage of farmers*[78] |
|---|---|---|---|
| Yodobashi-chō | 38,876 | 100 | 3.7 |
| Ōkubo | 22,596 | 400 | 3.9 |
| Naito-shinjuku | 16,952 | 40 | 2.9 |
| Totsuka-chō | 16,340 | 600 | 9.6 |
| Ochiai-mura | 7,736 | 200 | 20.3 |

The extremely low farmer percentages indicate the high degree of movement of urban population, especially in Yodobashi, Ōkubo, and Naito-shinjuku. Many were employed in small industries and shops. Naito-shinjuku continued to thrive as an area of brothels, as it had in the Edo era and even in the Meiji period when the signs were changed to "rooms for rent." In 1915 there were 288 brothels in its red-light district.[79] There were also twenty-two brokers operating in Naito-shinjuku, indicating that its stage of economic development was only semi-capitalistic. Shinjuku did not develop as the main commercial center of the urban residential sections in the hills west of the palace at this stage; the Yotsuya-ōyoko-cho and Kagurazaka districts, closer in, continued to perform this function until after the Great Earthquake in 1923.

In general, the absolute population of a city increases as one moves in concentric circles away from the center of the city, but the population density of specific sections increases as one approaches the center of the city. This held true between 1907 and 1919 when the central area of Tōkyō had a much higher population density than areas in the larger urban sector or the suburban areas where population density was lowest. We had occasion in the last chapter to remark that the urban area of Tōkyō in 1915 was circumscribed roughly by a circle drawn on a four-kilometer radius from Tōkyō Station. Townships along that circle in the western part of Tōkyō that registered population densities of over 40 persons per 1,000 *tsubo* (1.154 sq. mi.) with their density figures, are listed below:

| *Townships beyond 4 km. radius* | *No. of residents per 1,000 tsubo* |
|---|---|
| Nippori-machi | 114 |
| Shibuya | 103 |
| Naito-shinjuku | 101 |
| Shinagawa | 81 |
| Sugamo | 80 |
| Yodobashi | 78 |
| Ōsaki | 63 |
| Takinogawa | 55 |
| Takata | 55 |
| Ōkubo | 54 |
| Sendagaya | 54 |
| Totsuka | 53 |
| Yoyohata | 43 |

Townships beyond a similarly drawn circle with an eight-kilometer radius with more than 40 persons per 1,000 *tsubo* included:

| *Townships beyond 8 km. radius* | *No. of residents per 1,000 tsubo* |
|---|---|
| Ōji | 88 |
| Itabashi | 76 |
| Ōi | 72 |
| Setagaya | 55 |
| Iwabuchi | 46 |
| Meguro | 43 |
| Nakano | 40 |

There were no townships with over 40 persons per 1,000 *tsubo* twelve kilometers or more distant from the center point.

Industries and residential quarters accounted for most of the population increase in these areas. Government jobs, whether national, prefectural, or municipal, or even military, along with the manifold positions in private enterprises made up the white-collar class; in addition there were numerous factory workers and maids in the newer areas. Not a few of the laborers and maids came from the farms to escape near poverty and poor tenancy conditions.

Cleared lands suitable for housing lots experienced a sharp price rise as property demands intensified. In 1915 open fields in the suburban areas brought 20–30 yen per *tsubo* when sold, as against only 0.3 yen per *tsubo* realized annually in agricultural products, or a similar amount (0.3 yen–0.5 yen) if rented for cultivation by someone else. Farmers became excited by the prospects of selling their fields, thinking only of the immediate gains in sales transactions rather than the long-term security of agricultural production. Lands were sold to the highest bidders, rapidly transferring ownership of considerable properties to city dwellers. Without skills to enter industry, though, many of the farmers wound up as low wage earners in gardening, well-digging, or as day laborers.[80]

The population stratum in the western residential sector was composed almost entirely of salaried workers. The residential sections themselves were prevented from haphazard development by the fact that wealthier families had moved into these areas first and had seen, therefore, to basic community requirements such as land divisions, roads, drainage and sewage systems, water supply, and certain construction standards. Open areas providing fresh air and pleasant scenery had been one of the motivations for the selection of the areas by the wealthy residents, and these conditions were preserved to some extent in the new communities, filling in the spaces between homes of nobles and rich people in the following areas: Kita-shinagawa, Goten-yama, Hiraoka in Ōsaki, Sodegasaki, Shibuya-daikanyama, Shōtō-chō, Meguro-mura, Sendagaya, and Ochiai-mura.

Agricultural zones were forced to retreat by the advance of new residential communities. On the other hand, the increased population demanded a greater food supply from the farm villages in the more distant suburban areas. The common means of transport for agricultural products were man-drawn carts, and the maximum one-way distance allowing a return trip in a single day was about twenty kilometers (12.4 mi.). The following counties were within a 20-km. radius of central Tokyo: Ebara, Kita-tama, Toyotama, Kita-toshima, Minami-adachi, Kita-adachi, Higashi-katsushika, and Minami-katsushika.

Farmers within the 20-km. radius converted from cultivation of grain, grass, and soy for their own use to cultivation of green vegetables for commercial purposes. They devised methods of intensive farming to take advantage of seasons when the market prices were highest. The volume of gardening for supplying urban consumers increased notably; and some dairy farming was introduced.

Expansion of the city of Tōkyō not only absorbed farm areas, converting them into residential communities, then, but also absorbed farm villages as such, for their continued functions in agriculture. The farm communities were integrated into the organic whole of the metropolitan community as indispensable components of the total structure.

Social change was not limited to increased mobility, resettlement of urban communities, or even changes in social strata. There were significant developments in the socio-economic structures of the neighborhood communities and townships themselves.

The five-member household unit, *goningumi*, oriented to national administration ultimately, was abolished after the Meiji Restoration. But local administrative and social forms often remained intact. The traditional system of town elders, *machi-sōdai*, continued to function, as did landowners' associations (*jinushikai*), town managers (*sewanin*), justices of the peace (*toshiban*), young men's groups (*wakashū-kai*), and the local religious associations (*ujiko-shūdan*). These many patterns of town life carried over from the Edo era, or before.

A noteworthy movement in Tōkyō was the formation of self-government councils in the towns, called *chōnaikai*, meaning literally "association formed within the town." The councils were made up of men selected by local residents to work for the general welfare of the town and its citizens, and membership dues were paid. The *chōnaikai* gradually replaced the older forms of town management.

Government officials, military officers, and salarymen had little interest in community affairs in their residential areas. Home and office were completely separated, but their interests centered in their jobs in the downtown areas. Moreover, they tended to relocate more often and not sink deep roots in the community affairs. Laboring under demands for unswerving loyalty to employers, they had little time or reason to make contacts with neighbors, whose socio-economic conditions varied so much from their own anyway. Even the custom of erecting high walls around residences aided their tendency toward independence from community life.

Average family units in residential communities, especially those who earned their livings locally, had more time and made more effort to foster neighborhood contacts. Such people included landowners, merchants, and craftsmen, and laborers in small industries whose work brought them naturally into contacts with others living in the same area. Besides working relationships there were many other opportunities for social contacts, such as membership in a local army reserve unit, parent-teacher associations, groups of religious parishioners, use of public baths and communal wells or water faucets, not to mention casual strolls in the cool air of summer evenings, or simply game-playing in the neighbor streets. The *chōnaikai* emerged from the interlocking web of such relationships and fed on their nurture. Not a few feudal values were operative in the total system of these contacts.

The *chōnaikai* organized various meetings among residents that were mainly social gatherings, with objectives limited, for the most part, to needs and interests of the local communities. The town councils were responsible, for example, for organizing local shrines' festivals, night watches, public lighting, hygiene programs to deal with noise, dirt, and garbage disposal, as well as collecting and disposing of sewage. There were periodic functions like arranging for a hearty send-off for local men joining the army, or warm welcome parties for returning veterans. Seasonal preparations had to be arranged also in the June and December times of gifting-giving (*Chūgen* and *Seibo* respectively), which involved decorations for the towns' streets.

In the first two decades of the 20th century, the number of town councils in Tōkyō increased twelvefold: from 52 in 1902, to 624 in 1922. The increase was connected with the expansion of the city and of the residential areas, of course; but the immediate impetus for an increase in the number of town councils usually stemmed from local demands for voiding or revising some ordinance of the municipal, prefectural, or national governments, from some critical sanitation problem, or from the recruiting programs incumbent upon townships following the outbreak of war.

The town councils cannot be said to have emerged solely as spontaneous responses to local citizens' needs. They served also as the smallest units of municipal administration; the ward offices and police stations made full use of them at times for transmitting information and instructions to the neighborhood residents.

c. INDUSTRIAL ZONES. The central part of Tōkyō was given over to administrative organs and business firms, and the western hills to residential areas; large factories were not permitted in either of these sectors. Consequently, industries tended to develop in the lowlands east of the city's center where rivers and ports, in addition to flat lands suitable for factories, were available.

Industry had been promoted by the government from the very beginning, but large-scale expansion appeared, as we have seen, with the outbreak of World War I. Tōkyō was, to be sure, the major center of consumption in the nation, with supply routes developed to connect it with every region of the country, Chūbu, Kansai, Tōhoku, Hokkaidō, and so on. But the same transportation routes were equally suitable for transporting raw materials to factories, and for facilitating the flow of fresh labor supplies into the great city. With the nation's largest capital concentration near at hand, the conditions were quite ripe for industrial expansion in the city. In a twenty-year period from the turn of the century to 1919, the number of factories in Tōkyō increased twenty-one times, and the number of workers in factories expanded six times. The only places for these factories to go were in the suburban areas. Shoreline and river areas such as Arakawa were reclaimed and converted into industrial zones. Specific data on factory and laborer increases follows:

| *Year* | *Number of factories* | *Number of laborers* |
|---|---|---|
| 1897 | 333 | 30,022 |
| 1907 | 768 | 55,944 |
| 1919 | 7,233 | 188,786 |

Distribution of factories run by private enterprise and employees of these factories for the year 1919, according to city wards, was as follows:[81]

| *Ward or County (gun)* | *Order* | *No. of factories* | *Order* | *No. of employees* |
|---|---|---|---|---|
| Honjo | 1 | 1,113 | 2 | 27,892 |
| Fukagawa | 2 | 822 | 5 | 17,427 |
| Kyōbashi | 3 | 621 | 3 | 24,948 |
| Asakusa | 4 | 546 | 8 | 5,585 |
| Kita-toshima-gun | 5 | 483 | 4 | 21,142 |
| Minami-katsushika-gun | 6 | 438 | 1 | 32,699 |
| Shiba | 7 | 427 | 7 | 11,645 |

| | | | | |
|---|---|---|---|---|
| Shitaya | 8 | 414 | 11 | 4,122 |
| Kanda | 9 | 389 | 10 | 4,347 |
| Hongō | 10 | 347 | — | — |
| Koishikawa | 11 | 223 | 9 | 4,958 |
| Nihonbashi | 12 | 209 | — | — |
| Ebara-gun | — | — | 6 | 16,587 |

In this stage of industrial development in Tōkyō there were yet many factories in the lowland areas of urban Tōkyō, such as Honjo, Fukagawa, and Kyōbashi, where industry had been developed in the Edo era. But it is quite clear from the above data that there were many large factories in the suburban areas, as the number of workers is much larger for the suburban areas than for the urban districts. Asakusa and Fukagawa particularly were full of small factories, while in Ebara-gun and Minami-katsushika-gun there were located many large factories equipped with modern facilities.

Many of the small factories continued operating in the urban area even after development of large-scale production, taking advantage of locations near wholesalers, large retail stores, or larger factories for which they did subcontracted work, as they did not need special buildings or broad land areas. Larger factories, however, had little need of locating near markets, but did require more extensive land areas for specially constructed buildings, fuel and water tanks, and storing of raw materials. Consequently, they sought large tracts of land in the suburban districts where land costs were lower, and land or water transportation was available.

Home industries whose products could be produced more efficiently and cheaply by mass production methods dwindled in the modern period; some of their products were not adaptable to mass production techniques, however, and these forms of home industry persisted. Examples of some of them include: sewing Japanese-style apparel, hand-knit goods, embroidering, and special methods of spot-dyeing. Many side jobs were available also for folding printed material at printing shops and bookbinders' shops in Kanda and Koishikawa. Brushes were a special, exclusive home industry of Hongō.

Most of the home industries were concentrated in the Honjo, Fukagawa, and Asakusa districts, producing articles indicated in the list below:[82]

| *Products* | *Section or town* |
|---|---|
| Finishing sandal bottoms | Imado and Hashiba of Asakusa; Mikawashima, Ogu, Nippori, Honjo, and Fukagawa |
| Straps for sandals and clogs | Northern Asakusa |
| Straw mat covers (*nanbu omote*) | Asakusa-kameoka-chō |
| Artificial flowers, pasted cloth pictures (*oshie*), and toys | Asakusa and Honjo |
| Knit-work | Honjo |

| | |
|---|---|
| Assembling metal and celluloid toys | Nippori, Ogu, Mikawashima, Terajima, and Ōshima |
| Cloth and paper toys | Honjo, Fukagawa, and Asakusa |

Production methods of home industries were simple, needing no complicated machinery or power motors. Most of them filled subcontract orders for wholesalers or large stores, with various channels for distribution. In the majority of cases they were supplied with raw materials or semi-finished products for finishing by their wholesaler or retailer patrons, often on a consignment basis.

When the threat of replacement by large industries appeared, it was not simply because of greater efficiency in production techniques; ex-farmers were job-hungry, and wages ran lower in the large factories than in established home industries. The latter were forced to lower wages in order to survive by cutting production costs.[83] Thus, minor industries continue operating in the urban area of Tōkyō.

One of the first areas in which large industries began developing on the outskirts of the city was on the edge of the Honjo-Fukagawa section, called Kōtō, or "East River" section, as it was east of the Sumidagawa river. The Kōtō district already had the largest concentration of factories in Tōkyō, spread out over a sprawling tract of land, reclaimed from the sea in the middle of the 17th century under the Tokugawa shogunate, that was only three meters (about 10 ft.) above sea level. In Edo times the warehouses of the shogunate and villas of warriors were located here, along with the shops of agents dealing in rice, fertilizers, and lumber. Late in the Tokugawa era, there appeared a few cottage industries in the district manufacturing cast metal and porcelain wares.

Following the Meiji Restoration the Kōtō district was renewed as an industrial zone. In 1875 the Ministry of Industry built a cement plant in the area that was sold later to Asano Sōichiro, who renamed it for himself . There were built also the following factories: Kameido Mill of Ōji Paper Company, Tōkyō Chemical Fertilizer Company, and Nihon Sugar Refinery. Toward the end of the Meiji era (ended 1912) other large modern factories were constructed, such as: Tōkyō Spinning Company, Fuji Gas Spinning Company, Nisshin Spinning Company, and Tōkyō Railway Car and Locomotive Company. Power saws and other lumbering equipment were imported and installed from 1887 onward, replacing the manual operations of this industry in the Kōtō district.

The introduction of modernized industry into the Kōtō community aggravated certain social problems already in existence there. The Honjo and Fukagawa sections had slum districts even in the Edo era, catching the dispossessed folk pushed aside by expansion in that earlier period. The operators of wholesale houses and lumber yards generally provided simple meals and other minimum necessities to the slum dwellers, an old custom of mutual aid that enabled the poor to keep body and soul together, while assuring labor bosses of loyal workers when needed.

When the modern factories moved in, the master-subordinate and boss-slum dweller relationships were replaced by the more clear-cut employer-employee relationships of capitalist production. Factory executives, of course, were interested in low wages and low-cost transportation provided by nearby rivers and seaways. But loss of the mutual aid system threw the slum folk into great jeopardy.

Realizing that something had to be done, the factory owners made funds available for medical services, orphan care, and aid societies, around 1897 beginning with Fuji Gas Spinning Company and Tōyō Muslin Company. The services were extended, however, to people connected with their own companies, and not to the slum communities in general. The effort was a function internal to the smooth operation of industry.

Though business flourished after the Sino-Japanese and Russo-Japanese Wars, the number of destitute people in the Kōtō section increased sharply. The need for relief and social service agencies was recognized among wider segments of the citizenry. The municipal government set up relief facilities, and religious agencies established facilities for free lodging and meals, as well as an employment service.[84]

The housing accommodations of workers in the factories close by were not greatly removed from the slum conditions. They were usually company-built and owned tenement structures under surveillance of hired company supervisors, and had only poor lighting and ventilation. Two-storied dormitories within the factory compounds with only large rooms for many workers were common at first, though conditions were gradually improved to allow smaller rooms for fewer occupants.

In any event, the Kōtō district became full of workshops, factories, housing and slums. Further development was forced to move centrifugally to points farther out. Gradually there were built many factories of various sizes, small, medium and large, in a zone along the Arakawa Canal to the east outside the Honjo-Fukagawa area that included Senju, Sumida, Terajima, Azuma, Kameido, Ōshima, and Suna-machi of Minami-katsushika-gun (county). Among the many newly-developed factories were included modern plants such as the spinning mills of Tōkyō Dai-ichi and Kanegafuchi Spinning Companies, machine shops of Hitachi Works and Nihon Electric Bulb Company, and the Sumidagawa Iron Foundry. Population density in the industrial zone of Minami-katsushika county rose as high as that of the congested urban areas of Tōkyō, or of other densely populated sections like Honjo-Fukagawa and Kita-toshima county. The Minami-katsushika industrial belt emerged as one of the major centers of the spinning industry, with block after block of laborers' homes strung out among the factories.

Extensive residential areas had not developed during the Meiji period in the southern part of Kita-toshima county, that is in the Takinogawa, Arakawa, and Ōji areas on the Tōkyō side (southwest) of the Sumidagawa river that ran a northwest-southeast course just north of the urban area. In these lowlands between Akabane and Senju truck gardening had been promoted to supply the expanding needs of Tōkyō with such items as spring radishes from Mikawashima, summer radishes from Takinogawa, and long onions from Minami-senju. But commercial gardening areas in this district were converted into an industrial zone in the Taishō period.

The Ōji Paper Mill was built in the township with that name, the first paper mill in Japan, along with Dainihon Chemical Fertilizer Company, both large modern industrial plants. The government built several factories in this zone in 1919, which are listed below with data on the number of workers employed in each:

| *Factory* | *Number of workers* |
|---|---|
| Firearms Production Plant | 4,200 |
| Printing Bureau | 3,800 |
| Senju Spinning Mill | 1,200 |
| Powder Plant (explosives) | 1,500 |

These factories were all equipped with the latest production machinery.

Typical of the many other factories constructed in this area were the Tsunekawa Knitting Mill, Toyotama Paper Mill, and Tōyō Rag-processing Company.[85] Even more typical, however, was the process of converting farmlands in this area, and swamplands in the Minami-katsushika area, into an industrial belt along the northeastern edge of urban Tōkyō, just beyond the limits of land availability in the circle already urbanized.

Industrial expansion in the southern part of Tōkyō began with developments on reclaimed lands at the head of Tōkyō harbor in the central Kyōbashi district, and spread from there southward to the shores of the Shiba area, especially the district known as Shibaura by the harbor. Up to this point, industrial expansion was still within the limits of the urban area described by the imaginary 4-km. radius. But it was mostly heavy and machine industries that were being constructed along the southern harbor line, and space demands forced the expansion beyond the urban area into the coastal districts of Shinagawa and Ōi-machi. (This southern industrial belt-line can be visualized by thinking of the bayside edges of the present-day wards Chūō, Minato, and Shinagawa; although the Shinagawa portion was then Ebara-gun.) Later, the elongated industrial zone was extended into the Kawasaki city industrial area, linking up beyond that with the industrial zone of Yokohama, forming the extended Keihin (Tōkyō-Yokohama) Industrial Belt, approximately forty kilometers (25 mi.) long.

The starting point of industrial expansion southward was Tsukishima, a large island formed originally by silt and sand deposits of the Sumidagawa river just outside its mouth. Originally it was called Tsukuda-jima by fishermen settling there from Tsukuda-jima of Settsu. The northern part of the island was called Ishikawa-jima as it had been granted as a fiefdom to Ishikawa Shigemasa, captain of the shogunate fleet. The upper reaches of Ishikawa-jima, referred to simply as sections No. 1 and No. 2 (Ichigō-chi and Nigō-chi respectively), were filled in by reclamation crews about 1892–3.

Established by the Tokugawa shogunate in 1856, the Ishikawa-jima Shipyard was transferred to the Ministry of the Navy in 1872. In 1876 it was sold to Hirano Tomizo, who proceeded to develop it into a diversified heavy industry. It was the first shipbuilding yard operated by a civilian businessman, and remarkable expansion took place during the Sino-Japanese and Russo-Japanese Wars.

Production was not limited to ships alone; the many factories constructed on the Ishikawa-jima grounds produced locomotives and railway cars, machines, and steel frames for bridges. Kawasaki Shipyard was built in nearby Tsukiji soon after, heralding the growth of a whole complex of factories in this district that would produce many kinds of machines and metal products. The concentration of whole "families" of machine and metal factories in this district was its outstanding feature.[86]

To the south of the Kyōbashi area there were constructed many large-scale factories along the bayside of the Shiba district, that is, Shibaura, each with more than a hundred, or even several hundreds of workers, by 1901. Some of the earliest to build in this district were Shibaura Manufacturing Company, Oaki Shipyard, Nihon Electric Company, and Murai Brothers & Company. The rapid increase in the numbers of factories and workers in the Shibaura zone can be seen in the following figures:

| *Year* | *Number of factories* | *Number of workers* |
|---|---|---|
| 1904* | 70 | 405 |
| 1912 | 110 | 6,475 |
| 1919 | 427 | 11,645 |

(*before outbreak of the Russo-Japanese War)

In conjunction with formation of the Shibaura industrial zone, the riparian works begun at the mouth of the Sumidagawa river were extended south to include large tracts of reclaimed land for development of related groups of factories. Reclaimed areas were sold to factory owners at low prices as part of the industry promotion policy of the government, expediting rapid and substantial industrial construction in the Shibaura district.

During World War I a secondary industrial zone was developed along the Furukawa river running west from Shibaura toward Azabu. Small-sized factories in this secondary zone produced machines and tools under subcontracts of the larger industries, enabling the latter to keep production costs low while retaining some flexibility in management. That is, the large factories were able to expand or cut production rather quickly without immediate effects on their own production system.[87]

Industrial districts developed south of Shibaura in Shinagawa and Ōi-machi were beyond the limits of Tōkyō harbor proper, that is, openly exposed to Tōkyō Bay. They were also just outside the urban area of the capital, and possessed of a number of particularly advantageous aspects. The new train lines brought the Shinagawa-Ōi district into easy access of Yokohama's ports for receiving bulky cargoes of raw materials, or for shipping goods out to Tōkyō, other regions of the country, or overseas. Reclamation projects made large, level tracts of land available at low costs.

All the necessary factors for industrial expansion were met in this coastal area; but it was aggressively developed for the first time only during World War I.

In 1915 the government's Ministry of Railroads built a large workshop at Ōi on land reclaimed from the sea. By 1917 there were quite a number of factories with over one hundred employees each in various townships of the larger zone, such as:

| *Township* | *Company factories*[88] |
|---|---|
| Shinagawa | Sankyō Pharmaceutical Company, Morinaga Candy Company, Meiji Rubber Company, Nihon Paint Company, and Uchida Pharmaceutical Company |
| Ōsaki | Meidensha (elec.), Hoshi Pharmaceutical Company, and Fujikura Industrial Corporation |
| Ōi | Shinkō Wool Spinning Company and Nihon Optical Instrument Company |
| Ōmori | Tōkyō Gas Company and Nihon Special Steel Company |
| Kamata | Tōkyō Instrument Company and Niigata Steel Works. |
| Rokugō | Sanseido Cosmetics Company and Miyata Bicycle Company |

As large factories were constructed in the area, the towns and villages in the neighboring places were converted into residential zones for industrial workers. This added even greater pressure to the demand for additional space, pushing the industrial zones inevitably toward Kawasaki and Yokohama, to form the extended Keihin Industrial Belt.

d. Satellite Cities in the Encircling Area. The dynamic process by which a city expands into a metropolis begins with the centripetal concentration of capital resources and integrative organs inward toward the city's inner core. The enlarged functions and structures of the integrative organs absorb ever larger staffs who, with their families, cause a sharp rise in demands for living space and transit facilities. Provision of the transit facilities opens up the way for a reverse, centrifugal dispersion of integrative organs and population into the areas surrounding the city. Rural zones near the city are converted into industrial zones and residential districts, as we have just seen; or else, they turn to commercial farming as an integral part of the larger metropolitan way of life. The nucleus, inner urban, residential, industrial, and commercial districts are merged into a gigantic organic whole, a metropolitan structure held together in highly specialized and differentiated interdependence between component parts, by a system of total integration.

In some cases, the surrounding suburban areas are gradually absorbed into the larger city itself, constituting integral parts of its structure. On the other hand, some of the larger towns and cities in the vicinity of the metropolis are brought into interrelationships with the metropolis that integrate the satellite cities into the larger framework without extinguishing their identity as independent cities. Within the context of the mutually dependent relationships, the satellite cities undergo significant ecological and social changes.

*Yokohama:* Yokohama was developed initially as a base for export shipments of goods produced in the Kantō and Tōhoku regions, and for importing foreign goods required, especially in Tōkyō. It also had important functions in international politics and cultural exchange with other nations.

The proximity of Tōkyō was crucial to every phase of Yokohama's development; yet it is difficult to pinpoint exactly the precise level of interdependence. In addition to exercising controls over all national politics and being the largest center of consumption in the nation, Tōkyō had, as the preceding section amply demonstrates, become a massive production center as well. But goods to be exported overseas, for instance, did not always leave from the nearby port of Yokohama. A considerable volume of goods passed first by rail to Kōbe, and were then exported. Nonetheless, Yokohama most assuredly handled a vast amount of exports from Tōkyō. At the same time, all imports coming into Yokohama were not destined for Tōkyō; although, the proportion consumed in Tokyo must have been very large. Import procedures are quite complicated, and it is impossible to assess the precise ratio of Tōkyō-bound goods coming into Yokohama's docks.

As part of the overall expansion of Japan's economy, Yokohama's export-import trade advanced rapidly. Exports to the United States alone jumped ten times from 190 million yen in 1898 to 1,900 million yen following World War I.[89] To handle the bustling foreign trade, a large number of banks and overseas trading firms were built at an early stage in the heart of the city, establishing the nucleus around which the present city was formed.

Advantages in freight shipments by rail or sea fostered industrial development in the city; so, likewise, did the municipal office by enacting a law permitting tax-exemption for five years for new industries. There appeared many factories in Yokohama after World War I, producing such items as ships, electric wire and cables, machines, chemical products, foodstuffs and beverages. Production totals reached 249 million yen by 1919, and in 1920 the number of factories was 1,706, employing 33,065 workers.[90]

The steps through which Yokohama passed to its dual role as an industrial and export city are indicated in the following schedule:

| *Year* | *Municipal developments* |
|---|---|
| 1885 | Population of Yokohama=180,000. |
| 1901 | Two towns, two counties, and one village merged. |
| 1911 | One town and village added; municipal office was built. |
| 1913 | Prefectural office of Kanagawa Prefecture erected. |

| | |
|---|---|
| 1914 | Yokohama Station on Tōkaidō Line built. |
| 1917 | New pier constructed at Yokohama port. |
| 1919 | Main roads of city repaired following big fire. |
| 1920 | Population reached 570,000. |

These are but the bare essentials of the process in which a small port opened to foreign trade became a modern city for both industry and international trade.

To implement the functions shared by Tōkyō and Yokohama a greatly improved system of transportation and communications was developed. This gave the two cities together a two-member metropolitan-complex structure that reached out to absorb smaller cities in the combined vicinities of the two cities. The socio-economic conditions and structures of the surrounding cities were vastly altered in the process.

The criteria for determining suitable locations for industry were quite different after the large integratively-central cities developed, after rail and other transportation improved radically, and after the forms and sources of energy for driving industry's wheels were changed. Electric power was used mainly for practical, domestic purposes when it was first introduced into Japan. Electric motors were installed in some factories for driving machines after the Russo-Japanese War; but it was not until a sharp rise in coal prices occurred during World War I that utilization of electricity was expedited widely throughout all industries.

Compared to the various limiting conditions involved in both the installation and use of steam engines, electric power offers virtual freedom from any restrictions, whether time, quantity, or location. Factories equipped with electric motors increased very quickly, and once power lines were put up, there was nothing of the bother of repeatedly hauling coal in and ashes out. New factories could concentrate attention more exculsively on transportation facilities for receiving raw materials and delivering products, and for disposing of wastes deriving from production processes. Especially, the newer factories could move out to areas where land costs were low and no reclamation projects needed.

*Kawasaki:* Kawasaki was the highway station town between Shinagawa and Yokohama on the old Edo era highway, one of the famous Fifty-three Stations of the Tōkaidō. There were two official inns (*honjin*) and seventy-two private inns in the town in 1943.[91] Kawasaki became a major rest stop after stage coach and rickshaw services were introduced in the Meiji period, and traffic between Tōkyō and Yokohama increased considerably in this early phase of the modern era.

Completion of the Tōkyō-Yokohama railway in 1882 eliminated the need for a rest stop on so short a run. Situated right between two large centers of production, consumption, and export business, though, it was virtually inevitable that industries should flock to this convenient site. Propitiously placed in the mid-point of the Tōkyō-Yokohama urban complex, Kawasaki had the following factors operating in its favor as a suitable location for industry:

1. Both capital funds and plentiful manpower supply were available in the two urban centers north and south of this city.
2. Located on the shore of Tōkyō Bay, it had direct access to the sea for receiving raw materials and disposing of wastes.
3. With a station on the Tōkaidō trunk line it had ready access not only to the two neighboring cities, but to the provinces north and west as well.
4. Large tracts of land were available at lower costs than could be found in Tōkyō or Yokohama.

Kawasaki Salt Plant was built in 1907, followed soon by such important industrial installations as: Tōkyō Electric Company, Nihon Gramophone Company, Meiji Sugar Company, Nihon Steel Tube Company, and Tōkyō Wire Company. In the Taishō period, beginning in 1912, the following factories were constructed: Fuji Gas Spinning Company, Ajinomoto Company, Tōyō Steel Products Company, and Asano Cement Company. As is evident from the use of the name "Tōkyō" in so many of the company titles, these factories were all started by major enterprisers and financiers in the capital city. In 1916 a public works project was begun to open up an inland canal connecting Tōkyō and Yokohama.[92]

In 1898 the population of Kawasaki town was only 5,600; and when the plant and offices of Tōkyō Electric Company were built near the new Kawasaki Station, one could see little more than fields and swamps of the Sagami plain in all directions. But the conditions conducive to industrial development, including the plentiful water supply of Rokugogawa river for a larger population, made for very rapid progress that brought the population up to 37,000 by 1918.[93]

*Chiba:* The castle town of the Sakura domain ruling the Chiba peninsula was not located in the present city of Chiba, but inland some twenty kilometers by a crooked finger lake. Chiba town was a port for handling goods of this domain being shipped to Edo. There many shops of wholesalers in the town, that did a thriving business with producers in the districts of Shimōsa, Kazusa, and Awa (northern, central, and southern sections of the peninsula respectively). This town was brought within the range of the integrative activity of Tōkyō, but after a different pattern from that of Kawasaki. It was rather too far from Tōkyō for easy absorption at this stage, yet too close to escape some necessary role in the life of the capital metropolis.

Though not a former castle town, Chiba city was made the administrative center of the peninsula, the prefectural office being located there in 1873. There followed soon afterward a District Court and public schools. Then, the city was made also the locus of several military installations after the Russo-Japanese War, such as the First Railroad Regiment, an Army Infantry School, and a Quartermasters' Depot. Later in the Taishō era an Air Defense School was established in Chiba. It had at this juncture, then, several political, military, and commercial (wholesalers) functions.

The intermediate services of wholesalers was needed primarily because the chief means of transporting goods was by boat. The Samukawa port of Chiba city is said to have accommodated 240 steamers and 290 sailing vessels in a year, while Noborito harbor was visited by 2,100 sailing craft. Rail service was extended to Chiba in 1889 with completion of the Bōsō Line; and the sea transport function was abolished overnight. Local producers on the peninsula could deal more directly with Tōkyō wholesalers, depriving the Chiba middlemen of their function. This trend was fulfilled when another line, the Sōbu, was completed in 1904. On the other hand, the expanded population related to new government offices and military installations provided the thwarted wholesalers an opportunity to shift to retail operations, which many chose to do.[94]

Chiba was developed clearly as a satellite city, performing specialized functions on behalf of the capital city, such as military, political, land transport and products supply, and its population showed a modest growth on the basis of its satellite position. From 26,000 in 1898, the city grew to 33,000 in 1920; and it was reorganized as a municipality in 1921.

Other cities in the vicinity of Tōkyō developed as satellites, namely, Kawaguchi, Urawa, and Ōmiya on the Nakasendō route northwest, and Ichikawa and Matsudo just across Edogawa river toward Chiba, plus Tachikawa due west of the capital.

*Kawaguchi:* Kawaguchi had been a haven for an old metal casters guild during the Edo era. The guild was abolished in the Meiji reforms, but the skills were put to work in new factories utilizing modern smelting and casting tools. Stepped-up demands from the Tōkyō Arsenal during the Sino-Japanese and Russo-Japanese Wars drove production up, and with it the size of the city.

*Urawa:* Urawa was a relay station town on the Nakasendō highway with a reported total of houses numbering 208 in the Bunsei era (1818–29). It was chosen as the location of the prefectural office for Saitama Prefecture in 1869, at which time there were some 400 houses. Urawa Normal School was established there, introducing an educational function to the town. A railroad station on the line running northwest to Takasaki was built in 1883, and the population began to increase. Toward the end of the Meiji period (1912), there were 1,800 houses, and this number increased two or three times during the Taishō era, as some industry was started in this town. Following the Great Earthquake of 1923, Urawa was developed as a residential city for people working in Tōkyō.[95]

The others, Tachikawa, Ōmiya, Ichikawa and Matsudo were initially independent cities. Tachikawa and Ōmiya were developed as industrial zones of the larger integrative sphere of Tōkyō; Matsudo and Ichikawa served primarily as residential areas. Their independence was lost as they were converted into satellite towns with specialized functions.

All towns in the vicinity of Tōkyō were not drawn immediately within the integrative sphere of the emerging metropolis, whether by absorption or conversion to satellite status. However, the basic pattern was now established and it would be only the next generation before each of the other towns in the surrounding area would be made into a component part, or a functional affiliate (satellite), of the expanding network of integrative activity. The differentiation of specialized functions for separate cities and towns within the larger organic structure of an emerging metropolitan community was a process now well under way; and it was to continue for some time to come until Tōkyō became again the world's largest city.

(2) METROPOLITAN GROWTH IN ŌSAKA, KYŌTO, AND NAGOYA.
*Ōsaka:* Ōsaka lost its key place in the national economy as the chief supply center for the Kinki district, for Edo, and for most provinces after the Meiji directives took Japan off the silver standard, abolished the domains and therefore their warehouses in Ōsaka, and finally, declared a moratorium on all debts owed by the government to the powerful merchants of Ōsaka. The city was caught suddenly in a state of bankruptcy.

Almost as if to compensate Ōsaka for its monetary losses with intended irony, the government constructed its mint there in 1871, an operation of large-scale proportions predating most large-scale production anywhere else in the country. Then, in rapid succession rail links with major cities in the Kinki district were completed as follows:

| *Year* | *Section* |
|---|---|
| 1874 | Ōsaka—Kōbe |
| 1876 | Ōsaka—Kyōto |
| 1877 | Kyōto—Kōbe |

Following enactment of the stock exchange laws, the Ōsaka Stock Exchange was opened in 1878, and Ōsaka merchants began pouring their capital resources and talents into the development of new enterprises. Economic recovery in Ōsaka was also aided by the establishment of firms by foreign enterprises, such as Ōsaka Iron Works (English), Ōsaka Gas Company (American), and a number of match factories (Chinese). The city began a significant transformation from a center specializing in the gathering and distributing of goods, to one that would soon be a major production center itself.

In 1889 the railway connecting Tōkyō and Kōbe via Ōsaka was completed. The foundation was laid on which Ōsaka could develop into a modern city, and Ōsaka was recognized at that time as a municipality. With a revised administrative system, a key location with respect to transportation and communications, and a growing number of modern industries, Ōsaka was set upon the way to becoming the nation's second largest metropolis.

Industrial development in Ōsaka received its first major stimulus from the Sino-Japanese War. In the spinning industry alone it claimed over

40% of the operating spindleage in the country, with an annual production of one million yen. Until 1898 Ōsaka was, with Tōkyō and Kyōto, under the old "special cities" law; when this was cancelled in that year, Ōsaka assumed self-government as a municipality. Initial plans of the city government included a project for improving the facilities of Ōsaka's port. This work was finished in 1901, giving the city greater access to the prosperous foreign trade.

By 1897 both industrial and population expansion forced an extension of the city limits to include an area of fifty-five square kilometers (21.2 sq. mi.), or three and a half times its previous size. The most remarkable phase of industrial growth in the city was its spinning industry, which jumped quickly to more than ten million yen in annual productivity soon after the Sino-Japanese War, and under the further stimulus of the Russo-Japanese War had, by 1907, 927 mills employing 53,507 workers.[96] Department stores were established in the central area of the city to serve a rapidly expanding and increasingly urbanized population. Streetcar and electric train lines to the suburban areas were installed.

Like all other industrial centers in Japan, each war period brought an upward thrust in the economy of Ōsaka. This can be seen vividly in the upsurge in foreign trading, comparing the first and last years of World War I (1914–8), when Ōsaka experienced an unprecedented boom in foreign trading activity:

| *Year* | *Exports (yen)* | *Imports (yen)* |
|---|---|---|
| 1914 | 74,300,000 | 50,000,000 |
| 1918 | 400,000,000 | 100,000,000 |

Tōkyō's dominant position in the national economy up to this time was now shifted to the city of Ōsaka; the latter became once again the city that determined the movements of finance and economy in Japan.

Before development as a major industrial center Ōsaka's chief export item had been silk. The process of industrialization had diversified her production considerably; now there were factories for spinning, dyeing, and weaving, metal products, machines and tools, electrical goods, foodstuffs, beverages, and sundries.

Cotton production and exports made up a large portion of the city's industry and commerce, as the Japanese industries were capable in this period, not only of supplying all domestic needs, but also of entering into international markets. Cotton products were exported, to be sure, to Oriental markets in China, India, and the Southeast Asian island countries; but they went also to European and African countries where competition with European and American products was extremely keen. Nonetheless, the products of the cotton spinning industry took top place among all Japanese industrial products, and Ōsaka and Kōbe were the chief outports for the brisk export trade.

Ōsaka continued to expand at a rapid pace, as did neighboring cities and towns which were brought into its integrative scope. Not a little confusion was caused by the bifurcation of many citizens' lives, in that community and residential roots were in neighboring towns, while economic livelihood was based in Ōsaka itself. A second enlargement of the Ōsaka city limits was carried out in 1925, yielding an overall area of 181 square kilometers (69.7 sq. mi.), and a population of over two million people. With expanded administrative scope and authority, major reforms were expedited in many fields: improved water and sewage systems; road paving projects, and extension of streetcar lines; expansion of electric power supply and city lighting facilities; improved educational, public welfare, and other social facilities. Ōsaka became the sixth largest modern city in the world after this consolidation of the former urban area and the suburban areas in its immediate vicinity.

The business district was developed in the Kitahama and Koraibashi sections; retailers prospered along such streets as Shinsaibashi-suji, Gonda, Tenjinbashi-suji, Kujo, and Shinsekai. Amusement facilites were located in the Dōtonbori and Sennichimae sections. Industrial zones were extended in the western and northern parts of the city.

The population of Ōsaka continued growing after the second enlargement, expanding from 2.11 million to 2.99 million in the ten years following the 1925 expansion, or about 50% growth. However, decentralization of the city's population began about this time; population growth in the inner urban area was only 20% while new urban areas expanded in population by 80%.

A rather remarkable development of satellite cities can be seen in the Taishō period. In 1911 there were only two satellite cities with populations somewhere between 10,000 and 100,000; the number of satellite cities within that range increased to nineteen by 1920. As in the case of the satellite cities around Tōkyō, these cities were originally independent towns or farm villages; but they each took on specialized functions as they were absorbed into the outstretching integrative sphere of Ōsaka.

Surveyed briefly, the changes wrought in the satellite towns ringing Ōsaka in a wide arc swinging from Sakai on the shore of Ōsaka Bay south of Ōsaka around east, then to the fertile plain north of Ōsaka, were as follows:

*Sakai:* Its harbor unsuitable for large freighters, this old port town lost its former function; but its proximity to Ōsaka made it a natural site for development as an industrial zone. Craftsmen formerly engaged in firearms production as a secondary business were put into large-scale production of bicycle parts. Sakai also had factories for producing cutlery, woven fabrics and yarns.

*Fuse:* This small town due east of Ōsaka on the route to Nara was once a local center of home industries providing side jobs for farmers. Small and medium-sized factories were built here for production of metal nets and other metal products, machines, celluloid, rubber, furniture and stationery goods.

*Moriguchi:* A former highway station town on the road to Kyōto and a riverside port on the Yodogawa river, this town was developed for both industrial and residential purposes.

*Suita:* An out-of-the-way hamlet due north of Ōsaka beyond the Yodogawa river, Suita was chosen as the site of the Dainihon Beer Company's brewery, giving it a productive function within the Ōsaka sphere.

Toyonaka, Ikeda, and Minomo were towns in the vicinity of Suita that were developed as residential areas of salaried workers employed in Ōsaka. On the shore of Ōsaka Bay farther south than Sakai, Izumi-ōtsu Izumi-sano, and Kaizuka were developed as industrial zones for weaving and spinning.[97]

Construction of electric train lines connecting the satellite cities to Ōsaka and to each other during this period of development was nothing short of astounding. The sections completed, the railroad companies involved, and the years of completion are given below:

| *Year* | *Name of railway company* | *Section completed* |
|---|---|---|
| 1893 | Settsu R.R. Co. | Amagasaki—Ikeda |
| 1895 | Ōsaka R.R. Co. | Tennōji—Umeda |
| 〃 | Naniwa R.R. Co. | Katayama—Shijōnawate |
| 1900 | Hankaku R.R. Co. | Ikeda—Takarazuka |
| 〃 | Nankai R.R. Co. | Tennōji—Tenkajaya |
| 〃 | Kōya R.R. Co. | Shiomi—Nagano |
| 〃 | Kansai R.R. Co. | Tsunashima—Nagoya |
| 〃 | Hankaku R.R. Co. | Ōsaka—Fukuchiyama |
| 〃 | Nankai R.R. Co. | Ōsaka—Wakayama |
| 〃 | Hankaku R.R. Co. | Ōsaka—Shinmaizuru |

These many electric train lines were the threads with which the integrative web of the Ōsaka metropolitan community was spun.[98]

The movement toward specialized functions performed by distinct suburban and satellite communities within the larger metropolitan community was also greatly accelerated by the installation of the many rail lines. The centrifugal expansion of residential and industrial zones spilled over the boundaries of Ōsaka Prefecture (*Ōsaka-fu*) as such.

*Kōbe:* Major outport of the industrial complex centered in Ōsaka, Kōbe was utilized by Japanese and foreign firms alike. Shipbuilding and iron and steel production had been developed in Kōbe since the beginning of the Meiji period, and factories for producing camphor, matches, and rubber products were introduced from the middle of the Meiji period on. The foundation of industrial production in the city was laid by the beginning of the Taishō period, with the substantial assistance of expanded foreign trade. Endowed with an excellent natural port, the dock facilities were also completed by the Taishō era.

During World War I the expansion of foreign trade business in Kōbe was momentous, as per the following:

| Year | Amount of foreign trade (yen) |
| --- | --- |
| 1897 | 160,000,000 |
| 1918 | 1,223,000,000 |

The shortage of merchant vessels during World War I prompted construction of a number of new large-scale shipbuilding operations in Kōbe. The overall number of factories in the city expanded ten times in this period.[99]

New factories, and a harbor busy with ships of all nations, business companies built and enlarged again soon after completion, and warehouses full of cargoes with which forwarding agents busied themselves,—this was the new face of old Hyōgo, now Kōbe. Laborers and office workers were attracted in large numbers to the thriving city, giving Kōbe the highest rate of population increase among all large cities starting with more than 10,000 population, in the quarter century up to 1920. With a population of 190,000 in 1897, this figure mushroomed to 640,000 by 1920, an increase rate of 337%.

*Amagasaki:* Ōsaka and Kōbe formed a large two-component urban complex much the same as that formed by Tōkyō and Yokohama. Amagasaki was situated between the former cities just as Kawasaki was sandwiched in between the latter two cities. Hence, the criteria for locating industries in Amagasaki were almost the same as in the case of Kawasaki. It was blessed by a ready supply of capital funds close at hand, plenty of manpower and raw materials, plus the added advantage of easy disposal of waste materials from production processes.

Amagasaki had had traffic and transport functions in Edo times when it was the castle town of the Amagasaki domain, with an income of 50,000 *koku* and thriving fish markets and breweries. Its first ventures into the industrial revolution were made in spinning mills, metal products and glass-making industries.

Rails for the Tōkaidō Line were laid through Amagasaki in 1873 (Ōsaka-Kōbe section completed 1874), and in 1893 the Hankyū Line running parallel to it made direct connections at Amagasaki. A third parallel line between Ōsaka and Kōbe, the Hanshin Railway, was finished in 1905. These rail lines tied Amagasaki into the larger Ōsaka-Kōbe urban-industrial belt all the more tightly.

Amagasaki was converted thenceforth into a fully industrial city. A chemical industry was established at the outbreak of World War I, and by the end of the Taishō period there were factories for machine making, iron and steel foundries, and steam plants for electric power; most of these were built on lands reclaimed from the sea. Amagasaki was organized as a municipality in 1916, when its population reached 32,000, with 52 factories in the city. It was a major link in the Hanshin (Ōsaka-Kōbe) Industrial Belt.

*Nishinomiya:* This city was typical of another type of satellite center developed in the Ōsaka-Kōbe urban complex. Like Amagasaki, it too was situated between the two larger cities, but its development paralleled Amagasaki in few other respects.

Nishinomiya was famous for its breweries since the Muromachi era; its *sake* sold under the name *Nada-no-sake*, "*sake* brewed in Nada." The breweries remained in the modern period, but the rest of Nishinomiya was developed as a residential area for the large populations of Ōsaka and Kōbe, especially after completion of the network of lines in the Hanshin area around 1920. Higher income families began transferring their residences out to the pleasant surroundings of Nishinomiya, with lovely mountains in the background and the sea stretched out before it. It was a high class suburban area.

But this development was not due solely to individual initiative. The railway companies took considerable initiative in planning and constructing residential communities in the district. Apart from purely commercial interests on the part of the railway companies, there were serious limiting conditions operating against the development of suitable residential areas in either Ōsaka or Kōbe. Ōsaka was all lowlands, with no attractive hill sections like the western suburbs of Tōkyō. Kōbe was built on a narrow ledge between high mountains and Ōsaka Bay; there simply was no room for residential communities adequate for its swelling population. Finally, the rail networks completed between the two cities made it inevitable that certain districts like Nishinomiya become residential components of the Ōsaka-Kōbe metropolitan community.

*Kyōto:* Kyōto's ties with tradition and the fact that its temples and shrines constituted a large part of its functions as a city might have been disastrous had not the general elevation of the standard of living throughout the country made it possible for sightseeing and religious pilgrimages to flourish along with other activities in the country.

But Kyōto had also its traditional spinning and weaving industries which, if not large-scale, had an unchallenged reputation for quality and good taste. Efforts were made by the operators of the Nishijin silk factories to modernize production, by sending workers to France to receive training in new weaving techniques. In 1890 the Keage Steam Power Plant was built after drainage work was completed on Lake Biwa. Industrial development was fostered by a ready supply of electric power, and by institutions such as schools, experimental laboratories, labor unions, and a Chamber of Commerce.[100]

An unusual stimulus toward urban improvement came from Kyōto's ancient ties to the Imperial Household. The coronation ceremony for the Emperor Taishō in 1915 was performed in the Imperial Palace of Kyōto. The city officials issued municipal bonds to raise a special budget with which to dress up the city through widening roads, repairing drainage systems, and erecting public facilities such as hospitals.

Kyōto was not in a particularly convenient location with respect to transportation functions. Its prosperity came, rather, as a part of the general economic growth of the entire nation. Amalgamating some fifteen towns and villages in 1918, it almost doubled in size and population, as per the following:

| *Year* | *City area* | *Population* |
|---|---|---|
| 1897 | 3,123 sq. km. (1,205 sq. mi.) | 330,000 |
| 1920 | 6,043 sq. km. (2,332 sq. mi.) | 590,000 |

Though not on the scale of Tōkyō and Ōsaka, the foundations for development as a modern city were laid on the same terms as its sister cities.

*Nagoya:* A metropolitan community developed around Nagoya on the basis of traditional light industries of ceramics, and cotton and silk spinning, and through the construction of railways, port facilities, and new industries. It was the mid-point on the Tōkaidō trunk line between Tōkyō and Kōbe, and suburban lines were gradually installed. A cement plant was built in 1890, and a clock and watch factory in 1892. Watches and clocks were exported to Hong Kong, Vladivostok, and to cities in China and the Southeast Asian countries.

The port of Atsuta in central Nagoya was provided with modern facilities in 1907, and nearby towns such as Kana-machi and Koshika-mura were consolidated into the growing city. To its light industries were added, after World War I, heavy industries producing railway cars and locomotives, automobiles, and machines, as well as factories for chemical fertilizers. It could draw on the surrounding region for needed laborers, and the rail and port services provided for raw materials' supply and distribution of finished goods.

With a very favorable spectrum of conditions, Nagoya became the controlling center of the Chūbu (Central) Industrial Area, the nucleus of the economic circle located between and interacting with the larger Keihin and Hanshin Industrial Belts.[101]

*Regional Urban Development.*——

(1) NORTH KYŪSHŪ. There was a different mode of urban development from the patterns reviewed thus far, in the cluster of modern cities that emerged in North Kyūshū. These cities were founded on the basic industries of iron, steel and coal. The immediate source of coal was the Chikuhō Coal Fields in northern Kyūshū, though after the Russo-Japanese War iron ore and coal were shipped from Manchuria.

Yawata was perhaps the most spectacular city of the North Kyūshū cluster, in that it literally grew up around the Yawata Steel Mill built by the government. A small hamlet of slightly more than one thousand people before development as a factory town, its population reached 84,000 by 1917, at which time it was incorporated as a municipality. The port town serving Yawata was Wakamatsu, and it was only one of several cities in the area that developed through some direct or indirect function in the production or consumption of coal and iron ore. Others in the North

Kyūshū group were Tobata and Moji on the coast, and the old castle town of Kokura.

These cities were closely connected with each other, and all together constituted a rather large urban complex. They lacked, however, that character seen in the metropolitan communities described above, namely, a large nuclear city around which all other cities and towns took their respective places as component parts of a larger organic whole, totally integrated by the nuclear city.

*Yawata:* Yawata had only 1,229 people in 351 houses in 1889 when the administrative laws for towns and villages were applied. Under the impetus of victory in the Sino-Japanese War construction was begun on the government iron and steel works in 1897, with iron ores and coal imported from Manchuria through the nearby port of Wakamatsu, and from the neighboring Chikuhō Coal Fields; convenient access to the Kyūshū mines and the resources in China were the reasons for selecting Yawata for the government mills. It took three years and 14.7 million yen to complete construction, employing 1.8 million workers in the total project.

The large steel mill appeared abruptly in northern Kyūshū without any relation to local capital or initiative; all of a sudden, there was this large-scale, modern production system ready to operate. Its presence, however, bred development of other industries in the neighboring district and promoted development of the Chikuhō Coal Fields.[102]

In 1901 the No. 1 blast furnace of Yawata Iron and Steel Mill was put into operation successfully, and the other component parts of the mill were brought into production soon afterward. Production facilities were expanded as the government entered into heavier armaments programs. The estimated annual production of iron products follows:

| *Year* | *Estimated annual production (tons)* |
|---|---|
| 1906 | 180,000 |
| 1911 | 300,000 |
| 1916 | 650,000 |

The number and job distribution of employees for the year 1921 was as follows: executive managers, 912; clerical staff, 1,350; regular laborers, 15,949; and temporary laborers, an average 6,000 per day.

One of the ways the Yawata operations bred other industries was in the proliferation of small factories in the Yawata area doing subcontract work. Otherwise, banks and business firms established themselves in Yawata to serve the rapidly expanding population. Indeed, the rate of increase, more than 33 times in a generation, was the highest rate of population increase of all Japanese cities. In terms of absolute number, Yawata grew from only 3,014 people in 1897 to a population of 100,235 by 1920.

*Wakamatsu:* The growth of this port city was completely dependent upon the Yawata operations and development of the Chikuhō Coal Fields.

In the Edo era it had served the Kuroda fiefdom for sending and unloading commodity shipments. It was with the development of coal mining after the Meiji period began that it was developed as a modern port. The following companies were developed in order to obtain and use the coal deposits:

| *Year* | *Company* |
|---|---|
| 1890 | Wakamatsu Port Construction Company |
| 1891 | Chikuhō Industrial Railway Company |
| 1897 | Yawata Iron and Steel Mill |

Once the Yawata mill was in operation, Wakamatsu expanded rapidly as an export-import center.

Wakamatsu was authorized as an open port in 1904, restrictions on export business were removed in 1905, and import restrictions were cancelled in 1917. After these obstacles were cleared out of the way, foreign trade through Wakamatsu port improved considerably, consisting mainly of coal and iron products.

Most of the coal mined in the five counties of the Chikuhō district was shipped to Ōsaka, Kōbe, and Yokohama, although shipments sometimes went as far away as Shanghai or Hong Kong. Other products cleared through this port in the year 1919 were:

| *Goods exported* | *Amount of export* (*yen*) |
|---|---|
| Metal | 15,550 |
| Iron & steel products | 16,200 |
| Steamships and other vessels | 33,000 |

The city of Wakamatsu expanded as the demands for coal rose, and as it worked to improve its own port and other transportation facilities. The population figures and rates of increase for the period under review follow:

| *Year* | *Population* | *Rate of increase*(%)[103] |
|---|---|---|
| Early Meiji | 1,000 | —— |
| 1898 | 12,000 | 1,200 |
| 1920 | 49,336 | 411 |

*Tobata:* Originally a small fishing village, Tobata stood on a narrow neck of land across a strip of water from Wakamatsu to the west; Kokura lay along the shore to the east. Yawata was south of Tobata and Wakamatsu at the head of the inlet whose entrance they shared. Reclamation work had begun at the Tobata site late in the Tokugawa era to extend rice fields. By 1880 the reclaimed area was about three square kilometers (1.15 sq. mi.), but this was extended further by the Wakamatsu Port Construction Company and the Yawata Steel Mill, and businesses and factories were begun. In 1880 a number of small factories were built, such as a coal processing factory, an iron works, a coke producing plant, and a brick plant. Large-scale production did not begin until 1908 with construction of Meiji Spinning Company, followed by Tobata Casting Company in 1910, and Meiji Mining Company in 1919.

Fishing was ruined for Tobata by the dredging done in reclamation work, but some recompense came in the form of offices and banks set up to handle coal transactions and transportation needs. Tobata fulfilled industrial and port functions in the North Kyūshū urban complex. Its population expanded ten times between 1891 and 1920, from 3,319 to 33,824.[104]

*Kokura:* Kokura had been an important castle town of the Edo period because of its commanding position over the entrance to the Inland Sea of Seto, and the shogunate had made it a naval base for defense against possible foreign invasion, and to protect Yamaguchi domain. In 1845, two decades before the shogunate fell, there were 3,099 warriors and 13,091 townsmen in this castle center.

The Meiji government retained the military function of Kokura, and added certain commercial and transport functions. A brief timetable of developments might be:

| *Year* | *Agencies established in Kokura* |
|---|---|
| 1875 | Fourteenth Infantry Regiment stationed in Kokura |
| 1885 | Pier of Kokura port completed |
| 1891 | Railroad between Moji and Kurosaki completed, passing through Kokura |
| 1897 | Kokura incorporated as a municipality |
| 1912 | Streetcar lines installed |

Kokura acquired additional importance in the multiple functions of military, commerce, and transport under a policy that regarded North Kyūshū and Shimonoseki on the other side of the channel leading into the Inland Sea as a special zone in national defense and development.

An old cotton crepe industry developed first as a side business of warriors late in the Tokugawa era continued to thrive during the Meiji and Taishō eras, but it meant little for the development of the city itself. It was, rather, an iron foundry and army arsenal built there, with the extended use of coal and iron ore, that gave the city new life, in addition to its military, commercial, and transport functions.[105]

*Moji:* Reclamation work, new port facilities, and a southbound railway begun in 1889 by the Kyūshū Railway Company, all transformed Moji from a small fishing village into an industrial port city with a population of 29,000 by 1899. Its port was authorized to export five items through the coal dealers of the city, who received their coal from the Chikuhō Fields. Moji ranked with Wakamatsu in coal business by 1902, though it eventually lost most of the coal trade to the latter city.

There were large firms, banks, shipping companies, and warehouses which made use of Moji's port and rail services, especially after railroads were extended throughout more of Kyūshū island. Asano Cement, Dainihon Sugar, and Sakura Beer Companies put in modern installations in

Moji in the Meiji period, and these were activated considerably by the outbreak of World War I. Other large factories were built, helping to bring the population up to 72,111 by 1920.[106] In 1919 a long-term project for repairing and expanding Moji's port facilities was laid, with gigantic budgetary backing. Shorelines, roads, warehouses, and other facilities were also improved, making Moji a typical port city of western Japan.

(2) PIONEER CITIES IN HOKKAIDŌ. Not all cities developed "naturally," that is, evolving from older feudal cities of one kind or another. Some were planned and built according to schedule by the government. Yet they did not inherit much of a legacy of feudalism. These were the pioneer cities of Hokkaidō.

In developing the large island north of the main island of Honshū, the Japanese government saw a number of advantages; one was a defense line against any threat from Russia. A domestic advantage was the dispersion of surplus population to the undeveloped north country. Still another was the quest for new raw materials for industry. The government appointed a commissioner for the pioneer development of the north island, and actively backed him with road construction, government-built enterprises, subsidies of goods and money for settlers, and extension of rail facilities onto the island of Hokkaidō.

The city of Muroran, where iron and steel were produced, was the first city on the island to be incorporated as a municipality, in 1918. There were others which followed soon, in 1922, such as Sapporo, Hakodate, Otaru, Asahikawa, and Kushiro. All of these cities were pioneered under the government's Hokkaidō development program.

The pioneer cities drew on no traditions; they were settled and developed by peoples from many different provinces. They were truly pioneer cities. All the more, then, did the development of these cities depend on establishing transportation and communication facilities, and all the more natural that the process began close to the main island before penetrating later into remote places farther north.

*Hakodate:* Hakodate was a fishing base as early as 1793 when negotiations with Russia were first held there by the Tokugawa shogunate. Settlers from the Ōu district in the northern part of the main island developed a thriving seafoods business, exporting goods from Ezo-chi, as it was known before being renamed Hokkaidō in 1869.

Hakodate was under the direct rule of the *bakufu* after it was made an open port in 1854. Most of the fish caught in Hokkaidō were collected first in Hakodate for reshipment, and many foreign vessels frequented this port. This city also served as the administrative center for Hokkaidō, before the administrative offices were moved to Sapporo later in the Meiji period. Even then, its fishing, commerce, trade and transport functions flourished, and the population of Hakodate was 31,000 already in 1878.

After Japan acquired fishing rights in the Siberian waters from Russia in 1907, Hakodate became the base for extensive fishing operations in the

North Pacific Ocean. This activity helped breed other businesses and industries. In time merchants in Hakodate were able to extend their activities into the main island districts such as Tōhoku, Keihin, and Hanshin. Eventually their business extended to the Japan Sea side of the main island.

Foreign trade developed remarkably in conjunction with expansion in the fishing industry, as the figures below show:

| *Year* | *Amount of exports (yen)* | *Amount of imports (yen)* |
|---|---|---|
| 1907 | 3,400,000 | 2,800,000 |
| 1920 | 19,000,000 | 16,000,000 |

Hakodate's population expanded commensurately, as per the following:

| *Year* | *Population* | *Rate of increase (%) (over previous figure)* |
|---|---|---|
| 1878 | 30,000 | —— |
| 1897 | 73,000 | 243 |
| 1920 | 140,000 | 192 |

Hakodate was incorporated as a municipality in 1922.[107]

*Sapporo:* In Tokugawa times the area where Sapporo was to rise later was a wholly undeveloped territory of virgin forests. In 1855 the shogunate took over the territory for development as a defense zone, following the settlement of the boundary question over Sakhalin and the Kurile isles north of Hokkaidō, giving Russia the former and Japan the latter. Matsuura Takeshirō was sent by the *bakufu* to Sapporo in 1856, where he found only the Ainu aborigines and two ordinary Japanese families.

Sapporo was made the administrative center of Hokkaidō early in the Meiji era when the office of the Commissioner of Colonization was located there. Shima Yoshio, a low grade magistrate, was made the first commissioner, and his office was initially in Hakodate. In 1870 he was succeeded by Kuroda Kiyotaka, a Satsuma warrior who had fought in support of the pro-imperialist movement, defeating the last resistance put up by the pro-shogunal forces who had fled to Hakodate. He transferred the Colonization Office to Sapporo in 1871, and served as its Commissioner until its dissolution in 1882. A number of merchants followed the removal of the Colonization Office to Sapporo, leaving Hakodate and Fukuyama, castle town of the Matsumae house near Hakodate.

A major function of the Commissioner's office was to provide subsidies to farmers and merchants in the form of long-term loans, or in the case of farmers, partial advance payments were sometimes made against future crops. The function of this office served to strengthen the centrality of Sapporo as a regional integrative city.

Arable lands were offered to ex-samurai for settlement, a system called *tondenhei*. Around 1875–6 the government founded Sapporo Agricultural College, which later was expanded into Hokkaidō Imperial University. The first rail line was laid from Sapporo to Tekan in Otaru in 1880. In 1886 the government offered to guarantee interest payments on loans made in the interests of further development of Hokkaidō. Reimbursements of interest payments on business loans were made to Hokkaidō Linen Company, Hokkaidō Sugar Company, Hokkaidō Colliery and Railway Company, and Sapporo Beer Company.

Sapporo expanded in line with the general growth of capitalism and industry in Japan after the Sino-Japanese and Russo-Japanese Wars. By 1914 its population already totalled 98,000; and in the same year a Great Exhibition was held in the city. For this important event roads were repaired and constructed, and carriages were replaced by streetcars.[108]

During World War I the textile industry and especially linens showed notable growth. The following companies were founded in Sapporo: Tōyō Spinning Company (1917), Nihon Linen Spinning Company (1919), and Taishō Linen Spinning Company (1920).

*Otaru:* When Sakhalin Island was occupied by the Russians in 1806, the Tokugawa shogunate, through the Matsumae domain, took direct control of Otaru district in the next year to serve as a defense base. It was not developed as a commerical port until after the Meiji Restoration, when the villages of Shikinai and Tekan were built up in the area. The number of townships in Otaru gradually increased, giving an increasingly larger population to Otaru, as follows:

| *Year* | *Population of Otaru* |
|---|---|
| 1882 | 2,230 |
| 1897 | 54,966 |
| 1921 | 111,939 |

There were commercial ports in Hokkaidō before the Meiji era, such as Fukuyama on the southernmost tip of the island, and Esashi and Hakodate on the western and eastern coasts of the same peninsula. Restrictions on the operations of ports were loosened after the Meiji government came to power, and loans at low interest rates were made to fishermen in 1871 to rescue them from the high rates charged by private merchant-brokers.

In 1873 a government loan of 114,000 yen was made through the Office of Colonization to several shipping companies in Otaru to purchase a number of vessels. In 1878 a road connecting Sapporo and Otaru was completed, and in 1880 the rail line from Sapporo to Tekan in Otaru was finished. An ocean route between Otaru and Hakodate was opened the same year, and fishing was developed along the eastern (Kitami) and western (Teshio) coasts of the triangular northern part of Hokkaidō. The combination of these many factors promoted a substantial increase in the volume of goods concentrated and distributed in and through the city of Otaru.

Otaru was designated a special port for certain items in 1889, such as rice, wheat, coal, and sulphur, and it was made an open port. In the following year the railway from Sapporo was extended all the way south to Hakodate. This gave the city fairly good transportation facilities on land and sea, just at a time when industry in general was making considerable progress in Hokkaidō. These two factors together caused a great upsurge in the volume of goods handled in Otaru.

When transactions were opened up with traders in Sakhalin about 1893 or 1894, the quantity of goods loaded and unloaded at Otaru rose sharply again. Between 1898 and 1923 export-import tonnage nearly tripled from 1,328,662 to 3,609,325 tons. A number of industries were operated in Otaru itself, in such fields as oil, paper, rubber products, iron and steel, and breweries. The city streets were improved to accommodate heavier traffic as industry progressed in this important commercial port.[109]

*Asahikawa:* Conditions in the Asahikawa site before the Meiji era are not clearly known. Around 1885 the government decided to explore developmental possibilities in the Kamikawa district along the upper reaches of the Ishikarigawa river, that flows from headwaters mountains north of Mt. Daisetsu westward beyond present-day Asahikawa, then turns south through the Sorachi region before making a final westward course toward the open sea just north of Sapporo. Road construction was begun in that same year on an east-west road transversing Hokkaidō, from the Sorachi valley across the Kamikawa highlands to the Abashiri plain on the west coast near Shiretoko Peninsula jutting out into the Okhotsk Sea. This road was completed in 1890 and Asahikawa was born from this project. Some 400 soldiers were put to work on lands around Asahikawa-mura, and merchants set up shops in the frontier town to handle rice and other daily necessities, as it became the key center of Kamikawa regional development.

House lots were made availabe to settlers in 1890, and some 213 persons built houses and took up residence there. Population increased rapidly after a railway was built from the Sorachi Valley into Asahikawa in 1898, opening the way for many new settlers. Later railroads were extended to the northern tip of Hokkaidō called Sōya, and to the western tip called Kushiro. The intermediate functions of receiving and distributing goods in Asahikawa was greatly strengthened after these rail lines were completed.

The Headquarters of the Seventh Army Division was established in Asahikawa in 1902, attracting many more merchants and industrial operators. By the following year the facilities of this new urban center included: banks, companies, and factories; roads and bridges; improved housing structures; the city had its own electric power supply, and a telephone service was installed.

At the outbreak of World War I the price of farm goods rose sharply, which benefited Asahikawa considerably in its distributive role. By 1921 the city had some 141 business firms, both limited and unlimited corporations, as well as 119 factories including those producing *sake* and matches. Thus, industry, commerce, and military functions characterized this young pioneer city, which was incorporated in 1922.[110]

*Muroran:* Muroran was part of the Nanbu fief before the Tokugawa shogunate decided to exercise direct control over it. The new Meiji government established a district court in Hakodate in 1868, as part of the administrative office through which it intended to rule the entire territory of Hokkaidō. Hakodate was referred to as Hakodate-fu (i.e., prefecture of Hakodate) in this initial stage; and the Nanbu officials withdrew from public life. Ishikawa Kunimitsu, a member of the Date household, came to Muroran in this early phase of development to build up a base for colonization there. His efforts were, on the whole, a failure; his workers suffered many hardships and the colonization schedule was delayed considerably. Muroran was not able to develop much beyond a remote traffic junction with minor officials in residence, travelers' inns, and a few merchants' shops. There were about thirty ordinary Japanese families and thirteen Ainu families in the town. In 1873 the main road between Sapporo and Hakodate was completed, passing through Muroran. Its course ran south from Sapporo overland to Muroran, then west around Uchiura Bay to Mori on the south side of the bay; from there it transversed the eastern promontory of Oshima Peninsula due south to Hakodate. This road opened the way for further development of Muroran.

It was not easy to get immigrants to settle in Muroran, even though settlers' loans were available and wooden furniture and other household goods could be had at relatively low prices. Some 989 families did move into the new Muroran development in 1874. Although railroads were built in 1880 from Sapporo to Otaru westward, and to Horonai in the mining district to the east, no railway was installed to Muroran. There was only the road from Sapporo to Hakodate via Muroran, although the long way around Uchiura Bay could be by-passed by small vessels (100 tons) running between Muroran and Mori. Under such circumstances, it was most difficult to develop a prosperous market in Muroran.

A series of events did set the stage for further progress, however, and these were, in brief staccato fashion:

1887—Warrior families were resettled on arable lands in Muroran district.
1889—Coal mines in the mining districts of Yūbari and Sorachi to the north of Muroran were developed on a large scale.
1893—Steamer line opened from Aomori to Hakodate and Muroran.
1903—Muroran made an open treaty port.
1910—Pier built at Muroran accommodating 5,000–6,000 ton vessels.
1911—Steamships sailing a route from Kobe via Yokohama and Hakodate to Kushiro began dropping in at Muroran.

The last item in the above series made a big difference in developmental possibilities in Muroran, and it began soon thereafter to develop as an industrial city. In 1906 Japan Steel Mill had built a plant in Muroran.

After World War I, with the new transportation connections now available, this plant expanded into a large factory employing 2,200 regular workers, and 1,700 semi-permanent laborers by 1919. Hokkaidō Iron Foundry was built in Muroran in 1917. During the period from 1914 to 1916 between 100,000 and 140,000 tons of coal and 100,000 *koku* (1 million cu. ft.) of lumber were exported from Muroran to Southeast Asian countries. Banks and companies were established to fill out the structure of this industrial city, which was incorporated in 1918.[111]

Sharp population increases were experienced through the successive developmental phases outlined above, driving the small population of only 5,200 in 1896 up to 56,082 in 1920; this was an increase of eleven times in twenty-five years.

*Kushiro:* Kushiro was originally a fishing village on the shores of Kusurihama, where Ainu families serving under the Matsumae house lived. By the end of the Tokugawa period there were in Kushiro a *bakufu* office, watchhouse, wood and lumber warehouse, warehouse for miscanthus roofing supplies, storehouse for fishing tackle, blacksmith shop and other workshops, and 225 houses for the village residents. Some of the villagers had come from the Nanbu fief.

In 1869 a branch office of the Colonization Commission was placed in Kushiro, and immigrants were urged to settle there, including doctors and priests. The branch office offered to help with housing, and 174 families migrated from Hakodate. Telegraph service was installed in 1874, and special port privileges were granted in 1891. The branch office was expanded into a regional office in 1898, and Kushiro port was opened to foreign trade in 1899. The facilities of a functioning city were built up one by one.

Significant development came, however, after the railroad from Hakodate to Kushiro was completed in 1908. This gave this town the dual land-sea transportation advantages that proved so essential to large-scale development elsewhere. Kushiro became the central supply base for the Tokachi, Kitami, and Nemuro districts to the west, north, and east of it respectively. Its major shipments of export goods were lumber, farm products, and seafoods. Its population expanded from 2,600 in 1897 to a fifteenfold increase of 39,392 by 1920. Export trade in 1919 was valued at 19 million yen.[112]

(3) CENTERS OF TRADITIONAL INDUSTRIES. All of the cities discussed thus far fall within one of the following categories:

a. A feudal city converted into an industrial city with drastic changes in its municipal structure.

b. A city without any specific feudal age background that emerged as an industrial city because of suitable conditions of natural endowment or relation to transportation routes.

c. A pioneer city developed under specific plans and support of the government, as seen in the cities of Hokkaidō.

Not all modern cities in Japan fit into these categories, however; there were towns that had deep roots in the feudal tradition and social structure that were able to adjust to the demands of a modern industrial society without rejecting their heritage. These were towns and cities with traditional industries that could be easily adapted to modern capitalism, and especially to the new export activity. Such cities included Hamamatsu, Kiryū, Ashikaga, Hachiōji, Takata, and Kurume.

*Kiryū:* In the chapter dealing with the final phase of the Tokugawa shogunate we saw that the weaving techniques of Kyōto's Nishijin industry were transmitted as early as the 16th century to the town of Kiryū in the upper reaches of the Kantō plain, and that it became, as it were, the "Nishijin of Kantō." The Kiryū merchants worked hard to expand the range of marketing the Kiryū fabrics; and they worked hard at social stability too by seeing that the taxes due for all citizens were paid, even in advance, to keep down the troubles that so often erupted into rioting. When the shogunate began to fall, the Kiryū merchants cleverly treated both sides, anti- and pro-shogunate, with equal solicitation, hoping to preserve their business undamaged.

Kiryū's weaving industry was fostered as an early form of Japanese capitalism so that, when the fall of the shogunate threw other cities into confusion and economic recession, Kiryū was not hurt badly. Indeed, its merchants moved aggressively to enter into foreign trade and quickly assimilated forms of Western culture.

The Kiryū industries were also quick to make use of the government loans being offered to promote national wealth and strength. New rail lines gave the town access to wider markets: the Kiryū station on the Ryōmō Line was opened in 1882 (line runs east-west from Oyama in Tochigi Pref. to Takasaki in Gunma Pref.); a spur line to Ashio, site of Japan's most productive copper mining, was laid in 1912; and Kiryū station on the Tōbu Isesaki Line was built in 1913. These lines gave Kiryū access to surrounding districts as well as a connecting route with Tōkyō.

In the early stage of export activity, around 1882–3, Kiryū specialized in exports of traditional *habutae* silks to the U.S.A. By 1893 it was exporting silk prints to India and Australia. In the Taishō period silk and rayon blends were produced for export. Taking the year 1894 as a base of 100, the production scale for Kiryū shows only half the base, or 50, for 1887, but a production rating two and a half times the base level, or 257, by 1913.[113]

Another index to its industrial growth can be seen in the changes of population composition. Of all Kiryū families engaged in some production in 1875, only 18.5% were occupied in industrial production. By 1919 the percentage of industrial families increased to 50%. This took place within an overall population increase in Kiryū ranging from 19,000 in 1897 to 37,674 in 1920.[114] Kiryū was incorporated as a municipality in 1921.

*Ashikaga:* The textile industry of Ashikaga is known to be several centuries old. It is said that Ashikaga fabrics were presented in the dedication ceremony for the Great Buddha (*Daibutsu*) statue of Tōdaiji temple, although the date would be 752 if true. The report may well refer to later ceremonies connected with repairs following earthquakes or fires in the 9th, 12th, 16th and 17th centuries.

In any case, crepe silk and figured prints were produced in Ashikaga during the Bunka and Bunsei eras (1804–30 inclusive) to compete with Kiryū fabrics. The Ashikaga products are referred to as Kiryū fabrics because the Kiryū merchant brokers handled them for marketing. Ashikaga prints were sold to Dutch traders in 1860, the first silk exports from Japan in its history.

Kawafuji Weaving Mill was established in Ashikaga in 1871, and efforts were made at improving dyeing techniques since then. Jacquard looms were imported from France in 1877, greatly increasing production. Marketing was expedited, as in Kiryū, with the completion of the Ryōmō and Tōbu Lines in the area. There were 150 mills in Ashikaga in 1920, by which year the population had risen to 33,637, as against 18,000 in 1897. Like its neighbor Kiryū only nine miles away, Ashikaga was incorporated in 1921.[115]

*Hamamatsu:* As in Ashikaga the town of Hamamatsu had a small-scale weaving industry in the Edo era, though it was also a highway station town, being just midway between Edo and Kyōto on the Tōkaidō route. In 1743 its townsmen numbered 4,300. Toward the end of the Edo era local warriors were engaged in weaving to supplement diminishing incomes.

When the money economy penetrated into Hamamatsu the side jobs in cottage industries were converted into independent industries. In 1884 the Enshū Spinning Company was founded, equipped with imported machines. After the Sino-Japanese War business picked up considerably, and hand looms were replaced by treadle looms. Hamamatsu was not solely dependent upon weaving, however; factories for musical instruments, soft hats, paper and other goods were also constructed.

Banks were opened in the town after the Russo-Japanese War, and electric power was installed in 1904, followed by a town gas supply in 1909. Electric train lines servicing the suburban communities were provided, as Hamamatsu was transformed from a town with cottage industries into a city with large-scale industries using power-driven machinery in production.

The monopoly given Japan over Oriental markets by the outbreak of World War I opened new marketing channels for Hamamatsu fabrics in China, India, Singapore, Thailand, and even Turkey. The overt impetus to industry had commensurate effect on population growth. Data on mills, workers and population are given below:

| Year | Number of looms | Number of mills | Number of workers | Population |
|---|---|---|---|---|
| 1897 | — | — | — | 19,380 |
| 1912–6 | 1,500 | 76 | 3,111 | — |
| 1918–20 | 8,200 | 249 | 8,415 | 64,749 |

Mills and workers tripled in the interval 1916–20, while population tripled in the quarter-century shown. There were few cities that experienced so high a rate of population growth as did Hamamatsu.[116]

(4) Provincial Urban Centers. Our study has centered on gigantic metropolitan centers such as Tōkyō, Ōsaka, and others which performed a multiplicity of functions—political, economic, industrial, transport, military, cultural, and so on—and therefore maintained integrative spheres over whole regions of the nation, over the entire nation, and extending into international society. Such mammoth urban communities had in their integrative orbits suburban areas for residence and industry, and a string of satellite towns. Within the metropolitan areas were farming villages that were thoroughly oriented to commercial production of farm goods to supply the hungry markets of the great cities.

Regional cities that repeated the metropolitan mode on smaller scales have a second place in the order of cities. They too developed industries to fill out their wider ranges of socio-economic and political functions, enabling them to serve as integrative centers for a region, a prefecture, or other extended region.

Then there were cities with specialized functions, industry, trade, transport, or military, that could expand into large-scale urban operations because of the relation of their functions to wider national and international interests. These were the industrial cities, the cities around naval bases, and so on. They did not have the added range of integrative functions over immediately surrounding areas as did the large regional and national cities. Even so, it was surplus farm population that supplied the labor forces needed in these newly expanded cities. The structure of the industrial cities, though, remained comparatively simple and straightforward.

Not all cities managed to adopt specialized industrial functions, but acted mainly as minor cities in the integration of local areas. Most of these were former castle towns, where prefectural offices were placed in the modern period. Because the integrative areas were narrowly confined, population growth in local urban centers was quite slow. The larger the integrative sphere, the greater the interdependence upon other cities; therefore, these cities of only minor integrative range retained a greater degree of self-sufficiency than the large urban centers. They were located mainly in areas where industry was not developed on a large scale, principally in the Tōhoku and Hokuriku regions, where transportation advantages were also scarce.

Sendai, Morioka, Hirosaki, Akita, Aizu Wakamatsu, Yamagata,

Mito, Toyama, Takaoka, Kanazawa, Matsue, Tokushima, and Kumamoto are examples of this lower order of urban centers. Traditional elements remained operative in the social structures of these cities for a long time. The natural and social conditions of the districts in which these cities were located served to retard the growth of existing cities and to discourage the emergence of new cities. Thus the expansion of the above cities, whether in size, population, or multiplicity of functions, was relatively less than in the other cities reviewed in greater detail.

# Epilogue

In our systematic account of the developmental process of the Japanese city we have traced each succeeding stage from the pre-urban conditions of primitive society to the birth of the modern city, focusing especially on the structure and disintegration of the city late in the feudal age and on the emergence of the modern city in the industrial revolution that followed the Meiji transformation. The methods of analysis and synthesis employed and the urban theory evolved from this research, have been elaborated in detail in both Japanese and English. For this theoretical discussion we would again refer the reader to the earlier volumes, *Nihon Toshi no Shakai Riron* and *The Japanese City: A Sociological Analysis*, both published in 1963. We would like to conclude this volume, however, with a few comments on certain key issues that have been fundamental to the research undergirding it.

In most of the urban studies of the past we find a rather static depiction of the cultural structure or socio-economic conditions of the city. The city was generally treated as a fixed, discrete entity abstracted from the socio-cultural system of the larger national society. The need, as we saw it, was to grasp the overall socio-cultural system—on the largest scale, the total national society—within which the urban and rural sectors are found, and at the same time to focus on the urban and rural communities as sub-systems of the larger social system. When national society undergoes change, urban and rural communities are altered; when structural changes appear in the sub-systems, change is induced in the encompassing national society. Our analysis has centered, then, on the importance of these structural interrelationships. This has enabled us, we believe, to grasp more dynamically the reasons for the emergence of cities possessing specific structures and to account more fully for the cultural relativity seen in the existence of cities with different cultural configurations in various societies.

By dealing with the city as a sub-system of the larger society of the nation, not only are the mutual relations between cities and rural communities made clear, but the structural relations of various kinds of cities and rural communities to the capital city as the summit and center of national society come into proper perspective. It is this perspective that is particularly useful in seeing the essential character of the city as the locus of those political, economic, military, educational, religious and communications organs that perform the multiple functions through the exercise of power and authority that weld the total social system of the nation into a cohesive social order. A coordinated structural and functional framework overcomes the methodological deficiencies of both the oversimplified, static approach based on an urban-rural dichotomy, so widely criticized, and the approach oriented to an urban-rural continuum that developed later. Indeed, the way is opened up for a new dimension of urban analysis.

The various political, economic, military and other integrative organs are not only located in the city; they form its core. Because they serve to integrate a wide range of human behavior in the effective accomplishment of their social goals, it is of first importance that they be placed in a central location, allowing maximum accessibility to a wider region in terms of both time and expense. Secondly, the high degree of interdependence among specialized integrative organs demands their concentration in a city center. Thirdly, depending on the relative scale and standing of the organs in a given society, they have various status, roles, and reward systems which inevitably draw qualified personnel into the integrative organizations and, therefore, into the residential sectors of the city. The larger the city, the greater the concentration of large-scale organs in its center; and as functions become increasingly differentiated, the variety and number of organs multiply. The integrative activity of the large metropolitan communities naturally extends over far wider areas than that of lesser cities and towns and, consequently, the big cities attract even larger populations.

The expansion in scale and the increase in numbers and kinds of integrative organs depend in part, of course, on commensurate increases in productivity; but not on that alone. An equally important factor is the form and degree the exercise of power takes in a society. In Japan's history this was evident in the ability of the court officials in the ancient state and of the military leaders in the feudal order to acquire command over a large portion of agricultural production. Similarly, the unprecedented expansion of the modern Japanese city was based upon the bureaucracy's taxing authority and the financiers' accumulative powers with respect to both industrial and agricultural productivity.

As the integrating functions of large cities central to given regions expand, lesser cities and rural communities lose their self-sufficiency and resilience as distinct localities. Becoming sectors within central metropolitan complexes, their functions are further differentiated and specialized. Many local urban and rural communities are drawn into a high degree of organic relationship to the central metropolitan community of a given region. That is, they are included within the expanding integrative scope of the core city.

Using the concepts of integrative organs to trace the structural relationships of a larger social system and the functional relationships operative over a wide range of social activity, it is possible to break through the lack of precision deriving from former vague ideas of the city and to grasp urban phenomena more concretely and accurately. Moreover, one can comprehend more adequately the nature of change witnessed in urban phenomena.

The city consists of more than the coordination of integrative organs; it also involves the interrelationships of the socio-economic behavior of the people connected with these organs. These characteristics are most appropriately analyzed from the three related vantage points of human ecology, social organization and social controls, as Louis Wirth so ably demonstrated. This trilogy has, of course, been criticized by others, and we have made certain revisions in the light of our own investigations.

Yet, urban research is more than mere cataloging of data related to the city. It is more than contrasting urban with rural, or looking for continuity between these two sectors. The structural and functional interrelatedness of urban and rural communities and of these to large, central metropolitan communities compel us to concentrate on the integrative organs. By doing so, we can grasp the nature of the city as the coordinated functioning of integrative organs that makes the city both an agency of system-maintenance and an agency for inducing social change as well. The social dominance of the ruling class in and through the integrative organs becomes clear, as does the fact that the city is also the aggregate of the socio-economic realities of the people whose lives it embraces.

These are the basic outlines, then, of the analytical methods we have followed in this volume. The city is a massive and complex phenomenon, and the long history of urban development is not easily compressed into the limited confines of a single book. But this work represents our own attempt to appropriate the research efforts of many scholars, in America, Japan and elsewhere, and to organize the data of the Japanese city into as consistent a framework as possible. We have tried to encompass as much relevant factual data as possible, while systematizing it from as comprehensive a theoretical standpoint as we could. In the process, we have also tried to test the theories of others where relevant. If, in addition to providing a substantial amount of data hitherto unknown to the non-Japanese world, we have also been able to suggest new lines for theoretical inquiry, we shall be more than gratified.

# Bibliographical References

[Names of living authors are given in the western order in English, but in the Japanese order in characters.]


I

[1]Kunio Tanaka, *Yayoi-shiki Jōmon-shiki Sesshoku Bunka no Kenkyū*, (1944). *(A study in cultural contacts of Yayoi and Jōmon eras).
[田中国男・弥生式縄文式接触文化の研究]

[2]Teruya Esaka and Kaku Yoshida, "Kaigara-yama Kaizuka," *Kodai Bunka*, XIII, No. 9, (1942). *(The shell-mound of Mt. Kaizuka; The ancient culture).
[江坂輝弥・吉田格・貝柄山貝塚]

[3]Ichirō Kurata, "Gyokakubutsu Bunpai toshiteno Mondai," *Minzokugaku Kenkyū*, New I, Nos. 9, 10 & 12, (1943). *(Problems in shares in fishery; Study in ethnology).
[倉田一郎・魚獲物分配としての問題]

[4]Tadashi Saitō, "Genshi," *Nihon Zenshi*, I, 19, (Tōkyō University Press, Tōkyō, 1958). *(The primitive time; The history of Japan).
[斎藤　忠・原始]

[5]Tadaaki Ono, "Zenshi-jidai no Shūraku," *Rekishi Chiri Kōza*, (Asakura-shoten, Tokyo, 1957). *(Groups of dwellings in the pre-historic era; Lectures on history and geography).
[小野忠凞・先史時代の集落]

[6]Seiji Seino and Kanji Kanetaka, "Mikawanokuni Yoshiko Kaizukajin no Basshi oyobi Shiga-henkei no Fūshū ni tsuite," *Shizengaku Zasshi*, I, No, 3, (1929). *(Customs of dwellers of shell-mounds of Yoshiko [Shizuoka-ken] in pulling teeth and operation on teeth).
[清野清次・金高勘次・三河国吉胡貝塚人の抜歯及歯牙変形の風習に就て]

[7]Masao Suenaga, Yukio Kobayashi and Kenjirō Fujioka, "Yamato Karako Yayoi-shiki Iseki no Kenkyū," *Kōkogaku Kenkyū Hōkoku*, No. 16, (Kyōto Teikoku Daigaku Bungaku-bu). *(A study in the site of Karako, Nara-ken; A report on study in archaeology by the Department of Literature, Kyōto Imperial University).
[末永雅雄・小林行雄・藤岡謙次郎・大和唐古弥生式遺跡の研究]

[8]Nihon Kōkogaku Kyōkai, *Toro*, (Mainichi Shinbun Co., Tōkyō, 1954). *(The site of Toro; compiled by the Institute of Archaeology of Japan).
[日本考古学協会編・登呂]

[9]Yukio Kobayashi, *Nihon Kōkogaku Gaisetsu* (Sogen-sha, Tōkyō, 1951). *(A summary of archaeology in Japan).
[小林行雄・日本考古学概説]

[10]Heijirō Nakayama, "Ishi Hōchō Seizōsho-ato no Chikuzen Iizuka-shi ōaza Tateiwa aza Yakenosho Iseki," *Kōkogaku* V, No. 5, (1934). *(The remains of shops of stone cutlery in the site of Yakenosho, Tateiwa, Iizuka-shi, Fukuoka-ken).
[中山平次郎・石庖製造所址の筑前飯塚市大字立岩字焼ノ正遺跡]

[11]Utarō Yoshida, "Niizawa-mura Sekki-jidai Iseki Hōkoku," *Nara-ken Shiseki Chōsa Hōkoku*, No. 10, (1928). *(A report on the site of the stone age in Niizawa-mura; Survey reports on sites in Nara-ken).
[吉田宇太郎・新沢村石器時代遺跡報告]

[12]Rokuya Morimoto, "Seidōki no Chūzo—sono Shiryō no raretsuteki na Kisai," *Kōkogaku* IV, No. 4, (1933). *(Casting of bronze utensils, marshalling materials collected).
[森本六爾・青銅器の鋳造—其の資料の羅列的な記載]

[13]"Chikuzen Suku Shizen-iseki no Kenkyū," *Kōkogaku Kenkyū Hōkoku*, No. 11, (Kyōto Teikoku Daigaku Bungaku-bu, 1930). *(A study in the site of pre-historic age in Suku, Fukuoka-ken; Study in archaeology, Department of Literature, Kyōto Imperial University).
[筑前須玖史前遺跡の研究]

[14]Moriichi Gotō, "Kozuke-no-kuni Sawa-gōri Akabori-mura Imai Chausubako Kofun," *Teishitsu Hakubutsukan Gakuhō*, No. 6, (1933). *(The site of Chausubako, Imai, Akabori-mura, Sawa-gōri, Kōzuke-no-kuni; Bulletin of the Imperial Museum).
[後藤守一・上野国佐波郡赤堀村今井茶臼函古墳]

[15]Seiichi Wajima, "Tōkyō-shi-nai Shimura ni okeru Genshi-jidai Tateana no Chōsa Hōkoku," *Kōko Zasshi* XXVIII, No. 9, (1938). *(A survey report on the remains of pit dwellings of primitive times in the site of Shimura of Tōkyō).
[和島誠一・東京市内志村に於ける原始時代竪穴の調査報告]

[16]Kizaemon Ariga, "Nihon Jōdai no Ie to Sonraku," *Tōa Shakai Kenkyū*, 63–6. *(Houses and villages in ancient Japan).
[有賀喜左衛門・日本上代の家と村落]

[17]Shinobu Origuchi, *Kodai Kenkyū*, I, 191, (Chūōkōron-sha, Tōkyō, 1954). *(Ancient Studies).
[折口信夫・古代研究]

[18]Kichiji Nakamura, *Nihon Keizaishi*, 67–8, (Nihonhyōron-shinsha, Tōkyō, 1955–7). *(The economic history of Japan).
[中村吉治・日本経済史]

[19]———, *ibid.*, 67–71.
[中村吉治・日本経済史]

[20]Takeichirō Fukuo, *Nihon Kazoku-seido-shi* 12, (Yoshikawa-kōbunkan, Tōkyō, 1954). *(History of the family system in Japan).
[福尾猛市郎・日本家族制度史]

[21]Tadashi Saitō, *op. cit.*, 271–3.
[斎藤　忠・原始]

[22]Mataji Miyamoto, *Nihon Shōgyōshi Gairon*, 9–15, (Sekaishisō-sha, Kyōto, 1954). *(Outline of the history of commerce in Japan).
[宮本又次・日本商業史概論]

[23]Kijirō Satō, *Jōdai no Teito no Iseki*, 5–6, (Sankyō-shinsha, Tōkyō, 1940) *(The sites of ancient imperial capitals in Japan).
[佐藤喜次郎・上代の帝都の遺跡]

[24]Shigejirō Ōi, *Jōdai no Teito*, 53–4, (Ritsumeikan Press, Kyōto, 1944). *(Imperial capitals in ancient Japan).
[大井重二郎・上代の帝都]

[25]Noboru Ōrui and Masao Toba, *Nihon Jōkaku-shi*, 66, (Yūzankaku, Tōkyō, 1936). *(A history of castles in Japan).
[大類　伸・鳥羽正雄・日本城郭史]

[26]Teikichi Kita, *Teito*, 1–22, (Nihon Gakujutsu Fukyū Kai, Tōkyō, 1916). *(Imperial capitals).
[喜田貞吉・帝都]

[27]Shigejirō Ōi, *op. cit.*, 91–3.
[大井重二郎・上代の帝都]

II

[1]Ōsaka Shiritsu Daigaku, *Naniwa-gūchi no Kenkyū*, (Ōsaka Shiritsu University Naniwa-Gūchi Kenkyūkai, Ōsaka, 1958). *(A study in the capital of Naniwa by Ōsaka Municipal University).
[大阪市立大学・難波宮地の研究]

[2]Teikichi Kita, *Teito*, 66.
[喜田貞吉・帝都]

[3]Shigejirō Ōi, *Jōdai no Teito*, 153–4.
[大井重二郎・上代の帝都]

[4]Teikichi Kita, *op. cit.*, 144–88.
[喜田貞吉・帝都]

[5]Shūichi Kishiro, "Jōdai-toshi-seikatsu no Tenkai," *Shin Nihonshi*, (Fukumura-shoten, Tōkyō, 1953). *(Development of urban life in ancient times, New history of Japan; Nara and Heian Era.)
[木代修一・上代都市生活の展開]

[6]Goichi Sawada, *Narachō-jidai Minseikeizai no Sūteki-kenkyū*, Chapter XVII, (Settsu-bunko, Tōkyō, 1927). *(Numerical study in economy of common people in the Nara era).
[沢田吾一・奈良朝時代民政経済の数的研究]

[7]Shigejirō Ōi, *op. cit.*, 184–5.
[大井重二郎・上代の帝都]

[8]Katsu Sekino, *Nihon Jūtaku Shōshi*, 52, (Sagami-shobō, Tōkyō, 1942). *(A short history of Japanese residences).
[関野　克・日本住宅小史]

[9]Ijirō Fujishima, *Nihon no Kenchiku*, (Shibun-do, Tōkyō 1958). *(Architecture of Japan).
[藤島亥次郎・日本の建築]

[10]Akira Seki and Kazuo Aoki, "Heijōkyō," *Nihon Rekishi Kōza*, (Tōkyō University Press, Tōkyō, 1959). *(Lectures on Japanese history)
[関晃・青木和夫・平城京]

[11]———, *ibid.*
[関晃・青木和夫・平城京]

[12]———, *ibid.*
[関晃・青木和夫・平城京]

[13]Shūichi Kishiro, "Heijōkyō ni okeru Kōbō ni tsuite," *Shichō*, IV, No. 3. *(Workshops in Heijōkyō, Historical Tide).
[木代修一・平城京に於ける工房に就て]

[14]———, "Heijōkyō Toshi-seikatsu no Ichikōsatsu," *Shichō*, I, No. 3. *(A study in the urban life in Heijōkyō).
[木代修一・平城京都市生活の一考察]

[15]Shūichi Murayama, *Nihon Toshi-seikatsu no Genryū*, 3, (Seki-shoin, Kyōto, 1953). *(The origin of urban life in Japan).
[村山修一・日本都市生活の源流]

[16]Shūichi Kishiro, "Heijōkyō Toshiseikatsu no Ichikōsatsu," *Shichō*, I, No. 3.
[木代修一・平城京都市生活の一考察]

[17]Mataji Miyamoto, *Nihon Shōgyōshi Gairon*, 15–34, (Sekaishisō-sha, Kyōto 1954). *(Outline of the history of commerce in Japan).
[宮本又次・日本商業史概論]

[18]Keiji Misaka, *Kokubō Kokufu no Kenkyū*, *(Study in the defense of Kokufu).
[三坂圭治・国防国府の研究]

Kenjirō Fujioka, *Toshi to Kōtsuro no Rekishichiriteki Kenkyū*, 43–50, (Daimei-dō, Tōkyō, 1960) *(A historical and geographical study of the cities and traffic routes).
[藤岡謙次郎・都市と交通路の歴史地理的研究]

[19]Takeshi Kagamiyama, *Kitakyūshū no Kodai Iseki*, 143–96, (Shibun-dō, Tōkyō, 1956). *(Ancient sites in North Kyūshū).
[鏡山　猛・北九州の古代遺跡]

[20]Tadashi Saitō, "Saikin ni okeru Tojōshi no Kenkyū," *Nihon no Machi*, (Yuzankaku, Tōkyō, 1958). *(A recent study on sites of castles in old cities: Towns in Japan).
[斎藤　忠・最近に於ける都城址の研究]

[21]Tarō Sakamoto, *Jōdai Ekisei no Kenkyū*, 1–106, (Kokushi Kenkyū-sōsho, Tōkyō, 1928). *(Study of the station system of ancient times).
[坂本太郎・上代駅制の研究]

[22]Nobujirō Ōshima, *Nihon Kōtsūshi Gaisetsu*, 18–26, (Hōbun-kan, Tōkyō, 1953). *(A summarized history of traffic in Japan)
[大島延次郎・日本交通史概説]

[23]———, *Nihon Toshi Hattatsushi*, 152–6, (Hōbun-kan, Tōkyō, 1954). *(History of development of the Japanese city).
[大島延次郎・日本都市発達史]

[24]Goichi Sawada, *op. cit.*, 296.
[沢田吾一・奈良朝時代経済の数的研究]

[25]Teikichi Kita, *op. cit.*, 222–334.
[喜田貞吉・帝都]

[26]Tarō Wakamori, "Heian Jidai no Seiji," *Shin Nihon Shi*, (Inamura-shoten, Tōkyō, 1953). *(Politics in the Heian era; New history of Japan).
[和歌森太郎・平安時代の政治]

[27]Tatsusaburō Hayashiya, "Heiankyō no Keizaiteki Shichū," (Tōkyō University Press, Tōkyō, 1955), *(Economic support of Heiankyō).
[林屋辰三郎・平安京の経済的支柱]

[28]Shūichi Murayama, *Nihon Toshi-seikatsu no Genryū*, 38.
[村山修一・日本都市生活の源流]

[29]Tomohiko Harada, *Chūsei ni okeru Toshi no Kenkyū*, 143, (Kōdan-sha, Tōkyō, 1932). *(A study of the city of the Middle Ages).
[原田伴彦・中世に於ける都市の研究]

[30]Shūichi Murayama, *Heiankyō*, 516.
[村山修一・平安京]

[31]Teikichi Kita, *op. cit.*, 283–300.
[喜田貞吉・帝都]

Motoharu Fujita, *Heiankyō Hensenshi; Tojō-kō*, (Tōkō-shoin, Tōkyō, 1929). *(The history of Heiankyō; The capital).
[藤田元春・平安京変遷史・都城考]

[32]Katsu Sekino, *Nihon Jūtaku Shōshi*, 81–2, (Sagami-shobō, Tōkyō, 1942). *(A short history of Japanese residences.).
[関野　克・日本住宅小史]

[33]Kaneyuki Miura, *Hōseishi no Kenkyū*, 705–18, (Iwanami-shoten, Tōkyō, 1943–4). *(Study in the history of legislation).
[三浦周行・法制史の研究]

[34]Kunihiko Fujiki, "Heian Jidai no Fūzoku," *Kōza Nihon Fūzokushi*, (Yūzankaku, Tōkyō, 1959). *(Manners and customs in Heian era; Lectures on the history of Japanese manners and customs).
[藤木邦彦・平安時代の風俗]

[35]Takeshi Abe, "Heiankyō no Keizaikōzō," *Kokumin Seikatsu Shi Kenkyū* (Yoshikawa-kōbunkan, Tōkyō, 1959), *(Economic structure of Heiankyō; Study in the history of national life).
[阿部　猛・平安京の経済構造]

[36]———, *ibid.*
[阿部　猛・平安京の経済構造]

[37]SHŪICHI MURAYAMA, *Heiankyō*, 9–10.
[村山修一・平安京]

[38]TATSUSABURŌ HAYASHIYA, "Heiankyō ni okeru Juryō no Seikatsu," *Kodai Kokka no Kaitai*, (Tōkyō University Press, Tōkyō, 1955). *(The life of Juryō in Heiankyō; Disintegration of the ancient state).
[林屋辰三郎・平安京に於ける受領の生活]

[39]SHŪICHI MURAYAMA, *Nihon Toshi-seikatsu no Genryū*, 64–6, (Seki-shoin, Kyōto, 1953). *(The origin of urban life in Japan).
[村山修一・日本都市生活の源流]

[40]SOGORŌ UOZUMI, *Kyōto Shiwa*, 31–9, (Shōka-sha, Kyōto, 1936). *(Historical tales of Kyōto).
[魚澄惣五郎・京都史話]

[41]TEIKICHI KITA, *op. cit.*, 266–9.
[喜田貞吉・帝都]

[42]TAKESHI ABE, *op. cit.*
[阿部　猛・平安京の経済構造]

[43]TEIKICHI KITA, *op. cit.*, 266–7.
[喜田貞吉・帝都]

[44]SHŪICHI MURAYAMA, *Nihon Toshi-seikatsu no Genryū*, 47.
[村山修一・日本都市生活の源流]

[45]MATAJI MIYAMOTO, *Nihon Shōgyōshi Gairon*, 40–55, (Sekaishisō-sha, Kyōto, 1954). *(Outline of the history of commerce in Japan).
[宮本又次・日本商業史概論]

III

[1]KAMAKURA-SHI, *Kamakura Shishi; Sōsetsu-hen*, 325–6, (Kamakura-shishi Hensan Iinkai, Kamakura, 1956). *(The history of Kamakura; General features). I am indebted for most of my explanations on Kamakura to the references in this list by Mr. Kawakami (6) for population and social control and by Mr. Endo (2) for the organization of commerce and industry.
[鎌 倉 市・鎌倉市史総説編]

[2]MOTO-O ENDŌ, "Chūsei ni okeru Toshi Kamakura no Hattensō," *Rekishi Kyōiku*, VIII, No. 5. *(Development of Kamakura in the Middle Ages; Education in history).
[遠藤元男・中世に於ける都市鎌倉の発展相]

[3]——, *Chūsei Toshi-ron*, 112, (Hakuyō-sha, Tōkyō, 1940). *(Cities in the Middle Ages).
[遠藤元男・中世都市論]

[4]TAKAYA NAKAMURA, *Chūsei Sesōshi*, 52, (Yūzankaku, Tōkyō, 1949). *(Social conditions of the Middle Ages).
[中村孝也・中世世相史]

[5]MOTO-O ENDŌ, *op. cit.*
[遠藤元男・中世に於ける都市鎌倉の発展相]

[6]TASUKE KAWAKAMI, "Toshi to shite no Kamakura," *Shirin*, III, No. 4. *(Kamakura as a city).
[川上多助・都市としての鎌倉]

[7]MOTO-O ENDŌ, *op. cit.*
[遠藤元男・中世に於ける都市鎌倉の発展相]

[8]SHŪICHI MURAYAMA, *Nihon Toshi-seikatsu no Genryū*, 69–86.
[村山修一・日本都市生活の源流]

[9]TOSHIHIDE AKAMATSU, "Machi Za no Seiritsu ni tsuite," *Nihon Rekishi*, (Tōkyō University Press, 1962). *(Establishment of the *Za* cooperatives in towns; The history of Japan).
[赤松俊秀・町座の成立に就て]

[10]SHŪICHI MURAYAMA, *op. cit.*, 87–92,
[村山修一・日本都市生活の源流]

[11]———, *ibid.*, 92–3.
[村山修一・日本都市生活の源流]

[12]GEN ITABASHI, *Ōshū Hiraizumi*, 130–2, (Shibun-dō, Tōkyō, 1961).
[板橋　源・奥州平泉]

[13]NOBUJIRŌ ŌSHIMA, *Nihon Toshi Hattatsushi*, 110–11, (Hōbun-kan, Tōkyō, 1954). *(History of development of the Japanese city).
[大島延次郎・日本都市発達史]

[14]———, *Nihon Kōtsūshi Gaisetsu*, 45, (Hōbun-kan, Tōkyō, 1953). *(A summarized history of traffic in Japan).
[大島延次郎・日本交通史概説]

[15]——, *ibid.*
[大島延次郎・日本交通史概説]

[16]TAKAYA NAKAMURA, *op. cit.*, 60.
[中村孝也・中世世相史]

[17]RINTARŌ IMAI, "Chūsei ni okeru Bushi no Yashikichi," *Shakai Keizaishi*, I, No. 4. *(House lots of warriors in the Middle Ages; Socio-economic history).
[今井林太郎・中世に於ける武士の屋敷地]

[18]NOBORU ŌRUI and MASAO TOBA, *Nihon Jōkakushi*, 204–5, (Yūzankaku, Tōkyō, 1936). *(A history of castles in Japan).
[大類　伸・鳥羽正雄・日本城郭史]

[19]YUKIO ASAKA, "Chūsei no Shūraku," *Rekishi-chiri*, *(Living centers in the Middle Ages; Historical geography in Japan).
[浅香幸雄・中世の集落]

[20]———, *ibid.*
[浅香幸雄・中世の集落]

[21]TAKESHI TOYOTA, *Nihon no Hōkentoshi*, 50–2, (Iwanami-shoten, Tōkyō 1952). *(A history of feudal cities in Japan).
[豊田　武・日本の封建都市]

[22]———, *Chūsei Nihon Shōgyōshi no Kenkyū*, 112–8, (Iwanami-shoten, Tōkyō, 1952). *(Study in the history of commerce in the Middle Ages of Japan). This work contains precise descriptions of the distribution of markets.
[豊田　武・中世日本商業史の研究]

[23]TOMOHIKO HARADA, *Chūsei ni okeru Toshi no Kenkyū*, 24, (Kōdansha, Tōkyō, 1932). *(A study of the city of the Middle Ages).
[原田伴彦・中世に於ける都市の研究]

[24]TAKESHI TOYOTA, *op. cit.*, 28.
[豊田　武・日本の封建都市]

## IV

[1]SŌGORŌ UOZUMI, *Kyōto Shiwa*, 211–3, (Shōka-sha, Kyōto, 1936). *(Historical tales of Kyōto).
[魚澄惣五郎・京都史話]

[2]SHŪICHI MURAYAMA, *Nihon Toshi-seikatsu no Genryū*, 112, (Seki-shoin, Kyōto, 1953). *(The origin of urban life in Japan).
[村山修一・日本都市生活の源流]

[3]———, *ibid.*, 116–20.
[村山修一・日本都市生活の源流]

[4]———, *ibid.*, 127–32.
[村山修一・日本都市生活の源流]

[5]———, *ibid.*, 124–6.
[村山修一・日本都市生活の源流]

[6]TEIKICHI KITA, *Teito*, 275, (Nihon Gakujutsu Fukyū Kai, Tōkyō, 1916). *(Imperial capitals).
[喜田貞吉・帝都]

[7]TAKAYA NAKAMURA, *Chūsei Sesōshi*, 265. (Yūzankaku, Tōkyō, 1949). *(Social conditions of the Middle Ages).
[中村孝也・中世世相史]

[8]KAMAKURA-SHI, *Kamakura Shishi; Sōsetsu-hen*, 537–40, (Kamakura-shi-shi Hensan Iinkai, Kamakura, 1956–8). *(The history of Kamakura; General features).
[鎌 倉 市・鎌倉市史：総説篇]

[9]AKITSUGU ONO, "Chūsei ni okeru Nara Monzenmachi Ichiba," *Shigaku Zasshi*, XLV, No, 5. *(Markets in the temple town of Nara in the Middle Ages; Historical bulletin).
[小野晃嗣・中世に於ける奈良門前市場]

[10]TOMOHIKO HARADA, "Chūsei Jisha-shihai no Seikaku to sono Hensen," *Nihon Hōkentaiseika no Toshi to Shakai*, (Sanichi-shobō, Tōkyō). *(Changes in the nature of temple controls; City and society in the feudal system of Japan).
[原田伴彦・中世寺社支配の性格と其の変遷]

[11]UJI-YAMADA-SHI, *Uji-yamada Shishi*, I, 1–85, (Uji-yamada-shi, 1929). *(The history of Uji-yamada-shi).
[宇治山田市・宇治山田市史]

[12]TOMOHIKO HARADA, *Chūsei ni okeru Toshi no Kenkyū*, 136, (Kōdan-sha, Tōkyō, 1932) *(A study of the city in the Middle Ages).
[原田伴彦・中世に於ける都市の研究]

[13]NAGANO-SHI, *Nagano Shishi*, 12–78, (Nagano-shiyakusho, 1925). *(The history of Nagano).
[長 野 市・長野市史]

[14]TOMOHIKO HARADA, *Chūsei ni okeru Toshi no Kenkyū*, 134.
[原田伴彦・中世に於ける都市の研究]

[15]NOBUJIRŌ ŌSHIMA, *Nihon Toshi Hattatsushi*, 73, (Hōbun-kan, Tōkyō, 1954). *(History of development of the Japanese city).
[大島延次郎・日本都市発達史]

[16]SHINNOSUKE MAKINO, "Chūsei Jishamachi no Hattatsu," *Tochi oyobi Shūraku Shijo no Shomondai*, (Kawade-shobō, Tōkyō, 1938). *(Development of the temple town in the Middle Ages; Historical study in problems of the land and living centers).
[牧野信之助・中世寺社町の発達]

[17]KENJIRŌ FUJIOKA, "Jishamachi no Seikaku," *Jinbun Chiri*, I. *(The character of the temple towns; Cultural geography).
[藤岡謙次郎・寺社町の性格]

[18]SHINNOSUKE MAKINO, *Bukejidai Shakai no Kenkyū*, 376–407, (Tōkō-shoin, Tōkyō, 1928). *(Study of society in the age of feudalism).
[牧野信之助・武家時代社会の研究]

[19]KAZUO HIGO, *Miyaza no Kenkyū*, 579–80, (Tōkyō Bunrika University, Tokyo, 1938). *(Study in shrine cooperatives).
[肥後和男・宮座の研究]

[20]SHINNOSUKE MAKINO, *Bukejidai Shakai no Kenkyū*, 368–75.
[牧野信之助・武家時代社会の研究]

[21]TAKESHI TOYOTA, *Chūsei Nihon Shōgyōshi no Kenkyū*, 318, (Iwanami-shoten, Tōkyō, 1944). *(Study in the history of commerce in the Middle Ages).
[豊田　武・中世日本商業史の研究]

[22]———, *ibid.*, 320.
[豊田　武・中世日本商業史の研究]

[23]———, *ibid.*, 324.
[豊田　武・中世日本商業史の研究]

[24]Masao Toba, "Chūseimakki ni okeru Toshi no Hassei-katei," *Jinbun-chirigaku Nenpō, Toshichiri Kenkyū*, (Tōkō-shoin, Tōkyō, 1929). *(The process of urban development in the Late Middle Ages; Annual bulletin of cultural geography, study in urban geography).
[鳥羽正雄・中世末期に於ける都市の発生過程]

[25]Saitama-ken, *Saitama-ken Shi*, I, 440–41, (Saitama-ken Kyōiku Shinkō Kyōkai, 1951). *(Annals of Saitama-ken).
[埼 玉 県・埼玉県誌]

[26]Takeshi Toyota, *Nihon no Hōkentoshi*, 33, (Iwanami-shoten, Tōkyō, 1952). *(A history of feudal cities in Japan).
[豊田 武・日本の封建都市]

[27]Noboru Ōrui and Masao Toba, *Nihon Jōkakushi*, 419–32, (Yūzankaku, Tōkyō, 1936). *(A history of castles in Japan).
[大類 伸・鳥羽正雄・日本城郭史]

[28]Tomohiko Harada, *Chūsei ni okeru Toshi no Kenkyū*, 92, (Kōdansha, Tōkyō, 1932). *(A study of the city of the Middle Ages).
[原田伴彦・中世に於ける都市の研究]

[29]———, *ibid.*, 94.
[原田伴彦・中世に於ける都市の研究]

[30]Masaharu Kawai, "Jōkamachi Seiritsu no Mondai," *Daimyō Ryōkoku to Jōkamachi*, (Yanahara-shoten, Tōkyō, 1957). *(Formation of castle towns; Feudal domain and the castle town).
[河合正治・城下町成立の問題]

[31]Tomohiko Harada, "Chūsei—Chūsei Toshi no Kōsei," *Rekishi Chiri Kōza*, (Asakura-shoten, Tōkyō, 1957). *(The Middle Ages—structure of the city; Lectures on history and geography).
[原田伴彦・中世―中世都市の構成]

[32]Fujō Nomura, "Sengokujidai ni okeru Odawara Shakai," *Keizaishigaku.* *(Odawara society in the Age of Civil Wars; Socio-economic history).
[野村晋城・戦国時代に於ける小田原社会]

[33]Tomohiko Harada, "Sengoku Daimyō to Toshi Minshū," *Hōkentoshi no Kenkyū*, (Tōkyō University Press, Tōkyō, 1957). *(War lords in the Age of Civil Wars and common people in the city; Studies in feudal cities).
[原田伴彦・戦国大名と都市民衆]

[34]Tsunezo Araki, *Sengokujidai no Kōtsū*, 27–8, (Unebi-shobō, Tōkyō, 1943). *(Transportation in the Age of Civil Wars).
[新城常三・戦国時代の交通]

[35]Takeshi Toyota, *Nihon no Hōkentoshi*, 39–42.
[豊田 武・日本の封建都市]

[36]Noboru Ōrui and Masao Toba, *op. cit.*, 403.
[大類 伸・鳥羽正雄・日本城郭史]

[37]Hitoshi Ono, *Kinsei Jōkamachi no Kenkyū*, 29, (Shibun-dō, Tōkyō, 1928). *(Study in the castle town of the Edo period).
[小野 均・近世城下町の研究]

[38]Masao Toba, "Chūseimakki ni okeru Toshi no Hassei-katei," *Jinbun-chirigaku Nenpō, Toshichiri Kenkyū*, (Tōkō-shoin, Tōkyō, 1929). *(The process of urban development in the Late Middle Ages; Annual bulletin of cultural geography, study in urban geography).
[鳥羽正雄・中世末期に於ける都市の発生過程]

[39]Tsunezo Araki, *op. cit.*, 231.
[新城常三・戦国時代の交通]

[40]Tatsusaburo Hayashiya, "Machishū no Seiritsu," *Chūseibunka no Kichō*, (Tōkyō University Press, Tōkyō, 1960). *(Emergence of influential citizens; Foundation of culture in the Middle Ages).
[林屋辰三郎・町衆の成立]

41SHŪICHI MURAYAMA ,*op. cit.*, 293–4.
[村山修一・日本都市の源流]

42FUKUTARŌ NAGASHIMA, "Toshijichi no Genkai, Nara no Baai," *Shakai-keizai*, XVII, No. 3. *(Limits of self-government in the city, the case of Nara; Social economy).
[永島福太郎・都市自治の限界，奈良の場合]

43UJI-YAMADA-SHI, *Uji-yamada Shishi*, I, 96–102, (Uji-yamada-Shiyakusho, 1929). *(The history of Uji-yamada-shi).
[宇治山田市・宇治山田市史]

44TAKESHI TOYOTA, *Chūsei Nihon Shōgyōshi no Kenkyū*, 370–7, (Iwanami-shoten, Tokyo, 1952). *(Study in the history of commerce in the Middle Ages).
[豊田　武・中世日本商業史の研究]

45———, *Sakai*, 1–73, (Shibun-dō, Tōkyō, 1957).
[豊田　武・堺]

KANEYUKI MIURA, *Sakai Shishi*, I, II. (1929–1931). I am indebted to the above two authors for freely quoting materials in my descriptions.
[三浦周行・堺市史]

46TAKESHI TOYOTA, "Hirano to Sueyoshi Ke," *Rekishigaku Kenkyū*, III, No. 5. *(The Hirano and Sueyoshi families; Study in historiography).
[豊田　武・平野と末吉家]

V

1TOSHIKI IMAI, "Jōkamachi no Chiriteki-jōken," *Toshi Hattatsushi Kenkyū*, (Tōkyō University Press, Tōkyō, 1951). *(Geographical conditions of the castle town; Study in the development of the city).
[今井登志喜・城下町の地理的条件]

2TOMOHIKO HARADA, "Kinsei Toshi no Keisei," *Nihon Hōkentoshi Kenkyū*, (Tōkyō University Press, Tōkyō, 1957). *(Formation of the city in the Edo period; Study in the feudal cities in Japan).
[原田伴彦・近世都市の形成]

3KENJIRŌ FUJIOKA, "Nihon ni okeru Toshibunpu no Ritchi to Hensen," *Toshi Mondai* (Tōkyō-shisei-chosakai, Tōkyō). *(Changes in the distribution of Japan cities; Urban problems).
[藤岡謙次郎・日本に於ける都市分布の立地と変遷]

4ŌSAKA-SHI, *Ōsaka Shishi*, I, 14, (Ōsakashi-sanjikai, 1913). *(The history of Ōsaka).
[大 阪 市・大阪市史]

5TŌGO YOSHIDA, *Ishinshi Hakkō*, 25, (Fuzanbō, Tōkyō, 1911). *(Eight articles on the history of the Meiji Restoration).
[吉田東伍・維新史八講]

6NAOTARŌ SEKIYAMA, *Kinsei Nihon no Jinkōkōzō*, 153–86, (Yoshikawa-kōbunkan, Tōkyō, 1958). *(Population structure of Japan in the Edo period).
[関山直太郎・近世日本の人口構造]

7SHIGETOMO KŌDA, "Edo no Chōnin no Jinkō," *Shakai-keizai Shigaku*, VIII, No. 1. *(Townsmen population of Edo; Socio-economic history).
[幸田成友・江戸の町人の人口]

8TŌGO YOSHIDA, "Edo no Chiri," *Edo Jidaishi Ron* (Nihon Rekishichiri Gakkai, Tōkyō, 1915). *(Geography of Edo; History of Edo era).
[吉田東伍・江戸の地理]

9KANAZAWA-SHI, *Kanazawa-shi Kiyō*, 144–5, (Kanazawa-shiyakusho, 1923). *(Annals of Kanazawa).
[金 沢 市・金沢市紀要]

10NAGOYA-SHI, *Nagoya-shishi; Seiji-hen*, (Nagoya-shi, 1953–8). *(The history of Nagoya; Politics).
[名古屋市・名古屋市史]

11 KAGOSHIMA-SHI, *Kagoshima no Oitachi*, 310, (Kagoshima-shiyakusho, 1955). *(The history of Kagoshima).
[鹿児島市・鹿児島のおいたち]

12 MASAHARU KAWAI, "Jōkamachi Seiritsu no Mondai," *Daimyō Ryōkoku to Jōkamachi* (Yanahara-shoten, Tōkyō, 1957). *(Formation of castle towns; Feudal domain and the castle town).
[河合正治・城下町成立の問題]

13 OKAYAMA-SHI, *Okayama-shishi*, 21–32, (Okayama-shiyakusho, 1936). *(The history of Okayama).
[岡 山 市・岡山市史]

14 TAKESHI TOYOTA, *Nihon no Hōkentoshi*, 148, (Iwanami-shoten, Tōkyō, 1952). *(A history of feudal cities in Japan).
[豊田　武・日本の封建都市]

15 KŌTA KODAMA, *Shukueki*, 177–208, (Shibundō, Tōkyō, 1960). *(Highway stations).
[児玉幸多・宿駅]

16 RYŌICHI FURUTA, "Wagakuni Kinsei ni okeru Kokunai-kaiun no Hattatsu," *Keizaishi Kenkyū*. *(Development of domestic marine transportation in the feudal age in Japan; Study in the history of economy).
[古田良一・我国近世に於ける国内海運の発達]

17 EIJIRŌ HONJŌ, *Jinkō oyobi Jinkōmondai*, 98–158, (Nihonhyōron-sha, Tōkyō, 1930). *(Population and its problems).
[本庄栄治郎・人口及び人口問題]

18 TAKESHI TOYOTA, *op. cit.*, 7–8.
[豊田　武・日本の封建都市]

19 EIJIRŌ HONJŌ, *op. cit.*, 96–8.
[本床栄治郎・人口及び人口問題]

20 AKITSUGU ONO, "Kinseitoshi no Hattatsu," *Nihon Rekishi*, (Iwanami-shoten, Tokyo, 1930). *(Development of the cities in the Edo period; The history of Japan).
[小野晃嗣・近世都市の発達]

21 OGIŪ SORAI, "Taiheisaku," *Nihon Keizaisōsho*, III, 555, (Nihonkeizai-sōsho-kankōkai, Tōkyō, 1915). *(Peace policy; Library of Japanese economy).
[荻生徂徠・太平策]

22 ———, "Seidan," *Nihon Keizaisōsho*, III, 345, *(Political talks).
[荻生徂徠・政談]

23 SHIGETOMO KŌDA, *op. cit.*
[幸田成友・江戸の町人の人口]

24 NAOTARŌ SEKIYAMA, *op. cit.*, 221–2.
[関山直太郎・近世日本の人口構造]

25 KURUME-SHI, *Kurume-shishi*, I, 29–30, (Miki Toda, Tōkyō, 1894). *(The history of Kurume).
[久留米市・久留米市誌]

26 KŌCHI-SHI *Kōchi-shishi*, I, 368–9, (Kōchi-shishi-hensan Iinkai, 1958). *(The history of Kōchi).
[高 知 市・高知市史]

27 MATSUMOTO-SHI, *Matsumoto-shishi*, 766. (Matsumoto-shiyakusho, 1933). *(The history of Matsumoto).
[松 本 市・松本市史]

28 HIMEJI-SHI, *Himeji-shishi*, 5, (Harima-shidankai, 1919). *(The history of Himeji).
[姫 路 市・姫路市史]

29 FUKUI-SHI, *Fukui-shishi*, 19–24, (Fukui-shiyakusho, 1941). *(The history of Fukui).
[福 井 市・福井市史]

[30]ŌGAKI-SHI, *Ōgaki-shishi*, I, 56, 429, 520, (*Ōgaki-shi*, 1930). *(The history of Ōgaki).
[大 垣 市・大垣市史]

[31]TAKADA-SHI, *Takada-shishi*, 222–4, (Takada-shishi-hensan Iinkai, 1958). *(The history of Takada).
[高 田 市・高田市史]

[32]FUJIO SHIMOMURA, "Kinseitoshi no Mibunbetsu Jinkōkōsei ni tsuite," *Shakai-keizai-shigaku*, III, No. 9. *(Population structure according to status; Socio-economic history).
[下村富士男・近世都市の身分別人口構成に就て]

[33]GŌHEI ITŌ, *Chihōtoshi no Kenkyū*, 19, (Kokon-shoin, Tōkyō, 1954). *(Study of local cities).
[伊藤郷平・地方都市の研究]

[34]TAKESHI TOYOTA, *op. cit.*, 152.
[豊田 武・日本の封建都市]

[35]SUMIO TANIGUCHI, "Jōkamachi Okayama no Seiritsu," *Daimyō Ryōkoku to Jōkamachi*, (Yanahara-shoten, Kyōto, 1957). *(Establishment of the castle town of Okayama; Feudal domain and the castle town).
[谷口澄夫・城下町岡山の成立]

[36]YOSHIKO NAKABE, "Jōkamachi Takatsuki no Seiritsu," *Daimyō Ryōkoku to Jokamachi* (Yanahara-shoten, Kyōto, 1957). *(Establishment of the castle town of Takatsuki, Feudal domain and the castle town).
[中部よし子・城下町高槻の成立]

[37]KAZUHIKO YAMORI, "Jōkamachi no Jinkōkōsei," *Shirin*, XXXVII, No. 3. *(Population structure in the castle town; Historical essays).
[矢守一彦・城下町の人口構成]

[38]TAKEHIKO NISHIZAWA, "Kinsei Jōkamachi ni okeru Chōninkōzō," *Nihon no Machi* (Yūzankaku, Tōkyō, 1958). *(Structure of the townsmen in the castle town of the Edo period; Japanese towns).
[西沢武彦・近世城下町に於ける町人構造]

[39]TAKESHI TOYOTA, *op. cit.*, 152.
[豊田 武・日本の封建都市]

[40]HITOSHI ONO, *Kinsei Jōkamachi no Kenkyū*, 50–7, (Kokushikenkyu-sosho, Shibun-dō, Tōkyō, 1928). *(Study in the castle town of the Edo period).
[小野 均・近世城下町の研究]

[41]———, *ibid.*, 91–102.
[小野 均・近世城下町の研究]

[42]TAKESHI TOYOTA, "Jōkamachi no Kōzō to Kinō," *Nihon no Machi*, (Yūzankaku, Tōkyō, 1958). *(Structure and function of the castle town; Japanese towns).
[豊田 武・城下町の構造と機能]

[43]TOMOHIKO HARADA, "Chūseitoshi kara Kinseitoshi e no Tenkai," *Nihon Hōkentaiseika no Toshi to Shakai*, (Sanichi-shobō, Tōkyō, 1960). *(Transition from the medieval to the feudal city; City and society in the feudal system of Japan).
[原田伴彦・中世都市から近世都市への展開]

[44]MICHIO FUJIOKA, *Shiro to Jōkamachi*, 192, (Sōgen-sha, Tōkyō). *(The castle and its town).
[藤岡通夫・城と城下町]

[45]NOBORU ŌRUI, and MASAO TOBA, *Nihon Jōkakushi*, 550–5, (Yūzankaku, Tōkyō, 1936). *(A history of castles in Japan).
[大類 伸・鳥羽正雄・日本城郭史]

[46]DOBOKU GAKKAI, *Meiji-izen Nihon Dobokushi*, 1218–23, (Doboku Gakkai, Tōkyō, 1936). *(The history of civil engineering prior to the Meiji period).
[土木学会・明治以前日本土木史]

[47]KAZUHIKO YAMORI, "Jōkamachi no Jinkōkōsei", *Shirin* XXXVII, No. 2. *(Population structure in the castle town; Historical essays).
[矢守一彦・城下町の人口構成]

[48]AKITSUGU ONO, *op. cit.*
[小野晃嗣・近世都市の発達]

[49]TAKESHI TOYODA, *Nihon no Hōkentoshi*, 125.
[豊田　武・日本の封建都市]

[50]TOYOTOSHI MATSUMOTO, "Kochizu yorimita Edojidai-shotō ni okeru Kinsei-jōkamachi no Toshi-iki no Kōzo," *Chiri Hyōron*, XXX, No. 8. *(Structure of the urban area of the castle town in the early days of the Edo era—a study of old maps; Geographical review).
[松本豊寿・古地図よりみた江戸時代初頭における近世城下町の都市域の構造]

[51]HIROSHIMA-SHI, *Shinshū Hiroshima-shishi*, II, No. 205. (Hiroshima-shiyakusho, 1958). *(The newly compiled history of Hiroshima).
[広 島 市・新修広島市史]

[52]MASAHARU KAWAI, *op. cit.*
[河合正治・城下町成立の問題]

[53]HITOSHI ONO, *op. cit.*, 191–200.
[小野　均・近世城下町の研究]

[54]TAKESHI TOYOTA, *op. cit.*, 217–19.
[豊田　武・日本の封建都市]

[55]HITOSHI ONO, *op. cit.*, 216–20.
[小野　均・近世城下町の研究]

[56]———, *ibid.*, 147–52.
[小野　均・近世城下町の研究]

[57]———, *ibid.*, 155–74.
[小野　均・近世城下町の研究]

[58]MASUO MURAI, "Jōkashokuninmachi ni kansuru Ichi-kōsatsu," *Kokumin Seikatsushi* (Yoshikawa-kōbunkan, Tōkyō, 1959). *(A study in the towns of craftsmen in the castle town; A history of national life).
[村井益男・城下職人町に関する一考察]

[59]NOBORU ŌRUI, *Jōkaku no Kenkyū*, 149–58. (Tōkyō 1915). *(Study of castles).
[大類　伸・城郭の研究]

[60]TOMOHIKO HARADA, "Kinseitoshi to Mibunsei," *Nihon Hōkentoshi Kenkyū*, (Tōkyō University Press, Tōkyō, 1957). *(The city in the feudal age and the status system; Study in the feudal city of Japan).
[原田伴彦・近世都市と身分制]

[61]HIROSHIMA-SHI, *op. cit.*, I, No. 308.
[広 島 市・新修広島市]

[62]TAKESHI TOYOTA, *op. cit.*, 167. *(Histories of the cities compiled by Kagoshima-shi, Kanazawa-shi, Kokura-shi, Takada-shi, Hiroshima-shi, Imabari-shi and Fukui-shi respectively).
[豊田　武・日本の封建都市および鹿児島市史，金沢市史，小倉市史，高田市史，広島市史，今治市史，福井市史による]

[63]———, *op. cit.*, 168.
[豊田　武・日本の封建都市]

[64]TOMOHIKO HARADA, "Hōkentoshi no Jichisoshiki", *Nihon Hōkentaiseika no Toshi to Shakai* (Sanichi-shobō, Tōkyō, 1960). *(The system of self-government in the feudal city; City and society in the feudal system of Japan).
[原田伴彦・封建都市の自治組織]

[65]MAEBASHI-SHI, *Maebashi-shishi*, II, (Maebashi-shiyakusho, 1954). *(The history of Maebashi).
[前 橋 市・前橋市史]

[66]Tomohiko Harada, "Kinseizenki Toshiseikatsu Tenbyō," *Nihon Hōken-toshi Kenkyū*, (Tōkyō University Press, 1957). *(Sketches of urban life in the early Edo period; A study of the feudal city in Japan).
[原田伴彦・近世前期都市生活点描]

[67]Takehiko Nishizawa, "Kinsei-jōkamachi ni okeru Chōninmachi no Keizai," *Hōkentoshi no Shomondai* (Yūzankaku, Tōkyō, 1959). *(Economy in the town of common citizens in the castle town; Problems of the feudal city).
[西沢武彦・近世城下町に於ける町人町の経済]

[68]Takeshi Toyota, *op. cit.*, 225.
[豊田　武・日本の封建都市]

[69]Akitsugu Ono, *op. cit.*
[小野晃嗣・近世都市の発達]

[70]Hitoshi Ono, *op. cit.*, 242–3.
[小野　均・近世城下町の研究]

[71]Shin Fujisawa, "Shōhinryūtsū kara mita Jōkamachi Okayama to Zai," *Daimyō Ryōkoku to Jōkamachi* (Yanahara-shoten, Kyōto, 1957). *(The castle town of Okayama and its rural district from the view point of commodity exchange; Feudal domain and the castle town).
[藤沢　晋・商品流通からみた城下町岡山と在]

[72]Akitsugu Ono, *op. cit.*
[小野晃嗣・近世都市の発達]

[73]Hitoshi Ono, *op. cit.*, 277–80.
[小野　均・近世城下町の研究]

[74]Toshiaki Harada, *Kumamoto-ken no Rekishi*, 285, (Bunkaku-dō, 1957). *(The history of Kumamoto-ken).
[原田敏明・熊本県の歴史]

[75]Tomohiko Harada, "Kinsei Zaigōmachi no Rekishiteki Tenkai," *Nihon Hōkentoshi Kenkyū* (Tōkyō University Press, 1957). *(Historical development of feudal towns in rural districts; A study of the feudal city in Japan).
[原田伴彦・近世在郷町の歴史的展開]

[76]Masaru Kawamura and Shiro Kaiho, "Kinseishotō Higashikazusa ni okeru Zaikata Seiritsu no Ichijirei," *Hōkentoshi no Shomondai* (Yūzankaku, Tōkyō, 1959). *(An example of the establishment of a commercial center in the rural district of East Kazusa; Problems of the feudal cities).
[川村　優・海保四郎・近世初頭東上総に於ける在方成立の一事例]

[77]Hajime Komura, "Kinsei Zaigōmachi ichi, ni no Mondai—Echigo no kuni Kanbara-gun Kameta o tōshite," *Nihon no Machi* (Yūzankaku, Tōkyō, 1958). *(Some problems of rural towns in the Edo period—a study of Kameta of Kanbara-gun in Echigo; Japanese towns).
[小村　弌・近世在郷町一，二の問題　越後国蒲原郡亀田をとおして]

[78]Imabari Shiyakusho, *Imabari-shoshi*. (The history of Imabari-shi).
[今治市役所・今治小誌]

[79]Tomohiko Harada, "Kinsei Zaigōmachi no Rekishiteki Tenkai," *Nihon Hōkentoshi Kenkyū* (Tōkyō University Press, 1957). *(Historical development of feudal towns in rural districts; A study of the feudal city in Japan).
[原田伴彦・近世在郷町の歴史的展開]

[80]Hitoshi Ono, *op. cit.*, 251–3.
[小野　均・近世城下町の研究]

VI

[1]Ijin Ashida (Ed.), *Gofunai Bikō*, I, 27, (Yūzankaku, Tōkyō, 1933). *(Statistics of the city of Edo,).
[芦田偉人・御府内備考]

[2]HIROSHI SUGIYAMA, "Go-hōjō-jidai no Edo," *Hōkentoshi no Shomondai*, (Yūzankaku, Tōkyō, 1959). *(Edo in the later Hōjō period; Problems of the feudal cities).
[杉山　博・後北条時代の江戸]
[3]IJIN ASHIDA (Ed.), *op. cit.*, 36–8.
[芦田偉人・御府内備考]
[4]TŌKYŌ-TO, *Edo no Hattatsu*, 32, (Tōkyō-to, 1956). *(Development of the city of Edo).
[東 京 都・江戸の発達]
[5]———, *Kusei Enkaku*, 11–2, (Tōkyō-to, 1958). *(History of the ward system).
[東 京 都・区制沿革]
[6]CHIYODA-KU, *Chiyoda-kushi*, I, 413–21, (Chiyoda-kuyakusho, Tōkyō, 1960). *(History of Chiyoda-ku).
[千代田区・千代田区史]
[7]USABURŌ NAKAJIMA, *Kōjō*, 60, (Yūzankaku, Tōkyō, 1959). *(Imperial castle).
[中島卯三郎・皇城]
[8]YOSHIKUNI ŌKUMA, "Edo no 36 Mitsuke," *Edo Kenchiku Sōwa*, (Tōa-shuppansha, Tōkyō, 1948). *(Thirty-six Mitsuke in Edo; Architecture in Edo).
[大熊喜邦・江戸の三十六見附]
[9]———, "Edo Yonshuku," *Edo Kenchiku Banashi*, (Tōa-shuppansha, Tōkyō, 1953). *(Four relay stations in Edo; Discussion of Edo's Architecture).
[大熊喜邦・江戸四宿]
[10]SHINAGAWA-MACHI, *Shinagawa-chōshi*, I, 826–7, (Shinagawa-machi, Tōkyō, 1932). *(History of Shinagawa-machi).
[品 川 町・品川町史]
[11]SHINJUKU-KU, *Shinjuku-kushi*, 230–50, (Shinjuku-kuyakusho, Tōkyō, 1955). *(History of Shinjuku-ku).
[新 宿 区・新宿区史]
[12]ITABASHI-KU, *Itabashi-kushi*, 324, (Itabashi-kuyakusho, Tōkyō, 1954). *(History of Itabashi-ku).
[板 橋 区・板橋区史]
[13]ADACHI-KU, *Adachi-kushi*, 347, (Adachi-kuyakusho, Tōkyō, 1955). *(History of Adachi-ku).
[足 立 区・足立区史]
[14]ARAKAWA-KU, *Arakawa-kushi*, 485, (Arakawa-kuyakusho, Tōkyō, 1936). *(History of Arakawa-ku).
[荒 川 区・荒川区史]
[15]*Keichō Kenbunshū*, No. 5; *Edo Sōsho*, II, 26, (Edosōsho-kankōkai, Tōkyō, 1916). *(Keichō Review; Book of Edo).
[慶長見聞集]
[16]CHIYODA-KU, *op. cit.*, 441–2.
[千代田区・千代田区史]
[17]MASAO SUZUKI, "Shoki no Edo ni okeru Machi no Hensen to Jiin no Iten," *Hōkentoshi no Shomondai*, (Yūzankaku, Tōkyō, 1959). *(Changes in the towns of Edo in its early stage and the relocation of temples; Problems of the feudal cities).
[鈴木昌雄・初期の江戸に於ける町の変遷と寺院の移転]
[18]SHIGETOMO KŌDA, *Edo to Ōsaka*, 17, (Fuzan-bō, Tōkyō, 1942). *(Edo and Ōsaka).
[幸田成友・江戸と大阪]
[19]KENTARŌ NOMURA, *Edo*, 147, (Shibun-dō, Tōkyō, 1958).
[野村兼太郎・江戸]

[20]RYŌICHI FURUTA, *Higashimawari Kaiun oyobi Nishimawari Kaiun no Kenkyū*, 42. *(East-bound and west-bound shipping services).
[古田良一・東廻海運及び西廻海運の研究]

[21]KENTARŌ NOMURA, *op. cit.*, 149–50.
[野村兼太郎・江戸]

[22]CHŪŌ-KU, *Chūō-kushi*, I, 549, (Chūō-kuyakusho, Tōkyō, 1958). *(History of Chūō-ku).
[中 央 区・中央区史]

[23]———, *ibid.*, 382.
[中 央 区・中央区史]

[24]———, *ibid.*, 421–2.
[中 央 区・中央区史]

[25]TŌKYŌ-SHI, *Nihonbashi*, 107–8, (Nihonbashi-kenkyūkai, Tōkyō, 1935).
[東 京 市・日本橋]

[26]IKOKU SŌSHO, *Don Rodriguez Kenbunroku*, 17, (Yūshōdō, Tōkyō, 1966). *(Record of Travels in Japan by Don Rodriguez).
[異国叢書・ドン・ロドリゴ見聞録]

[27]———, *Zoku Edo Ōrai: Nihonbashi*, 209–10, (Nihonbashi-kenkyūkai, Tōkyō, 1935). *(Introduction to the city of Edo, continued: Nihonbashi).
[続江戸往来・日本橋]

[28]Tōkyō-shi, *op. cit.*, 209–10.
[東 京 市・日本橋]

[29]———, *ibid.*, 209–30.
[東 京 市・日本橋]

[30]———, *ibid.*, 231–48.
[東 京 市・日本橋]

[31]ASAKUSA-KU, *Asakusa-kushi*, I, 438–40, (Asakusa-kuyakusho, Tōkyō, 1913–4). *(Annals of Asakusa-ku).
[浅 草 区・浅草区誌]

[32]SHIGETOMO KŌDA, *op. cit.*
[幸田成友・江戸と大阪]

[33]*Edosuzume*, No. 12; *Edo Sōsho* VI, (Edosōsho-kankōkai, Tōkyō, 1916). *(Sparrows in Edo; Book of Edo).
[江戸叢書・江 戸 雀]

[34]IJIN ASHIDA (Ed.); *op. cit.*, 2.
[芦田偉人・御府内備考]

[35]TŌKYŌ-TO, *Edo no Hattatsu*, 117–21.
[東 京 都・江戸の発達]

[36]SHIGETOMO KŌDA, *op. cit.*, 91–4.
FUKKŌKYOKU CHŌKAN KANBŌ KEIKAKU-KA, *Edo no Kōtsu Un-yu Soshiki* (1942). *(Planning Section, Chamber of the Director, Bureau of Restoration of Tōkyō; Traffic and transportation system in the city of Edo).
[幸田成友・江戸と大阪] [復興局長官官房計画課・江戸の交通運輸組織]

[37]TŌKYŌ-TO, *Edo no Hattatsu*, 169–72.
[東 京 都・江戸の発達]

[38]KENJI DATE, "Edo ni okeru Shokō no Shōhi-seikatsu ni tsuite," *Rekishigaku Kenkyū*, IV, No. 4. *(Consumer activity of the feudal lords in the city of Edo; Study in History).
[伊達研次・江戸に於ける諸侯の消費生活に就て]

[39]———, *ibid.*
[伊達研次・江戸に於ける諸侯の消費生活に就て]

[40]IJIRŌ FUJIOKA, *Nihon no Kenchiku*, 202, (Shibun-dō, Tōkyō, 1958). *(Architecture of Japan).
[藤岡亥治郎・日本の建築]

41 Yoshikuni Ōkuma, "Edo no Jūtaku Kenchiku to Hōrei," *Tōkyō-fu Minsei Shiryō Kōenkai Sokki.* *(Houses in Edo and laws governing architecture; Record of lectures on civil government held by Tōkyō-fu).
[大熊喜邦・江戸の住宅建築と法令]

42 Tōkyō-to, *Edo no Hattatsu*, 77–80.
[東 京 都・江戸の発達]

43 Katsu Sekino, *Nihon Jūtaku Shōshi*, 87, (Sagami-shobō, Tōkyō, 1948). *(A short history of Japanese residences).
[関野　克・日本住宅小史]

44 Seiken Koji, *Edo Hanjōki*, III, (Yūzankaku, Tōkyō, 1939). *(Thriving city of Edo).
[静軒居士・江戸繁昌記]

45 Tasaburo Itō, *Bakuhan-taisei*, 18, (Kōbun-dō, Tōkyō, 1958). *(System of central and domain governments).
[伊東多三郎・幕藩体制]

46 Tarō Matsudaira, *Edojidai-seido no Kenkyū*, I, 382, (Bukeseido-kenkyūkai, Tōkyō, 1920). *(Study in the feudal system of the Edo era).
[松平太郎・江戸時代制度の研究]

47 Motoji Kurita, "Edojidai-shoki no Rōnin no Hassei," *Shakaigaku Zasshi* XXVII, XXVIII. *(Emergence of unemployed warriors in the early days of the Edo era).
[栗田元次・江戸時代初期の浪人の発生]

48 Yoshimiki Shinshi, "Bushi no Shakai-soshiki," *Kōza Nihon Fūzokushi*, II (Yūzankaku, Tokyo, 1926). *(Social organization of warriors; Lectures on the history of social conditions in Japan).
[進士慶幹・武士の社会組織]

49 Kiyoshi Inoue, *Nihon Joseishi*, 142, (Sanichi-shobō, Tōkyō, 1954). *(History of Japanese women).
[井上　清・日本女性史]

50 Kaneyuki Miura, *Kokushijō no Shakai-mondai*, 333, (Osanai-bunko, Tōkyō, 1920). *(Social problems in the history of Japan).
[三浦周行・国史上の社会問題]

51 Nihonbashi-ku, *Shinshū Nihonbashi-kushi*, 338, (Nihonbashi-kuyakusho, Tōkyō, 1937). *(Newly compiled history of Nihonbashi-ku).
[日本橋区・新修日本橋区史]

52 Takeichirō Fukuo, *Nihon Kazoku-seido-shi*, 168, (Yoshikawa-kōbunkan, Tōkyō, 1954). *(History of the family system in Japan).
[福尾猛市郎・日本家族制度史]

53 Masajiro Takikawa, *Nihon Shakaishi*, 317, (Kangen-sha, Tōkyō, 1948). *(Social history of Japan).
[滝川政次郎・日本社会史]

54 Kenji Date, *op. cit.*
[伊達研次・江戸に於ける諸侯の消費生活]

55 Eitarō Tamura, *Edo no Fūzoku: Chōnin-hen*, 30, (Yūzankaku, Tōkyō, 1960). *(Social conditions in Edo: Townsmen).
[田村栄太郎・江戸の風俗：町人篇]

56 ———, *ibid.*, 31–2.
[田村栄太郎・江戸の風俗：町人篇]

57 Shigetomo Kōda, "Fudasashi," *Mita Gakkai Zasshi*, IX, No. 8. *(Brokers handling rice as agents for the lords and *hatamoto;* Gazette of the Institute of Mita).
[幸田成友・札差]

58 Buyō Inshi, "Seji Kenbunroku Go no Maki," *Kinsei Shakai-keizai Sōsho*, I, 196, (Kaizō-sha, Tōkyō, 1920). *(Review of social happenings, Vol. 5; Library of social economy of the Edo period).
[武陽隠士・世事見聞録五ノ巻]

[59]MATAJI MIYAMOTO, *Kabunakama no Kenkyū*, 12–25, (Yūhikaku, Tōkyō, 1938). *(Study of the unions of merchants and craftsmen engaged in the same occupation).
[宮本又次・株仲間の研究]

[60]KENTARŌ NOMURA, *Edo*, 159–60, (Shibundō, Tōkyō, 1958).
[野村兼太郎・江戸]

[61]NOBUHIKO NAKAI, *Bakuhan-shakai to Shōhinryūtsū*, 97–100, (Hanawashobō, Tōkyō, 1961). *(Commodity exchange in feudal society).
[中井信彦・幕藩社会と商品流通]

[62]GITARO HIRANO, "Meiji-ishin no Kaikaku ni tomonau atarashii Kaikyu-bunka to shakaiteki Seijiundō," *Nihon Shihonshugi Hattatsushi Kōza*, (Iwanami-shoten, Tōkyō, 1932–3). *(New culture in the stratification of status following reformation in the Meiji Restoration and the socio-political movement; Lecture on the history of progress in capitalism in Japan).
[平野義太郎・明治維新の改革に伴う新しい階級文化と社会的政治運動]

[63]MOTO-O ENDŌ, *Shokunin no Rekishi*, 130, (Shibun-dō, Tōkyō). *(History of craftsmen).
[遠藤元男・職人の歴史]

[64]CHIYODA-KU, *Chiyoda-kushi*, I, 631, (Chiyoda-kuyakusho, Tōkyō, 1960). *(History of Chiyoda-ku).
[千代田区・千代田区史]

[65]BUYŌ INSHI, *op. cit.*, 209.
[武陽隠士・世事見聞録五ノ巻]

[66]EITARŌ TAMURA, *op. cit.*, 160–1.
[田村栄太郎・江戸の風俗：町人篇]

[67]KANEYUKI MIURA, *Hōseishi no Kenkyū*, I, 134, (Iwanami-shoten, Tōkyō, 1943). *(Study in the history of legislation).
[三浦周行・法制史の研究]

[68]SHIGETOMO KŌDA, "Danzaemon no Seikatsu," *Chūō Shidan*, II, No. 6. *(The life of Danzaemon; Central historical essays).
[幸田成友・弾左衛門の生活]

[69]BUYŌ INSHI, "Seji Kenbunroku, Shichi no Maki," *Kinsei Shakai-keizai Sōsho*, I, 271, (Kaizō-sha, Tōkyō, 1920). *(Review of social happenings, Vol. 7; Library of social economy of the Edo period).
[武陽隠士・世事見聞録七ノ巻]

[70]KANEYUKI MIURA, *op. cit.*, 1146.
[三浦周行・法制史の研究]

[71]MASAJIRO TAKIKAWA, *op. cit.*, 347.
[滝川政次郎・日本社会史]

[72]TAITŌ-KU, *Taitō-kushi*, 1, 320, (Taitō-kuyakusho, Tōkyō, 1955). *(History of Taitō-ku).
[台 東 区・台東区史]

[73]———, *ibid.* 348–57.
[台 東 区・台東区史]

[74]EITARŌ TAMURA, *op. cit.*, 213.
[田村栄太郎・江戸の風俗：町人篇]

[75]TŌKYŌ-TO, *Edo no Hattatsu*, 73.
[東 京 都・江戸の発達]

[76]CHŪŌ-KU, *Chūō-kushi*, I, 252, (Chūō-kuyakusho, Tōkyō, 1069). *(History of Chūō-ku).
[中 央 区・中央区史]

[77]TŌKYŌ-TO, *Kusei Enkaku*, 2-3, (Tōkyō-to, 1958). *(History of the ward system).
[東 京 都・区制沿革]

[78]———, *ibid*., 6.
[東 京 都・区制沿革]
[79]SHIGETOMO KŌDA, "Edo no Shisei," *Nihon Rekishi*, (Iwanami-shoten, Tōkyō, 1934). *(The municipal system of Edo; The history of Japan).
[幸田成友・江戸の市制]
[80]CHŪŌ-KU, *op. cit*., 314.
[中 央 区・中央区史]
[81]SHIGETOMO KŌDA, "Edo no Shisei."
[幸田成友・江戸の市制]
[82]CHŪŌ-KU, *op. cit*., 323–30.
[中 央 区・中央区史]
[83]TŌKYŌ-SHI, *Nihonbashi*, 128.
[東 京 市・日本橋]
[84]———, *ibid*.
[東 京 市・日本橋]
[85]TŌKYŌ-TO, *Kusei Enkaku*, 16–7.
[東 京 都・区制沿革]
[86]SHIGETOMO KŌDA, "Edo no Shisei."
[幸田成友・江戸の市制]
[87]KENTARŌ NOMURA, *op. cit*., 83–4.
[野村兼太郎・江戸]
[88]TŌKYŌ-TO, *Kusei Enkaku*, 23–6.
[東 京 都・区制沿革]
[89]RYŌICHI FURUTA, *Higashimawari Kaiun oyobi Nishimawari Kaiun no Kenkyū*, 42. *(East-bound and west-bound shipping services).
[古田良一・東廻海運及び西廻海運の研究]
[90]MATAJI MIYAMOTO, *Ōsaka*, 90, (Shibun-dō, Tōkyō, 1957).
[宮本又次・大阪]
[91]———, *ibid*., 117.
[宮本又次・大阪]
[92]ŌSAKA-SHI, *Ōsaka-shishi*, I, 165–71, (Ōsaka-shi Sanjikai, Tōkyō, 1913). *(History of Ōsaka).
[大 阪 市・大阪市史]
[93]EIJIRŌ HONJŌ, *Jinkō oyobi Jinkōmondai*, 98–102, (Nihonhyōron-sha, Tōkyō, 1930). *(Population and its problems).
[本庄栄治郎・人口及び人口問題]
[94]SHIGETOMO KŌDA, *Edo to Ōsaka*, 45, (Fuzan-bō, Tōkyō, 1942). *(Edo and Ōsaka).
[幸田成友・江戸と大阪]
[95]ŌSAKA-SHI, *op. cit*., 314.
[大 阪 市・大阪市史]
[96]SHIGETOMO KŌDA, *Edo to Ōsaka*, 40.
[幸田成友・江戸と大阪]
[97]MATAJI MIYAMOTO, *Ōsaka*, 17.
[宮本又次・大阪]
[98]TAKESHI TOYOTA, *Nihon no Hōkentoshi*, 180, (Iwanami-shoten, Tōkyō, 1952). *(A history of feudal cities in Japan).
[豊田 武・日本の封建都市]
[99]ŌSAKA-SHI, *op. cit*., 316.
[大 阪 市・大阪市史]

VII

[1]KENTARŌ NOMURA, *Goningumi-chō no Kenkyū*, 65–6, (Yūhikaku, Tōkyō, 1943). *(Study of registration books of the five-family groups).
[野村兼太郎・五人組帳の研究]

[2]KŌTA KODAMA, "Hida Shirakawa-mura no Daikazoku-seido to sono Keizaiteki-kiso," *Kinseishakai no Kenkyū*, (Sōbunsha, Tōkyō, 1960). *(The large family system in Shirakawa-mura of Hida and its economic foundation; Study of Tokugawa society).
[児玉幸多・飛驒白川村の大家族制度と其の経済的基礎]

[3]TOSHIO KOJIMA, *Nihon Hōken Nōgyōshi*, 263 ff. (Kōwa-shobō, Tōkyō, 1948). *(History of agriculture in the feudal era of Japan).
[古島敏雄・日本封建農業史]

[4]YOSHIJI NAKAMURA, *Nihon Shakaishi*, 318, (Yūhikaku, Tōkyō, 1956). *(Social history of Japan).
[中村吉治・日本社会史]

[5]SHIN-EN SATŌ, *Keizai Yōroku*, 27, (Iwanami-shoten, Tōkyō, 1928). *(Economic report).
[佐藤信淵・経済要録]

[6]GITARŌ HIRANO, "Meiji-ishin no Kaikaku ni tomonau atarashii Kaikyu," *Nihon Shihonshugi Hattatsushi Kōza* (Iwanami-shoten, Tōkyō, 1932–3). *(New social classes after the Meiji Restoration; Lectures on the history of progress in capitalism in Japan).
[平野義太郎・明治維新の改革に伴う新しい階級]

[7]TŌGO YOSHIDA, *Ishinshi Hakkō*, 25, (Fuzan-bō, Tōkyō, 1911). *(Eight articles on the history of the Meiji Restoration).
[吉田東伍・維新史八講]

[8]NAOTARŌ SEKIYAMA, *Kinsei Nihon no Jinkō-kōzō*, 123, (Yoshikawa-kōbunkan, Tōkyō, 1958). *(Population structure of Japan in the Edo period).
[関山直太郎・近世日本の人口構造]

[9]KENTARŌ NOMURA, *Nihon Keizaishi*, 317, (Yūhikaku, Tōkyō, 1957). *(The economic history of Japan).
[野村兼太郎・日本経済史]

[10]EIJIRŌ HONJŌ, *Jinkō oyobi Jinkōmondai*, 109–57, (Nihonhyōron-sha, Tōkyō, 1930). *(Population and its problems).
[本庄栄治郎・人口及び人口問題]

[11]SHIGETOMO KŌDA, "Edo no Chōnin no Jinkō," *Shakai-keizai Shigaku*, VIII, No. 1. *(Townsmen population of Edo; Socio-economic history).
[幸田成友・江戸の町人の人口]

[12]EIJIRŌ HONJŌ, *op. cit.*, 79–86.
[本庄栄治郎・人口及び人口問題]

[13]IWAO KUROMASA, "Hyakushō Ikki Gaikan oyobi Nenpyō," *Keizaishi Kenkyū*, XVII, No. 3. *(Summary of peasants revolts with a chronological table; Study in economic history).
[黒正　巌・百姓一揆概鑑及び年表]

[14]OKAYAMA-SHI, *Okayama-shihsi*, 2132–34, (Okayama-shiyakusho). *(History of Okayama).
[岡 山 市・岡山市史]

[15]FUKUI-SHI, *Fukui-shishi*, I, 19–34, (Fukui-shiyakusho, 1941). *(History of Fukui).
[福 井 市・福井市史]

[16]ŌGAKI-SHI, *Ōgaki-shishi*, I, 56, 429, 520, (Ōgaki-shi, 1930). *(History of Ōgaki).
[大 垣 市・大垣市史]

[17]KANAZAWA-SHI, *Kanazawa-shishi* (Kanazawa-shi, 1952). *(History of Kanazawa).
[金 沢 市・金沢市史]

[18]HAMAMATSU-SHI, *Hamamatsu-shishi*, 361, (Hamamatsu-shiyakusho, 1957). *(History of Hamamatsu).
[浜 松 市・浜松市史]

[19]WAKAMATSU-SHI, *Wakamatsu-shishi*, 414, (Wakamatsu-shiyakusho, 1941–2). *(History of Wakamatsu).
[若 松 市・若松市史]

[20]TAKADA-SHI, *Takada-shishi*, 222–3, (Takada-shishi-hensan Iinkai, 1958). *(History of Takada).
[高 田 市・高田市史]

[21]TOTTORI-SHI, *Tottori-shishi*, 194, (Tottori-shiyakusho, 1943). *(History of Tottori).
[鳥 取 市・鳥取市史]

[22]HIMEJI-SHI, *Himeji-shishi*, 4–5, (Harima-shidankai, Himeji, 1919). *(History of Himeji).
[姫 路 市・姫路市史]

[23]UEDA-SHI, *Ueda-shishi*, II, 233–6, (Ueda-shiyakusho, 1949). *(History of Ueda).
[上 田 市・上田市史]

[24]KŌFU-SHI, *Kōfu-shishi*, 214–7, (Kōfu-shiyakusho, 1964). *(History of Kōfu).
[甲 府 市・甲府市史]

[25]IMABARI-SHI, *Imabari-shishi*, 36, (Imabari-shi, 1963). *(History of Imabari).
[今 治 市・今治市史]

[26]KAGOSHIMA-SHI, *Kagoshima no Oitachi*, 31, (Kagoshima-shiyakusho, 1955). *(History of Kagoshima).
[鹿児島市・鹿児島のおいたち]

[27]KURUME-SHI, *Kurume-Shishi*, I, 29–30, (Kurume-shiyakusho, 1932). *(History of Kurume).
[久留米市・久留米市誌]

[28]TOYAMA-SHI, *Toyama-shishi*, 55, (Toyama-shiyakusho, 1909). *(History of Toyama).
[富 山 市・富山市史]

[29]NAGAOKA-SHI, *Nagaoka-shishi*, 331, (Nagaoka-shiyakusho, 1931). *(History of Nagaoka).
[長 岡 市・長岡市史]

[30]TAKASAKI-SHI, *Takasaki-shishi*, I, 173, (Takasaki-shi, 1927). *(History of Takasaki).
[高 崎 市・高崎市史]

[31]MATSUMOTO-SHI, *Matsumoto-shishi*, I, 766–72, (Matsumato-shiyakusho, 1933). *(History of Matsumoto).
[松 本 市・松本市史]

[32]———, *ibid.*, 776.
[松 本 市・松本市史]

[33]KŌCHI-SHI, *Kōchi-shishi*, I, 368–9, (Kōchi-shishi-hensan Iinkai, 1958). *(History of Kōchi).
[高 知 市・高知市史]

[34]KANAZAWA-SHI, *Kanazawa-shi Kiyō*, 144–5, (Kanazawa-shiyakusho, 1924). *(Chronicle of Kanazawa).
[金 沢 市・金沢市紀要]

[35]EIJIRŌ HONJŌ, *op. cit.*, 101–2.
[本庄栄治郎・人口及び人口問題]

[36]SAKAI-SHI, *Sakai-shishi*, 4-6, (Sakai-shiyakusho, 1929–31). *(History of Sakai).
[堺　　市・堺市史]

[37]NAGASAKI-SHI, *Nagasaki Shisei 65 Nenshi*, 328, (Nagasaki-shiyakusho, 1928). *(A sixty-five year history of Nagasaki's municipal system).
[長 崎 市・長崎市制六十五年史]

[38]NIIGATA-SHI, *Niigata-shishi*, 91, (Niigata-shi, 1933). *(History of Niigata).
[新 潟 市・新潟市史]

[39]SHIMONOSEKI-SHI, *Shimonoseki-shishi*, (Shimonoseki-shishi-hensan Iinkai 1958). *(History of Shimonoseki).
[下 関 市・下関市史]

[40]ONOMICHI-SHI, *Onomichi-shishi*, I, 100, (Onomichi-shiyakusho, 1939). *(History of Onomichi).
[尾 道 市・尾道市史]

[41]KŌBE-SHI, *Kōbe-shishi*, (Kōbe-shiyakusho, 1921–3). *(History of Kōbe).
[神 戸 市・神戸市史]

[42]TOMOHIKO HARADA, "Kinseikōki no Toshi Kasōmin," *Nihon Hōkentai-seika no Toshi to Shakai* (Sanichi-shobō, Tōkyō, 1960). *(Low class residents in the city of the late feudal age; City and society in the feudal system of Japan).
[原田伴彦・近世後期の都市下層民]

[43]———, "Kinsei Toshi Sōjō Oboegaki," *Nihon Hōkentoshi Kenkyū* (Tōkyō University Press, 1957). *(Memorandum on urban riots in feudal cities; Study of the feudal city in Japan).
[原田伴彦・近世都市騒擾覚書]

[44]UEDA-SHI, *Ueda-shishi*, II, 135–45, (Ueda-shiyakusho, 1949). *(History of Ueda).
*Koagata-gunshi Yohen*, 783–801. *(Articles on the history of Koagata county).
[上 田 市・上田市史] [小県郡史余篇]

[45]FUKUI-SHI, *Fukui-shishi*, I, 206–11, (Shisei 50-shunen Kinenkai, Fukui, 1941) *(History of Fukui).
*Fukui-kenshi*, II, 519. *(History of Fukui prefecture).
[福 井 市・福井市史] [福井県史]

[46]UJI-YAMADA-SHI, *Uji-yamada-shishi*, I, 186, (Uji-yamada-shi, 1929). *(History of Uji-yamada).
[宇治山田市・宇治山田市史]

[47]TOMOHIKO HARADA, "Kinsei Toshi Sōjō Oboegaki," *Nihon Hōkentoshi Kenkyū* (Tōkyō University Press, Tokyo, 1957). *(Memorandum on urban riots in feudal cities; Study of the feudal city in Japan).
[原田伴彦・近世都市騒擾覚書]

[48]*Aomori Enkakushi*, I, 683. (Aomori-shiyakusho-shishi-hensankai, 1910). *(History of Aomori).
[青森沿革史]

[49]NIIGATA-SHI, *Niigata-shishi*, II, 675–965, (Niigata-shishi-henshubu, 1933). *(History of Niigata).
[新 潟 市・新潟市史]
RYŪSUKE SHIBUKI, "Niigata Sōdō Oboegaki," *Rekishi Hyōron*, 31. *(Memorandum on revolts in Niigata; Historical review).
[渋木隆介・新潟騒動覚書]

[50]TAITŌ-KU, *Taitō-kushi*, I, 512–16, (Taitō-kuyakusho, Tokyo, 1955). *(History of Taitō ward).
[台 東 区・台東区史]

[51]ŌSAKA-SHI, *Ōsaka-shishi*, II, 481–519, (Ōsaka-shi Sanjikai, 1913). *(History of Ōsaka-shi).
[大 阪 市・大阪市史]

[52]TOMOHIKO HARADA, "Kinsei Toshi Sōjō Oboegaki," *Nihon Hōkentoshi Kenkyū* (Tōkyō University Press, Tokyo, 1957). *(Memorandum on urban riots in feudal cities; Study of the feudal city in Japan).
[原田伴彦・近世都市騒擾覚書]

[53]TAKESHI TOYOTA, *Nihon no Hōkentoshi*, 280, (Iwanami-shoten, Tōkyō, 1952). *(A history of feudal cities in Japan).
[豊田　武・日本の封建都市]

[54]TOMOHIKO HARADA, "Kinsei Zaigōmachi no Rekishiteki Tenkai," *Nihon Hōkentoshi Kenkyū* (Tōkyō University Press, Tōkyō 1957). *(Historical development of feudal towns in rural districts; Study of the feudal city in Japan).
[原田伴彦・近世在郷町の歴史的展開]

[55]ŌSAKA-SHI, *Ōsaka-shishi*, II, 576–86, (Ōsaka-shi Sanjikai, 1913). *(History of Ōsaka).
[大 阪 市・大阪市史]

[56]MATAJI MIYAMOTO, *Kabunakama no Kenkyū*, 320–2, (Yūhikaku, Tōkyō, 1938). *(Study of the unions of merchants and craftsmen engaged in the same occupation).
[宮本又次・株仲間の研究]

[57]CHIYODA-KU, *Chiyoda-kushi*, II, 23–6, (Chiyoda-kuyakusho, Tōkyō, 1960). *(History of Chiyoda-ku).
[千代田区・千代田区史]

[58]CHŪŌ-KU, *Chūō-kushi*, I, 564, (Chūō-kuyakusho, Tōkyō, 1958). *(History of Chūō-ku).
[中 央 区・中央区史]

[59]ŌSAKA-SHI, *op. cit.*, 721–6.
[大 阪 市・大阪市史]

[60]SEIZAN MATSUURA, *Kinoene Yawa*, I, 267, (Hakubun-kan, Tōkyō, 1892). *(Stories of Kinoene).
[松浦静山・甲子夜話]

[61]*Sendai no Rekishi*, 134–6, (Sendai-shiyakusho, 1950–6). *(History of Sendai). AKIRA ŌSHIMA, "Sendai ni okeru Kakyūbushi no Shukōgyōka," *Rekishigaku Kenkyū*, II, No. 5. *(Introduction of handicraft into the households of low class warriors in Sendai; Historical studies).
[仙台の歴史] [大島　昭・仙台に於ける下級武士の手工業化]

[62]FUKUI-SHI, *op. cit.*, 743.
[福 井 市・福井市史]

[63]HAMAMATSU-SHI, *Hamamatsu Hattatsushi*, 34, (Hamamatsu-shiyakusho, Kikakushitsu, 1954–5). *(History of development of the city of Hamamatsu).
[浜 松 市・浜松発達史]

[64]TAKAOKA-SHI, *Takaoka-shishi*, I, (Takaoka-shishi-hensan Iinkai, 1959). *(History of Takaoka).
[高 岡 市・高岡市史]

[65]SEIZABURŌ SHINOBU, *Kinsei Nihon Sangyōshi*, 3–28, (Nihonhyōron-sha, Tokyo, 1942). *(History of industry in feudal Japan).
[信夫清三郎・近世日本産業史]

[66]KIRYŪ-SHI, *Kiryū-shishi*, II, 52, (Kiryū-shishi-hensan Iinkai, 1958). *(History of Kiryū).
[桐 生 市・桐生市史]

[67]GORŌ ISHIBASHI, "Ishinzengo ni okeru Gaikokubōeki ni tsuite," *Shirin*, VII, No. 3. *(Foreign trade in Japan before and after the Meiji Restoration; Historical essays).
[石橋五郎・維新前後に於ける外国貿易に就いて]

[68]YOKOHAMA-SHI, *Yokohama-shishikō*, *Sangyō-hen*, 7, (Yokohama-shiyakusho, 1931–3). *(History of Yokohama, industry).
[横 浜 市・横浜市史稿産業篇]

[69]GORŌ ISHIBASHI, *op. cit.*
[石橋五郎・維新前後に於ける外国貿易に就て]

[70]JŪBE HASHIMOTO, *Kiitobōeki no Hensen*, 26–7. *(Transitions in overseas silk trade).
[橋本重兵衛・生糸貿易の変遷]

[71]TŌKYŌ SHŌKŌKAIGISHO, *Tōkyō Shōkōkaigisho Yōkenroku*, *Gōgai Furoku*. *(Records of important affairs compiled by the Chamber of Commerce

and Industry of Tōkyō, supplementary edition with appendix).
[東京商工会議所・東京商工会議所要件録号外附録]

[72]ŌSAKA-SHI, *Ōsaka-shishi*, II, 940–1, (Ōsaka-shi Sanjikai, 1913–5). *(History of Ōsaka).
[大 阪 市・大阪市史]

[73]SHINAGAWA-MACHI, *Shinagawa-chōshi*, II, 562–70, (Shinagawa-machi-yakuba, Tōkyō, 1932). *(History of Shinagawa-township).
[品 川 町・品川町史]

[74]CHIYODA-KU, *Chiyoda-kushi*, 125–6, (Chiyoda-kuyakusho, Tōkyō, 1960). *(History of Chiyoda-ku).
[千代田区・千代田区史]

[75]SHŪICHIRO ONUKI, *Seien Kaikoroku*, I, 75, (Seien Kaikoroku Kankōkai, Tokyo, 1927). *(Seien's memoirs).
[小貫修一郎・青淵回顧録]

[76]TŌKYŌ-TO, *Shichū Torishimari Enkaku*, 23–5, (Tōkyō-to, 1955). *(Survey of the police system in the city of Tōkyō).
[東 京 都・市中取締沿革]

[77]———, *ibid.*, 26–61.
[東 京 都・市中取締沿革]

[78]NORIHIKO FUJISAWA, "Meiji-jidai no Fūzoku," *Fūzoku Kōza*, (Yūzan-kaku, Tōkyō, 1959). *(Social conditions in the Meiji era; Lectures on social conditions).
[藤沢衛彦・明治時代の風俗]

[79]TŌKYŌ-TO, *Edo kara Tōkyō e no Tenkai*, 51–5, (Tōkyō-to, 1953). *(Transition from Edo to Tōkyō).
[東 京 都・江戸から東京への展開]

VIII

[1]TAKESHI OSATAKE, *Ishinzengo ni okeru Rikkenshisō*, (Bunkaseikatsu-kenkyu-kai, Tokyo, 1925). *(Constitutional ideas prior to and shortly after the Meiji Restoration).
[尾佐竹猛・維新前後に於ける立憲思想]

[2]*Meiji-shiyō*, II, 118, (Shūshi-kyoku, 1876). *(Summary history of the Meiji period).
[明治史要]

[3]*Dajōkan-fukoku*, No. 170. *(Edicts of the *Dajōkan*).
[太政官布告一七〇号]

[4]TAKEO FUJITA, *Nihon Chihō-zaisei-seido no Seiritsu*, 131–227, (Iwanami Shoten, Tōkyō, 1941). *(Formation of local financial systems in Japan).
[藤田武夫・日本地方財政制度の成立]

[5]TEIJIRO UEDA, "Nihon ni okeru Kabushiki-kaisha no Kigen," *Shōgaku Kenkyū*, II, No. 3. *(The origin of joint-stock corporations in Japan; Study of commerce).
[上田貞次郎・日本に於ける株式会社の起源]

[6]HYOE ŌUCHI and TAKAO TSUCHIYA, *Meijizenki Zaiseikeizai Shiryōshūsei*, VIII, 475, (Kaizō-sha, Tokyo, 1933). *(References in the history of financial economy in the early Meiji period).
[大内兵衛, 土屋喬雄・明治前期財政経済史料集成]

[7]TAKAO TSUCHIYA, "Nihon-shihonshugi no Keiei Shiteki-kenkyū," 171, (Kō-bundō, Tōkyō, 1961). *(Historical study of management in Japanese capitalism).
[土屋喬雄・日本資本主義の経営史的研究]

[8]J. C. ABEGGLEN and HIROSHI MANNARI, "Nihon Sangyō no Shidōshasō no Gakureki," *Bessatsu Chūōkōron*, (1963). *(Educational backgrounds of leading figures in Japanese industry; Special issue of the Central Review, Winter, 1963).
[J. C. アベグレン・万成博・日本産業の指導者層の学歴]

MONBUSHŌ, *Nihon no Seichō to Kyōiku*, 37, (Monbushō, Tōkyō, 1962). *(Ministry of Education: Education and the development of Japan).
[文 部 省・日本の成長と教育]

[9]EIJIRŌ HONJŌ, *Shiteki-kenkyū Nihon no Keizai to Shisō*, 192ff, (Hoshino-shoten, Kyōto, 1943). *(Historical study of Japanese thought and economy).
[本庄栄治郎・史的研究日本の経済と思想]

[10]HYOE ŌUCHI and TAKAO TSUCHIYA, *op. cit.*, VII, 301 ff.
[大内兵衛，土屋喬雄・明治前期財政経済史料集成]

[11]GITARŌ HIRANO, "Meiji Ishin no Kaikaku ni tomonau atarashii Kaikyū," *Nihon Shihonshugi Hattatsushi Kōza* (Iwanami-shoten, Tōkyō, 1932–3). *(New social classes after the Meiji Restoration; Lectures on the history of progress in capitalism in Japan).
[平野義太郎・明治維新の改革に伴う新しい階級]

[12]TAKAO TSUCHIYA, *Zaibatsu o kizuita Hitobito*, 22–3, (Kōbundō, Tōkyō, 1955). *(Those who built the *zaibatsu*).
[土屋喬雄・財閥を築いた人々]

[13]———, *Nihon no Seishō*, 24, (Keizai Ōraisha, Tōkyō, 1956). *(Political affiliations of Japanese business).
[土屋喬雄・日本の政商]

[14]"Gendai Kōtsū no Hattatsu," *Kōtsū Kenkyū Shiryō*, No. 37. *(Development of traffic and transportation in the modern era; Traffic and transportation references).
[現代交通の発達・交通研究資料]

[15]NAOTARŌ SEKIYAMA, *Nihon Jinkōshi*, 230, (Shikai-shobō, Tōkyō, 1942). *(History of population in Japan).
[関山直太郎・日本人口史]

[16]EIJIRŌ HONJŌ, *Jinkō oyobi Jinkōmondai*, 226, (Nihonhyōron-sha, Tōkyō, 1930). *(Population and its problems).
[本庄栄治郎・人口及び人口問題]

[17]NAOTARŌ SEKIYAMA, *op. cit.*
*Teikoku Tōkei Nenkan*. *(Statistical yearbook of imperial Japan).
[関山直太郎・日本人口史] [帝国統計年鑑]

[18]RYŌ KOBATA, "Kyūjōkamachi no Keikan," *Chirizōsho*, No. 7. *(Introduction to old castle towns; Library of geography).
[小葉田亮・旧城下町の景観]

[19]TAKESHI TOYOTA, "Hōkentoshi kara Kindaitoshi e," *Toshimondai*, XLVIII, No. 1. *(From the feudal city to the modern city; Urban Problems).
[豊田 武・封建都市から近代都市へ]

[20]ŌSAKA-SHI, *Ōsaka-shishi*, I, 57–70, (Ōsaka-shi Sanjikai, 1913–5). *(History of Osaka).
[大 阪 市・大阪市史]

[21]NAGOYA-SHI, *Nagoya-shishiyo* (Nagoya-shiyakusho, 1953–5). *(Short history of Nagoya).
[名古屋市・名古屋市史要]

[22]FUKUI-SHI, *Fukui-shishi*, I (Fukui-shiyakusho, 1941). *(History of Fukui).
[福 井 市・福井市史]

[23]MICHI KASHIWABARA and SHIGETSUGU NISHIDA, *Tsu-shishi*, 308, (Tsu-shiyakusho, 1965). *(History of Tsu).
[柏原ミチ，西田重嗣・津市史]

[24]MATSUMOTO-SHI, *Matsumoto-shishi*, II, (Matsumoto-shiyakusho, 1933). *(History of Matsumoto).
[松 本 市・松本市史]

[25]SENDAI-SHI, *Sendai-shishi* (Sendai-shi, 1929). *(History of Sendai).
[仙 台 市・仙台市史]

[26]KUMAMOTO-SHI, *Kumamoto-shishi* (Kumamato-shiyakusho, 1932). *(History of Kumamoto).
[熊 本 市・熊本市史]
[27]KŌFU-SHI, *Kōfu Ryakushi* (Kōfu-shi, 1918). *(Short history of Kōfu).
[甲 府 市・甲府略志]
[28]ISHIKAWA-KEN, *Ishikawa-kenshi*, IV, 4, (Kanazawa-shi, 1927, 33). *(History of Ishikawa prefecture).
[石 川 県・石川県史]
[29]WAKAYAMA-SHI, *Wakayama-shishiyō* (Wakayama-shi, 1920). *(A short history of Wakayama).
[和歌山市・和歌山市史要]
[30]TAKATA-SHI, *Takata-shishi*, II, 43, (Takata-shishi-hensan Iinkai, 1958). *(History of Takata).
[高 田 市・高田市史]
[31]YOKOHAMA-SHI, *Yokohama-shishi* (Yokohamashi-shiryō-chōsa Iinkai). *(History of Yokohama).
[横 浜 市・横浜市史]
[32]KŌBE-SHI, *Shisei Yōran*, (Kōbeshi-bunshoka, 1934). *(History of Kōbe).
[神 戸 市・市勢要覧]
[33]NAGASAKI-SHI, *Nagasaki Shisei 65 Nenshi*, (Nagasaki-shiyakusho Somubu Chōsatōkei-ka, 1956). *(A sixty-five years history of Nagasaki's municipal system).
[長 崎 市・長崎市政六十五年史]
[34]HAKODATE-SHI, *Hakodate-shishi*, (Kanzaburō Sato, 1935). *(History of Hakodate).
[函 館 市・函館市誌]
[35]YOKOSUKA-SHI, *Yokosuka-shishi*, (Yokosuka-shishi-hensan Iinkai, 1957). *(History of Yokosuka).
[横須賀市・横須賀市史]
[36]KURE-SHI, *Kure-shishi* (Kure-shiyakusho, 1924). *(History of Kure).
[呉 市・呉市史]
[37]SASEBO-SHI, *Sasebo-shishi* (Sasebo-shi Shi-chōshitsu Chōsaka, 1955–7). *(History of Sasebo).
[佐世保市・佐世保市史]
[38]KŌTA KODAMA, *Shukueki* (Shibun-dō, Tōkyō, 1950). *(Highway stations).
[児玉幸多・宿駅]
[39]NOBUJIRŌ ŌSHIMA, *Nihon Toshi Hattatsushi*, 124–37, (Hōbun-kan, Tōkyō 1954). *(History of development of the Japanese city).
[大島延次郎・日本都市発達史]
[40]CHIYODA-KU, *Chiyoda-kushi*, II, 278, (Chiyoda-kuyakusho, 1958). *(History of Chiyoda-ku).
[千代田区・千代田区史]
[41]ISO-O ABE, *Toshimondai*, 196, (Waseda University Press, Tōkyō). *(Problems of the city).
[安部磯雄・都市問題]
[42]USABURŌ NAKAJIMA, *Kōjō*, 67, (Yūzankaku, Tōkyō, 1959). *(Imperial castle).
[中島卯三郎・皇城]
[43]———, *ibid.*, 41.
[中島卯三郎・皇城]
[44]SHŪICHIRŌ ONUKI, *Seien Kaikoroku*, I, 383–94, (Seien Kaikoroku Kankōkai, Tōkyō, 1927). *(Seien's memoirs).
[小貫修一郎・青淵回顧録]
[45]CHŪŌ-KU, *Chūō-kushi*, II, 317, (Chūō-kuyakusho, 1958). *(History of Chūō-ku).
[中 央 区・中央区史]

[46]———, *ibid.*, 307–28.
[中 央 区・中央区史]
[47]———, *ibid.*, 329.
[中 央 区・中央区史]
[48]MITSUKOSHI HONTEN, *Mitsukoshi no Ayumi* (Mitsukoshi. Tōkyō, 1954). *(Mitsukoshi's past).
[三越本店・三越のあゆみ]
[49]SHIROKIYA, *Shirokiya 300 nen-shi* (Shirokiya, Tōkyō, 1947). *(History of Shirokiya for three hundred years).
[白 木 屋・白木屋三百年史]
[50]———, *ibid.*, 269–70.
[白 木 屋・白木屋三百年史]
[51]YASUNOSUKE IRIE, "Tōkyō Beikoku Shōhin Torihikisho," *Meiji Shōkōshi*, (Hōchi Shinbunsha, Tōkyō, 1911). *(Rice and commodity exchange of Tōkyō; History of commerce and industry in the Meiji period).
[入江保之助・東京米穀商品取引所]
[52]BUEI NAKANO, *Kabushiki Torihikisho* (Hōchi Shinbunsha, Tōkyō, 1911). *(Stock Exchange).
[中野武営・株式取引所]
[53]SHŪHEI UNO, "Atarashii Shūdan-seikatsu," *Meiji Bunkashi*, 552, (Yōyō-sha, 1958). *(New patterns of group behavior; History of culture in the Meiji period).
[宇野修平・新しい集団生活]
[54]KEIŌGIJUKU, *Keiōgijuku Sotsugyōsei-meibo* (Keiō Univ., Tōkyō, 1884). *(List of the graduates of Keiōgijuku).
[慶応義塾・慶応義塾卒業生名簿]
[55]TŌKYŌ-FU, *Meiji Jūgonen Tōkyō-fu Tōkeisho*, (Tokyō-fu, 1883). *(Statistics of Tōkyō-fu in Meiji 15 [1882]).
[東 京 府・明治十五年東京府統計書]
[56]CHŪŌ-KU, *op. cit.*, 387–98
[中 央 区・中央区史]
[57]YOKOYAMA-CHŌ and BAKURŌ-CHŌ, *Yokoyama-chō Bakurō-chōshi*, 200–4, (Yokoyama-chō Bakurō-chō Tonya Renmei, Tōkyō, 1952). *(History of Yokoyama-chō and Bakurō-chō).
[横山町馬喰町・横山町馬喰町史]
[58]TŌKYŌ-FU, *op. cit.*
[東 京 府・明治十五年東京府統計書]
[59]———, *Ginza Renga-gai Kensetsu-shimatsu*, 95–255, (Tōkyō-to, 1955). *(Report on brick construction along the Ginza).
[東 京 府・銀座煉瓦街建設始末]
[60]———, *ibid.*, 102–3.
[東 京 府・銀座煉瓦街建設始末]
[61]KENJIRŌ HIRAYAMA, *Tōkyō Fūzokushi*, I, (Kazama-shobō, Tōkyō, 1961). *(Social conditions of Tōkyō: Chapters in social conditions, Library of historical material of culture in the Meiji period).
[平山鏗二郎・東京風俗誌]
[62]TAITŌ-KU, *Taitō-kushi*, I, 981–1040, (Taitō-kuyakusho, Tokyo, 1955). *(History of Taitō-ku).
[台 東 区・台東区史]
[63]———, *ibid.* 722–8.
[台 東 区・台東区史]
[64]FUKUTARŌ OKUI, "Meiji Tōkyō no Seikaku," *Mitagakkai Zasshi*, XLVI, No. 6. *(Characteristics of Tōkyō in the Meiji period; Bulletin of the Institute of Mita).
[奥井復太郎・明治東京の性格]

[65]SHINAGAWA-MACHI, *Shinagawa-chōshi* II, 1013–29, (Shinagawa-machi-yakuba, Tōkyō, 1932). *(History of Shinagawa township).
[品 川 町・品川町史]
[66]———, *ibid.*, 769.
[品 川 町・品川町史]
[67]SHINJUKU-KU, *Shinjuku-kushi*, 619, (Shinjuku-kuyakusho, 1955). *(History of Shinjuku-ku)
[新 宿 区・新宿区史]
[68]ARAKAWA-KU, *Arakawa-kushi*, II, 298–314, (Arakawa-kuyakusho, Tōkyō, 1936). *(History of Arakawa-ku).
[荒 川 区・荒川区史]
[69]ADACHI-KU, *Adachi-kushi*, 935, (Adachi-kuyakusho, Tōkyō, 1955). *(History of Adachi-ku).
[足 立 区・足立区史]
[70]ITABASHI-KU, *Itabashi-kushi* (Itabashi-kuyakusho, Tōkyō, 1954). *(History of Itabashi-ku).
[板 橋 区・板橋区史]
[71]TŌKYŌ-FU, *Tokyo-fushi Gyōsei-hen*, III, 1–9, (Tōkyō-fu, 1936). *(Chapters on administration, History of Tōkyō-fu).
[東 京 府・東京府史行政篇]
[72]GENNOSUKE YOKOYAMA, *Nihon no Kasōshakai*, 71, (Iwanami-shoten, Tōkyō, 1949). *(Lower class society in Japan).
[横山源之助・日本の下層社会]
[73]CHIYODA-KU, *Chiyoda-kushi*, 355–70, (Chiyoda-kuyakusho, Tōkyō, 1958). *(History of Chiyoda-ku).
[千代田区・千代田区史]
[74]TAKEJIRŌ WATANABE, *Marunouchi Ima to Mukashi*, 14–34, (Fuzan-bō, Tōkyō, 1941). *(Marunouchi, past and present).
[渡辺武次郎・丸の内今と昔]
[75]TŌKYŌ GAS CO., *Tōkyō Gas 70-nenshi*, 1–46, (Tōkyō Gas Co., Tōkyō, 1956). *(History of Tōkyō Gas Co. for seventy years).
[東京瓦斯株式会社・東京瓦斯七十年史]
[76]TŌKYŌ DENTŌ K.K., *Tōkyō Dentō Kabushikikaisha Kaigyō 50-nenshi*, 1–72, (Tōkyō Dentō K.K., Tōkyō, 1936). *(History of Tōkyō Electric Light Co. for fifty years).
[東京電燈株式会社・東京電燈株式会社開業五十年史]
[77]MASAJIRŌ TAKIKAWA, *Nihon Shakaishi*, 247, (Kangen-sha, Tōkyō, 1948). *(Social history of Japan).
[滝川政次郎・日本社会史]
[78]OTOHIKO HAGIWARA, *Tōkyō Kaika Hanjōshi* (Hatsuetsu Shorin, Tōkyō, 1874). *(Flourishing city of Tokyo after the Meiji Restoration in the process of introducing civilization into the country).
[荻原乙彦・東京開化繁昌誌]
[79]NŌSHŌMUSHŌ, *Kōgyō Iken Sho*, (Nōshōmushō, Tōkyō, 1884). *(Ministry of Agriculture and Commerce: Official opinion on promoting the development of industry).
[農商務省・興業意見書]
[80]TAKAO TSUCHIYA and SABURŌ OKAZAKI, *Nihon Shihonshugi Hattatsushi Gaisetsu*, (Yūhi-kaku, Tōkyō, 1937). *(Summary of the history of development of capitalism in Japan).
[土屋喬雄，岡崎三郎・日本資本主義発達史概説]
[81]ŌKURASHŌ KIROKU-KYOKU, *Meiji Hachinen Shokuinroku*, (Ōkurashō, Tōkyō, 1875). *(Bureau of Archives, Ministry of Finance: Blue book for Meiji 8 [1875]).
[大蔵省記録局・明治八年職員録]

[82]OTOHIKO HAGIWARA, *op. cit.*
[荻原乙彦・東京開化繁昌誌]

[83]KEITARŌ MIYAMOTO, "Jūkyo to Seikatsu," *Meiji Bunkashi* (Yōyō-sha, Tōkyō, 1955). *(Homes and living patterns; History of culture in Meiji period).
[宮本馨太郎・住居と生活]

[84]TAKEICHIRŌ FUKUO, *Nihon Kazoku-seido-shi*, 218–30, (Yoshikawa-kōbunkan, Tōkyō, 1954). *(History of the family system in Japan).
[福尾猛市郎・日本家族制度史]

[85]YOKOYAMA-CHŌ and BAKURŌ-CHŌ, *op. cit.*, 221–38.
[横山町馬喰町・横山町馬喰町史]

[86]———, *ibid.*, 206–12.
[横山町馬喰町・横山町馬喰町史]

[87]KENJIRŌ HIRAYAMA, *op. cit.*, II.
[平山鏗二郎・東京風俗誌]

[88]GENNOSUKE YOKOYAMA, *op. cit.*, 78–88.
[横山源之助・日本の下層社会]

[89]———, *ibid.*, 28–9.
[横山源之助・日本の下層社会]

[90]KENJIRŌ HIRAYAMA, *op. cit.*
[平山鏗二郎・東京風俗誌]

[91]TOSHIMI TAKEUCHI, "Toshi to Sonraku," *Meiji Bunkashi* (Yōyō-sha, Tōkyō, 1955). *(City and village; History of culture in Meiji period).
[竹内利美・都市と村落]

## IX

[1]TŌYŌ KEIZAI SHINPŌSHA, "Naichi Kōjōsū narabi ni Jūgyōshasū Shokkōsū Nenpyō, *Meiji Taishō Kokusei Sōran*, (Tōyō Keizai Shinpōsha, Tōkyō, 1927). *(Oriental Economist, Comprehensive statistics of Japan in the Meiji and Taishō period; chronological tables of number of factories, number of workers and number of employees in the factories in Japan, excluding colonies).
[東洋経済新報社・内地工場数ならびに従業者数職工数年表・明治大正国勢総覧]

[2]YŪZŌ YAMADA, "Seisan Kokumin Shotoku," *Nihon Kokumin Shotoku Suikeishiryō*, (Tōyō Keizai Shinpōsha, Tōkyō, 1951). *(Estimated national income; National income data).
[山田雄三・生産国民所得・日本国民所得推計資料]

[3]———, *ibid.*
[山田雄三・生産国民所得・日本国民所得推計資料]

[4]MORITARŌ YAMADA, *Nihon Shihonshugi Bunseki*, 33, (Iwanami-shoten, Tōkyō, 1934). *(Analysis of capitalism in Japan).
[山田盛太郎・日本資本主義分析]

[5]TŌYŌ KEIZAI SHINPŌSHA, *op. cit.*
[東洋経済新報社・明治大正国勢総覧]

[6]*Chūgai Shōgyō Shinpō*, January 7, 1899. *(Chūgai Commercial News).
[中外商業新報]

[7]TAKAO TSUCHIYA, *Zoku Nihon Keizaishi Gaiyō*, 280, (Iwanami-shoten, Tōkyō, 1939). *(Outline of the economic history of Japan, continued).
[土屋喬雄・続日本経済史概要]

[8]MITSUHAYA KAINISHI *et al.*, *Nihon ni okeru Shihonshugi no Hattatsu*, 50, (Tōkyō University Press, Tōkyō, 1958). *(Development of capitalism in Japan).
[楫西光速他・日本に新ける資本主義の発達]

[9]KAMEKICHI TAKAHASHI, *Nihon Shihonshugi Hattatsushi*, 254, (Nihonhyōron-

sha, Tōkyō, 1928). *(The history of development of capitalism in Japan).
[高橋亀吉・日本資本主義発達史]

[10]Mitsuhaya Kainishi, *Zoku Nihon Shihonshugi Hattatsushi*, 7–8, (Yūhikaku, Tōkyō, 1957).*(History of development of Japanese capitalism, continued).
[楫西光速・続日本資本主義発達史]

[11]Okazaki, Kainishi and Kuramochi, *Nihon Shihonshugi Hattatsushi Nenpyō; Tōkeihyō*, 51, (Yūhi-kaku, Tokyō, 1954–7). *(Chronological and statistical tables of the history of development of capitalism in Japan).
[岡崎・楫西・倉持・日本資本主義発達史年表統計表]

[12]Tōyō Keizai Shinpōsha, *op. cit.*
[東洋経済新報社・明治大正国勢総覧]

[13]Kiichi Mori, *Nihon Kōgyō Kōseishi*, 373–4, (Itō-shoten, Tōkyō, 1943). *(History of industrial structures in Japan).
[森　喜一・日本工業構成史]

[14]Takao Tsuchiya, *op. cit.*, 321.
[土屋喬雄・続日本経済史概要]

[15]Mitsuhaya Kainishi, *Zoku Nihon Shihonshugi Hattatsushi*, 13, (Yūhikaku, Tōkyō, 1957). *(History of development of Japanese capitalism, continued).
[楫西光速・続日本資本主義発達史]

[16]Asahi Shinbunsha, *Nihon Keizaitōkei Sōkan* (Asahi Shinbunsha, Tōkyō, 1916). *(Asahi: Statistics of the Japanese economy).
[朝日新聞社・日本経済統計総観]

[17]Ōkurashō, *Kinyūjijō Sankōsho* (Ōkurashō, Tōkyō, 1922). *(Ministry of Finance: References for financial matters).
[大蔵省・金融事情参考書]

[18]Yūzō Yamada, *op. cit.*
[山田雄三・生産国民所得・日本国民所得推計資料]

[19]______, "Seisan Kokuminshotoku Hitori-atari-shotoku," *Nihon Kokuminshotoku Suikeishiryō*, (Tōyō Keizai Shinpōsha, Tōkyō, 1951). *(Estimated per capita incomes in Japan; National income data).
[山田雄三・生産国民所得一人当所得・日本国民所得推計資料]

[20]______, "Sangyōbetsu Jinkō," *Nihon Kokuminshotoku Suikeishiryō*, (Tōyō-Keizai Shinpōsha, Tōkyō, 1951). *(Population classified by industries).
[山田雄三・産業別人口・日本国民所得推計資料]

[21]Tōyō Keizai Shinpōsha, "Naichi Jinkō Niman-ijō Toshi Chōson betsu Jinkō Setaisū Mai-gokanen Nentaishōhyō," *Meiji Taishō Kokusei Sōran*, (Tōyō Keizai Shinpōsha, Tōkyō, 1927). *(Chronological table for every five years indicating the number of families living in same houses, and population in cities with population over 20,000, towns and villages, excluding the colonies).
[東洋経済新報社・内地人口二万以上都市町村別人口世帯数毎五ヶ年年対照表・明治大正国勢総覧]

[22]______, "Naichi Kōsakumenseki Kaikyūbetsu nōkakosū oyobi Hyakubunhi Ruinenhyō," *Meiji Taisho Kokusei Sōran*, (Tōyō Keizai Shinpōsha, Tōkyō, 1927). *(Chronological tables of cultivated land areas, number of houses of farmers classified by stratum and percentages, excluding the colonies).
[東洋経済新報社・内地耕作面積階級別農家戸数別及び百分比累年表・明治大正国勢総覧]

[23]Eitarō Noro, *Nihon Shihonshugi Hattatsushi*, 86, (Iwanami-shoten, Tōkyō, 1954). *(History of the development of capitalism in Japan).
[野呂栄太郎・日本資本主義発達史]

[24]Tōyō Keizai Shinpōsha, "Naichimai Sakutsuketanbetsu oyobi Jisshūdaka," *Meiji Taishō Kokusei Sōran*, (Tōyō Keizai Shinpōsha, Tōkyō, 1927). *(Area of cultivated land planted with rice in *tan* and actual rice crops, excluding

the colonies).
[東洋経済新報社・内地米作付段別及び実収高・明治大正国勢総覧]

[25]TAKAO TSUCHIYA and SABURŌ OKAZAKI, *Nihon Shihonshugi Hattatsushi Gaisetsu*, 476, Shakaimondai Kōza, (Yūhikaku, Tōkyō, 1937). *(Summary of the history of development of capitalism in Japan).
[土屋喬雄・岡崎三郎・日本資本主義発達史概説]

[26]KAMEKICHI TAKAHASHI, "Mitsubishi Ōkokuron," *Chūōkōron*, (1929). *(The kingdom of Mitsubishi; Central review).
[高橋亀吉・三菱王国論]

[27]HIROSHI HIGUCHI, *Nihon Zaibatsu no Kenkyū*, 1 (Mito-shoten, Tōkyō, 1948). *(Study of financial cliques in Japan).
[樋口 弘・日本財閥の研究]

[28]KAMEKICHI TAKAHASHI, *Nihon Shihonshugi Hattatsushi*, 280.
[高橋亀吉・日本資本主義発達史]

[29]TAKAO TSUCHIYA, *Zoku Ninon Keizaishi Gaiyō*, 364.
[土屋喬雄・続日本経済史概要]

[30]KAMEKICHI TAKAHASHI, *Nihon Zaibatsu no Kaibō*, 8–12, (Chūōkōron-sha, Tōkyō, 1930) *(Analysis of financial cliques in Japan).
[高橋亀吉・日本財閥の解剖]

[31]———, "Mitsui Ōkokuron," *Chūōkōron*, (1929). *(The kingdom of Mitsui).
[高橋亀吉・三井王国論]

[32]———, "Mitsubishi Ōkokuron,"
[高橋亀吉・三菱王国論]

[33]JUN'ICHIRŌ ŌTSU, *Dainihon Kenseishi*, III, 551–2. (Hōbun-kan, Tōkyō, 1927). *(The history of constitutionalism in Great Japan).
[大津淳一郎・大日本憲政史]

[34]*Ōsaka Ginkō Tsūshinroku*, No. 147, 1919. *(Records on communication in banks of Ōsaka).
[大阪銀行通信録]

[35]J.C. ABEGGLEN and HIROSHI MANNARI, "Nihon Sangyō no Shidōshasō no Gakureki," *Bessatsu Chūōkōron*, (1963). *(Educational backgrounds of leading figures in Japanese industry; Special issue of the Central Review, Winter, 1963).
[J.C. アベグレン・万成博・日本産業の指導者層の学歴]

[36]MONBUSHŌ, *Nihon no Seichō to Kyōiku*, (Monbushō, Tōkyō, 1962). *(Ministry of Education: Education and the development of Japan).
[文 部 省・日本の成長と教育]

[37]GENNOSUKE YOKOYAMA, *Nihon no Kasōshakai* (Iwanami-shoten, Tōkyō, 1949). *(Lower class society in Japan).
[横山源之助・日本の下層社会]

[38]KIYOSHI INOUE, *Nihon Kindaishi*, 29–130, (Gōdō-shuppansha, Tōkyō, 1957). *(The modern history of Japan).
[井上 清・日本近代史]

[39]NŌSHŌMUSHŌ, *Shokkōjijō*, I, 24 (Tōkyō, 1893). *(Ministry of Agriculture and Commerce: Conditions of workers in Japan).
[農商務省・職工事情]

[40]NŌSHŌMUSHŌ, *ibid.*
[農商務省・職工事情]

[41]KIYOSHI INOUE, *op. cit.*, 237.
[井上 清・日本近代史]

[42]NAIKAKU TŌKEIKYOKU, *Teikoku Tōkei Nenkan* (1921). *(Statistical Bureau of the Cabinet: Statistical yearbook of imperial Japan).
[内閣統計局・帝国統計年鑑]

[42]*Tōkyō Asahi Shinbun* May 3, (1920).
[東京朝日新聞]

[44]KIYOSHI INOUE, *op. cit.*, 260–1.
[井上　清・日本近代史]

[45]*Chūgai Shōgyō Shinpō*, October 19, (1910). *(Chūgai Commercial News).
[中外商業新報]

[46]MITSUHAYA KAINISHI, *Zoku Nihon Shihonshugi Hattatsushi*, 89.
[楫西光速・続日本資本主義発達史]

[47]*Nihon Tōkei Nenkan: Teikoku Tōkei Nenkan;* EIJIRŌ HONJŌ, *Jinkō oyobi Jinkōmondai*.
[日本統計年鑑] [帝国統計年鑑] [本庄栄治郎・人口及び人口問題]

[48]TŌYŌ KEIZAI SHINPŌSHA, "Bunkanjinin oyobi Nenpōgaku Ruinenhyō," *Meiji Taishō Kokuseisōran*, (Tōyō Keizai Shinpōsha, Tōkyō, 1926). *(Tables of numbers of government officials and their annual incomes)
[東洋経済新報社・文官人員及び年俸額累年表・明治大正国勢総覧]

[49]KIYOAKI TSUJI, *Nihon Kanryōsei no Kenkyū*, 58, (Kōbundō, Tōkyō, 1955). *(Study on bureaucracy in Japan).
[辻　清明・日本官僚制の研究]

[50]TŌKYŌ-FU, "Kaisha Shihonkinbetsu," *Taishō 8 nen Tōkyō-fu Tōkeisho*, 1922. *(Statistical tables of capital holdings by companies, Tōkyō statistical yearbook, Taishō 8 [1919]).
[東 京 府・会社資本金別]

[51]TŌYŌ KEIZAI SHINPŌSHA, "Zenkoku Sōkatsu Tegatakōkandaka oyobi Fuwataritegata Tsukibetsuhyō," (Tōkyō, 1927). *(Amount of bank clearings of Meiji and Taishō eras.).
[東洋経済新報社・全国総括手形交換高及不渡手形月別表]

[52]TŌKYŌ-FU, *Tōkyō-fushi, Gyōsei-hen*, III, 682–3. (Tōkyō, 1936). *(History of Tōkyō-fu: Administration).
[東 京 府・東京府史: 行政篇]

[53]YOSHIE MATSUNARI *et al.*, *Nihon no Sarari-man*, 32, (Aoki-shoten, Tōkyō, 1958).*(Salarymen in Japan).
[松成義衛他・日本のサラリーマン]

[54]TŌKYŌ-FU, "Kaisha Shihonkinbetsu."
[東 京 府・会社資本金別]

[55]TAKEJIRŌ WATANABE, *Marunouchi Ima to Mukashi*, 23–45, (Fuzanbō, Tōkyō, 1941). *(Marunouchi, past and present).
[渡辺武次郎・丸の内今と昔]

[56]TŌKYŌ-FU, "Kaisha Shihonkinbetsu."
[東 京 府・会社資本金別]

[57]———, *ibid.*
[東 京 府・会社資本金別]

[58]NIHONBASHI-KU, *Shinshū Nihonbashi-kushi*, 724, (Nihonbashi-kuyakusho, Tōkyō, 1938). *(Newly-compiled history of Nihonbashi-ku).
[日本橋区・新修日本橋区史]

[59]TŌKYŌ-FU, *Tokyo-fushi*, 537.
[東 京 府・東京府史]

[60]CHŪŌ-KU, *Chūō-kushi*, II, 778, (Chūō-kuyakusho, Tōkyō, 1958). *(History of Chūō-ku).
[中 央 区・中央区史]

[61]MICHITOSHI ODANAI, *Teito to Kinkō*, 169–72, (Ōkura-kenkyūsho, 1918). *(Metropolis and suburbs).
[小田内通敏・帝都と近郊]

[62]CHŪŌ-KU, *op cit.*, 402.
[中 央 区・中央区史]

[63]NIHONBASHI-KU, *op. cit.*, 779–81.
[日本橋区・新修日本橋区史]

[64]———, *ibid.*
[日本橋区・新修日本橋区史]

[65]MITSUKOSHI HONTEN, *Mitsukoshi no Ayumi*, (Mitsukoshi, Tōkyō, 1954). *(Mitsukoshi's past).
[三越本店・三越のあゆみ]

[66]NIHONBASHI-KU, *op. cit.*, 710.
[日本橋区・新修日本橋区史]
SHIROKIYA, *Shirokiya 300 nen-shi*, (Shirokiya, Tōkyō. 1947). *(History of Shirokiya for three hundred years).
[白 木 屋・白木屋三百年史]

[67]KYŌBASHI-KU, *Kyōbashi-kushi*, 121–6, (Kyōbashi-kuyakusho, Tōkyō, 1937–42). *(History of Kyōbashi-ku).
[京 橋 区・京橋区史]

[68]HARUNOSUKE ISHIZUMI, *Ginza Kaibōzu*, 121–6, (*Social anatomy of the Ginza).
[石角春之助・銀座解剖図]

[69]MICHIZŌ NISHIKAWA, *Tōkyō no Hattatsushi*, 163–5, (Toshibunka-kenkyūkai, Tōkyō. 1950). *(Development of Tōkyō).
[西川迪造・東京の発達史]

[70]———, *ibid.*, 123.
[西迪川造・東京の発達史]

[71]TŌKYŌ-FU, *Tōkyō-shi Tōkeihyō*, (Tōkyō-fu, Tōkyō 1882–1920). *(Statistical tables of Tōkyō).
[東 京 府・東京市統計表]

[72]KEISHICHŌ KEISATSURENSHŪJO, *Tōkyō-fushi*, (1921). *(History of Tōkyō-Prefecture).
[警視庁警察練習所・東京府史]

[73]MINATO-KU, *Minato-kushi*, 584, (Minato-kuyakusho, Tōkyō, 1960). *(History of Minato-ku).
[港　　区・港区史]

[74]TŌKYŌ-SHI SHAKAIKYOKU, *Tōkyōshinai no Saimin ni kansuru Chōsa*, (1920). *(Survey on the slums in Tōkyō).
[東京市社会局・東京市内の細民に関する調査]

[75]SAWA SEIMUCHŌSASHO, *Tōkyōshinai ni okeru Takuchigai Tochichōsasho*, (1920). *(Survey report of non-residential sections in Tōkyō).
[沢政務調査所・東京市内に於ける宅地外土地調査書]

[76]MINATO-KU, *op. cit.*, 488, 494.
[港　　区・港区史]

[77]MICHITOSHI ODANAI, *op. cit.*, 214.
[小田内通敏・帝都と近郊]

[78]TŌKYŌ-SHI, *Dai 18 kai Tōkyō-shi Tōkeihyō*, (Tōkyō-shiyakusho, Tōkyō, 1922). *(Statistical tables of Tōkyō-shi, No. 18).
]東 京 市・第十八回東京市統計表]

[79]SHINJUKU-KU, *Shinjuku-kushi*, *Shiryōtōkei-hen*, 2, (Shinjuku-kuyakusho, Tōkyō, 1955). *(History of Shinjuku-ku, Statistics).
[新 宿 区・新宿区史]

[80]MICHITOSHI ODANAI, *op. cit.*, 87
[小田内通敏・帝都と近郊]

[81]TŌKYŌ-FU, *Shisetsu Kōjō no Ichi*, (Tōkyō-fu, 1922). *(Location of privately-owned industries in Tōkyō).
[東 京 府・私設工場の位置]

[82]TŌKYŌ-FU, *Tōkyō-fushi*, III, 60.
[東 京 府・東京府史]

[83]KYŌBASHI-KU, *op. cit.*, 745–57.
[京 橋 区・京橋区史]

[84]KŌTŌ-KU, *Kōtō-kushi*, 666–77, (Kōtō-kuyakusho, Tōkyō, 1957). *(History of Kōtō-ku).
[江 東 区・江東区史]
[85]TŌKYŌ-FU NŌSHŌ-KA. *Tōkyō-fu Kōjo-ichiran*, (1919). *(Table of factories in Tōkyō).
[東京府農商課・東京府工場一覧]
[86]KYŌBASHI-KU, *op. cit.*, 720–4
[京 橋 区・京橋区史]
[87]MINATO-KU, *op. cit.*, 363–414.
[港 区・港区史]
[88]SHINAGAWA-MACHI, *Shinagawa-chōshi*, 938, (Shinagawa-machiyakuba, Tokyo, 1932). *(History of Shinagawa township).
[品 川 町・品川町史]
[89]YOKOHAMA-SHI, *Yokohama-shi Yōran*, 59, (Yokohama-shiyakusho, 1921). (History of Yokohama).
[横 浜 市・横浜市要覧]
[90]———, *ibid.*, 68–73.
[横 浜 市・横浜市要覧]
[91]KAWASAKI-SHI, *Kawasaki-shishi*, *Tsūshihen*, 172, (Kawasaki-shiyakusho, 1938). *(General history of Kawasaki).
[川 崎 市・川崎市史：通史篇]
[92]———, *ibid.*, 812.
[川 崎 市・川崎市史]
[93]TŌKYŌ SHIBAURA DENKI K.K., *Tōkyō Denki Kabushikikaisha 50 nen-shi*, 107, (1940). *(Fifty years' history of Tōkyō Electric Company).
[東京芝浦電気株式会社・東京電気株式会社五十年史]
[94]CHIBA-SHI, *Chiba-shishi*, 241–68, (1953). *(History of Chiba).
[千 葉 市・千葉市史]
[95]URAWA-SHI, *Urawa-shisei 20 nen-shi*, 50–82, (1955). *(History of Urawa).
[浦 和 市・浦和市制二十年史]
[96]ŌSAKA-SHI, *Ōsaka-shi Yōran*, (1952). *(Handbook of Ōsaka)
[大 阪 市・大阪市要覧]
[97]MATAJI MIYAMOTO, *Ōsaka hattatsushi*, (1955). *(Growth of Ōsaka).
[宮本又次・大阪発達史]
[98]ŌSAKA-SHI, *Ōsaka-shishi*, I, 259, (Nihonhyōron-sha, Tōkyō, 1933–5). *(History of Ōsaka).
[大 阪 市・大阪市史]
[99]KŌBE-SHI, *Kōbe-shishi*. *(History of Kōbe).
[神 戸 市・神戸市史]
[100]KYŌTO-SHI, *Kyōto-shishi*, (1944–8). *(History of Kyōto).
[京 都 市・京都市史]
[101]NAGOYA-SHI, *Nagoya-shishi*, (1942); *Nagoya 70 nen-shi*, 20–108. *(History of Nagoya; Seventy-years' history of Nagoya).
[名古屋市・名古屋市史・名古屋七十年史]
[102]YAWATA-SHI, *Yawata-shisei Yōran*, (1924). *(Handbook of Yawata).
[八 幡 市・八幡市政要覧]
[103]WAKAMATSU-SHI, *Wakamatsu-shishi*, (1941–2). *(History of Wakamatsu).
[若 松 市・若松市史]
[104]TOBATA-SHI, *Tobata-shi Shōshi*, (1939). *(Short history of Tobata).
[戸 畑 市・戸畑市小史]
[105]KOKURA-SHI, *Kokura-shishi*, (1921, 1955). *(History of Kokura).
[小 倉 市・小倉市史]
[106]KANMON KEIZAI KENKYŪKAI. *Kanmon Keizai*, II, 1–16. *(Economy of Kanmon).
[関門経済]

[107]HAKODATE-SHI, *Hakodate-shishi*, (1911). *(History of Hakodate).
[函 館 市・函館市誌]
[108]SAPPORO-SHI, *Sapporo-shishi*, *Sangyō Keizai-hen*, 167–88, (1953–8). *(History of Sapporo, industrial economy).
[札 幌 市・札幌市史]
[109]OTARU-SHI, *Otaru-shishi*, (1923–4). *(History of Otaru).
[小 樽 市・小樽市史]
[110]ASAHIKAWA-SHI, *Asahikawa-shishi*, (1957). *(History of Asahikawa).
[旭 川 市・旭川市史]
[111]MURORAN-SHI, *Shinpen Muroran-shishi*, (1955). *(Revised history of Muroran).
[室 蘭 市・新篇室蘭市史]
[112]KUSHIRO-SHI, *Kushiro-shishi*, (1944). *(History of Kushiro).
[釧 路 市・釧路市史]
[113]KIRYŪ-SHI, *Kiryū-shishi*, II, 556, (1948). *(History of Kiryū).
[桐 生 市・桐生市史]
[114]———, *ibid.*, 547.
[桐 生 市・桐生市史]
[115]ASHIKAGA-SHI, *Ashikaga-shishi*, (1928). *(History of Ashikaga).
[足 利 市・足利市史]
[116]HAMAMATSU-SHI, *Hamamatsu-shishi*, (1957). *(History of Hamamatsu).
[浜 松 市・浜松市史]

# INDEX

[City, town, and village names are marked with an asterisk. See initial page references for the meaning of untranslated Japanese terms in italics.]

E



F

**P**

## R



## S

T

Z